Barron's How to Prepare for the Graduate Management Admission Test
GMAT
Revised Edition

by
EUGENE D. JAFFE, M.B.A., Ph.D.
Associate Professor and
Director of the Management Training Center,
Bar-Ilan University, Israel
Formerly Professor of Marketing,
Graduate School of Business, St. John's University

and

STEPHEN HILBERT, Ph.D.
Associate Professor of Mathematics
Ithaca College

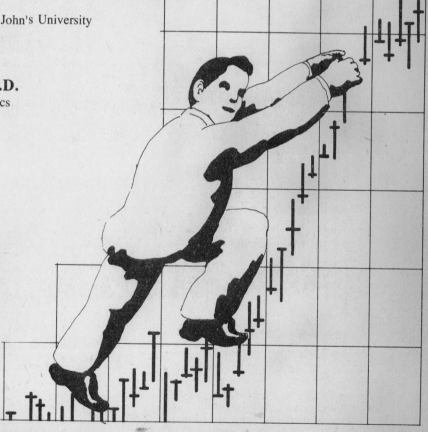

Barron's
Educational Series, Inc. / Woodbury, New York

All inquiries should be addressed to:

Barron's Educational Series, Inc.
113 Crossways Park Drive
Woodbury, New York 11797

Library of Congress Catalog Card No. 78–31875

International Standard Book No. 0–8120–2024–3

Library of Congress Cataloging in Publication Data

Jaffe, Eugene D
  Barron's how to prepare for the graduate management admission test (GMAT).

  1. Business education—Examinations, questions,
etc. I. Hilbert, Stephen, joint author. II. Title.
III. Title: How to prepare for the graduate manage-
ment admission test (GMAT).
HF1118.J33   1979   371.2′64   78–31875
ISBN 0–8120–2024–3

PRINTED IN THE UNITED STATES OF AMERICA

Table of Contents

For Liora, Iris and Nurit

Preface

Barron's How to Prepare for the Graduate Management Admission Test (GMAT) is designed to assist students planning to take the official Graduate Management Admission Test administered by the Educational Testing Service of Princeton, New Jersey. Since the results of the GMAT are used by many graduate schools of business as a means for measuring the qualifications of their applicants, it is important that the prospective student do as well as he possibly can on this exam. His admission to business school may well depend on it.

A study guide, although not able to guarantee a perfect score, can provide a good deal of assistance in test preparation by enabling the student to become familiar with the material he will encounter on the exam and supplying him with ample opportunity for practice and review. With this in mind, we have developed a study guide that goes further than the simple simulation of the official GMAT in its effort to offer a sound basis of test preparation. Besides containing six practice tests with questions (and answers) similar to those the student will encounter on the actual exam, it offers invaluable advice on *how* to prepare for the exam, ranging from a general discussion of the purpose and various formats of the GMAT to a step-by-step program of subject analysis and review designed to help the student discover his weak points and take measures to correct them.

Review sections for each subject area appearing on the exam have been especially developed to meet the specific needs of students who may feel a deficiency in any of these areas. Each review provides both an explanation of the material and exercises for practice work. The six practice exams included in the guide have self-scoring tables to help the student evaluate his results and check his progress. All answers to the test questions are fully explained to ensure complete understanding. A glossary of business terms, a general vocabulary list, and a list of business schools requiring the GMAT add to the value of this guide as a means of preparation for this important test.

The authors would also like to extend their appreciation to Mrs. Susan Hilbert and Ms. Dawn Murcer for their excellent job in typing the manuscript, to Professor Shirley Hockett for several helpful discussions, and to Professor Justin Longenecker for his generous advice.

How to Use This Guide

The step-by-step study program appearing below outlines the recommended study plan you should follow when preparing for the GMAT. By making use of this procedure, you will be able to take full advantage of the material presented in this guide.

1. Familiarize yourself with the purpose and general format of the GMAT (Chapter I).

2. Study the analysis of each type of question on the exam (Chapter II).

3. Take the GMAT Diagnostic Test and use the Self-scoring Table at the end of the test to evaluate your results.

4. Study the review sections (Chapter IV), spending more time on areas where you scored poorly on the Diagnostic Test.

5. Take the five sample GMAT tests and evaluate your results after completing each one.

6. Review again any areas you discover you are still weak in after you have evaluated your test results.

7. Use the General Vocabulary List and Glossary of Business Terms to help increase your knowledge of word meanings and supplement your review.

Acknowledgments

The authors gratefully acknowledge the kindness of all organizations concerned with granting us permission to reprint passages, charts, and graphs. The copyright holders and publishers of quoted passages are listed on this and the following pages.

Sources and permissions for charts and graphs appear on the appropriate pages throughout the book through the courtesy of the following organizations: the New York Times Company; U.S. Department of Labor; Dow Jones & Company, Inc.; U.S. Department of Health, Education, and Welfare; United Nations Economics Bulletin for Europe; Social Security Bulletin, Statistical Abstract of the U.S., U.S. Department of Commerce, Bureau of Economic Analysis; Federal Reserve Bank of New York; European Economic Community; U.S. Department of Commerce, Bureau of the Census; New York State Department of Labor; Federal Power Commission; U.S. Treasury Department; U.S. Bureau of Labor Statistics; Institute of Life Insurance; and the Statistical Abstract of Latin America.

Page 15, Sample Passage: Maynard and Davis, *Sales Management,* © 1957, reprinted by permission of John Wiley & Sons, Inc., New York.

Page 10, Sample Passage: Reprinted with permission of the author, Virgil Thomson.

Page 502, Passage 1: *Trade Policy Toward Low-Income Countries,* copyright 1967 by the Committee for Economic Development.

Page 527, Passage 2: reprinted with permission from Cruickshank and Davis, *Cases in Management* (Homewood, Ill.: Richard D. Irwin, Inc., 1954 c.).

Page 84, Passage 2: from *The Social Bond,* by Robert A. Nisbet. Copyright © 1970 by Alfred A. Knopf, Inc. Reprinted by permission of the publisher.

Page 86, Example 2: "Skye, Lonely Scottish Isle," *Newark Sunday News,* June 9, 1968, C 16, Sec. 2.

Page 88, Example 4: David Gunter, "Kibbutz Life Growing Easier," *Newark News,* May 6, 1968, p. 5.

Page 93, Example 2: Reprinted with permission from "Understanding Foreign Policy," by Saul K. Padover, *Public Affairs Pamphlet #280.* Copyright, Public Affairs Committee, Inc.

Page 95, Exercise A: from *New Students and New Places* by the Carnegie Commission on Higher Education. Copyright 1971 The Carnegie Foundation for the Advancement of Teaching. Used with permission of McGraw-Hill Book Company.

Page 106, Exercise E: Marina Gazzo and Catherine Browne, "Venice Rising," *European Community,* November-December, 1975, pp. 15–16.

Page 441, Passage 1: *Improving Executive Development in the Federal Government,* copyright 1964 by the Committee for Economic Development.

Page 442, Passage 2: from *Legal Aspects of Marketing* by Marshall C. Howard. Copyright 1964 by McGraw-Hill Book Company. Used with permission of McGraw-Hill Book Company.

Page 443, Passage 3: Harold B. Scott, "Government Policies and Attitude Toward U.S.-East European and Mainland China Trade," in Arvind A. Phatak, (ed.), *Building Business Bridges To Eastern Europe And Mainland China,* Temple University, Bureau of Economic and Business Research, 1972.

Page 468, Passage 2: from *Basic Problems in Marketing Management* by Edwin C. Greif. © 1967 by Wadsworth Publishing Company, Inc., Belmont, California 94002. Reprinted by permission of the publisher.

Page 44, Passage 2: reprinted with permission from Cruickshank and Davis, *Cases in Management* (Homewood, Ill.: Richard D. Irwin, Inc., 1954 c.).

Page 574, Passage 1: Maynard and Davis, *Sales Management,* © 1957, reprinted by permission of John Wiley & Sons, Inc., New York.

Page 577, Passage 2: reprinted by permission of The World Publishing Company from *Basic Marketing* by Robert S. Raymond. Copyright © 1967 by Robert S. Raymond.

Page 27, Passage 1: Petra Karin Kelly, "Cancer A European Conquest?" *European Community,* April-May, 1976, pp. 23–24.

Page 29, Passage 2: Walter Sturdivant, "Loch Ness Monster," *European Community,* April-May, 1976, pp. 36–37.

Page 33, Passage 4: Reprinted from *The Bible on Broadway* by Arthur T. Buch © Arthur T. Buch

ONE

AN INTRODUCTION TO THE GMAT

The most productive approach to undertaking the actual study and review necessary for any examination is first to determine the answers to some basic questions: What? Where? When? and How? In this case, what is the intent of the Graduate Management Admission Test (GMAT)? What does it measure? Where and when is the exam given? And most important, how can the candidate specifically prepare himself to demonstrate aptitude and ability to study business at the graduate level?

The following discussion centers on the purpose behind the Graduate Management Admission Test and presents a study program to follow in preparing for this exam, including a special section to acquaint you with the general format and procedure used on the GMAT.

The Purpose of the GMAT

The purpose of the GMAT is to measure the candidate's ability to *think systematically* and to employ the *reading and analytical skills* that he has acquired throughout his years of schooling. The types of questions that are used to test this ability are discussed in the next chapter. It should be noted that the test does not aim to measure the student's knowledge of *specific business or academic subjects*. No specific business experience is necessary, nor will any specific academic subject area be covered. The candidate is assumed to have knowledge of basic algebra, geometry, and arithmetic.

In effect, the GMAT provides college admission officials with an *objective* measure of academic abilities to supplement subjective criteria used in the selection process, such as interviews, grades, and references. In other words, the test is used as a means for measuring ability other than college grades. Suppose you are an average student in a college with high grading standards. Your overall grade average may be lower than that of a student from a college with lower grading standards. The GMAT allows you and the other student to be tested under similar conditions using the same grading standard. In this way, a more accurate picture of all-around ability can be established.

Where to Apply

Information about the exact dates of the exam, fees, testing locations, and a test registration form can be found in the GMAT Bulletin of Information for Candidates published by ETS. You can obtain a copy by writing:

Graduate Management Admission Test
Educational Testing Service
Box 966
Princeton, New Jersey 08540

The Graduate Management Admission Test (GMAT) is generally given in November, January, March, and July. Since the majority of business schools send out their acceptances in the spring, it is wise to take this exam as early as possible to ensure that the schools you are applying to receive your scores in time.

The Test Format

In recent years the GMAT has contained seven types of questions — Reading Recall, Mathematics, Verbal Aptitude, Data Sufficiency, Business Judgment, Reading Comprehension and Writing Ability. The following chart gives the format of several recent GMAT exams. Notice that not all types of questions may appear on each exam and some types may be repeated. It is obviously impossible to predict the format of future exams but in recent years most exams have contained Reading Recall, Mathematics, Business Judgment and Data Sufficiency sections along with some of the other types.

Type A

SECTION	TYPE OF QUESTION	NUMBER OF QUESTIONS	TIME (MIN.)
I	Reading Recall	reading only	15
II	Answer questions on Reading	30	20
III	Mathematics	55	75
	10 minute break		
IV	Business Judgment	20	20
V	Data Sufficiency	15	15
VI	Verbal	25	15
VII	Business Judgment	20	20
VIII	Reading Comprehension OR Data Sufficiency OR Mathematics OR Writing Ability	25	30
TOTAL		190	3 Hours, 30 Minutes

Type B

SECTION	TYPE OF QUESTION	NUMBER OF QUESTIONS	TIME (MIN.)
I	Reading Recall	read only	15
II	Answer questions on Reading	30	20
III	Mathematics	55	75
	10 minute break		
IV	Verbal Aptitude	40	20
V	Data Sufficiency	15	15
VI	Repeat of one of the above OR Business Judgment OR Reading Comprehension	25	25
VII	Repeat of one of the above	40	35
TOTAL		205	3 Hours, 25 Minutes

NOTE: Format and timing are subject to change.

Type C

SECTION	TYPE OF QUESTION	NUMBER OF QUESTIONS	TIME (MIN.)
I	Reading Comprehension	25	30
II	Math Ability (No Graphs)	30	40
III	Business Judgment	25	20
IV	Data Sufficiency	30	30
V	Writing Ability	25	15
VI	Business Judgment	25	20
VII	Logical Reasoning OR Analysis of Explanations OR Case Evaluation	20–40	25–30
TOTAL		180–200	Approx. 3 Hours

Type D

SECTION	TYPE OF QUESTION	NUMBER OF QUESTIONS	TIME (MIN.)
I	Reading Comprehension	25	30
II	Math Ability (No Graphs)	30	40
III	Business Judgment	25	20
IV	Data Sufficiency	15	15
V	Writing Ability	35	20
VI	Business Judgment	20	25
VII	Case Evaluation OR Analysis of Explanations	40	30
TOTAL		190	3 Hours

Each section of the GMAT must be completed within a specified time limit. If you should finish the section before the allotted time has elapsed, you must spend the remaining time working on that section *only*. You may *not* work on other sections of the test at all. It is a good idea to have a watch with you during the exam so that you can keep track of how much time you have and budget it accordingly.

Specific directions telling you exactly how to answer the questions appear at the beginning of each section of the exam. Keep in mind that although the directions for answering the sample questions in this guide are designed to simulate as closely as possible those on the actual test, the format of the test you take may vary. Therefore, it is important that you read the directions on the actual test very carefully before attempting to answer the questions. You also should be certain of the exact time limit you are allowed.

How to Prepare for the GMAT

You should now be aware of the purpose of the GMAT and have a general idea of the format of the test. With this basic information, you are in the position to begin your study and review. The rest of this guide represents a study plan which will enable you to prepare for the GMAT. If used properly, it will help you diagnose your weak areas and take steps to remedy them.

Begin your preparation by becoming as familiar as possible with the various types of questions that appear on the exam. The analysis of typical GMAT questions in the next chapter is designed for this purpose. When you feel you understand this material completely, take the Diagnostic Test that follows and evaluate your results on the self-scoring table provided at the end of the test. (An explanation of how to use these tables appears below.) A low score in any area indicates that you should spend more time reviewing that particular material. Study the review section for that area until you feel you have mastered it and then take one of the sample GMATs at the back of the book. Continue this pattern of study until you are completely satisfied with your performance. For best results, try to simulate exam conditions as closely as possible when taking sample tests.

The Self-scoring Tables

The self-scoring tables for each sample test in this guide can be used as a means of evaluating your weaknesses in particular subject areas and should give you a rough estimate of how you will do when you take the actual test.

After completing a sample test, first determine the number of *correct* answers you had for each section. Next, subtract *one-fourth* the number of *wrong* answers for each part from the number of correct answers. This is done to compensate for guessing. For example, suppose that in section 1 of a certain test you answered 24 out of 30 questions correctly. This means that you had 6 incorrect responses (30 minus 24). Subtract $\frac{1}{4}$ of 6 ($1\frac{1}{2}$) from 24 to obtain a final score of $22\frac{1}{2}$. Record this score in the appropriate score box in the Self-scoring Table as shown below.

Self-scoring Table

PART	SCORE	RANK
1	$22\frac{1}{2}$	GOOD
2		
3		
4		
5		
6		

Then, compare this score with those contained in the Self-scoring Scale. Insert the rank, either POOR, FAIR, GOOD, or EXCELLENT, in the appropriate box in the Self-scoring Table.

Self-scoring Scale

PART	POOR	FAIR	GOOD	EXCELLENT
1	0–15	16–21	22–25	26–30
2	0–29	30–40	41–47	48–55
3	0–20	21–28	29–34	35–40
4	0–7	8–10	11–12	13–15
5	0–10	11–14	15–16	17–20
6	0–18	19–25	26–30	31–35

A rank of FAIR or POOR in any area indicates that you need to spend more time reviewing that material.

Scaled Scores

(for a GMAT test with 195 questions)

Your GMAT score will be some number between 200 and 800. The scores on the GMAT are scaled so that scores above 700 or below 250 are unusual and most scores (about 2/3) fall between 400 and 600. The rules below will give you a method for converting your raw score on a practice exam into a scaled score. This is not the same procedure that the GMAT uses but it should give you some idea of what your scaled score would be on the exam. Note that your raw score on an exam is the number of correct answers minus one fourth of the incorrect answers.

Now use the following rules to convert your raw score into a scaled score.

RAW SCORE	RULES FOR SCALED SCORE
15 or less	250
between 15 and 65	250 plus 3 times raw score minus 15
between 65 and 165	400 plus 2 times raw score minus 65
between 165 and 185	600 plus 5 times raw score minus 165
between 185 and 195	700 plus 10 times raw score minus 185

EXAMPLE:

Raw score is 142.5
(A)   Raw score is between 65 and 165
(B)   Raw score minus 65 = 77.5
(C)   Scaled Score is $400 + 2(77.5) = 400 + 155 = 555$

If your scaled scores are low on the first practice exams you take, don't get discouraged. Your scaled score should improve on the later practice exams after you have used the various reviews to strengthen your weaknesses. The tests were made hard. That way you can discover your weaknesses and try to correct them. Giving you easy practice tests is not the way to study for a difficult exam. Remember that on the GMAT itself you shouldn't expect to be able to answer every single question. Don't worry about that. To maximize your score you want to answer as many questions as you can *correctly* in the given amount of time. Don't forget to clock yourself on the practice exams.

TWO
AN ANALYSIS OF TYPICAL GMAT QUESTIONS

A logical first step in preparing for the GMAT is to become as familiar as possible with the types of questions that usually appear on this exam. The following analysis of typical GMAT questions explains the purpose behind each type and the best method for answering it. Samples of the questions with a discussion of their answers are also presented. More detailed discussions and reviews for each type of question are presented elsewhere in this book.

Reading Recall

The purpose of these questions is to test your ability to understand and remember *main points* and *significant details* contained in material you have read and to determine how well you can draw inferences from this material. Generally, each Reading Recall section contains three passages of several paragraphs each. You are allowed 15 minutes to read all three passages. After this time has elapsed you are given another 20 minutes to answer questions based on these passages. You may not refer to the passages while answering the questions, but instead must rely on your memory to supply the desired information.

The best way to approach the Reading Recall question is to concentrate as much as possible on the *significant details* in the passages. A good method for fixing these ideas in your memory is to underline main points as you read. Try to budget your time so that you can cover all the material during the allotted 15 minutes. If you finish all three passages before time is called, you will be able to use the material you have underlined as a means of quick review.

The following passage will give you an idea of the format of the Reading Recall section. As you read, underline what you believe to be the main ideas presented. Limit your reading time to 7 minutes. Spend another 7 minutes answering the questions that follow, remembering not to refer back to the passage for assistance. When you have finished, compare your responses with the analysis of answers provided at the end.

Sample Passage

Part A: TIME—7 minutes

Some economists believe that the United States can be utilized as a "land bridge" for the shipment of containerized cargo between Europe and the Far East. Under the land-bridge concept, containerized freight traveling between Europe and the Far East would be shipped by ocean carrier to the United States East Coast, unloaded and placed on special railway flatcars, and shipped via railroad to a West Coast port. At this port, the containers would then be loaded on ships bound to a Far East port of entry. This procedure would be reversed for material traveling in the opposite direction. Thus, a land transportation system would be substituted for marine transportation during part of the movement of goods between Europe and the Far East.

If a land-bridge system of shipment were deemed feasible and competitive with alternative methods, it would open a completely new market for both United States steamship lines and railroads. At present, foreign lines carry all Far East–Europe freight. American carriers get none of this trade, and the all-water route excludes the railroads.

The system established by a land-bridge could also serve to handle goods now being shipped between the United States West Coast and Europe, or goods shipped between the Far East and the United States Gulf and East Coasts. Currently, there are 20 foreign lines carrying West Coast freight to Europe via the Panama Canal, but not one United States line. Thus, in addition to the land-bridge getting this new business for the railroads, it also gives the United States East Coast ships an opportunity to compete for this trade.

While this method of shipment will probably not add to the labor requirements at East and West Coast piers, it does have the potential of absorbing some of the jobs that the containerization of current cargo has eliminated or could eliminate. Thus, the possibility of creating new jobs for longshoremen is not an expected benefit of such a system, but it will most certainly create other labor requirements. The land-bridge concept has the potential of offering new job openings for United States railway workers and seamen. In addition, there would be expansion of labor requirements for people in the shipbuilding and container manufacturing business.

By making United States rail transportation an export service, the land-bridge system would have a favorable effect on our balance of payments. Such a system also has the potential of relieving the United States government of part of the burden it now bears in the form of subsidies to the shipping industry. The federal government subsidizes the construction and operation of scheduled vessels. Some 52 percent of the income from their operation comes from the government in that these ships are used for all our military and other government-related export shipments. The land-bridge requirement for scheduled sailings could effect a shift from the use of these subsidized lines for shipment of government goods to commercial cargo of the land bridge. This would then open some of the lucrative government business to the unscheduled, unsubsidized lines.

QUESTIONS TO

Sample Passage

Part B: TIME — 7 minutes

DIRECTIONS: Answer the following questions pertaining to information contained in the passage you have just read. You may not turn back to this passage for assistance.

Ⓐ Ⓑ Ⓒ Ⓓ Ⓔ 1. According to the passage, if a land-bridge system were feasible, it would

    (A) create employment in the bridge-building industry
    (B) decrease the amount of air freight
    (C) create a new market for steamship lines and railroads
    (D) make American railroads more efficient
    (E) increase foreign trade

2. The author implies that which of the following would be provided employment by Ⓐ Ⓑ Ⓒ Ⓓ Ⓔ
the development of a land-bridge?

   I. Longshoremen
  II. U.S. railway workers
 III. U.S. seamen

(A) I only
(B) III only
(C) I and II only
(D) II and III only
(E) I, II, and III

3. According to the passage, the major alternative to a U.S. land-bridge is the Ⓐ Ⓑ Ⓒ Ⓓ Ⓔ

(A) Panama Canal
(B) Suez Canal
(C) air-freight system
(D) all land route
(E) military transport system

4. The passage states that a land-bridge would improve United States Ⓐ Ⓑ Ⓒ Ⓓ Ⓔ

(A) foreign trade
(B) balance of payments
(C) railroad industry
(D) international relations
(E) gold reserves

5. A land-bridge would *not* Ⓐ Ⓑ Ⓒ Ⓓ Ⓔ

(A) aid U.S. steamship lines
(B) handle goods shipped between Europe and the Far East
(C) create new jobs for longshoremen
(D) supply new business for U.S. railroads
(E) create business for unscheduled shipping lines

Answers and Analysis

The sample passage with main points underlined appears below:

   Some economists believe that the United States can be utilized as a ''land bridge'' for the shipment of containerized cargo between Europe and the Far East. Under the land-bridge concept, containerized freight traveling between Europe and the Far East would be shipped by ocean carrier to the United States East Coast, unloaded and placed on special railway flatcars, and shipped via railroad to a West Coast port. At this port, the containers would then be loaded on ships bound to a Far East port of entry. This procedure would be reversed for material traveling in the opposite direction. Thus, a land transportation system would be substituted for marine transportation during part of the movement of goods between Europe and the Far East.

   If a land-bridge system of shipment were deemed feasible and competitive with alternative methods, it would open a completely new market for both United States steamship lines and railroads. At present, foreign lines carry all Far East-Europe freight. American carriers get none of this trade and the all-water route excludes the railroads.

The system established by a land-bridge could also serve to handle goods now being shipped between the United States West Coast and Europe, or goods shipped between the Far East and the United States Gulf and East Coasts. Currently, there are 20 foreign lines carrying West Coast freight to Europe via the Panama Canal, but not one United States line. Thus, in addition to the land-bridge getting this new business for the railroads, it also gives the United States East Coast ships an opportunity to compete for this trade.

While this method of shipment will probably not add to the labor requirements at East and West Coast piers, it does have the potential of absorbing some of the jobs that the containerization of current cargo has eliminated or could eliminate. Thus, the possibility of creating new jobs for longshoremen is not an expected benefit of such a system, but it will most certainly create other labor requirements. The land-bridge concept has the potential of offering new job openings for United States railway workers and seamen. In addition, there would be expansion of labor requirements for people in the shipbuilding and container manufacturing business.

By making United States rail transportation an export service, the land-bridge system would have a favorable effect on our balance of payments. Such a system also has the potential of relieving the United States government of part of the burden it now bears in the form of subsidies to the shipping industry. The federal government subsidizes the construction and operation of scheduled vessels. Some 52 percent of the income from their operation comes from the government in that these ships are used for all our military and other government-related export shipments. The land-bridge requirement for scheduled sailings could effect a shift from the use of these subsidized lines for shipment of government goods to commercial cargo of the land bridge. This would then open some of the lucrative government business to the unscheduled, unsubsidized lines.

ANSWERS TO PART B:

1. (C)   2. (D)   3. (A)   4. (B)   5. (C)

ANALYSIS:

1.   (C) See paragraph 2.

2.   (D) See paragraph 4.

3.   (A) Paragraph 3 discusses use of the Panama Canal as a route for freight lines.

4.   (B) See paragraph 5.

5.   (C) See paragraph 4. It specifically states that longshoremen wouldn't benefit.

Reading Comprehension

The Reading Comprehension section tests your ability to analyze written information, and it includes passages from the humanities, the social sciences, and the physical and biological sciences. It differs from the Reading Recall section not only in the subject matter covered but also by the fact that you are allowed to refer to the passages while answering the questions.

The typical Reading Comprehension section consists of three or four passages with a total of 25 questions which must be completed in 30 minutes. An alternate section could have a time limit of 25 minutes.

The following passage will give you an idea of the format of the Reading Comprehension section. Read the passage through and then answer the questions, making sure to leave yourself enough time to complete them all.

Sample Passage

TIME—10 minutes

Political theories have, in fact, very little more to do with musical creation than electronic theories have. Both merely determine methods of distribution. The exploitation of these methods is subject to political regulation, is quite rigidly regulated in many countries. The revolutionary parties, both in Russia and elsewhere, have
(5)   tried to turn composers on to supposedly revolutionary subject-matter. The net result for either art or revolution has not been very important. Neither has official fascist music accomplished much either for music or for Italy or Germany.

Political party-influence on music is just censorship anyway. Performances can be forbidden and composers disciplined for what they write, but the creative stimulus
(10)   comes from elsewhere. Nothing really "inspires" an author but money or food or love.

That persons or parties subventioning musical uses should wish to retain veto power over the works used is not at all surprising. That our political masters (or our representatives) should exercise a certain negative authority, a censorship, over
(15)   the exploitation of works whose content they consider dangerous to public welfare is also in no way novel or surprising. But that such political executives should think to turn the musical profession into a college of political theorists or a bunch of hired propagandists is naïve of them. Our musical civilization is older than any political party. We can deal on terms of intellectual equality with acoustical engineers, with
(20)   architects, with poets, painters, and historians, even with the Roman clergy if necessary. We cannot be expected to take very seriously the inspirational dictates of persons or of groups who think they can pay us to get emotional about ideas. They can pay us to get emotional all right. Anybody can. Nothing is so emotion-producing as money. But emotions are factual; they are not generated by ideas. On the con-
(25)   trary, ideas are generated by emotions; and emotions, in turn, are visceral states produced directly by facts like money and food and sexual intercourse. To have any inspirational quality there must be present facts or immediate anticipations, not pie-in-the-sky.

Now pie-in-the-sky has its virtues as a political ideal, I presume. Certainly most
(30)   men want to work for an eventual common good. I simply want to make it quite clear that ideals about the common good (not to speak of mere political necessity) are not very stimulating subject-matter for music. They don't produce visceral movements the way facts do. It is notorious that musical descriptions of hell, which is something we can all imagine, are more varied and vigorous than the placid banal-
(35)   ities that even the best composers have used to describe heaven; and that all composers do better on really present matters than on either matters like love and hatred and hunting and war and dancing around and around.

The moral or all this is that the vetoing of objective subject-matter is as far as political stimulation or censorship can go in advance. Style is personal and emo-
(40)   tional, not political at all. And form or design, which is impersonal, is not subject to any political differences of opinion.

1. The author is making a statement of   Ⓐ Ⓑ Ⓒ Ⓓ Ⓔ

    I.   Intellectual freedom
   II. Apolitical musicians
  III. Emotional honesty

  (A) I only
  (B) II only
  (C) I and II only
  (D) I and III only
  (E) I, II, and III

2. The tone of the author in the passage is   Ⓐ Ⓑ Ⓒ Ⓓ Ⓔ

  (A) exacting
  (B) pessimistic
  (C) critical
  (D) optimistic
  (E) fatalistic

3. The author's reaction to political influence on music is one of   Ⓐ Ⓑ Ⓒ Ⓓ Ⓔ

  (A) surprise
  (B) disbelief
  (C) resignation
  (D) deference
  (E) rancor

4. It is the author's belief that censors of musical composition are   Ⓐ Ⓑ Ⓒ Ⓓ Ⓔ

  (A) evil
  (B) naïve
  (C) dangerous
  (D) stupid
  (E) fascist

5. It can be inferred that the author is a   Ⓐ Ⓑ Ⓒ Ⓓ Ⓔ

  (A) musician or composer
  (B) politician
  (C) journalist
  (D) historian
  (E) educator

6. The author maintains that composers are motivated by   Ⓐ Ⓑ Ⓒ Ⓓ Ⓔ

  (A) facts
  (B) money
  (C) politics
  (D) social customs
  (E) the public welfare

Answers to Sample Passages:

1. **(D)**   2. **(C)**   3. **(C)**   4. **(B)**   5. **(A)**   6. **(B)**

Analysis:

1. **(D)** The author is arguing that musicians will not conform to any control over their creativity. Thus, they want to be intellectually free and emotionally honest. It does not mean that they could not be active in politics (apolitical).

2. **(C)** The author is critical of attempts to censor the arts, especially music.

3. **(C)** The author does not find censorship surprising (line 13), nor does he take it seriously (line 21). He is resigned to attempts at censorship, although he does not believe it can control creativity.

4. **(B)** See line 18.

5. **(A)** The use of the third party form "we" and "us" implies that the writer is a musician or composer.

6. **(B)** The author states that composers are motivated by money, or food, or love. See lines 10, 23–24.

Verbal Aptitude

This section of the GMAT is designed to test your ability to grasp the meanings of words and to determine the relationships that exist between words and ideas in a given situation. Verbal aptitude thus reflects your capacity for communication and understanding, and is a basic measure of your vocabulary range.

The Verbal Aptitude section of the exam usually consists of three types of questions: antonyms, analogies, and sentence completions. The following discussion will give you an idea of how to approach each of these types when you encounter them on the exam.

Antonyms

An antonym is a word that is opposite in meaning to another word. For example, an antonym for *good* would be *bad*. On the exam you are given a key word printed in capital letters accompanied by five lettered choices. You must select the lettered word that comes closest to being *opposite* in meaning to the capitalized word. Your choice should be a word that corresponds in tense or part of speech to the key word. Try the following sample question.

BUILD: (A) destroy (B) deceive (C) furnish (D) demur (E) depart   Ⓐ Ⓑ Ⓒ Ⓓ Ⓔ

ANSWER: (*A*) destroy

ANALYSIS: Build is a verb in the present tense meaning to construct. (B) deceive means to trick, (C) furnish means to equip, (D) demur means to hesitate, and (E) depart means to leave. Clearly, (A) destroy, meaning to demolish, is the word that is opposite in meaning to the key word, build.

Word-Pair Relationships

In the context of the GMAT a word-pair relationship, or analogy, can be defined as a similarity existing between two given sets of words. An example of this would be the statement BOY : GIRL :: man : woman (read boy is to girl as man is to woman). The similarity between the two word-pairs should be apparent.

You are asked to select from five lettered word-pairs the combination which has a similar relationship to the key word-pair (stem) which appears in capital letters. When making your selection, you should first establish the type of relationship (rationale) existing between the key words. (In the example BOY : GIRL this can be stated as A is the male counterpart of B.) After the rationale of the key word has been determined, a corresponding word-pair can be logically located among the choices.

Try the sample question below.

RITUAL : WORSHIP :: (A) meal : recipe (B) paragon : person (C) protocol : diplomacy (D) geography : geology (E) medicine : magic   Ⓐ Ⓑ Ⓒ Ⓓ Ⓔ

ANSWER: (*C*) protocol : diplomacy

ANALYSIS: The rationale of the stem can be stated as A is the ceremony associated with B. Since protocol is the ceremony associated with diplomacy, the most similar word-pair is (C).

Sentence Completions

These questions require you to complete a sentence by selecting from five alternatives the word or set of words which when inserted into blanks in the given sentence best complete the meaning of that sentence. Look for key words in the sentence that will supply hints to the missing words. Make sure to choose only those words which are *logical* in the context of the sentence and also *grammatically* correct.

Try the sample questions below, choosing the set of words that best completes the meaning of the sentence.

SAMPLE 1:

In economics, inflation is sometimes defined as too much _____ chasing after too few _____.
Ⓐ Ⓑ Ⓒ Ⓓ Ⓔ

(A) money . . . goods
(B) production . . . dollars
(C) output . . . supplies
(D) productivity . . . workers
(E) advertising . . . consumers

ANSWER: (*A*) money . . . goods

ANALYSIS: In this sentence the desired information is a definition of inflation (the key word). Choices (B) through (E) may all be eliminated because they don't supply this information. Choice (A) clearly completes the meaning of the sentence.

SAMPLE 2:

A strike is taken as a last resort, only when other _____ fail.
Ⓐ Ⓑ Ⓒ Ⓓ Ⓔ

(A) excuses
(B) companies
(C) adjustments
(D) measures
(E) admonitions

ANSWER: (*D*) measures

ANALYSIS: Strike is the key word here. In the context of the sentence, the answer will be a word describing a strike. Of the five alternatives, measures is the only logical choice.

Writing Ability

The Writing Ability section tests your knowledge of college-level basic English grammar. To succeed in this section, you are required to have a command of sentence structure including tense and mood, subject and verb agreement, proper case and parallel structure, and other basics. No attempt is made to test for punctuation, spelling or capitalization. Each question consists of a sentence with four parts (words or phrases) underlined. These parts are labeled A, B, C, and D. There is also a fifth choice, No error, labeled E. You must choose the part of the sentence that is incorrect and blacken the corresponding letter on your answer sheet. If there are no incorrect parts, blacken letter E.

The following questions will give you an idea of the type of Writing Ability questions to expect. For each, choose the underlined word or phrase that is incorrect and blacken the appropriate letter in the answer grid.

After the fire whistle <u>blew and signaled</u> lunch time, the foreman told <u>Joe and I</u> <u>that we</u>   Ⓐ Ⓑ Ⓒ Ⓓ Ⓔ
                     A   B   C
would have to return early to finish <u>pouring the foundation.</u> <u>No error</u>
                                         D   E

ANSWER: **(B)**

ANALYSIS: *I* should be *me*; me is the objective case and in this instance is the object of the verb *told*.

<u>In order</u> to identify a bird, <u>one must note</u> <u>it's peculiar markings</u> <u>and then find</u> a bird   Ⓐ Ⓑ Ⓒ Ⓓ Ⓔ
   A   B   C   D
with similar markings in a guidebook. <u>No error</u>
                                      E

ANSWER: **(C)**

ANALYSIS: *it's* should be *its; it's* is a contraction of *it is,* not the possessive form that is needed here.

Business Judgment

The objective of the Business Judgment section is to test your ability to analyze business situations and draw subsequent conclusions about them. On this section you are asked to read a passage discussing various aspects of a business situation leading to the need for a decision. After you complete the passage, you are given two sets of questions to answer.

The first set, data evaluation, contains a number of factors relating to the passage which you must evaluate as being a *major objective,* a *major factor,* a *minor factor,* a *major assumption,* or an *unimportant issue* in the decision-making process. The second set, data application, contains general questions each requiring selection of the answer that comes closest to describing an objective or objectives in the passage. You are permitted to refer to the passage while answering the questions.

As in the Reading Recall passages, it is helpful to underline main points as you read. However, when reading the Business Judgment passages, you should concentrate on defining decision-making factors that fit into the categories for evaluation in the data evaluation questions.

Read the sample passage below, underlining what you feel to be

1. Major Objectives
2. Major Factors
3. Minor Factors
4. Major Assumptions
5. Unimportant Issues

After you have finished, answer the questions that follow. Allow yourself 12 minutes to complete the entire exercise. You may consult the passage for assistance.

Sample Passage

TIME — 12 minutes

Early in 1953, the soft drink world began to watch an interesting experiment, the introduction of soft drinks in cans. Grocery outlets up to that time had enjoyed about one-half of all sales, but it was felt that if the new package was successful, local bottling plants might give way to great central plants, possibly operated by companies with established names in the grocery fields, with shipments being made in carload lots. Local bottlers faced a great decision. If the change were to prove permanent, they should perhaps hasten to add can-filling machines lest they lose their market. Coca Cola, Canada Dry, White Rock, and many other bottlers experimented with the new plan. An eastern chain put out privately branded cans.

A basic limitation was a cost factor of about three cents per can, whereas bottle cost was but a fraction of a cent, since a bottle averaged about twenty-four round trips. It was, however, known that at that time about one-third of all beer sales were made in cans and furthermore, that other beverages had paved the way for consumer acceptance of a canned product. Beer prices normally were from three to four times those of soft drinks.

Many leaders in the industry felt that it might well be that consumer advertising emphasizing the convenience of using a nonreturnable package might offset both habit and the extra cost to the consumer. One of the principal bottling companies undertook a rather large-scale market research project to find useful guides to future action.

Sample Data Evaluation Questions

DIRECTIONS: Evaluate each of the following factors used in decision-making which relate to the passage you have just read by selecting

(A) for a *Major Objective* — the result desired by the executive;

(B) for a *Major Factor* — a primary consideration, spelled out in the passage, that influences the decision;

(C)　for a *Minor Factor*—a less important consideration in the decision;

(D)　for a *Major Assumption*—a conclusion reached by the executive not necessarily supported by the factors present;

(E)　for an *Unimportant Issue*—a consideration not directly related to the problem.

1.　Introduction of soft drinks in cans

2.　A large-scale market research project

3.　Cost of soft drinks in cans

4.　Grocery outlets accounted for one-half of sales

5.　The beer market was smaller than that of soft drinks

Sample Data Application Question

DIRECTIONS:　Answer the following question using information contained in the passage.

6.　Which of the following reasons are given for one of the bottling companies to launch a market research project?

I.　Desire to corner the soft-drink market

II.　Determine whether consumers would be willing to pay a higher price for canned soft-drinks

III.　Test consumer reaction to canned soft-drinks

(A)　I only
(B)　III only
(C)　I and II only
(D)　II and III only
(E)　I, II, and III

Answers and Analysis

The sample passage with suggested underlining appears below.

Early in 1953, the soft drink world began to watch an interesting experiment, the introduction of soft drinks in cans. Grocery outlets up to that time had enjoyed about one-half of all sales, but it was felt that if the new package was successful, local bottling plants might give way to great central plants, possibly operated by companies with established names in the grocery fields, with shipments being made in carload lots. Local bottlers faced a great decision. If the change were to prove permanent, they should perhaps hasten to add can-filling machines lest they lose their market. Coca Cola, Canada

Dry, White Rock, and many other bottlers experimented with the new plan. An eastern chain put out privately branded cans.

A basic limitation was a cost factor of about three cents per can, whereas bottle cost was but a fraction of a cent, since a bottle averaged about twenty-four round trips. It was, however, known that at that time about one-third of all beer sales were made in cases, and furthermore, that other beverages had paved the way for consumer acceptance of a canned product. Beer prices normally were from three or four times those of soft drinks.

Many leaders in the industry felt that it might well be that consumer advertising emphasizing the convenience of using a nonreturnable package might offset both habit and the extra cost to the consumer. One of the principal bottling companies undertook a rather large-scale market research project to find useful guides to future action.

Answers to Data Evaluation Questions:

1. (A) 2. (B) 3. (B) 4. (C) 5. (E)

Analysis:

1. (A) The introduction of soft drinks in cans is certainly the *Major Objective* here and the major decision to be made; the major outcome would be consumer acceptance of canned soft drinks.

2. (B) The market research project will gather information allowing management to make a decision; without such information, presumably, no decision could be reached. Therefore, the project is a *Major Factor*.

3. (B) The cost of canned soft drinks is a *Major Factor* in making the decision because it is crucial to consumer acceptance. If the soft drinks are priced too high, consumers may not be willing to purchase them.

4. (C) Grocery stores are related to the issue of whether consumers would accept the new product and thus a *Minor Factor*. If consumers accept the project, grocery stores would have to stock the item.

5. (E) It does not state in the passage that the "beer market was smaller than that of soft drinks." Therefore, the only possible answer to this question is (E), *Unimportant Issue*.

Answer to Data Application Question

ANSWER: (*D*) II and III only.

ANALYSIS: The correct answer is (D) because the passage states that some of the major uncertainties as to whether to offer canned soft drinks is their high cost and the purchasing habits of consumers, i.e., whether they would prefer canned soft drinks and be willing to pay a premium (high) price for them. Alternative (A), I only, is factually incorrect since no mention is made that the bottler in question desires to "corner the market," but rather to obtain some answers to the central problem—that of consumer reaction to canned soft drinks.

Mathematics

The Mathematics section of the GMAT is designed to test your ability to work with numbers. There are a variety of questions in this section dealing with the basic principles of arithmetic, algebra and geometry. These questions may take the form of word problems or require straight calculation. In addition, many questions involving the interpretation of tables and graphs are usually included.

The typical Mathematics section consists of 55 questions that must be answered within a time limit of 75 minutes. Often a shorter section of perhaps 35 questions with a 40 minute time limit will also appear on an exam. Although the majority of questions are not that difficult, it is not always possible to answer all of them within the allotted time. For this reason, you should be aware of certain procedures that will help you make the most of the time you have.

Strategy for GMAT Mathematics Questions

In order to maximize your score on this section, you must answer all the questions you can. *Don't waste time* on a question you can't figure out in a minute or two. You will score better if you answer 2 or 3 easy questions in the time it takes to answer one difficult one. Since the last questions may be easier than the first questions, try to *budget your time* so that you will have a chance to try each question.

Don't waste time on *unnecessary calculations*. If you can answer the question by *estimating* or doing a rough calculation, the time you save can be used to answer other questions. Keep this in mind especially when considering problems that involve tables and graphs. In many cases you can make estimates which will simplify your calculations and still be accurate enough to answer the question. Using estimates is a skill that can turn a good score into an excellent one.

For line and bar graphs, use your pencil as a ruler. It is more accurate than simply "eyeballing" columns which are not adjacent.

You should understand that random guessing will not help your score on these sections, since a percentage of your wrong answers is subtracted from your correct answers. If you can eliminate all but two of the answers for a particular question, it will probably help your score to guess an answer for that question.

Solve the sample questions below, allowing yourself 12 minutes to complete all of them. As you work, try to make use of the above strategy. Any figure that appears with a problem is drawn as accurately as possible to provide information that may help in answering the question. All numbers used are real numbers.

Sample Mathematics Questions

TIME—12 minutes

1. Ⓐ Ⓑ Ⓒ Ⓓ Ⓔ   1. A train travels from Albany to Syracuse a distance of 120 miles at the average rate of 50 miles per hour. The train then travels back to Albany from Syracuse. The total

traveling time of the train is 5 hours and 24 minutes. What was the average rate of speed of the train on the return trip to Albany?

(A) 60 mph
(B) 48 mph
(C) 40 mph

(D) 50 mph
(E) 35 mph

2. A parking lot charges a flat rate of X dollars for any amount of time up to two hours, and $\frac{1}{6}X$ for each hour or fraction of an hour after the first two hours. How much does it cost to park for 5 hours and 15 minutes? 2. Ⓐ Ⓑ Ⓒ Ⓓ Ⓔ

(A) $3X$
(B) $2X$
(C) $1\frac{2}{3}X$

(D) $1\frac{1}{2}X$
(E) $1\frac{1}{6}X$

Use the following table for questions 3–5.

Number of Students by major in State University		
	1950	1970
Division of Business	990	2,504
Division of Sciences	350	790
Division of Humanities	1,210	4,056
Division of Engineering	820	1,600
Division of Agriculture	630	1,050
TOTAL	4,000	10,000

3. From 1950 to 1970, the change in the percentage of university students enrolled in Engineering was 3. Ⓐ Ⓑ Ⓒ Ⓓ Ⓔ
(A) roughly no change
(B) an increase of more than 4%
(C) an increase of more than 1% but less than 4%
(D) a decrease of more than 4%
(E) a decrease of more than 1% but less than 4%

4. The number of students enrolled in Business in 1970 divided by the number of Business students in 1950 is 4. Ⓐ Ⓑ Ⓒ Ⓓ Ⓔ
(A) almost 3
(B) about 2.5
(C) roughly 2
(D) about 1
(E) about 40%

5. By 1970 how many of the divisions had an enrollment greater than 200% of the enrollment of that division in 1950? 5. Ⓐ Ⓑ Ⓒ Ⓓ Ⓔ

(A) 0
(B) 1
(C) 2

(D) 3
(E) 4

Use the graph below for questions 6 and 7.

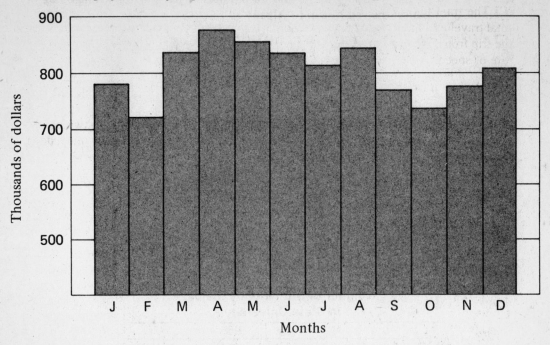

The graph gives monthly sales of the XYZ corporation in thousands of dollars for each month in 1970.

ⒶⒷⒸⒹⒺ   **6.** In what month were sales the least?

    (A) January   (D) December
    (B) February   (E) March
    (C) October

ⒶⒷⒸⒹⒺ   **7.** Which of the following statements are true?

    I. Of Spring, Summer, and Fall, Spring was the season which had the highest total sales.

    II. Sales in April were greater than the combined sales of January and February.

    III. The greatest change in sales occurred between August and September.

    (A) I only   (D) II and III
    (B) I and II   (E) I and III
    (C) II only

Answers and Analysis

ANSWERS:

1. **(C)**	4. **(B)**	7. **(A)**
2. **(C)**	5. **(D)**	
3. **(D)**	6. **(B)**	

ANALYSIS:

1. **(C)** The train took $120/50 = 2\frac{2}{5}$ hours to travel from Albany to Syracuse. Since the total traveling time of the train was $5\frac{2}{5}$ hours, it must have taken the train 3 hours for the trip from Syracuse to Albany. Since the distance traveled is 120 miles, the average rate of speed on the return trip to Albany was $(1/3)(120)$ mph $= 40$ mph.

2. **(C)** It costs X for the first 2 hours. If you park 5 hours and 15 minutes there are 3 hours and 15 minutes left after the first 2 hours. Since this time is charged at the rate of $X/6$ for each hour or fraction thereof, it costs $4(X/6)$ for the last 3 hours and 15 minutes. Thus the total is $X + \frac{4}{6}X = 1\frac{2}{3}X$.

3. **(D)** Since $820/4{,}000 = .205$, the percentage of university students enrolled in Engineering in 1950 was 20.5%; since $1.600/10.000 = .16$, the percentage in 1970 was 16%. Thus the percentage of university students enrolled in Engineering was 4.5% less in 1970 than it was in 1950.

4. **(B)** In 1950 there were 990 Business students and in 1970 there were 2,504. Since $(2.5)(1{,}000) = 2{,}500$, the correct answer is thus (B) about 2.5. Note that this is an easy way to save yourself time. Instead of dividing 990 into 2,504 to find the exact answer, simply use numbers close to the original numbers to get an estimate. In many cases this gives enough information to answer the question and saves valuable time.

5. **(D)** If a division in 1970 has more than 200% of the number of students it had in 1950 that means that the number of students more than doubled between 1950 and 1970. Therefore simply double each entry in the 1950 column and if this is less than the corresponding entry in the 1970 column, that division has more than 200% of the number of students it had in 1950. Since $(2)(990) = 1980$ which is less than 2,504, the number of Business students more than doubled. Since $(2)(1{,}210) = 2{,}420$ which is less than 4,056, Humanities more than doubled, and because $(2)(350) = 700$ which is less than 790, Sciences more than doubled. Engineering did not double in size because $(2)(820) = 1640$ which is larger than 1,600. Also since $(2)(630) = 1{,}260$, which is larger than 1,050, the number of Agricultural students in 1970 was less than 200% of the number of Agricultural students in 1950. Therefore three of the divisions (Business, Humanities, and Sciences) more than doubled between 1950 and 1970.

6. **(B)** Use your pencil as a ruler to compare February to October; the other answers are obviously wrong.

7. **(A)** June and March were about the same; May was a little larger than August and April was much greater than July; so Spring sales were higher than Summer sales. It is easy to see Spring sales were higher than Fall sales. Therefore, statement I is true. (Use your pencil as a substitute for a ruler to compare columns which are not next to each other.) Since April sales were about $900,000 and sales in February and January were each larger than $700,000, the combined sales in January and February were larger than $1,400,000. Therefore, statement II is false. Between August and September the change was roughly $50,000 but between February and March the change was more than $100,000. Thus statement III is false.

Data Sufficiency

This section of the GMAT is designed to test your reasoning ability. Like the Mathematics section, it requires a basic knowledge of the principles of arithmetic, algebra, and geometry. Each Data Sufficiency question consists of a mathematical problem and two statements containing information relating to it. You must decide whether the problem can be solved by using information from (A) the first statement alone but not the second alone, (B) the second statement alone but not the first alone, (C) both statements together but not each separately (D) either of the statements alone, or (E) neither of the statements together. Generally, you are allowed one minute to answer each question. Thus, if a section contains 15 questions, it will be 15 minutes in length. As in the Mathematics section, time is of the utmost importance. Approaching Data Sufficiency problems properly will help you use this time wisely.

Always keep in mind the fact that you are never asked to supply an answer for the problem; you need only determine if there is sufficient data available to find the answer. Therefore, *don't waste time figuring out the exact answer*. Once you know whether or not it is possible to find the answer with the given information you are through. If you spend too much time doing unnecessary work on one question you may not be able to finish the entire section.

Because of the nature of these questions, it may be possible in certain instances to improve your score by making an educated guess. If, for example, you know that the first statement alone is sufficient but are not sure about the second one alone, you are already limited to just two choices—(A) the first statement alone but not the second statement alone is sufficient, or (D) either of the statements alone is sufficient. The same holds true if you are sure that the second statement alone is sufficient but are uncertain of the first statement. Since you get one point for each correct answer and only lose $\frac{1}{4}$ of a point for an incorrect answer, you won't run the risk of substantially lowering your score by guessing.

Read the following directions carefully and then try the sample Data Sufficiency questions below. Allow yourself 6 minutes total time. All numbers used are real numbers. A figure given for a problem is intended to provide information consistent with that in the question, but not necessarily consistent with the additional information contained in the statements.

Sample Data Sufficiency Questions

TIME—6 minutes

DIRECTIONS: Each of the following problems has a question and two statements which are labeled (1) and (2). Use the data given in (1) and (2) together with other available information (such as the number of hours in a day, the definition of *clockwise*, mathematical facts, etc.) to decide whether the statements are *sufficient* to answer the question. Then choose

- (A) if you can get the answer from (1) alone but not from (2) alone;
- (B) if you can get the answer from (2) alone but not from (1) alone;
- (C) if you can get the answer from (1) and (2) together, although neither statement by itself suffices;
- (D) if statement (1) alone suffices *and* statement (2) alone suffices;
- (E) if you cannot get the answer from statements (1) and (2) together, but need even more data.

Ⓐ Ⓑ Ⓒ Ⓓ Ⓔ 1. A rectangular field is 40 yards long. Find the area of the field.

- (1) A fence around the entire boundary of the field is 140 yards long.
- (2) The field is more than 20 yards wide.

2. Is X a number greater than zero?

    (1) $X^2 - 1 = 0$
    (2) $X^3 + 8 = 0$

3. An industrial plant produces bottles. In 1961 the number of bottles produced by the plant was twice the number produced in 1960. How many bottles were produced altogether in the years 1960, 1961 and 1962?

    (1)   In 1962 the number of bottles produced was 3 times the number produced in 1960.
    (2)   In 1963 the number of bottles produced was one half the total produced in the years 1960, 1961, and 1962.

4. A man 6 feet tall is standing near a light on the top of a pole. What is the length of the shadow cast by the man?

    (1)   The pole is 18 feet high.
    (2)   The man is 12 feet from the pole.

5. Find the length of RS if z is 90° and $PS = 6$.

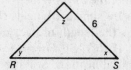

    (1) $PR = 6$
    (2) $x = 45°$

6. Working at a constant rate and by himself, it takes worker U 3 hours to fill up a ditch with sand. How long would it take for worker V to fill up the same ditch working by himself?

    (1)   Working together but at the same time U and V can fill in the ditch in 1 hour 52½ minutes.
    (2)   In any length of time worker V fills in only 60% as much as worker U does in the same time.

7. Did John go to the beach yesterday?

    (1)   If John goes to the beach, he will be sunburned the next day.
    (2)   John is sunburned today.

Answers and Analysis

ANSWERS:

1.	**(A)**	4.	**(C)**
2.	**(B)**	5.	**(D)**
3.	**(E)**	6.	**(D)**
		7.	**(E)**

ANALYSIS:

1. **(A)** The area of a rectangle is the length multiplied by the width. Since you know the length is 40 yards, you must find out the width in order to solve the problem. Since statement (2) simply says the width is greater than 20 yards you can not find out the exact width using (2). So (2) alone is not sufficient. Statement (1) says the length of a fence around the entire boundary of the field is 140 yards. The length of this fence is the perimeter of the rectangle, the sum of twice the length and twice the width. If we replace the length by 40 in $P = 2L + 2W$ we have $140 = 2(40) + 2W$ and solving for W yields $2W = 60$, or $W = 30$ yards. Hence the area is $(40)(30) = 1200$ square yards. Thus (1) alone is sufficient but (2) alone is not.

2. **(B)** Statement (1) means $X^2 = 1$, but there are two possible solutions to this equation, $X = 1$, $X = -1$. Thus using (1) alone you can not deduce whether X is positive or negative. Statement (2) means $X^3 = -8$ but there is only one possible (real) solution to this, $X = -2$. Thus X is not greater than zero which answers the question. And (2) alone is sufficient.

3. **(E)** T, the total produced in the three years, is the sum of $P_0 + P_1 + P_2$, where P_0 is the number produced in 1960, P_1 the number produced in 1961, and P_2 the number produced in 1962. You are given that $P_1 = 2P_0$. Thus $T = P_0 + P_1 + P_2 = P_0 + 2P_0 + P_2 = 3P_0 + P_2$. So we must find out P_0 and P_2 to answer the question. Statement (1) says $P_2 = 3P_0$; thus by using (1) if we can find the value of P_0 we can find T. But (1) gives us no further information about P_0. Statement (2) says T equals the number produced in 1963, but it does not say what this number is. Since there are no relations given between production in 1963 and production in the individual years 1960, 1961, or 1962 you can not use (2) to find out what P_0 is. Thus (1) and (2) together are not sufficient.

4. **(C)** Sometimes it may help to draw a picture. By proportions or by similar triangles the height of the pole, h, is to 6 feet as the length of the shadow, s, + the distance to the pole, x, is to s. So $h/6 = (s + x)/s$. Thus $hs = 6s + 6x$ by cross-multiplication. Solving for s gives $hs - 6s = 6x$, or $s(h - 6) = 6x$, or, finally we have $s = 6x/(h - 6)$. Statement (1) says $h = 18$; thus $s = 6x/12 = x/2$, but using (1) alone we can not deduce the value x. Thus (1) alone is not sufficient. Statement (2) says x equals 12; thus, using (1) and (2) together we deduce $s = 6$, but using (2) alone all we can deduce is that $s = 72/(h - 6)$, which cannot be solved for s unless we know h. Thus using (1) and (2) together we can deduce the answer but (1) alone is not sufficient nor is (2) alone.

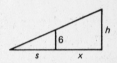

5. **(D)** Since z is a right angle, $(RS)^2 = (PS)^2 + (PR)^2$, so $(RS)^2 = (6)^2 + (PR)^2$, and RS will be the positive square root of $36 + (PR)^2$. Thus if you can find the length of PR the problem is solved. Statement (1) says $PR = 6$, thus $(RS)^2 = 36 + 36$, so $RS = 6\sqrt{2}$. Thus (1) alone is sufficient. Statement (2) says $x = 45°$ but since the sum of the angles in a triangle is $180°$ and z is $90°$ then $y = 45°$. So x and y are equal angles and that means the sides opposite x and opposite y must be equal or $PS = PR$. Thus $PR = 6$ and $RS = 6\sqrt{2}$ so (2) alone is also sufficient.

6. **(D)** (1) says U and V together can fill in the ditch in $1\frac{7}{8}$ hours. Since U can fill in the ditch in 3 hours, in 1 hour he can fill in one-third of the ditch. Hence, in $1\frac{7}{8}$ hours U would fill in $(1/3)(15/8) = \frac{5}{8}$ of the ditch. So V fills in $\frac{3}{8}$ of the ditch in $1\frac{7}{8}$ hours. Thus V would take $(8/3)(15/8) = 5$ hours to fill in the ditch working by himself. Therefore statement (1) alone is sufficient. According to statement (2) since U fills the ditch in 3 hours, V will fill $\frac{3}{5}$ of the ditch in 3 hours. Thus V will take 5 hours to fill in the ditch working by himself.

7. **(E)** Obviously, neither statement alone is sufficient. John *could* have gotten sunburned at the beach, but he might have gotten sunburned somewhere else. Therefore (1) and (2) together are not sufficient. This is an example of a conditional statement. Conditional statements are explained in the Logic Review.

Answer Sheet — Diagnostic Test

Section I — Reading Comprehension

1. Ⓐ Ⓑ Ⓒ Ⓓ Ⓔ
2. Ⓐ Ⓑ Ⓒ Ⓓ Ⓔ
3. Ⓐ Ⓑ Ⓒ Ⓓ Ⓔ
4. Ⓐ Ⓑ Ⓒ Ⓓ Ⓔ
5. Ⓐ Ⓑ Ⓒ Ⓓ Ⓔ
6. Ⓐ Ⓑ Ⓒ Ⓓ Ⓔ

7. Ⓐ Ⓑ Ⓒ Ⓓ Ⓔ
8. Ⓐ Ⓑ Ⓒ Ⓓ Ⓔ
9. Ⓐ Ⓑ Ⓒ Ⓓ Ⓔ
10. Ⓐ Ⓑ Ⓒ Ⓓ Ⓔ
11. Ⓐ Ⓑ Ⓒ Ⓓ Ⓔ
12. Ⓐ Ⓑ Ⓒ Ⓓ Ⓔ

13. Ⓐ Ⓑ Ⓒ Ⓓ Ⓔ
14. Ⓐ Ⓑ Ⓒ Ⓓ Ⓔ
15. Ⓐ Ⓑ Ⓒ Ⓓ Ⓔ
16. Ⓐ Ⓑ Ⓒ Ⓓ Ⓔ
17. Ⓐ Ⓑ Ⓒ Ⓓ Ⓔ
18. Ⓐ Ⓑ Ⓒ Ⓓ Ⓔ

19. Ⓐ Ⓑ Ⓒ Ⓓ Ⓔ
20. Ⓐ Ⓑ Ⓒ Ⓓ Ⓔ
21. Ⓐ Ⓑ Ⓒ Ⓓ Ⓔ
22. Ⓐ Ⓑ Ⓒ Ⓓ Ⓔ
23. Ⓐ Ⓑ Ⓒ Ⓓ Ⓔ
24. Ⓐ Ⓑ Ⓒ Ⓓ Ⓔ
25. Ⓐ Ⓑ Ⓒ Ⓓ Ⓔ

Section II — Mathematics

26. Ⓐ Ⓑ Ⓒ Ⓓ Ⓔ
27. Ⓐ Ⓑ Ⓒ Ⓓ Ⓔ
28. Ⓐ Ⓑ Ⓒ Ⓓ Ⓔ
29. Ⓐ Ⓑ Ⓒ Ⓓ Ⓔ
30. Ⓐ Ⓑ Ⓒ Ⓓ Ⓔ
31. Ⓐ Ⓑ Ⓒ Ⓓ Ⓔ
32. Ⓐ Ⓑ Ⓒ Ⓓ Ⓔ

33. Ⓐ Ⓑ Ⓒ Ⓓ Ⓔ
34. Ⓐ Ⓑ Ⓒ Ⓓ Ⓔ
35. Ⓐ Ⓑ Ⓒ Ⓓ Ⓔ
36. Ⓐ Ⓑ Ⓒ Ⓓ Ⓔ
37. Ⓐ Ⓑ Ⓒ Ⓓ Ⓔ
38. Ⓐ Ⓑ Ⓒ Ⓓ Ⓔ
39. Ⓐ Ⓑ Ⓒ Ⓓ Ⓔ

40. Ⓐ Ⓑ Ⓒ Ⓓ Ⓔ
41. Ⓐ Ⓑ Ⓒ Ⓓ Ⓔ
42. Ⓐ Ⓑ Ⓒ Ⓓ Ⓔ
43. Ⓐ Ⓑ Ⓒ Ⓓ Ⓔ
44. Ⓐ Ⓑ Ⓒ Ⓓ Ⓔ
45. Ⓐ Ⓑ Ⓒ Ⓓ Ⓔ
46. Ⓐ Ⓑ Ⓒ Ⓓ Ⓔ
47. Ⓐ Ⓑ Ⓒ Ⓓ Ⓔ

48. Ⓐ Ⓑ Ⓒ Ⓓ Ⓔ
49. Ⓐ Ⓑ Ⓒ Ⓓ Ⓔ
50. Ⓐ Ⓑ Ⓒ Ⓓ Ⓔ
51. Ⓐ Ⓑ Ⓒ Ⓓ Ⓔ
52. Ⓐ Ⓑ Ⓒ Ⓓ Ⓔ
53. Ⓐ Ⓑ Ⓒ Ⓓ Ⓔ
54. Ⓐ Ⓑ Ⓒ Ⓓ Ⓔ
55. Ⓐ Ⓑ Ⓒ Ⓓ Ⓔ

Section III — Business Judgment

56. Ⓐ Ⓑ Ⓒ Ⓓ Ⓔ
57. Ⓐ Ⓑ Ⓒ Ⓓ Ⓔ
58. Ⓐ Ⓑ Ⓒ Ⓓ Ⓔ
59. Ⓐ Ⓑ Ⓒ Ⓓ Ⓔ
60. Ⓐ Ⓑ Ⓒ Ⓓ Ⓔ
61. Ⓐ Ⓑ Ⓒ Ⓓ Ⓔ

62. Ⓐ Ⓑ Ⓒ Ⓓ Ⓔ
63. Ⓐ Ⓑ Ⓒ Ⓓ Ⓔ
64. Ⓐ Ⓑ Ⓒ Ⓓ Ⓔ
65. Ⓐ Ⓑ Ⓒ Ⓓ Ⓔ
66. Ⓐ Ⓑ Ⓒ Ⓓ Ⓔ
67. Ⓐ Ⓑ Ⓒ Ⓓ Ⓔ

68. Ⓐ Ⓑ Ⓒ Ⓓ Ⓔ
69. Ⓐ Ⓑ Ⓒ Ⓓ Ⓔ
70. Ⓐ Ⓑ Ⓒ Ⓓ Ⓔ
71. Ⓐ Ⓑ Ⓒ Ⓓ Ⓔ
72. Ⓐ Ⓑ Ⓒ Ⓓ Ⓔ
73. Ⓐ Ⓑ Ⓒ Ⓓ Ⓔ

74. Ⓐ Ⓑ Ⓒ Ⓓ Ⓔ
75. Ⓐ Ⓑ Ⓒ Ⓓ Ⓔ
76. Ⓐ Ⓑ Ⓒ Ⓓ Ⓔ
77. Ⓐ Ⓑ Ⓒ Ⓓ Ⓔ
78. Ⓐ Ⓑ Ⓒ Ⓓ Ⓔ
79. Ⓐ Ⓑ Ⓒ Ⓓ Ⓔ
80. Ⓐ Ⓑ Ⓒ Ⓓ Ⓔ

Section IV — Data Sufficiency

81. Ⓐ Ⓑ Ⓒ Ⓓ Ⓔ
82. Ⓐ Ⓑ Ⓒ Ⓓ Ⓔ
83. Ⓐ Ⓑ Ⓒ Ⓓ Ⓔ
84. Ⓐ Ⓑ Ⓒ Ⓓ Ⓔ
85. Ⓐ Ⓑ Ⓒ Ⓓ Ⓔ
86. Ⓐ Ⓑ Ⓒ Ⓓ Ⓔ
87. Ⓐ Ⓑ Ⓒ Ⓓ Ⓔ

88. Ⓐ Ⓑ Ⓒ Ⓓ Ⓔ
89. Ⓐ Ⓑ Ⓒ Ⓓ Ⓔ
90. Ⓐ Ⓑ Ⓒ Ⓓ Ⓔ
91. Ⓐ Ⓑ Ⓒ Ⓓ Ⓔ
92. Ⓐ Ⓑ Ⓒ Ⓓ Ⓔ
93. Ⓐ Ⓑ Ⓒ Ⓓ Ⓔ
94. Ⓐ Ⓑ Ⓒ Ⓓ Ⓔ

95. Ⓐ Ⓑ Ⓒ Ⓓ Ⓔ
96. Ⓐ Ⓑ Ⓒ Ⓓ Ⓔ
97. Ⓐ Ⓑ Ⓒ Ⓓ Ⓔ
98. Ⓐ Ⓑ Ⓒ Ⓓ Ⓔ
99. Ⓐ Ⓑ Ⓒ Ⓓ Ⓔ
100. Ⓐ Ⓑ Ⓒ Ⓓ Ⓔ
101. Ⓐ Ⓑ Ⓒ Ⓓ Ⓔ
102. Ⓐ Ⓑ Ⓒ Ⓓ Ⓔ

103. Ⓐ Ⓑ Ⓒ Ⓓ Ⓔ
104. Ⓐ Ⓑ Ⓒ Ⓓ Ⓔ
105. Ⓐ Ⓑ Ⓒ Ⓓ Ⓔ
106. Ⓐ Ⓑ Ⓒ Ⓓ Ⓔ
107. Ⓐ Ⓑ Ⓒ Ⓓ Ⓔ
108. Ⓐ Ⓑ Ⓒ Ⓓ Ⓔ
109. Ⓐ Ⓑ Ⓒ Ⓓ Ⓔ
110. Ⓐ Ⓑ Ⓒ Ⓓ Ⓔ

Section V — Writing Ability

111. Ⓐ Ⓑ Ⓒ Ⓓ Ⓔ
112. Ⓐ Ⓑ Ⓒ Ⓓ Ⓔ
113. Ⓐ Ⓑ Ⓒ Ⓓ Ⓔ
114. Ⓐ Ⓑ Ⓒ Ⓓ Ⓔ
115. Ⓐ Ⓑ Ⓒ Ⓓ Ⓔ
116. Ⓐ Ⓑ Ⓒ Ⓓ Ⓔ

117. Ⓐ Ⓑ Ⓒ Ⓓ Ⓔ
118. Ⓐ Ⓑ Ⓒ Ⓓ Ⓔ
119. Ⓐ Ⓑ Ⓒ Ⓓ Ⓔ
120. Ⓐ Ⓑ Ⓒ Ⓓ Ⓔ
121. Ⓐ Ⓑ Ⓒ Ⓓ Ⓔ
122. Ⓐ Ⓑ Ⓒ Ⓓ Ⓔ

123. Ⓐ Ⓑ Ⓒ Ⓓ Ⓔ
124. Ⓐ Ⓑ Ⓒ Ⓓ Ⓔ
125. Ⓐ Ⓑ Ⓒ Ⓓ Ⓔ
126. Ⓐ Ⓑ Ⓒ Ⓓ Ⓔ
127. Ⓐ Ⓑ Ⓒ Ⓓ Ⓔ
128. Ⓐ Ⓑ Ⓒ Ⓓ Ⓔ

129. Ⓐ Ⓑ Ⓒ Ⓓ Ⓔ
130. Ⓐ Ⓑ Ⓒ Ⓓ Ⓔ
131. Ⓐ Ⓑ Ⓒ Ⓓ Ⓔ
132. Ⓐ Ⓑ Ⓒ Ⓓ Ⓔ
133. Ⓐ Ⓑ Ⓒ Ⓓ Ⓔ
134. Ⓐ Ⓑ Ⓒ Ⓓ Ⓔ
135. Ⓐ Ⓑ Ⓒ Ⓓ Ⓔ

Section VI — Mathematics

136. Ⓐ Ⓑ Ⓒ Ⓓ Ⓔ
137. Ⓐ Ⓑ Ⓒ Ⓓ Ⓔ
138. Ⓐ Ⓑ Ⓒ Ⓓ Ⓔ
139. Ⓐ Ⓑ Ⓒ Ⓓ Ⓔ
140. Ⓐ Ⓑ Ⓒ Ⓓ Ⓔ
141. Ⓐ Ⓑ Ⓒ Ⓓ Ⓔ

142. Ⓐ Ⓑ Ⓒ Ⓓ Ⓔ
143. Ⓐ Ⓑ Ⓒ Ⓓ Ⓔ
144. Ⓐ Ⓑ Ⓒ Ⓓ Ⓔ
145. Ⓐ Ⓑ Ⓒ Ⓓ Ⓔ
146. Ⓐ Ⓑ Ⓒ Ⓓ Ⓔ
147. Ⓐ Ⓑ Ⓒ Ⓓ Ⓔ

148. Ⓐ Ⓑ Ⓒ Ⓓ Ⓔ
149. Ⓐ Ⓑ Ⓒ Ⓓ Ⓔ
150. Ⓐ Ⓑ Ⓒ Ⓓ Ⓔ
151. Ⓐ Ⓑ Ⓒ Ⓓ Ⓔ
152. Ⓐ Ⓑ Ⓒ Ⓓ Ⓔ
153. Ⓐ Ⓑ Ⓒ Ⓓ Ⓔ

154. Ⓐ Ⓑ Ⓒ Ⓓ Ⓔ
155. Ⓐ Ⓑ Ⓒ Ⓓ Ⓔ
156. Ⓐ Ⓑ Ⓒ Ⓓ Ⓔ
157. Ⓐ Ⓑ Ⓒ Ⓓ Ⓔ
158. Ⓐ Ⓑ Ⓒ Ⓓ Ⓔ
159. Ⓐ Ⓑ Ⓒ Ⓓ Ⓔ
160. Ⓐ Ⓑ Ⓒ Ⓓ Ⓔ

Section VII — Logical Reasoning

161. Ⓐ Ⓑ Ⓒ Ⓓ Ⓔ
162. Ⓐ Ⓑ Ⓒ Ⓓ Ⓔ
163. Ⓐ Ⓑ Ⓒ Ⓓ Ⓔ

164. Ⓐ Ⓑ Ⓒ Ⓓ Ⓔ
165. Ⓐ Ⓑ Ⓒ Ⓓ Ⓔ
166. Ⓐ Ⓑ Ⓒ Ⓓ Ⓔ
167. Ⓐ Ⓑ Ⓒ Ⓓ Ⓔ

168. Ⓐ Ⓑ Ⓒ Ⓓ Ⓔ
169. Ⓐ Ⓑ Ⓒ Ⓓ Ⓔ
170. Ⓐ Ⓑ Ⓒ Ⓓ Ⓔ
171. Ⓐ Ⓑ Ⓒ Ⓓ Ⓔ

172. Ⓐ Ⓑ Ⓒ Ⓓ Ⓔ
173. Ⓐ Ⓑ Ⓒ Ⓓ Ⓔ
174. Ⓐ Ⓑ Ⓒ Ⓓ Ⓔ
175. Ⓐ Ⓑ Ⓒ Ⓓ Ⓔ

THREE
GMAT DIAGNOSTIC TEST

Now that you have become familiar with the various types of questions appearing on the GMAT and have had a chance to sample each type, you probably have an idea of what to expect from an actual exam. The next step, then, is to take a sample test to see how you do.

The diagnostic test that follows has been designed to resemble the format of recent GMATs. When taking it, try to simulate actual test conditions as closely as possible. For example, you may want to time yourself as you work on each section so that you don't go over the allotted time limit for that section. After you have completed the test, check your answers and use the self-scoring chart to evaluate the results. Use these results to determine which review sections you should spend the most time studying before you attempt the 5 sample GMATs at the end of the book. To assist you in your review, all answers to mathematics questions are keyed so that you can easily refer to the section in the Mathematics Review that discusses the material covered in a particular question.

Diagnostic Test

Section I   Reading Recall

TIME: 30 minutes

DIRECTIONS: This part contains four reading passages. You are to read each one carefully. When answering the questions, you *will* be able to refer to the passages. The questions are based on what is *stated* or *implied* in each passage. You have thirty minutes to complete this section.

Passage 1:

In Aachen, Germany, and environs, many children have been found to have an unusually high lead content in their blood and hair. The amount of lead in the children tested has risen above the amount found in workers in heavy-metal industries. The general public is no longer surprised that the lead has been traced to Stol-
(5) berg near Aachen: Stolberg is surrounded by brass foundaries and slag heaps which supply building materials to construct schoolyards and sports halls.

This is but one example. In today's Europe, cancer stricken children outnumber adults with the disease. And in the United States cancer kills more children between the ages of one and four than any other disease.

(10)   When Dr. John W. Gofman, professor of medical physics at the University of California and a leading nuclear critic, speaks of "ecocide" in his adversary view of nuclear technology, he means the following: A large nuclear plant like that in Kalkar, the Netherlands, would produce about 200 pounds of plutonium each year. One pound, released into the atmosphere, could cause 9 billion cases of lung cancer.
(15) This waste product must be stored for 500,000 years before it is of no further danger to man. In the anticipated reactor economy, it is estimated that there will be 10,000 tons of this material in western Europe, of which one tablespoonful of plutonium-239 represents the official maximum permissible body burden for 200,000 people. Rather than being biodegradable, plutonium destroys biological properties.

(20)   In 1972 the U.S. Occupational Safety and Health Administration ruled that the asbestos level in the work place should be lowered to 2 fibers per cubic centimeter of air, but the effective date of the ruling has been delayed until now. The International Federation of Chemical and General Workers' Unions report that the 2 fiber standard was based primarily on one study of 290 men at a British asbestos factory.
(25) But when the workers at the British factory had been reexamined by another physician, 40–70 percent had x-ray evidence of lung abnormalities. According to present medical information at the factory in question, out of a total of 29 deaths thus far, seven were caused by lung cancer and three by mesothelima, a cancer of the lining of the chest-abdomen. An average European or American worker comes into con-
(30) tact with six million fibers a day. And when this man returns home at night, samples of this fireproof product are on his clothes, in his hair, in his lunchpail. "We are now, in fact, finding cancer deaths within the family of the asbestos worker," states Dr. Irving Salikoff, of the Mount Sinai Medical School in New York

It is now also clear that vinyl chloride, a gas from which the most widely used
(35) plastics are made, causes a fatal cancer of the blood-vessel cells of the liver. However, the history of the research on vinyl chloride is, in some ways, more disturbing than the "Watergate cover-up." "There has been evidence of potentially serious disease among polyvinyl chloride workers for 25 years that has been incompletely appreciated and inadequately approached by medical scientists and by regulatory
(40) authorities," summed up by Dr. Salikoff in the *New Scientist*. At least 17 workers have been killed by vinyl chloride because research over the past 25 years was not followed up. And for over 10 years, workers have been exposed to concentrations of vinyl chloride 10 times the "safe limit" imposed by Dow Chemical Company. In the United Kingdom, a threshold limit value was set after the discovery of the causal
(45) link with osteolysis, but the limit was still higher than that set by Dow Chemical. The Germans set a new maximum level in 1970, but also higher than that set by Dow. No other section of U.S. or European industry has followed Dow's lead.

1. Which of the following titles best describes the contents of the passage?

    (A) *The Problems of Nuclear Physics*
    (B) *Advanced Technology and Cancer*
    (C) *Occupational Diseases*
    (D) *Cancer in Germany*
    (E) *The Ecology of Cancer*

2. The author provides information that would answer which of the following questions?

    (A) What sort of legislation is needed to prevent cancer?
    (B) Should nuclear plants be built?
    (C) What are some causes of lung cancer?
    (D) What are the pros and cons of nuclear energy?
    (E) Which country has the lowest incidence of occupational disease?

3. According to the author, all the following are causes of lung cancer *except*

    (A) plutonium
    (B) asbestos
    (C) vinyl chloride
    (D) osteolysis
    (E) lead

4. The style of the passage is mainly

    (A) argumentative
    (B) emotional
    (C) factual
    (D) clinical
    (E) supportive

5. It can be inferred from the passage that

    (A) industrialization must be halted to prevent further spread of cancer-producing agents
    (B) only voluntary, industry-wide application of anti-pollution devices can halt cancer
    (C) workers are partly to blame for the spread of disease because of poor work habits
    (D) more research is needed into the causes of cancer before further progress can be made
    (E) tougher legislation is needed to set lower limits of worker exposure to harmful chemicals and fibers

6. Some workers have been killed by harmful pollutants because

    (A) they failed to take the required precautions and safety measures
    (B) not enough research has been undertaken to find solutions to the pollution problem
    (C) available research was not followed up
    (D) production cannot be halted
    (E) factory owners have failed to provide safety equipment

Passage 2:

   The Great Glen is a 100-mile-long rift valley stretching across the Scottish High-lands from the Moray Firth in the northeast to the Firth of Lorne in the southwest, thus forming a natural link between the North Sea and the Atlantic Ocean. It is the result of a sideways slippage of the earth, a northeast-southwest trending fault of the
(5) Caledonian mountain system. During the Ice Age, Scotland was literally shoved

down into the earth, and when the ice melted, the sea rose for a time, then ceased. But the land kept on rising, some 50 feet above sea level, sealing off bodies of water from the oceans and leaving bizarre, white beaches about the edges of medieval forestry.

(10)   Loch Ness, the largest freshwater lake in the British Isles and the third largest in Europe, is the principal basin of the Great Glen. It receives a quantum runoff from neighboring glens—Glen Affric, Glen Cannich, Glen Moriston, Glen Farrar, Glen Urquhart—so that the water level may rise as much as 24 inches in an hour. Any

(15) possible underground passage from the loch to the North Sea has long ago been dammed by some two miles of river-brought silt, thus changing the original sea loch into a fresh-water lake. It has no curving outlines made by an indented shore or shallow bays; but, instead, its riparian walls slice straight down, giving the appearance of an enormous ditch widening to 1.5 miles and extending approximately 23

(20) miles from Inverness in the North to Fort Augustus at the southern end, where the Caledonian Canal continues on into the Atlantic. Its depth exceeds 700 feet over much of its length, with the deepest point so far discovered of 975 feet. The loch never freezes and acts like an inland Gulf Stream on its immediate environs, giving off in winter a vast amount of heat collected in the summer months. The coldest

(25) water remains at a fairly constant 42 degrees, warm enough to provide a home for literally millions of migrating eels, which, according to ichthyologists, have made their home here instead of going to the sea. Along the rocky shoreline a reddish brown algae adheres to the stones, and in the shallows around the mouths of tributary rivers and burns is an abundance of freshwater weeds and organic detritus—all

(30) a possible food source for eels, brown trout, salmon, and sticklebacks. Hence, the biomass of the loch is thought sufficient to support a population of large animals.

The loch inherits its name from the Greek water goddess Nesa, whose spirit was thought to cause the many "unnatural" occurrences in the area. If "Ness" is given a feminine diminutive ending, it becomes "Nessie"—the sobriquet for the Loch Ness Monster. The scientific name of *Nessiteras rhombopteryx* has been applied to Nessie

(35) by Sir Peter Scott, head of the world Wildlife Foundation and chancellor of Birmingham University. The word *Nessiteras* combines the name of the loch with the Greek word *teras*, genitive of *teratos*, which means a "marvel or wonder . . . arousing awe, amazement, and often fear." The word *rhombopteryx* is a combination of

(40) the Greek *rhombos*, meaning a diamond or rhomboid shape, and the Greek *pteryx*, meaning fin or wing. The name does not link the species to any animal or group of animals known to science but applies specifically to the creature first recorded by St. Columba in 565 A.D. From a zoological point of view, to base a name on photographs rather than the remains of an animal is quite unsatisfactory, however justi-

(45) fied by the urgency to protect an endangered species and therefore permitted by the International Code of Zoological Nomenclature.

In 1933 dynamite charges shook the loch-side, tumbling boulders, tree limbs, earth, and scree into the lake. For a year the blasting intermittently continued as steam shovels chuffed and gnawed their way through the forest, gradually surround-

(50) ing the once tranquil shoreline with the fresh macadam of a scenic highway. Such violent activity sent reverberations down through the waters beneath Fort Augustus, down into the deep holes off Urquhart Bay, and down into the shallows around Dores, Foyers, and Invermoriston. After the day's work a quietude descended, but only for an uncertain time. Then something that looked like a hump of sorts, per-

(55) haps only a wave or floating log (surely one that had been blasted that morning) or an upturned boat, would appear, drift, and disappear beneath a gibbous moon.

7. It can be assumed from the passage that the Loch Ness "monster" was thought to have been

   (A) observed in 1933
   (B) observed in 565 A.D.
   (C) created during the ice age
   (D) fabricated during the Middle Ages
   (E) fabricated in Greek mythology

8. Evidence supporting the Loch Ness "monster" hypothesis—as implied in the passage —is best exemplified by which of the following?

   (A) photographs taken of the creature
   (B) the lake's organic contents which are suitable for such animals
   (C) a mild water temperature
   (D) observations by zoologists
   (E) none of the above

9. According to the passage, the surface area of Loch Ness is

   (A) 700 square miles
   (B) 800 square miles
   (C) 975 square miles
   (D) 2000 square miles
   (E) none of the above

10. The author is mainly concerned with

    (A) debunking the idea of a sea monster
    (B) describing the origins of Loch Ness
    (C) providing evidence of a sea monster
    (D) Greek mythology
    (E) Scottish glens

11. When the author uses the word *ichthyologists* in line 26, he is referring to

    (A) a Scottish clan
    (B) zoologists who study fish
    (C) conservationists
    (D) wildlife experts
    (E) geologists

12. Which of the following can be inferred from the passage?

    (A) Loch Ness is a popular tourist resort.
    (B) Scotland's climate is very harsh.
    (C) dynamite charges sealed off Noch Ness from the sea.
    (D) the inhabitants of Loch Ness are endangered species and protected by law.
    (E) none of the above can be inferred.

Passage 3:

It is easy to accept Freud as an applied scientist, and, indeed he is widely regarded as the twentieth century's master clinician. However, in viewing Marx as an applied social scientist the stance needed is that of a Machiavellian operationalism. The ob-

jective is neither to bury nor to praise him. The assumption is simply that he is bet-
(5) ter understood for being understood as an applied sociologist. This is in part the
clear implication of Marx's *Theses on Feurbach*, which culminate in the resounding
11th thesis: "The philosophers have only interpreted the world in different ways;
the point, however, is to change it." This would seem to be the tacit creed of applied
scientists everywhere.

(10)   Marx is no Faustian, concerned solely with understanding society, but a Prome-
thean who sought to understand it well enough to influence and to change it. He was
centrally concerned with the social problems of a lay group, the proletariat, and
there can be little doubt that his work is motivated by an effort to reduce their suffering, as he saw it. His diagnosis was that their increasing misery and alienation
(15) engendered endemic class struggle; his prognosis claimed that this would culminate
in revolution; his therapeutic prescription was class consciousness and active struggle.

Here, as in assessing Durkheim or Freud, the issue is not in whether this analysis
is empirically correct or scientifically adequate. Furthermore, whether or not this
formulation seems to eviscerate Marx's revolutionary core, as critics on the left may
(20) charge, or whether the formulation provides Marx with a new veneer of academic
respectability, as critics on the right may allege, is entirely irrelevant from the present standpoint. Insofar as Marx's or any other social scientist's work conforms to a
generalized model of applied social science, insofar as it is professionally oriented
to the values and social problems of laymen in his society, he may be treated as an
(25) applied social scientist.

Despite Durkheim's intellectualistic proclivities and rationalistic pathos, he was
too much the product of European turbulence to turn his back on the travail of his
culture. "Why strive for knowledge of reality, if this knowledge cannot aid us in
life," he asked. "Social science," he said, "can provide us with rules of action for the
(30) future." Durkheim, like Marx, conceived of science as an agency of social action,
and like him was professionally oriented to the values and problems of laymen in
his society. Unless one sees that Durkheim was in some part an applied social scientist, it is impossible to understand why he concludes his monumental study of
Suicide with a chapter on "Practical Consequences," and why, in the *Division of*
(35) *Labor*, he proposes a specific remedy for anomie.

Durkheim is today widely regarded as a model of theoretic and methodologic sophistication, and is thus usually seen only in his capacity as a pure social scientist.
Surely this is an incomplete view of the man who regarded the *practical* effectiveness of a science as its principal justification. To be more fully understood, Durk-
(40) heim also needs to be seen as an applied sociologist. His interest in religious beliefs
and organization, in crime and penology, in educational methods and organization,
in suicide and anomie, are not casually chosen problem areas. Nor did he select
them only because they provided occasions for the development of his theoretical
orientation. These areas were in his time, as they are today, problems of indigenous
(45) interest to applied sociologists in Western society, precisely because of their practical significance.

13. Which of the following best describes the author's conception of an applied social
scientist?

(A) a professional who listens to people's problems
(B) a professional who seeks social action and change
(C) a student of society
(D) a proponent of class struggle
(E) none of the above

14. According to the author, which of the folowing did Marx and Durkheim have in common?

    (A) a belief in the importance of class struggle
    (B) a desire to create a system of social organization
    (C) an interest in penology
    (D) regard for the practical application of science
    (E) a sense of the political organization of society

15. It may be inferred from the passage that the applied social scientist would be interested in all of the following subjects *except*

    (A) the theory of mechanics
    (B) how to make workers more efficient
    (C) rehabilitation of juvenile delinquents
    (D) reduction of social tensions
    (E) industrial safety

16. According to the passage, applied social science can be distinguished from pure social science by which of the following characteristics?

    (A) practical significance
    (B) universal application
    (C) cultural pluralism
    (D) objectivity
    (E) none of the above

17. Which of the following best summarizes the author's main point?

    (A) Marx and Durkheim were similar in their thoughts.
    (B) Freud, Marx and Durkheim were social scientists.
    (C) philosophers (among others) who are regarded as theoreticians, can also be regarded as empiricists.
    (D) Marx and Durkheim were in reality social scientists because they were concerned with the solution of social problems.
    (E) pure and applied sciences have the same objectives.

18. Marx, mentioned in the passage, is best known for his treatise on

    (A) philosophy
    (B) political economy
    (C) music
    (D) art
    (E) sociology

Passage 4:

    Morally and culturally, American society as reflected in our TV programs, our theatrical fare, our literature and art appears to have hit bottom.
    Gen. David Sarnoff felt prompted to issue a statement in defense of the TV industry. He pointed out that there was much good in its programs that was being
(5) overlooked while its occasional derelictions were being overly stressed. It struck me that what he was saying about TV applied to other aspects of American culture as well, particularly to the theatrical productions.

Without necessarily resting on his conviction that the good outweighed the bad in American cultural activity, I saw further implications in Gen. Sarnoff's declaration. (10) Audiences needed to be sensitized more and more to the positive qualities of the entertainment and cultural media. In addition, through such increased public sensitivity producers would be encouraged to provide ever more of the fine, and less of the sordid.

Here is where questions arise. If the exemplary aspects of TV are not being rec-(15) ognized, what is the reason for such a lack of appreciation? Similarly, and further, if the theatre, including in this term the legitimate stage, on and off Broadway as well as the moving pictures, has large measures of goodness, truth and beauty which are unappreciated, how are we to change this situation?

All in all, what should be done to encourage and condone the good, and to dis-(20) courage and condemn the unsavory in the American cultural pattern?

These are serious and pressing questions—serious for the survival of the American Way of Life, and pressing for immediate and adequate answers. Indeed the simple truth is that the face that America shows the world affects seriously the future of democracy all over the globe.

(25) Since the theatre in its broadest sense is a large aspect of American culture—its expression as well as its creation—I saw the urgent importance of bringing the worthwhile elements in the American Theatre to the fore. Especially was this importance impressed on me when I realized how much Hollywood was involved in exporting American life to the world, and how much Broadway with all its theatres (30) meant to the modern drama.

Then the thought of the Bible came to me in this connection. Was not the Bible the basis of Western civilization as far as morals are concerned? Why not use the Bible as guide and touchstone, as direction and goal in the matter of the cultural achievements of Western society? Thus was born "The Bible on Broadway."

(35) The birth of the idea accomplished, rearing it brought the usual difficulties of raising a child—albeit in this case a "brain" one. There was first the fact that the Bible, although the world's best seller, is not the world's best read book. Second was the current impression that "message-plays" must necessarily be dull and unpopular. What a combination! The Bible unknown, and Broadway (in the sense of (40) theatre with an idea) unpopular!

Still, I was drawn to the project of a series of lectures on the Bible and the contemporary theatre. What if the Bible is not well known? Teach it! Plays with a dull message? All plays by reason of their being works of art have been created by their authors' selection and ordering of experience. As such, plays are proponents of (45) ideas— and certainly they are not meant to be uninteresting.

Thus fortified, I turned to the subject of the Bible and the contemporary theatre and found it indeed appealing and full of interesting nuances.

That there are spiritual, even religious ideas, in the contemporary theatre should be no cause for wonderment. It is well known that the drama had its origin in re-(50) ligion. The Greeks, the Romans, as well as the early Hebrews, all had forms of the drama which among the first two developed into our classical plays.

In the Middle Ages, it was the Church in the Western World that produced the morality and mystery plays. With such a long history it is not surprising to find an affinity between the Bible and the Theatre.

19. The author is primarily concerned with
    (A) the declining pattern of morality in America
    (B) promoting American theatre
    (C) how the Bible illuminates contemporary theatre
    (D) comparing the theatre with other art forms
    (E) preserving the "American Way of Life"

20. With which of the following statements regarding the theatre would the author most likely agree?
    (A) The theatre does not reflect American culture.
    (B) Critics of American cultural life are biased.
    (C) While entertainment media can be criticized, they contain much wholesome material.
    (D) The advertising media are largely to blame for criticisms leveled at the theatre.
    (E) The Bible should be used as a source for entertainment ideas.

21. Which of the following statements best reflects the author's own ideas?

    (A) American art forms have degenerated to a new low.
    (B) The good outweighs the bad in American cultural activity.
    (C) American culture has positive content, but it is not appreciated by the public.
    (D) Only the Biblical content of American theatre has positive meaning.
    (E) American theatre is currently dull and unpopular.

22. The author implies that he will deal with which of the following questions?

    I.   What is the reason for the lack of appreciation of the theatre?
    II. To what extent have Bible themes been used in or influenced American theatrical productions?
    III. What should be done to encourage the good in American culture?

    (A) I only
    (B) II only
    (C) I and II only
    (D) I and III only
    (E) I, II and III

23. It can be inferred from the passage that the author's background might be in all of the following occupations *except*

    (A) theologian
    (B) thespian
    (C) obstreperous
    (D) writer
    (E) interlocutor

24. The author implies that if the public is made aware of the positive qualities of American entertainment, it will

  I. demand more high quality entertainment
  II. demand less base quality entertainment
  III. attend programs more often

  (A) I only
  (B) II only
  (C) I and II only
  (D) I and III only
  (E) I, II and III

25. When the author uses the expression the "Bible as guide and touchstone" in line 33, he probably means

  (A) the interrelationship of the Bible and the "American Way of Life"
  (B) an academic approach to researching the theatre and religion
  (C) the relationship of Biblical concepts to basic ideas and values contained in theatrical productions
  (D) the use of the Bible as a guide to everyday life
  (E) the Bible as a source of inspiration for all

If there is still time remaining, you may review the questions in this section only.
You may not turn to any other section of the test.

Section II Mathematics

DIRECTIONS: Solve each of the following problems; then indicate the correct answer on the answer sheet. [On the actual test you will be permitted to use any space available on the examination paper for scratch work.]

NOTE: A figure that appears with a problem is drawn as accurately as possible so as to provide information that may help in answering the question. Numbers in this test are real numbers.

TIME: 40 minutes

26. If the length of a rectangle is increased by 20% and the width is decreased by 20%, then the area

(A) decreases by 20%
(B) decreases by 4%
(C) stays the same
(D) increases by 10%
(E) increases by 20%

27. If it is 250 miles from New York to Boston and 120 miles from New York to Hartford, what percentage of the distance from New York to Boston is the distance from New York to Hartford?

(A) 12
(B) 24
(C) 36
(D) 48
(E) 52

28. The lead in a mechanical pencil is 5 inches long. After pieces $\frac{1}{8}$ of an inch long, $1\frac{3}{4}$ inches long, and $1\frac{1}{12}$ inches long are broken off, how long is the lead left in the pencil?

(A) 2 in.
(B) $2\frac{1}{24}$ in.
(C) $2\frac{1}{12}$ in.
(D) $2\frac{1}{4}$ in.
(E) $2\frac{1}{2}$ in.

29. It costs $1.00 each to make the first thousand copies of a record and it costs x dollars to make each subsequent copy. How many dollars will it cost to make 4800 copies of a record?

(A) 1,000
(B) 4800
(C) $4800x$
(D) $1000x + 3800$
(E) $1,000 + 3800x$

30. If a worker makes 4 boxes of labels in $1\frac{2}{3}$ hours, how many boxes of labels can he make in 50 minutes?

(A) 2
(B) $2\frac{1}{3}$
(C) $2\frac{2}{3}$
(D) $2\frac{5}{6}$
(E) 3

31. If $x + y = 3$ and $y/x = 2$, then y is equal to

(A) 0
(B) $\frac{1}{2}$
(C) 1
(D) $\frac{3}{2}$
(E) 2

32. A store buys paper towels for $9.00 a carton, each carton containing 20 rolls. The store sells a roll of paper towels for 50¢. About what percent of the cost is the selling price of a roll of paper towels?

(A) 11
(B) 89
(C) 100
(D) 111
(E) 119

33. A history book weighs 2.4 pounds. 12 copies of the history book and 8 copies of an English book together weigh 42.8 pounds. How much will one copy of the English book weigh?

(A) 1 pound
(B) 1.4 pounds
(C) 1.75 pounds
(D) 2.88 pounds
(E) 14 pounds

34. A car goes 15 miles on a gallon of gas when it is driven at 50 miles per hour. When the car is driven at 60 miles per hour it only goes 80% as far. How far will it travel on a gallon of gas at 60 miles per hour?

(A) 12 miles
(B) 13.5 miles
(C) 16.5 miles
(D) 18.75 miles
(E) 20 miles

35. If $x + y = z$ and x and y are positive, then which of the following statements can be inferred?

I. $x < y$
II. $x < z$
III. $x < 2z$

(A) I only
(B) II only
(C) I and III only
(D) II and III only
(E) I, II, and III

36. If it costs x cents to produce a single sheet of paper for the first 800 sheets and if every subsequent sheet costs $x/15$ cents, how much will it cost to produce 5,000 sheets of paper?

(A) 800x¢
(B) 1,080x¢
(C) 1,400x¢
(D) 2,430x¢
(E) 3,500x¢

37. If in 1967, 1968, and 1969 a worker received 10% more in salary each year than he did the previous year, how much more did he receive in 1969 than in 1967?

    (A) 10%
    (B) 12%
    (C) 19%
    (D) 20%
    (E) 21%

38. If factory A turns out a cars an hour and factory B turns out b cars every 2 hours, how many cars will both factories turn out in 8 hours?

    (A) $a + b$
    (B) $8a$
    (C) $8b$
    (D) $8a + 4b$
    (E) $8a + 8b$

39. If John makes a box every 5 minutes and Tim takes 7 minutes to make a box, what will be the ratio of the number of boxes produced by John to the number of boxes produced by Tim if they work 5 hours and 50 minutes?

    (A) 5 to 6
    (B) 5 to 7
    (C) 6 to 5
    (D) 7 to 5
    (E) 2 to 1

40. If a store sells $3\frac{1}{4}$ crates of lettuce on Monday, $2\frac{1}{6}$ on Tuesday, $4\frac{1}{2}$ on Wednesday, and $1\frac{2}{3}$ on Thursday, how many crates has the store sold altogether?

    (A) 10
    (B) $11\frac{1}{2}$
    (C) $11\frac{7}{12}$
    (D) $11\frac{3}{4}$
    (E) $12\frac{1}{3}$

41. If $x + y > 4$ and $x < 3$, then $y > 1$ is true

    (A) always
    (B) only if $x < 0$
    (C) only if $x > 0$
    (D) only if $x = 0$
    (E) never

42. If 50 apprentices can finish a job in 4 hours and 30 journeymen can finish the same job in $4\frac{1}{2}$ hours, how much of the job should be completed by 10 apprentices and 15 journeymen in one hour?

    (A) $\frac{1}{9}$
    (B) $\frac{29}{180}$
    (C) $\frac{26}{143}$
    (D) $\frac{1}{5}$
    (E) $\frac{39}{121}$

43. If 40% of all women are voters and 52% of the population are women, what percent of the population are women voters?

    (A) 18.1
    (B) 20.8
    (C) 26.4
    (D) 40
    (E) 52

44. If a bus can travel 15 miles on a gallon of gas, how many gallons of gas will it use to travel 200 miles?

(A) 10

(B) $12\frac{1}{2}$

(C) $13\frac{1}{3}$

(D) 15

(E) $20\frac{1}{5}$

45. A tank contains 10 gallons of water. If a pump takes $15 - \frac{x}{10}$ minutes to pump one gallon of water out of the tank, how many minutes will it take for the pump to empty the tank?

(A) x

(B) $15 - 10x$

(C) $150 - 10x$

(D) $150 - x$

(E) $15 - 10x$

46. A company makes a profit of 6% on its first $1,000 of sales each day, and 5% on all sales in excess of $1,000 for that day. How many dollars in profit will the company make in a day when sales are $6,000?

(A) $250

(B) $300

(C) $310

(D) $320

(E) $360

47. If 15 men working independently and at the same rate can manufacture 27 baskets in an hour, how many baskets would 45 men working independently and at the same rate manufacture in 40 minutes?

(A) 27

(B) 35

(C) 40

(D) 54

(E) 81

48. If one elevator can lift 2 tons in 5 minutes and another elevator can lift 3 tons in 7 minutes, how many minutes will it take to lift 20 tons using both elevators?

(A) 12

(B) $16\frac{4}{7}$

(C) $18\frac{3}{26}$

(D) 21

(E) $24\frac{4}{29}$

49. A field is rectangular and its width is $\frac{1}{3}$ as long as its length. What is the area of the field if the length of the field is 120 yards?

(A) 480 square yards

(B) 2,400 square yards

(C) 4,800 square yards

(D) 5,000 square yards

(E) 7,200 square yards

50. If the price of steak is currently $1.00 a pound, and the price triples every 6 months, how long will it be until the price of steak is $81.00 a pound?

(A) 1 year
(B) 2 years
(C) 2 ½ years

(D) 13 years
(E) 13 ½ years

51. If $\frac{x}{y} = \frac{2}{3}$, then $\frac{y^2}{x^2}$ is

(A) $\frac{4}{9}$

(B) $\frac{2}{3}$

(C) $\frac{3}{2}$

(D) $\frac{9}{4}$

(E) $\frac{5}{2}$

52. The entry following a_n in a sequence is determined by the rule $(a_n-1)^2$. If 1 is an entry in the sequence the next three entries are

(A) 0, −1, 2
(B) 0, −1, 1
(C) 0, 1, 2

(D) 2, 3, 4
(E) 0, 1, 0

53. An employer pays 3 workers X, Y, and Z a total of $610 a week. X is paid 125% of the amount Y is paid and 80% of the amount Z is paid. How much does X make a week?

(A) $150
(B) $175
(C) $180

(D) $195
(E) $200

54. What is the maximum number of points of intersection of two circles which have unequal radii?

(A) none
(B) 1
(C) 2

(D) 3
(E) infinite

55. If the area of a rectangle is equal to the area of a square, then the perimeter of the rectangle

(A) is ½ the perimeter of the square
(B) equal to the perimeter of the square
(C) equal to twice the perimeter of the square
(D) equal to the square root of the perimeter of the square
(E) none of the above

If there is still time remaining, you may review the questions in this section only.
You may not turn to any other section of the test.

Section III   Business Judgment

TIME: 20 minutes

DIRECTIONS: Read the following two passages. After you have completed each of them you will be asked to answer two sets of questions. The first of these, data evaluation, involves determining the importance of specific factors included in the passage. The second, data application, consists of general questions relating to the passage. When answering questions, you may consult the passage.

Passage 1:

The unclear economic situation into which the economy of this developing country has drifted has caused considerable uneasiness to both local industrialists and their employees, and to present and potential foreign investors. The seemingly firm course set by the now nearly defunct price-wage-tax restraint has faltered. As a result, the ABC Corporation was reconsidering its previous plans to invest in the country. Its management cited some of the following reasons for its decision to reevaluate its investment plans.

The chain of events which started with the government's apparent decision on a policy of economic slowdown via an increase of taxes has resulted in an unprecedented wave of price rises in the form of an additional cost of living allowance. That the business community will not accede to these requests has been hinted at by the Manufacturer's Association.

Compounding the current situation is the perennial tightness of capital and the galloping interest rates, which are from 17 to 18 percent; though "regular" clients can receive credit at 15 to 15 ½ percent.

One positive result of all of this may be an increase in the relative profitability of exports which are heavily supported by the government. Efforts to increase exports and foreign investments are in full swing as the various committees of the Investment Board bring their influence to bear. Nevertheless, foreign investors have proved cautious at this stage and are not rushing to transfer dollars to this country while the economic situation still seeks direction.

Some firm helmsmanship is required at this juncture on the part of government leaders, who must guide both industry and labor into an era of social peace and economic development. At the same time they seek a solution to the many economic and social problems facing the country.

Data Evaluation Questions

DIRECTIONS: Evaluate each of the following factors used in decision-making which relate to the passage you have just read by selecting

- (A)   for a *Major Objective*—the result desired by the executive;

- (B)   for a *Major Factor*—a primary consideration, spelled out in the passage, that influences the decision;

- (C)   for a *Minor Factor*—a less important consideration in the decision;

- (D)   for a *Major Assumption*—a conclusion reached by the executive not necessarily supported by the factors present;

- (E)   for an *Unimportant Issue*—a consideration not directly related to the problem.

56. Poor economic situation

57. ABC Corporation's investment plans

58. Economic slowdown

59. Foreign companies are reluctant to invest

60. Government efforts to increase foreign investment

61. Cost of living allowance

Data Application Questions

DIRECTIONS: Answer each of the following questions using information contained in the passage.

62. The economic slowdown was caused by

   I.   A lack of foreign investment
  II.   Militant labor unions
 III.   Government economic policy

  (A) I only
  (B) III only
  (C) I and II only
  (D) II and III only
  (E) I, II and III

63. Despite the economic situation, the government

   I.   Remained optimistic
  II.   Continued to waste capital
 III.   Encouraged foreign investment

  (A) I only
  (B) III only
  (C) I and II only
  (D) II and III only
  (E) I, II, and III

64. The government's economic policy had resulted in increased

   I.   Taxes
  II.   Prices
 III.   Investment

  (A) I only
  (B) III only
  (C) I and II only
  (D) II and III only
  (E) I, II, and III

65. A positive result of the government's economic policy was an increase in

   I. Wages
   II. Foreign investment
   III. Relative profitability of exports

   (A) I only
   (B) III only
   (C) I and II only
   (D) II and III only
   (E) I, II, and III

66. The additional cost of living allowance resulted in

   I. Inflation
   II. Lower wages
   III. Social unrest

   (A) I only
   (B) III only
   (C) I and II only
   (D) II and III only
   (E) I, II, and III

67. The government's economic policy may not be accepted by

   I. The Manufacturer's Association
   II. Foreign investors
   III. The Investment Board

   (A) I only
   (B) III only
   (C) I and II only
   (D) II and III only
   (E) I, II, and III

Passage 2:

The home office of the Hiram Insurance Company was divided into several departments, each consisting of over 200 persons. This problem concerns Department K, which employs mostly skilled men.

Almost every man within the department works without direct supervision, although each is under the general supervision of a section head. Each employee has definite duties to perform and definite lines of responsibility. These duties do not necessarily follow any definite sequence throughout the day, although the work must be completed on schedule.

The head of Department K retired, and no qualified successor was available in the department. Finally the management hired a man from another company. This man had satisfactory over-all qualifications, but his experience was in a position which was different from the one to which he was appointed. In general, the employees opposed selection of the new department head, because they felt some of their own number were qualified.

Shortly after becoming head of the department, the new executive issued a directive through his assistant that effective immediately each employee within the department would account for his time hour for hour throughout the working day. Each person would give this time report to his section head, who would in turn send a report to the department head.

The reaction was immediate and negative. A majority of the working force were intelligent men of high caliber who had been with the Hiram Insurance Company from ten to thirty years. Their judgment on utilization of time during the day had seldom before been questioned. The younger employees and those who had been with the organization only a short time took the attitude, "I will not observe the directive. I will resign first." The older men, and those who had only a few years until retirement, took a strongly negative attitude toward the directive, refusing to accept it for its apparent lack of reason. They argued that they never had reported their time, that other departments did not now have to report time, and that Department K would not become an exception to the rule.

The section heads had no recourse other than to report to the new department head that the men refused to co-operate with the directive. The department head threatened to tender his resignation to his superior, the vice-president, effective at once.

The president of the Hiram Insurance Company received word of the trouble from the vice-president. The president immediately intervened and supposedly settled the matter by soothing hot tempers with a diplomatic speech to the section heads. He then dropped the matter completely. The department head felt then that he was left with no recourse but to require compliance with his directive. Many employees still did not report their time, and their section heads asked the department head what should be done.

Data Evaluation Questions

DIRECTIONS: Evaluate each of the following factors used in decision-making which relate to the passage you have just read by selecting

- (A) for a *Major Objective*—the result desired by the executive;
- (B) for a *Major Factor*—a primary consideration, spelled out in the passage, that influences the decision;
- (C) for a *Minor Factor*—a less important consideration in the decision;
- (D) for a *Major Assumption*—a conclusion reached by the executive not necessarily supported by the factors present;
- (E) for an *Unimportant Issue*—a consideration not directly related to the problem.

68. Department K head and subordinate relations

69. The work force was of high caliber

70. The company has several departments

71. Employees have no direct supervision

72. The head of Department K retired

73. Department K employs 200 people

Data Application Questions

DIRECTIONS: Answer each of the following questions using information contained in the passage.

74. According to the passage, which of the following employees threatened to resign?

    I. The new department head
    II. Section heads
    III. The vice-president

    (A) I only
    (B) III only
    (C) I and II only
    (D) II and III only
    (E) I, II, and III

75. A new department head was needed because the previous one

    I. Was fired
    II. Was promoted
    III. Retired

    (A) I only
    (B) III only
    (C) I and II only
    (D) II and III only
    (E) I, II, and III

76. The president's talk to section heads

    I. Solved the company's problem
    II. Soothed "hot tempers"
    III. Delayed a solution

    (A) I only
    (B) III only
    (C) I and II only
    (D) II and III only
    (E) I, II, and III

77. Department K personnel refused to accept time reports because

    I.   They resented the new department head
    II. Other departments did not have time reports
   III. They never had to report time before

    (A) I only
    (B) III only
    (C) I and II only
    (D) II and III only
    (E) I, II, and III

78. It can be inferred from the passage that the department head's difficulties with his subordinates was due to

    I.   A lack of communication
    II. His promotion from outside the company
   III. His poor mannerisms

    (A) I only
    (B) III only
    (C) I and II only
    (D) II and III only
    (E) I, II, and III

79. The new executive demanded that time sheets be sent to the

    I.   Company president
    II. Section head
   III. Department head

    (A) I only
    (B) III only
    (C) I and II only
    (D) II and III only
    (E) I, II, and III

80. The new department head was hired from outside the company because

    I.   He had held a similar position in another company
    II. He had previously worked for an insurance company
   III. No qualified personnel existed in the department

    (A) I only
    (B) III only
    (C) I and II only
    (D) II and III only
    (E) I, II, and III

Section IV Data Sufficiency

TIME: 30 minutes

DIRECTIONS: Each of the following problems has a question and two statements which are labeled (1) and (2). Use the data given in (1) and (2) together with other available information (such as the number of hours in a day, the definition of *clockwise*, mathematical facts, etc.) to decide whether the statements are *sufficient* to answer the question. Then fill in space

(A) if you can get the answer from (1) alone but not from (2) alone;

(B) if you can get the answer from (2) alone but not from (1) alone;

(C) if you can get the answer from (1) and (2) together, although neither statement by itself suffices;

(D) if statement (1) alone suffices *and* statement (2) alone suffices;

(E) if you cannot get the answer from statements (1) and (2) together, but need even more data.

All numbers used in this section are real numbers. A figure given for a problem is intended to provide information consistent with that in the question, but not necessarily with the additional information contained in the statements.

81. A piece of wood 5 feet long is cut into three smaller pieces. How long is the longest of the three pieces?

(1) One piece is 2 feet, 7 inches long.
(2) One piece is 7 inches longer than another piece and the third piece is 5 inches long.

82. *AC* is a diameter of the circle. *ACD* is a straight line. What is the value of *x*?

(1) $AB = BC$
(2) $x = 2y$

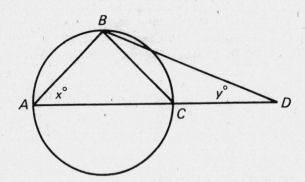

83. What is the value of *y*?

(1) $x + 2y = 6$
(2) $y^2 - 2y + 1 = 0$

84. Two pipes, A and B, empty into a reservoir. Pipe A can fill the reservoir in 30 minutes by itself. How long will it take for pipe A and pipe B together to fill up the reservoir.

(1) By itself, pipe B can fill the reservoir in 20 minutes.
(2) Pipe B has a larger cross-sectional area than pipe A.

85. AB is perpendicular to CO. Is A or B closer to C?

(1) OA is less than OB.
(2) $ACBD$ is not a parallelogram.

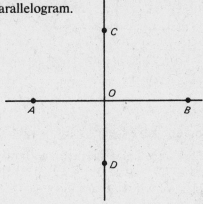

86. Is xy greater than 1? x and y are both positive.

(1) x is less than 1.
(2) y is greater than 1.

87. Does $x = y$?

(1) $z = u$
(2) $ABCD$ is a parallelogram.

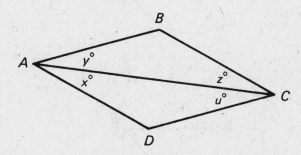

88. Train T leaves town A for town B and travels at a constant rate of speed. At the same time train S leaves town B for town A and also travels at a constant rate of speed. Town C is between A and B. Which train is traveling faster?

(1) Train S arrives at town C before train T.
(2) C is closer to A than to B

89. Does $x = y$?

    (1) BD is perpendicular to AC.
    (2) AB is equal to BC.

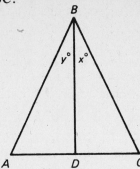

90. What is the value of $x + y$?

    (1) $x - y = 4$
    (2) $3x + 3y = 4$

91. Did the *XYZ* Corporation have higher sales in 1968 or in 1969?

    (1) In 1968 the sales were twice the average (arithmetic mean) of the sales in 1968, 1969, and 1970.
    (2) In 1970, the sales were three times those in 1969.

92. *AB* and *CD* are both chords of the circle with center *O*. Which is longer, *AB* or *CD*?

    (1) Arc *AEB* is smaller than arc *CFD*.
    (2) The area of the circular segment *CAEBD* is larger than the area of circular segment *ACFDB*.

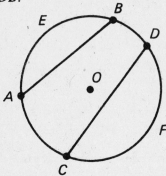

93. Is *ABCD* a square?

    (1) BC is perpendicular to AD.
    (2) $BE = EC$.

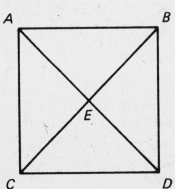

94. *k* is an integer. Is *k* divisible by 12?

  (1) *k* is divisible by 4.
  (2) *k* is divisible by 3.

95. How far is it from *A* to *B?*

  (1) It is 15 miles from *A* to *C*.
  (2) It is 25 miles from *C* to *B*.

96. Was Melissa Brown's novel published?

  (1) If Melissa Brown's novel was published she would receive at least $1,000 in royalties during 1978.
  (2) Melissa Brown's income for 1978 was over $1,000.

97. Is *x* an even integer? Assume *n* and *p* are integers.

  (1) $x = (n+p)^2$
  (2) $x = 2n+10p$

98. Did the price of lumber rise by more than 10% last year?

  (1) Lumber exports increased by 20%.
  (2) The amount of timber cut decreased by 10%.

99. Find the value of *z* if $x = 3$.

  (1) $z = (x + 3)^4$
  (2) $z = 2x + y$

100. What was the price of a dozen eggs during the 15th week of the year 1977?

  (1) During the first week of 1977 the price of a dozen eggs was 75¢.
  (2) The price of a dozen eggs rose 1¢ a week every week during the first four months of 1977.

101. Is *DE* parallel to *BC? DB = AD*.

  (1) $AE = EC$
  (2) $DB = EC$

102. There are two drains in the bottom of a water tank. If drain 1 is opened and drain 2 is closed a full tank will be empty in 15 minutes. How long will it take to empty a full tank if drain 1 and drain 2 are both opened?

  (1) If drain 1 is closed and drain 2 is opened it takes 20 minutes to empty a full tank.
  (2) In 3 minutes as much water flows through drain 1 as flows through drain 2 in 4 minutes.

103. Is $x > y$?

  (1) $\dfrac{x}{y} = \dfrac{5}{4}$
  (2) $x^2 > y^2$

104. Does every bird fly?

(1) Tigers do not fly.
(2) Ostriches do not fly.

105. Find $x + 2y$.

(1) $x - y = 12$
(2) $3x - 3y = 36$

106. Did the price of energy rise last year?

(1) If the price of energy rose last year then the price of food would rise this year.
(2) The price of food rose this year.

107. How much was a certain Rembrandt painting worth in Jan. 1971?

(1) In Jan. 1977 the painting was worth $2,000,000.
(2) Over the ten years 1968–1977 the painting increased in value by 10% each year.

108. A sequence of numbers a_1, a_2, a_3, . . . is given by the rule $a_n^2 = a_{n+1}$. Does 3 appear in the sequence?

(1) $a_1 = 2$
(2) $a_5 = 32$

109. Is AB greater than AC?

(1) $z > x$
(2) $AC > AD$

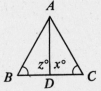

110. x and y are integers that are both less than 10. Is x greater than y?

(1) x is a multiple of 3.
(2) y is a multiple of 2.

If there is still time remaining, you may review the questions in this section only.
You may not turn to any other section of the test.

Section V Writing Ability

TIME: 30 minutes

DIRECTIONS: The following section contains a number of sentences with four *underlined* words or phrases. These sentences may have errors in grammar, tense, usage, diction (choice of words), idiom or structure. Choose the one *underlined* word or phrase that must be changed to make the sentence correct (for standard written English), and blacken the space provided to the right of the question. If you find no mistakes in a sentence, mark space E for *No error*; no sentence will contain more than one error. Note: Assume that all parts of the sentence that are not underlined are correct and cannot be changed.

111. The negotiators were enthused about the good prospects for peace. No error
      A   B   C   D   E

112. The tasks of the director are greater than the manager. No error
      A   B   C   D   E

113. The boy did not want to get off of the fence. No error
              A   B   C D   E

114. The pianist is a person with great promise and who should be encouraged. No error
                  A   B   C   D   E

115. An outstanding characteristic of each student, was their ability to complete the
                                      A   B   C
      exam on time. No error
           D   E

116. After he found a campsite, a bear followed Paul into the woods. No error
            A   B   C   D   E

117. If I would have arrived sooner, I would not have missed the fun. No error
         A   B   C   D   E

118. Our department was monitored by three supervisors, Sam, Bill and I. No error
      A   B   C D   E

119. The risks to the workers in contracting work-related diseases seems very great.
                 A   B   C   D
      No error
      E

120. To comprehend well, a student must read frequently. No error
                     A B   C   D   E

121. The day progressed very quietly, fishing and eating at a picnic. No error
      A   B   C   D   E

122. When I was a small boy, my father took me to the movies. No error
           A B   C   D   E

123. To join the club, a deposit must be made in advance. No error
      A B   C   D   E

124. It is not clear whether these are post-factum interpretations or something felt by the
    $\underline{\hspace{1cm}}$ $\underline{\hspace{1cm}}$ $\underline{\hspace{1cm}}$
     A   B   C
children at the time. No error
$\underline{\hspace{1cm}}$ $\underline{\hspace{1cm}}$
     D   E

125. Only once before have I met a musician who was so ready to help a student.
                   $\underline{\hspace{1cm}}$ $\underline{\hspace{1cm}}$ $\underline{\hspace{1cm}}$
                    A B   C   D
No error
$\underline{\hspace{1cm}}$
     E

126. My aunt, whom we admire almost too much, has given we boys ten dollars each
           $\underline{\hspace{1cm}}$ $\underline{\hspace{1cm}}$ $\underline{\hspace{1cm}}$
                  A   B   C
to spend at the fair tomorrow. No error
$\underline{\hspace{1cm}}$ $\underline{\hspace{1cm}}$
     D   E

127. When I showed my mother the suit I had selected, she objected to me buying it;
           $\underline{\hspace{1cm}}$ $\underline{\hspace{1cm}}$ $\underline{\hspace{1cm}}$
              A   B   C
she said it was too expensive. No error
$\underline{\hspace{1cm}}$ $\underline{\hspace{1cm}}$
     D   E

128. In her note the teacher asked the principal to give some chalk from his supply
    $\underline{\hspace{1cm}}$ $\underline{\hspace{1cm}}$
     A   B
room to whomever of us boys would go down to pick it up. No error
         $\underline{\hspace{1cm}}$ $\underline{\hspace{1cm}}$ $\underline{\hspace{1cm}}$
              C   D   E

129. New York City with it's many suburbs has been called America's fabulous metrop-
    $\underline{\hspace{1cm}}$ $\underline{\hspace{1cm}}$
          A   B
olis, its dirtiest city, and its most exciting place for a brief vacation. No error
       $\underline{\hspace{1cm}}$ $\underline{\hspace{1cm}}$ $\underline{\hspace{1cm}}$
          C   D   E

130. Abraham Lincoln's Gettysburg Address has been called a model of brevity, the
           $\underline{\hspace{1cm}}$ $\underline{\hspace{1cm}}$
                    A   B
greatest short speech that anyone has ever delivered, and a speech worth more than
$\underline{\hspace{1cm}}$ $\underline{\hspace{1cm}}$
          C   D
a longer one would have been. No error
                              $\underline{\hspace{1cm}}$
                                 E

131. Please ask whoever you wish to serve as a fourth member of the board I am ap-
           $\underline{\hspace{1cm}}$ $\underline{\hspace{1cm}}$ $\underline{\hspace{1cm}}$
              A   B   C
pointing to study the pollution situation in your county. No error
                                           $\underline{\hspace{1cm}}$ $\underline{\hspace{1cm}}$
                                              D   E

132. The United Nations has performed many useful tasks through its various commis-
    $\underline{\hspace{1cm}}$ $\underline{\hspace{1cm}}$
          A   B
sions although there are representatives on these commissions whom everyone knows
                 $\underline{\hspace{1cm}}$ $\underline{\hspace{1cm}}$
                    C   D
are Communists. No error
     $\underline{\hspace{1cm}}$
          E

133. The Nobel Prize for Literature has been awarded to John Steinbeck, who's novels

$\underset{A}{\qquad}$ $\underset{B}{\qquad}$

are now considered among the greatest which have been written in the United States

$\underset{C}{\qquad}$ $\underset{D}{\qquad}$

in the twentieth century. No error

$\underset{E}{\qquad}$

134. Even though we know that we are exercising our rights under the United States

$\underset{A}{\qquad}$ $\underset{B}{\qquad}$

Constitution, Gail and myself are arrested every time we picket police headquarters.

$\underset{C}{\qquad}$ $\underset{D}{\qquad}$

No error

$\underset{E}{\qquad}$

135. When the final story has been written for that final newspaper sometime in the future,

$\underset{A}{\qquad}$ $\underset{B}{\qquad}$

you can be sure that it's substance will be some violent act that has occurred.

$\underset{C}{\qquad}$ $\underset{D}{\qquad}$

No error

$\underset{E}{\qquad}$

If there is still time remaining, you may review the questions in this section only.
You may not turn to any other section of the test.

Section VI Business Judgment

TIME: 20 minutes

DIRECTIONS: Read the following two passages. After you have completed each of them you will be asked to answer two sets of questions. The first of these, data evaluation, involves determining the importance of specific factors included in the passage. The second, data application, consists of general questions relating to the passage. When answering questions, you may consult the passage.

Passage 1:

Brooks and Company is a food manufacturer established in 1850. Until very recently, its major product lines consisted of tomato specialties, such as catsup, pickles, and barbecue sauces. Its consumer products business accounted for 40% of sales; the balance consisted of institutional sales to restaurants, hospitals, and the armed forces. The company has advertised to the institutional market but never to final (household) consumers.

In 1977 the company introduced a new line of Italian specialty products aimed at the final consumer market. The line was composed of a number of prepared pasta dishes, such as spaghetti, lasagne, and ravioli. Each package contained all of the necessary ingredients (except meat) including seasoned tomato sauce, cheese, and noodles.

The idea for the line of Italian pasta products was conceived by Joe Brooks, son of the company president. Joe's enthusiasm for the product idea was quickly picked up by other executives. The president had married an Italian woman after World War I and their only child, Joe, was born in Naples. Because they lacked the Neapolitan background, William Johnson, production manager, and Carl Voght, treasurer, approved of the idea on less emotional grounds. Johnson saw in the Italian line certain production possibilities that fitted in well with the company's existing facilities. Mr. Voght had long argued for some type of expansion which would enable the company to pull out of a number of financial problems associated with its inability to attract outside capital.

Many planning meetings were held throughout the summer. These meetings were attended by both the Brookses, Johnson, and Voght. Charles Welch, an administrative assistant to the president, was instructed to sit in on the sessions after he returned from vacation on August 1. He acted as informal secretary for the group. The original thinking of the committee was that the product line should be introduced at the beginning of the fall food merchandising season, which started about October 1. This deadline, however, subsequently proved to be unrealistic. Production of the first items in the line did not get underway until September 30 and packaging difficulties prohibited introducing the product before mid-December.

In July the problems involved in the product introduction were not foremost in the planners' thoughts. Many hours were spent discussing the name of the product line. Finally, the name *Velsuvio* was adopted as a compromise, but without enthusiasm from Joe Brooks, who believed that a name such as *Valencia* better described the gourmet image that he thought the line should express. With the exception of the name, the younger Brooks directed most of the decisions related to the marketing program. From the beginning, he argued that there were already plenty of "middle class" spaghetti products on the grocers' shelves. What was needed, he believed, was a prestige—even a "gourmet"—line. The popularity of higher-priced Italian restaurants in many cities convinced young Brooks of the opportunity to market a prestige line of Italian food specialties.

Early in the planning it was decided not to limit distribution to those regional markets in which Brooks had previously established its reputation. National distribution would be undertaken from the beginning. It was planned that the *Velsuvio* line would be marketed in all major food chains except those handling only private or controlled brands. Sales to chain headquarters would be made by food brokers handling gourmet products rather than by brokers used to the handling of high-volume canned goods.

For the first time in its experience, Brooks planned to undertake an extensive consumer advertising program. A small Los Angeles advertising agency with some experience in handling food products was appointed. However, by the time the agency had been selected and oriented to the marketing program, the time remaining before the scheduled intro-duction did not allow for the preparation of magazine advertisements or filmed television commercials. In order to break into the consumer market at the time of the scheduled product introduction on October 1, a consumer advertising program using newspapers, live television commercials, and radio was prepared. Except for the product introduction pe-riod, however, relatively little thought was given during the summer planning sessions to the total amount of money required to support the new product with consumer advertising.

A number of circumstances combined to prevent the introduction of the product in October as originally planned. No one had assumed personal responsibility for package design, and production was held up three weeks while the company waited for supplies of packaging materials. Brooks was forced to move very rapidly to obtain a package, and he was the first to admit that the result was neither very well designed functionally nor at-tractive from a promotional point of view. Time was short, however, and there was no choice but to use this package or abandon the project for the present season and possibly altogether, depending on competitive conditions.

The product was finally launched in mid-December. However, by February, two major competitors began marketing similar products. By mid-year, Brooks' product sales were so poor that the company discontinued the new line.

Data Evaluation Questions

DIRECTIONS: Evaluate each of the following factors used in decision-making which relate to the passage you have just read by selecting

  (A) for a *Major Objective*—the result desired by the executive;

  (B) for a *Major Factor*—a primary consideration, spelled out in the passage, that influences the decision;

  (C) for a *Minor Factor*—a less important consideration in the decision;

  (D) for a *Major Assumption*—a conclusion reached by the executive not necessarily sup-ported by the factors present;

  (E) for an *Unimportant Issue*—a consideration not directly related to the problem.

136. Existing production facilities

137. Consumer acceptance of the *Velsuvio* line

138. Company growth and expansion

139. Brooks and Company is over 100 years old

140. Brooks' experience in the sale of consumer products

141. The popularity of higher-priced Italian restaurants in the U.S.

Data Application Questions

DIRECTIONS: Answer each of the following questions using information contained in the passage.

142. Initial sales of the new product line were disappointing because of

    I.   Organizational problems
    II. Lack of advertising objectives
    III. Poor package design

  (A) I only
  (B) III only
  (C) I and II only
  (D) II and III only
  (E) I, II, and III

143. It can be inferred from the passage that Brooks and Company is

    I.   Consumer oriented
    II. Progressive
    III. Organizationally deficient

  (A) I only
  (B) III only
  (C) I and II only
  (D) II and III only
  (E) I, II, and III

144. Brooks' advertising campaign was ill-conceived because of the

    I.   Inexperienced advertising agency
    II. Delay in the preparation of commercials
    III. Company's decision not to use TV commercials

  (A) I only
  (B) III only
  (C) I and II only
  (D) II and III only
  (E) I, II, and III

145. The name of the new product line was selected by

    I. The president's son
   II. A consumer panel
  III. The company committee

  (A) I only
  (B) III only
  (C) I and II only
  (D) II and III only
  (E) I, II, and III

146. According to the passage, it was planned to introduce the new product line

    I. About October 1
   II. At the beginning of the fall food merchandising season
  III. Mid-December

  (A) I only
  (B) III only
  (C) I and II only
  (D) II and III only
  (E) I, II, and III

147. Analyzing the passage, it can be concluded that Brooks and Company's greatest weakness was in the area of

    I. Consumer marketing
   II. Production
  III. Public relations

  (A) I only
  (B) III only
  (C) I and II only
  (D) II and III only
  (E) I, II, and III

148. The marketing program for the new product line was mainly directed by

    I. The marketing manager
   II. The planning committee
  III. The president's son

  (A) I only
  (B) III only
  (C) I and II only
  (D) II and III only
  (E) I, II, and III

Passage 2:

"Is that the final survey, Hermann?" Rudolf Grossmann asked his marketing director, Hermann Goldring. It was. As soon as Grossmann read it he knew that a decision on the company's future policy could no longer be delayed.

Grossmann had become chairman and chief executive of Swiss transmission manufacturer Johannes Pökel SA a few months previously.

Two years before his appointment Pökel had recognized that as the European car market became saturated the opportunities for growth in its long-established business of car transmission production were becoming limited. Moreover, as competition became more intense, profit margins declined.

Pökel's board had decided to enter another area of technology. Under the guidance of Grossmann's predecessor it had enlarged its research and development (R&D) facilities several times and started developing a transmission unit for electric cars.

The unit was intended to overcome one of the major problems of electric vehicles, the fact that they cannot as yet carry enough power to propel them at high speeds for long periods. It was designed to convert electric current into kinetic energy and recapture some of that energy through a system of magnetic fields.

The company was so pleased with the initial success of its development efforts that, despite the fact that it was dangerously close to going into debt, it began to look for other research projects where it might make a breakthrough.

It toyed with designs for car engine computerization, a radar device for preventing collisions and a method of projecting speed and other essential information onto the windshield.

The R&D facility grew accordingly, sucking in ever more funds and becoming the major hope for success of the board and senior management. Only Goldring had voiced disquiet at the proportion of funds being diverted from developing the company's basic transmission product into new areas with an uncertain future.

Even when the electric car transmission system ran into difficulties under road tests no one was seriously worried. The problem was one of materials technology. It was felt that it could be solved with more research.

Finally, even when some members of the board had begun to be aware that the company was spending heavily in an effort to avoid losses, Grossmann had been given no definite brief to cut back on R&D when he replaced the previous chief executive. He had been invited in to look around and make his recommendations.

First, he had commissioned a survey of the potential markets for all the projects on the R&D drawing boards. The results of the survey had now been placed on his desk.

The report made it obvious that the company's original estimate of the timing of future demands for the electric car was unrealistic. In addition, there was now serious doubt whether electric vehicles would ever make a real impact on the market. Other technologies, such as hydrogen power, showed rather more promise.

Second, Grossmann, in opposition to Pökel's brilliant but often overoptimistic director of research, had instituted an outside technical audit of R&D. This had concluded that Pökel had so many projects on hand that it had spread its resources far too thinly. Quite apart from marketing considerations, the prospect of success in any one of them was doubtful.

Grossman felt that in one sense he had no choice. He had to rationalize R&D. He had to cut back on the speculative projects and concentrate on one or two. But he had a very difficult choice.

Because it had starved the transmission business of development funds, Pökel had already fallen behind competitors in the constant minor improvements that make one transmission system sell better than its rivals. If Grossmann switched most or all of the development money back into transmissions the company would still find it difficult to catch up. It would also have lost the opportunity of a breakthrough into a more profitable new product line. At best it would be back where it started.

Data Evaluation Questions

DIRECTIONS: Evaluate each of the following factors used in decision-making which relate to the passage you have just read by selecting

- (A)   for a *Major Objective*—the result desired by the executive;

- (B)   for a *Major Factor*—a primary consideration, spelled out in the passage, that influences the decision;

- (C)   for a *Minor Factor*—a less important consideration in the decision;

- (D)   for a *Major Assumption*—a conclusion reached by the executive not necessarily supported by the factors present;

- (E)   for an *Unimportant Issue*—a consideration not directly related to the problem.

149. Johannes Pökel SA is based in Switzerland

150. R&D costs

151. Optimization of R&D investment

152. Materials technology

153. Declining profit margins

Data Application Questions

DIRECTIONS: Answer each of the following questions using information contained in the passage.

154. Which of the following describes the Pökel SA Company?

  I.   Marketing-oriented
 II.   Planning-oriented
III.   Product-oriented

- (A)   I only
- (B)   III only
- (C)   I and II only
- (D)   II and III only
- (E)   I, II, and III

155. Pökel SA's problems with the electric car transmission were due to

    I.   Technical difficulties
   II.   Uncertain demand
 III.   Export constraints

  (A) I only
  (B) III only
  (C) I and II only
  (D) II and III only
  (E) I, II, and III

156. Grossmann was brought into the company to

    I.   Specifically cut R&D spending
   II.   Improve the company's production facilities
 III.   Make recommendations for the R&D program

  (A) I only
  (B) III only
  (C) I and II only
  (D) II and III only
  (E) I, II, and III

157. Grossmann's predecessor felt that the electric car transmission problem could be solved by

    I.   Increased research
   II.   Market testing
 III.   Cutting production costs

  (A) I only
  (B) III only
  (C) I and II only
  (D) II and III only
  (E) I, II, and III

158. Grossmann's first act as chief executive was to

    I.   Computerize all new product design
   II.   Rationalize all R&D projects
 III.   Order a market survey of R&D projects

  (A) I only
  (B) III only
  (C) I and II only
  (D) II and III only
  (E) I, II, and III

159. A survey showed that Pökel SA had

   I.   Too many R&D projects
  II.   Spread its resources too thinly
 III.   Erred in its estimate of demand for the electric car

  (A) I only
  (B) III only
  (C) I and II only
  (D) II and III only
  (E) I, II, and III

160. It can be inferred from the passage that if Grossmann chooses to invest in speculative ventures, he has which of the following alternatives?

   I.   The one with the most obvious market potential
  II.   The one whose technical problems are the easiest and least costly to solve
 III.   The one which stockholders would be sure to approve

  (A) I only
  (B) III only
  (C) I and II only
  (D) II and III only
  (E) I, II, and III

If there is still time remaining, you may review the questions in this section only.
You may not turn to any other section of the test.

Section VII Logical Reasoning

TIME: 20 minutes

DIRECTIONS: This type of question asks you to judge the reasoning used in sentences or short paragraphs. Sometimes every choice will be a possible answer to the question. However, you must decide which one is the best. Best means that you are not forced to make any improbable, extra, or contradictory assumptions. The ideas contained in these passages may be controversial but you are only being tested on your ability to analyze the reasoning used.

161. All the short people I have seen are underweight. It is obvious that all short people don't get enough to eat.

   The author's conclusion would be false if which of the following statements were true?

   (A) Some tall people were underweight.
   (B) All tall people were overweight.
   (C) All short people exercise.
   (D) Some short people were overweight.
   (E) Some short people live in large houses.

162. All the birds I have observed can fly so every bird probably can fly.

   Which of the following is closest to the type of reasoning used in the above statement?

   (A) All trees I have seen have branches so every tree probably has leaves.
   (B) All the birds I have observed can fly so every bird probably has feathers.
   (C) All the houses I have seen have shingled roofs so probably every house has a shingled roof.
   (D) All the chairs I have seen have a wooden frame so wood is probably the best material for the frame of a chair.
   (E) Since all the shepherds that I know of use dogs, dogs must be a useful antidote for loneliness.

163. You ask me whether I favor a tax on oil imports. The decline of the dollar is certainly a serious indicator of weakness in the economy. Taxing oil imports might strengthen the dollar. However, the tax could also lead to inflationary pressures. Thus like many economic issues we must make a choice and the question could be considered political.

   The weakness in the economist's answer is

   (A) No one cares about the strength of the dollar.
   (B) She hasn't answered the question.
   (C) She can't be sure the tax will cause inflation.
   (D) Economics does not deal with choices.
   (E) The tax on oil imports will never pass Congress.

Questions 164–165 refer to missing portions of the following paragraph. For each question choose the answer which best completes the meaning of the paragraph.

The amount of compensation a person receives should be related to the importance of his/her work. Saving lives is more important than providing diversion so 164. It is incongruous that people who provide a few hours of entertainment are paid vast amounts of money while people who provide life-saving assistance must struggle to provide adequate food and shelter for their families. The value our society places on occupations is not proportional to their actual 165.

164. (A) T.V. newscasters should be paid more than doctors.
 (B) Teachers should be paid as much as professional athletes.
 (C) Firemen should be paid more than opera singers.
 (D) Surgeons should make more than the president of the U.S.
 (E) Ambulance drivers should be paid more than nurses.

165. (A) worth
 (B) danger
 (C) charisma
 (D) training
 (E) difficulty

166. All humans are mortal. Some of the French are human. Which of the following statements can be deduced from the two above statements?

 (A) Some humans are immortal.
 (B) A few of the French are immortal.
 (C) At least one of the French is mortal.
 (D) All the French are mortal.
 (E) All the French are human.

167. Every time the rainmaker performed his ritual it rained within twelve hours. He must be able to make it rain. Which of the following statements would weaken the author's conclusion the most?

 (A) The rainmaker accepted money for performing his ritual.
 (B) The rainmaker only performed his ritual when the sky was cloudy and dark.
 (C) The rainmaker was only hired after a long period of low moisture.
 (D) The rainmaker was not a certified meteorologist.
 (E) The rainmaker lived in the desert.

168. People who live in the desert don't know how to swim. Some sailers don't know how to swim.

 Which of the following statements can be deduced from the two above statements?

 I. Some sailors live in the desert.
 II. Some people who live in the desert are sailors.
 III. Some sailors don't live in the desert.

 (A) I only
 (B) II only
 (C) III only
 (D) I and II only
 (E) none of I, II, and III.

169. Everybody wants to save money. When I see a book offered at 50% less than its usual price, I buy it and I know I have saved money.

The author's conclusion follows from his initial statements only if which of the following statements is true?

(A) The author was only willing to pay $20 for the book.
(B) The author would have bought the book at the usual price.
(C) The author reads the book.
(D) The author enjoys the book.
(E) Most people do want to save money.

170. (1) As a family's income rises the percentage of income which is saved decreases. (2) Our family had more income this year than last year, but we saved $100 more this year than last year.

These two statements do not contradict each other because which of the following statements is true?

(A) Statement (1) is false.
(B) Statement (2) is false.
(C) Percentage saved can decrease but the amount saved can still increase.
(D) Statement (2) is particular but statement (1) is general.
(E) The first statement refers to some families but not all families.

171. The internal combustion engine in an automobile is more efficient at high speed than at low speed. So one would expect a car to get better mileage at high speed than at low speed if all other things were equal. However, all other things are not equal.

Which of the following statements best completes the thought in the passage?

(A) An air-conditioner is a drain on mileage.
(B) The price of gasoline has gone up recently.
(C) In fact, tire wear increases at high speed.
(D) The drag caused by air resistance increases so much as the speed increases that gas mileage is lower at high speeds.
(E) At higher speeds the gear ratio in the transmission is lower so that the engine is able to drive the car further.

Questions 172–173

There is a movement to have the United States call a second Constitutional Convention. Although at first glance this seems to be a very democratic approach to the problems we face, it presents some difficulties. Does anyone believe that the current political system will produce leaders who are the equivalent of Washington, Jefferson, Madison, and the other Founding Fathers? Can we be sure that the Bill of Rights would not be tampered with? Would special interests be able to control the selection of delegates? It seems to me that having another Constitutional Convention would be like opening Pandora's box again.

172. Which of the following arguments does the author use to attack the idea of a new Constitutional Convention?

    I.   Our political leadership is weaker today than when the Constitution was written.

    II.   Television has made the electorate apathetic.

    III.   The size of the electorate has increased greatly since the Constitution was adopted.

(A) I only
(B) II only
(C) III only
(D) I and II only
(E) I, II, and III

173. The author's method of attacking the idea of a new Constitutional Convention is to
(A) State consequences which would necessarily follow if a new convention were held.
(B) Give reasons why the convention would not be able to meet.
(C) Give possible reasons why the convention might produce undesirable results.
(D) Show that the convention would be extremely expensive.
(E) State that only extreme democrats would favor the proposal.

174. Any investment involves a certain degree of risk. Gambling also involves risk. Since gamblers are just another type of investor it is unfair to make this kind of investment illegal.

    The author's initial statements lead to his conclusion only if which of the following is also true?

(A) Gambling is illegal.
(B) Some types of investments are legal.
(C) Gambling is an investment.
(D) No other types of risky behavior are illegal.
(E) The state should protect its citizens from risk.

175. If a person spends more money than he has, he will go bankrupt. In the same way, if a country spends more money than it possesses in gold then it will go bankrupt.

    Which of the following principles is the author using as the basis for this argument?

(A) What is true for an individual is true for a nation.
(B) All nations should return to the gold standard.
(C) The bankruptcy laws are unfair.
(D) People should not use credit.
(E) If a statement is true for a nation it must be true for every citizen of that nation.

If there is still time remaining, you may review the questions in this section only.
You may not turn to any other section of the test.

Answers

Section I   Reading Comprehension

1. (B)	8. (A)	15. (A)	21. (C)
2. (C)	9. (E)	16. (A)	22. (B)
3. (D)	10. (B)	17. (D)	23. (C)
4. (C)	11. (B)	18. (B)	24. (C)
5. (E)	12. (E)	19. (C)	25. (C)
6. (C)	13. (B)	20. (C)	
7. (B)	14. (D)		

Section II   Mathematics

(Numbers in parentheses indicate the section in the Mathematics Review where material concerning the question is discussed.)

26. (B) (I-4)	34. (A) (II-3)	42. (B) (II-3)	50. (B) (II-6)
27. (D) (I-4)	35. (D) (II-7)	43. (B) (II-4)	51. (D) (I-2, I-8)
28. (B) (I-2)	36. (B) (II-3)	44. (C) (I-2)	52. (E) (II-6, II-1)
29. (E) (II-3)	37. (E) (I-4)	45. (D) (II-3)	53. (E) (II-3)
30. (A) (II-5)	38. (D) (II-1)	46. (C) (I-4)	54. (C) (III-6)
31. (E) (II-2)	39. (D) (II-5)	47. (D) (II-5)	55. (E) (III-7)
32. (D) (I-4)	40. (C) (I-2)	48. (E) (II-3)	
33. (C) (II-3)	41. (A) (II-7)	49. (C) (III-7, II-3)	

Section III   Business Judgment

56. (B)	63. (B)	70. (E)	77. (E)
57. (A)	64. (C)	71. (B)	78. (C)
58. (B)	65. (B)	72. (B)	79. (D)
59. (C)	66. (A)	73. (E)	80. (B)
60. (E)	67. (C)	74. (A)	
61. (B)	68. (A)	75. (B)	
62. (B)	69. (C)	76. (D)	

Section IV   Data Sufficiency

81.	(D)	89.	(C)	97.	(B)	105.	(E)
82.	(A)	90.	(B)	98.	(E)	106.	(E)
83.	(B)	91.	(A)	99.	(A)	107.	(C)
84.	(A)	92.	(D)	100.	(C)	108.	(D)
85.	(A)	93.	(E)	101.	(A)	109.	(A)
86.	(E)	94.	(C)	102.	(D)	110.	(E)
87.	(C)	95.	(E)	103.	(E)		
88.	(C)	96.	(E)	104.	(B)		

Section V   Writing Ability

111.	(B)	118.	(D)	125.	(C)	132.	(D)
112.	(D)	119.	(D)	126.	(B)	133.	(B)
113.	(D)	120.	(E)	127.	(C)	134.	(C)
114.	(C)	121.	(A)	128.	(C)	135.	(C)
115.	(B)	122.	(E)	129.	(B)		
116.	(C)	123.	(C)	130.	(A)		
117.	(A)	124.	(E)	131.	(B)		

Section VI   Business Judgment

136.	(B)	143.	(B)	150.	(B)	157.	(A)
137.	(D)	144.	(C)	151.	(A)	158.	(B)
138.	(A)	145.	(B)	152.	(C)	159.	(B)
139.	(E)	146.	(C)	153.	(B)	160.	(C)
140.	(B)	147.	(A)	154.	(B)		
141.	(D)	148.	(B)	155.	(C)		
142.	(E)	149.	(E)	156.	(B)		

Section VII   Logical Reasoning

161.	(D)	165.	(A)	169.	(B)	173.	(C)
162.	(C)	166.	(C)	170.	(C)	174.	(C)
163.	(B)	167.	(B)	171.	(D)	175.	(A)
164.	(C)	168.	(E)	172.	(A)		

Analysis

Section I   Reading Comprehension

1. **(B)** The passage deals with the harmful effects of certain production processes on workers and others.

2. **(C)** This answer is clear from the passage in lines 20-33.

3. **(D)** Osteolysis is not mentioned as a cause. (A) can be found in lines 12-13; (B) in lines 20; (C) in line 34; and (E) in line 2.

4. **(C)** The author does not argue for remedial action in the passage, but merely presents the facts of cancer-producing, occupational hazards.

5. **(E)** This is implied in lines 40ff. Existing legislated-maximum levels of vinyl chloride exposure are higher than that set by Dow Chemical, and apparently higher than a medically permissible safe limit.

6. **(C)** The passage relates that at least 17 workers were killed because of the failure by authorities to follow up on available research. See lines 40-41.

7. **(B)** The passage states that "a creature" was first observed by St. Columba in 565 A.D. See line 43.

8. **(A)** The statement beginning on line 43 indicates that the name of the monster is based on a specific shape and form (as discussed in lines 32ff) taken from a description of the animal.

9. **(E)** In line 19 the dimensions of the lake are given as approximately 23 miles long, with a maximum width of 1.5 miles. However, we do not have the measurements of other widths which could vary significantly. Therefore, we can not determine the area.

10. **(B)** Most of the passage deals with the origins of Loch Ness and only incidentally with the so-called "monster" within.

11. **(B)** Ichthyologists are zoologists who study fish.

12. **(E)** None can be inferred from the passage.

13. **(B)** Line 7 quotes Marx as saying that philosophers only want to interpret the world, when what should be done is to change it. Change, the author states on line 8, is the "creed of applied scientists everywhere."

14. **(D)** Durkheim also highly regarded the application of science rather than theoretical constructs alone. See line 38.

15. **(A)** Items (B) through (E) deal with *applied* problems which are the main concern of the social scientist, according to the passage.

16. **(A)** See lines 38-40.

17. **(D)** This point is stressed in lines 5, 12, 17ff, 30, 32, 38, and 44ff.

18. **(B)** Marx is best known for his political-economic work, *Das Kapital*.

19. **(C)** While the author is concerned with the moral and cultural aspects of American society (lines 1, 21-25), his major concern is to show how the Bible has been used as a guide for some theatrical productions and thus demonstrate that there is much morally and culturally worthwhile in that entertainment medium. See especially lines 31-35, 48ff.

20. **(C)** This central theme of the author's concern is contained in lines 3-12.

21. **(C)** Statements (A) and (B) were not originally voiced by the author, but rather by Gen. Sarnoff. See lines 1-2, 8-9. Statements (D) and (E) are taken out of context. See lines 32-40. Statement (C) reflects the author's own ideas. See lines 14-19.

22. **(B)** Question I is found in lines 14-18, question III in lines 19-20. However, the author does not present evidence that he intends to answer them. Only answers to question II are implied throughout. See lines 41-47.

23. **(C)** The author does not state his background or profession, but it might be any of the above except (C) which is an adjective for noisy.

24. **(C)** Both these questions are implied in lines 10-13.

25. **(C)** Taken in context with the sentence, (C) is the most probable answer. See lines 32-34.

Section II   Mathematics

26. **(B)** Let L be the original length and W the original width. The new length is 120% of L which is $(1.2)L$; the new width is 80% of W which is $(.8)W$. The area of a rectangle is length times width, so the original area is LW and the new area is $(1.2)(L)(.8)W$ or $(.96)LW$. Since the new area is 96% of the original area, the area has decreased by 4%.

27. **(D)** The distance from New York to Hartford divided by the distance from New York to Boston is $\frac{120}{250}$ or .48, and $.48 = 48\%$.

28. **(B)** The amount broken off is $\frac{1}{8} + 1\frac{3}{4} + 1\frac{1}{12}$ inches. Since $\frac{1}{8} + 1\frac{3}{4} + 1\frac{1}{12} = \frac{3}{24} + \frac{42}{24} + \frac{26}{24} = \frac{71}{24}$ and the lead was 5 inches long to begin with, the amount left $= 5 - \frac{71}{24} = \frac{120}{24} - \frac{71}{24} = \frac{49}{24} = 2\frac{1}{24}$ inches.

29. **(E)** The first 1,000 copies cost $1 each; so altogether they will cost $1,000. The remaining 3,800 copies $(4,800 - 1,000)$ cost x dollars each; so their cost is $3,800x. Therefore, the total cost of all 4,800 copies is $1,000 + $3,800x.

30. **(A)** Since $1\frac{2}{3}$ hours is 100 minutes, 50 minutes is $\frac{1}{2}$ of $1\frac{2}{3}$ hours. Therefore, he should make half as much in 50 minutes as he does in $1\frac{2}{3}$ hours. Since he made 4 boxes in $1\frac{2}{3}$ hours, he makes 2 boxes in 50 minutes.

31. **(E)** Since $\frac{y}{x} = 2$, $y = 2x$. Therefore, $x + y = x + 2x = 3x$ which equals 3. So $3x = 3$, which means $x = 1$. Thus, $y = 2$ because $y = 2x$.

32. **(D)** Since there are 20 rolls in a carton and a carton costs $9, each roll costs $\frac{1}{20}$ of $9 which is 45¢. The roll sells for 50¢, so the selling price divided by the cost is $\frac{50}{45} = \frac{10}{9}$ which is about 111%. (or divide the total income by the total cost: $\frac{20 \times .50}{9} = \frac{10}{9} = 111\%$.)

33. **(C)** 12 copies of the history book weigh $(12)(2.4)$ or 28.8 pounds. Since the total weight of the books is 42.8 pounds, the weight of the English books is $42.8 - 28.8$ or 14 pounds. Therefore, each English book weighs $\frac{14}{8}$ or 1.75 pounds.

34. **(A)** Let x be the number of miles the car travels on a gallon of gas when driven at 60 miles an hour. Then 80% of 15 is x; so $\frac{4}{5} \cdot 15 = x$ and $x = 12$.

35. **(D)**

STATEMENT I cannot be inferred since if $x = 2$ and $y = 1$, then x and y are positive but x is not less than y.

STATEMENT II is true since $x + y = z$ and y is positive so $x < z$.

STATEMENT III is true. z is positive since it is the sum of two positive numbers and so $z < 2z$. Since we know $x < z$ and $z < 2z$, then $x < 2z$.

Therefore, only STATEMENTS II and III can be inferred.

36. **(B)** The first 800 sheets cost $800x$ ¢. The remaining 4,200 sheets cost $\frac{x}{15}$ ¢ apiece which comes to $(4,200)\left(\frac{x}{15}\right)$¢ or $280x$ ¢. Therefore, the total cost of the 5,000 sheets of paper is $800x$ ¢ $+ 280x$ ¢, which is $1,080x$ ¢.

37. **(E)** Let S denote the worker's salary in 1967. In 1968 he received 110% of S which is $(1.1)S$, and in 1969 he received 110% of $(1.1)S$ which is $(1.1)(1.1)S$ or $1.21\ S$. Therefore, he received 21% more in 1969 than he did in 1967.

38. **(D)** Factory A turns out $8a$ cars in 8 hours. Since factory B turns out b cars in 2 hours, it turns out $4b$ cars in 8 hours. Therefore, the total is $8a + 4b$.

39. **(D)** In 35 minutes John makes 7 boxes and Tim makes 5. The required ratio, 7 to 5, is constant no matter how long they work.

40. **(C)** The total number of crates sold is $3\frac{1}{4} + 2\frac{1}{6} + 4\frac{1}{2} + 1\frac{2}{3}$ which is equal to $\frac{39}{12} + \frac{26}{12} + \frac{54}{12} + \frac{20}{12} = \frac{139}{12} = 11\frac{7}{12}$. A shorter method would be to add the integral parts of each of the numbers $3 + 2 + 4 + 1 = 10$. Next add the fractional parts $\frac{1}{4} + \frac{1}{6} + \frac{1}{2} + \frac{2}{3}$. Using 12 as a common denominator you get $\frac{(3+2+6+8)}{12}$ which is $\frac{19}{12} = 1\frac{7}{12}$. Therefore, the answer is $10 + 1\frac{7}{12} = 11\frac{7}{12}$.

41. **(A)** If $x + y$ exceeds 4 and x is less than 3, it is clear that y must exceed 1.

42. **(B)** Since 10 is $\frac{1}{5}$ of 50, the 10 apprentices should do $\frac{1}{5}$ as much work as 50 apprentices. 50 apprentices did the job in 4 hours, so in 1 hour 50 apprentices will do $\frac{1}{4}$ of the job.

43. **(B)** 40% of the 52% of the population who are women are voters. So $(.40)(.52) = .2080 = 20.8\%$ of the population are women voters.

44. **(C)** The amount of gas needed for a bus to travel 200 miles if the bus travels 15 miles on a gallon is $\frac{200}{15}$ or $13\frac{1}{3}$ gallons.

45. **(D)** The time required to pump 10 gallons of water out of the tank is $(10)\left(15 - \frac{x}{10}\right)$ which equals $150 - x$ minutes.

46. **(C)** The profit is 6% of $1,000 plus 5% of $6,000 − $1,000 which is $(.06)(\$1,000) + (.05)(\$5,000)$. Therefore, the profit equals $60 + $250 which is $310.

47. **(D)** Since the number of baskets manufactured in an hour is proportional to the number of workers, $\frac{15}{45} = \frac{27}{x}$, where x is the number of baskets manufactured by 45 men in an hour. Therefore, x is 81. Since 40 minutes is $\frac{2}{3}$ of an hour, 45 men will make $\frac{2}{3}$ of 81 or 54 baskets in 40 minutes.

48. **(E)** The first elevator lifts $\frac{2}{5}$ of a ton per minute and the second elevator lifts $\frac{3}{7}$ of a ton per minute, so both elevators together will lift $\frac{2}{5} + \frac{3}{7} = \frac{29}{35}$ of a ton per minute. Therefore, using both elevators it will take $\frac{20}{29/35} = \frac{35}{29} \times 20 = \frac{700}{29}$ or $24\frac{4}{29}$ minutes to lift 20 tons.

49. **(C)** Since the width is $\frac{1}{3}$ of the length and the length is 120 yards, the width of the field is 40 yards. The area of a rectangle is length times width, so the area of the field is 120 yards times 40 yards, which is 4,800 square yards.

50. **(B)** The price will be $3.00 a pound 6 months from now and $9.00 a pound a year from now. The price is a geometric progression of the form 3^j where j is the number of 6 month periods which have passed. Since $3^4 = 81$, after 4 six month periods, the price will be $81.00 a pound. Therefore, the answer is two years, since 24 months is 2 years.

51. **(D)** Since $\frac{x}{y} = \frac{2}{3}$, $\frac{y}{x}$, which is the reciprocal of $\frac{x}{y}$, must be equal to $\frac{3}{2}$. Also, $\frac{y^2}{x^2}$ is equal to $\left(\frac{y}{x}\right)^2$, so $\frac{y^2}{x^2}$ is equal to $\frac{9}{4}$.

52. **(E)** Starting with $a_n = 1$ the rule $(a_n - 1)^2 = (1 - 1)^2 = 0^2 = 0$ so the next entry is 0. Using 0 as a_n gives $(0 - 1)^2 = (-1)^2 = 1$ so the second entry is 1. Since using 1 as a_n gives 0 as the next entry, the entries after 1 should be 0,1,0.

53. **(E)** X is paid 125%, or $\frac{5}{4}$ of Y's salary, so Y makes $\frac{4}{5}$ of what X makes. X makes 80% or $\frac{4}{5}$ of Z's salary, so Z makes $\frac{5}{4}$ of what X makes. Thus, the total salary of X, Y, and Z is the total of X's salary, $\frac{4}{5}$ of X's salary and $\frac{5}{4}$ X's salary. Therefore, the total is $\frac{61}{20}$ of X's salary. Since the total of the salaries is $610, X makes $\frac{20}{61}$ of $610, or $200.

54. **(C)** Since the radii are unequal, the circles cannot be identical, thus (E) is incorrect. If two circles intersect in 3 points they must be identical, so (D) is also incorrect. Two different circles can intersect in 2 points without being identical, so (C) is the correct answer.

55. **(E)** Let L be the length and W be the width of the rectangle, and let S be the length of a side of the square. It is given that $LW = S^2$. A relation must be found between $2L + 2W$ and $4S$. It is possible to construct squares and rectangles so that (A), (B), (C), or (D) is false, so (E) is correct. For example, if the rectangle is a square, then the two figures are identical and (A), (C) and (D) are false. If the rectangle is not equal to a square, then the perimeter of the rectangle is larger than the perimeter of the square, so (B) is also false.

Section III   Business Judgment

56. **(B)** The poor economic situation was a *Major Factor* leading to the ABC Corporation's reconsidering its investment plans.

57. **(A)** The *Major Objective* or result sought by the company was another look at its previous decision to invest.

58. **(B)** The economic slowdown was a *Major Factor* in the company's decision to reconsider.

59. **(C)** That other foreign companies were also reluctant to invest was a *Minor Factor* entering into ABC's decision to invest.

60. **(E)** That the government sought to attract foreign investment was an *Unimportant Issue* to ABC. Its major concern was the state of the economy and the effect on its plans.

61. **(B)** The ABC Corporation is concerned with all factors that will affect its profitability if it invests in the country. Increased cost of living allowances paid to workers will increase its wage bill and adversely affect profits. Thus, this is a *Major Factor*.

62. **(B)** See paragraph 2: The economic slowdown was caused by deliberate government action.

63. **(B)** See paragraph 4: The government still encouraged foreign investment.

64. **(C)** See paragraph 2: Government economic policy resulted in increased prices and taxes.

65. **(B)** See paragraph 4: Only the relative profitability of exports was a positive consequence of the government's economic policy.

66. **(A)** See paragraph 2: The cost of living allowance (paid to workers) led to higher wage costs and directly to higher prices.

67. **(C)** Only the Investment Board was not mentioned as being wary of the new economic policy.

68. **(A)** This case illustrates problems of company discipline and inter-executive relationships. It is replete with miscues on the part of the new department head as well as top management. The major problem is not whether subordinates in Department K will accede to their supervisors' requests to fill out time sheets but whether their relationships with the new department head are not irreparably damaged. This, then, is the *Major Objective;* a restoration of discipline in Department K.

69. **(C)** That the employees are of high caliber is a *Minor Factor* with regard to the issue of discipline, although it might have been a more important factor in the original decision to demand that time sheets be used.

70. **(E)** That the company has several departments certainly has no bearing on the issues at hand and is an *Unimportant Issue.*

71. **(B)** Apparently the fact employees worked without any *direct* supervision strongly motivated them against the acceptance of any procedure that would change the status quo. This is in effect what the new department head's directive would do.

72. **(B)** Another major grievance of the employees was that management went outside the company to hire a replacement for the retired department head. This is certainly a *Major Factor* that top management should have considered more carefully before making their decision—and now that it has been made—a solution must be found.

73. **(E)** The number of employees is an *Unimportant Issue.*

74. **(A)** See paragraph 6: The new department head threatened to resign.

75. **(B)** See paragraph 3: The head of Department K retired.

76. **(D)** While the passage states (in paragraph 3) that the president's talk soothed "hot tempers," it is clear that it also delayed a decision of what to do next. Many employees still did not report their time, and presumably the new department head's threat to resign still stood.

77. **(E)** See paragraph 5: All of these are given. Employees resented the new department head because he was hired from outside the company; they never had to fill out time sheets and neither did other departments.

78. **(C)** We know nothing about his mannerisms; but his communication with subordinates leaves something to be desired. Apparently he did not consult with them before issuing his directive.

79. **(D)** See paragraph 4.

80. **(B)** See paragraph 3: No qualified successor was available in the department. The man was hired even though his experience was in a different position. No mention was made of his working previously for an insurance company.

Section IV Data Sufficiency

81. **(D)**

STATEMENT (1) alone is sufficient. 2 feet 7 inches is more than half of 5 feet, so the piece which is 2 feet 7 inches long must be longer than the other two pieces put together.

STATEMENT (2) alone is sufficient. Since one piece is 5 inches long, the sum of the lengths of the remaining two pieces is 4 feet, 7 inches. Since one piece is 7 inches longer than the other, $L + (L + 7 \text{ in.}) = 4$ ft. 7 in., where L is the length of the smaller of the two remaining pieces. Solving the equation yields $L + 7$ in. as the length of the longest piece.

82. **(A)** Since AC is a diameter, angle ABC is inscribed in a semicircle and is therefore a right angle.

STATEMENT (1) alone is sufficient since it implies the two other angles in the triangle must be equal. Since the sum of the angles of a triangle is 180°, we can deduce that $x = 45$.

STATEMENT (2) alone is not sufficient. There is no information about the angle ABD; so STATEMENT (2) cannot be used to find the angles of triangle ABD.

83. **(B)**

STATEMENT (2) alone is sufficient. $y^2 - 2y + 1$ equals $(y - 1)^2$, so the only solution to $(y - 1)^2 = 0$ is $y = 1$.

STATEMENT (1) alone is not sufficient. $x + 2y = 6$ implies $y = 3 - \frac{x}{2}$, but there is no data given about the value of x.

84. **(A)**

STATEMENT (1) alone is sufficient. Pipe A fills up $\frac{1}{30}$ of the reservoir per minute. STATEMENT (1) says pipe B fills up $\frac{1}{20}$ of the reservoir per minute, so A and B together fill up $\frac{1}{20} + \frac{1}{30}$ or $\frac{5}{60}$ or $\frac{1}{12}$ of the reservoir. Therefore, together pipe A and pipe B will take 12 minutes to fill the reservoir.

STATEMENT (2) alone is not sufficient. There is no information about how long it takes pipe B to fill the reservoir.

85. **(A)**

STATEMENT (1) alone is sufficient. Draw the lines AC and BC; then AOC and BOC are right triangles, since AB is perpendicular to CO. By the Pythagorean theorem, $(AC)^2 = (AO)^2 + (CO)^2$ and $(BC)^2 = (OB)^2 + (CO)^2$; so if AO is less than OB, then AC is less than BC.

STATEMENT (2) alone is not sufficient. There is no restriction on where the point D is.

86. **(E)**

STATEMENTS (1) and (2) together are not sufficient. If $x = \frac{1}{2}$ and $y = 3$, then xy is greater than 1, but if $x = \frac{1}{2}$ and $y = \frac{3}{2}$, then xy is less than 1.

87. **(C)**

STATEMENT (1) alone is not sufficient. By choosing B and D differently we can have

either $x = y$ or $x \neq y$ and still have $z = u$.

STATEMENT (2) alone is not sufficient. It implies that $x = z$ and $y = u$, but gives no information to compare x and y. STATEMENTS (1) and (2) together, however, yield $x = y$.

88. **(C)**

STATEMENT (1) alone is not sufficient. If town C were closer to B, even if S were going slower than T, S could arrive at C first. But if you also use STATEMENT (2), then train S must be traveling faster than train T, since it is further from B to C than it is from A to C.

So STATEMENTS (1) and (2) together are sufficient.

STATEMENT (2) alone is insufficient since it gives no information about the trains.

89. **(C)**

STATEMENT (2) alone is not sufficient, since D can be any point if we assume only STATEMENT (2).

STATEMENT (1) alone is not sufficient. Depending on the position of point C, x and y can be equal or unequal. For example, in both of the following triangles BD is perpendicular to AC.

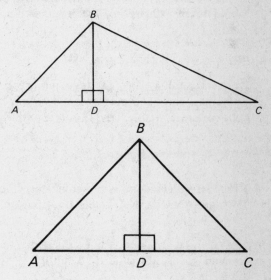

If STATEMENTS (1) and (2) are both true, then $x = y$. The triangles ABD and BDC are both right triangles with two pairs of corresponding sides equal; the triangles are therefore congruent and $x = y$.

90. (B)

STATEMENT (2) alone is sufficient, since $3x + 3y$ is $3(x + y)$. (Therefore, if $3x + 3y = 4$, then $x + y = {}^4\!/_3$.)

STATEMENT (1) alone is not sufficient, since you need another equation besides $x - y = 4$ to find the values of x and y.

91. (A)

STATEMENT (1) alone is sufficient. We know that the total of sales for 1968, 1969, and 1970 is three times the average and that sales in 1968 were twice the average. Then the total of sales in 1969 and 1970 was equal to the average. Therefore, sales were less in 1969 than in 1968.

STATEMENT (2) alone is insufficient, since it does not relate sales in 1969 to sales in 1968.

92. (D)

Since the length of the arc of the circle is proportional to the length of the chord connecting the endpoints, STATEMENT (1) alone is sufficient.

STATEMENT (2) alone is sufficient, since the areas of the circular segments are proportional to the squares of the lengths of the chord.

93. (E)

STATEMENTS (1) and (2) together are not sufficient, since the points A and D can be moved and STATEMENTS (1) and (2) still be satisfied.

94. (C)

STATEMENT (1) alone is not sufficient, since 24 and 16 are both divisible by 4 but only 24 is divisible by 12.

STATEMENT (2) alone is not sufficient, since 24 and 15 are divisible by 3 but 15 is not divisible by 12.

STATEMENT (1) implies that $k = 4m$ for some integer m. If you assume STATEMENT (2), then since k is divisible by 3, either 4 or m is divisible by 3. Since 4 is not divisible by 3, m must be. Therefore, $m = 3j$, where j

is some integer and $k = 4 \times 3j$ or $12j$. So k is divisible by 12. Therefore, STATEMENTS (1) and (2) together are sufficient.

95. (E)

STATEMENTS (1) and (2) together are not sufficient, because there is no information about the location of C relative to the locations of A and B.

96. (E) Obviously a single statement is not sufficient. However, since Ms. Brown could have other sources of income, even both statements together are not sufficient. If you answered (C) you are making the additional assumption that Ms. Brown's only source of income was royalties from the novel.

97. (B) An even integer is an integer divisible by 2. Since $2n + 10p$ is 2 times $(n + 5p)$ using (2) lets you deduce that x is even. (1) by itself is not sufficient. If n were 2 and p were 3, $(n + p)^2$ would be 25 which is not even, but by choosing n to be 2 and p to be 4, $(n + p)^2$ is 36 which is even.

98. (E) Both statements give facts that *might* explain why the price of lumber rose. However, even using both statements you can't deduce what happened to the price of lumber.

99. (A) Since you know $x = 3$, statement (1) alone is sufficient. However, since no information is given about the value of y, statement (2) is insufficient.

100. (C) You need (1) to know what the price was at the beginning of 1977. Using (2) you could then compute the price during the fifteenth week. Either statement alone is insufficient. You should not actually compute the price since it would only waste time.

101. (A) (1) alone is sufficient since the line connecting the midpoints of 2 sides of a triangle is parallel to the third side. (2) alone is insufficient. In an isosceles triangle statement (2) would imply that ED is parallel to BC, but in a non-isosceles triangle, (2) would imply that ED and BC are not parallel.

102. **(D)** (1) alone is sufficient. For example, with both drains open, $\frac{1}{15} + \frac{1}{20}$ of the tank would be emptied each minute. You should not waste any time solving the problem. Remember, you only have to decide whether there is enough information to let you answer the question.

   (2) alone is also sufficient. You can deduce (1) from (2) and from the fact that drain 1 alone takes 15 minutes to empty the tank, and we just saw that (1) alone is sufficient.

103. **(E)** If you answered incorrectly you probably assumed that x and y were positive. If $x = 5$ and $y = 4$, then (1) and (2) are both true and $x > y$. However, if $x = -5$ and $y = -4$, (1) and (2) are both true but $x < y$.

104. **(B)** (2) alone is sufficient since ostriches are birds. (1) alone is not sufficient since tigers are not birds.

105. **(E)** Since the equation in (2) has exactly the same solutions as the equation in (1), $(3 (x - y) = 3x - 3y$ and $3 (12) = 36)$, you can't determine x and y even by using both (1) and (2). If $x = 12$ and $y = 0$, then (1) and (2) are true and $x + 2 y = 12$, but if $x = 6$ and $y = -6$, (1) and (2) are again true but $x + 2y = -6$.

106. **(E)** (1) and (2) are not sufficient. The price of food could rise for other reasons besides the price of energy rising.

107. **(C)** (1) alone is obviously insufficient. To use (2) you need to know what the painting was worth at some time between 1968 and 1977. So (2) alone is insufficient, but by using (1) and (2) together you can figure out the worth of the painting in Jan. 1971.

108. **(D)** (1) alone is sufficient since the rule enables you to compute all successive values once you know a_1. Also the rule and (1) tell you that the numbers in the sequence will always increase. Thus since $a_2 = 4$, 3 will never appear. In the same way, by using (2) and the rule you can determine $a_1, a_2, a_3,$ and a_4 and then a_6, etc.

109. **(A)** (1) alone is sufficient. If $z > x$ then the side opposite angle ABC is larger than the side opposite angle ACB. (2) alone is insufficient since D can be anywhere between B and C, so you can't decide whether AD is larger or smaller than AB.

110. **(E)** If $x = 9$ and $y = 8$, then (1) and (2) would be true and $x > y$. However, if $x = 6$ and $y = 8$, (1) and (2) would still be true although $x < y$.

Section V   Writing Ability

111. **(B)** Enthused is the colloquial (substandard) form of enthusiastic.

112. **(D)** Tasks and manager are being compared in this sentence rather than the director and manager. A possible correct form is: The tasks of the director are greater than the *manager's*.

113. **(D)** The proper form is *off*, not *off of*.

114. **(C)** In parallel writing, adjectives should be balanced with adjectives, phrases with phrases, etc. In this sentence, the who clause is incorrect. *And* is a conjunction connecting two ideas about the pianist. For parallel construction *she* (or he) is correct: The pianist is a person with great promise and *she* should be encouraged.

115. **(B)** The pronoun *their* does not agree in number with its antecedent (*each* student). The proper form is *his* (or her).

116. **(C)** The problem in this sentence is that the reference to the antecedent is unclear. *He* can refer to the bear or Paul. A better version would be: After he found a campsite, *Paul was followed by a bear* into the woods.

117. **(A)** Improper tense. The correct form is: If I had. . . .

118. **(D)** The pronoun I is in the subjective or nominative case, and when used, must be in the same case as the noun or pronoun that it

explains (apposition). However, the pronoun in this sentence should be in the objective case (object of *supervisors*). The correct form is *me*.

119. **(D)** Verbs must agree in number with their subjects. The plural subject (*risks*) must have a plural verb (*seem*).

120. **(E)** No error.

121. **(A)** This is an example of a dangling participle: *playing* and *eating* should not refer to *day*, but to the subject *we*. For example: We spent the day very quietly, fishing and eating at a picnic.

122. **(E)** No error.

123. **(C)** In this sentence it seems as if the deposit is joining the club, because of a dangling infinitive phrase. The phrase should modify a person, i.e.: To join the club, *you* must make a deposit in advance.

124. **(E)** No error.

125. **(C)** Proper diction avoids excess subordination, or the inclusion of unnecessary words or phrases that add nothing to the theme or idea of a sentence. In this sentence, "who was" should be eliminated.

126. **(B)** *we* should be *us*, because it is the indirect object of the verb *has given*.

127. **(C)** *me* should be *my*, because the possessive case is used with the gerund; the object of the preposition is *buying* and not *me*.

128. **(C)** *whomever* should be *whoever*, because it is the subject of *would go*.

129. **(B)** *it's* should be *its*, because possessive case of *it* never has an apostrophe.

130. **(A)** *Lincolns* should be *Lincoln's*; this is a possessive, not a plural.

131. **(B)** *whoever* should be *whomever*; objective case needed; object of *wish*.

132. **(D)** *whom* should be *who*; subject of verb *are*.

133. **(B)** *who's* should be *whose*; who's is a contraction of *who is*.

134. **(C)** *myself* should be *I*; I, subject of *are arrested*; *myself* is a reflexive pronoun.

135. **(C)** *it's* should be *its*; possessive pronoun never has an apostrophe.

Section VI   Business Judgment

136. **(B)** A major consideration of the production manager to endorse the new product was that it "fit in well" with existing production facilities. See paragraph 3.

137. **(D)** The company's decision to market the new product line was *a priori* based on the assumption that it would be purchased by consumers. However, nowhere in the passage is there mention of any consumer research to buttress this assumption.

138. **(A)** A *major objective* of the new product launch was to generate sales needed to expand the company and enable it to solve some of its financial problems. See paragraph 3.

139. **(E)** The age of the company is unimportant to its success.

140. **(B)** This fact convinced the president's son of the need for a gourmet line of Italian food products. See paragraph 5.

141. **(D)** The company's experience in the sale of consumer products was limited to the West Coast and the Southwest.

142. **(E)** All these were mentioned as constraints to the sale of the line.

143. **(B)** The company had a poor organizational structure. This is evidenced by (1) poor planning and advertising, (2) lack of responsibility for package design, (3) poor production planning, and (4) absence of coordination of the marketing, production, and design functions.

144. **(C)** The selected advertising agency had little experience with food products, and the preparation of magazine advertisements and filmed TV commercials was delayed. See paragraph 7.

145. **(B)** No mention was made of any consumer research. The president's son objected to the selected name, which was determined by the committee.

146. **(C)** It was decided to launch the new line at the beginning of the fall food merchandising season, which was about October 1. See paragraph 4.

147. **(A)** Before introducing the new line, 60% of the company's sales were to the institutional market; thus its experience in marketing to the final consumer was limited. Moreover, no evidence was given that even hinted at any consumer research to compensate for this deficiency.

148. **(B)** This is mentioned in paragraph 5: "With the exception of the name, the younger Brooks directed most of the decisions relating to the marketing program."

149. **(E)** The nationality and location of the company have no relation to the problem.

150. **(B)** The increased cost of R&D is a *Major Factor* influencing the decision; the company is near debt because of these costs and the number of projects has caused a dispersion of its resources.

151. **(A)** Grossmann's major task as a decision maker is to allocate the company's resources on those R&D projects which can capitalize on the company's strength's in the car transmission manufacturing field.

152. **(C)** It is true that the difficulties of the electric car transmission system were due to materials technology. But this is only one facet of the overall problem of R&D allocation.

153. **(B)** Pökel SA's declining profit was a symptom of increased competition, but also of poor product planning. It is a primary consideration in the major decision of R&D rationalization.

154. **(B)** Pökel SA is a product-oriented company. Its strategy has been to invest heavily in R&D in the hope of developing innovative new products, with the expectations that they will be accepted by consumers. If it were consumer-oriented, it would have studied market trends first. The company is certainly not planning-oriented, given the manner in which management allocated R&D funds.

155. **(C)** The electric car transmission had road test difficulties and its future was unknown. See paragraphs 8 and 9.

156. **(B)** Grossmann was asked to "look around and make recommendations." See paragraph 10.

157. **(A)** The passage states that it "was felt that it [transmission problem] could be solved with more research." See paragraph 9.

158. **(B)** Grossmann first "commissioned a survey of the potential markets for all the projects on the R&D drawing boards." See paragraph 11.

159. **(B)** Grossmann commissioned two studies. The first, a market survey (paragraphs 11 and 12), found that the "company's original estimate of the timing of future demand for the electric car was unrealistic." The second study was a technical audit of R&D. This study concluded items I and II in question 159.

160. **(C)** Alternative III is vague. No mention was made of the role of stockholders in the decision-making process. If Grossmann decides to invest in speculative ventures, he may select from the first two alternatives.

Section VII   Logical Reasoning

161. **(D)** (A) and (B) are obviously incorrect since they don't say anything about short people. (C) gives another reason for what the author observed but it does not contradict the author's statement. (E) might cast doubt on the author's statement but you must make the extra assumption that people who live in large houses will get enough to eat. People who are overweight probably get enough to eat so (D) is the best choice.

162. **(C)** The given statement uses inductive reasoning. You observe that a certain statement is true every time you check it so you conclude that the statement is probably true all the time. (C) is in exactly the same form as the original statement. (A) and (B) deal with observing one attribute and forming a conclusion about a *different* attribute. (D) and (E) start with an observation and then supply a *reason* for the attribute.

163. **(B)** The point of the passage is supposed to be whether or not she favors a tax on oil imports. She has simply ducked the issue.

164. **(C)** (A) contradicts the author's point. The occupations in (E) do not fit the contrast that the author is trying to establish. Although the author would probably agree with (B), it says that two occupations should be equally compensated and the author is trying to establish pay differentials. (D) does not fit the contrast established in the first part of the sentence since the presidency is usually not considered as providing diversion.

165. **(A)** The main point of the passage is that compensation should be related to importance of work performed. (B), (C), (D), and (E) are other possibilities for deciding compensation but they don't fit the author's point of view.

166. **(C)** (A) contradicts the first statement. (B) does not follow from the statements, since saying some of the French are mortal does not imply that the rest of the French must be immortal. (C) follows since the French who are human must be mortal. (D) and (E) are true statements but they do *not* follow from the two statements because *some* is not the same as *all*.

167. **(B)** (B) gives another possible reason for the fact that it rained soon after the ritual. (C) is a weaker possibility because it does not give information about how likely it was to rain soon. (A), (D), and (E) have no relation to the facts observed.

168. **(E)** The fact that two classes of objects can be described by the same adjective does not imply that the classes overlap. For example, fire engines are red and some blankets are red, but fire engines are not blankets and blankets are not fire engines. So I and II can't be deduced. III is probably true but it cannot be deduced from the two statements.

169. **(B)** The author doesn't save money unless he originally intended to spend more than he actually spent. (A) and (E) are irrelevant. (C) and (D) give information which might answer the question whether the author should have bought the book, but you would need to make additional assumptions to obtain the conclusion.

170. **(C)** (C) explains how both statements can be true. For example, 5% of a million is much more than 10% of one hundred. (A) and (B) simply tell the truth of each statement and not whether or not they contradict each other. (D) describes each type of statement but that does not explain why they would not contradict each other. (E) might explain any contradiction but there is no reason why it should be true.

171. **(D)** (D) fits best because it contrasts with the statements about efficiency. (E) seems to continue the argument but the word *however* indicates a contrast to the previous statements. (A), (B), and (C) do not continue the thought about gas mileage in terms of the engine.

172. **(A)** If the author is using II or III, several other assumptions must be made to link them to the reasons given in the paragraph.

173. **(C)** (B), (D), and (E) can easily be eliminated. (A) is a possibility but the passage does not give consequences, only things that *might* happen, so (C) is the best answer.

174. **(C)** Just because investing and gambling are risky does not mean they are the same. The conclusion depends on the statement that gambling is a type of investment. Since the

argument concludes that gambling should be legal, the actual legal status of gambling is not used in the argument. Thus (A) is incorrect. (B) and (D) are incorrect since they would strengthen the conclusion *if* gambling were an investment, but the argument depends on the idea that gambling is an investment. (E) is incorrect since it contradicts the idea that gambling should be legal.

175. **(A)** The argument generalizes from an individual to a nation, so (A) is correct. (E) is incorrect since it uses the general case to obtain information about a specific case. (B), (C), and (D) are incorrect since they simply expand on parts of the argument. They are not the basis of the argument.

Evaluating Your Score

Tabulate your score for each section of the Diagnostic Test according to the directions on pages 4–5 and record the results in the Self-scoring Table below. Then find your rank for each score on the Self-scoring Scale and record it in the appropriate blank.

Self-scoring Table

PART	SCORE	RANK
1		
2		
3		
4		
5		
6		
7		

Self-scoring Scale

ACHIEVEMENT

PART	POOR	FAIR	GOOD	EXCELLENT
1	0–12	13–17	18–21	22–25
2	0–15	16–21	22–25	26–30
3	0–12	13–17	18–21	22–25
4	0–15	16–21	22–25	26–30
5	0–12	13–17	18–21	22–25
6	0–12	13–17	18–21	22–25
7	0–7	8–10	11–12	13–15

The following Review sections cover material for each type of question on the GMAT. Spend more time studying those sections for which you had a rank of FAIR or POOR on the Diagnostic Test.

To obtain an approximation of your actual GMAT score, see page 5.

FOUR
REVIEW AND PRACTICE
FOR THE GMAT

By taking the Diagnostic Test and evaluating your results, you now have an indication of what your strong and weak points are. Your next step is to begin a more intensive review of test material, concentrating particularly on those areas in which you rated FAIR or POOR, but also covering material you did well on so that you will be certain you fully understand all of the topics.

Study the following sections carefully and do the practice exercises that are provided. The *Reading Comprehension Review* will also assist you in preparing for both Reading Recall and Reading Comprehension as well as Business Judgment questions. For further business review, use the *Glossary of Business Terms* in the following chapter. Mathematics and Data Sufficiency are covered in the *Mathematics Review* which is keyed to answers for sample tests for easy reference. The *Logic Review* contains a discussion of principles of logic that can be applied to many areas of the exam. In the same manner the *General Vocabulary List* not only supplements the *Verbal Aptitude Review* but also presents words appearing throughout the GMAT.

READING COMPREHENSION AND RECALL REVIEW

A large proportion of the GMAT is designed to test your ability to comprehend material contained in reading passages. The Reading Recall sections of the exam are concerned with determining how well you remember the main points and significant details in the material you have read and also your capacity for drawing inferences from this material. After you have read the material you are *not* allowed to turn back to the passages in order to answer the questions. Reading Comprehension sections, on the other hand, do *allow* you to turn back to the passages when answering the questions. However, many of the questions may be based on what is *implied* in the passages, rather than what is explicitly stated. Your ability to draw inferences from the material is critical to successful completing this section.

The objective of the Business Judgment areas is to test your ability to analyze business situations and draw subsequent conclusions about them. In each case, success depends on the extent of your reading comprehension skills. The following discussion is designed to help you formulate an approach to reading passages that will enable you to better understand the material you will be asked to read on the GMAT. Practice exercises at the end of this review will give you an opportunity to try out this approach.

Basic Reading Skills

A primary skill necessary for good reading comprehension and recall is the understanding of the meanings of individual words. Knowledge of a wide and diversified vocabulary enables you to detect subtle differences in sentence meaning that may hold the key to the meaning of an entire paragraph or passage. For this reason, it is important that you familiarize yourself with as many words as possible. The *General Vocabulary List* in Chapter five is a good place to begin.

A second reading skill to be developed is the ability to discover the central theme of a passage. By making yourself aware of what the entire passage is about, you are in a position to relate what you read to this central theme, logically picking out the main points and significant details as you go along. Although the manner in which the central theme is stated may vary from passage to passage, it can usually be found in the title (if one is presented), in the "topic sentence" of a paragraph in shorter passages, or in longer passages, by reading several paragraphs.

A third essential skill is the capacity to organize mentally how the passage is put together and determine how each part is related to the whole. This is the skill you will have to use to the greatest degree on the GMAT where you must pick out significant and insignificant factors, remember main details, and relate information you have read to the central theme.

In general, a mastery of these three basic skills will provide you with a solid basis for better reading comprehension wherein you will be able to read carefully to draw a conclusion from the material, decide the meanings of words and ideas presented and how they in turn affect the meaning of the passage, and recognize opinions and views that are expressed.

Applying Basic Reading Skills

The only way to become adept at the three basic reading skills outlined above is to practice using the techniques involved as much as possible. Studying the meanings of new words you encounter, not only in the vocabulary lists in this Guide but also in all your reading material, will soon help you establish a working knowledge of many words. In the same manner, making an effort to locate topic sentences, general themes, and specific details in material you read will enable you to improve your skills in these areas. The following drills will help. After you have read through them and answered the questions satisfactorily, you can try the longer practice exercises at the end.

Finding the Topic Sentence

The term "topic sentence" is used to describe the sentence that gives the key to an entire paragraph. Usually the topic sentence is found in the beginning of a paragraph. However, there is no absolute rule. A writer may build his paragraph to a conclusion, putting the key sentence at the end. Here is an example in which the topic sentence is located at the beginning:

EXAMPLE 1:

The world faces a serious problem of overpopulation. Right now many people starve from lack of adequate food. Efforts are being made to increase the rate of food production, but the number of people to be fed increases at a faster rate.

The idea is stated directly in the opening sentence. You know that the passage will be about "a serious problem of overpopulation." Like a heading or caption, the topic sentence sets the stage or gets your mind ready for what follows in that paragraph.

Before you try to locate the topic sentence in a paragraph you must remember that this technique depends upon reading and judgment. Read the whole passage first. Then try to decide which sentence comes closest to expressing the main point of the paragraph. Do not worry about the position of the topic sentence in the paragraph; look for the most important statement. Find the idea to which all the other sentences relate.

Try this passage yourself to identify the topic sentence:

EXAMPLE 2:

During the later years of the American Revolution, the Articles of Confederation government was formed. This government suffered severely from a lack of power. Each state distrusted the others and gave little authority to the central or federal government. The Articles of Confederation produced a government which could not raise money from taxes, prevent Indian raids, or force the British out of the United States.

What is the topic sentence? Certainly the paragraph is about the Articles of Confederation. However, is the key idea in the first sentence or in the second sentence? In this instance, the *second* sentence does a better job of giving you the key to this paragraph — the lack of power that describes the Articles of Confederation. The sentences that complete the paragraph relate more to the idea of "lack of power" than to the time when the government was formed. Don't assume that the topic sentence is always the first sentence of a paragraph. Try this:

EXAMPLE 3:

There is a strong relation between limited education and low income. Statistics show that unemployment rates are highest among those adults who attended school the fewest years. Most jobs in a modern industrial society require technical or advanced training. The best pay goes with jobs that demand thinking and decisions based on knowledge. A few people manage to overcome their limited education by personality or a "lucky break." However, studies of lifetime earnings show that the average high school graduate earns more than the average high school dropout, who in turn earns more than the average adult who has not finished eighth grade.

Here, the first sentence contains the main idea of the whole paragraph. One more example should be helpful:

EXAMPLE 4:

They had fewer men available as soldiers. Less than one third of the railroads and only a small proportion of the nation's industrial production was theirs. For most of the war their coastline was blockaded by Northern ships. It is a tribute to Southern leadership and the courage of the people that they were not defeated for four years.

In this case you will note that the passage builds up to its main point. The topic sentence is the last one. Practice picking out the topic sentences in other material you read until it becomes an easy skill.

Finding the General Theme

A more advanced skill is the ability to read several paragraphs and relate them to one general theme or main idea. The procedure involves careful reading of the entire passage and deciding which idea is the central or main one. You can tell you have the right idea when it is most frequent, most important, or every sentence relates to it. As you read the next passage note the *underlined* parts.

EXAMPLE 1:

True democracy means direct <u>rule by the people</u>. A good example can be found in a modern town meeting in many small New England towns. All citizens aged twenty-one or over may vote. <u>They not only vote for officials, but they also get together to vote on local laws</u> (or ordinances). The small size of the town and the limited number of voters make this possible.

In the cities, voters cast ballots <u>for officials who get together to make the laws</u>. Because the voters do not make the laws directly, <u>this system is called indirect democracy or representative government</u>. There is no problem of distance to travel, but it is difficult to run a meeting with hundreds of thousands of citizens.

Representation of voters and a direct voice in making laws are more of a problem in state or national governments. <u>The numbers of citizens and the distances to travel make representative government the most practical way</u> to make laws.

Think about the passage in general and the underlined parts in particular. Several examples discuss voting for officials and making laws. In the first paragraph both of these are done by the voters. The second paragraph describes representative government in which voters elect officials who make laws. The last paragraph emphasizes the problem of size and numbers and says that representative government is more practical. In the following question, put all these ideas together.

 The main theme of this passage is that

    (A)   the United States is not democratic
    (B)   citizens cannot vote for lawmakers
    (C)   representative government does not make laws
    (D)   every citizen makes laws directly
    (E)   increasing populations lead to less direct democracy

The answer is choice (E). Choices (B), (C), and (D) can be eliminated because they are not true of the passage. Choice (A) may have made you hesitate a little. The passage makes comments about *less direct* democracy, but it never says that representative government is *not democratic*.

The next 3 passages offer further practice in finding the main theme. Answer the question following each example and check the analysis to make sure you understand.

EXAMPLE 2:

Skye, 13 miles off the northwest coast of Scotland, is the largest and most famous of the Hebrides. Yet fame has neither marred its natural beauty nor brought affectation to its inhabitants. The scene and the people are almost as they were generations ago.

The first sight that impresses the visitor to Skye is its stark beauty. This is not beauty of the usual sort, for the island is not a lush green "paradise." It is, on the other hand, almost devoid of shrubbery. Mountains, moorlands, sky, and sea combine to create an overpowering landscape. Endless stretches of rocky hills dominate the horizon. Miles of treeless plains meet the eye. Yet this scene has a beauty all its own.

And then cutting into the stark landscape are the fantastic airborne peaks of the Cuillins, rising into the clear skies above. The Cuillins are the most beloved mountains in Scotland and are frequently climbed. Their rugged, naked grandeur, frost-sculptured ridges and acute peaks even attracted Sir Edmund Hilary.

The main idea of this passage is   Ⓐ Ⓑ Ⓒ Ⓓ Ⓔ

(A)   the sky over Skye
(B)   the lack of trees on Skye
(C)   the natural beauty of Skye
(D)   the lack of affectation on Skye
(E)   the Cuillins in the skies of Skye

All of the answers have some truth to them. The problem is to find the *best* answer. Four of the choices are mentioned in the passage only by a small comment. But choice (C) is throughout every part of the passage. The clue to the correct answer was the frequency or how often the same theme was covered.

EXAMPLE 3:

Trade exists for many reasons. No doubt it started from a desire to have something different. Men also realized that different men could make different products. Trade encouraged specialization, which led to improvement in quality.

Trade started from person to person, but grew to involve different towns and different lands. Some found work in transporting the goods or selling them. Merchants grew rich as the demand for products increased. Craftsmen were able to sell more products at home and abroad. People in general had a greater variety of things to choose.

The knowledge of new products led to an interest in the lands which produced them. More daring persons went to see other lands. Others stayed at home, but asked many questions of the travellers. As people learned about the products and the conditions in other countries, they compared them with their own. This often led to a desire for better conditions or a hope for a better life. Trade was mainly an economic force, but it also had other effects.

The general theme of the passage deals with how

(A)   trade makes everyone rich
(B)   trade divides the world
(C)   products are made
(D)   trade changes people's lives
(E)   people find new jobs

This is not easy as you may feel that all the choices are good. Most of them were mentioned in some part of the passage. However, you must select the *best* choice. If you had trouble, let us analyze the passage.

Paragraph one emphasizes a "desire for something different" and "improvement." The second paragraph refers to "found work," "merchants grew rich," "craftsmen sell more," and "greater variety of things to choose." The third paragraph covers "interest in the lands," "compared them with their own," "desire for better conditions" and "better life." All these are evidence of the same general theme of how trade brings changes in the lives of people. Choice (D) is the best answer.

Choice (A) is tempting because of the comment on merchants getting rich. However, this idea is not found all through the passage. Choice (B) may catch the careless thinker. Trade does not divide the world, even though the passage talks about dividing jobs. Choice (C) is weak. Some comment is made about making products, but not in all parts of the passage. Choice (E) is weak for the same reason as choice (C).

EXAMPLE 4:

The enormous problems of turning swamps and desert into fields and orchards, together with the ideal of share-and-share-alike, gave birth to the kibbutz.

In those days, the kibbutz member had to plow the fields with a rifle slung over his shoulder.

Today security is still a factor in the kibbutz. Shelters are furrowed into the ground along every walk among the shade trees, near the children's house, where all the young children of the kibbutz live, and near the communal dining room.

But the swamps have been conquered, and the desert is gradually becoming green. And while kibbutz members once faced deprivation and a monotonous diet, today they reap the harvest of hard work and success.

One such kibbutz is Dorot, at the gateway to the Negev desert and typical of the average size Israeli communal settlement.

Life on the kibbutz has become more complex through growth and prosperity. While once the land barely yielded enough for a living, Dorot, like many other kibbutzim, now exports some of its crops. It also has become industrialized, another trend among these settlements. Dorot has a factory which exports faucets to a dozen countries, including the United States.

Ⓐ Ⓑ Ⓒ Ⓓ Ⓔ   The main theme of this article is

- (A) faucets are a sign of growth and prosperity in the kibbutz
- (B) with the solving of agricultural problems the kibbutz has become a more complex society
- (C) since security is a problem for the kibbutz, it has become industrialized
- (D) Dorot is the prosperous gateway to the Negev desert
- (E) kibbutzim are good places to live because they are located in swamps and deserts

Choice (A) receives brief mention at the end of the passage. It is an idea in the passage, but certainly not the general idea of the passage. Choice (D) is the same kind of answer as choice (A)—it is too specific a fact. Choice (E) is unrelated to the passage. We now have choices (B) and (C) as possible answers. Choice (C) seems reasonable until you analyze it. Did the need for security *cause* the industrialization? Or are there better examples of how life has become more complex now that agricultural problems have been solved? The evidence leans more to choice (B).

In summary, in order to find the general theme:

1. Read at your normal speed
2. Locate the topic sentence in each paragraph
3. Note ideas that are frequent or emphasized
4. Find the idea to which most of the passage is related

Finding Logical Relationships

In order to fully understand the meaning of a passage, you must first look for the general theme and then relate the ideas and opinions found in the passage to this general theme. In this way, you can determine not only what is important but also how the ideas interrelate to form the whole. From this understanding, you will be better able to answer questions that refer to the passage.

As you read the following passages, look for general theme and supporting facts, words or phrases that signal emphasis or shift in thought, and the relation of one idea to another.

EXAMPLE 1:

The candidate who wants to be elected pays close attention to statements and actions that will make the voters see him favorably. In ancient Rome candidates wore pure white togas (the Latin word *candidatus* means "clothed in white") to indicate that they were pure, clean, and above any "dirty work." However, it is interesting to note that such a toga was not worn after election.

In more modern history, candidates allied themselves with political parties. Once a voter knows and favors the views of a certain political party, he may vote for anyone with that party's label. Nevertheless, divisions of opinion develop so that today there is a wide range of candidate views in any major party.

1. From the first paragraph the best of these conclusions is that after an election   Ⓐ Ⓑ Ⓒ Ⓓ Ⓔ

   (A) all candidates are dishonest
   (B) candidates do not have to use the toga as a symbol
   (C) candidates do not change their ideas
   (D) officials are always honest
   (E) policies always change

You noted the ideas about a candidate in Rome. You saw the word "however" signal a shift in ideas or thinking. Now the third step rests with your judgment. You cannot jump to a conclusion; you must see which conclusion is reasonable or fair. Choices (A), (D), and (E) should make you wary. They say "all" or "always" which means without exception. The last sentence is not that strong or positive. Choices (B) and (C) must be considered. There is nothing in the paragraph that supports the fact that candidates do not change their ideas. This forces you into choice (B) as the only statement logically related to what the paragraph said.

2. A fair statement is that most candidates from the same political party today are likely to

Ⓐ Ⓑ Ⓒ Ⓓ Ⓔ

(A) have the same views
(B) be different in every view
(C) agree on almost all points
(D) agree on some points and disagree on others
(E) agree only by accident

Here again, the burden rests on your judgment after following ideas and word clues. The paragraph makes the point that there is a wide range of views. That eliminates choice (A). Choice (B) is not logical because the candidates would not likely be in the same party if they disagree on every view. The remaining choices are different degrees of agreement. Choice (E) is weak because candidates are too interested to arrive at agreement only by accident. The wide range mentioned seems to oppose choice (C) and favor choice (D) as a little more likely. You may say that choice (C) sounds pretty good. Again we stress that *you are picking the very best choice*, not just a good choice. This is what we mean by reflecting carefully on all possibilities and selecting the best available choice.

EXAMPLE 2:

In 1812 Napoleon had to withdraw his forces from Russia. The armies invaded successfully and reached the city of Moscow. There was no question of French army disloyalty or unwillingness to fight. As winter came, the Russian army moved out of the way, leaving a wasted land and burned buildings. Other conquered European nations seized upon Napoleon's problems in Russia as their chance to rearm and to break loose from French control.

Ⓐ Ⓑ Ⓒ Ⓓ Ⓔ

According to the passage, the main reason for Napoleon's withdrawal from Russia was the

(A) disloyalty of the French troops
(B) Russian winter
(C) burned buildings
(D) planned revolts in other countries
(E) Russian army

In this passage, only choice (A) is totally incorrect. Choice (E) is very weak because the Russian army was not able to stop the invasion. The choices narrow to which is the best of (B), (C), and (D). It seems that all three answers are supported by the passage. There needs to be some thought and judgment by you. Which of these could be overcome easily and which could be the strongest reason for Napoleon leaving Russia? The burned buildings could be overcome by the troops making other shelters. The Russian winter was severe and the army did not want to face it. However, marching out of Russia in the winter was also a great problem. Napoleon probably would have stayed in Moscow except for a more serious problem—the loss of control he had established over most of Europe, thus, answer (D) is best.

EXAMPLE 3:

By 1915 events of World War I were already involving the United States and threatening its neutrality. The sinking of the British liner *Lusitania* in that year by a German submarine caused great resentment among Americans. Over a hundred United States citizens were killed in the incident. President Wilson had frequently deplored the use of submarines by Germany against the United States. Since the U.S. was neutral, it was not liable to acts of war by another nation.

However, Wilson resolved to represent the strong feeling in the country (notably in the Midwest) and in the Democratic Party that U.S. neutrality should be maintained. He felt that the United States should have "peace with honor," if possible.

There were also people, mostly in the East, that wanted to wage a preventive war against Germany. Such men as Theodore Roosevelt bitterly attacked Wilson as one who talked a great deal but did nothing.

By 1917 Germany again used unrestricted submarine warfare and Wilson broke off relations with Germany. In February British agents uncovered the Zimmerman Telegram. This was an attempt by the German ambassador to Mexico to involve that nation in a war against the United States. And in March several American merchant ships were sunk by German submarines. His patience at an end, Wilson at last took the position of a growing majority of Americans and asked Congress to declare war on Germany. Thus, United States entered World War I.

1. This passage tries to explain that   1. Ⓐ Ⓑ Ⓒ Ⓓ Ⓔ

   (A) Wilson wanted the U.S. to go to war against Germany
   (B) Wilson tried to avoid war with Germany
   (C) Germany wanted the U.S. to enter the war
   (D) Other nations were pressuring U.S. to enter the war
   (E) Mexico was our main enemy

2. We can conclude from the passage that most citizens of United States in 1917 were   2. Ⓐ Ⓑ Ⓒ Ⓓ Ⓔ

   (A) totally opposed to war with Germany
   (B) in favor of war before Wilson was
   (C) willing to accept war after Wilson persuaded them
   (D) neutral
   (E) trying to avoid war

3. The last event in the series of happenings that led to a declaration of war against   3. Ⓐ Ⓑ Ⓒ Ⓓ Ⓔ
Germany was the

   (A) Zimmerman Telegram
   (B) attacks on U.S. merchant ships
   (C) Wilson's war message to Congress
   (D) change of public opinion
   (E) sinking of the *Lusitania*

In question 1, the key is to note Wilson's actions discussed in paragraph two. Near the end of the passage there is a phrase about "his patience at end." These describe a man who was trying to avoid a conflict as in answer choice (B).

Question 2 rests on two ideas. There was a change in the feeling of the American people about war. The other idea is whether Wilson changed to lead them or he responded after he felt that they had changed. The phrase "took the position of a growing majority of Americans" tells us that Wilson followed the change in opinion as in answer choice (B).

In question 3, you need to check the sequence of events. A declaration of war followed the president's request.

Making Inferences

An inference is not stated. It is assumed by the reader from something said by the writer. An inference is the likely or probable conclusion rather than the direct logical one. It usually involves an opinion or viewpoint that the writer wants the reader to follow or assume. In another kind of inference the reader figures out the author's opinion even though it is not stated. The clues are generally found in which facts are presented and in the choice of words and phrases. Opinion is revealed by its one-sided nature in which no opposing facts are given. It is shown further by "loaded" words that reveal feelings.

It is well worth noting that opinionated writing is often more interesting than straight factual accounts. Some writers are very colorful, forceful, or amusing in presenting their views. You should understand that there is nothing wrong with reading opinion. You should read varied opinions, but know that they are opinions. Then make up your own mind.

Not every writer will insert his opinion obviously. However, you can get clues from how often the same idea is said (frequency), whether arguments are balanced on both sides (fairness), and the choice of wording (emotional or loaded words). Look for the clues in this next passage.

EXAMPLE 1:

Slowly but surely the great passenger trains of the United States have been fading from the rails. Short-run commuter trains still rattle in and out of the cities. Between major cities you can still find a train, but the schedules are becoming less frequent. The Twentieth Century Limited, The Broadway Limited, and other luxury trains that sang along the rails at 60 to 80 miles an hour are no longer running. Passengers on other long runs complain of poor service, old equipment, and costs in time and money. The long distance traveller today accepts the noise of jets, the congestion at airports, and the traffic between airport and city. A more elegant and graceful way is becoming only a memory.

1. Ⓐ Ⓑ Ⓒ Ⓓ Ⓔ 1. With respect to the reduction of long run passenger trains, this writer expresses

    (A) regret   (D) elation
    (B) pleasure   (E) anger
    (C) grief

Before you choose the answer, you must assume what the writer's feeling is. He does not actually state his feeling, but clues are available so that you may infer what it is. Choices (B) and (D) are impossible, because he gives no word that shows he is pleased by the change. Choice (C) is too strong as is choice (E). Choice (A) is the most reasonable inference to make. He is sorry to see the change. He is expressing regret.

2. Ⓐ Ⓑ Ⓒ Ⓓ Ⓔ 2. The author seems to feel that air travel is

    (A) costly   (D) crude
    (B) slow   (E) uncomfortable
    (C) streamlined

Here we must be careful because he says very little about air travel. However, his one sentence about it presents three negative or annoying points. The choice now becomes fairly clear.

EXAMPLE 2:

When the United States started at the end of the eighteenth century, it was a small and weak country, made up mostly of poor farmers. Foreign policy, reflecting this domestic condition, stressed "no entangling alliances." The State Department then had a staff of less than half a dozen persons, whose total salary was $6,600 (of which $3,500 went to the Secretary of State), and a diplomatic service budget (July, 1790) of $40,000. Militarily, too, the country was insignificant. The first United States army, soon after the American Revolution, was made up of one captain (John Doughty) and 80 men. Clearly, the United States did not consider itself a real power and was not taken seriously by the rest of the world.

It was not until immense changes took place INSIDE the United States that the country began to play an important role in foreign affairs. By the beginning of the twentieth century, the United States had ceased to be a predominantly agricultural nation and had become an industrial one. Its population had grown more than 30 times its original number. George Washington was president of 3,000,000 Americans; Theodore Roosevelt, of 100,000,000.

1. A small country today cannot expect to play an important part in world affairs unless it

    (A) has wealth
    (B) has powerful allies
    (C) is strong internally
    (D) is none of the above
    (E) is all of the above

1. Ⓐ Ⓑ Ⓒ • Ⓓ Ⓔ

(NOTE: This is a slightly different style of question. You must look at each of the answer choices in (A)–(C). As you consider the passage and what it suggests for a small country today, you add your own knowledge. Each of the answer choices in (A)–(C) makes good sense. Therefore, answer choice (E) is the best answer because it includes all of the good ones in (A)–(C). Again, this is not designed to trick you. The purpose of such a question is to be sure that you have read all the choices before you have made a selection of the best one.)

2. The writer seems to think that the main factor in making the United States a world power was

    (A) industrialization
    (B) passing of time
    (C) growth of population
    (D) the presidency of Theodore Roosevelt
    (E) avoiding entangling alliances

2. Ⓐ Ⓑ Ⓒ Ⓓ Ⓔ

The passage does not answer the question directly. You must infer or assume what is meant by the author. However, there is a clue in the author's comment that changes inside a country make a big difference in its foreign policy. The big internal changes noted are population and industrial power. By drawing on your knowledge and by interpreting the passage, you will be led to choice (A) for this question.

In Example 3 you will find three short statements by three different writers. The questions will require that you make inferences about each writer and then make comparisons of one against the other two.

EXAMPLE 3:

Writer I

No nation should tolerate the slacker who will not defend his country in time of war. The so-called conscientious objector is a coward who accepts the benefits of his country but will not accept the responsibility. By shirking his fair share, he forces another person to assume an unfair burden.

Writer II

A democratic nation should have room for freedom of conscience. Religious training and belief may make a man conscientiously opposed to participation in war. The conscientious objector should be permitted to give labor service or some form of non-combat military duty. His beliefs should be respected.

Writer III

The rights of the conscientious objector should be decided by each individual. No government should dictate to any person or require him to endanger his life if the person, in conscience, objects. There need be no religious basis. It is enough for a free individual to think as he pleases and to reject laws or rules to which he conscientiously objects.

1. Ⓐ Ⓑ Ⓒ Ⓓ Ⓔ   **1.**   A balanced opinion on this subject is presented by

     (A)   Writer I
     (B)   Writer II
     (C)   Writer III
     (D)   all of the writers
     (E)   none of the writers

2. Ⓐ Ⓑ Ⓒ Ⓓ Ⓔ   **2.**   We can conclude that the writer most likely to support a person who refuses any military service is

     (A)   Writer I
     (B)   Writer II
     (C)   Writer III
     (D)   all of the writers
     (E)   none of the writers

3. Ⓐ Ⓑ Ⓒ Ⓓ Ⓔ   **3.**   An authoritarian person is most likely to agree with

     (A)   Writer I
     (B)   Writer II
     (C)   Writer III
     (D)   all of the writers
     (E)   none of the writers

Look for clues in the language or choice of words that are loaded with feeling such as "slacker," "so-called," and "shirking" by Writer I and "dictate," "endanger," and "as he pleases" by Writer III. Compare them with the language used by Writer II. The second help is to connect what these writers say with views you have heard or read. We are not asking you to take any of these opinions. You are using your skill in reading what the writers think and adding it to your own knowledge. Then you make logical or related inferences.

Now that you have spent time reviewing the three basic skills you should master for better reading comprehension ability, try the practice exercises that follow. Answers to these exercises appear after Exercise C. You should also try to spend time using this reading approach as you read other material not related to the GMAT.

Practice Exercises

The following five reading passages are similar to those found on the GMAT. The first three are Reading Recall sections; the latter two, Reading Comprehension. You should read each one and then answer the questions that follow according to the directions. Remember that in Reading Recall sections you cannot refer to the passage while answering the questions. Also, on the actual exam you are asked to read three or four Reading Recall passages before answering the questions. Passages are separated here for practice purposes.

Reading Recall

EXERCISE A

TOTAL TIME: 12 minutes

Part A: TIME — 5 minutes

DIRECTIONS: This part contains a reading passage. You will have 5 minutes to study the passage and 7 minutes to answer questions based on it. When answering the questions you will *not* be allowed to refer back to the passage.

For the most part, American institutions of higher education managed to expand their resources and facilities to absorb the rapidly increasing numbers of students seeking to enroll in the 1960s. Students who could not qualify for the most selective four-year institutions were admitted to less selective four-year institutions or to two-year colleges. Only toward the end of the decade were there signs of serious stresses and strains resulting from financial stringency in both public and private institutions.

The outlook for smooth absorption of the increased numbers of students who will be seeking higher education in the 1970s is at present very uncertain. Campus unrest, which is leading some state legislatures to "punish" public institutions of higher education by withholding funds and which is causing some alumni and other private donors to hold back on gifts to colleges and universities, may abate somewhat if we withdraw from the Indochina war, but most sophisticated observers do not expect unrest to disappear on campuses. Cutbacks in federal government support of higher education may prove to be temporary if a decline in military expenditures facilitates increased appropriations for education and other social services. But a more persistent problem is likely to be the fiscal stringency faced by state and local governments (with the latter representing a significant source of financing of two-year colleges).

Appropriations for higher education must compete at state and local levels with rapidly rising expenditures for welfare, elementary and secondary education, and other public services. State and local governments face serious difficulties in meeting these mounting costs because they tend to rely heavily on sales taxes and, in the case of local governments, property taxes—taxes yielding revenues that tend to rise less rapidly than personal income. In contrast, the tax revenues of the federal government, which rely in large part on personal and corporate income taxes, tend to rise more rapidly than personal income.

In fact, from the perspective of the fall of 1971, it appears likely that higher education will *not* be in a position to absorb the increased numbers of students seeking admission in the 1970s without greatly increased federal government support, along the lines recommended by the Carnegie Commission. In the absence of such increased federal government support, students and their parents in both public and private institutions will have to meet an increased proportion of the rising costs of education through greatly increased tuition and fees. That requirement will be to the detriment of enrollment of many students from low-income families and even of a good many students from middle-income families, and public institutions may continue to be forced to turn away qualified applicants on an increased scale.

Assuming, however, that adequate funds are forthcoming from public sources, that growth is not inhibited by changes in the demand for college graduates or by structural changes in higher education, and that the age distribution of students does not change very much, enrollment trends in the 1970s and the following two decades will be determined by (1) changes in the rate of growth of the college-age population and (2) a continuation of the long-run upward trend in enrollment rates, which in turn primarily reflects the influence of three interrelated and overlapping factors: (a) the upward trend in high school graduation rates, (b) the rise in real per-capita income, and (c) changes in the occupational structure which result in an increased demand for persons holding academic degrees.

How will enrollment be distributed among types of institutions in future years? If changes in the 1970s reflect the shifts that occurred from 1963 to 1970, the most rapid growth of enrollment to 1980 is likely to occur in the two-year institutions. Their enrollment will increase 70 percent and may be expected to increase these institutions' share of total enrollment from 28 to 31 percent. Most of this growth will occur in the public two-year colleges, which are likely to account for 96 percent of all enrollment in two-year institutions in 1980, as compared with 94 percent in 1970.

The comprehensive colleges are also estimated to experience rapid growth. Although their enrollment is likely to increase 58 percent in the 10-year period, their share of the total is projected to rise only from 31 to 32 percent. This estimate would be only slightly altered if, as seems likely, some of the public liberal arts colleges were to broaden their programs so that they would be entitled to classification as comprehensive colleges by 1980.

Interestingly, the projections suggest that the most slowly growing group of institutions will be the doctoral-granting institutions, although they will experience a substantial 37 percent increase in enrollment. But their share of the total is likely to fall from 30 to about 27 percent. Moreover, the more prestigious the institution, the less rapid the rate of enrollment growth is likely to be. This reflects the fact that the less prestigious doctoral-granting institutions tend to be younger, and thus in an earlier and more rapid stage of development.

If there is still time remaining, review the passage until all 5 minutes have elapsed.
Do not look at Part B until that time.

Part B: TIME — 7 minutes

DIRECTIONS: Answer the following questions pertaining to information in the passage you have just read. You may not turn back to that passage for assistance.

1. According to the passage, American institutions of higher education   1. Ⓐ Ⓑ Ⓒ Ⓓ Ⓔ

   (A) failed to absorb all applicants in the 1960s
   (B) were financially strained
   (C) expanded their resources and facilities
   (D) worsened academically
   (E) increased in number

2. According to the author, the outlook for absorption of increased numbers of students   2. Ⓐ Ⓑ Ⓒ Ⓓ Ⓔ
   is

   (A) favorable   (D) optimistic
   (B) doubtful   (E) plausible
   (C) uncertain

3. It is stated in the passage that enrollment trends in the 1970s will be influenced by   3. Ⓐ Ⓑ Ⓒ Ⓓ Ⓔ

   (A) costs of education
   (B) changes in the rate of growth of educational institutions
   (C) changes in the educational system
   (D) changes in the rate of growth of college-age population
   (E) none of the above

4. Another factor mentioned by the author that can influence enrollment trends is   4. Ⓐ Ⓑ Ⓒ Ⓓ Ⓔ

   (A) changes in the demand for college graduates
   (B) attitudes of high school students
   (C) the general economic climate
   (D) growth of the service industry
   (E) the future of extra-curricular college activities

5. It can be inferred that the author believes that increased federal support   5. Ⓐ Ⓑ Ⓒ Ⓓ Ⓔ

   (A) should be welcomed only as a last resort
   (B) is essential to support increased enrollment
   (C) should be used only in public institutions
   (D) could lead to higher income taxes
   (E) would result in higher tuition costs

6. The author states that campus unrest has caused   6. Ⓐ Ⓑ Ⓒ Ⓓ Ⓔ

   (A) a decline in enrollment
   (B) disruption of classes
   (C) a decline in gift-giving to colleges
   (D) student support for the Indochina war
   (E) increased costs for police protection

7. Ⓐ Ⓑ Ⓒ Ⓓ Ⓔ 7. The author believes that campus unrest is

(A) a passing phenomenon
(B) of little effect on enrollment
(C) unlikely to disappear quickly
(D) of little consequence
(E) the work of a minority

8. Ⓐ Ⓑ Ⓒ Ⓓ Ⓔ 8. It is the author's opinion that higher education will

(A) not be able to absorb increased enrollments without more federal support
(B) face a decrease in demand for a college degree
(C) rely on higher personal and corporate income taxes
(D) experience quite substantial enrollment increases
(E) be affected by a changing labor market for Ph.D's

9. Ⓐ Ⓑ Ⓒ Ⓓ Ⓔ 9. According to the passage. enrollment in two-year institutions will

(A) increase by 70 percent
(B) increase by 20 percent
(C) remain somewhat stable
(D) decline slightly
(E) decline rapidly

10. Ⓐ Ⓑ Ⓒ Ⓓ Ⓔ 10. The most slowly growing group of institutions will be

(A) comprehensive colleges
(B) four-year colleges
(C) doctoral-granting institutions
(D) two-year colleges
(E) private colleges

EXERCISE B

TOTAL TIME: 12 minutes

Part A: TIME — 5 minutes

DIRECTIONS: This part contains a reading passage. You will have 5 minutes to study the passage and 7 minutes to answer questions based on it. When answering the questions you will *not* be allowed to refer back to the passage.

On August 15. 1971. the President announced a far-reaching New Economic Policy designed to check the rise in prices and wages. strengthen the Nation's external economic position and stimulate economic activity at home. To curb the rate of inflation. prices. wages. and rents were subjected to a 90-day freeze. which was followed by a comprehensive but more flexible system of controls. To improve the Nation's balance of payments, the President suspended the convertibility of the dollar into gold and other reserve assets and imposed a temporary 10-percent surcharge on imports. And to strengthen the domestic economy, the President proposed, in addition to these measures, a fiscal package whose stimulus came from a set of tax cuts, which were passed by the Congress in December in somewhat altered form.

Results of the new program were visible in varying degrees by the end of the year. They were most apparent in the slowdown of price and wage increases during the freeze. On the international front the major industrial countries agreed to a realignment of currencies more favorable to the U.S. competitive position and to prompt discussions concerning trade barriers and long-term monetary reform. The strong upsurge in the purchases of automobiles from mid-August through November was partly a result of the proposed removal of the Federal excise tax, but much of it was apparently an attempt by consumers to buy automobiles before prices were increased in the post-freeze period. Perhaps the most significant effect of the combined package was the impact on public confidence. From mid-August to the end of the year, there was slow but steady improvement in confidence that the rate of inflation was subsiding and the pace of the economic recovery was gathering strength.

The decision to embark on the New Economic Policy (NEP) came from an increasing awareness in the Administration that the ambitious goals it had set in the beginning of the year were not being met. Progress in the fight against inflation was proceeding too slowly, and its future success was uncertain. At the same time, the recovery was also progressing, but not fast enough to cut the rate of unemployment. More crucial than either of these for the timing of the decisions was the serious weakening of the dollar in international markets. As the summer wore on, there were no signs of a resolution of the financial crisis that in May caused the Swiss franc and the Austrian schilling to be revalued and the German mark and the Netherlands guilder to be set free to float in value. In the second quarter, the U.S. balance of payments on the official reserve transactions basis had recorded a deficit of $23 billion at a seasonally adjusted annual rate, and in July and August pressure against the dollar reached enormous proportions. Funds totalling $3.7 billion moved into foreign official reserve accounts in the week ended August 15. The time had come to deal decisively with the international financial problem that had persisted for at least a dozen years despite the efforts of four successive Administrations.

If there is still time remaining, review the passage until all 5 minutes have elapsed.
Do not look at Part B until that time.

Part B: TIME—7 minutes

DIRECTIONS: Answer the following questions pertaining to information in the passage you have just read. You may not turn back to that passage for assistance.

1. A provision of the President's New Economic Policy was

    (A) wage and price controls
    (B) increased income taxes
    (C) a surcharge on exports
    (D) reduced tariffs
    (E) devaluation of the dollar

1. Ⓐ Ⓑ Ⓒ Ⓓ Ⓔ

2. Ⓐ Ⓑ Ⓒ Ⓓ Ⓔ 2. Imports were subjected to a

(A) 90-day freeze
(B) system of price controls
(C) quota system
(D) 10-percent surcharge
(E) most-favored nation basis

3. Ⓐ Ⓑ Ⓒ Ⓓ Ⓔ 3. The decision to embark on the NEP came about because of

(A) public pressure
(B) devaluation of the dollar
(C) an act of Congress
(D) slowdown of inflation
(E) failure to meet the Administration's economic goals

4. Ⓐ Ⓑ Ⓒ Ⓓ Ⓔ 4. What currencies were set free to float in value?

(A) dollar
(B) Swiss franc
(C) German mark
(D) British pound
(E) Italian lira

5. Ⓐ Ⓑ Ⓒ Ⓓ Ⓔ 5. The international financial problem had persisted for

(A) 12 years
(B) 4 years
(C) 12 months
(D) 2 years
(E) since World War II

6. Ⓐ Ⓑ Ⓒ Ⓓ Ⓔ 6. Increased automobile purchases in the United States were the result of

(A) rising incomes
(B) a surge in car imports
(C) removal of the Federal excise tax
(D) significant body restyling
(E) unknown factors

7. Ⓐ Ⓑ Ⓒ Ⓓ Ⓔ 7. The President suspended the convertibility of the dollar into gold to improve the country's

(A) monetary system
(B) balance of payments
(C) dollar reserves
(D) foreign exchange holdings
(E) scarce resources

8. Ⓐ Ⓑ Ⓒ Ⓓ Ⓔ 8. As a result of the President's NEP, the passage states that the public's confidence

(A) waned
(B) showed little change
(C) showed no change
(D) showed slow but steady improvement
(E) greatly increased

9. During the period under discussion in the passage, unemployment

    (A) declined
    (B) increased
    (C) stayed about the same
    (D) was not mentioned in the passage
    (E) was mentioned without comment

        9. Ⓐ Ⓑ Ⓒ Ⓓ Ⓔ

10. Which of the following men was President during the time period under discussion?

        10. Ⓐ Ⓑ Ⓒ Ⓓ Ⓔ

    (A) Kennedy   (D) Johnson
    (B) Roosevelt   (E) Truman
    (C) Nixon

EXERCISE C

TOTAL TIME: 12 minutes

Part A: TIME — 5 minutes

DIRECTIONS: This part contains a reading passage. You will have 5 minutes to study the passage and 7 minutes to answer questions based on it. When answering the questions you will *not* be allowed to refer back to the passage.

The sudden and summary demise of the SST program supplied final evidence of a process that started in the mid-sixties; our generation stands, at present, at one of the sharp turning points of human culture characterized by fairly general rejection of an old value system.

We grew up in a world that regarded material progress through technological improvement as the main glory of our times. We learned to admire our productive machinery as a generator of greater self-fulfillment by freeing us from the toil of past generations. We interpreted the conquest of distance through rapid transportation as a way of creating freer and better understanding among the inhabitants of our planet. As our younger generation has taken stock of our hopes and actual accomplishments, however, it has found that a world built on technology is a hollow one. Our expectations were too utopian and, therefore, our actual achievements have lost the creditability of our ideals.

A new orientation is emerging. It does not build its hopes on the more efficient creation of goods and services as the ultimate answer to miseries. Instead, it regards technology as a source of our ills rather than the solution to them. The factories, once visited by streams of admiring townfolk, now stand in the public eye as the source of pollution. Supersonic planes are no longer the embodiment of the ultimate conquest of distance. The important element of their existence is now the nuisance of their noise. Automation is no longer valued as the source of leisure time; it draws criticism as the creator of structural unemployment.

Middle-aged men are ill advised to argue their ideological-social beliefs with the younger generation. As value systems replace each other, being "right" or "wrong" loses most of its meaning. Demography itself assures the ultimate domination by the younger generation; the young will outlive us.

There is, however, room for rational analysis in the economic impact of this change in cultures. The SST case has proven it; the preferences of the alienated are now a strong enough factor to determine the contractions and expansions of the public purse.

There can be little doubt that their attitudes as citizens, as consumers and even as investors will have a crucial impact upon the economic structure.

Mankind has experienced recurrent trouble in dealing with the intricacies of advanced civilizations. Saint Augustine's Christian purism was a rejection of Roman sophistication. Calvin's puritanistic views represented deep distrust of Renaissance worldliness. Jean Jacques Rousseau's XVIII century turn to natural life expressed the reservations of a sensitive man to complexities beyond his understanding. High moments of civilization have a general tendency to produce counter-cultures and alienated reactions: a yearning for a world with fewer complexities and closer to the intimate scale of man's own life.

Life at present abounds with similar symptoms. Leading schools report a growing interest among graduating collegians for careers in farming. Clothing styles among the young, a good indicator of cultural change, reflect a taste for the simple, non-commercial product. The traditionalist tweedy line is being replaced by items from the Army and Navy surplus store. Girls turn to home sewing and create their own styles inspired by folkloric elements. Over-urbanized vacation spots are losing out to wandering and camping. "Roughing it" is now in style. The rediscovery of nature mixes well with the embracement of conservationist causes. The latter, formerly a conservative movement among the landed gentry against the intrusion of new elements, is now a mass issue.

If there is still time remaining, review the passage until all 5 minutes have elapsed. Do not look at Part B until that time.

Part B: TIME — 7 minutes

DIRECTIONS: Answer the following questions pertaining to information in the passage you have just read. You may not turn back to that passage for assistance.

1. Ⓐ Ⓑ Ⓒ Ⓓ Ⓔ **1.** An appropriate title for the passage could be

   (A) *Youth in Rebellion*
   (B) *Demographics of Youth*
   (C) *Dethroning Technology*
   (D) *Demise of the SST*
   (E) *Old and New Ideologies*

2. Ⓐ Ⓑ Ⓒ Ⓓ Ⓔ **2.** The demise of the SST is indicative of

   (A) an upsurge of patriotism
   (B) rejection of technology if it is a source of ills
   (C) a misunderstanding of progress
   (D) costly failures
   (E) rebellious youth

3. Ⓐ Ⓑ Ⓒ Ⓓ Ⓔ **3.** Progress, according to the passage, used to mean

   (A) establishment of science-based industry
   (B) an increase in material goods
   (C) better transportation
   (D) greater self-fulfillment
   (E) more wealth

4. The author states that automation is viewed by young people as a(n)   4. Ⓐ Ⓑ Ⓒ Ⓓ Ⓔ

   (A) potential source of leisure time
   (B) labor saving device
   (C) aid to economic growth
   (D) creator of structural unemployment
   (E) complement to technology

5. Some colleges report that graduates have taken a growing interest in   5. Ⓐ Ⓑ Ⓒ Ⓓ Ⓔ

   (A) politics   (D) farming
   (B) sewing   (E) auto mechanics
   (C) transportation

6. The desire by youth for a simpler life closer to nature is expressed by the term   6. Ⓐ Ⓑ Ⓒ Ⓓ Ⓔ

   (A) conservationism   (D) purism
   (B) counter-culture   (E) conservatism
   (C) renaissance

7. Which historical person desired a return to the "natural life"?   7. Ⓐ Ⓑ Ⓒ Ⓓ Ⓔ

   (A) Rousseau   (D) Saint Augustine
   (B) Calvin   (E) Luther
   (C) Saint Simon

8. The author believes that the older generation should   8. Ⓐ Ⓑ Ⓒ Ⓓ Ⓔ

   (A) not argue their ideological beliefs with the young generation
   (B) take on the beliefs of the young generation
   (C) take a "business as usual" attitude
   (D) try to persuade young people to be more conservative
   (E) take no action at all

9. According to the passage, young people will have an impact on the economy   9. Ⓐ Ⓑ Ⓒ Ⓓ Ⓔ
because of all the following except

   (A) they will comprise a large number of the population
   (B) they will influence investment
   (C) their incomes will rise
   (D) they have more voting power
   (E) they are more militant

10. In general, the passage points out that attitudes and values of the youth generation   10. Ⓐ Ⓑ Ⓒ Ⓓ Ⓔ
are

   (A) basically the same as their parents
   (B) influenced by what they learn in college
   (C) basically different from that of their parents
   (D) volatile, in that they change every year or two
   (E) favorably disposed to conspicuous consumption

Reading Comprehension

EXERCISE D

TIME: 9 minutes

DIRECTIONS: This part contains a reading passage. You are to read it carefully. When answering the questions, you *will* be able to refer to the passages. The questions are based on what is *stated* or *implied* in the passage. You have nine minutes to complete this part.

Above all colonialism was hated for its explicit assumption that the civilizations of colonized peoples were inferior. Using slogans like *The White Man's Burden* and *La Mission Civilicatrice* Europeans asserted their moral obligation to impose their way of life on those endowed with inferior cultures. This orientation was
(5) particularly blatant among the French. In the colonies, business was conducted in French. Schools used that language and employed curricula designed for children in France. One scholar suggests that Muslim children probably learned no more about the Maghreb than they did about Australia. In the Metropole, intellectuals discoursed on the weakness of Arabo-Islamic culture. A noted historian accused Islam
(10) of being hostile to science. An academician wrote that Arabic—the holy language of religion, art and the Muslim sciences—is "more of an encumbrance than an aid to the mind. It is absolutely devoid of precision." There was of course an element of truth in the criticisms. After all, Arab reformists had been engaging in self-criticism for decades. Also, at least some Frenchmen honestly believed they were help-
(15) ing the colonized. A Resident General in Tunisia, for example, told an assemblage of of Muslims with sincerity, "We shall distribute to you all that we have of learning; we shall make you a party to everything that makes for the strength of our intelligence." But none of this could change or justify the cultural racism in colonial ideologies. To the French, North Africans were only partly civilized and could be saved
(20) only by becoming Frenchmen. The reaction of the colonized was of course to defend his identity and to label colonial policy, in the words of Algerian writer Malek Hadad, "cultural asphyxia." Throughout North Africa, nationalists made the defense of Arabo-Islamic civilization a major objective, a value in whose name they demanded independence. Yet the crisis of identity, provoked by colonial experiences, has not
(25) been readily assured and lingers into the post-colonial period. A French scholar describes the devasting impact of colonialism by likening it to "the role played for us (in Europe) by the doctrine of original sin." Frantz Fanon, especially in his *Studies in a Dying Colonialism,* well expresses the North African perspective.

Factors producing militant and romantic cultural nationalism are anchored in
(30) time. Memories of colonialism are already beginning to fade and, when the Maghreb has had a few decades in which to grow, dislocations associated with social change can also be expected to be fewer. Whether this means that the cultural nationalism characteristic of the Maghreb today will disappear in the future cannot be known. But a preoccupation with identity and culture and an affirmation of Arabism and Islam
(35) have characterized the Maghreb since independence and these still remain today important elements in North African life.

A second great preoccupation in independent North Africa is the promotion of a modernist social revolution. The countries of the Maghreb do not pursue development in the same way and there have been variations in policies within each coun-
(40) try. But all three spend heavily on development. In Tunisia, for example, the goverment devotes 20–25% of its annual budget to education and literacy has climbed from 15% in 1956 to about 50% today. A problem, however, is that such advances

are not always compatible with objectives flowing from North African nationalism.
In Morocco, for instance, when the government decided to give children an "Arab"
(45)   education, it was forced to limit enrollments because, among other things, most
Moroccans had been educated in French and the country consequently had few
teachers qualified to teach in Arabic. Two years later, with literacy rates declining,
this part of the Arabization program was postponed. The director of Arabization declared, "We are not fanatics; we want to enter the modern world."

1. Which of the following titles best describes the content of the passage?   1. Ⓐ Ⓑ Ⓒ Ⓓ Ⓔ

     (A) *Education in the Levant*
     (B) *Nationalism in North Africa*
     (C) *Civilization in the Middle East*
     (D) *Muslim Science*
     (E) *Culture and Language*

2. Which of the following is *not* used by the author in the presentation of his arguments?   2. Ⓐ Ⓑ Ⓒ Ⓓ Ⓔ

     (A) Colonialism demoralized the local inhabitants.
     (B) Colonialism produced an identity crisis.
     (C) Cultural nationalism will soon disappear.
     (D) Decolonization does not always run smoothly.
     (E) Colonialists assumed that local cultures were inferior.

3. The author's attitude toward colonialism is best described as one of   3. Ⓐ Ⓑ Ⓒ Ⓓ Ⓔ

     (A) sympathy
     (B) intolerance
     (C) objectivity
     (D) hostility
     (E) ambivalence

4. Which of the following does the author mention as evidence for cultural colonialism?   4. Ⓐ Ⓑ Ⓒ Ⓓ Ⓔ

     (A) Native children learned little about local culture.
     (B) Science was not taught in the Arabic language.
     (C) Colonial policy was determined in France.
     (D) Colonialists spent little on development.
     (E) Native teachers were not employed in public schools.

5. The author provides information that would answer which of the following questions?   5. Ⓐ Ⓑ Ⓒ Ⓓ Ⓔ

     (A) What was the difference between French and German attitudes toward their colonies?
     (B) Why did Europeans impose their way of life on their colonies?
     (C) Why was colonialism bad?
     (D) Why was colonialism disliked?
     (E) When did colonialism end in North Africa?

EXERCISE E

TIME: 9 minutes

DIRECTIONS: This part contains a reading passage. You are to read it carefully. When answering the questions, you *will* be able to refer to the passages. The questions are based on what is *stated* or *implied* in the passage. You have nine minutes to complete this part.

Man and nature were the culprits as Venice sank hopelessly—or so it seemed—into the 177 canals on which the city is built. While nature's work took ages, man's work was much quicker and more brutal. But now man is using his ingenuity to save what he had almost destroyed. The sinking has been arrested and Venice
(5)   should start rising again, like an oceanic phoenix from the canals.

The saving of Venice is the problem of the Italian Government of course, but Venice is also a concern for Europe. And it happened that in the second half of 1975 Italy was in the chair of the European Council of Ministers. But the EC as such has no program for the salvation of Venice. "The Community is not a cultural
(10)   community," explained one Commission official. "There are some areas where it just does not have competence, the preservation of historical landmarks being one of them." So the efforts to save Venice have taken on a worldwide, rather than a Community-wide dimension.

Industrialization of the Porto Marghera area brought economic benefits to Venice,
(15)   but it also raped the city as growing air and water pollution began to take their toll on the priceless works of art and architecture. The danger of the imminent disappearance of Venice's cultural heritage was first brought to public attention in November 1966 when tides rose over six feet to flood Venice's canals and squares. Since then, various national and international organizations have sought ways and
(20)   means to halt the destruction of the "queen of the Adriatic," though no one program has proved wholly satisfactory.

The US "Save Venice" group and the British "Venice in Peril" committee were formed to raise money for the restoration of priceless works of art and monuments. In 1967 the United Nations Educational, Scientific and Cultural Organization (UN-
(25)   ESCO) took on the task of helping to save Venice by setting up a joint international advisory committee with the Italian Government. Such distant lands as Pakistan, no stranger to aid programs itself, joined in the effort, giving UNESCO a gift of 10,000 postage stamps for "Venice in Peril." Even a group of famous cartoonists felt moved to draw attention to the fact that "Venice must be saved" and organized an exhibit
(30)   in 1973, with the Council of Europe in Strasbourg, France, and this year a ballet festival drew people and funds to Venice.

Though Venice, the city of bridge-linked islands, was built in the Fifth Century, the land on which it was built has been sinking "naturally" for a billion years. Movements of the earth's crust have caused the very slow and gradual descent of
(35)   the Po Valley. And nature's forces aren't easily countered. Each year, Venice has been sinking about one millimeter into the lagoon which holds this Adriatic jewel. To add to Venice's peril, the slow melting of the polar cap causes the level of the sea to rise another millimeter. If nothing is done to reverse nature's work, Venice is doomed to be another Atlantis, lost for ever beneath the murky sea.

(40)   Man's part in the sink-Venice movement has been for reasons mainly economic. For the last 400 years, the population of Venice has been drifting toward the mainland to escape the isolation and incovenience of living on a series of islets. Between 1951 and 1971, Venice lost 63,000 inhabitants. To curtail this migration, new, artificial land areas, on the Dutch model, were added to the old Venice. Venice's orig-
(45)   inal builders had not been far-sighted enough and set the ground level at only a few inches above what they expected to be the maximum tides. The combination of reclaimed land and Porto Marghera industrialization have "squeezed" the lagoon until its waters have no place to go but . . . up.

As Porto Marghera grows as an industrial port, and more and deeper channels
(50)   are added for larger ships, currents become faster and dikes make the ravaging tides

even more violent. The "acqua alta" has always been a problem for Venice, but with increased industrialization, flooding has become more frequent, sometimes occurring 50 times a year. Added to the violent "scirocco" that blows up to 60 miles an hour, Venice is rendered all the more vulnerable.

(55) Yet Venice is not crumbling. Despite the visible decay caused by repeated floods and despite pollution that peels the stucco off the palazzi and eats away at their bottom-most steps, the structures are solid. The Rialto Bridge still stands safely on its ancient foundations supported by 6000 piles.

And something has been done to stop the damage done by water. Indeed, one (60) simple measure has proved to work miracles. The ban on pumping from the thousands of artesian wells in and around the city—an easy source of water, but also a folly that caused a further descent of 5 millimeters a year—has been so effective that Venice should rise an inch in the next twenty years.

1. According to the passage, Venice should rise approximately how many inches during the next century?   1. Ⓐ Ⓑ Ⓒ Ⓓ Ⓔ

    (A) one
    (B) five
    (C) ten
    (D) twenty
    (E) thirty

2. The author's point of view is that Venice   2. Ⓐ Ⓑ Ⓒ Ⓓ Ⓔ

    (A) cannot be saved from destruction
    (B) is in danger of imminent disappearance
    (C) is doomed to become another "Atlantis"
    (D) can be saved, but much work is necessary
    (E) must become a member of the EC

3. Which of the following conditions has *not* contributed to Venice's peril?   3. Ⓐ Ⓑ Ⓒ Ⓓ Ⓔ

    (A) movement of the earth's crust
    (B) natural causes
    (C) melting of the polar cap
    (D) industrialization
    (E) shipping on the canals

4. According to the passage, which of the following figures best indicates the year when Venice first began sinking?   4. Ⓐ Ⓑ Ⓒ Ⓓ Ⓔ

    (A) 400
    (B) 1400
    (C) 1960
    (D) 1970
    (E) 1975

5. The author feels that Venice is an example of   5. Ⓐ Ⓑ Ⓒ Ⓓ Ⓔ

    (A) a lost city like Atlantis
    (B) uncontrolled conditions
    (C) a combination of natural and human destruction
    (D) international neglect
    (E) benign concern by international agencies

Answers and Analysis

EXERCISE A

1. **(C)** See paragraph 1, line 1: ". . . American institutions of higher education managed to expand their resources and facilities. . . ."

2. **(C)** Paragraph 2, see line 1: "The outlook for smooth absorption of the increased numbers of students in the 1970s is at present very uncertain."

3. **(D)** See paragraph 5, item 1: "changes in the rate of growth of the college age population."

4. **(A)** See paragraph 5, item c: "changes in the occupational structure which result in an increased demand for persons holding academic degrees."

5. **(B)** See paragraph 5, line 1, and also paragraph 4, line 1: ". . . it appears likely that higher education will *not* be in a position to absorb the increased numbers of students seeking admission in the 1970s without greatly increased federal government support. . . ."

6. **(C)** See paragraph 2, line 2: "Campus unrest . . . is leading some state legislatures [to withhold] funds . . . and . . . is causing some alumni to hold back on gifts. . . ."

7. **(C)** See paragraph 2: ". . . most sophisticated observers do not expect unrest to disappear. . . ."

8. **(A)** See the explanation to question 5 above.

9. **(A)** This figure is given in paragraph 6.

10. **(C)** See paragraph 8, line 1: ". . . the most slowly growing group of institutions will be the doctoral-granting. . . ."

EXERCISE B

1. **(A)** This is inferred in paragraph 1, line 1, and specifically mentioned in line 2.

2. **(D)** Also mentioned in paragraph 1: ". . . the President . . . imposed a temporary 10-percent surcharge on imports."

3. **(E)** See paragraph 3, line 1: "The decision to embark on the NEP came from. . . ." and following.

4. **(C)** See paragraph 3: ". . . the German mark and the Netherlands guilder to be set free to float in value."

5. **(A)** See the last line of the passage: ". . . the international financial problem that had persisted for at least a dozen years. . . ."

6. **(C)** Paragraph 2: "The strong upsurge in the purchases of automobiles . . . was partly a result of the proposed removal of the Federal excise tax. . . ."

7. **(B)** Paragraph 1: "To improve the Nation's balance of payments. the President suspended the convertibility of the dollar into gold. . . ."

8. **(D)** See paragraph 2: ". . . the most significant effect of the combined package [i.e. the NEP] was the impact on public confidence."

9. **(C)** Paragraph 3: "Progress in the fight against inflation was proceeding too slowly, and its future success was uncertain."

10. **(C)** Obviously President Nixon. since the NEP was announced in August. 1971. See paragraph 1. line 1.

EXERCISE C

1. **(C)** The passage deals with the supposed rejection of technology and material progress by youth.

2. **(B)** See for example. paragraph 3: ". . . it regards technology as a source of our ills. . . ."

3. **(B)** See paragraph 2: "We grew up in a world that regarded material progress through technological improvement. . . ."

4. **(D)** See paragraph 3: "Automation . . . draws criticism as the creator of structural unemployment."

5. **(D)** See paragraph 7. line 2.

6. **(B)** This is expressed in paragraph 6. last line.

7. **(A)** See paragraph 6.

8. **(A)** See paragraph 4: "Middle-aged men are ill-advised to argue . . . with the younger generation."

9. **(E)** These reasons are found in paragraphs 4 and 5.

10. **(C)** The youth have apparently rejected the value systems of their parents. as exemplified by the issues raised in the passage.

EXERCISE D

1. **(B)** Clearly, the subject of the passage is one of nationalism. This is given in the statement on line 1, "Above all colonialism was hated. . . ," and in lines 22ff and 29ff.

2. **(C)** Choice (E) is given in lines 1–2, (D) in lines 42–43, (B) in lines 24–25, and (A) is implied throughout; while the opposite of (C) is found in lines 34–36.

3. **(C)** The author neither supports nor condones it, explicitly or implicitly. He is not ambivalent to the subject, but treats it with scholarly objectivity.

4. **(A)** This is mentioned in lines 6–8. The fact that children were taught very little about their own culture and history gave rise to cultural colonialism.

5. **(D)** This theme begins on line 1 and continues throughout much of the passage.

EXERCISE E

1. **(B)** See lines 60–63. One inch per twenty years.

2. **(D)** Venice can be saved, but much work is necessary. See lines 3–5.

3. Answer (A) appears in line 34, (B) in 33, (C) in 37, and (D) in lines 49–53. Choice **(E)** is not mentioned.

4. **(A)** In lines 32–33 it is stated that the land on which Venice is situated has been sinking for a billion years; therefore, the year 400 comes closest of all the choices.

5. **(C)** The theme is given in the first line and repeated in lines 33, 37, 40, 46, 47, and 53.

VERBAL APTITUDE REVIEW

The Verbal Aptitude section of the GMAT usually contains three parts — antonyms, word-pair relationships, and sentence completions — each designed to test your ability to grasp the meanings of words and to determine the relationships that exist between words and ideas in a given situation. Success with this section depends largely on your grasp of a wide range of vocabulary and your understanding of how to answer each type of question. A discussion of these questions with practice exercises for further review follows. You will also benefit by using the *General Vocabulary List* starting on page 257 to familiarize yourself with as many new words as possible.

Antonyms

You will recall that an antonym is a word that is *opposite* in meaning to another word as, for example, *fat* is an antonym for *thin*. On the exam you are given a key word printed in capital letters followed by five lettered choices. You must select the lettered word that comes closest to being *opposite* in meaning to the capitalized word.

There are two main points to remember in approaching questions of this type. First, when choosing the antonym for a key word, be sure that both words correspond in tense (present to present, past to past, etc.) or part of speech (noun to noun, adverb to adverb, etc.). Otherwise, your choice won't be a true opposite. Second, a large command of vocabulary is essential for success with antonym questions. You must know the meanings of all five choices and the key word in order to determine which choice is correct. Keeping these points in mind, try the following practice exercises. Answers are given after Exercise D.

Practice Exercises

Antonyms

EXERCISE A

DIRECTIONS: For each question below, select the lettered word or phrase that comes closest to being *opposite* in meaning to the word appearing in capital letters. Be sure to consider all meanings carefully.

1. ABOMINATE: (A) love (B) loathe (C) abhor (D) despise (E) attach

   1. Ⓐ Ⓑ Ⓒ Ⓓ Ⓔ

2. RAVENOUS: (A) famished (B) nibbling (C) sated (D) starving (E) unsatisfied

   2. Ⓐ Ⓑ Ⓒ Ⓓ Ⓔ

3. PITHY: (A) central (B) federal (C) homogeneous (D) tautological (E) gregarious

   3. Ⓐ Ⓑ Ⓒ Ⓓ Ⓔ

4. ADAMANT: (A) yielding (B) primitive (C) elementary (D) primeval (E) inflexible

   4. Ⓐ Ⓑ Ⓒ Ⓓ Ⓔ

5.Ⓐ Ⓑ Ⓒ Ⓓ Ⓔ **5.** EPHEMERAL: (A) evergreen (B) deciduous (C) biennial (D) everlasting (E) tactile

6.Ⓐ Ⓑ Ⓒ Ⓓ Ⓔ **6.** SYNTHETIC: (A) cosmetics (B) artificial (C) plastic (D) viscous (E) natural

7.Ⓐ Ⓑ Ⓒ Ⓓ Ⓔ **7.** VIVACIOUS: (A) animated (B) dramatic (C) versatile (D) phlegmatic (E) vigilant

8.Ⓐ Ⓑ Ⓒ Ⓓ Ⓔ **8.** AUDACITY: (A) quivering (B) cowardice (C) conciseness (D) patricide (E) bravado

9.Ⓐ Ⓑ Ⓒ Ⓓ Ⓔ **9.** IRASCIBLE: (A) pictorial (B) piscatorial (C) bellicose (D) cranky (E) good-natured

10.Ⓐ Ⓑ Ⓒ Ⓓ Ⓔ **10.** BUCOLIC: (A) citified (B) rustic (C) intoxicated (D) sick (E) healthy

11.Ⓐ Ⓑ Ⓒ Ⓓ Ⓔ **11.** INFINITESIMAL: (A) everlasting (B) colossal (C) picayune (D) microscopic (E) telescopic

12.Ⓐ Ⓑ Ⓒ Ⓓ Ⓔ **12.** GELID: (A) lurid (B) torpid (C) torrid (D) piebald (E) vapid

13.Ⓐ Ⓑ Ⓒ Ⓓ Ⓔ **13.** CIRCUITOUS: (A) diameter (B) direct (C) roundabout (D) labyrinth (E) radius

14.Ⓐ Ⓑ Ⓒ Ⓓ Ⓔ **14.** PROVINCIAL: (A) urbane (B) governmental (C) local (D) rural (E) native

15.Ⓐ Ⓑ Ⓒ Ⓓ Ⓔ **15.** CLANDESTINE: (A) open (B) daylight (C) miasma (D) pugnacious (E) banal

16.Ⓐ Ⓑ Ⓒ Ⓓ Ⓔ **16.** ABHOR: (A) detest (B) absolve (C) accuse (D) bedizen (E) adore

17.Ⓐ Ⓑ Ⓒ Ⓓ Ⓔ **17.** FLAMBOYANT: (A) decorated (B) apparition (C) plain (D) female (E) terse

18.Ⓐ Ⓑ Ⓒ Ⓓ Ⓔ **18.** REDUNDANT: (A) tautological (B) repeated (C) curt (D) voluble (E) opulent

19.Ⓐ Ⓑ Ⓒ Ⓓ Ⓔ **19.** IMPOVERISHED: (A) impecunious (B) affluent (C) rococo (D) iniquitous (E) pendent

20.Ⓐ Ⓑ Ⓒ Ⓓ Ⓔ **20.** OBSEQUIOUS: (A) fawning (B) servile (C) supercilious (D) improper (E) first

21. DISCRETE: (A) wise (B) foolish (C) unkempt (D) separate (E) continuous   21.Ⓐ Ⓑ Ⓒ Ⓓ Ⓔ

22. FATUOUS: (A) inane (B) thin (C) witty (D) planned (E) stout   22.Ⓐ Ⓑ Ⓒ Ⓓ Ⓔ

23. AMENABLE: (A) responsive (B) intractable (C) indifferent (D) agreeable (E) correct   23.Ⓐ Ⓑ Ⓒ Ⓓ Ⓔ

24. FALLACIOUS: (A) erroneous (B) faulty (C) accurate (D) afraid (E) plucky   24.Ⓐ Ⓑ Ⓒ Ⓓ Ⓔ

25. ALTRUISM: (A) honesty (B) tolerance (C) bigotry (D) thievery (E) selfishness   25.Ⓐ Ⓑ Ⓒ Ⓓ Ⓔ

EXERCISE B

DIRECTIONS: For each question below, select the lettered word or phrase that comes closest to being *opposite* in meaning to the word appearing in capital letters. Be sure to consider all meanings carefully.

1. INDIFFERENT: (A) curious (B) varied (C) uniform (D) alike (E) uninquisitive   1.Ⓐ Ⓑ Ⓒ Ⓓ Ⓔ

2. COHESIVE: (A) attached (B) detached (C) associated (D) affiliated (E) sticky   2.Ⓐ Ⓑ Ⓒ Ⓓ Ⓔ

3. INSIPID: (A) tasty (B) silly (C) angry (D) active (E) emaciated   3.Ⓐ Ⓑ Ⓒ Ⓓ Ⓔ

4. DISCORD: (A) noise (B) amity (C) irritation (D) scrap (E) use   4.Ⓐ Ⓑ Ⓒ Ⓓ Ⓔ

5. PRIORITY: (A) anxiety (B) irregular (C) subsequence (D) pious (E) impious   5.Ⓐ Ⓑ Ⓒ Ⓓ Ⓔ

6. CRABBED: (A) fished (B) saccharine (C) sour (D) apple (E) orange   6.Ⓐ Ⓑ Ⓒ Ⓓ Ⓔ

7. CORROBORATION: (A) proof (B) arrest (C) invalidation (D) alibi (E) alias   7.Ⓐ Ⓑ Ⓒ Ⓓ Ⓔ

8. DECORUM: (A) ribaldry (B) balladry (C) high collar (D) solo (E) freedom   8.Ⓐ Ⓑ Ⓒ Ⓓ Ⓔ

9. Ⓐ Ⓑ Ⓒ Ⓓ Ⓔ **9.** VIVACIOUS: (A) surgery (B) awake (C) girlish (D) inactive (E) boyish

10. Ⓐ Ⓑ Ⓒ Ⓓ Ⓔ **10.** INGENUOUS: (A) clever (B) stupid (C) naive (D) young (E) sophisticated

11. Ⓐ Ⓑ Ⓒ Ⓓ Ⓔ **11.** ALLEVIATE: (A) allow (B) aggravate (C) instigate (D) belittle (E) refuse

12. Ⓐ Ⓑ Ⓒ Ⓓ Ⓔ **12.** OBSOLETE: (A) automobile (B) fancy (C) free (D) renovated (E) old

13. Ⓐ Ⓑ Ⓒ Ⓓ Ⓔ **13.** BLASÉ: (A) indifferent (B) awed (C) afraid (D) cultured (E) worldly

14. Ⓐ Ⓑ Ⓒ Ⓓ Ⓔ **14.** SANGUINE: (A) bloody (B) gloomy (C) happy (D) thin (E) red-faced

15. Ⓐ Ⓑ Ⓒ Ⓓ Ⓔ **15.** LANGUID: (A) pusillanimous (B) indifferent (C) sad (D) vigorous (E) motley

16. Ⓐ Ⓑ Ⓒ Ⓓ Ⓔ **16.** RESPITE: (A) recess (B) intermission (C) exertion (D) friendly (E) angry

17. Ⓐ Ⓑ Ⓒ Ⓓ Ⓔ **17.** OBLOQUY: (A) shame (B) fame (C) name (D) colloquy (E) inquiry

18. Ⓐ Ⓑ Ⓒ Ⓓ Ⓔ **18.** PLACATE: (A) nettle (B) label (C) soothe (D) reply (E) retaliate

19. Ⓐ Ⓑ Ⓒ Ⓓ Ⓔ **19.** COMPLACENT: (A) satisfied (B) agreeable (C) nasty (D) querulous (E) asking

20. Ⓐ Ⓑ Ⓒ Ⓓ Ⓔ **20.** ASSENT: (A) save (B) inquire (C) resent (D) introduce (E) disavow

21. Ⓐ Ⓑ Ⓒ Ⓓ Ⓔ **21.** HUSBANDRY: (A) munificence (B) wife (C) frugality (D) matrimony (E) widower

22. Ⓐ Ⓑ Ⓒ Ⓓ Ⓔ **22.** NOISOME: (A) quiet (B) salubrious (C) eager (D) foul (E) deodorant

23. Ⓐ Ⓑ Ⓒ Ⓓ Ⓔ **23.** PERMANENT: (A) indifferent (B) tardy (C) mutable (D) improper (E) disheveled

24. Ⓐ Ⓑ Ⓒ Ⓓ Ⓔ **24.** COVETOUS: (A) unfinished (B) uncovered (C) undesirous (D) birdlike (E) plying

25. Ⓐ Ⓑ Ⓒ Ⓓ Ⓔ **25.** CORPOREAL: (A) sergeant (B) private (C) commissioned officer (D) spiritual (E) boatswain

EXERCISE C

DIRECTIONS: For each question below, select the lettered word or phrase that comes closest to being *opposite* in meaning to the word appearing in capital letters. Be sure to consider all meanings carefully.

1. ZEALOT: (A) heretic (B) hypocrite (C) person who is careless (D) person who is rich (E) person who is indifferent   1. Ⓐ Ⓑ Ⓒ Ⓓ Ⓔ

2. ABSTEMIOUS: (A) fastidious (B) punctilious (C) pusillanimous (D) dissipated (E) prodigal   2. Ⓐ Ⓑ Ⓒ Ⓓ Ⓔ

3. SATIETY: (A) starvation (B) dissatisfaction (C) unfeigned (D) lowest class (E) grandeur   3. Ⓐ Ⓑ Ⓒ Ⓓ Ⓔ

4. DECIDUOUS: (A) undecided (B) hesitant (C) evergreen (D) annual (E) perennial   4. Ⓐ Ⓑ Ⓒ Ⓓ Ⓔ

5. INNOCUOUS: (A) large (B) toxic (C) spotless (D) impeccable (E) sober   5. Ⓐ Ⓑ Ⓒ Ⓓ Ⓔ

6. GERMANE: (A) Teutonic (B) healthful (C) irrelevant (D) massive (E) puny   6. Ⓐ Ⓑ Ⓒ Ⓓ Ⓔ

7. EGREGIOUS: (A) notorious (B) splendid (C) abortive (D) maturing (E) birdlike   7. Ⓐ Ⓑ Ⓒ Ⓓ Ⓔ

8. NEPOTISM: (A) midnight (B) partiality (C) impartiality (D) dawn (E) noon   8. Ⓐ Ⓑ Ⓒ Ⓓ Ⓔ

9. AUTONOMOUS: (A) magnanimous (B) ambiguous (C) exiguous (D) dependent (E) operated by hand   9. Ⓐ Ⓑ Ⓒ Ⓓ Ⓔ

10. EXCULPATE: (A) pardon (B) destroy (C) create (D) convict (E) admonish   10. Ⓐ Ⓑ Ⓒ Ⓓ Ⓔ

11. EARTHY: (A) pithy (B) salty (C) watery (D) refined (E) moldy   11. Ⓐ Ⓑ Ⓒ Ⓓ Ⓔ

12. CONTENTIOUS: (A) pacific (B) bellicose (C) satisfied (D) dissatisfied (E) hungry   12. Ⓐ Ⓑ Ⓒ Ⓓ Ⓔ

13. GAINSAY: (A) deny (B) lose money (C) audit (D) applaud (E) affirm   13. Ⓐ Ⓑ Ⓒ Ⓓ Ⓔ

14.Ⓐ Ⓑ Ⓒ Ⓓ Ⓔ **14.** AMELIORATE: (A) harden (B) coarsen (C) aggravate (D) improve (E) scrape

15.Ⓐ Ⓑ Ⓒ Ⓓ Ⓔ **15.** IGNOMINIOUS: (A) disgraceful (B) erudite (C) scholarly (D) incognito (E) laudatory

16.Ⓐ Ⓑ Ⓒ Ⓓ Ⓔ **16.** EVANESCENT: (A) permanent (B) incandescent (C) ephemeral (D) putrid (E) perfunctory

17.Ⓐ Ⓑ Ⓒ Ⓓ Ⓔ **17.** CORPULENT: (A) sallow (B) partnership (C) emaciated (D) entrepreneur (E) red-blooded

18.Ⓐ Ⓑ Ⓒ Ⓓ Ⓔ **18.** JOCUND: (A) round (B) flat (C) jocular (D) jugular (E) melancholy

19.Ⓐ Ⓑ Ⓒ Ⓓ Ⓔ **19.** HIBERNAL: (A) Irish (B) estival (C) English (D) festival (E) wintry

20.Ⓐ Ⓑ Ⓒ Ⓓ Ⓔ **20.** EBULLIENT: (A) intoxicated (B) placid (C) effervescent (D) gregarious (E) jovial

21.Ⓐ Ⓑ Ⓒ Ⓓ Ⓔ **21.** ASSUAGE: (A) meat (B) abate (C) individual (D) irritate (E) demonstrate

22.Ⓐ Ⓑ Ⓒ Ⓓ Ⓔ **22.** INDIGENOUS: (A) alien (B) digestible (C) comestible (D) pleased (E) irate

23.Ⓐ Ⓑ Ⓒ Ⓓ Ⓔ **23.** DEARTH: (A) birth (B) scantiness (C) abundance (D) bright (E) morning

24.Ⓐ Ⓑ Ⓒ Ⓓ Ⓔ **24.** DELETERIOUS: (A) sane (B) intoxicated (C) sober (D) wholesome (E) adding

25.Ⓐ Ⓑ Ⓒ Ⓓ Ⓔ **25.** FELL: (A) downed (B) risen (C) propitious (D) cruel (E) officer

EXERCISE D

DIRECTIONS: For each question below, select the lettered word or phrase that comes closest to being *opposite* in meaning to the word appearing in capital letters. Be sure to consider all meanings carefully.

1.Ⓐ Ⓑ Ⓒ Ⓓ Ⓔ **1.** EXEMPLARY: (A) deplorable (B) imitative (C) good (D) conduct (E) addition

2.Ⓐ Ⓑ Ⓒ Ⓓ Ⓔ **2.** CHOLERIC: (A) red (B) serene (C) severe (D) stern (E) irritable

3. BAROQUE: (A) commoner (B) boat (C) rococo (D) simple (E) stupid   3. Ⓐ Ⓑ Ⓒ Ⓓ Ⓔ

4. DILETTANTE: (A) amateur (B) professional (C) late (D) early (E) advancing   4. Ⓐ Ⓑ Ⓒ Ⓓ Ⓔ

5. AMORPHOUS: (A) diaphanous (B) translucent (C) organized (D) opaque (E) chaotic   5. Ⓐ Ⓑ Ⓒ Ⓓ Ⓔ

6. CAPRICIOUS: (A) whimsical (B) consistent (C) goatlike (D) honest (E) hypocritical   6. Ⓐ Ⓑ Ⓒ Ⓓ Ⓔ

7. SALUBRIOUS: (A) healthy (B) plagued (C) rustic (D) fashioned (E) miasmic   7. Ⓐ Ⓑ Ⓒ Ⓓ Ⓔ

8. DISPARITY: (A) equality (B) aspersion (C) allusion (D) equanimity (E) suture   8. Ⓐ Ⓑ Ⓒ Ⓓ Ⓔ

9. APOTHEGM: (A) perpendicular (B) pithy statement (C) prolix statement (D) terse statement (E) letter   9. Ⓐ Ⓑ Ⓒ Ⓓ Ⓔ

10. CHARY: (A) lavish (B) malevolent (C) insinuating (D) sparing (E) irritable   10. Ⓐ Ⓑ Ⓒ Ⓓ Ⓔ

11. CANDOR: (A) hypocrisy (B) ingenuousness (C) sweetmeat (D) pleasure (E) velocity   11. Ⓐ Ⓑ Ⓒ Ⓓ Ⓔ

12. EQUIVOCATE: (A) lie (B) whisper (C) balance (D) tell truth (E) be unequal   12. Ⓐ Ⓑ Ⓒ Ⓓ Ⓔ

13. ESTRANGED: (A) reconciled (B) separated (C) foreign (D) traded (E) embarrassed   13. Ⓐ Ⓑ Ⓒ Ⓓ Ⓔ

14. PRETENTIOUS: (A) real (B) excusing (C) modest (D) unpardonable (E) typical   14. Ⓐ Ⓑ Ⓒ Ⓓ Ⓔ

15. SUB ROSA: (A) under the rose (B) clandestinely (C) fashionable (D) open (E) simple   15. Ⓐ Ⓑ Ⓒ Ⓓ Ⓔ

16. SUBSERVIENT: (A) obsequious (B) omnipresent (C) oligarchy (D) haughty (E) miserly   16. Ⓐ Ⓑ Ⓒ Ⓓ Ⓔ

17. UNTENABLE: (A) rented (B) maintainable (C) occupied (D) permanent (E) picayune   17. Ⓐ Ⓑ Ⓒ Ⓓ Ⓔ

18. Ⓐ Ⓑ Ⓒ Ⓓ Ⓔ **18.** HERBIVOROUS: **(A)** ravenous **(B)** omnivorous **(C)** carnivorous **(D)** voracious **(E)** veracious

19. Ⓐ Ⓑ Ⓒ Ⓓ Ⓔ **19.** OPULENCE: **(A)** glamor **(B)** sobriety **(C)** badinage **(D)** penury **(E)** petulance

20. Ⓐ Ⓑ Ⓒ Ⓓ Ⓔ **20.** THRENODY: **(A)** elegy **(B)** eulogy **(C)** ballade **(D)** paean **(E)** epic

21. Ⓐ Ⓑ Ⓒ Ⓓ Ⓔ **21.** VAUNTED: **(A)** lauded **(B)** belittled **(C)** crept **(D)** worried **(E)** wicked

22. Ⓐ Ⓑ Ⓒ Ⓓ Ⓔ **22.** CEDE: **(A)** yield **(B)** harvest **(C)** annex **(D)** examine **(E)** mimic

23. Ⓐ Ⓑ Ⓒ Ⓓ Ⓔ **23.** OBFUSCATE: **(A)** clarify **(B)** magnify **(C)** intensify **(D)** belittle **(E)** becloud

24. Ⓐ Ⓑ Ⓒ Ⓓ Ⓔ **24.** CONCAVE: **(A)** hollow **(B)** solid **(C)** convex **(D)** complex **(E)** broken

25. Ⓐ Ⓑ Ⓒ Ⓓ Ⓔ **25.** PRECIPITATE: **(A)** wary **(B)** steep **(C)** audacious **(D)** masterly **(E)** conquered

Answer Key

Antonyms

EXERCISE A			EXERCISE B			EXERCISE C			EXERCISE D		
1. A	11. B	21. E	1. A	11. B	21. A	1. E	11. D	21. D	1. A	11. A	21. B
2. C	12. C	22. C	2. B	12. D	22. B	2. D	12. A	22. A	2. B	12. D	22. C
3. D	13. B	23. B	3. A	13. B	23. C	3. A	13. E	23. C	3. D	13. A	23. A
4. A	14. A	24. C	4. B	14. B	24. C	4. C	14. C	24. D	4. B	14. C	24. C
5. D	15. A	25. E	5. C	15. D	25. D	5. B	15. E	25. C	5. C	15. D	25. A
6. E	16. E		6. B	16. C		6. C	16. A		6. B	16. D	
7. D	17. C		7. C	17. B		7. B	17. C		7. E	17. B	
8. B	18. C		8. A	18. A		8. C	18. E		8. A	18. C	
9. E	19. B		9. D	19. D		9. D	19. B		9. C	19. D	
10. A	20. C		10. E	20. E		10. D	20. B		10. A	20. D	

Word-Pair Relationships

The purpose of this type of question, also known as an analogy, is to test your ability to determine relationships existing between pairs of words. This may involve finding a relationship between a tangible situation and a more abstract grouping or it may center around synonyms, antonyms, cause and effect, or other areas.

On the GMAT you are given a pair of words printed in capital letters and five other lettered pairs. You must select the pair of words from among the five lettered choices that best matches the relationship of the first pair. For example:

TREE : FOREST :: (A) daisy : meadow (B) grass : lawn (C) wheat : field (D) flower : garden (E) frog : pond

The first step in finding the answer to a word-pair relationship problem is to determine the relationship (rationale) existing between the initial word-pair. In this instance it is that a forest would not exist without trees. Looking at the choices you can see that B is the correct answer because a lawn would not exist without grass — TREE is to FOREST as *grass* is to *lawn*. The other choices are not satisfactory because a meadow can exist without daisies, a field can exist without wheat, gardens don't necessarily have to have flowers (e.g., vegetable garden), and ponds don't need frogs to exist.

Consider the following example:

POSSESS : LOSE :: (A) hesitate : advance (B) cease : recur (C) undertake : perform (D) continue : desist (E) produce : supply

The initial words are opposite in meaning. Therefore, you can immediately eliminate choices C and E as they represent synonyms. Choice A is poor because hesitate and advance aren't clear opposites. Choice B is better, but the concept of repetition in recur is not found in lose. Choice D is the best answer — POSSESS is to LOSE as *continue* is to *desist*.

As has been noted, there are many possible relationships that can exist between words. The following list presents some of the more common ones you may encounter.

1. Worker and article created

    carpenter : house
    writer : book
    composer : symphony

2. Worker and tool used

    carpenter : saw
    writer : typewriter
    surgeon : scalpel

3. Tool and object worked on

    pencil : paper
    saw : wood

4. The act the tool does to the object it works on

    saw : wood (cuts)
    knife : bread (cuts)
    brake : car (stops)

5. Time sequence

> early : late
> dawn : twilight
> sunrise : sunset

6. Cause and effect

> germ : disease
> carelessness : accident
> explosion : debris

7. Degree of intensity

> tepid : hot
> joy : ecstasy
> admiration : love

8. Class — species

> furniture : chair
> insect : grasshopper
> mammal : whale
> dog : poodle

9. Type — characteristic

> cow : herbivorous
> tiger : carnivorous

10. Grammatical relationships

> I : mine (first person nominative case : first person possessive case)
> wolf : vulpine (noun : adjective)
> have : had (present tense : past tense)
> alumnus : alumni (masculine singular noun : masculine plural noun)

11. Synonyms

> lie : prevaricate
> kind : benevolent

12. Antonyms

> never : always
> love : hate
> fancy : plain
> real : fictional

13. Homonyms

> hour : our
> their : there
> wear : where

14. Rhyming

> had : bad
> some : come
> fall : tall

15. Person and thing he seeks

>   alchemist : gold
>   prospector : gold

16. Person and thing he learns to avoid

>   child : fire
>   pilot : reef

17. Part to the whole

>   soldier : regiment
>   star : constellation

18. Sex

>   duck : drake
>   bull : cow

The following exercises will give you more practice in solving word-pair relationships. Use the *General Vocabulary List* to find the meanings of any words you don't know. Answers to all exercises are located after Exercise D.

Practice Exercises

Word-Pair Relationships

EXERCISE A

DIRECTIONS: For each question below, determine the relationship between the pair of capitalized words and then select the lettered pair of words which have a similar relationship to the first pair.

1. QUIXOTIC : FEASIBLE :: (A) sudden : workable (B) theoretical : practical (C) fashionable : efficient (D) precise : practicable (E) sad : adept

    1. Ⓐ Ⓑ Ⓒ Ⓓ Ⓔ

2. DEBATE : FORENSIC :: (A) drama : histrionic (B) opera : spoken (C) concerto : harmonizing (D) argument : domestic (E) novel : original

    2. Ⓐ Ⓑ Ⓒ Ⓓ Ⓔ

3. ANTHOLOGY : POEMS :: (A) antipasto : hors d'oeuvres (B) volume : book (C) encyclopedia : words (D) thesaurus : synonyms (E) medley : arrangement

    3. Ⓐ Ⓑ Ⓒ Ⓓ Ⓔ

4. ANHYDROUS : SATURATED :: (A) dry : wet (B) sweet : wet (C) cloying : full (D) stolid : liquid (E) physics : chemistry

    4. Ⓐ Ⓑ Ⓒ Ⓓ Ⓔ

5. Ⓐ Ⓑ Ⓒ Ⓓ Ⓔ   5. WINE : GRAPES :: (A) champagne : raisins (B) liquor : intoxicating (C) vineyard : winery (D) whiskey : hops (E) vodka : potatoes

6. Ⓐ Ⓑ Ⓒ Ⓓ Ⓔ   6. NOTABLE : NOTORIOUS :: (A) philanthropic : benevolent (B) philandering : pleasant (C) heinous : atrocious (D) nefarious : secret (E) philanthropic : miserly

7. Ⓐ Ⓑ Ⓒ Ⓓ Ⓔ   7. ENTREPRENEUR : LABORER :: (A) profits : wages (B) arbitrator : capitalist (C) mediator : conflict (D) moonlighting : worker (E) capitalism : communism

8. Ⓐ Ⓑ Ⓒ Ⓓ Ⓔ   8. MORPHINE : SEDATES :: (A) drug : addicts (B) liquor : intoxicates (C) medicine : soothes (D) oil : smears (E) bandage : heals

9. Ⓐ Ⓑ Ⓒ Ⓓ Ⓔ   9. *HAMLET* : SOLILOQUY :: (A) *Macbeth* : tragedy (B) trust : monopoly (C) *Rigoletto* : quartet (D) *Othello* : jealousy (E) play : act

10. Ⓐ Ⓑ Ⓒ Ⓓ Ⓔ   10. CONTINENT : IMMORAL :: (A) land : evil (B) dissolute : lascivious (C) wanton : restrained (D) shore : reef (E) conscience : sin

11. Ⓐ Ⓑ Ⓒ Ⓓ Ⓔ   11. MENDICANT : IMPECUNIOUS :: (A) critic : quizzical (B) complainer : petulant (C) hat : askew (D) liar : poor (E) philanthropist : prodigal

12. Ⓐ Ⓑ Ⓒ Ⓓ Ⓔ   12. APOSTATE : RELIGION :: (A) loyal : faith (B) traitor : country (C) renegade : Indian (D) vital : church (E) disloyal : colonies

13. Ⓐ Ⓑ Ⓒ Ⓓ Ⓔ   13. DERMATOLOGIST : SKIN :: (A) paleontologist : statues (B) genealogist : genes (C) cardiologist : heart (D) astrologist : future (E) psychologist : insanity

14. Ⓐ Ⓑ Ⓒ Ⓓ Ⓔ   14. SEE : EYES :: (A) grapple : iron (B) grasp : hands (C) lisp : speech (D) limp : limbs (E) sneeze : nostrils

15. Ⓐ Ⓑ Ⓒ Ⓓ Ⓔ   15. CYNOSURE : BRILLIANT :: (A) student : attentive (B) map : legible (C) rock : large (D) word : common (E) magnet : attractive

16. Ⓐ Ⓑ Ⓒ Ⓓ Ⓔ   16. NUMERATOR : DENOMINATOR :: (A) fraction : decimal (B) divisor : quotient (C) ratio : proportion (D) dividend : divisor (E) top : bottom

17. Ⓐ Ⓑ Ⓒ Ⓓ Ⓔ   17. NOISOME : GARBAGE :: (A) liquid : perfume (B) heavy : metal (C) loud : music (D) warmth : snow (E) fragrant : incense

18. SAD : DOLOROUS :: (A) rich : wealthy (B) smart : smattering (C) grief : healthy (D) giver : free (E) gratitude : frugal   18. Ⓐ Ⓑ Ⓒ Ⓓ Ⓔ

19. SCHOOL : TUITION :: (A) game : loss (B) lawyer : client (C) hospital : insurance (D) church : tithe (E) library : fine   19. Ⓐ Ⓑ Ⓒ Ⓓ Ⓔ

20. DISSERTATION : IDEAS :: (A) propaganda : facts (B) novel : theme (C) poem : emotions (D) play : acting (E) essay : novel   20. Ⓐ Ⓑ Ⓒ Ⓓ Ⓔ

21. NAIVE : INGENUOUS :: (A) ordinary : ingenious (B) old : wise (C) simple : kind (D) eager : reserved (E) sophisticated : urbane   21. Ⓐ Ⓑ Ⓒ Ⓓ Ⓔ

22. TERMAGANT : SHREW :: (A) anteater : mouse (B) virago : scold (C) supporter : nag (D) single : married (E) male : female   22. Ⓐ Ⓑ Ⓒ Ⓓ Ⓔ

23. CLOUD : STORM :: (A) container : contained (B) portent : disaster (C) cumulus : gale (D) thunder : lightning (E) rain : wind   23. Ⓐ Ⓑ Ⓒ Ⓓ Ⓔ

24. CONDUIT : WATER :: (A) pump : oil (B) behavior : liquid (C) artery : blood (D) wire : sound (E) electricity : television   24. Ⓐ Ⓑ Ⓒ Ⓓ Ⓔ

25. BREAD : OVEN :: (A) ceramics : kiln (B) silo : corn (C) pottery : wheel (D) iron : furnace (E) cake : stove   25. Ⓐ Ⓑ Ⓒ Ⓓ Ⓔ

EXERCISE B

DIRECTIONS: For each question below, determine the relationship between the pair of capitalized words and then select the lettered pair of words which have a similar relationship to the first pair.

1. LATITUDE : EQUATOR :: (A) direction : declension (B) weight : length (C) warp : woof (D) longitude : International Date Line (E) north pole : Arctic Circle   1. Ⓐ Ⓑ Ⓒ Ⓓ Ⓔ

2. ANTIMACASSAR : SOFA :: (A) rug : floor (B) table : chair (C) door : window (D) picture : frame (E) pillow : bed   2. Ⓐ Ⓑ Ⓒ Ⓓ Ⓔ

3. PERIMETER : ADDITION :: (A) arithmetic : geometric (B) exponential : quadratic (C) linear : logarithmic (D) triangle : sphere (E) area : multiplication   3. Ⓐ Ⓑ Ⓒ Ⓓ Ⓔ

4. Ⓐ Ⓑ Ⓒ Ⓓ Ⓔ   **4.** ACTUARY : INSURANCE :: (A) librarian : school (B) historian : dates (C) veterinarian : animal husbandry (D) agronomist : agreement (E) vegetarian : meat

5. Ⓐ Ⓑ Ⓒ Ⓓ Ⓔ   **5.** ISOLATIONIST : ALOOF :: (A) altruist : selfish (B) pessimist : mournful (C) scholar : proud (D) bigot : tolerant (E) segregationist : gregarious

6. Ⓐ Ⓑ Ⓒ Ⓓ Ⓔ   **6.** WATER : CONDUIT :: (A) electricity : magnet (B) elevator : shaft (C) shell : rifle (D) noise : cannon (E) soda : bottle

7. Ⓐ Ⓑ Ⓒ Ⓓ Ⓔ   **7.** PLAINTIFF : DEFENDANT :: (A) court : law (B) injured : accused (C) judge : jury (D) district attorney : lawyer (E) nobleman : serf

8. Ⓐ Ⓑ Ⓒ Ⓓ Ⓔ   **8.** EXPLOSIVE : VOLCANO :: (A) cold : mountain (B) arid : desert (C) humid : valley (D) misty : morning (E) fertile : plain

9. Ⓐ Ⓑ Ⓒ Ⓓ Ⓔ   **9.** BIZARRE : EXOTIC :: (A) stage : dancer (B) commonplace : routine (C) wild : tame (D) ordinary : exceptional (E) lively : livid

10. Ⓐ Ⓑ Ⓒ Ⓓ Ⓔ   **10.** DOCTOR : DISEASE :: (A) psychiatrist : maladjustment (B) teacher : pupils (C) scholar : knowledge (D) judge : crime (E) lawyer : law

11. Ⓐ Ⓑ Ⓒ Ⓓ Ⓔ   **11.** SHOWER : DELUGE :: (A) irritation : rage (B) April : May (C) passion : affection (D) surprise party : exceptional (E) flow : surge

12. Ⓐ Ⓑ Ⓒ Ⓓ Ⓔ   **12.** DRAMA : PLAYWRIGHT :: (A) act : actor (B) words : author (C) poetics : poet (D) review : critic (E) opera : musician

13. Ⓐ Ⓑ Ⓒ Ⓓ Ⓔ   **13.** ALWAYS : NEVER :: (A) often : rarely (B) frequently : occasionally (C) constantly : frequently (D) intermittently : casually (E) occasionally : constantly

14. Ⓐ Ⓑ Ⓒ Ⓓ Ⓔ   **14.** PRESIDENT : POPE :: (A) elected : chosen (B) ballot : smoke (C) proclamation : bull (D) temporal : secular (E) leader : religion

15. Ⓐ Ⓑ Ⓒ Ⓓ Ⓔ   **15.** PERMANENT : EVANESCENT :: (A) durable : fleeting (B) lasting : glittering (C) eternal : everlasting (D) hairdo : bleach (E) wave : scene

16. Ⓐ Ⓑ Ⓒ Ⓓ Ⓔ   **16.** ORNITHOLOGIST : BIRDS :: (A) aquarium : fish (B) anthropologist : insects (C) archeologist : artifacts (D) architect : buildings (E) botanist : animals

17. VERBS : ACTION :: (A) nouns : amplification (B) pronouns : demonstration (C) adjectives : modification (D) adverbs : connection (E) prepositions : definition

17. Ⓐ Ⓑ Ⓒ Ⓓ Ⓔ

18. OAFISH : ASTUTE :: (A) net : gun (B) ocean : mountain (C) wise : smart (D) lake : thorough (E) simpleton : sage

18. Ⓐ Ⓑ Ⓒ Ⓓ Ⓔ

19. SUGGEST : DEMAND :: (A) deny : request (B) affection : consolation (C) hint : blunder (D) give : receive (E) take : grab

19. Ⓐ Ⓑ Ⓒ Ⓓ Ⓔ

20. VINDICABLE : REPREHENSIBLE :: (A) mild : serious (B) bitter : sad (C) mild : sad (D) solid : porous (E) vivid : dull

20. Ⓐ Ⓑ Ⓒ Ⓓ Ⓔ

21. MULTIPLICATION : DIVISION :: (A) increase : decrease (B) zero : infinity (C) calculate : estimate (D) digit : series (E) integers : numbers

21. Ⓐ Ⓑ Ⓒ Ⓓ Ⓔ

22. ABAB CDCD EFEF GG : ABBA ABBA CDE CDE :: (A) Italian : Petrarchan (B) Milton : Wordsworth (C) Shakespeare : Wordsworth (D) ballad : sonnet (E) Miltonic : Petrarchan

22. Ⓐ Ⓑ Ⓒ Ⓓ Ⓔ

23. TRIANGLE : QUADRILATERAL :: (A) plane : solid (B) pentagon : hexagon (C) rectangle : octagon (D) cone : cube (E) regular : irregular

23. Ⓐ Ⓑ Ⓒ Ⓓ Ⓔ

24. FINE : IMPRISONMENT :: (A) sentence : judgment (B) bail : bond (C) jury : judge (D) magistrate : judge (E) misdemeanor : felony

24. Ⓐ Ⓑ Ⓒ Ⓓ Ⓔ

25. EINSTEIN : RELATIVITY :: (A) Aristotle : calculus (B) Newton : gravity (C) Pasteur : biology (D) Edison : mechanics (E) Galileo : chemistry

25. Ⓐ Ⓑ Ⓒ Ⓓ Ⓔ

EXERCISE C

DIRECTIONS: For each question below, determine the relationship between the pair of capitalized words and then select the lettered pair of words which have a similar relationship to the first pair.

1. LIQUEFY : PETRIFY :: (A) water : stone (B) soften : frighten (C) cash in : strengthen (D) solvent : rich (E) insolvent : bankrupt

1. Ⓐ Ⓑ Ⓒ Ⓓ Ⓔ

2. BELT : TROUSERS :: (A) braces : garters (B) trunk : tree (C) pillar : society (D) cables : trolley (E) cables : bridge

2. Ⓐ Ⓑ Ⓒ Ⓓ Ⓔ

3.Ⓐ Ⓑ Ⓒ Ⓓ Ⓔ **3.** GASOLINE : PETROL :: (A) motor : car (B) engine : trunk (C) light : heavy (D) elevator : lift (E) refined : crude

4.Ⓐ Ⓑ Ⓒ Ⓓ Ⓔ **4.** RHYTHM : RHYME :: (A) poet : versifier (B) accent : sound (C) prose : poetry (D) versification : scansion (E) blank verse : free verse

5.Ⓐ Ⓑ Ⓒ Ⓓ Ⓔ **5.** SCHOLAR : ENTREPRENEUR :: (A) books : superstition (B) learning : studying (C) university : laboratory (D) knowledge : profits (E) knowledge : research

6.Ⓐ Ⓑ Ⓒ Ⓓ Ⓔ **6.** NECTAR : AMBROSIA :: (A) frankincense : myrrh (B) vegetable : fruit (C) taste : smell (D) goddess : god (E) drink : food

7.Ⓐ Ⓑ Ⓒ Ⓓ Ⓔ **7.** MUSLIN : BROCADE :: (A) ornate : decorated (B) simple : torn (C) gaudy : rich (D) plain : figured (E) multicolored : variegated

8.Ⓐ Ⓑ Ⓒ Ⓓ Ⓔ **8.** DERIVATION : LEXICOGRAPHER :: (A) evolution : biologist (B) origin : typographer (C) politics : anarchist (D) laws : court (E) foundation : roofer

9.Ⓐ Ⓑ Ⓒ Ⓓ Ⓔ **9.** EPAULET : SHOULDER :: (A) medal : chest (B) knapsack : back (C) sash : window (D) sword : scabbard (E) decoration : uniform

10.Ⓐ Ⓑ Ⓒ Ⓓ Ⓔ **10.** SHEEP : WOOL :: (A) fodder : animal (B) otter : fur (C) flax : cotton (D) animal : vegetable (E) stupid : good

11.Ⓐ Ⓑ Ⓒ Ⓓ Ⓔ **11.** NAIL : PUNCTURE :: (A) sword : scabbard (B) scalpel : incision (C) easel : picture (D) needle : sew (E) tire : flat

12.Ⓐ Ⓑ Ⓒ Ⓓ Ⓔ **12.** MISDEMEANOR : FELONY :: (A) imprisonment : bail (B) joy : ecstasy (C) gale : breeze (D) judge : magistrate (E) coward : criminal

13.Ⓐ Ⓑ Ⓒ Ⓓ Ⓔ **13.** SECRET SERVICE : F.B.I. :: (A) soldier : army (B) local : national (C) treasury : justice (D) policemen : detectives (E) open : undercover

14.Ⓐ Ⓑ Ⓒ Ⓓ Ⓔ **14.** FATUOUS : INANE :: (A) clever : inchoate (B) querulous : picayune (C) fatal : mordant (D) portentous : significant (E) cloying : viscous

15.Ⓐ Ⓑ Ⓒ Ⓓ Ⓔ **15.** LUNGS : BLOOD :: (A) heart : circulation (B) arteries : veins (C) carburetor : car (D) glands : secretions (E) carburetor : gasoline

16. SCALES : JUSTICE :: (A) weights : measures (B) markets : courts (C)   16. Ⓐ Ⓑ Ⓒ Ⓓ Ⓔ
torch : liberty (D) laurel : peace (E) balance : right

17. DIAPHANOUS : CACOPHONOUS :: (A) twofold : multiple (B) sheer :   17. Ⓐ Ⓑ Ⓒ Ⓓ Ⓔ
transparent (C) sheer : opaque (D) harmonious : discordant (E) transparent
: noisy

18. BLEEDING : TOURNIQUET :: (A) drowning : resuscitation (B) sun-   18. Ⓐ Ⓑ Ⓒ Ⓓ Ⓔ
stroke : fatigue (C) traffic : red light (D) coughing : elixir (E) disease :
microbe

19. DETRITUS : GLACIERS :: (A) ice : icebergs (B) thaw : cold (C) silt   19. Ⓐ Ⓑ Ⓒ Ⓓ Ⓔ
: rivers (D) sediment : bottom (E) dregs : society

20. EXCULPATE : INCRIMINATE :: (A) exonerate : involve (B) free :   20. Ⓐ Ⓑ Ⓒ Ⓓ Ⓔ
fine (C) blame : criticize (D) blame : pardon (E) excuse : free

21. TRUMPET : BRASS :: (A) drums : hide (B) bugle : bronze (C) cello :   21. Ⓐ Ⓑ Ⓒ Ⓓ Ⓔ
string (D) orchestra : band (E) horn : metal

22. SANDPAPER : ABRASIVE :: (A) polish : floors (B) pumice : emulsion   22. Ⓐ Ⓑ Ⓒ Ⓓ Ⓔ
(C) gasoline : refined (D) oil : lubricant (E) gratuity : irritant

23. ALBEIT : ALTHOUGH :: (A) preposition : conjunction (B) conjunction   23. Ⓐ Ⓑ Ⓒ Ⓓ Ⓔ
: conjunction (C) conjunction : preposition (D) adjective : conjunction (E)
conjunction : adverb

24. HABITS : INSTINCTS :: (A) work : play (B) training : heredity (C)   24. Ⓐ Ⓑ Ⓒ Ⓓ Ⓔ
acquired : cultivated (D) natural : unusual (E) birds : animals

25. AMBULATORY : BEDRIDDEN :: (A) wheelchair : bed (B) healthy :   25. Ⓐ Ⓑ Ⓒ Ⓓ Ⓔ
sick (C) strong : weak (D) broken arm : broken limb (E) free : confined

EXERCISE D

DIRECTIONS: For each question below, determine the relationship between the pair of
capitalized words and then select the lettered pair of words which have a similar relationship
to the first pair.

1. PARIAH : FAVORITE :: (A) nephew : son (B) hypnotism : comatose   1. Ⓐ Ⓑ Ⓒ Ⓓ Ⓔ
(C) sycophant : obsequious (D) ostracism : nepotism (E) chosen : accepted

2. Ⓐ Ⓑ Ⓒ Ⓓ Ⓔ **2.** GOLF : HOLES :: (A) badminton : feather (B) football : kick (C) baseball : innings (D) tennis : net (E) swimming : pool

3. Ⓐ Ⓑ Ⓒ Ⓓ Ⓔ **3.** INFANCY : SENILITY :: (A) conclusion : climax (B) incipient : critical (C) dawn : dusk (D) day : night (E) January : October

4. Ⓐ Ⓑ Ⓒ Ⓓ Ⓔ **4.** TIRADE : ABUSIVE :: (A) monologue : lengthy (B) aphorism : boring (C) prologue : precedent (D) encomium : laudatory (E) critique : insolent

5. Ⓐ Ⓑ Ⓒ Ⓓ Ⓔ **5.** GOOSE : GANDER :: (A) lion : lioness (B) shark : sharkskin (C) duck : drake (D) male : female (E) master : slave

6. Ⓐ Ⓑ Ⓒ Ⓓ Ⓔ **6.** BUSHEL : POTATOES :: (A) container : fruit (B) ounce : coal (C) wood : cord (D) point : diamond (E) bricks : mortar

7. Ⓐ Ⓑ Ⓒ Ⓓ Ⓔ **7.** PADDLE : CANOE :: (A) engine : train (B) auto : motor (C) oar : row (D) walk : run (E) steer : rudder

8. Ⓐ Ⓑ Ⓒ Ⓓ Ⓔ **8.** THERMOMETER : TEMPERATURE :: (A) minute : time (B) gauge : pressure (C) calendar : year (D) stopwatch : speed (E) barometer : air current

9. Ⓐ Ⓑ Ⓒ Ⓓ Ⓔ **9.** SYNTHESIS : CONSTRUCTION :: (A) artificial : building (B) dissection : analysis (C) excuse : denial (D) inductive : logical (E) artificial : true

10. Ⓐ Ⓑ Ⓒ Ⓓ Ⓔ **10.** PLEBISCITE : UKASE :: (A) vote : musical instrument (B) lack : abundance (C) public : ruler (D) written : oral (E) cancel : construct

11. Ⓐ Ⓑ Ⓒ Ⓓ Ⓔ **11.** IAMBIC : DACTYLIC :: (A) poem : essay (B) accent : sound (C) two : three (D) rhythm : hand (E) anapest : trochee

12. Ⓐ Ⓑ Ⓒ Ⓓ Ⓔ **12.** PARTNERSHIP : CORPORATION :: (A) two : many (B) local : national (C) agreement : conspiracy (D) conspiracy : plot (E) unlimited : limited

13. Ⓐ Ⓑ Ⓒ Ⓓ Ⓔ **13.** INKBLOT : EYE CHART :: (A) blurs : letters (B) blotter : spectacles (C) physician : specialist (D) psychiatrist : optometrist (E) oculist : ophthalmologist

14. TULIP : ZINNIA :: (A) Dutch : Swiss (B) garden : meadow (C) bulb :   14.Ⓐ Ⓑ Ⓒ Ⓓ Ⓔ
seed (D) annual : perennial (E) flower : grass

15. LIGAMENTS : BONES :: (A) fat : muscles (B) invertebrates : verte-   15.Ⓐ Ⓑ Ⓒ Ⓓ Ⓔ
brates (C) tear : fracture (D) invertebrates : mammals (E) heart : arm

16. LIKE : AS :: (A) conjunction : conjunction (B) conjunction : preposition   16.Ⓐ Ⓑ Ⓒ Ⓓ Ⓔ
(C) me : I (D) me : me (E) comparison : contrast

17. DEBATER : LARYNGITIS :: (A) actor : applause (B) doctor : diagnosis   17.Ⓐ Ⓑ Ⓒ Ⓓ Ⓔ
(C) writer : paper (D) pedestrian : lameness (E) swimmer : wet

18. DAFFODILS : TREES :: (A) spring : summer (B) fish : frogs (C) lake :   18.Ⓐ Ⓑ Ⓒ Ⓓ Ⓔ
meadow (D) snakes : grass (E) garden : orchard

19. KNIGHT : SHIELD :: (A) fencer : saber (B) soldier : carbine (C)   19.Ⓐ Ⓑ Ⓒ Ⓓ Ⓔ
welder : goggles (D) mechanic : wrench (E) lord : escutcheon

20. FURLONG : MILE :: (A) second : hour (B) degree : thermometer (C)   20.Ⓐ Ⓑ Ⓒ Ⓓ Ⓔ
foot : yard (D) ounce : pound (E) pint : gallon

21. SECURITY COUNCIL : ASSEMBLY :: (A) veto : no veto (B) Senate :   21.Ⓐ Ⓑ Ⓒ Ⓓ Ⓔ
House of Representatives (C) United Nations : League of Nations (D) strong :
weak (E) unpopular : popular

22. CONVICTION : INTELLECT :: (A) speech : propaganda (B) belief :   22.Ⓐ Ⓑ Ⓒ Ⓓ Ⓔ
religion (C) facts : statistics (D) court : home (E) persuasion : emotion

23. BEREAVED : CONDOLENCES :: (A) guilty : accusation (B) faulty :   23.Ⓐ Ⓑ Ⓒ Ⓓ Ⓔ
eraser (C) robbed : insurance (D) victorious : wealth (E) destitute : charity

24. MERCURY : VENUS :: (A) furthest : nearest (B) asteroid : planet (C)   24.Ⓐ Ⓑ Ⓒ Ⓓ Ⓔ
Roman : Greek (D) speed : love (E) martial : marital

25. BRUSH : PAINT :: (A) hammer : nail (B) polish : floor (C) trowel :   25.Ⓐ Ⓑ Ⓒ Ⓓ Ⓔ
cement (D) match : fire (E) rake : lawn

Answer Key

Word-Pair Relationships

EXERCISE A			EXERCISE B			EXERCISE C			EXERCISE D		
1. B	11. B	21. E	1. D	11. A	21. B	1. A	11. B	21. C	1. D	11. C	21. A
2. A	12. B	22. B	2. A	12. D	22. C	2. E	12. B	22. D	2. C	12. E	22. E
3. D	13. C	23. B	3. E	13. A	23. B	3. D	13. C	23. B	3. C	13. D	23. E
4. A	14. B	24. C	4. C	14. C	24. E	4. B	14. D	24. B	4. D	14. C	24. D
5. E	15. E	25. A	5. B	15. A	25. B	5. D	15. E	25. E	5. C	15. C	25. C
6. E	16. D		6. B	16. C		6. E	16. C		6. D	16. C	
7. A	17. E		7. B	17. C		7. D	17. E		7. A	17. D	
8. B	18. A		8. B	18. E		8. A	18. C		8. B	18. E	
9. C	19. D		9. B	19. E		9. A	19. C		9. B	19. C	
10. C	20. C		10. A	20. A		10. B	20. A		10. C	20. E	

Sentence Completions

This type of question is designed to test your skills in vocabulary *usage* and your ability to recognize consistency among the elements in a sentence. You are given a sentence in which one or two words have been omitted. You must select from five lettered choices the word or words that when inserted in the sentence blanks best completes the meaning of the sentence.

In effect, these questions are a form of reading comprehension. If you are able to recognize the implication of a sentence, you will be able to choose the words that relate to this implication. At times your knowledge of a particular fact may help you choose the correct answer, but for the most part you must depend upon your ability to understand and use language. For this reason you should make sure you understand the *usage* of all vocabulary words you learn.

When answering sentence completion questions, look for key words to assist you in determining the idea being expressed in each sentence. Consider the following examples.

Ⓐ Ⓑ Ⓒ Ⓓ Ⓔ   Because the enemy had a reputation for engaging in sneak attacks, we were ＿＿＿ on the alert.

(A) inevitably
(B) frequently
(C) constantly

(D) evidently
(E) occasionally

The key words here are *sneak attacks* and *alert*. The missing word refers to the degree of alertness necessary for protection against sneak attacks. Since one must always be on the alert when faced with the possibility of sneak attacks, choice C, constantly, is the best answer. Choices B and E can be eliminated because neither indicates steady alertness. Choices A and D are possible answers, but C is the best choice.

Ⓐ Ⓑ Ⓒ Ⓓ Ⓔ   ＿＿＿ has introduced the tremendous problem of the ＿＿＿ of the hundreds of workers replaced by machines.

(A) Specialization . . . relocation
(B) Automation . . . retraining
(C) Unemployment . . . education

(D) Disease . . . recovery
(E) Machinery . . . training

In this sentence the key words are *problem* and *replaced by machines.* Choice B, automation . . . retraining and Choice E, machinery . . . training, both pertain to machines. Choice B, however, is better because *automation* implies replacing by machines and *retraining* states the problem resulting from this replacement. The other choices don't fit into the context of the sentence.

The following exercises will help you become more adept at sentence completions. Answers to the exercises appear after Exercise D.

Practice Exercises

Sentence Completions

EXERCISE **A**

DIRECTIONS: For each sentence below, select the lettered word or set of words which, when inserted in the sentence blanks, best completes the meaning of that sentence.

1. The literary artist, concerned solely with the creation of a book or story as close to perfection as his powers will permit, is generally a quiet individual, contemplative, _____.

   1. Ⓐ Ⓑ Ⓒ Ⓓ Ⓔ

   (A) effuse
   (B) somnolent
   (C) retiring
   (D) poetic
   (E) gregarious

2. He was so _____ at tying fishermen's flies that he was asked to demonstrate his technique at sports fairs and exhibitions.

   2. Ⓐ Ⓑ Ⓒ Ⓓ Ⓔ

   (A) applicable
   (B) adroit
   (C) fancy
   (D) gauche
   (E) impressed

3. No punishment is too severe for such an _____ crime; it is almost impossible to understand its enormity.

   3. Ⓐ Ⓑ Ⓒ Ⓓ Ⓔ

   (A) avaricious
   (B) apposite
   (C) exemplary
   (D) arbitrary
   (E) egregious

4. He was so convinced that people were driven by _____ motives that he could not believe that anyone could be unselfish.

   4. Ⓐ Ⓑ Ⓒ Ⓓ Ⓔ

   (A) selfless
   (B) personal
   (C) altruistic
   (D) ulterior
   (E) intrinsic

5. Ⓐ Ⓑ Ⓒ Ⓓ Ⓔ 5. When the infant displayed signs of illness, the anxious parents called in a ____.

(A) podiatrist   (D) pedagogue
(B) pediatrician   (E) plagiarist
(C) practitioner

6. Ⓐ Ⓑ Ⓒ Ⓓ Ⓔ 6. I can recommend him for this position because I have always found him ____ and reliable.

(A) voracious   (D) valorous
(B) veracious   (E) mendacious
(C) vindictive

7. Ⓐ Ⓑ Ⓒ Ⓓ Ⓔ 7. No hero of ancient or modern times can surpass the Indian with his lofty contempt of death and the ____ with which he sustained the cruelest affliction.

(A) assent   (D) concern
(B) fortitude   (E) reverence
(C) guile

8. Ⓐ Ⓑ Ⓒ Ⓓ Ⓔ 8. Sitting so close to the ____ section of the orchestra, I found that the incessant beating of the drums gave me a headache.

(A) string   (D) percussion
(B) brass   (E) front
(C) wind

9. Ⓐ Ⓑ Ⓒ Ⓓ Ⓔ 9. I could not wish for a more ____ occasion on which to announce my plans for enlarging our establishment.

(A) ominous   (D) pronounced
(B) propitious   (E) portentous
(C) magnificent

10. Ⓐ Ⓑ Ⓒ Ⓓ Ⓔ 10. We ask for ____ from others, yet we are never merciful ourselves.

(A) clemency   (D) selectivity
(B) culpability   (E) consideration
(C) sincerity

11. Ⓐ Ⓑ Ⓒ Ⓓ Ⓔ 11. To prevent a repetition of this dreadful occurrence, we must discover the ____ element in the food that was served.

(A) unknown   (D) tawdry
(B) toxic   (E) heinous
(C) benign

12. Ⓐ Ⓑ Ⓒ Ⓓ Ⓔ 12. The concept of ____ grouping of people with similar interests and abilities was very popular among educators.

(A) segregated   (D) homogeneous
(B) integrated   (E) congruent
(C) heterogeneous

13. His theories were so ____ that few could see what he was trying to establish.　13.Ⓐ Ⓑ Ⓒ Ⓓ Ⓔ

(A) logical
(B) erudite
(C) scholarly
(D) theoretical
(E) nebulous

14. When I first began to study words in families. I was unaware that *protagonist* was the opposite of *antagonist*, that ____ was the opposite of *zenith*.　14.Ⓐ Ⓑ Ⓒ Ⓓ Ⓔ

(A) *apex*
(B) *rood*
(C) *solstice*
(D) *nadir*
(E) *hegira*

15. Your ____ attitude will alienate any supporters you may have won to your cause.　15.Ⓐ Ⓑ Ⓒ Ⓓ Ⓔ

(A) fascinating
(B) humanitarian
(C) logical
(D) truculent
(E) tortuous

16. We do not mean to be disrespectful when we refuse to follow the advice of our ____ leader.　16.Ⓐ Ⓑ Ⓒ Ⓓ Ⓔ

(A) venerable
(B) respectful
(C) famous
(D) gracious
(E) dynamic

17. I fail to understand why there is such a ____ atmosphere; we have lost a battle, not a war.　17.Ⓐ Ⓑ Ⓒ Ⓓ Ⓔ

(A) funereal
(B) blatant
(C) giddy
(D) sanguine
(E) haughty

18. When he recited the passage by ____. he revealed that he was reproducing ____ without understanding their meaning.　18.Ⓐ Ⓑ Ⓒ Ⓓ Ⓔ

(A) sounds – meaning
(B) sounds – pronunciation
(C) effects – cause
(D) rote – sounds
(E) ideas – message

19. Something that is ____ is not ____ .　19.Ⓐ Ⓑ Ⓒ Ⓓ Ⓔ

(A) trite – boring
(B) violent – vivid
(C) common – a cliché
(D) elastic – resilient
(E) hackneyed – original

20. When he realized that he had been induced to sign the contract by ____ , he threatened to institute legal proceedings to ____ the agreement.　20.Ⓐ Ⓑ Ⓒ Ⓓ Ⓔ

(A) force – nullify
(B) innuendo – negate
(C) chicanery – cancel
(D) flattery – liquidate
(E) hypnotism – validate

21.Ⓐ Ⓑ Ⓒ Ⓓ Ⓔ   **21.** An individual who is ____ is incapable of ____.

         (A)   fettered—flight   (D)   militant—fear
         (B)   modest—shame   (E)   ambitious—failure
         (C)   penurious—thought

22.Ⓐ Ⓑ Ⓒ Ⓓ Ⓔ   **22.** His ____ was so marked that I teasingly suggested that he had seen a ____.

         (A)   clumsiness—vision   (D)   separation—lawyer
         (B)   pallor—spectre   (E)   visage—ghost
         (C)   demeanor—physician

23.Ⓐ Ⓑ Ⓒ Ⓓ Ⓔ   **23.** A ____ statement is an ____ comparison.

         (A)   sarcastic—unfair   (D)   metaphorical—implied
         (B)   blatant—overt   (E)   bellicose—ardent
         (C)   sanguine—inherent

24.Ⓐ Ⓑ Ⓒ Ⓓ Ⓔ   **24.** The hostess attempted to ____ a romantic atmosphere that would bring the two young people together in ____.

         (A)   simulate—conflict   (D)   contrive—matrimony
         (B)   expand—fealty   (E)   present—collusion
         (C)   introduce—cacophony

25.Ⓐ Ⓑ Ⓒ Ⓓ Ⓔ   **25.** Old legends of extinct religions come down to us as ____ and ____.

         (A)   romance—chivalry   (D)   predictions—prophecies
         (B)   myths—fables   (E)   miracles—epiphanies
         (C)   dreams—visions

EXERCISE B

DIRECTIONS: For each sentence below, select the lettered word or set of words which, when inserted in the sentence blanks, best completes the meaning of that sentence.

1.Ⓐ Ⓑ Ⓒ Ⓓ Ⓔ   **1.** As I recall my plane trip around the world last July and August, I think my greatest difficulty was the adjustment to the different ____ served with the food in the various cities we visited.

         (A)   ingredients   (D)   grades
         (B)   condiments   (E)   varieties
         (C)   qualities

2.Ⓐ Ⓑ Ⓒ Ⓓ Ⓔ   **2.** After several ____ attempts to send the missile into space, the spacecraft was finally launched successfully.

         (A)   abortive   (D)   preliminary
         (B)   difficult   (E)   excellent
         (C)   experimental

3. He worked _____ at his task for weeks before he felt satisfied that the results would   3.Ⓐ Ⓑ Ⓒ Ⓓ Ⓔ
justify his long effort.

(A) occasionally   (D) assiduously
(B) regularly   (E) intermittently
(C) patiently

4. His book was marred by the many _____ remarks, which made us forget his main   4.Ⓐ Ⓑ Ⓒ Ⓓ Ⓔ
theme.

(A) inappropriate   (D) opinionated
(B) humorous   (E) slanted
(C) digressive

5. Overindulgence _____ character as well as physical stamina.   5.Ⓐ Ⓑ Ⓒ Ⓓ Ⓔ

(A) strengthens   (D) maintains
(B) stimulates   (E) provides
(C) debilitates

6. He was not _____ and preferred to be alone most of the time.   6.Ⓐ Ⓑ Ⓒ Ⓓ Ⓔ

(A) antisocial   (D) cordial
(B) gracious   (E) handsome
(C) gregarious

7. The reasoning in this editorial is so _____ that we cannot see how anyone can be   7.Ⓐ Ⓑ Ⓒ Ⓓ Ⓔ
deceived by it.

(A) coherent   (D) specious
(B) special   (E) chauvinistic
(C) cogent

8. Since you have failed three of the last four tests, you cannot afford to be _____ about   8.Ⓐ Ⓑ Ⓒ Ⓓ Ⓔ
passing for the term.

(A) courteous   (D) passive
(B) relevant   (E) indolent
(C) sanguine

9. You are afraid to attack him directly; you, therefore, are resorting to _____ .   9.Ⓐ Ⓑ Ⓒ Ⓓ Ⓔ

(A) guile   (D) innuendo
(B) effrontery   (E) condemnation
(C) criticism

10. His _____ remarks are often embarrassing because of their frankness.   10.Ⓐ Ⓑ Ⓒ Ⓓ Ⓔ

(A) sarcastic   (D) urbane
(B) sadistic   (E) ingenuous
(C) frank

11.Ⓐ Ⓑ Ⓒ Ⓓ Ⓔ **11.** The pioneers' greatest asset was not their material wealth but their _____.

  (A) fortitude   (D) companions
  (B) simplicity   (E) possessions
  (C) largesse

12.Ⓐ Ⓑ Ⓒ Ⓓ Ⓔ **12.** Your _____ tactics may compel me to cancel the contract because the job must be finished on time.

  (A) dilatory   (D) infamous
  (B) offensive   (E) confiscatory
  (C) obstructive

13.Ⓐ Ⓑ Ⓒ Ⓓ Ⓔ **13.** Some students are _____ and want to take only the courses for which they see immediate value.

  (A) theoretical   (D) foolish
  (B) stupid   (E) opinionated
  (C) pragmatic

14.Ⓐ Ⓑ Ⓒ Ⓓ Ⓔ **14.** Because I find that hot summer weather _____ me and leaves me very tired, I try to leave the city every August and go to Maine.

  (A) irritates   (D) boils
  (B) bores   (E) disturbs
  (C) enervates

15.Ⓐ Ⓑ Ⓒ Ⓓ Ⓔ **15.** Americans do not feel that _____ obedience and implicit submission to the will of another is necessary in order to maintain good government.

  (A) titular   (D) verbal
  (B) blind   (E) stark
  (C) partial

16.Ⓐ Ⓑ Ⓒ Ⓓ Ⓔ **16.** Because his occupation required that he work at night and sleep during the day, he had an exceptionally _____ complexion.

  (A) ghastly   (D) plain
  (B) ruddy   (E) pallid
  (C) livid

17.Ⓐ Ⓑ Ⓒ Ⓓ Ⓔ **17.** It is almost impossible at times to capture the _____ of words when we translate them into a foreign language.

  (A) implications   (D) connotations
  (B) meanings   (E) essence
  (C) denotations

18. As ____ head of the organization. he attended social functions and civic meetings   18. Ⓐ Ⓑ Ⓒ Ⓓ Ⓔ
but had no ____ in the formulation of company policy.

   (A) titular – voice   (D) real – competition
   (B) complete – vote   (E) actual – superior
   (C) titular – pride

19. Unlike the Shakespearean plays. the "closet dramas" of the nineteenth century were   19. Ⓐ Ⓑ Ⓒ Ⓓ Ⓔ
meant to be ____ rather than ____ .

   (A) seen – acted   (D) sophisticated – urbane
   (B) read – acted   (E) produced – acted
   (C) quiet – loud

20. The collapse of the financial empire set up by the small group was more than a ____;   20. Ⓐ Ⓑ Ⓒ Ⓓ Ⓔ
it affected millions of small ____ .

   (A) threat – men   (D) disaster – homeowners
   (B) vision – speculators   (E) calamity – prospectors
   (C) debacle – investors

21. Employers who retire people who are willing and able to continue working should   21. Ⓐ Ⓑ Ⓒ Ⓓ Ⓔ
realize that ____ age is not an effective ____ in determining whether an individual
is capable of working.

   (A) physical – barrier   (D) chronological – criterion
   (B) chronological – factor   (E) declining – standard
   (C) intellectual – criterion

22. Her true feelings ____ themselves in her sarcastic asides; only then was her ____   22. Ⓐ Ⓑ Ⓒ Ⓓ Ⓔ
revealed.

   (A) concealed – sweetness   (D) developed – anxiety
   (B) manifested – bitterness   (E) grieved – charm
   (C) hid – sarcasm

23. To ____ is to try to ____ an individual.   23. Ⓐ Ⓑ Ⓒ Ⓓ Ⓔ

   (A) gainsay – corrupt   (D) proselytize – convert
   (B) evacuate – dismiss   (E) inhibit – frighten
   (C) exhume – bury

24. When I listened to his cogent arguments, all my ____ were ____ and I was forced   24. Ⓐ Ⓑ Ⓒ Ⓓ Ⓔ
to agree with his point of view.

   (A) senses – stimulated   (D) questions – asked
   (B) doubts – confirmed   (E) doubts – dispelled
   (C) friends – present

25. Ⓐ Ⓑ Ⓒ Ⓓ Ⓔ 25. She was _____ because her plans had gone _____.

    (A) pleased — awry   (D) importunate — splendidly
    (B) imminent — efficiently   (E) distraught — awry
    (C) foiled — well

EXERCISE C

DIRECTIONS: For each sentence below, select the lettered word or set of words which, when inserted in the sentence blanks, best completes the meaning of that sentence.

1. Ⓐ Ⓑ Ⓒ Ⓓ Ⓔ 1. The ties that bind us together in common activity are so _____ that they can disappear at any moment.

    (A) tentative   (D) consistent
    (B) tenuous   (E) tenacious
    (C) restrictive

2. Ⓐ Ⓑ Ⓒ Ⓓ Ⓔ 2. I did not anticipate reading such an _____ discussion of the international situation in the morning newspaper; normally, such a treatment could be found only in scholarly magazines.

    (A) erudite   (D) overt
    (B) arrogant   (E) analytical
    (C) ingenious

3. Ⓐ Ⓑ Ⓒ Ⓓ Ⓔ 3. We need more men of culture and enlightenment; we have too many _____ among us.

    (A) boors   (D) pragmatists
    (B) students   (E) philosophers
    (C) philistines

4. Ⓐ Ⓑ Ⓒ Ⓓ Ⓔ 4. The Trojan War proved to the Greeks that cunning and _____ were often more effective than military might.

    (A) treachery   (D) wisdom
    (B) artifice   (E) beauty
    (C) strength

5. Ⓐ Ⓑ Ⓒ Ⓓ Ⓔ 5. His remarks were filled with _____, which sounded lofty but presented nothing new to the audience.

    (A) aphorisms   (D) adages
    (B) platitudes   (E) symbols
    (C) bombast

6. Ⓐ Ⓑ Ⓒ Ⓓ Ⓔ 6. Achilles had his _____, Hitler had his Elite Corps.

    (A) myrmidons   (D) myriads
    (B) antagonists   (E) anchorites
    (C) arachnids

7. In order to photograph ____ animals, elaborate flashlight equipment is necessary.   7. Ⓐ Ⓑ Ⓒ Ⓓ Ⓔ

   (A) predatory   (D) live
   (B) wild   (E) rare
   (C) nocturnal

8. He was deluded by the ____ who claimed he could cure all diseases with his miracle   8. Ⓐ Ⓑ Ⓒ Ⓓ Ⓔ
machine.

   (A) salesman   (D) doctor
   (B) inventor   (E) practitioner
   (C) charlatan

9. The attorney protested that the testimony being offered was not ____ to the case and   9. Ⓐ Ⓑ Ⓒ Ⓓ Ⓔ
asked that it be stricken from the record as irrelevant.

   (A) favorable   (D) beneficial
   (B) coherent   (E) germane
   (C) harmful

10. Automation threatens mankind with an increased number of ____ hours.   10. Ⓐ Ⓑ Ⓒ Ⓓ Ⓔ

   (A) meager   (D) complex
   (B) useless   (E) idle
   (C) active

11. I was so bored with the verbose and redundant style of that writer that I welcomed   11. Ⓐ Ⓑ Ⓒ Ⓓ Ⓔ
the change to the ____ style of this author.

   (A) prolix   (D) logistical
   (B) consistent   (E) tacit
   (C) terse

12. Such doltish behavior was not expected from so ____ an individual.   12. Ⓐ Ⓑ Ⓒ Ⓓ Ⓔ

   (A) exasperating   (D) enigmatic
   (B) astute   (E) democratic
   (C) cowardly

13. Disturbed by the ____ nature of the plays being presented, the Puritans closed the   13. Ⓐ Ⓑ Ⓒ Ⓓ Ⓔ
theaters in 1642.

   (A) mediocre   (D) salacious
   (B) fantastic   (E) witty
   (C) moribund

14. John left his position with the company because he felt that advancement was based   14. Ⓐ Ⓑ Ⓒ Ⓓ Ⓔ
on ____ rather than on ability.

   (A) chance   (D) superciliousness
   (B) seniority   (E) maturation
   (C) nepotism

15. Ⓐ Ⓑ Ⓒ Ⓓ Ⓔ   **15.** He became quite overbearing and domineering once he had become accustomed to the _____ shown to soldiers by the natives; he enjoyed his new sense of power.

       (A)   ability   (D)   culpability
       (B)   domesticity   (E)   insolence
       (C)   deference

16. Ⓐ Ⓑ Ⓒ Ⓓ Ⓔ   **16.** Epicureans live for the _____ of their senses.

       (A)   mortification   (D)   gravity
       (B)   removal   (E)   lassitude
       (C)   gratification

17. Ⓐ Ⓑ Ⓒ Ⓓ Ⓔ   **17.** I grew more and more aware of Iago's _____ purpose as I watched him plant the seeds of suspicion in Othello's mind.

       (A)   noble   (D)   insincere
       (B)   meritorious   (E)   hypocritical
       (C)   fell

18. Ⓐ Ⓑ Ⓒ Ⓓ Ⓔ   **18.** Her reaction to his proposal was _____; she rejected it _____.

       (A)   inevitable – vehemently   (D)   sympathetic – angrily
       (B)   subtle – violently   (E)   garrulous – tersely
       (C)   clever – obtusely

19. Ⓐ Ⓑ Ⓒ Ⓓ Ⓔ   **19.** _____ is the mark of the _____.

       (A)   Timorousness – hero   (D)   Trepidation – coward
       (B)   Thrift – impoverished   (E)   Vanity – obsequious
       (C)   Avarice – philanthropist

20. Ⓐ Ⓑ Ⓒ Ⓓ Ⓔ   **20.** If you carry this _____ attitude to the conference, you will _____ any supporters you may have at this moment.

       (A)   belligerent – delight   (D)   supercilious – attract
       (B)   truculent – alienate   (E)   ubiquitous – alienate
       (C)   conciliatory – defer

21. Ⓐ Ⓑ Ⓒ Ⓓ Ⓔ   **21.** It hurt my pride to be forced to _____ a person who always insulted me; nevertheless, I tried to _____ him.

       (A)   rebuke – condign   (D)   repudiate – evaluate
       (B)   respect – avenge   (E)   intimidate – redeem
       (C)   propitiate – conciliate

22. Ⓐ Ⓑ Ⓒ Ⓓ Ⓔ   **22.** Because _____ is such an unsightly disease, its victims have frequently been shunned.

       (A)   leprosy   (D)   poverty
       (B)   cancer   (E)   tuberculosis
       (C)   halitosis

23. I am not attracted by the _____ life of the _____, always wandering through the   23. Ⓐ Ⓑ Ⓒ Ⓓ Ⓔ
countryside, begging for charity.

(A) proud – almsgiver
(B) noble – philanthropic
(C) urban – hobo
(D) natural – philosopher
(E) peripatetic – vagabond

24. The sugar dissolved in the water _____; finally all that remained was an almost _____   24. Ⓐ Ⓑ Ⓒ Ⓓ Ⓔ
residue on the bottom of the glass.

(A) quickly – lumpy
(B) immediately – fragrant
(C) gradually – imperceptible
(D) subsequently – glassy
(E) spectacularly – opaque

25. It is foolish to vent your spleen on an _____ object; still, you make _____ enemies   25. Ⓐ Ⓑ Ⓒ Ⓓ Ⓔ
that way.

(A) inanimate – fewer
(B) immobile – bitter
(C) interesting – curious
(D) insipid – fewer
(E) humane – more

EXERCISE D

DIRECTIONS: For each sentence below, select the lettered word or set of words which, when
inserted in the sentence blanks, best completes the meaning of that sentence.

1. Architects travel to Greece and _____ to study the Parthenon and the Pantheon.   1. Ⓐ Ⓑ Ⓒ Ⓓ Ⓔ

(A) Cyprus
(B) Turkey
(C) France
(D) Spain
(E) Italy

2. The discoveries of science often are a mixed blessing; on the one hand they give us   2. Ⓐ Ⓑ Ⓒ Ⓓ Ⓔ
valuable pesticides that enable the farmer to grow more abundant crops and on the
other hand they _____ the benefits by destroying the balance of nature.

(A) compromise
(B) misplace
(C) mollify
(D) damage
(E) counteract

3. If we _____ these experienced people to positions of unimportance because of their   3. Ⓐ Ⓑ Ⓒ Ⓓ Ⓔ
political persuasions, we shall lose the services of valuably trained personnel.

(A) define
(B) propel
(C) relegate
(D) constrict
(E) detract

4. Ⓐ Ⓑ Ⓒ Ⓓ Ⓔ **4.** His ___ directions misled us; we did not know which of the two roads to take.

  (A) foolish
  (B) complicated
  (C) extenuating
  (D) ambiguous
  (E) arbitrary

5. Ⓐ Ⓑ Ⓒ Ⓓ Ⓔ **5.** I am afraid that you will have to alter your ___ views in the light of the tragic news that has just arrived.

  (A) roseate
  (B) tragic
  (C) contrary
  (D) narrow
  (E) dour

6. Ⓐ Ⓑ Ⓒ Ⓓ Ⓔ **6.** You were frightened by a concept that you ___ in your own mind.

  (A) accepted
  (B) idealized
  (C) sought
  (D) externalized
  (E) created

7. Ⓐ Ⓑ Ⓒ Ⓓ Ⓔ **7.** Although there are ___ outbursts of gunfire, we can report that the major rebellion has been suppressed.

  (A) bitter
  (B) heinous
  (C) meager
  (D) nocturnal
  (E) sporadic

8. Ⓐ Ⓑ Ⓒ Ⓓ Ⓔ **8.** He was guided by ___ rather than by ethical considerations.

  (A) expediency
  (B) precepts
  (C) morality
  (D) consequence
  (E) sophistry

9. Ⓐ Ⓑ Ⓒ Ⓓ Ⓔ **9.** We now know that what constitutes practically all matter is empty space; relatively enormous ___ in which revolve with lightning velocity infinitesimal particles so small that they have never been seen or photographed.

  (A) seas
  (B) particles
  (C) areas
  (D) skies
  (E) voids

10. Ⓐ Ⓑ Ⓒ Ⓓ Ⓔ **10.** To be ___ is to be without ___.

  (A) credulous – gullibility
  (B) considerate – incredibility
  (C) belligerent – pugnacity
  (D) maudlin – tenacity
  (E) gullible – skepticism

11. Ⓐ Ⓑ Ⓒ Ⓓ Ⓔ **11.** His listeners enjoyed his ___ wit but his victims often ___ at its satire.

  (A) lugubrious – suffered
  (B) taut – smiled
  (C) bitter – smarted
  (D) lugubrious – smiled
  (E) trenchant – winced

12. An occasional _____ remark spoiled the _____ that made the paper memorable.　12. Ⓐ Ⓑ Ⓒ Ⓓ Ⓔ

    (A) trite – clichés   (D) urbane – sophistication
    (B) colloquial – verisimilitude (E) jocund – gaiety
    (C) hackneyed – originality

13. Unlike the carefully weighed and _____ compositions of Dante, Goethe's writings　13. Ⓐ Ⓑ Ⓒ Ⓓ Ⓔ
have always the sense of _____ and enthusiasm.

    (A) inspired – vigor   (D) planned – immediacy
    (B) spontaneous – immediacy (E) developed – construction
    (C) contrived – languor

14. In Homer's work, Achilles is the _____ of Greek warriors; Odysseus _____ the　14. Ⓐ Ⓑ Ⓒ Ⓓ Ⓔ
shrewd man.

    (A) epitome – abhors   (D) prototype – eschews
    (B) antithesis – exemplifies (E) adversary – abhors
    (C) paragon – exemplifies

15. _____ enables us to know the past and to use it in preparing for the future.　15. Ⓐ Ⓑ Ⓒ Ⓓ Ⓔ

    (A) Beauty   (D) Antiquity
    (B) Truth   (E) Thought
    (C) Language

16. Victims of glaucoma find that their _____ vision is impaired and that they can no　16. Ⓐ Ⓑ Ⓒ Ⓓ Ⓔ
longer see objects not directly in front of them.

    (A) peripatetic   (D) ocular
    (B) peripheral   (E) perspicacious
    (C) periphrastic

17. The child's earliest words deal with concrete objects and actions; it is much later that　17. Ⓐ Ⓑ Ⓒ Ⓓ Ⓔ
he is able to grapple with _____.

    (A) decisions   (D) opponents
    (B) abstractions   (E) mathematics
    (C) maxims

18. It is regrettable that the author saved many of his most brilliant lines for the _____;　18. Ⓐ Ⓑ Ⓒ Ⓓ Ⓔ
by that time, most of the audience had left.

    (A) ingenue   (D) curtain
    (B) epilogue   (E) book
    (C) climax

19. Ⓐ Ⓑ Ⓒ Ⓓ Ⓔ **19.** It would be difficult for one so _____ to be led to believe that all men are equal and that we must disregard race, color, and creed.

(A) emotional
(B) broadminded
(C) tolerant

(D) intolerant
(E) democratic

20. Ⓐ Ⓑ Ⓒ Ⓓ Ⓔ **20.** The _____ of our civilization from an agricultural society to today's complex industrial world was accompanied by upheaval and, all too often, war.

(A) adjustment
(B) migration
(C) phasing

(D) metamorphosis
(E) route

21. Ⓐ Ⓑ Ⓒ Ⓓ Ⓔ **21.** To be _____ is to be _____.

(A) petulant – agreeable
(B) turbid – swollen
(C) torpid – sluggish

(D) turgid – clear
(E) evergreen – deciduous

22. Ⓐ Ⓑ Ⓒ Ⓓ Ⓔ **22.** Man is essentially a _____ animal and tends to _____ others.

(A) selfish – resent
(B) vicarious – work with
(C) maudlin – belittle

(D) perverse – adopt
(E) gregarious – associate with

23. Ⓐ Ⓑ Ⓒ Ⓓ Ⓔ **23.** Singers have a definite advantage over musicians who play an instrument; they can appeal to us through _____ as well as _____.

(A) personality – charm
(B) emotions – sounds
(C) thoughts – ideas

(D) ideas – music
(E) sight – personality

24. Ⓐ Ⓑ Ⓒ Ⓓ Ⓔ **24.** Because the inspector gave the plant a _____ examination, he _____ many defects.

(A) semiannual – uncovered
(B) significant – neglected
(C) perfunctory – overlooked

(D) pertinent – unveiled
(E) routine – discovered

25. Ⓐ Ⓑ Ⓒ Ⓓ Ⓔ **25.** The playwright was known not for his original ideas but for his _____ of ideas that had been propounded by others.

(A) invention
(B) reiteration
(C) consideration

(D) enlightenment
(E) rejection

Answer Key

Sentence Completions

EXERCISE A			EXERCISE B			EXERCISE C			EXERCISE D		
1. C	11. B	21. A	1. B	11. A	21. D	1. B	11. C	21. C	1. E	11. E	21. C
2. B	12. D	22. B	2. A	12. A	22. B	2. A	12. B	22. A	2. E	12. C	22. C
3. E	13. E	23. D	3. D	13. C	23. D	3. C	13. D	23. E	3. C	13. D	23. D
4. D	14. D	24. D	4. C	14. C	24. E	4. B	14. C	24. C	4. D	14. C	24. C
5. B	15. D	25. B	5. C	15. B	25. E	5. B	15. C	25. A	5. A	15. C	25. B
6. B	16. A		6. C	16. E		6. A	16. C		6. E	16. B	
7. B	17. A		7. D	17. D		7. C	17. C		7. E	17. B	
8. D	18. D		8. C	18. A		8. C	18. A		8. A	18. B	
9. B	19. E		9. D	19. B		9. D	19. D		9. E	19. D	
10. A	20. C		10. E	20. C		10. D	20. B		10. E	20. D	

Writing Ability Review

Writing ability questions test your knowledge of college-level basic English grammar. To succeed in this section, you are required to have a command of sentence structure including tense and mood, subject and verb agreement, pronoun and antecedent agreement, proper case and parallel structure, and other basics. No attempt is made to test for punctuation, spelling or capitalization.

The best preparation for this test has been your exposure to English classes in both high school and college. Reading texts and supplementary books in other classes, as well as writing term papers, should also have added to your knowledge of standard English grammar. Additional preparation for this test may be had by reviewing any basic college grammar text in the fundamentals of English.

In general, when taking this section of the test:

1. Remember that each sentence may contain only *one* error, and that the error *must* be an *underlined* word or phrase.

2. Carefully read the entire sentence, considering each underlined part in context.

3. Look first for such items as tense sequences (using two different tenses in one sentence) and agreement between pronoun and antecedent.

Before answering the questions, read the directions carefully. The following is an example of the procedure for answering Writing Ability questions.

DIRECTIONS: The following section contains a number of sentences with four *underlined* words or phrases. These sentences may have errors in grammar, tense, usage, diction (choice of words), idiom or structure. Choose the one *underlined* word or phrase that must be changed to make the sentence correct (for standard written English), and blacken the space provided to the right of the question. If you find no mistakes in a sentence, mark space Ⓔ for *no error;* no sentence will contain more than one error.

Note: Assume that all parts of the sentence that are not underlined are correct and cannot be changed.

Sample Questions

The wear and tear on the body is a medical problem. No error
     A   B   C   D   E

Answer: **(E)** No error. Since both subjects are joined by the word "and," and since they are considered as a single thing, we use the single verb form *is*. (subject and verb agreement)

This review contains a guide to the essential points of English grammar and diction, including sample questions and detailed answers. The questions are illustrative of those found on the actual test.

Grammar

Tense

Verbs indicate time and therefore have tense. Time has three dimensions: past, present and future. Basically, there are five tense forms in general use:

(1) PRESENT: "The student *studies* his lessons very well."

(2) PAST: "The student *studied* his lessons very well."

(3) FUTURE: "The student *will study* his lessons very well."

(4) PERFECT PRESENT: "*Has* the student *studied* his lessons very well?"

(5) PERFECT PAST: "The student *had studied* his lessons before going to bed."

The following questions illustrate the rules of tense. Answer them following the directions above.

Practice Exercise

Tense

1. The parliamentarians cheered as the speaker entered. No error
            A   B   C   D   E

2. I had stopped playing ball three weeks ago because I became ill. No error
        A   B   C   D   E

3. He approached the counter and pays for his meal. No error
    A   B   C   D   E

4. You have to remember that not all people were honest and not above reproach.
            A   B   C   D
   No error
   E

5. A ball was thrown through the window but no one seen where it came from. No error
         A   B C D   E

6. The boys digged for hidden treasure, but found nothing. No error
         A B   C   D   E

7. The day was very warm, so I hoped to have played ball. No error
                   A B   C   D   E

8. My wife and I travel by train many times in the past. No error
           A B C   D   E

9. If the policeman would have arrived earlier, he would have seen the accident.
                    A   B   C   D
   No error
   E

10. Jogging through the streets, he passed many incredulous onlookers. No error
      A   B   C   D   E

Answers and Analysis

Tense

1. **(E)** No error. The past tense *entered* is correct, following *cheered*.

2. **(E)** No error. The verb tense (past) in the subordinate clause indicates a time period before the main verb, *had stopped*, which is in the past perfect tense.

3. **(C)** Tenses do not agree in this sentence. *Pays* is in the present tense, but should agree with the past tense *approached*. The correct form is *paid*.

4. **(C)** Inconsistent shift of tense from present in the main clause to past in the subordinate clause. A better structure is: "You have to remember that not all people *are honest* and not above reproach."

5. **(D)** *Seen* is the wrong tense; *saw* is the correct form.

6. **(A)** *Dig* is an irregular verb; its past tense is *dug*.

7. **(C)** *To play* is the correct form of the verb. The subject is hoping to do something in the future. *Have played* indicates something in the past.

8. **(B)** Since the action took place in the past, the past tense (*traveled*) or the perfect present tense (*have traveled*) would be correct.

9. **(A)** *Would have* is incorrect. It should not be used in place of *had*. The sentence should read: "If the policeman *had* arrived earlier, he would have seen the accident."

10. **(E)** No error. The present participle, *jogging*, expresses action occurring at the same time as the verb *passed*.

Agreement

There are two main rules involving agreement: (1) a verb must agree in number with its subject, and (2) a pronoun must agree in number with its antecedent (a word to which the pronoun refers). To put these rules into practice, a helpful exercise is to locate the subject and its verb or the pronoun and its antecedent in each sentence and try to form a relationship between them. To illustrate:

The *elevator goes* down (singular subject, singular verb).

The *elevators go* down (plural subject, plural verb).

The *student* writes *his* own dissertation (singular antecedent, singular pronoun).

The *students* write *their* own dissertations (plural antecedent, plural pronoun).

Visually forming relationships among the subject and verb (elevator—goes, elevators —go) and antecedent and pronoun (student—his, students—their) helps to avoid errors in agreement and can save time on a test.

Pronoun and Antecedent Agreement

A pronoun refers to another word called an antecedent. Antecedents are words such as *somebody, everyone, no one, everybody, each, either,* and *sort*. Pronouns which take the place of (refer to) antecedents are words such as *his, their,* and *its*. A major problem in usage is that a pronoun must agree in number with its antecedent. A singular antecedent must take a singular pronoun; a plural antecedent must take a plural pronoun.

The *students* write *their* own dissertations. (plural antecedent, plural pronoun).

EXAMPLES: "The *students* (plural antecedent) waited for the professor to address *them* (plural pronoun)."

"*Each* (singular antecedent) professor has *his* (singular pronoun) particular method of instruction."

Apply the above rules in answering the following questions.

Practice Exercise

Agreement

1. Our favorite teacher and friend have gone. No error
   A   B   C   D   E

2. The plant manager, like many workers, were very experienced in safety precautions.
                        A   B   C   D

   No error
   E

3. The entire community was saddened to hear of the mayor's sudden resignation.
          A   B   C   D

   No error
   E

4. Economics is a subject which many students take. No error
             A   B   C   D   E

5. Each supervisor and subordinate were to prepare their reports independently.
      A   B   C   D

   No error
   E

6. Neither the teacher nor the students were introduced to their dean. No error
          A   B   C   D   E

7. When husbands and wives both work, they may not have enough time for their chil-
                          A   B   C   D

   dren. No error
         E

8. Each takes their turn standing guard every night. No error
      A   B   C   D   E

9. The captain is the only one of the players who have attended team practice regularly.
             A   B   C   D

   No error
   E

10. Every teacher and student have been told to come to class promptly. No error
       A   B   C   D   E

11. We found that everyone had finished their work. No error
       A   B   C   D   E

12. The foreman and supervisor inspected their plant workshop. No error
                A   B   C   D   E

13. Neither the foreman nor supervisor inspected their plant workshop. No error
        A   B   C   D   E

14. Either the teacher or the assistant will bring their books. No error
        A   B   C   D   E

15. Each man and woman will prepare his or her report. No error
      A   B   C   D   E

16. Neither the students nor the teacher was aware of his problem. No error
    A   B   C   D   E

17. The group is waiting for their plane to Alaska. No error
    A   B   C   D   E

18. We completed our work to ensure that everyone will receive his paycheck. No error
                  A   B   C   D   E

19. The remainder of the students will receive their certificates next month. No error
        A   B   C   D   E

20. Neither of the teachers had their notes duplicated in sufficient number. No error
        A   B   C   D   E

Answers and Analysis

Agreement

1. **(C)** In this sentence there is only one person or subject—*teacher and friend*. This is a compound subject, but is treated as singular since it is only one person. The correct form of the verb is *has*.

2. **(B)** Since the subject of the sentence, *plant manager*, is singular, the verb should be singular too. The correct form of the verb here is *was*. Do not be confused by the plural, *workers*, in the parenthetical expression following the subject.

3. **(E)** No error. Collective nouns such as *community, family,* etc., are regarded as singular and therefore take singular verbs.

4. **(E)** No error. Nouns representing an organized field of knowledge usually ending in *-ics* (*statistics, economics,* etc.) take the singular form. If these same nouns refer to an activity, they are considered plural. An example of the latter: "The economics of the proposed building site *were* satisfactory."

5. **(C)** When a singular subject is preceded by *each* and joined by *and* to another singular subject, they are treated as singular units and the verb in the sentence is singular (to agree with *each*). This is an exception to the rule that subjects joined by *and* are usually plural.

6. **(E)** No error. In this sentence, two antecedents, *teacher* and *students*, are joined by the word *nor*. Since one antecedent is singular and the other plural, the question is whether the pronoun should be plural *their* or singular *his*. In such a sentence structure, the rule is that the pronoun agrees with the number of the *nearest* antecedent (*students*).

7. **(E)** No error. The plural pronoun *their* agrees with its antecedent *husbands and wives*.

8. **(C)** *Each* is the subject and takes a singular verb (*takes*) and a singular pronoun (*his*).

9. **(C)** The antecedent of *who* is the word *one*, not the plural word *players*. Therefore, since *who* is singular the verb should be *has attended*, also the singular form.

10. **(B)** The same rule applies here as in question 5 above. Although two singular subjects have been joined by the word *and*, they are treated as a single unit because they are preceded by the word *every*. The singular form of the verb, *has been*, is the correct form.

11. **(D)** A singular antecedent, *everyone*, must be referred to by a singular pronoun, *his*.

12. **(E)** No error. The antecedents *foreman* and *supervisor* are considered plural because they are joined by *and*. Note that they are not preceded by words such as *each* or *every*.

13. **(D)** Two or more singular antecedents joined by *or* or *nor* are followed by a singular pronoun, *his*.

14. **(D)** The same rule applies here as in question 13. The pronoun should be *his*.

15. **(D)** While technically correct (singular antecedent followed by singular pronoun), if two antecedents have different genders, the conventional style is to use the masculine pronoun.

16. **(E)** No error. This is similar to question 23. However, when a sentence contains both a singular and a plural antecedent, the pronoun agrees with the number of the nearest antecedent (in this case, singular).

17. **(C)** Since the collective noun is singular, the pronoun must also be singular (*its*).

18. **(E)** No error. The singular pronoun *everyone* takes a singular antecedent, *his*.

19. **(E)** No error. A pronoun referring to a collective unit or noun will be singular or plural depending on the number of the antecedent. Since *students* is plural, the antecedent *their* agrees in number.

20. **(C)** The antecedent *neither* takes a singular form, hence its antecedent must agree in number. In this case, *her* is the correct pronoun.

Proper Case and Parallel Structure

Case

The case of a noun or a pronoun indicates its relationship to other parts of a sentence. In general, pronouns have three cases—*nominative*, *objective* and *possessive*. The table below shows the form a pronoun may take in each case.

Nominative	I	you	he she it	we	they	who whoever
Objective	me	you	him her	us	them	whom whomever
Possessive	my mine	your yours	her, hers his its	our ours	their theirs	whose

NOMINATIVE CASE

Personal pronouns such as *I, you, he, she, it, we, they, who, whoever* are in the *nominative* case and are used when the pronoun is the subject of the verb—"*He* and *they* studied in the same school"; in apposition to a noun or pronoun—"Two students—Fred and *I*— are in the top five percent of our class"; or as a complement to the verb *to be*—"It was *he* at the door."

OBJECTIVE CASE

The pronoun forms of the *objective* case are *me, us, her, him, them, whom, whomever.* This form is used to indicate the object of a verb or preposition—"Give the book to *me*"; or to indicate the object when the verb is omitted—"Martha could play guitar better than *him.*"

POSSESSIVE CASE

In the *possessive* case, pronoun forms are *my, mine, our, ours, your, yours, her, hers, his, its, their, theirs, those.* This case is used before nouns to determine relationship—"That was *his* car"; in gerund phrases—"*My* disappearing caused much confusion"; or independently as subjects, objects, and complements of verbs—"*Whose* is this?"; "*Theirs* is a beautiful relationship"; "There are some clothes of *mine.*"

Parallel Structure

If a sentence is composed of two or more parts consisting of similar ideas or meanings, all parts should have the same structure. This is true of nouns, participles, infinitives, and clauses. The following examples illustrate parallel structure.

NOUNS	not parallel	He enjoys football, baseball, and the playing of tennis.
	parallel	He enjoys *football, baseball,* and *tennis.*
PARTICIPLES	not parallel	The door was opened by the doorman and then someone else closed it.
	parallel	The door was *opened* by the doorman and *closed* by someone else.
INFINITIVES	not parallel	Anna wanted to cook, to sew, and do some gardening.
	parallel	Anna wanted *to cook, to sew,* and *to garden.*
CLAUSES	not parallel	Looking at the painting, Lou saw that the sky was green, there was blue grass, and yellow trees were in the background.
	parallel	Looking at the painting, Lou saw *that the sky was green, that the grass was blue,* and *that the background trees were yellow.*

The following exercise makes use of the above rules.

1. I read in the newspaper that in Nigeria they grow large tomatoes. No error
   A   B   C   D   E

2. To master the proper backstroke, the breathing must be carefully controlled. No error.
            A   B   C   D   E

3. While one part of the TV program carried the football game, the other part shows
        A   B   C
   the training of the teams. No error
        D   E

4. It was he who traveled the distance in half the time. No error
   A B C D   E

5. The teacher appreciates whomever volunteers in class. No error
               A   B   C   D   E

6. <u>My</u> mathematics teacher is one person <u>who</u> I shall always respect. <u>No error</u>
   A   B   C D   E

7. <u>He</u> told the teacher <u>who</u> <u>had</u> given <u>him</u> the correct answers. <u>No error</u>
   A   B C   D   E

8. <u>Almost</u> <u>every day</u> the laboratory assistant <u>helps</u> Fred and <u>I.</u> <u>No error</u>
    A   B   C   D E

9. The musician is a man <u>with</u> great promise and <u>who</u> should be <u>encouraged</u> to continue
                          A   B   C

   <u>his work.</u> <u>No error</u>
     D   E

10. The professor, <u>whom</u> <u>we</u> <u>all respect,</u> is <u>retiring</u> in two months. <u>No error</u>
               A   B   C   D   E

Answers and Analysis

Proper Case and Parallel Structure

1. **(C)** The use of the personal pronoun *they* in an impersonal sense should be avoided. This sentence should read: "I read in the newspaper that large tomatoes are grown in Nigeria."

2. **(B)** In this sentence, it seems as if the breathing is doing the swimming. The problem here is the dangling phrase which must be given a word to modify; "To master the proper backstroke, the swimmer must carefully control his breathing."

3. **(C)** This is a complex sentence with one main clause (the TV program) and one subordinate clause (the training sequence). However, the error is in tense. The main clause is in the past tense, while the subordinate clause is in the present. This subordinate clause should also be in the past tense, "the other part *showed.* . . ."

4. **(E)** No error. *He* is the subject complement, and *who* is the subject of *traveled.*

5. **(B)** The subject of a clause is written in the nominative case. Therefore, *whomever* should be *whoever.*

6. **(C)** The pronoun is the object of *respect* and should take the objective form *whom.*

7. **(E)** No error. *Who* is the subject of the verb *had given* and is in the nominative case.

8. **(D)** Since the pronoun is the object of the verb *helps*, it takes the objective form *me.*

9. **(A)** The second pronoun *who* is not parallel to the word *with.* The sentence should read: "The musician is a man *who has* great promise and who should be encouraged . . . ."

10. **(E)** No error. *Whom* is the object of the verb *respect* and therefore is in the objective case.

Diction

Proper communication—whether through speech or writing—depends upon the correct choice of words. Generally, specific and concise wording is preferred to general or vague usage. For example:

Engineers working as grade A designers will take notice that as of January 1, in the course of their employment, their pay will increase by 10 percent.

This sentence is wordy and vague. It would be better understood if written:

Grade A engineers will receive a 10 percent increase in pay commencing January 1.

With the more precise usage of words in the second sentence, the meaning immediately becomes clearer.

The Dictionary

As we have seen, a prerequisite to good diction is the proper use of words. A major aid in selecting what words to use is the dictionary. A dictionary is not only a collection of words, it is also a source of information about these words. Any good English dictionary provides the etymology (derivation or origin) of a word, its meaning, its preferred spelling and part of speech, and various other facts. Students can consult either an unabridged dictionary (which includes nearly all the words in the language), or the abridged, shorter version. The following excerpt from *Webster's New World Dictionary* will help you understand how to use this reference aid.

```
                          part of
      spelling pronunciation speech  word derivation
          ↓          ↓        ↓   ↓
        anx·ious (ank'sh s, an'-), adj.[<L. angere, choke],
                    1. worried; uneasy; apprehensive.
      definitions   2. causing anxiety.
                    3. eagerly wishing.—
                    anx'ious·ly, adv. — anx'ious·ness, n.
                              ↑
                         inflected forms
```

From *Webster's New World Dictionary*. (Cleveland, OH: World Publishing Company, 1963).

Spelling and Pronunciation

The spelling of the word is shown first. In words of two or more syllables, the syllables are separated by a dot. The pronunciation of *anxious* is shown by the symbols in parentheses, with the stress indicated by a stroke (/). In some dictionaries a bold stroke indicates the primary stress, while a lighter stroke indicates a secondary, or weak stress. The symbol ə, called a *schwa* (from the International Phonetic Alphabet), is used to indicate natural, weakened, or dulled vowels.

Parts of Speech and Word Derivation

The part of speech of the word is given after the pronunciation; here, *anxious* is an adjective (adj.). The symbol < (in brackets) means "derived from." The L. means *Latin*, and so, *anxious* is derived from the Latin word *angere*, "to choke."

Definitions

Webster's New World Dictionary gives word definitions in this order: (1) the standard, general sense of the word, and (2) colloquial, slang, dialectical, archaic, and obsolete senses. Check the guide in the dictionary you use for an explanation of the order of the definitions.

Inflected Forms

The inflected forms of the word are given last. For *anxious* there is *anxiously* (adverb) and *anxiousness* (noun). This is also where synonyms, antonyms and other related words are often given.

Common Errors of Word Usage

The Use of Colloquial (Informal) Words

Although colloquialisms appear in most dictionaries, they should be avoided in formal writing or speech. They may be used informally. The following sentences are illustrations of this.

INFORMAL: This is *sure* a delightful concert.

FORMAL: This is *indeed* a delightful concert.

INFORMAL: We have a long *way* to travel.

FORMAL: We have a long *distance* to travel.

INFORMAL: Our teacher was *plenty* good today.

FORMAL: Our teacher was *very* good today.

Illiteracies (Nonstandard and Substandard) and Slang Words

Although substandard words like *ain't* and *they's* are found in some dictionaries, they are usually used by uneducated people. Slang, on the other hand, may be used on informal occasions, but should be avoided in formal writing. Examples are as follows:

NONSTANDARD: Do you think we *had ought* paid attention to the policeman?

STANDARD: Do you think we *should have* paid attention to the policeman?

SUBSTANDARD: We should have gone *irregardless* of the hour.

STANDARD: We should have gone *regardless* of the hour.

SLANG: The supervisor received an *invite* to the manager's home.

STANDARD: The supervisor received an *invitation* to the manager's home.

Glossary of Usage

This glossary contains some additional words which may appear on your GMAT Writing Ability tests. Note which words are illiterate or substandard.

AD, LAB, PHONE. These words are informal short forms of advertisement, laboratory, and telephone.

AIN'T. Nonstandard for *am not, are not, is not, have. Ain't* should not be used on the college level.

ALRIGHT. Alright is the substandard spelling of *all right.*

AMONG, BETWEEN. *Among* is used to designate a group, generally two or more persons or objects. For example: "Debate the problem *among* yourselves." The word *between* refers to two persons or objects, e.g.: "He was found *between* the university and the concert hall." However, *between* can also refer to more than two objects when each is treated individually, e.g.: "The signed protocol was *between* the three nations in Asia."

AND, ETC. *and* used with *etc*. is redundant because *etc*. used alone means "and so forth."

ANYWHERES. Dialectical form of *anywhere*.

AS TO. Substandard for *about*.

BUT WHAT. Informal form of *that*.

CAN'T HARDLY, COULDN'T HARDLY. Substandard form of *can hardly*, *could hardly*. The substandard forms are also double negatives.

COMPLECTED. Colloquial for *complexioned*. The standard form is: "He is light-complexioned."

COULD OF, MIGHT OF. Nonstandard forms of *could have* and *might have*.

ENTHUSE. Substandard form of the verb *to show enthusiasm*.

EXPECT. Informal for *suppose* or *think*. "We *suppose* he arrived on time." not "We *expect* he arrived on time."

FEWER, LESS. *Fewer* indicates number; *less* refers to amount, quantity, or degree. "*Fewer workers* (not *less*) were promoted." "I made *less* profit on this job."

HAD OUGHT. Nonstandard form of *ought*. "We *ought* (not *had ought*) to commence the meeting."

INVITE. Slang for *invitation*.

IRREGARDLESS. Nonstandard for *regardless*.

KIND OF. Informal for *almost, somewhat*. "The president was *somewhat* (not *kind of*) apprehensive about his forthcoming speech."

LIKE, AS, AS IF. The use of *like* in a well-known commercial is informal: ". . . cigarette tastes *like* it should." The standard form is "tastes *as* it should."

LOT, LOTS OF. Informal for *many, much*.

NOHOW. Nonstandard for *not at all*.

OFF OF. Informal for *off*, as in: "Get *off* (not *off of*) the stairs."

PLENTY. Informal for *very, extremely*. "The speaker was *very* (not *plenty*) good."

REAL. Informal for *very, extremely*. "The speaker was *very* (not *real*) good."

SOME. Informal for *wonderful, extraordinary, remarkable*. "The speaker delivered a *remarkable* speech," not "The speaker delivered *some* speech."

THAT THERE, THIS HERE. Nonstandard for *that, this*.

WAYS. Informal for *way*. "I traveled a long *way* (not *ways*) to school."

WOULD OF. Nonstandard form of *would have*, as in: "I *would have* (not *would of*) liked to attend the concert."

MATHEMATICS REVIEW

The Mathematics and Data Sufficiency areas of the GMAT require a working knowledge of mathematical principles, including an understanding of the fundamentals of algebra, geometry, and arithmetic, and the ability to interpret graphs. The following review covers these areas thoroughly and if used properly, will prove helpful in preparing for the mathematical parts of the GMAT.

Read through the review carefully. You will notice that each topic is keyed for easy reference. Use the key number next to each answer given in the Sample Tests to refer to those sections in the review that cover material you may have missed and therefore will need to spend more time on.

I. Arithmetic

I-1. Whole Numbers

1-1
The numbers 0,1,2,3, . . . are called whole numbers or *integers*. So 75 is an integer but $4\frac{1}{3}$ is not an integer.

1-2
If the integer k divides m evenly, then we say *m is divisible by k* or *k is a factor of m*. For example, 12 is divisible by 4, but 12 is not divisible by 5. 1,2,3,4,6,12 are all factors of 12.

If k is a factor of m, then there is another integer n such that $m = k \times n$; in this case, m is called a *multiple of k*.

Since $12 = 4 \times 3$, 12 is a multiple of 4 and also 12 is a multiple of 3. 5,10,15, and 20 are all multiples of 5 but 15 and 5 are not multiples of 10.

Any integer is a multiple of each of its factors.

1-3
Any whole number is divisible by itself and by 1. If p is a whole number greater than 1, which has *only p* and 1 as factors, then p is called a *prime number*. 2,3,5,7,11,13,17,19 and 23 are all primes. 14 is not a prime since it is divisible by 2 and by 7.

A whole number which is divisible by 2 is called an *even* number; if a whole number is not even, then it is an *odd* number. 2,4,6,8,10 are even numbers, and 1,3,5,7 and 9 are odd numbers.

A collection of numbers is *consecutive* if each number is the successor of the number which precedes it. For example, 7,8,9 and 10 are consecutive, but 7,8,10,13 are not. 4,6,8,10 are consecutive even numbers. 7,11,13,17 are consecutive primes. 7,13,19,23 are not consecutive primes since 11 is a prime between 7 and 13.

1-4

> Any whole number can be written as a product of factors which are prime numbers.

To write a number as a *product of prime factors:*

(A) Divide the number by 2 if possible; continue to divide by 2 until the factor you get is not divisible by 2.

(B) Divide the result from (A) by 3 if possible; continue to divide by 3 until the factor you get is not divisible by 3.

(C) Divide the result from (B) by 5 if possible; continue to divide by 5 until the factor you get is not divisible by 5.

(D) Continue the procedure with 7,11, and so on, until all the factors are primes.

EXAMPLE 1:   Express 24 as a product of prime factors.

(A) $24 = 2 \times 12$, $12 = 2 \times 6$, $6 = 2 \times 3$ so $24 = 2 \times 2 \times 2 \times 3$. Since each factor (2 and 3) is prime, $24 = 2 \times 2 \times 2 \times 3$.

EXAMPLE 2:   Express 252 as a product of primes.

(A) $252 = 2 \times 126$, $126 = 2 \times 63$ and 63 is not divisible by 2, so $252 = 2 \times 2 \times 63$.

(B) $63 = 3 \times 21$, $21 = 3 \times 7$ and 7 is not divisible by 3. Since 7 is a prime, then $252 = 2 \times 2 \times 3 \times 3 \times 7$ and all the factors are primes.

1-5

A number m is a *common multiple* of two other numbers k and j if it is a multiple of each of them. For example, 12 is a common multiple of 4 and 6, since $3 \times 4 = 12$ and $2 \times 6 = 12$. 15 is not a common multiple of 3 and 6, because 15 is not a multiple of 6.

A number k is a *common factor* of two other numbers m and n if k is a factor of m and k is a factor of n.

The *least common multiple* (L.C.M.) of two numbers is the smallest number which is a common multiple of both numbers. To find the least common multiple of two numbers k and j:

(A) Write k as a product of primes and j as a product of primes.

(B) If there are any common factors *delete* them in *one* of the products.

(C) Multiply the remaining factors; the result is the least common multiple.

EXAMPLE 1:   Find the L.C.M. of 12 and 11.

(A) $12 = 2 \times 2 \times 3, 11 = 11 \times 1$.
(B)   There are no common factors.
(C)   The L.C.M. is $12 \times 11 = 132$.

EXAMPLE 2:   Find the L.C.M. of 27 and 63.

(A) $27 = 3 \times 3 \times 3, 63 = 3 \times 3 \times 7$.
(B) $3 \times 3 = 9$ is a common factor so delete it once.
(C)   The L.C.M. is $3 \times 3 \times 3 \times 7 = 189$.

You can find the L.C.M. of a collection of numbers in the same way except that if in step (B) the common factors are factors of more than two of the numbers, then delete the common factor in *all but one* of the products.

EXAMPLE 3:   Find the L.C.M. of 27, 63 and 72.

(A) $27 = 3 \times 3 \times 3, 63 = 3 \times 3 \times 7, 72 = 2 \times 2 \times 2 \times 3 \times 3$.
(B)   Delete 3×3 from two of the products.
(C)   The L.C.M. is $3 \times 7 \times 2 \times 2 \times 2 \times 3 \times 3 = 21 \times 72 = 1,512$.

I–2.   Fractions

2–1

A FRACTION is a number which represents a ratio or division of two whole numbers (integers). A fraction is written in the form $\frac{a}{b}$. The number on the top, a, is called the numerator; the number on the bottom, b, is called the denominator. The denominator tells how many equal parts there are (for example, parts of a pie); the numerator tells how many of these equal parts are taken. For example, $\frac{5}{8}$ is a fraction whose numerator is 5 and whose denominator is 8; it represents taking 5 of 8 equal parts, or dividing 8 into 5.

A fraction can not have 0 as a denominator since division by 0 is not defined.
A fraction with 1 as the denominator is the same as the whole number which is its numerator. For example, $\frac{12}{1}$ is 12, $\frac{0}{1}$ is 0.

If the numerator and denominator of a fraction are identical, the fraction represents 1. For example, $\frac{3}{3} = \frac{9}{9} = \frac{13}{13} = 1$. Any whole number, k, is represented by a fraction with a numerator equal to k times the denominator. For example, $\frac{18}{6} = 3$, and $\frac{30}{5} = 6$.

2-2

Mixed Numbers. A mixed number consists of a whole number and a fraction. For example, $7\frac{1}{4}$ is a mixed number; it means $7 + \frac{1}{4}$ and $\frac{1}{4}$ is called the fractional part of the mixed number $7\frac{1}{4}$. Any mixed number can be changed into a fraction:

(A) Multiply the whole number by the denominator of the fraction.
(B) Add the numerator of the fraction to the result of step A.
(C) Use the result of step B as the numerator and use the denominator of the fractional part of the mixed number as the denominator. This fraction is equal to the mixed number.

EXAMPLE 1:   Write $7\frac{1}{4}$ as a fraction.

(A) $4 \cdot 7 = 28$
(B) $28 + 1 = 29$
(C)   so $7\frac{1}{4} = \frac{29}{4}$.

A fraction whose numerator is larger than its denominator can be changed into a mixed number.

(A) Divide the denominator into the numerator; the result is the whole number of the mixed number.
(B) Put the remainder from step A over the denominator; this is the fractional part of the mixed number.

EXAMPLE 2:   Change $\frac{35}{8}$ into a mixed number.

(A) Divide 8 into 35; the result is 4 with a remainder of 3.
(B) $\frac{3}{8}$ is the fractional part of the mixed number.
(C) So $\frac{35}{8} = 4\frac{3}{8}$.

We can regard any whole number as a mixed number with 0 as the fractional part. For example, $\frac{18}{6} = 3$.

> In calculations with mixed numbers, change the mixed numbers into fractions.

2–3

Multiplying Fractions. To multiply two fractions, multiply their numerators and divide this result by the product of their denominators.

> In word problems, *of* usually indicates multiplication.

EXAMPLE: John saves $\frac{1}{3}$ of $240. How much does he save?

$$\frac{1}{3} \cdot \frac{240}{1} = \frac{240}{3} = \$80, \text{ the amount John saves.}$$

2–4

Dividing Fractions. One fraction is a *reciprocal* of another if their product is 1. So $\frac{1}{2}$ and 2 are reciprocals. To find the reciprocal of a fraction, simply interchange the numerator and denominator (turn the fraction upside down). This is called *inverting* the fractions. So when you invert $\frac{15}{17}$ you get $\frac{17}{15}$. When a fraction is inverted the inverted fraction and the original fraction are reciprocals. Thus $\frac{15}{17} \cdot \frac{17}{15} = \frac{255}{255} = \frac{1}{1} = 1$.

To divide one fraction (the dividend) by another fraction (the divisor), invert the divisor and multiply.

EXAMPLE 1: $\frac{5}{6} \div \frac{3}{4} = \frac{5}{6} \cdot \frac{4}{3} = \frac{20}{18}$

EXAMPLE 2: A worker makes a basket every $\frac{2}{3}$ hour. If the worker works for $7\frac{1}{2}$ hours, how many baskets will he make? We want to divide $\frac{2}{3}$ into $7\frac{1}{2}$, $7\frac{1}{2} = \frac{15}{2}$, so we want to divide $\frac{15}{2}$ by $\frac{2}{3}$. Thus

$$\frac{15}{2} \div \frac{2}{3} = \frac{15}{2} \cdot \frac{3}{2} = \frac{45}{4} = 11\frac{1}{4} \text{ baskets.}$$

2–5

Dividing and Multiplying by the Same Number. Since multiplication or division by 1 does not change the value of a number, you can multiply or divide any fraction by 1 and the fraction will remain the same. Remember that $\frac{a}{a} = 1$ for any non-zero number a. Therefore, if you multiply or divide any fraction by $\frac{a}{a}$, the result is the same as if you multiplied the numerator and denominator by a or divided the numerator and denominator by a.

If you multiply the numerator and denominator of a fraction by the same non-zero number the fraction remains the same.

If you divide the numerator and denominator of any fraction by the same non-zero number, the fraction remains the same.

Consider the fraction $\frac{3}{4}$. If we multiply 3 by 10 and 4 by 10, then $\frac{30}{40}$ must equal $\frac{3}{4}$.

When we multiply fractions, if any of the numerators and denominators have a common factor (see page 135 for factors) we can divide each of them by the common factor and the fraction remains the same. This process is called *cancelling* and can be a great time-saver.

EXAMPLE: Multiply $\frac{4}{9} \cdot \frac{75}{8}$. Since 4 is a common factor of 4 and 8, divide 4 and 8 by 4 getting $\frac{4}{9} \cdot \frac{75}{8} = \frac{1}{9} \cdot \frac{75}{2}$. Since 3 is a common factor of 9 and 75 divide 9 and 75 by 3 to get $\frac{1}{9} \cdot \frac{75}{2} = \frac{1}{3} \cdot \frac{25}{2}$. So $\frac{4}{9} \cdot \frac{75}{8} = \frac{1}{3} \cdot \frac{25}{2} = \frac{25}{6}$.

2–6

Equivalent Fractions. Two fractions are equivalent or equal if they represent the same ratio or number. In the last section, you saw that if you multiply or divide the numerator and denominator of a fraction by the same non-zero number the result is equivalent to the original fraction. For example, $\frac{7}{8} = \frac{70}{80}$ since $70 = 10 \times 7$ and $80 = 10 \times 8$.

> *In the test there will only be five choices, so your answer to a problem may not be the same as any of the given choices.* You may have to express a fraction as an equivalent fraction.

To find a fraction with a known denominator equal to a given fraction:

(A) divide the denominator of the given fraction into the known denominator;
(B) multiply the result of (A) by the numerator of the given fraction; this is the numerator of the required equivalent fraction.

EXAMPLE: Find a fraction with denominator 30 which is equal to $\frac{2}{5}$:

(A) 5 into 30 is 6;
(B) $6 \cdot 2 = 12$ so $\frac{12}{30} = \frac{2}{5}$.

2–7

Reducing a Fraction to Lowest Terms. A fraction has been reduced to lowest terms when the numerator and denominator have no common factors.

For example, $\frac{3}{4}$ is reduced to lowest terms, but $\frac{3}{6}$ is not because 3 is a common factor of 3 and 6.

> To reduce a fraction to lowest terms, cancel all the common factors of the numerator and denominator. (Cancelling common factors will not change the value of the fraction.)

For example, $\frac{100}{150} = \frac{10 \cdot 10}{10 \cdot 15} = \frac{10}{15} = \frac{5 \cdot 2}{5 \cdot 3} = \frac{2}{3}$. Since 2 and 3 have no common factors, $\frac{2}{3}$ is $\frac{100}{150}$ reduced to lowest terms. A fraction is equivalent to the fraction reduced to lowest terms.

If you write the numerator and denominator as products of primes, it is easy to cancel all the common factors.

$$\frac{63}{81} = \frac{3 \cdot 3 \cdot 7}{3 \cdot 3 \cdot 3 \cdot 3} = \frac{7}{9}$$

2–8
Adding Fractions. If the fractions have the same denominator, then the denominator is called a *common denominator*. Add the numerators, and use this sum as the new numerator with the common denominator as the denominator of the sum.

EXAMPLE 1: $\frac{5}{12} + \frac{3}{12} = \frac{5+3}{12} = \frac{8}{12} = \frac{2}{3}$

EXAMPLE 2: Jim uses 7 eggs to make breakfast and 8 eggs for supper. How many dozen eggs has he used? 7 eggs are $\frac{7}{12}$ of a dozen and 8 eggs are $\frac{8}{12}$ of a dozen. He used $\frac{7}{12} + \frac{8}{12} = \frac{7+8}{12} = \frac{15}{12} = \frac{5}{4} = 1\frac{1}{4}$ dozen eggs.

If the fractions don't have the same denominator, you must first find a common denominator. Multiply all the denominators together; the result is a common denominator.

EXAMPLE: To add $\frac{1}{2} + \frac{2}{3} + \frac{7}{4}$, $2 \cdot 3 \cdot 4 = 24$ is a common denominator.

There are many common denominators; the smallest one is called the *least common denominator*. For the previous example, 12 is the least common denominator.

Once you have found a common denominator, express each fraction as an equivalent fraction with the common denominator, and add as you did for the case when the fractions had the same denominator.

EXAMPLE: $\frac{1}{2} + \frac{2}{3} + \frac{7}{4} = ?$

(A) 24 is a common denominator.

(B) $\frac{1}{2} = \frac{12}{24}, \frac{2}{3} = \frac{16}{24}, \frac{7}{4} = \frac{42}{24}.$

(C) $\frac{1}{2} + \frac{2}{3} + \frac{7}{4} = \frac{12}{24} + \frac{16}{24} + \frac{42}{24} = \frac{12 + 16 + 42}{24} = \frac{70}{24} = \frac{35}{12}.$

2–9

Subtracting Fractions. When the fractions have the same denominator, subtract the numerators and place the result over the denominator.

EXAMPLE: $\frac{3}{5} - \frac{2}{5} = \frac{3 - 2}{5} = \frac{1}{5}$

When the fractions have different denominators

(A) Find a common denominator.
(B) Express the fractions as equivalent fractions with the same denominator.
(C) Subtract.

EXAMPLE: $\frac{3}{5} - \frac{2}{7} = ?$

(A) A common denominator is $5 \cdot 7 = 35$.

(B) $\frac{3}{5} = \frac{21}{35}, \frac{2}{7} = \frac{10}{35}.$

(C) $\frac{3}{5} - \frac{2}{7} = \frac{21}{35} - \frac{10}{35} = \frac{21 - 10}{35} = \frac{11}{35}.$

2–10

Complex Fractions. A fraction whose numerator and denominator are themselves fractions is called a *complex fraction*. For example $\frac{2/3}{4/5}$ is a complex fraction. A complex fraction can always be simplified by dividing the fraction.

EXAMPLE 1: $\frac{2}{3} \div \frac{4}{5} = \frac{\cancel{2}^{1}}{3} \cdot \frac{5}{\cancel{4}_{2}} = \frac{1}{3} \cdot \frac{5}{2} = \frac{5}{6}$

EXAMPLE 2: It takes $2\frac{1}{2}$ hours to get from Buffalo to Cleveland traveling at a constant rate of speed. What part of the distance is traveled in $\frac{3}{4}$ of an hour?

$\frac{3/4}{2\,1/2} = \frac{3/4}{5/2} = \frac{3}{4} \cdot \frac{2}{5} = \frac{3}{2} \cdot \frac{1}{5} = \frac{3}{10}$ of the distance.

I-3. Decimals

3-1

A collection of digits (the digits are 0,1,2, . . . ,9) after a period (called the decimal point) is called a *decimal fraction*. For example, .503, .5602, .32, and .4 are all decimal fractions.

Every decimal fraction represents a fraction. To find the fraction a decimal fraction represents:

(A) Take the fraction whose denominator is 10 and whose numerator is the first digit to the right of the decimal point.

(B) Take the fraction whose denominator is 100 and whose numerator is the second digit to the right of the decimal point.

(C) Take the fraction whose denominator is 1,000 and whose numerator is the third digit to the right of the decimal point.

(D) Continue the procedure until you have used each digit to the right of the decimal place. The denominator in each step is 10 times the denominator in the previous step.

(E) The *sum* of the fractions you have obtained in (A), (B), (C), and (D) is the fraction that the decimal fraction represents.

EXAMPLE 1: Find the fraction .503 represents.

(A) $\frac{5}{10}$

(B) $\frac{0}{100}$

(C) $\frac{3}{1000}$

(D) All the digits have already been used.

(E) So $.503 = \frac{5}{10} + \frac{0}{100} + \frac{3}{1000} = \frac{500}{1000} + \frac{0}{1000} + \frac{3}{1000} = \frac{503}{1000}$.

EXAMPLE 2: What fraction does .78934 represent?

(A) $\frac{7}{10}$

(B) $\frac{8}{100}$

(C) $\frac{9}{1000}$

(D) $\frac{3}{10,000}, \frac{4}{100,000}$

(E) So $.78934 = \frac{7}{10} + \frac{8}{100} + \frac{9}{1000} + \frac{3}{10,000} + \frac{4}{100,000} = \frac{78,934}{100,000}$.

Notice that the denominator of the last fraction you obtain in step (D) is a common denominator for all the previous denominators. Since each denominator is 10 times the previous one, the denominator of the final fraction of part (D) will be the product of r copies of 10 multiplied together (called 10^r) where r is the number of digits which appear in the decimal fraction. Therefore, a decimal fraction represents a fraction whose denominator is 10^r where r is the number of digits in the decimal fraction and whose numerator is the number represented by the digits of the decimal fraction.

EXAMPLE 3: What fraction does .5702 represent?

There are 4 digits in .5702. Therefore, the denominator is $10 \times 10 \times 10 \times 10 = 10,000$, and the numerator is 5,702. Therefore, $.5702 = \dfrac{5,702}{10,000}$.

> *You can add any number of zeros to the right of a decimal fraction without changing its value.*

EXAMPLE: $.3 = \dfrac{3}{10} = \dfrac{30}{100} = .30 = .30000 = \dfrac{30,000}{100,000} = .300000000 \ldots$

3–2

We call the first position to the right of the decimal point the tenths place, since the digit in that position tells you how many tenths you should take. (It is the numerator of a fraction whose denominator is 10.) In the same way, we call the second position to the right the hundredths place, the third position to the right the thousandths, and so on. This is similar to the way whole numbers are expressed, since 568 means $5 \times 100 + 6 \times 10 + 8 \times 1$. The various digits represent different numbers depending on their position: the first place to the left of the decimal point represents units, the second place to the left represents tens, and so on.

The following diagram may be helpful:

```
T  H  T  U   T  H  T
H  U  E  N   E  U  H
O  N  N  I . N  N  O
U  D  S  T   T  D  U
S  R     S   H  R  S
A  E         S  E  A
N  D            D  N
D  S            T  D
S               H  T
                S  H
                   S
```

Thus, 5,342.061 means 5 thousands + 3 hundreds + 4 tens + 2 + 0 tenths + 6 hundredths + 1 thousandth.

3–3

A DECIMAL is a whole number plus a decimal fraction; the decimal point separates the whole number from the decimal fraction. For example, 4,307.206 is a decimal which represents 4,307 added to the decimal fraction .206. A decimal fraction is a decimal with zero as the whole number.

3–4

A fraction whose denominator is a multiple of 10 is equivalent to a decimal. The denominator tells you the last place that is filled to the right of the decimal point. Place the decimal point in the numerator so that the last place to the right of the decimal point corresponds to the denominator. If the numerator does not have enough digits, add the appropriate number of zeros *before* the numerator.

EXAMPLE 1:   Find the decimal equivalent of $\frac{5,732}{100}$.

Since the denominator is 100, you need two places to the right of the decimal point so $\frac{5,732}{100} = 57.32$.

EXAMPLE 2:   What is the decimal equivalent of $\frac{57}{10,000}$?

The denominator is 10,000, so you need 4 decimal places. Since 57 only has two places, we add two zeros in front of 57; thus, $\frac{57}{10,000} = .0057$.

Do not make the error of adding the zeros to the right instead of to the left of 57; .5700 means $\frac{5,700}{10,000}$ not $\frac{57}{10,000}$.

3–5

Adding Decimals.   Decimals are much easier to add than fractions. To add a collection of decimals:

(A)   Write the decimals in a column with the decimal points vertically aligned.

(B)   Add enough zeros to the right of the decimal point so that every number has an entry in each column to the right of the decimal point.

(C)   Add the numbers in the same way as whole numbers.

(D)   Place a decimal point in the sum so that it is directly beneath the decimal points in the decimals added.

EXAMPLE 1:   How much is $5 + 3.43 + 16.021 + 3.1$?

(A)   5
       3.43
      16.021
    + 3.1

(B)   5.000
       3.430
      16.021
    + 3.100

(C)   5.000
       3.430
      16.021
    + 3.100

(D)   27.551   The answer is **27.551**.

EXAMPLE 2: If John has $.50, $3.25, and $6.05, how much does he have altogether?

$$\begin{array}{r} \$ \ .50 \\ 3.25 \\ + \ 6.05 \\ \hline \$9.80 \end{array}$$ So John has $9.80.

3-6

Subtracting Decimals. To subtract one decimal from another:

(A) Put the decimals in a column so that the decimal points are vertically aligned.

(B) Add zeros so that every decimal has an entry in each column to the right of the decimal point.

(C) Subtract the numbers as you would whole numbers.

(D) Place the decimal point in the result so that it is directly beneath the decimal points of the numbers you subtracted.

EXAMPLE 1: Solve 5.053 − 2.09.

(A) $$\begin{array}{r} 5.053 \\ - \ 2.09 \\ \hline \end{array}$$ (B) $$\begin{array}{r} 5.053 \\ - \ 2.090 \\ \hline \end{array}$$

(C) $$\begin{array}{r} 5.053 \\ - \ 2.090 \\ \hline \end{array}$$

(D) 2.963   The answer is **2.963.**

EXAMPLE 2: If Joe has $12 and he loses $8.40, how much money does he have left?

Since $12.00 − $8.40 = $3.60, he has $3.60 left.

3-7

Multiplying Decimals. Decimals are multiplied like whole numbers. *The decimal point of the product is placed so that the number of decimal places in the product is equal to the total of the number of decimal places in all of the numbers multiplied.*

EXAMPLE 1: What is (5.02)(.6)?

(502)(6) = 3012. There were 2 decimal places in 5.02 and 1 decimal place in .6, so the product must have $2 + 1 = 3$ decimal places. Therefore, (5.02)(.6) = 3.012.

EXAMPLE 2: If eggs cost $.06 each, how much should a dozen eggs cost?

Since (12)(.06) = .72, a dozen eggs should cost $.72.

> **Computing Tip.** To multiply a decimal by 10, just move the decimal point to the right one place; to multiply by 100, move the decimal point two places to the right and so on.

EXAMPLE: $9,983.456 \times 100 = 998,345.6$

3-8

Dividing Decimals. To divide one decimal (the dividend) by another decimal (the divisor):

(A) Move the decimal point in the divisor to the right until there is no decimal fraction in the divisor (this is the same as multiplying the divisor by a multiple of 10).

(B) Move the decimal point in the dividend the same number of places to the right as you moved the decimal point in step (A).

(C) Divide the result of (B) by the result of (A) as if they were whole numbers.

(D) The number of decimal places in the result (quotient) should be equal to the number of decimal places in the result of step (B).

EXAMPLE 1: Divide .05 into 25.155.

(A) Move the decimal point two places to the right in .05; the result is 5.

(B) Move the decimal point two places to the right in 25.155; the result is 2515.5.

(C) Divide 5 into 25155; the result is 5031.

(D) Since there was one decimal place in the result of (B); the answer is 503.1.

The work for this example might look like this:

$$\begin{array}{r} 503.1 \\ .05\overline{)25.15\,5} \end{array}$$

You can always check division by multiplying.

$$(503.1)(.05) = 25.155 \text{ so we were correct.}$$

If you write division as a fraction, example 1 would be expressed as $\dfrac{25.155}{.05}$.

You can multiply both the numerator and denominator by 100 without changing the value of the fraction, so

$$\frac{25.155}{.05} = \frac{25.155 \times 100}{.05 \ \times 100} = \frac{2515.5}{5.}.$$

So step (A) and (B) always change the division of a decimal by a decimal into the division by a whole number.

To divide a decimal by a whole number, divide them as if they were whole numbers. Then place the decimal point in the quotient so that the quotient has as many decimal places as the decimal (the dividend).

EXAMPLE 2: $\dfrac{55.033}{1.1} = \dfrac{550.33}{11.} = 50.03.$

EXAMPLE 3:   If oranges cost 6¢ each, how many oranges can you buy for $2.52?

$$6¢ = \$.06,$$

so the number of oranges is

$$\frac{2.52}{.06} = \frac{252}{6} = 42.$$

Computing Tip.   To divide a decimal by 10, move the decimal point *to the left* one place; to divide by 100, move the decimal point two places to the left, and so on.

EXAMPLE: Divide 5,637.6471 by 1,000.

The answer is 5.6376471, since to divide by 1,000 you move the decimal point 3 places to the left.

3–9

Converting a Fraction into a Decimal.   To convert a fraction into a decimal, divide the denominator into the numerator. For example, $\dfrac{3}{4} = \dfrac{3.00}{4} = .75.$ Some fractions give an infinite decimal when you divide the denominator into the numerator, for example, $\dfrac{1}{3} = .333 \ldots$ where the three dots mean you keep on getting 3 with each step of division. $.333 \ldots$ is an *infinite decimal*.

If a fraction has an infinite decimal, use the fraction in any computation.

EXAMPLE 1:   What is $\dfrac{2}{9}$ of $3,690.90?

Since the decimal for $\dfrac{2}{9}$ is $.2222 \ldots$ use the fraction $\dfrac{2}{9}$.
$\dfrac{2}{9} \times \$3,690.90 = 2 \times \$410.10 = \$820.20.$

You should know the following decimal equivalents of fractions:

$\frac{1}{100} = .01$	$\frac{1}{6} = .1666\ldots$
$\frac{1}{50} = .02$	$\frac{1}{5} = .2$
$\frac{1}{40} = .025$	$\frac{1}{4} = .25$
$\frac{1}{25} = .04$	$\frac{1}{3} = .333\ldots$
$\frac{1}{20} = .05$	$\frac{3}{8} = .375$
$\frac{1}{16} = .0625$	$\frac{2}{5} = .4$
$\frac{1}{15} = .0666\ldots$	$\frac{1}{2} = .5$
$\frac{1}{12} = .0833\ldots$	$\frac{5}{8} = .625$
$\frac{1}{10} = .1$	$\frac{2}{3} = .666\ldots$
$\frac{1}{9} = .111\ldots$	$\frac{3}{4} = .75$
$\frac{1}{8} = .125$	$\frac{7}{8} = .875$

$$\frac{3}{2} = 1.5$$

Any decimal with . . . is an infinite decimal.

I–4.   Percentage

4–1

PERCENTAGE is another method of expressing fractions or parts of an object. Percentages are expressed in terms of hundredths, so 100% means 100 hundredths or 1. 50% would be 50 hundredths or $\frac{1}{2}$.

A decimal is converted to a percentage by multiplying the decimal by 100. Since multiplying a decimal by 100 is accomplished by moving the decimal point two places to the right, *you convert a decimal into a percentage by moving the decimal point two places to the right.* For example, .134 = 13.4%.

If you wish to convert a percentage into a decimal, you divide the percentage by 100. There is a shortcut for this also. To divide by 100 you move the decimal point two places to the left.

Therefore, *to convert a percentage into a decimal, move the decimal point two places to the left.* For example, 24% = .24.

A fraction is converted into a percentage by changing the fraction to a decimal and then changing the decimal to a percentage. A percentage is changed into a fraction by first converting the percentage into a decimal and then changing the decimal to a fraction. You should know the following fractional equivalents of percentages:

$$1\% = \frac{1}{100} \qquad 25\% = \frac{1}{4} \qquad 80\% = \frac{4}{5}$$

$$2\% = \frac{1}{50} \qquad 33\frac{1}{3}\% = \frac{1}{3} \qquad 83\frac{1}{3}\% = \frac{5}{6}$$

$$4\% = \frac{1}{25} \qquad 37\frac{1}{2}\% = \frac{3}{8} \qquad 87\frac{1}{2}\% = \frac{7}{8}$$

$$5\% = \frac{1}{20} \qquad 40\% = \frac{2}{5} \qquad 100\% = 1$$

$$8\frac{1}{3}\% = \frac{1}{12} \qquad 50\% = \frac{1}{2} \qquad 120\% = \frac{6}{5}$$

$$10\% = \frac{1}{10} \qquad 60\% = \frac{3}{5} \qquad 125\% = \frac{5}{4}$$

$$12\frac{1}{2}\% = \frac{1}{8} \qquad 62\frac{1}{2}\% = \frac{5}{8} \qquad 133\frac{1}{3}\% = \frac{4}{3}$$

$$16\frac{2}{3}\% = \frac{1}{6} \qquad 66\frac{2}{3}\% = \frac{2}{3} \qquad 150\% = \frac{3}{2}$$

$$20\% = \frac{1}{5} \qquad 75\% = \frac{3}{4}$$

Note, for example, that $133\frac{1}{3}\% = 1.33\frac{1}{3} = 1\frac{1}{3} = \frac{4}{3}$.

When you compute with percentages, it is usually easier to change the percentages to decimals or fractions.

EXAMPLE 1: A company has 6,435 bars of soap. If the company sells 20% of its bars of soap, how many bars of soap did it sell?

Change 20% into .2. Thus, the company sold $(.2)(6,435) = 1287.0 = 1,287$ bars of soap. An alternative method would be to convert 20% to $\frac{1}{5}$. Then, $\frac{1}{5} \times 6,435 = 1,287$.

EXAMPLE 2: In a class of 60 students, 18 students received a grade of B. What percentage of the class received a grade of B?

$\frac{18}{60}$ of the class received a grade of B. $\frac{18}{60} = \frac{3}{10} = .3$ and $.3 = 30\%$, so 30% of the class received a grade of B.

EXAMPLE 3: If the population of Dryden was 10,000 in 1960 and the population of Dryden increased by 15% between 1960 and 1970, what was the population of Dryden in 1970?

The population increased by 15% between 1960 and 1970, so the increase was (.15)(10,000) which is 1,500. The population in 1970 was 10,000 + 1,500 = 11,500.

A quicker method: the population increased 15%, so the population in 1970 is 115% of the population in 1960. Therefore, the population in 1970 is 115% of 10,000 which is (1.15)(10,000) = 11,500.

4–2

Interest and Discount. Two of the most common uses of percentages are in interest and discount problems.

The rate of interest is usually given as a percentage. The basic formula for interest problems is:

$$\boxed{\text{INTEREST} = \text{AMOUNT} \times \text{TIME} \times \text{RATE}}$$

You can assume the rate of interest is the annual rate of interest unless the problem states otherwise; so you should express the time in years.

EXAMPLE 1: How much interest will $10,000 earn in 9 months at an annual rate of 6%?

9 months is $\frac{3}{4}$ of a year and $6\% = \frac{3}{50}$, so using the formula, the interest is $10,000

$\times \frac{3}{4} \times \frac{3}{50} = \$50 \times 9 = \$450.$

EXAMPLE 2: What annual rate of interest was paid if $5,000 earned $300 in interest in 2 years?

Since the interest was earned in 2 years, $150 is the interest earned in one year. $\frac{150}{5,000} = .03 = 3\%$, so the annual rate of interest was 3%.

This type of interest is called *simple interest*.

There is another method of computing interest called *compound interest*. In computing compound interest, the interest is periodically added to the amount (or principal) which is earning interest.

EXAMPLE 3: What will $1,000 be worth after three years if it earns interest at the rate of 5% compounded annually?

Compounded annually means that the interest earned during one year is added to the amount (or principal) at the end of each year. The interest on $1,000 at

5% for one year is $(1,000)(.05) = $50. So you must compute the interest on $1,050(not $1,000) for the second year. The interest is $(1,050)(.05) = $52.50. Therefore, during the third year interest will be computed for $1,102.50. During the third year the interest is $(1,102.50)(.05) = $55.125 = $55.13. Therefore, after 3 years the original $1,000 will be worth $1,157.63.

If you calculated simple interest on $1,000 at 5% for three years, the answer would be $(1,000)(.05)(3) = $150. Therefore, using simple interest, $1,000 is worth $1,150 after 3 years. Notice that this is not the same as the money was worth using compound interest.

You can assume that interest means simple interest unless a problem states otherwise.

The basic formula for discount problems is:

$$\boxed{\text{DISCOUNT} = \text{COST} \times \text{RATE OF DISCOUNT}}$$

EXAMPLE 1:   What is the discount if a car which cost $3,000 is discounted 7%?

The discount is $3,000 × .07 = $210.00 since 7% = .07.

If we know the cost of an item and its discounted price, we can find the rate of discount by using the formula

$$\text{rate of discount} = \frac{\text{cost} - \text{price}}{\text{cost}}.$$

EXAMPLE 2.   What was the rate of discount if a boat which cost $5,000 was sold for $4,800?

Using this formula, we find that the rate of discount equals

$$\frac{5,000 - 4,800}{5,000} = \frac{200}{5,000} = \frac{1}{25} = .04 = 4\%.$$

After an item has been discounted once, it may be discounted again. This procedure is called *successive* discounting.

EXAMPLE 3:   A bicycle originally cost $100 and was discounted 10%. After three months it was sold after being discounted 15%. How much was the bicycle sold for?

After the 10% discount the bicycle was selling for $100(.90) = $90. An item which costs $90 and is discounted 15% will sell for $90(.85) = $76.50, so the bicycle was sold for $76.50.

Notice that if you added the two discounts of 10% and 15% and treated the successive discounts as a single discount of 25%, your answer would be that the bicycle sold for $75, which is incorrect. Successive discounts are *not* identical to a single discount of the sum of the discounts. The previous example shows that successive discounts of 10% and 15% are not identical to a single discount of 25%.

I-5. Rounding off Numbers

5-1

Many times an approximate answer can be found more quickly and may be more useful than the exact answer. For example, if a company had sales of $998,875.63 during a year, it is easier to remember that the sales were about $1 million.

Rounding off a number to a decimal place means finding the multiple of the representative of that decimal place which is closest to the original number. Thus, rounding off a number to the nearest hundred means finding the multiple of 100 which is closest to the original number. Rounding off to the nearest tenth means finding the multiple of $\frac{1}{10}$ which is closest to the original number. After a number has been rounded off to a particular decimal place, all the digits to the right of that particular decimal place will be zero.

EXAMPLE 1:   Round off 9,403,420.71 to the nearest hundred.

You must find the multiple of one hundred which is closest to 9,403,420.71.

The answer is 9,403,400.

To round off a number to the rth decimal place:

- (A) Look at the digit in the place to the right of the rth place;
- (B) *If the digit is 0,1,2,3, or 4, change all the digits in places to the right of the rth place to 0* to round off the number.
- (C) *If the digit is 5,6,7,8, or 9, add 1 to the digit in the rth place and change all the digits in places to the right of the rth place to 0* to round off the number.

For example, the multiple of 100 which is closest to 5,342.1 is 5,300. Most problems dealing with money are rounded off if the answer contains a fractional part of a cent. This is common business practice.

EXAMPLE 2:   If 16 donuts cost $1.00, how much should three donuts cost?

Three donuts should cost $\frac{3}{16}$ of $1.00. Since $\frac{3}{16} \times 1. = .1875$, the cost would be $.1875. In practice, you would round it up to $.19 or 19¢.

Rounding off numbers can help you get quick, approximate answers. Since many questions require only rough answers, you can save time on the test by rounding off numbers.

EXAMPLE 3: If 5,301 of the 499,863 workers employed at the XYZ factory don't show up for work on Monday, about what percentage of the workers don't show up?

(A) 1 (B) 2 (C) 3 (D) 4 (E) 5

You can quickly see that the answer is (A) by rounding off both numbers to the nearest thousand before you divide, because $\frac{5,000}{500,000} = \frac{1}{100} = .01 = 1\%$. The exact answer is $\frac{5,301}{499,863} = .010604$, but it would take much longer to get an exact answer.

EXAMPLE 4: Round off 43.79 to the nearest tenth.

The place to the right of tenths is hundredths, so look in the hundredths place. Since 9 is bigger than 5, add 1 to the tenths place. Therefore, 43.79 is 43.8 rounded off to the nearest tenth.

If the digit in the rth place is 9 and you need to add 1 to the digit to round off the number to the rth decimal place, put a zero in the rth place and add 1 to the digit in the position to the left of the rth place. For example, 298 rounded off to the nearest 10 is 300; 99,752 to the nearest thousand is 100,000.

I–6. Signed Numbers

6–1

A number preceded by either a plus or a minus sign is called a SIGNED NUMBER. For example, $+5$, -6, -4.2, and $+\frac{3}{4}$ are all signed numbers. If no sign is given with a number, a plus sign is assumed; thus, 5 is interpreted as $+5$.

Signed numbers can often be used to distinguish different concepts. For example, a profit of $10 can be denoted by $+\$10$ and a loss of $10 by $-\$10$. A temperature of 20 degrees below zero can be denoted $-20°$.

6–2

Signed numbers are also called DIRECTED NUMBERS. You can think of numbers arranged on a line, called a number line, in the following manner:

Take a line which extends indefinitely in both directions, pick a point on the line and call it 0, pick another point on the line to the right of 0 and call it 1. The point to the right of 1 which is exactly as far from 1 as 1 is from 0 is called 2, the point to the right of 2 just as far from 2 as 1 is from 0 is called 3, and so on. The point halfway between 0 and 1 is called $\frac{1}{2}$, the point halfway between $\frac{1}{2}$ and 1 is called $\frac{3}{4}$. In this way, you can identify any whole number or any fraction with a point on the line.

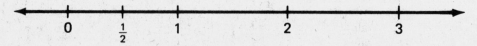

All the numbers which correspond to points to the right of 0 are called *positive numbers*. The sign of a positive number is +.

If you go to the left of zero the same distance as you did from 0 to 1, the point is called -1; in the same way as before, you can find $-2, -3, -\frac{1}{2}, -\frac{3}{2}$ and so on.

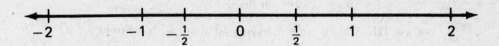

All the numbers which correspond to points to the left of zero are called *negative numbers*. Negative numbers are signed numbers whose sign is $-$. For example, $-3, -5.15, -.003$ are all negative numbers.

> 0 is neither positive nor negative; any nonzero number is positive or negative but not both. So $-0 = 0$.

6-3

Absolute Value. The absolute value of a signed number is the distance of the number from 0. The absolute value of any nonzero number is *positive*. For example, the absolute value of 2 is 2; the absolute value of -2 is 2. The absolute value of a number a is denoted by $|a|$, so $|-2| = 2$. The absolute value of any number can be found by dropping its sign, $|-12| = 12$, $|4| = 4$. *Thus* $|-a| = |a|$ *for any number a.* The only number whose absolute value is zero is zero.

6-4

Adding Signed Numbers.

Case I. Adding numbers with the _same sign:_

(A) The sign of the sum is the same as the sign of the numbers being added.
(B) Add the absolute values.
(C) Put the sign from step (A) in front of the number you obtained in step (B).

EXAMPLE 1:   What is $-2 + (-3.1) + (-.02)$?

(A) The sign of the sum will be $-$.
(B) $|-2| = 2$, $|-3.1| = 3.1$, $|-.02| = .02$, and $2 + 3.1 + .02 = 5.12$.
(C) The answer is -5.12.

Case II. Adding *two* numbers with _different signs:_

(A) The sign of the sum is the sign of the number which is largest in absolute value.
(B) Subtract the absolute value of the number with the smaller absolute value from the absolute value of the number with the larger absolute value.
(C) The answer is the number you obtained in step (B) preceded by the sign from part (A).

EXAMPLE 2: How much is $-5.1 + 3$?

  (A) The absolute value of -5.1 is 5.1 and the absolute value of 3 is 3, so the sign of the sum will be $-$.

  (B) 5.1 is larger than 3, and $5.1 - 3 = 2.1$.

  (C) The sum is -2.1.

Case III. Adding *more than two* numbers with *different signs:*

  (A) Add all the positive numbers; the result is positive (this is Case I).

  (B) Add all the negative numbers; the result is negative (this is Case I).

  (C) Add the result of step (A) to the result of step (B), by using Case II.

EXAMPLE 3: Find the value of $5 + 52 + (-3) + 7 + (-5.1)$.

  (A) $5 + 52 + 7 = 64$.

  (B) $-3 + (-5.1) = -8.1$.

  (C) $64 + (-8.1) = 55.9$, so the answer is 55.9.

EXAMPLE 4: If a store made a profit of \$23.50 on Monday, lost \$2.05 on Tuesday, lost \$5.03 on Wednesday, made a profit of \$30.10 on Thursday, and made a profit of \$41.25 on Friday, what was its total profit (or loss) for the week? Use $+$ for profit and $-$ for loss.

The total is $23.50 + (-2.05) + (-5.03) + 30.10 + 41.25$ which is $94.85 + (-7.08) = 87.77$. So the store made a profit of \$87.77.

6-5

Subtracting Signed Numbers. When subtracting signed numbers:

  (A) Change the sign of the number you are subtracting (the subtrahend).

  (B) <u>Add</u> the result of step (A) to the number being subtracted from (the minuend) using the rules of the preceding section.

EXAMPLE 1: Subtract 4.1 from 6.5.

  (A) 4.1 becomes -4.1.

  (B) $6.5 + (-4.1) = 2.4$.

EXAMPLE 2: What is $7.8 - (-10.1)$?

  (A) -10.1 becomes 10.1.

  (B) $7.8 + 10.1 = 17.9$.

So we subtract a negative number by adding a positive number with the same absolute value, and we subtract a positive number by adding a negative number of the same absolute value.

6-6

Multiplying Signed Numbers.

Case I. Multiplying two numbers:

(A) Multiply the absolute values of the numbers.
(B) If both numbers have the same sign, the result of step (A) is the answer, i.e. the product is positive. If the numbers have different signs, then the answer is the result of step (A) with a minus sign.

EXAMPLE 1: $(-5)(-12) = ?$

(A) $5 \times 12 = 60$
(B) Both signs are the same, so the answer is 60.

EXAMPLE 2: $(4)(-3) = ?$

(A) $4 \times 3 = 12$
(B) The signs are different, so the answer is -12. You can remember the sign of the product in the following way:

$$(-)(-) = +$$
$$(+)(+) = +$$
$$(-)(+) = -$$
$$(+)(-) = -$$

Case II. Multiplying more than two numbers:

(A) Multiply the first two factors using Case I.
(B) Multiply the result of (A) by the third factor.
(C) Multiply the result of (B) by the fourth factor.
(D) Continue until you have used each factor.

EXAMPLE 3: $(-5)(4)(2)(-\frac{1}{2})(\frac{3}{4}) = ?$

(A) $(-5)(4) = -20$
(B) $(-20)(2) = -40$
(C) $(-40)(-\frac{1}{2}) = 20$
(D) $(20)(\frac{3}{4}) = 15$, so the answer is 15.

The sign of the product is + if there are no negative factors or an even number of negative factors. The sign of the product is − if there are an odd number of negative factors.

6-7

Dividing Signed Numbers.
Divide the absolute values of the numbers; the sign of the quotient is determined by the same rules as you used to determine the sign of a product. Thus,

$$+ \div + = +$$
$$- \div - = +$$
$$+ \div - = -$$
$$- \div + = -$$

EXAMPLE 1: Divide 53.2 by -4.

53.2 divided by 4 is 13.3. Since one of the numbers is positive and the other negative, the answer is -13.3.

EXAMPLE 2: $\dfrac{-5}{-2} = \dfrac{5}{2}$

I-7. Averages and Medians

7-1

Mean. The *average* or *arithmetic mean* of a collection of N numbers is the result of dividing the sum of all the numbers in the collection by N.

EXAMPLE 1: The scores of 9 students on a test were 72, 78, 81, 64, 85, 92, 95, 60, and 55. What was the average score of the students?

Since there are 9 students, the average is the total of all the scores divided by 9. So the average is $\dfrac{1}{9}$ of $(72 + 78 + 81 + 64 + 85 + 92 + 95 + 60 + 55)$, which is $\dfrac{1}{9}$ of (682) or $75\frac{7}{9}$.

EXAMPLE 2: The temperature at noon in Coldtown, U.S.A. was 5° on Monday, 10° on Tuesday, 2° below zero on Wednesday, 5° below zero on Thursday, 0° on Friday, 4° on Saturday, and 1° below zero on Sunday. What was the average temperature at noon for the week?

Use negative numbers for the temperatures below zero. The average temperature is the average of 5, 10, −2, −5, 0, 4 and −1, which is $\dfrac{5 + 10 + (-2) + (-5) + 0 + 4 + (-1)}{7} = \dfrac{11}{7} = 1\frac{4}{7}$. Therefore, the average temperature at noon for the week is $1\frac{4}{7}°$.

EXAMPLE 3: If the average annual income of 10 workers is $15,665 and two of the workers each made $20,000 for the year, what is the average annual income of the remaining 8 workers?

The total income of all 10 workers is 10 times the average income which is $156,650. The two workers made a total of $40,000, so the total income of the remaining 8 workers was $156,650 − $40,000 = $116,650. Therefore, the average annual income of the 8 remaining workers is $\dfrac{\$116,650}{8} = \$14,581.25$.

7-2

The Median. The number which is in the middle if the numbers in a collection of numbers are arranged in order is called the *median*. In example 1 above, the median score was 78, and in example 2, the median temperature for the week was 0. Notice that the medians were different from the averages. In example 3, we don't have enough data to find the median although we know the average.

In general, the median and the average of a collection of numbers are different.

If the number of objects in the collection is even, the median is the average of the two numbers in the middle of the array. For example, the median of 64, 66, 72, 75, 76, and 77 is the average of 72 and 75 which is 73.5.

I-8. Powers, Exponents, and Roots

8-1

If b is any number and n is a whole number greater than 0, b^n means the product of n factors each of which is equal to b. Thus,

$$b^n = b \times b \times b \times \cdots \times b \text{ where there are } n \text{ copies of } b.$$

If $n = 1$, there is only one copy of b so $b^1 = b$. Here are some examples,

$$2^5 = 2 \times 2 \times 2 \times 2 \times 2 = 32, \ (-4)^3 = (-4) \times (-4) \times (-4) = -64, \ \frac{3^2}{4} = \frac{3 \times 3}{4} = \frac{9}{4},$$

$$1^n = 1 \text{ for any } n, \ 0^n = 0 \text{ for any } n.$$

b^n is read as "b raised to the nth power." b^2 is read "b squared." b^2 is always greater than 0 (positive) if b is not zero, since the product of two negative numbers is positive. b^3 is read "b cubed," b^3 can be negative or positive.

You should know the following squares and cubes:

$1^2 = 1$	$8^2 = 64$
$2^2 = 4$	$9^2 = 81$
$3^2 = 9$	$10^2 = 100$
$4^2 = 16$	$11^2 = 121$
$5^2 = 25$	$12^2 = 144$
$6^2 = 36$	$13^2 = 169$
$7^2 = 49$	$14^2 = 196$
	$15^2 = 225$
$1^3 = 1$	$3^3 = 27$
$2^3 = 8$	$4^3 = 64$
	$5^3 = 125$

If you raise a fraction, $\dfrac{p}{q}$, to a power, then $\left(\dfrac{p}{q}\right)^n = \dfrac{p^n}{q^n}$. For example,

$$\left(\frac{5}{4}\right)^3 = \frac{5^3}{4^3} = \frac{125}{64}.$$

EXAMPLE 1:   If the value of an investment triples each year, what percent of its value today will the investment be worth in 4 years?

The value increases by a factor of 3 each year. Since the time is 4 years, there will be four factors of 3. So the investment will be worth $3 \times 3 \times 3 \times 3 = 3^4$ as much as it is today. $3^4 = 81$, so the investment will be worth 8,100% of its value today in four years.

8–2

Exponents. In the expression b^n, b is called the base and n is called the *exponent*. In the expression 2^5, 2 is the base and 5 is the exponent. The exponent tells how many factors there are.

The *two basic formulas for problems involving exponents* are:

(A) $b^n \times b^m = b^{n+m}$
(B) $a^n \times b^n = (a \cdot b)^n$

(A) and (B) are called *laws of exponents.*

EXAMPLE 1:   What is 6^3?

$$\text{Since } 6 = 3 \times 2,\ 6^3 = 3^3 \times 2^3 = 27 \times 8 = 216.$$
$$\text{or}$$
$$6^3 = 6 \times 6 \times 6 = 216.$$

EXAMPLE 2:   Find the value of $2^3 \times 2^2$.

Using (A), $2^3 \times 2^2 = 2^{2+3} = 2^5$ which is 32. You can check this, since $2^3 = 8$ and $2^2 = 4$; $2^3 \times 2^2 = 8 \times 4 = 32$.

8–3

Negative Exponents. $b^0 = 1$ *for any nonzero number b.* By one of the laws of exponents (A) above, $b^n \times b^0$ should be $b^{n+0} = b^n$. If we still want (A) to be true, then b^0 must be 1. (NOTE: 0^0 is not defined.)

Using the law of exponents once more, you can define b^{-n} where n is a positive number. If (A) holds, $b^{-n} \times b^n = b^{-n+n} = b^0 = 1$, so $b^{-n} = \dfrac{1}{b^n}$. *Multiplying by b^{-n} is the same as dividing by b^n.*

EXAMPLE 1:

$$2^{-3} = \frac{1}{2^3} = \frac{1}{8}$$

$$2^0 = 1$$

EXAMPLE 2:

$$\left(\frac{1}{2}\right)^{-1} = \frac{1}{1/2} = 2$$

EXAMPLE 3:   Find the value of $\dfrac{6^4}{3^3}$.

$$\frac{6^4}{3^3} = \frac{(3 \cdot 2)^4}{3^3} = \frac{3^4 \cdot 2^4}{3^3} = 3^4 \times 2^4 \times 3^{-3} = 3^4 \times 3^{-3} \times 2^4 = 3^1 \times 2^4 = 48.$$

8-4

Roots. If you raise a number d to the nth power and the result is b, then d is called the nth root of b, which is usually written $\sqrt[n]{b} = d$. Since $2^5 = 32$, then $\sqrt[5]{32} = 2$. The second root is called the square root and is written $\sqrt{}$; the third root is called the cube root. If you read the columns of the table on page 159 from right to left, you have a table of square roots and cube roots. For example, $\sqrt{225} = 15$; $\sqrt{81} = 9$; $\sqrt[3]{64} = 4$.

There are two possibilities for the square root of a positive number; the positive one is called the square root. Thus we say $\sqrt{9} = 3$ although $(-3) \times (-3) = 9$.

Since the square of any nonzero number is positive *the square root of a negative number is not defined as a real number.* Thus $\sqrt{-2}$ is not a real number. There are cube roots of negative numbers. $\sqrt[3]{-8} = -2$, because $(-2) \times (-2) \times (-2) = -8$.

You can also write roots as exponents; for example,

$$\sqrt[n]{b} = b^{1/n}; \text{ so } \sqrt{b} = b^{1/2}, \sqrt[3]{b} = b^{1/3}.$$

Since you can write roots as exponents, formula (B) above is especially useful.

$a^{1/n} \times b^{1/n} = (a \cdot b)^{1/n}$ or $\sqrt[n]{a \times b} = \sqrt[n]{a} \times \sqrt[n]{b}$. This formula is the basic formula for simplifying square roots, cube roots and so on. *On the test you must state your answer in a form which matches one of the choices given.*

EXAMPLE 1: $\sqrt{54} = ?$

Since $54 = 9 \times 6$, $\sqrt{54} = \sqrt{9 \times 6} = \sqrt{9} \times \sqrt{6}$. Since $\sqrt{9} = 3$, $\sqrt{54} = 3\sqrt{6}$.

You can not simplify by adding square roots unless you are taking square roots of the same number. For example,

$$\sqrt{3} + 2\sqrt{3} - 4\sqrt{3} = -\sqrt{3}, \text{ but } \sqrt{3} + \sqrt{2} \text{ is not equal to } \sqrt{5}.$$

EXAMPLE 2: Simplify $6\sqrt{12} + 2\sqrt{75} - 3\sqrt{98}$.

Since $12 = 4 \times 3$, $\sqrt{12} = \sqrt{4 \times 3} = \sqrt{4} \times \sqrt{3} = 2\sqrt{3}$;
$75 = 25 \times 3$, so $\sqrt{75} = \sqrt{25} \times \sqrt{3} = 5\sqrt{3}$;
and $98 = 49 \times 2$, so $\sqrt{98} = \sqrt{49} \times \sqrt{2} = 7\sqrt{2}$.
Therefore, $6\sqrt{12} + 2\sqrt{75} - 3\sqrt{98} = 6 \times 2\sqrt{3} + 2 \times 5\sqrt{3} - 3 \times 7\sqrt{2} = 12\sqrt{3} + 10\sqrt{3} - 21\sqrt{2} = 22\sqrt{3} - 21\sqrt{2}$.

EXAMPLE 3: Simplify $27^{1/3} \times 8^{1/3}$.

$27^{1/3} = \sqrt[3]{27} = 3$ and $8^{1/3} = 2$, so $27^{1/3} \times 8^{1/3} = 3 \times 2 = 6$. Notice that 6 is $\sqrt[3]{216}$ and $27^{1/3} \times 8^{1/3} = (27 \times 8)^{1/3} = 216^{1/3}$.

II. Algebra

II–1. Algebraic Expressions

1–1

Often it is necessary to deal with quantities which have a numerical value which is unknown. For example, we may know that Tom's salary is twice as much as Joe's salary. If we let the value of Tom's salary be called T and the value of Joe's salary be J, then T and J are numbers which are unknown. However, we do know that the value of T must be twice the value of J, or $T = 2J$.

T and $2J$ are examples of algebraic expressions. An algebraic expression may involve letters in addition to numbers and symbols; however, *in an algebraic expression a letter always stands for a number*. Therefore, you can multiply, divide, add, subtract and perform other mathematical operations on a letter. Thus, x^2 would mean x times x. Some examples of algebraic expressions are: $2x + y$, $y^3 + 9y$, $z^3 - 5ab$, $c + d + 4$, $5x + 2y(6x - 4y + z)$. When letters or numbers are written together without any sign or symbol between them, multiplication is assumed. Thus $6xy$ means 6 times x times y. $6xy$ is called a term; terms are separated by $+$ or $-$ signs. The expression $5z + 2 + 4x^2$ has three terms, $5z$, 2, and $4x^2$. Terms are often called monomials (mono = one). If an expression has more than one term, it is called a *polynomial*, (poly = many). The letters in an algebraic expression are called *variables* or *unknowns*. When a variable is multiplied by a number, the number is called the *coefficient* of the variable. So in the expression $5x^2 + 2yz$, the coefficient of x^2 is 5, and the coefficient of yz is 2.

1–2

Simplifying Algebraic Expressions. *Since there are only five choices of an answer given for the test questions, you must be able to recognize algebraic expressions which are equal.* It will also save time when you are working problems if you can change a complicated expression into a simpler one.

Case I. Simplifying expressions which don't contain parentheses:

(A) Perform any multiplications or divisions before performing additions or subtractions. Thus, the expression $6x + y \div x$ means add $6x$ to the quotient of y divided by x. Another way of writing the expression would be $6x + \dfrac{y}{x}$. This is not the same as $\dfrac{6x + y}{x}$.

(B) The order in which you multiply numbers and letters in a term does not matter. So $6xy$ is the same as $6yx$.

(C) The order in which you add terms does not matter; for instance, $6x + 2y - x = 6x - x + 2y$.

(D) If there are roots or powers in any terms, you may be able to simplify the term by using the laws of exponents. For example, $5xy \cdot 3x^2y = 15x^3y^2$.

(E) Combine like terms. *Like terms* (or similar terms) are terms which have exactly the same letters raised to the same powers. So x, $-2x$, $\frac{1}{3}x$ are like terms. For example, $6x - 2x + x + y$ is equal to $5x + y$. In combining like terms, you simply add or subtract the coefficients of the like terms, and the result is the coefficient of that term in the simplified expression. In our example above, the coefficients of x were $+6$, -2, and $+1$; since $6 - 2 + 1 = 5$ the coefficient of x in the simplified expression is 5.

(F) Algebraic expressions which involve divisions or factors can be simplified by using the techniques for handling fractions and the laws of exponents. Remember dividing by b^n is the same as multiplying by b^{-n}.

EXAMPLE 1: $3x^2 - 4\sqrt{x} + \sqrt{4x} + xy + 7x^2 = ?$

(D) $\sqrt{4x} = \sqrt{4}\sqrt{x} = 2\sqrt{x}.$

(E) $3x^2 + 7x^2 = 10x^2, -4\sqrt{x} + 2\sqrt{x} = -2\sqrt{x}.$

The original expression equals $3x^2 + 7x^2 - 4\sqrt{x} + 2\sqrt{x} + xy$. Therefore, the simplified expression is $10x^2 - 2\sqrt{x} + xy$.

EXAMPLE 2: Simplify $\dfrac{21x^4y^2}{3x^6y}$.

(F) $\dfrac{21}{3}x^4y^2x^{-6}y^{-1}.$

(B) $7x^4x^{-6}y^2y^{-1}.$

(D) $7x^{-2}y$, so the simplified term is $\dfrac{7y}{x^2}$.

EXAMPLE 3: Write $\dfrac{2x}{y} - \dfrac{4}{x}$ as a single fraction.

(F) A common denominator is xy so $\dfrac{2x}{y} = \dfrac{2x \cdot x}{y \cdot x} = \dfrac{2x^2}{xy}$, and $\dfrac{4}{x} = \dfrac{4y}{xy}$.

$$\text{Therefore, } \frac{2x}{y} - \frac{4}{x} = \frac{2x^2}{xy} - \frac{4y}{xy} = \frac{2x^2 - 4y}{xy}$$

Case II. Simplifying expressions which have parentheses:

The first rule is to perform the operations inside parentheses first. So $(6x + y) \div x$ means divide the sum of $6x$ and y by x. Notice that $(6x + y) \div x$ is different from $6x + y \div x$.

The main rule for getting rid of parentheses is the distributive law, which is expressed as $a(b + c) = ab + ac$. In other words, if any monomial is followed by an expression contained in a parenthesis, then *each* term of the expression is multiplied by the monomial. Once we have gotten rid of the parentheses, we proceed as we did in Case I.

EXAMPLE 4: $2x(6x - 4y + 2) = (2x)(6x) + (2x)(-4y) + (2x)(2) = 12x^2 - 8xy - 4x.$

If an expression has more than one set of parentheses, get rid of the *inner parentheses first* and then *work out* through the rest of the parentheses.

EXAMPLE 5: $2x - (x + 6(x - 3y) + 4y) = ?$

To remove the inner parentheses we multiply $6(x - 3y)$ getting $6x - 18y$. Now we have $2x - (x + 6x - 18y + 4y)$ which equals $2x - (7x - 14y)$. Distribute the minus sign (multiply by -1), getting $2x - 7x - (-14y) = -5x + 14y$. Sometimes brackets are used instead of parentheses.

EXAMPLE 6:   Simplify $-3x\left[\dfrac{1}{2}(3x - 2y) - 2(x(3 + y) + 4y)\right]$

$$= -3x\left[\dfrac{1}{2}(3x - 2y) - 2(3x + xy + 4y)\right]$$

$$= -3x\left[\dfrac{3}{2}x - y - 6x - 2xy - 8y\right]$$

$$= -3x\left[-\dfrac{9}{2}x - 2xy - 9y\right]$$

$$= \dfrac{27}{2}x^2 + 6x^2y + 27xy.$$

1-3

Adding and Subtracting Algebraic Expressions.   Since algebraic expressions are numbers, they can be added and subtracted.

> *The only algebraic terms which can be combined are like terms.*

EXAMPLE 1: $(3x + 4y - xy^2) + (3x + 2x(x - y)) = ?$

The expression $= (3x + 4y - xy^2) + (3x + 2x^2 - 2xy)$, removing the inner parentheses;

$\qquad = 6x + 4y + 2x^2 - xy^2 - 2xy$, combining like terms.

EXAMPLE 2: $(2a + 3a^2 - 4) - 2(4a^2 - 2(a + 4)) = ?$

It equals $(2a + 3a^2 - 4) - 2(4a^2 - 2a - 8)$, removing inner parentheses;

$= 2a + 3a^2 - 4 - 8a^2 + 4a + 16$, removing outer parentheses;

$= -5a^2 + 6a + 12$, combining like terms.

1-4

Multiplying Algebraic Expressions.   When you multiply two expressions, you multiply *each term of the first by each term of the second.*

EXAMPLE 1: $(b - 4)(b + a) = b(b + a) - 4(b + a) = ?$

$$= b^2 + ab - 4b - 4a.$$

EXAMPLE 2: $(2h - 4)(h + 2h^2 + h^3) = ?$

$$= 2h(h + 2h^2 + h^3) - 4(h + 2h^2 + h^3)$$
$$= 2h^2 + 4h^3 + 2h^4 - 4h - 8h^2 - 4h^3$$
$$= -4h - 6h^2 + 2h^4, \text{ which is the product.}$$

If you need to multiply more than two expressions, multiply the first two expressions, then multiply the result by the third expression, and so on until you have used each factor. Since algebraic expressions can be multiplied, they can be squared, cubed, or raised to other powers.

EXAMPLE 3: $(x - 2y)^3 = (x - 2y)(x - 2y)(x - 2y).$

Since $(x - 2y)(x - 2y) = x^2 - 2yx - 2yx + 4y^2$
$$= x^2 - 4xy + 4y^2,$$

$$(x - y)^3 = (x^2 - 4xy + 4y^2)(x - 2y)$$
$$= x(x^2 - 4xy + 4y^2) - 2y(x^2 - 4xy + 4y^2)$$
$$= x^3 - 4x^2y + 4xy^2 - 2x^2y + 8xy^2 - 8y^3$$
$$= x^3 - 6x^2y + 12xy^2 - 8y^3.$$

The order in which you multiply algebraic expressions does not matter. Thus $(2a + b)(x^2 + 2x) = (x^2 + 2x)(2a + b).$

1–5

Factoring Algebraic Expressions.   If an algebraic expression is the product of other algebraic expressions, then the expressions are called factors of the original expression. For instance, we claim that $(2h - 4)$ and $(h + 2h^2 + h^3)$ are factors of $-4h - 6h^2 + 2h^4$. We can always check to see if we have the correct factors by multiplying; so by example 2 above we see that our claim is correct. We need to be able to factor algebraic expressions in order to solve quadratic equations. It also can be helpful in dividing algebraic expressions.

First remove any monomial factor which appears in every term of the expression.

Some examples:

$$3x + 3y = 3(x + y): 3 \text{ is a monomial factor.}$$
$$15a^2b + 10ab = 5ab(3a + 2): 5ab \text{ is a monomial factor.}$$
$$\frac{1}{2}hy - 3h^3 + 4hy = h\left(\frac{1}{2}y - 3h^2 + 4y\right),$$

$$= h\left(\frac{9}{2}y - 3h^2\right): h \text{ is a monomial factor.}$$

You may also need to factor expressions which contain squares or higher powers into factors which only contain linear terms. (Linear terms are terms in which variables are raised only to the first power.) The first rule to remember is that since $(a + b)(a - b) = a^2 + ba - ba - b^2 = a^2 - b^2$, the difference of two squares can always be factored.

EXAMPLE 1:   Factor $(9m^2 - 16)$.

$9m^2 = (3m)^2$ and $16 = 4^2$, so the factors are $(3m - 4)(3m + 4)$.

Since $(3m - 4)(3m + 4) = 9m^2 - 16$, these factors are correct.

EXAMPLE 2:   Factor $x^4y^4 - 4x^2$.

$x^4y^4 = (x^2y^2)^2$ and $4x^2 = (2x)^2$, so the factors are $x^2y^2 + 2x$ and $x^2y^2 - 2x$.

You also may need to factor expressions which contain squared terms and linear terms, such as $x^2 + 4x + 3$. The factors will be of the form $(x + a)$ and $(x + b)$. Since $(x + a)(x + b) = x^2 + (a + b)x + ab$, you must look for a pair of numbers a and b such that $a \cdot b$ is the numerical term in the expression and $a + b$ is the coefficient of the linear term (the term with exponent 1).

EXAMPLE 3:   Factor $x^2 + 4x + 3$.

You want numbers whose product is 3 and whose sum is 4. Look at the possible factors of three and check whether they add up to 4. Since $3 = 3 \times 1$ and $3 + 1$ is 4, the factors are $(x + 3)$ and $(x + 1)$. Remember to check by multiplying.

EXAMPLE 4:   Factor $y^2 + y - 6$.

Since -6 is negative, the two numbers a and b must be of opposite sign. Possible pairs of factors for -6 are -6 and $+1$, 6 and -1, 3 and -2, and -3 and 2. Since $-2 + 3 = 1$, the factors are $(y + 3)$ and $(y - 2)$. So $(y + 3)(y - 2) = y^2 + y - 6$.

EXAMPLE 5:   Factor $a^3 + 4a^2 + 4a$.

Factor out a, so $a^3 + 4a^2 + 4a = a(a^2 + 4a + 4)$. Consider $a^2 + 4a + 4$; since $2 + 2 = 4$ and $2 \times 2 = 4$, the factors are $(a + 2)$ and $(a + 2)$. Therefore, $a^3 + 4a^2 + 4a = a(a + 2)^2$.

If the term with the highest exponent has a coefficient unequal to 1, divide the entire expression by that coefficient. For example, to factor $3a^3 + 12a^2 + 12a$, factor out a 3 from each term, and the result is $a^3 + 4a^2 + 4a$ which is $a(a + 2)^2$. Thus, $3a^3 + 12a^2 + 12a = 3a(a + 2)^2$.

There are some expressions which can not be factored, for example, $x^2 + 4x + 6$. In general, if you can't factor something by using the methods given above, don't waste a lot of time on the question. Sometimes you may be able to check the answers given to find out what the correct factors are.

1-6

Division of Algebraic Expressions.   The main things to remember in division are:

(1) When you divide a sum, you can get the same result by dividing each term and adding quotients. For example, $\dfrac{9x + 4xy + y^2}{x} = \dfrac{9x}{x} + \dfrac{4xy}{x} +$

$\dfrac{y^2}{x} = 9 + 4y + \dfrac{y^2}{x}$.

(2) You can cancel common factors, so the results on factoring will be helpful. For example, $\dfrac{x^2 - 2x}{x - 2} = \dfrac{x(x - 2)}{x - 2} = x$.

You can also divide one algebraic expression by another using long division.

EXAMPLE 1: $(15x^2 + 2x - 4) \div 3x - 1$.

$$
\begin{array}{r}
5x + 2 \\
3x - 1 \overline{\smash{)}15x^2 + 2x - 4} \\
\underline{15x^2 - 5x} \\
7x - 4 \\
\underline{6x - 2} \\
x - 2
\end{array}
$$

So the answer is $5x + 2$ with a remainder of $x - 2$. You can check by multiplying,

$(5x + 2)(3x - 1) = 15x^2 + 6x - 5x - 2$

$ = 15x^2 + x - 2;$ now add the remainder $x - 2$

and the result is $15x^2 + x - 2 + x - 2 = 15x^2 + 2x - 4$.

Division problems where you need to use (1) and (2) are more likely than problems involving long division.

II-2. Equations

2-1

AN EQUATION is a statement that says two algebraic expressions are equal. $x + 2 = 3, 4 + 2 = 6, 3x^2 + 2x - 6 = 0, x^2 + y^2 = z^2, \dfrac{y}{x} = 2 + z$, and $A = LW$ are all examples of equations. We will refer to the algebraic expressions on each side of the equals sign as the left side and the right side of the equation. Thus, in the equation $2x + 4 = 6y + x$, $2x + 4$ is the left side and $6y + x$ is the right side.

2-2

If we assign specific numbers to each variable or unknown in an algebraic expression, then the algebraic expression will be equal to a number. This is called *evaluating* the expression. For example, if you evaluate $2x + 4y^2 + 3$ for $x = -1$ and $y = 2$, the expression is equal to $2(-1) + 4 \cdot 2^2 + 3 = -2 + 4 \cdot 4 + 3 = 17$.

If we evaluate each side of an equation and the number obtained is the same for each side of the equation, then the specific values assigned to the unknowns are called a *solution of the equation*. Another way of saying this is that the choices for the unknowns satisfy the equation.

EXAMPLE 1:   Consider the equation $2x + 3 = 9$.

If $x = 3$, then the left side of the equation becomes $2 \cdot 3 + 3 = 6 + 3 = 9$, so both sides equal 9, and $x = 3$ is a solution of $2x + 3 = 9$. If $x = 4$, then the left side is $2 \cdot 4 + 3 = 11$. Since 11 is not equal to 9, $x = 4$ is *not* a solution of $2x + 3 = 9$.

EXAMPLE 2:   Consider the equation $x^2 + y^2 = 5x$.

If $x = 1$ and $y = 2$, then the left side is $1^2 + 2^2$ which equals $1 + 4 = 5$. The right side is $5 \cdot 1 = 5$, since both sides are equal to 5, $x = 1$ and $y = 2$ is a solution.

If $x = 5$ and $y = 0$, then the left side is $5^2 + 0^2 = 25$ and the right side is $5 \cdot 5 = 25$, so $x = 5$ and $y = 0$ is also a solution.

If $x = 1$ and $y = 1$, then the left side is $1^2 + 1^2 = 2$ and the right side is $5 \cdot 1 = 5$. Therefore, since $2 \neq 5$, $x = 1$ and $y = 1$ is not a solution.

There are some equations which *do not have any solutions which are real numbers*. Since the square of any real number is positive or zero, the equation $x^2 = -4$ does not have any solutions which are real numbers.

2–3

Equivalence.   One equation is *equivalent* to another equation, if they have exactly the same solutions. The basic idea in solving equations is to transform a given equation into an equivalent equation whose solutions are obvious.

The two main tools for solving equations are:

(A)   If you add or subtract the same algebraic expression to or from *each side* of an equation, the resulting equation is equivalent to the original equation.
(B)   If you multiply or divide both sides of an equation by the same *nonzero* algebraic expression, the resulting equation is equivalent to the original equation.

The most common type of equation is the linear equation with only one unknown. $6z = 4z - 3$, $3 + a = 2a - 4$, $3b + 2b = b - 4b$, are all examples of linear equations with only one unknown.

Using (A) and (B), you can solve a linear equation in one unknown in the following way:

(1)   Group all the terms which involve the unknown on one side of the equation and all the terms which are purely numerical on the other side of the equation. This is called *isolating the unknown*.
(2)   Combine the terms on each side.
(3)   Divide each side by the coefficient of the unknown.

EXAMPLE 1: Solve $6x + 2 = 3$ for x.

(1) Using (A) subtract 2 from each side of the equation. Then $6x + 2 - 2 = 3 - 2$ or $6x = 3 - 2$.

(2) $6x = 1$.

(3) Divide each side by 6. Therefore, $x = \dfrac{1}{6}$.

You should always check your answer in the original equation.

$$\text{Since } 6\left(\frac{1}{6}\right) + 2 = 1 + 2 = 3, \ x = \frac{1}{6} \text{ is a solution.}$$

EXAMPLE 2: Solve $3x + 15 = 3 - 4x$ for x.

(1) Add $4x$ to each side and subtract 15 from each side; $3x + 15 - 15 + 4x = 3 - 15 - 4x + 4x$.

(2) $7x = -12$.

(3) Divide each side by 7, so $x = \dfrac{-12}{7}$ is the solution.

CHECK:

$$3\left(\frac{-12}{7}\right) + 15 = \frac{-36}{7} + 15 = \frac{69}{7} \text{ and } 3 - 4\left(\frac{-12}{7}\right) = 3 + \frac{48}{7} = \frac{69}{7}.$$

If you do the same thing to each side of an equation, the result is still an equation but it may not be equivalent to the original equation. Be especially careful if you square each side of an equation. For example, $x = -4$ is an equation; square both sides and you get $x^2 = 16$ which has both $x = 4$ and $x = -4$ as solutions. *Always check your answer in the original equation.*

If the equation you want to solve involves square roots, get rid of the square roots by squaring each side of the equation. Remember to check your answer since squaring each side does not always give an equivalent equation.

EXAMPLE 3: Solve $\sqrt{4x + 3} = 5$.

Square both sides: $(\sqrt{4x + 3})^2 = 4x + 3$ and $5^2 = 25$, so the new equation is $4x + 3 = 25$. Subtract 3 from each side to get $4x = 22$ and now divide each side by 4. The solution is $x = \dfrac{22}{4} = 5.5$. Since $4(5.5) + 3 = 25$ and $\sqrt{25} = 5$, $x = 5.5$ is a solution to the equation $\sqrt{4x + 3} = 5$.

If an equation involves fractions, multiply through by a common denominator and then solve. Check your answer to make sure you did not multiply or divide by zero.

EXAMPLE 4: Solve $\dfrac{3}{a} = 9$ for a.

Multiply each side by a: the result is $3 = 9a$. Divide each side by 9, and you obtain $\dfrac{3}{9} = a$ or $a = \dfrac{1}{3}$. Since $\dfrac{3}{1/3} = 3 \cdot 3 = 9$, $a = \dfrac{1}{3}$ is a solution.

You may be asked to solve two equations in two unknowns. Use one equation to solve for one unknown in terms of the other; now change the second equation into an equation in only one unknown which can be solved by the methods of the preceding section.

EXAMPLE 1:   Solve for x and y: $\begin{cases} \dfrac{x}{y} = 3 \\ 2x + 4y = 20. \end{cases}$

The first equation gives $x = 3y$. Using $x = 3y$, the second equation is $2(3y) + 4y = 6y + 4y$ or $10y = 20$, so $y = \dfrac{20}{10} = 2$. Since $x = 3y$, $x = 6$.

CHECK:

$$\frac{6}{2} = 3, \text{ and } 2 \cdot 6 + 4 \cdot 2 = 20, \text{ so } x = 6 \text{ and } y = 2 \text{ is a solution.}$$

EXAMPLE 2:   If $2x + y = 5$ and $x + y = 4$, find x and y.

Since $x + y = 4$, $y = 4 - x$, so $2x + y = 2x + 4 - x = x + 4 = 5$ and $x = 1$. If $x = 1$, then $y = 4 - 1 = 3$. So $x = 1$ and $y = 3$ is the solution.

CHECK:

$$2 \cdot 1 + 3 = 5 \text{ and } 1 + 3 = 4.$$

Sometimes we can solve two equations by adding them or by subtracting one from the other. If we subtract $x + y = 4$ from $2x + y = 5$ in example 2, we have $x = 1$. However, the previous method will work in cases when the addition method does not work.

2–5

Solving Quadratic Equations.   If the terms of an equation contain squares of the unknown as well as linear terms, the equation is called *quadratic*. Some examples of quadratic equations are $x^2 + 4x = 3$, $2z^2 - 1 = 3z^2 - 2z$, and $a + 6 = a^2 + 6$.

To solve a quadratic equation:

(A)   Group all the terms on one side of the equation so that the other side is *zero*.
(B)   Combine the terms on the nonzero side.
(C)   Factor the expression into linear expressions.
(D)   Set the linear factors equal to zero and solve.

The method depends on the fact that if a product of expressions is zero then at least one of the expressions must be zero.

EXAMPLE 1:   Solve $x^2 + 4x = -3$.

(A) $x^2 + 4x + 3 = 0$
(C) $x^2 + 4x + 3 = (x + 3)(x + 1) = 0$
(D) So $x + 3 = 0$ or $x + 1 = 0$. Therefore, the solutions are $x = -3$ and $x = -1$.

CHECK:

$$(-3)^2 + 4(-3) = 9 - 12 = -3$$
$$(-1)^2 + 4(-1) = 1 - 4 = -3, \text{ so } x = -3 \text{ and } x = -1$$
are solutions.

A quadratic equation will usually have 2 different solutions, but it is possible for a quadratic to have only one solution or even no solution.

EXAMPLE 2:   If $2z^2 - 1 = 3z^2 - 2z$, what is z?

(A) $0 = 3z^2 - 2z^2 - 2z + 1$
(B) $z^2 - 2z + 1 = 0$
(C) $z^2 - 2z + 1 = (z - 1)^2 = 0$
(D) $z - 1 = 0$ or $z = 1$

CHECK:

$$2 \cdot 1^2 - 1 = 2 - 1 = 1 \text{ and } 3 \cdot 1^2 - 2 \cdot 1 = 3 - 2 = 1,$$
so $z = 1$ is a solution.

Equations which may not look like quadratics may be changed into quadratics.

EXAMPLE 3:   Find a if $a - 3 = \dfrac{10}{a}$.

Multiply each side of the equation by a to obtain $a^2 - 3a = 10$, which is quadratic.

(A) $a^2 - 3a - 10 = 0$
(C) $a^2 - 3a - 10 = (a - 5)(a + 2)$
(D) So $a - 5 = 0$ or $a + 2 = 0$.

Therefore, $a = 5$ and $a = -2$ are the solutions.

CHECK:

$$5 - 3 = 2 = \frac{10}{5} \text{ so } a = 5 \text{ is a solution.}$$

$$-2 - 3 = -5 = \frac{10}{-2} \text{ so } a = -2 \text{ is a solution.}$$

You can also solve quadratic equations by using the *quadratic formula*. The quadratic formula states that the solutions of the quadratic equation

$$ax^2 + bx + c = 0 \text{ are } x = \frac{1}{2a}[-b + \sqrt{b^2 - 4ac}] \text{ and } x = \frac{1}{2a}[-b - \sqrt{b^2 - 4ac}].$$

This is usually written $x = \dfrac{1}{2a}[-b \pm \sqrt{b^2 - 4ac}]$. Use of the quadratic formula would replace steps (C) and (D).

EXAMPLE 4: Find x if $x^2 + 5x = 12 - x^2$.

(A) $x^2 + 5x + x^2 - 12 = 0$
(B) $2x^2 + 5x - 12 = 0$

So $a = 2$, $b = 5$ and $c = -12$. Therefore, using the quadratic formula, the solutions are $x = \frac{1}{4}[-5 \pm \sqrt{25 - 4 \cdot 2 \cdot (-12)}] = \frac{1}{4}[-5 \pm \sqrt{25 + 96}] = \frac{1}{4}[-5 \pm \sqrt{121}]$. So we have $x = \frac{1}{4}[-5 \pm 11]$. The solutions are $x = \frac{3}{2}$ and $x = -4$.

CHECK:

$$\left(\frac{3}{2}\right)^2 + 5 \cdot \frac{3}{2} = \frac{9}{4} + \frac{15}{2} = \frac{39}{4} = 12 - \frac{9}{4} = 12 - \left(\frac{3}{2}\right)^2$$
$$(-4)^2 + 5(-4) = 16 - 20 = -4 = 12 - 16 = 12 - (-4)^2$$

NOTE: If $b^2 - 4ac$ is negative, then the quadratic equation $ax^2 + bx + c = 0$ has no real solutions because negative numbers do not have real square roots.

The quadratic formula will always give you the solutions to a quadratic equation. If you can factor the equation, factoring will usually give you the solution in less time. Remember, you want to answer as many questions as you can in the time given. So factor if you can. If you don't see the factor immediately, then use the formula.

II-3. Word Problems

3-1

The general method for solving word problems is to translate them into algebraic problems. The quantities you are seeking are the unknowns, which are usually represented by letters. The information you are given in the problem is then turned into equations. Words such as "is," "was," "are," and "were" mean equals, and words like "of" and "as much as" mean multiplication.

EXAMPLE 1: A coat was sold for $75. The coat was sold for 150% of the cost of the coat. How much did the coat cost?

You want to find the cost of the coat. Let C be the cost of the coat. You know that the coat was sold for $75 and that $75 was 150% of the cost. So $75 = 150\%$ of C or $75 = 1.5C$. Solving for C you get $C = \frac{75}{1.5} = 50$, so the coat cost $50.

CHECK:

$$(1.5) \$50 = \$75.$$

EXAMPLE 2: Tom's salary is 125% of Joe's salary; Mary's salary is 80% of Joe's salary. The total of all three salaries is $61,000. What is Mary's salary?

Let M = Mary's salary, J = Joe's salary and T = Tom's salary. The first sentence says $T = 125\%$ of J or $T = \frac{5}{4}J$, and $M = 80\%$ of J or $M = \frac{4}{5}J$. The second sentence says that $T + M + J = \$61{,}000$. Using the information from the first sentence, $T + M + J = \frac{5}{4}J + \frac{4}{5}J + J = \frac{25}{20}J + \frac{16}{20}J + J = \frac{61}{20}J$. So $\frac{61}{20}J = 61{,}000$; solving for J you have $J = \frac{20}{61} \times 61{,}000 = 20{,}000$. Therefore, $T = \frac{5}{4} \times \$20{,}000 = \$25{,}000$ and $M = \frac{4}{5} \times \$20{,}000 = \$16{,}000$.

CHECK:

$$\$25{,}000 + \$16{,}000 + \$20{,}000 = \$61{,}000.$$

So Mary's salary is \$16,000.

EXAMPLE 3: Steve weighs 25 pounds more than Jim. The combined weight of Jim and Steve is 325 pounds. How much does Jim weigh?

Let S = Steve's weight in pounds and J = Jim's weight in pounds. The first sentence says $S = J + 25$, and the second sentence becomes $S + J = 325$. Since $S = J + 25$, $S + J = 325$ becomes $(J + 25) + J = 2J + 25 = 325$. So $2J = 300$ and $J = 150$. Therefore, Jim weighs 150 pounds.

CHECK:

If Jim weighs 150 pounds, then Steve weighs
175 pounds and $150 + 175 = 325$.

EXAMPLE 4: A carpenter is designing a closet. The floor will be in the shape of a rectangle whose length is 2 feet more than its width. How long should the closet be if the carpenter wants the area of the floor to be 15 square feet?

The area of a rectangle is length times width, usually written $A = LW$, where A is the area, L is the length, and W is the width. We know $A = 15$ and $L = 2 + W$. Therefore, $LW = (2 + W)\,W = W^2 + 2W$; this must equal 15. So we need to solve $W^2 + 2W = 15$ or $W^2 + 2W - 15 = 0$. Since $W^2 + 2W - 15$ factors into $(W + 5)(W - 3)$, the only possible solutions are $W = -5$ and $W = 3$. Since W represents a width, -5 cannot be the answer; therefore the width is 3 feet. The length is the width plus two feet, so the length is 5 feet. Since $5 \times 3 = 15$, the answer checks.

3–2

Distance Problems. A common type of word problem is a distance or velocity problem. The basic formula is

$$\boxed{\text{DISTANCE TRAVELED} = \text{RATE} \times \text{TIME.}}$$

The formula is abbreviated $d = rt$.

EXAMPLE 1: A train travels at an average speed of 50 miles per hour for $2\frac{1}{2}$ hours and then travels at a speed of 70 miles per hour for $1\frac{1}{2}$ hours. How far did the train travel in the entire 4 hours?

The train traveled for $2\frac{1}{2}$ hours at an average speed of 50 miles per hour, so it traveled $50 \times \frac{5}{2} = 125$ miles in the first $2\frac{1}{2}$ hours. Traveling at a speed of 70 miles per hour for $1\frac{1}{2}$ hours, the distance traveled will be equal to $r \times t$ where $r = 70$ m.p.h. and $t = 1\frac{1}{2}$, so the distance is $70 \times \frac{3}{2} = 105$ miles. Therefore, the total distance traveled is $125 + 105 = 230$ miles.

EXAMPLE 2: The distance from Cleveland to Buffalo is 200 miles. A train takes $3\frac{1}{2}$ hours to go from Buffalo to Cleveland and $4\frac{1}{2}$ hours to go back from Cleveland to Buffalo. What was the average speed of the train for the round trip from Buffalo to Cleveland and back?

The train took $3\frac{1}{2} + 4\frac{1}{2} = 8$ hours for the trip. The distance of a round trip is $2(200) = 400$ miles. Since $d = rt$ then 400 miles $= r \times 8$ hours. Solve for r and you have $r = \dfrac{400 \text{ miles}}{8 \text{ hours}} = 50$ miles per hour. Therefore the average speed is 50 miles per hour.

The speed in the formula is the average speed. If you know that there are different speeds for different lengths of time, then you must use the formula more than once, as we did in example 1.

3–3

Work Problems. In this type of problem you can always assume all workers in the same category work at the same rate. The main idea is: If it takes k

workers 1 hour to do a job then *each worker does* $\frac{1}{k}$ *of the job in an hour* or he works at the rate of $\frac{1}{k}$ of the job per hour. If it takes m workers h hours to finish a job then each worker does $\frac{1}{m}$ of the job in h hours so he does $\frac{1}{h}$ of $\frac{1}{m}$ in an hour. Therefore, each worker *works at the rate of* $\frac{1}{mh}$ *of the job per hour.*

EXAMPLE 1: If 5 men take an hour to dig a ditch, how long should it take 12 men to dig a ditch of the same type?

Since 5 workers took an hour, each worker does $\frac{1}{5}$ of the job in an hour. So 12 workers will work at the rate of $\frac{12}{5}$ of the job per hour. Thus if T is the time it takes for 12 workers to do the job, $\frac{12}{5} \times T = 1$ job and $T = \frac{5}{12} \times 1$, so

$$T = \frac{5}{12} \text{ hours or 25 minutes.}$$

EXAMPLE 2: Worker A takes 8 hours to do a job. Worker B takes 10 hours to do the same job. How long should it take worker A and worker B working together, but independently, to do the same job?

Worker A works at a rate of $\frac{1}{8}$ of the job per hour, since he takes 8 hours to finish the job. Worker B finished the job in 10 hours, so he works at a rate of $\frac{1}{10}$ of the job per hour. Therefore, if they work together they should complete $\frac{1}{8} + \frac{1}{10} = \frac{18}{80} = \frac{9}{40}$, so they work at a rate of $\frac{9}{40}$ of the job per hour together. So if T is the time it takes them to finish the job, $\frac{9}{40}$ of the job per hour $\times T$ hours must equal 1 job. Therefore,

$$\frac{9}{40} \times T = 1 \text{ and } T = \frac{40}{9} = 4\frac{4}{9} \text{ hours.}$$

EXAMPLE 3: There are two taps, tap 1 and tap 2, in a keg. If both taps are opened, the keg is drained in 20 minutes. If tap 1 is closed and tap 2 is open, the keg will be drained in 30 minutes. If tap 2 is closed and tap 1 is open, how long will it take to drain the keg?

Tap 1 and tap 2 together take 20 minutes to drain the keg, so together they drain the keg at a rate of $\frac{1}{20}$ of the keg per minute. Tap 2 takes 30 minutes to drain the keg by itself, so it drains the keg at the rate of $\frac{1}{30}$ of the keg per minute. Let r be the rate at which tap 1 will drain the keg by itself. Then $\left(r + \frac{1}{30} \right)$ of the keg per minute is the rate at which both taps together will drain the keg, so $r + \frac{1}{30} = \frac{1}{20}$. Therefore, $r = \frac{1}{20} - \frac{1}{30} = \frac{1}{60}$, and tap 1 drains the keg at the rate of $\frac{1}{60}$ of the keg per minute, so it will take 60 minutes or 1 hour for tap 1 to drain the keg if tap 2 is closed.

II-4. Counting Problems

4-1

An example of the first type of counting problem is: 50 students signed up for both English and Math. 90 students signed up for either English or Math. If 25 students are taking English but not taking Math, how many students are taking Math but not taking English?

In these problems, "either . . . or . . ." means you can take both, so the people taking both are counted among the people taking either Math or English.

You must avoid counting the same people twice in these problems. The formula is:

the number taking English or Math = the number taking English + the number taking Math − the number taking both.

You have to subtract the number taking both subjects since they are counted once with those taking English and counted again with those taking Math.

A person taking English is either taking Math or not taking Math, so there are $50 + 25 = 75$ people taking English, 50 taking English and Math and 25 taking English but not taking Math. Since 75 are taking English, $90 = 75 +$ number taking Math $- 50$; so there are $90 - 25 = 65$ people taking Math. 50 of the people taking Math are taking English so $65 - 50$ or 15 are taking Math but not English.

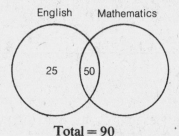

Total = 90

The figure shows what is given. Since 90 students signed up for English or Mathematics, 15 must be taking Mathematics but not English.

EXAMPLE 1: In a survey, 60% of those surveyed owned a car and 80% of those surveyed owned a T.V. If 55% owned both a car and a T.V., what percent of those surveyed owned a car or a T.V. or both?

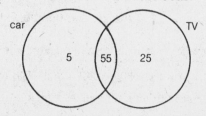

The basic formula is:

people who own a car or a T.V. = people who own a car
+ people who own a T.V. − people who own both a car and a T.V.

So the people who own a car or a T.V. = 60% + 80% − 55% = 85%. Therefore, 85% of the people surveyed own either a car or a T.V.

If we just add 60% and 80% the result is 140% which is impossible. This is because the 55% who own both are counted twice.

4–2

> If an event can happen in m different ways, and each of the m ways is followed by a second event which can occur in k different ways, then the first event can be followed by the second event in $m \cdot k$ different ways. This is called the *fundamental principle of counting*.

EXAMPLE 1:   If there are 3 different roads from Syracuse to Binghamton and 4 different roads from Binghamton to Scranton, how many different routes are there from Syracuse to Scranton which go through Binghamton?

There are 3 different ways to go from Syracuse to Binghamton. Once you are in Binghamton, there are 4 different ways to get to Scranton. So using the fundamental principle of counting, there are $3 \times 4 = 12$ different ways to get from Syracuse to Scranton going through Binghamton.

EXAMPLE 2:   A club has 20 members. They are electing a president and a vice president. How many different outcomes of the election are possible? (Assume the president and vice president must be different members of the club.)

There are 20 members, so there are 20 choices for president. Once a president is chosen, there are 19 members left who can be vice president. So there are $20 \cdot 19 = 380$ different possible outcomes of the election.

II–5.   Ratio and Proportion

5–1

Ratio.   A ratio is a comparison of two numbers by division. The ratio of a to b is written as $a{:}b = \dfrac{a}{b} = a \div b$. We can handle ratios as fractions, since a ratio is a fraction. In the ratio $a{:}b$, a and b are called the *terms* of the ratio. *Since* a:b *is a fraction,* b *can never be zero.* The fraction $\dfrac{a}{b}$ is usually different from the fraction $\dfrac{b}{a}$ $\left(\text{for example } \dfrac{3}{2} \text{ is not the same as } \dfrac{2}{3}\right)$ so *the order of the terms in a ratio is important.*

EXAMPLE 1: If an orange costs 20¢ and an apple costs 12¢, what is the ratio of the cost of an orange to the cost of an apple?

The ratio is $\frac{20¢}{12¢} = \frac{5}{3}$ or 5:3. Notice that the ratio of the cost of an apple to the cost of an orange is $\frac{12¢}{20¢} = \frac{3}{5}$ or 3:5. So the order of the terms is important.

A ratio is a number, so if you want to find the ratio of two quantities they must be expressed in the same units.

EXAMPLE 2: What is the ratio of 8 inches to 6 feet?

Change 6 feet into inches. Since there are 12 inches in a foot, 6 feet = 6 × 12 inches = 72 inches. So the ratio is $\frac{8 \text{ inches}}{72 \text{ inches}} = \frac{1}{9}$ or 1:9. If you regard ratios as fractions, the units must cancel out. In example 2, if you did not change units the ratio would be $\frac{8 \text{ inches}}{6 \text{ feet}} = \frac{4}{3}$ inches/feet, which is not a number.

If two numbers measure different quantities, their quotient is usually called a rate. For example, $\frac{50 \text{ miles}}{2 \text{ hours}}$ which equals 25 miles per hour is a rate of speed.

5-2

Proportion. A proportion is a statement that two ratios are equal. For example, $\frac{3}{12} = \frac{1}{4}$ is a proportion; it could also be expressed as 3:12 = 1:4 or 3:12 :: 1:4.

In the proportion $a:b = c:d$, the terms on the outside, (a and d), are called the *extremes,* and the terms on the inside, (b and c), are called the *means.* Since $a:b$ and $c:d$ are ratios, b and d are both different from zero, so $bd \neq 0$. Multiply each side of $\frac{a}{b} = \frac{c}{d}$ by bd; you get $(bd)\left(\frac{a}{b}\right) = ad$ and $(bd)\left(\frac{c}{d}\right) = bc$. Since $bd \neq 0$, the proportion $\frac{a}{b} = \frac{c}{d}$ is equivalent to the equation $ad = bc$. This is usually expressed in the following way.

In a proportion the product of the extremes is equal to the product of the means.

EXAMPLE 1: Find x if $\frac{4}{5} = \frac{10}{x}$.

In the proportion $\frac{4}{5} = \frac{10}{x}$, 4 and x are the extremes and 5 and 10 are the means, so $4x = 5 \cdot 10 = 50$.

Solve for x and we get $x = \frac{50}{4} = 12.5$.

Finding the products ad and bc is also called _cross-multiplying the proportion:_ $\frac{a}{b} \diagdown \frac{c}{d}$. So cross-multiplying a proportion gives two equal numbers. The proportion $\frac{a}{b} = \frac{c}{d}$ is read "a is to b as c is to d."

EXAMPLE 2:   Two numbers are in the ratio 5:4 and their difference is 10. What is the larger number?

Let m and n be the two numbers. Then $\frac{m}{n} = \frac{5}{4}$ and $m - n = 10$. Cross-multiply the proportion and you get $5n = 4m$ or $n = \frac{4}{5}m$. So $m - n = m - \frac{4}{5}m = \frac{1}{5}m = 10$ and $m = 50$, which means $n = \frac{4}{5} \cdot 50 = 40$. Therefore, the larger number is 50.

CHECK:

$$\frac{50}{40} = \frac{5}{4} \text{ and } 50 - 40 = 10.$$

Two variables, a and b, are _directly proportional_ if they satisfy a relationship of the form $a = kb$, where k is a number. The distance a car travels in two hours and its average speed for the two hours are directly proportional, since $d = 2s$ where d is the distance and s is the average speed expressed in miles per hour. Here $k = 2$. Sometimes the word _directly_ is omitted, so a and b are proportional means $a = kb$.

EXAMPLE 3:   If m is proportional to n and $m = 5$ when $n = 4$, what is the value of m when $n = 18$?

There are two different ways to work the problem.

I.   Since m and n are directly proportional, $m = kn$; and $m = 5$ when $n = 4$, so $5 = k \cdot 4$ which means $k = \frac{5}{4}$. Therefore, $m = \frac{5}{4}n$. So when $n = 18$,

$m = \frac{5}{4} \cdot 18 = \frac{90}{4} = 22.5$.

II. Since m and n are directly proportional, $m = kn$. If n' is some value of n, then the value of m corresponding to n' we will call m', and $m' = kn'$. So $\frac{m}{n} = k$ and $\frac{m'}{n'} = k$; therefore, $\frac{m}{n} = \frac{m'}{n'}$ is a proportion. Since $m = 5$ when $n = 4$, $\frac{m}{n} = \frac{5}{4} = \frac{m'}{18}$. Cross-multiply and we have $4m' = 90$ or

$m' = \frac{90}{4} = 22.5$.

If two quantities are proportional, you can always set up a proportion in this manner.

EXAMPLE 4: If a machine makes 3 yards of cloth in 2 minutes, how many yards of cloth will the machine make in 50 minutes?

The amount of cloth is proportional to the time the machine operates. Let y be the number of yards of cloth the machine makes in 50 minutes; then $\frac{2 \text{ minutes}}{50 \text{ minutes}} = \frac{3 \text{ yards}}{y \text{ yards}}$, so $\frac{2}{50} = \frac{3}{y}$. Cross multiply, and you have $2y = 150$, so $y = 75$. Therefore, the machine makes 75 yards of cloth in 50 minutes.

Since a ratio is a number, the units must cancel; so put the numbers which measure the same quantity in the same ratio.

Any two units of measurement of the same quantity are directly proportional.

EXAMPLE 5: How many ounces are there in $4\frac{3}{4}$ pounds?

Let x be the number of ounces in $4\frac{3}{4}$ pounds. Since there are 16 ounces in a pound, $\frac{x \text{ ounces}}{16 \text{ ounces}} = \frac{4\frac{3}{4} \text{ pounds}}{1 \text{ pound}}$. Cross-multiply to get $x = 16 \cdot 4\frac{3}{4} = 16 \cdot \frac{19}{4} = 76$; so $4\frac{3}{4}$ pounds = 76 ounces.

You can always change units by using a proportion. You should know the following measurements:

LENGTH:	1 foot = 12 inches
	1 yard = 3 feet
AREA:	1 square foot = 144 square inches
	1 square yard = 9 square feet
TIME:	1 minute = 60 seconds
	1 hour = 60 minutes
	1 day = 24 hours
	1 week = 7 days
	1 year = 52 weeks
VOLUME:	1 quart = 2 pints
	1 gallon = 4 quarts
WEIGHT:	1 ounce = 16 drams
	1 pound = 16 ounces
	1 ton = 2000 pounds

EXAMPLE 6: On a map, it is $2\frac{1}{2}$ inches from Harrisburg to Gary. The actual distance from Harrisburg to Gary is 750 miles. What is the actual distance from town A to town B if they are 4 inches apart on the map?

Let d miles be the distance from A to B; then $\frac{2\frac{1}{2} \text{ inches}}{4 \text{ inches}} = \frac{750 \text{ miles}}{d \text{ miles}}$. Cross-multiply and we have $\left(2\frac{1}{2}\right)d = 4 \times 750 = 3,000$, so $d = \frac{2}{5} \times 3,000 = 1,200$.

Therefore, the distance from A to B is 1,200 miles. Problems like this one are often called scale problems.

Two variables, a and b, are *indirectly proportional* if they satisfy a relationship of the form $k = ab$, where k is a number. So the average speed of a car and the time it takes the car to travel 300 miles are indirectly proportional, since $st = 300$ where s is the speed and t is the time.

EXAMPLE 7: m is indirectly proportional to n and $m = 5$ when $n = 4$. What is the value of m when $n = 18$?

Since m and n are indirectly proportional, $m \cdot n = k$, and $k = 5 \cdot 4 = 20$ because $m = 5$ when $n = 4$. Therefore, $18m = k = 20$, so $m = \frac{20}{18} = \frac{10}{9}$ when $n = 18$.

Other examples of indirect proportion are work problems (see page 174).

If two quantities are directly proportional, then when one increases, the other increases. If two quantities are indirectly proportional when one quantity increases, the other decreases.

5–3
It is also possible to compare three or more numbers by a ratio. The numbers A, B, and C are in the ratio 2:4:3 means $A:B = 2:4$, $A:C = 2:3$, and $B:C = 4:3$. The order of the terms is important. $A:B:C$ is read A is to B is to C.

EXAMPLE 1:   What is the ratio of Tom's salary to Martha's salary to Anne's salary if Tom makes $15,000, Martha makes $12,000 and Anne makes $10,000?

The ratio is 15,000:12,000:10,000 which is the same as 15:12:10. You can cancel a factor which appears in *every* term.

EXAMPLE 2:   The angles of a triangle are in the ratio 5:4:3; how many degrees are there is the largest angle?

The sum of the angles in a triangle is 180°. If the angles are $a°$, $b°$, and $c°$, then $a + b + c = 180$, and $a:b:c: = 5:4:3$. You could find b in terms of a since $\frac{a}{b} = \frac{5}{4}$ and c in terms of a since $\frac{a}{c} = \frac{5}{3}$ and then solve the equation for a.

A quicker method for this type of problem is:

(1)   Add all the numbers, so $5 + 4 + 3 = 12$.
(2)   Use each number as the numerator of a fraction whose denominator is the result of step (1), getting $\frac{5}{12}, \frac{4}{12}, \frac{3}{12}$.
(3)   Each quantity is the corresponding fraction (from step (2)), of the total.

Thus

$a = \frac{5}{12}$ of 180 or 75, $b = \frac{4}{12}$ of 180 or 60, and $c = \frac{3}{12}$ of 180 or 45.
So the largest angle is 75°.

CHECK:

$$75:60:45 = 5:4:3 \text{ and } 75 + 60 + 45 = 180.$$

II–6. Sequence and Progressions

6–1

A SEQUENCE is an ordered collection of numbers. For example, 2,4,6,8,10, . . . is a sequence. 2,4,6,8,10 are called the *terms* of the sequence. We identify the terms by their position in the sequence; so 2 is the first term, 8 is the 4th term and so on. The dots mean the sequence continues; you should be able to figure out the succeeding terms. In the example, the sequence is the sequence of even integers, and the next term after 10 would be 12.

EXAMPLE 1:   What is the eighth term of the sequence 1,4,9,16,25, . . . ?

Since $1^2 = 1$, $2^2 = 4$, $3^2 = 9$, the sequence is the sequence of squares of integers, so the eighth term is $8^2 = 64$.

6–2

An *arithmetical progression* is a sequence of numbers with the property that the *difference* of any two consecutive numbers is always the same. The numbers 2,6,10,14,18,22, . . . constitute an arithmetical progression, since each term is 4 more than the term before it. 4 is called the common difference of the progression.

If d is the common difference and a is the first term of the progression, then the nth term will be $a + (n - 1)d$. So a progression with common difference 4 and initial term 5 will have $5 + 6(4) = 29$ as its 7th term. You can check your answer. The sequence would be 5,9,13,17,21,25,29, . . . so 29 is the seventh term.

A sequence of numbers is called a *geometric progression* if the *ratio* of consecutive terms is always the same. So 3,6,12,24,48, . . . is a geometric progression since $\frac{6}{3} = 2 = \frac{12}{6} = \frac{24}{12} = \frac{48}{24}$, ... *The nth term of a geometric series is ar^{n-1}* where a is the first term and r is the common ratio. If a geometric progression started with 2 and the common ratio was 3, then the fifth term should be $2 \cdot 3^4 = 2 \cdot 81 = 162$. The sequence would be 2,6,18,54,162, . . . so 162 is indeed the fifth term of the progression.

We can quickly add up the first n terms of a geometric progression which starts with a and has common ratio r. *The formula for the sum of the first n terms is $\frac{ar^n - a}{r - 1}$* when $r \neq 1$. (If $r = 1$ all the terms are the same so the sum is na.)

EXAMPLE 1:   Find the sum of the first 7 terms of the sequence 5,10,20,40, ...

Since $\frac{10}{5} = \frac{20}{10} = \frac{40}{20} = 2$, the sequence is a geometric sequence with common ratio 2. The first term is 5, so $a = 5$ and the common ratio is 2. The sum of the first seven terms means $n = 7$, thus the sum is

$$\frac{5 \cdot 2^7 - 5}{2 - 1} = 5(2^7 - 1) = 5(128 - 1) = 5 \cdot 127 = 635.$$

CHECK:

The first seven terms are 5,10,20,40,80,160,320, and $5 + 10 + 20 + 40 + 80 + 160 + 320 = 635$.

II-7. Inequalities

7-1

A number is positive if it is greater than 0, so 1, $\frac{1}{1000}$, and 53.4 are all positive numbers. Positive numbers are signed numbers whose sign is +. If you think of numbers as points on a number line (see section 6, page 155), positive numbers correspond to points to the right of 0.

A number is negative if it is less than 0. $-\frac{4}{5}$, -50, and $-.0001$ are all negative numbers. Negative numbers are signed numbers whose sign is $-$. Negative numbers correspond to points to the left of 0 on a number line.

0 is the only number which is neither positive nor negative.

$a > b$ means the number a is greater than the number b, that is $a = b + x$ where x is a positive number. If we look at a number line, $a > b$ means a is to the right of b. $a > b$ can also be read as b is less than a, which is also written $b < a$. For example, $-5 > -7.5$ because $-5 = -7.5 + 2.5$ and 2.5 is positive.

The notation $a \leq b$ means a is less than or equal to b, or b is greater than or equal to a. For example, $5 \geq 4$; also $4 \geq 4$. $a \neq b$ means a is not equal to b.

> If you need to know whether one fraction is greater than another fraction, put the fractions over a common denominator and compare the numerators.

EXAMPLE 1: Which is larger, $\frac{13}{16}$ or $\frac{31}{40}$?

A common denominator is 80.

$\frac{13}{16} = \frac{65}{80}$, and $\frac{31}{40} = \frac{62}{80}$;

since $65 > 62$,

$\frac{65}{80} > \frac{62}{80}$,

so $\frac{13}{16} > \frac{31}{40}$.

7-2

Inequalities have certain properties which are similar to equations. We can talk about the left side and the right side of an inequality, and we can use algebraic expressions for the sides of an inequality. For example, $6x < 5x + 4$. A value for an unknown *satisfies an inequality*, if when you evaluate each side of the inequality the numbers satisfy the inequality. So if $x = 2$, then $6x = 12$ and $5x + 4 = 14$ and since $12 < 14$, $x = 2$ satisfies $6x < 5x + 4$. Two inequalities are equivalent if the same collection of numbers satisfies both inequalities.

The following basic principles are used in work with inequalities:

(A) Adding the same expression to *each* side of an inequality gives an equivalent inequality (written $a < b \Leftrightarrow a + c < b + c$ where $\Leftrightarrow$ means equivalent).

(B) Subtracting the same expression from *each* side of an inequality gives an equivalent inequality ($a < b \Leftrightarrow a - c < b - c$).

(C) Multiplying or dividing *each* side of an inequality by the same *positive* expression gives an equivalent inequality ($a < b \Leftrightarrow ca < cb$ for $c > 0$).

(D) Multiplying or dividing each side of an inequality by the same *negative* expression *reverses* the inequality ($a < b \Leftrightarrow ca > cb$ for $c < 0$).

(E) If both sides of an inequality have the same sign, inverting both sides of the inequality *reverses* the inequality.

$$0 < a < b \Leftrightarrow 0 < \frac{1}{b} < \frac{1}{a}$$

$$a < b < 0 \Leftrightarrow \frac{1}{b} < \frac{1}{a} < 0$$

(F) If two inequalities are of the same type (both greater or both less), adding the respective sides gives the same type of inequality.

$$(a < b \text{ and } c < d, \text{ then } a + c < b + d)$$

Note that the inequalities are *not* equivalent.

(G) If $a < b$ and $b < c$ then $a < c$.

EXAMPLE 1: Find the values of x for which $5x - 4 < 7x + 2$.

Using **principle** (B) subtract $5x + 2$ from each side, so $(5x - 4 < 7x + 2) \Leftrightarrow -6 < 2x$. Now use **principle** (C) and divide each side by 2, so $-6 < 2x \Leftrightarrow -3 < x$.

So any x greater than -3 satisfies the inequality. It is a good idea to make a spot check. -1 is > -3; let $x = -1$ then $5x - 4 = -9$ and $7x + 2 = -5$. Since $-9 < -5$, the answer is correct for at least the particular value $x = -1$.

EXAMPLE 2: Find the values of a which satisfy $a^2 + 1 > 2a + 4$.

Subtract $2a$ from each side, so
$(a^2 + 1 > 2a + 4) \Leftrightarrow a^2 - 2a + 1 > 4$.
$a^2 - 2a + 1 = (a - 1)^2$ so
$a^2 - 2a + 1 > 4 \Leftrightarrow (a - 1)^2 > 2^2$.

We need to be careful when we take the square roots of inequalities. If $q^2 > 4$ and if $q > 0$, then $q > 2$; but if $q < 0$, then $q < -2$. We must look at two cases in example 2. First, if $(a - 1) \geq 0$ then

$(a - 1)^2 > 2^2 \Leftrightarrow a - 1 > 2$ or $a > 3$.
If $(a - 1) < 0$ then $(a - 1)^2 > 2^2 \Leftrightarrow a - 1 < -2 \Leftrightarrow a < -1$.
So the inequality is satisfied if $a > 3$ or if $a < -1$.

CHECK:

$$(-2)^2 + 1 = 5 > 2(-2) + 4 = 0, \text{ and } 5^2 + 1 = 26 > 14 = 2 \cdot 5 + 4.$$

Some inequalities are not satisfied by *any* real number. For example, since $x^2 \geq 0$ for all x, there is no real number x such that $x^2 < -9$.

You may be given an inequality and asked whether other inequalities follow from the original inequality. You should be able to answer such questions by using principles (A) through (G).

If there is any property of inequalities you can't remember, try out some specific numbers. If $x < y$, then what is the relation between $-x$ and $-y$? Since $4 < 5$ but $-5 < -4$, the relation is probably $-x > -y$, which is true by (D).

Probably the most common mistake is forgetting to reverse the inequalities if you multiply or divide by a negative number.

III. Geometry

III-1. Angles

1-1

If two straight lines meet at a point they form an *angle*. The point is called the *vertex* of the angle and the lines are called the *sides* or *rays* of the angle. The sign for angle is $\angle$ and an angle can be denoted in the following ways:

(A) $\angle ABC$ where B is the vertex, A is a point on one side, and C a point on the other side.

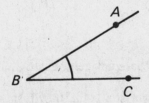

(B) $\angle B$ where B is the vertex.

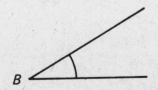

(C)   ∠1 or ∠x where x or 1 is written inside the angle.

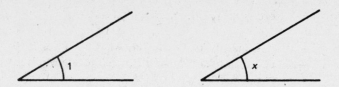

Angles are usually measured in degrees. We say that an angle equals x degrees, when its measure is x degrees. Degrees are denoted by °. An angle of 50 degrees is 50°. $60' = 1°$, $60'' = 1'$ where ′ is read minutes and ″ is read seconds.

1–2

Two angles are *adjacent* if they have the same vertex and a common side and one angle is not inside the other.

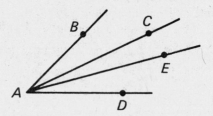

∠BAC and ∠CAD are adjacent, but ∠CAD and ∠EAD are not adjacent.

If two lines intersect at a point, they form 4 angles. The angles opposite each other are called *vertical* angles. ∠1 and ∠3 are vertical angles. ∠2 and ∠4 are vertical angles.

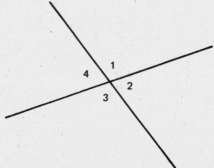

Vertical angles are equal,

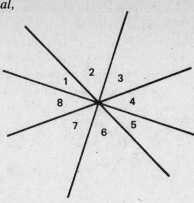

so $\angle 1 = \angle 5$, $\angle 2 = \angle 6$, $\angle 3 = \angle 7$, $\angle 4 = \angle 8$.

1–3

A straight angle is an angle whose sides lie on a straight line. *A straight angle equals 180°.*

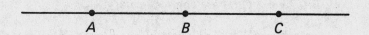

$\angle ABC$ is a straight angle.

If the sum of two adjacent angles is a straight angle, then the angles are *supplementary* and each angle is the supplement of the other.

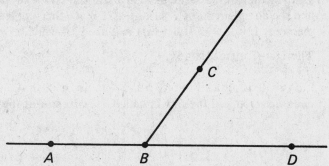

$\angle ABC$ and $\angle CBD$ are supplementary.

If an angle of $x°$ and an angle of $y°$ are supplements, then $x + y = 180$.

If two supplementary angles are equal, they are both *right angles*. A right angle is half of a straight angle. A right angle = 90°.

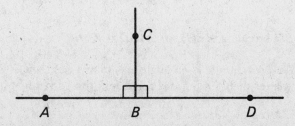

$\angle ABC = \angle CBD$ and they are both right angles. A right angle is denoted by ㄴ. When 2 lines intersect and all four of the angles are equal, then each of the angles is a right angle.

If the sum of two adjacent angles is a right angle, then the angles are *complementary* and each angle is the complement of the other.

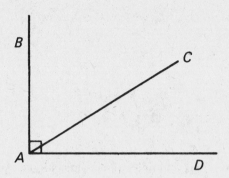

$\angle BAC$ and $\angle CAD$ are complementary.

If an angle of $x°$ and an angle of $y°$ are complementary, then $x + y = 90$.

EXAMPLE 1: If the supplement of angle x is three times as much as the complement of angle x, how many degrees is angle x?

Let d be the number of degrees in angle x; then the supplement of x is $(180 - d)°$, and the complement of x is $(90 - d)°$. Since the supplement is 3 times the complement, $180 - d = 3(90 - d) = 270 - 3d$ which gives $2d = 90$, so $d = 45$.

Therefore, angle x is $45°$.

If an angle is divided into two equal angles by a straight line, then the angle has been *bisected* and the line is called the *bisector* of the angle.

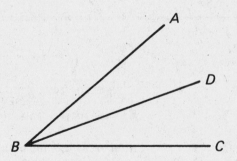

BD bisects $\angle ABC$; so $\angle ABD = \angle DBC$.

An *acute angle* is an angle less than a right angle. An *obtuse* angle is an angle greater than a right angle, but less than a straight angle.

∠1 is an acute angle, and ∠2 is an obtuse angle.

III–2. Lines

2–1

A line is understood to be a straight line. A line is assumed to extend indefinitely in both directions. *There is one and only one line between two distinct points.* There are two ways to denote a line:

(1) (A) by a single letter: *l* is a line;

l

(2) (B) by two points on the line: *AB* is a line.

A   B

A *line segment* is the part of a line between two points called *endpoints*. A line segment is denoted by its endpoints.

A   B

AB is a line segment. If a point *P* on a line segment is equidistant from the endpoints, then *P* is called the *midpoint* of the line segment.

A   P   B   *P* is the midpoint of *AB* if the length of *AP* =

the length of *PB*. Two line segments are equal if their lengths are equal; so $AP = PB$ means the line segment *AP* has the same length as the line segment *PB*.

When a line segment is extended indefinitely in one direction, it is called a *ray*. A ray has one endpoint.

AB is a ray which has *A* as its endpoint.

2-2

P is a *point of intersection* of two lines if *P* is a point which is on both of the lines. *Two different lines can not have more than one point of intersection,* because there is only one line between two points.

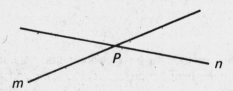

P is the point of intersection of *m* and *n*. We also say *m and n intersect at P*.

Two lines in the same plane are parallel if they do not intersect no matter how far they are extended.

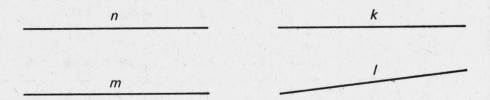

m and *n* are parallel, but *k* and *l* are not parallel since if *k* and *l* are extended they will intersect. Parallel lines are denoted by the symbol ‖; so *m* ‖ *n* means *m* is parallel to *n*.

If two lines are parallel to a third line, then they are parallel to each other.

If a third line intersects two given lines, it is called a *transversal*. A transversal and the two given lines form eight angles. The four inside angles are called *interior* angles. The four outside angles are called *exterior* angles. If two angles are on opposite sides of the transversal they are called *alternate* angles.

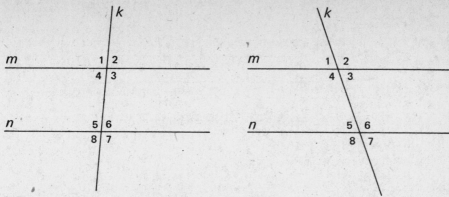

k is a transversal of the lines m and n. Angles 1, 2, 7, and 8 are the exterior angles, and angles 3, 4, 5, and 6 are the interior angles. $\angle 4$ and $\angle 6$ are an example of a pair of alternate angles. $\angle 1$ and $\angle 5$, $\angle 2$ and $\angle 6$, $\angle 3$ and $\angle 7$, and $\angle 4$ and $\angle 8$ are pairs of *corresponding* angles.

If two parallel lines are intersected by a transversal then:

(1) Alternate interior angles are equal.
(2) Corresponding angles are equal.
(3) Interior angles on the same side of the transversal are supplementary.

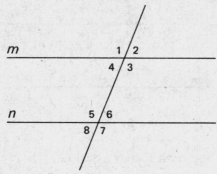

If we use the fact that vertical angles are equal, we can replace "interior" by "exterior" in (1) and (3).

m is parallel to n implies:

(1) $\angle 4 = \angle 6$ and $\angle 3 = \angle 5$
(2) $\angle 1 = \angle 5$, $\angle 2 = \angle 6$, $\angle 3 = \angle 7$ and $\angle 4 = \angle 8$
(3) $\angle 3 + \angle 6 = 180°$ and $\angle 4 + \angle 5 = 180°$

The reverse is also true. Let m and n be two lines which have k as a transversal.

(1) If a pair of alternate interior angles are equal, then m and n are parallel.
(2) If a pair of corresponding angles are equal, then m and n are parallel.
(3) If a pair of interior angles on the same side of the transversal are supplementary, then m is parallel to n.

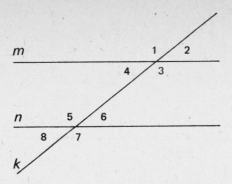

If $\angle 3 = \angle 5$, then $m \parallel n$. If $\angle 4 = \angle 6$ then $m \parallel n$. If $\angle 2 = \angle 6$ then $m \parallel n$. If $\angle 3 + \angle 6 = 180°$, then $m \parallel n$.

EXAMPLE 1:   If m and n are two parallel lines and angle 1 is 60°, how many degrees is angle 2?

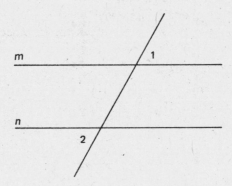

Let $\angle 3$ be the vertical angle equal to angle 2.

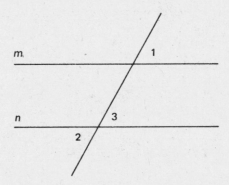

$\angle 3 = \angle 2$. Since m and n are parallel, corresponding angles are equal. Since $\angle 1$ and $\angle 3$ are corresponding angles, $\angle 1 = \angle 3$. Therefore, $\angle 1 = \angle 2$, and $\angle 2$ equals 60° since $\angle 1 = 60°$.

2–3

When two lines intersect and all four of the angles formed are equal, the lines are said to be *perpendicular*. If two lines are perpendicular, they are the sides of right angles whose vertex is the point of intersection.

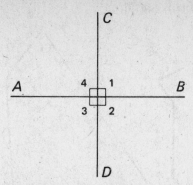

AB is perpendicular to CD, and angles 1, 2, 3, and 4 are all right angles. $\perp$ is the symbol for perpendicular; so $AB \perp CD$.

If two lines in a plane are perpendicular to the same line, then the two lines are parallel.

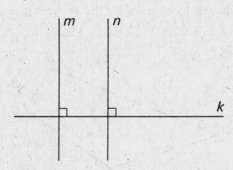

$m \perp k$ and $n \perp k$ implies that $m \parallel n$.

If *any one* of the angles formed when two lines intersect is a right angle, then the lines are perpendicular.

III-3. Polygons

A POLYGON is a closed figure in a plane which is composed of line segments which meet only at their endpoints. The line segments are called *sides* of the polygon, and a point where two sides meet is called a *vertex* (plural *vertices*) of the polygon.

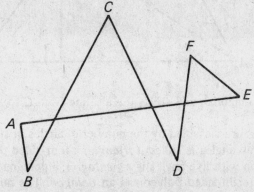

$ABCDEF$ is not a polygon since the line segments intersect at points which are not endpoints.

Some examples of polygons are:

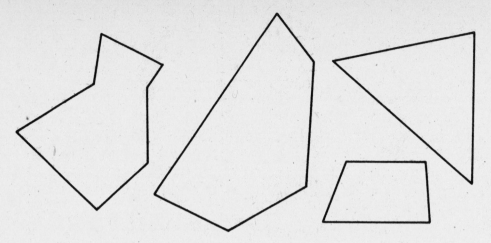

A polygon is usually denoted by the vertices given in order.

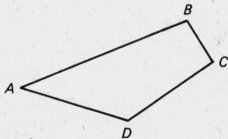

ABCD is a polygon.

A *diagonal* of a polygon is a line segment whose endpoints are nonadjacent vertices. The *altitude* from a vertex *P* to a side is the line segment with endpoint *P* which is perpendicular to the side.

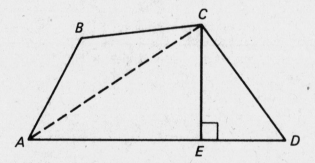

AC is a diagonal, and *CE* is the altitude from *C* to *AD*.

Polygons are classified by the number of angles or sides they have. A polygon with three angles is called a *triangle;* a four-sided polygon is a *quadrilateral;* a polygon with five angles is a *pentagon;* a polygon with six angles is a *hexagon;* an eight-sided polygon is an *octagon*. The number of angles is always equal to the number of sides in a polygon, so a six-sided polygon is a hexagon. The term *n*-gon refers to a polygon with *n* sides.

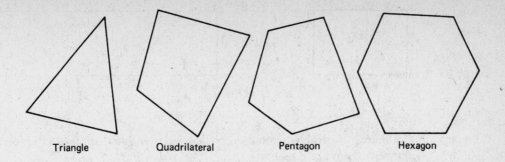

Triangle   Quadrilateral   Pentagon   Hexagon

If the sides of a polygon are all equal in length and if all the angles of a polygon are equal, the polygon is called a *regular* polygon.

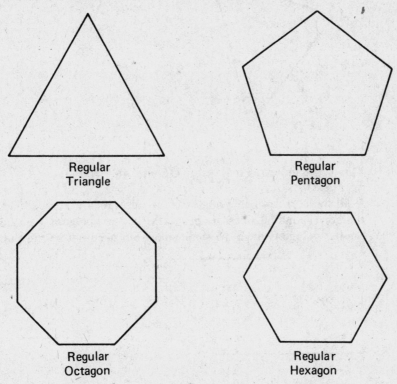

Regular
Triangle

Regular
Pentagon

Regular
Octagon

Regular
Hexagon

If the corresponding sides and the corresponding angles of two polygons are equal, the polygons are *congruent*. Congruent polygons have the same size and the same shape.

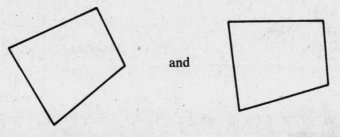

and

are congruent but

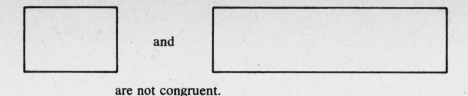

are not congruent.

In figures for problems on congruence, sides with the same number of strokes through them are equal.

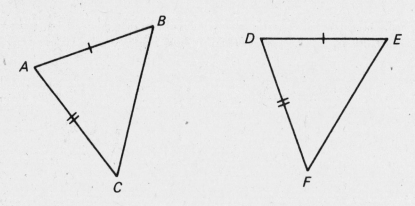

This figure indicates that $AB = DE$ and $AC = DF$.

If all the corresponding angles of two polygons are equal and the lengths of the corresponding sides are proportional, the polygons are said to be *similar*. Similar polygons have the same shape but need not be the same size.

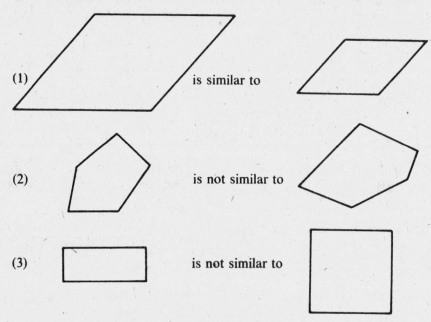

In (3) the corresponding angles are equal, but the corresponding sides are not proportional.

The sum of all the angles of an n-gon is $(n-2)180°$. So the sum of the angles in a hexagon is $(6-2)180° = 720°$.

III–4. Triangles

4–1

A TRIANGLE is a 3-sided polygon. If two sides of a triangle are equal, it is called *isosceles*. If all three sides are equal, it is an *equilateral* triangle. If all of the sides have different lengths, the triangle is *scalene*. When one of the angles in a triangle is a right angle, the triangle is a *right triangle*. If one of the angles is obtuse we have an *obtuse triangle*. If all the angles are acute, the triangle is an *acute triangle*.

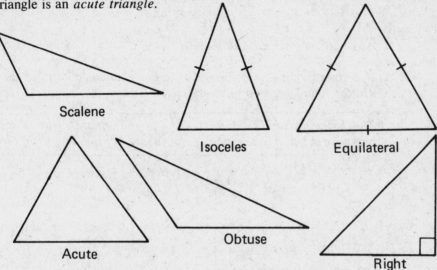

The symbol for a triangle is △; so △*ABC* means a triangle whose vertices are *A*, *B*, and *C*.

> *The sum of the angles in a triangle is 180°.*

The sum of the lengths of any two sides of a triangle must be longer than the remaining side.

If two angles in a triangle are equal, then the lengths of the sides opposite the equal angles are equal. If two sides of a triangle are equal, then the angles opposite the two equal sides are equal. In an equilateral triangle all the angles are equal and each angle = 60°. If each of the angles in a triangle is 60°, then the triangle is equilateral.

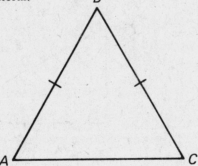

If *AB* = *BC*, then ∠*BAC* = ∠*BCA*.

If one angle in a triangle is larger than another angle, the side opposite the larger angle is longer than the side opposite the smaller angle. If one side is longer than another side, then the angle opposite the longer side is larger than the angle opposite the shorter side.

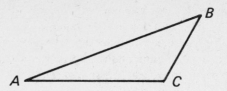

$AB > AC$ implies $\angle BCA > \angle ABC$.

In a right triangle, the side opposite the right angle is called the *hypotenuse*, and the remaining two sides are called *legs*.

> The Pythagorean Theorem states that *the square of the length of the hypotenuse is equal to the sum of the squares of the lengths of the legs.*

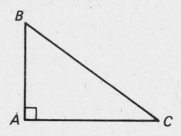

$(BC)^2 = (AB)^2 + (AC)^2$

If $AB = 4$ and $AC = 3$ then $(BC)^2 = 4^2 + 3^2 = 25$ so $BC = 5$. If $BC = 13$ and $AC = 5$, then $13^2 = 169 = (AB)^2 + 5^2$. So $(AB)^2 = 169 - 25 = 144$ and $AB = 12$.

If the lengths of the three sides of a triangle are a, b, and c and $a^2 = b^2 + c^2$, then the triangle is a right triangle where a is the length of the hypotenuse.

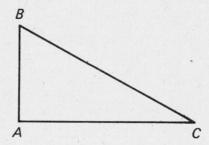

If $AB = 8$, $AC = 15$, and $BC = 17$, then since $17^2 = 8^2 + 15^2$, $\angle BAC$ is a right angle.

4–2

CONGRUENCE. Two triangles are congruent, if two pairs of corresponding sides and the corresponding *included* angles are equal. This is called *Side-Angle-Side* and is denoted by S.A.S.

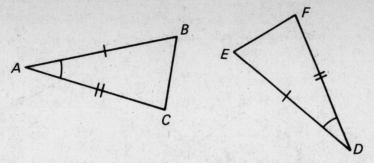

AB = DE, AC = DF and ∠*BAC* = ∠*EDF* imply that △*ABC* ≅ △*DEF*. ≅ means congruent.

Two triangles are congruent if two pairs of corresponding angles and the corresponding *included* side are equal. This is called *Angle-Side-Angle* or A.S.A.

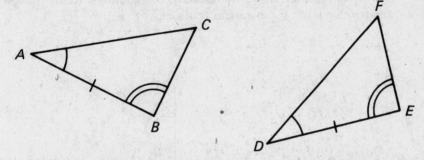

If *AB = DE*, ∠*BAC* = ∠*EDF*, and ∠*CBA* = ∠*FED* then △*ABC* ≅ △*DEF*.

If all three pairs of corresponding sides of two triangles are equal, then the triangles are congruent. This is called *Side-Side-Side* or S.S.S.

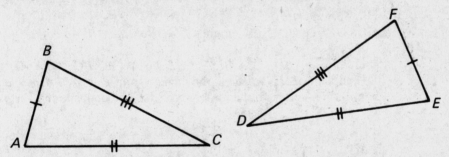

AB = EF, AC = ED, and *BC = FD* imply that △*ABC* ≅ △*EFD*.

Because of the Pythagorean Theorem, if any two corresponding sides of two right triangles are equal, the third sides are equal and the triangles are congruent.

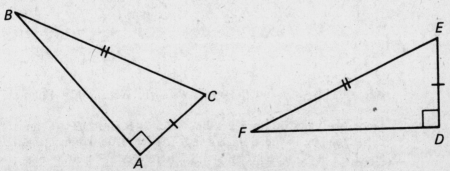

AC = DE and *BC = EF* imply △*ABC* ≅ △*DFE*.

In general, if two corresponding sides of two triangles are equal, we cannot infer that the triangles are congruent.

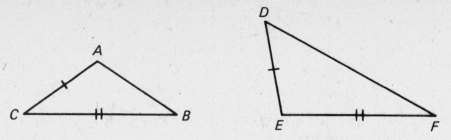

$AC = DE$ and $CB = EF$, but the triangles are not congruent.

If two sides of a triangle are equal, then the altitude to the third side divides the triangle into two congruent triangles.

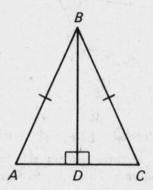

$AB = BC$ and $BD \perp AC$ implies $\triangle ADB \cong \triangle CDB$.

Therefore, $\angle ABD = \angle CBD$, so BD bisects $\angle ABC$. Since $AD = DC$, D is the midpoint of AC so BD is the median from B to AC. A *median* is the segment from a vertex to the midpoint of the side opposite the vertex.

EXAMPLE 1: $EF = ?$

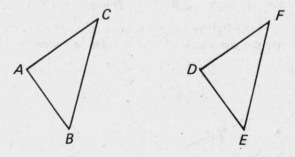

$AB = 4$, $AC = 4.5$ and $BC = 6$, $\angle BAC = \angle EDF$, $DE = 4$ and $DF = 4.5$

Since two pairs of corresponding sides (AB and DE, AC and DF) and the corresponding included angles ($\angle BAC$, $\angle EDF$) are equal, the triangles ABC and DEF are congruent by S.A.S. Therefore, $EF = BC = 6$.

4–3

Similarity. *Two triangles are similar if all three pairs of corresponding angles are equal.* Since the sum of the angles in a triangle is 180°, it follows that if two corresponding angles are equal, the third angles must be equal.

If you draw a line which passes through a triangle and is parallel to one of the sides of the triangle, the triangle formed is similar to the original triangle.

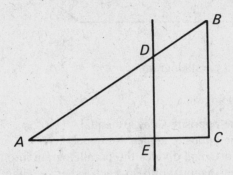

If $DE \parallel BC$ then $\triangle ADE \sim \triangle ABC$. The symbol $\sim$ means similar.

EXAMPLE 1:   A man 6 feet tall casts a shadow 4 feet long; at the same time a flagpole casts a shadow which is 50 feet long. How tall is the flagpole?

The man with his shadow and the flagpole with its shadow can be regarded as the pairs of corresponding sides of two similar triangles.

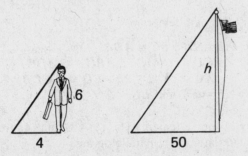

Let h be the height of the flagpole. Since corresponding sides of similar triangles are proportional, $\frac{4}{50} = \frac{6}{h}$. Cross-multiply getting $4h = 6 \cdot 50 = 300$; so $h = 75$. Therefore, the flagpole is 75 feet high.

III–5. Quadrilaterals

A QUADRILATERAL is a polygon with four sides. The sum of the angles in a quadrilateral is 360°. If the opposite sides of a quadrilateral are parallel, the figure is a *parallelogram*.

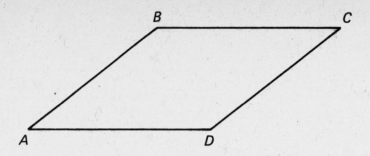

ABCD is a parallelogram.

In a parallelogram:

(1) The opposite sides are equal.
(2) The opposite angles are equal.
(3) A diagonal divides the parallelogram into two congruent triangles.
(4) The diagonals bisect each other. (A line *bisects* a line segment if it intersects the segment at the midpoint of the segment.)

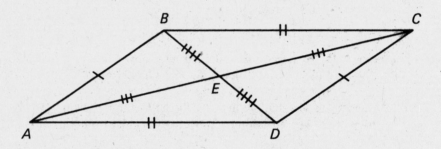

ABCD is a parallelogram.

(1) $AB = DC, BC = AD$.
(2) $\angle BCD = \angle BAD, \angle ABC = \angle ADC$.
(3) $\triangle ABC \cong \triangle ADC, \triangle ABD \cong \triangle CDB$.
(4) $AE = EC$ and $BE = ED$.

If *any* of the statements (1), (2), (3) and (4) are true for a quadrilateral, then the quadrilateral is a parallelogram.

If all of the sides of a parallelogram are equal, the figure is called a *rhombus*.

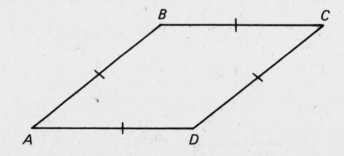

ABCD is a rhombus.

The diagonals of a rhombus are perpendicular.

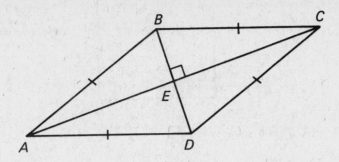

$BD \perp AC;\ \angle BEC = \angle CED = \angle AED = \angle AEB = 90°.$

If all the angles of a parallelogram are right angles, the figure is a *rectangle*.

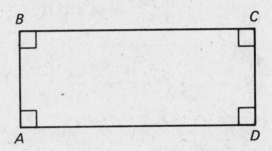

ABCD is a rectangle.

Since the sum of the angles in a quadrilateral is 360°, if *all* the angles of a quadrilateral are equal then the figure is a rectangle. The diagonals of a rectangle are equal. The length of a diagonal can be found by using the Pythagorean Theorem.

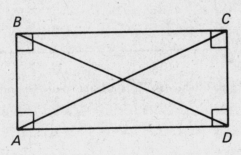

If *ABCD* is a rectangle, $AC = BD$ and $(AC)^2 = (AD)^2 + (DC)^2$.

If all the sides of a rectangle are equal, the figure is a *square*.

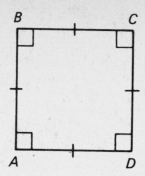

ABCD is a square.

If all the angles of a rhombus are equal, the figure is a square. The length of the diagonal of a square is $\sqrt{2}\,s$ where s is the length of a side.

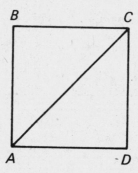

In square *ABCD*, $AC = (\sqrt{2})AD$.

A quadrilateral with two parallel sides and two sides which are not parallel is called a *trapezoid*. The parallel sides are called *bases*, and the non-parallel sides are called *legs*.

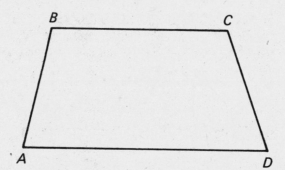

If $BC \parallel AD$ then *ABCD* is a trapezoid; *BC* and *AD* are the bases.

III–6. Circles

A CIRCLE is a figure in a plane consisting of all the points which are the same distance from a fixed point called the *center* of the circle. A line segment from any point on the circle to the center of the circle is called a *radius* (plural: radii) of the circle. All radii of the same circle have the same length.

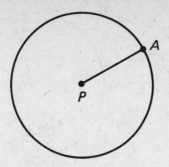

This circle has center *P* and radius *AP*.

A circle is **denoted** by a single letter, usually its center. Two circles with the same center are *concentric*.

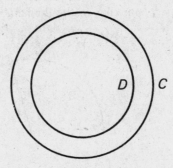

C and *D* are concentric circles.

A line segment whose endpoints are on a circle is called a *chord*. A chord which passes through the center of the circle is a *diameter*. *The length of a diameter is twice the length of a radius.* A diameter divides a circle into two congruent halves which are called *semicircles*.

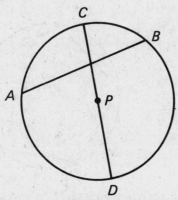

P is the center of the circle.
AB is a chord and *CD* is a diameter.

A diameter which is perpendicular to a chord bisects the chord.

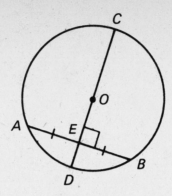

O is the center of this circle and $AB \perp CD$; then $AE = EB$.

If a line intersects a circle at one and only one point, the line is said to be a *tangent* to the circle. The point common to a circle and a tangent to the circle is called the *point of tangency*. The radius from the center to the point of tangency is perpendicular to the tangent.

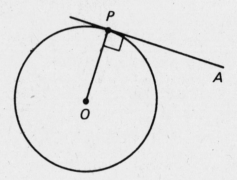

AP is tangent to the circle with center O. P is the point of tangency and $OP \perp PA$.

A polygon is *inscribed* in a circle if all of its vertices are points on the circle.

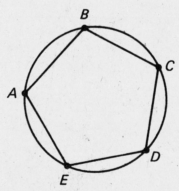

$ABCDE$ is an inscribed pentagon.

An angle whose vertex is a point on a circle and whose sides are chords of the circle is called an *inscribed angle*. An angle whose vertex is the center of a circle and whose sides are radii of the circle is called a *central angle*.

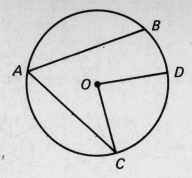

∠*BAC* is an inscribed angle.
∠*DOC* is a central angle.

An *arc* is a part of a circle.

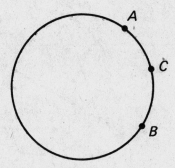

ACB is an arc. Arc *ACB* is written $\overparen{ACB}$.

If two letters are used to denote an arc, they represent the smaller of the two possible arcs. So $\overparen{AB} = \overparen{ACB}$.

An arc can be measured in degrees. The entire circle is 360°; thus an arc of 120° would be ⅓ of a circle.

A central angle is equal in measure to the arc it intercepts.

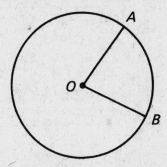

∠*AOB* = $\overparen{AB}$

An inscribed angle is equal in measure to ½ the arc it intercepts.

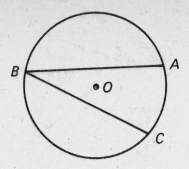

$\angle ABC = \frac{1}{2} \widehat{AC}$.

An angle inscribed in a semicircle is a *right angle*.

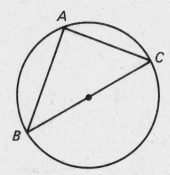

If BC is a diameter, then $\angle BAC$ is inscribed in a semicircle; so $\angle BAC = 90°$.

III–7. Area and Perimeter

7–1

The area A of a square equals s^2, where s is the length of a side of the square. Thus, $A = s^2$.

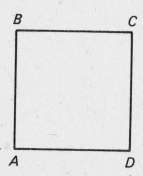

If $AD = 5$ inches, the area of square $ABCD$ is 25 square inches.

The area of a rectangle equals length times width; if L is the length of one side and W is the length of a perpendicular side, then the area $A = LW$.

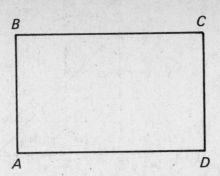

If $AB = 5$ feet and $AD = 8$ feet, then the area of rectangle $ABCD$ is 40 square feet.

The area of a parallelogram is base × height; $A = bh$, where b is the length of a side and h is the length of an altitude to the base.

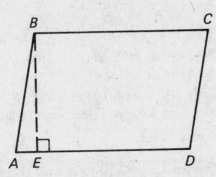

If $AD = 6$ yards and $BE = 4$ yards, then the area of the parallelogram $ABCD$ is $6 \cdot 4$ or 24 square yards.

The area of a trapezoid is the (average of the bases) × height. $A = [(b_1 + b_2)/2]h$ where b_1 and b_2 are the lengths of the parallel sides and h is the length of an altitude to one of the bases.

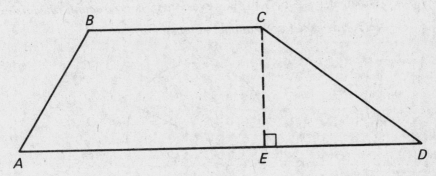

If $BC = 3$ miles, $AD = 7$ miles, and $CE = 2$ miles, then the area of trapezoid $ABCD$ is $[(3 + 7)/2] \cdot 2 = 10$ square miles.

The area of a triangle is $\frac{1}{2}$ (base × height); $A = \frac{1}{2} bh$, where b is the length of a side and h is the length of the altitude to that side.

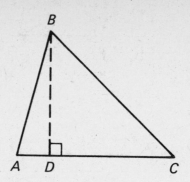

If $AC = 5$ miles and $BD = 4$ miles, then the area of the triangle is $\frac{1}{2} \times 5 \times 4 = 10$ square miles.

Since the legs of a right triangle are perpendicular to each other, the area of a right triangle is one-half the product of the lengths of the legs.

EXAMPLE 1:   If the lengths of the sides of a triangle are 5 feet, 12 feet, and 13 feet, what is the area of the triangle?

Since $5^2 + 12^2 = 25 + 144 = 169 = 13^2$, the triangle is a right triangle and the legs are the sides with lengths 5 feet and 12 feet. Therefore, the area is $\frac{1}{2} \times 5 \times 12 = 30$ square feet.

If we want to find the area of a polygon which is not of a type already mentioned, we break the polygon up into smaller figures such as triangles or rectangles, find the area of each piece, and add these to get the area of the given polygon.

The area of a circle is πr^2 where r is the length of a radius. Since $d = 2r$ where d is the length of a diameter, $A = \pi \left(\frac{d}{2} \right)^2 = \pi \frac{d^2}{4}$. π is a number which is approximately $\frac{22}{7}$ or 3.14; however, there is *no fraction which is exactly equal to π. π is called an irrational number.*

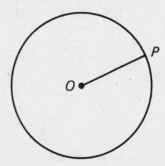

If $OP = 2$ inches, then the area of the circle with center O is $\pi 2^2$ or 4π square inches. The portion of the plane bounded by a circle and a central angle is called a *sector* of the circle.

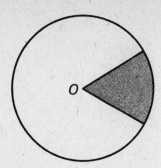

The shaded region is a sector of the circle with center O. The area of a sector with central angle $n°$ in a circle of radius r is $\frac{n}{360}\pi r^2$.

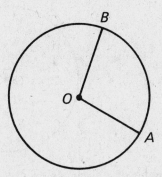

If $OB = 4$ inches and $\angle BOA = 100°$, then the area of the sector is $\frac{100}{360}\pi \cdot 4^2 =$ $\frac{5}{18} \cdot 16\pi = \frac{40}{9}\pi$ square inches.

7–2

The *perimeter* of a polygon is the sum of the lengths of the sides.

EXAMPLE 1: What is the perimeter of a regular pentagon whose sides are 6 inches long?

A pentagon has 5 sides. Since the pentagon is regular, all sides have the same length which is 6 inches. Therefore, the perimeter of the pentagon is 5×6 which equals 30 inches or 2.5 feet.

The *perimeter of a rectangle* is $2(L + W)$ where L is the length and W is the width.
The *perimeter of a square is 4s* where s is the length of a side of the square.

The *perimeter of a circle* is called the *circumference* of the circle. The *circumference of a circle is πd or $2\pi r$*, where d is the length of a diameter and r is the length of a radius.

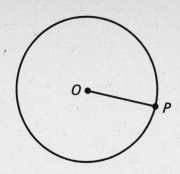

If O is the center of a circle and $OP = 5$ feet, then the circumference of the circle is $2 \times 5\pi$ or 10π feet.

The length of an arc of a circle is $(n/360)\,\pi d$ where the central angle of the arc is $n°$.

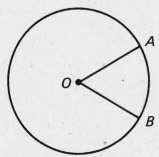

If O is the center of a circle where $OA = 5$ yards and $\angle AOB = 60°$, then the length of arc AB is $\dfrac{60}{360}\pi \times 10 = \dfrac{10}{6}\pi = \dfrac{5}{3}\pi$ yards.

EXAMPLE 2: How far will a wheel of radius 2 feet travel in 500 revolutions? (Assume the wheel does not slip.)

The diameter of the wheel is 4 feet; so the circumference is 4π feet. Therefore, the wheel will travel $500 \times 4\pi$ or $2,000\pi$ feet in 500 revolutions.

III–8. Volume and Surface Area

8–1

The volume of a rectangular prism or box is length times width times height.

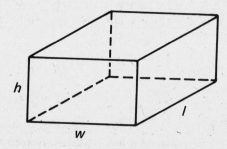

$$V = lwh$$

EXAMPLE 1: What is the volume of a box which is 5 feet long, 4 feet wide, and 6 feet high?

The volume is $5 \times 4 \times 6$ or 120 cubic feet.

If each of the faces of a rectangular prism is a congruent square, then the solid is a *cube*. The volume of a cube is the length of a side (or edge) cubed.

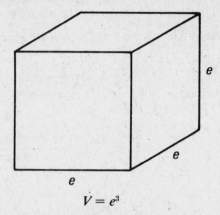

$$V = e^3$$

If the side of a cube is 4 feet long, then the volume of the cube is 4^3 or 64 cubic feet.

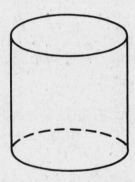

This solid is a circular cylinder. The top and the bottom are congruent circles. Most tin cans are circular cylinders. The volume of a circular cylinder is the product of the area of the circular base and the height.

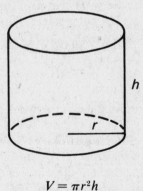

$$V = \pi r^2 h$$

EXAMPLE 2: A circular pipe has a diameter of 10 feet. A gallon of oil has a volume of 2 cubic feet. How many gallons of oil can fit into 50 feet of the pipe?

Think of the 50 feet of pipe as a circular cylinder on its side with a height of 50 feet and a radius of 5 feet. Its volume is $\pi \cdot 5^2 \cdot 50$ or $1,250\pi$ cubic feet. Since a gallon of oil has a volume of 2 cubic feet, 50 feet of pipe will hold $1,250\pi/2$ or 625π gallons of oil.

A *sphere* is the set of points in space equidistant from a fixed point called the center. The length of a segment from any point on the sphere to the center is called the radius of the sphere. *The volume of a sphere of radius r is $\frac{4}{3}\pi r^3$.*

$$V = \frac{4}{3}\pi r^3$$

The volume of a sphere with radius 3 feet is $\frac{4}{3}\pi 3^3 = 36\pi$ cubic feet.

8-2

The surface area of a rectangle prism is $2LW + 2LH + 2WH$ where L is the length, W is the width, and H is the height.

EXAMPLE 1:   If a roll of wallpaper covers 30 square feet, how many rolls are needed to cover the walls of a rectangular room 10 feet long by 8 feet wide by 9 feet high?

We have to cover the surface area of the walls which equals $2(10 \times 9 + 8 \times 9)$ or $2(90 + 72)$ or 324 square feet. (Note that the product omits the area of the floor or the ceiling.) Since a roll covers 30 square feet, we need $\frac{324}{30} = 10\frac{4}{5}$ rolls.

The surface area of a cube is $6e^2$ where e is the length of an edge.

The area of the circular part of a cylinder is called the lateral area. The lateral area of a cylinder is $2\pi rh$. If we unroll the circular part, we get a rectangle whose dimensions are the circumference of the circle and the height of the cylinder. The total surface area is $2\pi rh + 2\pi r^2$.

EXAMPLE 2:   How much tin is needed to make a tin can in the shape of a circular cylinder whose radius is 3 inches and whose height is 5 inches?

The area of both the bottom and top is $\pi \cdot 3^2$ or 9π square inches. The lateral area is $2\pi \cdot 3 \cdot 5$ or 30π square inches. Therefore, we need $9\pi + 9\pi + 30\pi$ or 48π square inches of tin.

III–9. Coordinate Geometry

In coordinate geometry, every point in the plane is associated with an ordered pair of numbers called *coordinates*. Two perpendicular lines are drawn; the horizontal line is called the *x*-axis and the vertical line is called the *y*-axis. The point where the two axes intersect is called the *origin*. Both of the axes are number lines with the origin corresponding to zero (see I–6.) Positive numbers on the *x*-axis are to the right of the origin, negative numbers to the left. Positive numbers on the *y*-axis are above the origin, negative numbers below the origin. The coordinates of a point P are (x,y) if P is located by moving *x* units along the *x*-axis from the origin and then moving *y* units up or down. *The distance along the x-axis is always given first.*

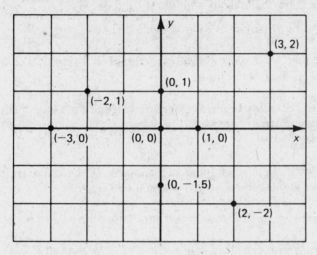

The numbers in parentheses are the coordinates of the point. Thus "$P = (3,2)$" means that the coordinates of P are $(3,2)$. *The distance between the point with coordinates (x,y) and the point with coordinates (a,b) is* $\sqrt{(x-a)^2 + (y-b)^2}$. You should be able to answer most questions by using the distance formula.

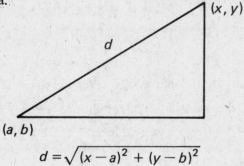

$$d = \sqrt{(x-a)^2 + (y-b)^2}$$

EXAMPLE 1:   Is $ABCD$ a parallelogram? $A = (3,2)$, $B = (1,-2)$, $C = (-2,1)$, $D = (1,5)$.

The length of AB is $\sqrt{(3-1)^2+(2-(-2))^2} = \sqrt{2^2+4^2} = \sqrt{20}$. The length of CD is $\sqrt{(-2-1)^2+(1-5)^2} = \sqrt{(-3)^2+(-4)^2} = \sqrt{25}$. Therefore, $AB \neq CD$, so $ABCD$

cannot be a parallelogram, since in a parallelogram the lengths of opposite sides are equal.

Geometry problems occur frequently in the data sufficiency questions. *If you are not provided with a diagram, draw one for yourself.* Think of any conditions which will help you answer the question; perhaps you can see how to answer a different question which will lead to an answer to the original question. It may help to draw in some diagonals, altitudes, or other auxiliary lines in your diagram.

IV. Tables and Graphs

IV-1. Tables

General Hints. You *must* know how to interpret tables and graphs to score well on the Mathematics part of the test. In some recent tests, about half of the questions in the sections on mathematics have dealt with charts and graphs.

(A) Make sure to look at the *entire* table or graph.

(B) Figure out what *units* the table or graph is using. Make sure to express your answer in the correct units.

(C) Look at the possible answers before calculating. Since many questions only call for an approximate answer, it may be possible to round off (see I–5) saving time and effort.

(D) Don't confuse decimals and percentages. If the units are percentages, then an entry of .2 means .2% which is equal to .002.

(E) In inference questions, only the information given can be used.

(F) See if the answer makes sense.

EXAMPLE: (Refer to the table on page 217.)

1. Ⓐ Ⓑ Ⓒ Ⓓ Ⓔ 1. What percent of the babies born in the U.S. in 1947 died before the age of 1 year?

(A) 3.22   (D) 32.2
(B) 4.7   (E) 47
(C) 26.7

To find a percentage, use the information given in the rate columns. The rate is given *per thousand*. In 1947 the rate was 32.2 per thousand which is $\frac{32.2}{1000} = .0322$ or 3.22%. So the correct answer is (A). If you assumed incorrectly that the rate was per hundred, you would get the incorrect answer (D); if you looked in the wrong column you might get (B) or (E) as your answer.

2. Ⓐ Ⓑ Ⓒ Ⓓ Ⓔ 2. Which state had the most infant deaths in 1940?

(A) California   (D) Pennsylvania
(B) New Mexico   (E) Texas
(C) New York

INFANT DEATHS (UNDER 1 YEAR OF AGE) AND RATES PER 1,000 LIVE BIRTHS, BY STATES: 1940 TO 1950

STATE	NUMBER OF INFANT DEATHS					RATE PER 1,000 LIVE BIRTHS				
	1940	1947	1948	1949	1950	1940	1947	1948	1949	1950
United States	110,984	119,173	113,169	111,531	103,825	47.0	32.2	32.0	31.3	29.2
Alabama	3,870	3,301	3,228	3,345	3,044	61.5	37.5	37.8	39.6	36.8
Arizona	983	973	1,083	1,034	953	85.5	50.8	56.4	51.0	45.8
Arkansas	1,810	1,445	1,363	1,539	1,209	47.0	29.5	28.4	33.7	26.5
California	4,403	7,233	6,885	6,574	6,115	39.2	29.4	28.6	26.8	25.0
Colorado	1,270	1,234	1,267	1,153	1,167	60.4	37.5	38.4	35.1	34.4
Connecticut	868	1,150	1,026	943	886	34.0	25.2	24.3	23.1	21.8
Delaware	217	239	214	224	235	47.7	31.0	29.5	30.4	30.7
District of Columbia	554	691	531	576	603	49.3	31.9	25.5	29.1	30.4
Florida	1,818	2,285	2,103	2,088	2,078	53.8	38.2	35.3	33.8	32.1
Georgia	3,744	3,251	3,169	3,101	3,064	57.8	34.2	34.2	33.3	33.5
Idaho	506	478	481	431	434	42.9	29.4	29.8	27.0	27.1
Illinois	4,398	5,672	5,123	5,195	4,868	35.3	28.9	27.7	27.4	25.6
Indiana	2,595	2,949	2,760	2,746	2,520	42.1	30.6	29.8	29.1	27.0
Iowa	1,636	1,817	1,610	1,591	1,555	36.5	28.5	26.6	25.7	24.8
Kansas	1,106	1,251	1,151	1,136	1,130	38.3	28.1	26.9	25.9	25.7
Kentucky	3,387	2,971	3,073	3,139	2,616	53.1	37.1	39.8	41.2	34.9
Louisiana	3,268	2,773	2,779	2,810	2,639	64.3	37.2	37.9	37.2	34.6
Maine	810	853	706	713	650	53.2	35.7	32.0	32.5	30.9
Maryland	1,590	1,794	1,537	1,636	1,465	49.1	31.6	28.8	30.5	27.0
Massachusetts	2,458	3,027	2,613	2,347	2,240	37.5	28.1	26.8	24.5	23.3
Michigan	4,032	5,080	4,639	4,545	4,230	40.7	31.5	30.0	28.9	26.3
Minnesota	1,758	2,165	1,959	1,893	1,889	33.2	28.6	26.9	25.6	25.1
Mississippi	2,869	2,448	2,474	2,631	2,385	54.4	36.8	37.9	39.6	36.7
Missouri	2,885	2,929	2,585	2,563	2,510	46.9	32.5	30.3	30.0	29.2
Montana	537	484	461	457	441	46.5	32.1	30.7	29.7	28.2
Nebraska	792	894	835	761	796	36.0	27.8	26.8	24.1	25.0
Nevada	109	134	147	118	139	51.7	33.2	39.8	32.1	37.9
New Hampshire	341	399	361	333	282	40.9	30.1	29.1	27.9	24.5
New Jersey	2,121	2,965	2,585	2,534	2,467	35.5	27.9	26.5	26.0	25.2
New Mexico	1,488	1,379	1,438	1,408	1,211	100.6	67.9	70.1	65.1	54.8
New York	7,297	9,123	8,258	7,878	7,429	37.2	28.2	27.3	26.1	24.7
North Carolina	4,631	3,938	3,858	4,113	3,674	57.6	34.9	35.3	38.1	34.5
North Dakota	593	523	487	517	453	45.1	30.6	29.4	30.7	26.6
Ohio	4,744	5,817	5,693	5,315	4,990	41.4	29.5	30.5	28.1	26.8
Oklahoma	2,238	1,733	1,731	1,531	1,514	49.9	32.3	34.4	30.8	30.2
Oregon	585	895	897	869	812	33.2	24.7	25.5	24.6	22.5
Pennsylvania	7,404	7,741	6,442	6,567	6,126	44.7	31.1	28.4	29.2	27.6
Rhode Island	410	522	444	395	450	37.9	28.2	26.3	24.0	27.8
South Carolina	3,042	2,352	2,331	2,283	2,220	68.2	39.5	40.4	39.0	38.6
South Dakota	466	511	525	448	473	38.7	30.9	32.0	26.0	26.6
Tennessee	2,954	3,144	3,098	3,331	2,961	53.5	36.3	37.7	40.2	36.4
Texas	8,675	8,161	9,131	8,628	7,630	68.3	41.1	46.2	42.7	37.4
Utah	539	545	568	535	503	40.4	25.1	27.4	25.3	23.7
Vermont	309	303	271	301	221	44.5	31.2	28.9	32.4	24.5
Virginia	3,335	3,142	3,163	3,162	2,836	58.5	36.6	38.5	38.1	34.6
Washington	992	1,643	1,537	1,530	1,522	35.2	28.1	27.5	27.1	27.3
West Virginia	2,269	2,091	2,108	2,082	1,822	53.7	38.0	40.2	39.6	36.1
Wisconsin	2,046	2,476	2,148	2,202	2,121	37.3	29.5	26.3	26.5	25.7
Wyoming	232	249	293	280	247	44.7	34.0	39.5	37.4	32.5

Source: Department of Health, Education, and Welfare, Public Health Service, National Office of Vital Statistics; annual report, *Vital Statistics of the United States.*

Source: Statistical Abstract of the U.S. 1957

Look in the numbers column under 1940. Only Texas had more than 8,000 in 1940, so the correct answer is (E). New Mexico had a *higher rate*, but the question asked for the *highest amount. Make sure you answer the question which is asked.*

3. Ⓐ Ⓑ Ⓒ Ⓓ Ⓔ   3. Which of the following statements can be inferred from the table?

    I. In 1950 less than $\frac{1}{20}$ of the babies born in the U.S. died before the age of 1 year.
    II. The number of infant deaths in the U.S. decreased from 1945 to 1950.
    III. More than 5% of the infant deaths in the U.S. in 1950 occurred in California.
    IV. The number of infant deaths in North America in 1950 was less than 150,000.

    (A) I only
    (B) II only
    (C) I and III only
    (D) I, III, IV only
    (E) I, II, III, IV

Analysis:

Statement I can be inferred since $\frac{1}{20}$ of $1,000 = 50$ which exceeds the rate per thousand of 29.2 in 1950.

Statement II can't be inferred since the table has no information about 1945. Infant deaths decreased between 1940 and 1950, but that doesn't mean they decreased between 1945 and 1950.

Statement III can be inferred from the table. The total number of infant deaths in 1950 was 103,825, and 6,115 occurred in California. A calculation of 6,115/103,825 could be made, but it is much quicker to find 5% of 103,825 which is 5,191. Since 6,115 is greater than 5,191, more than 5% of the infant deaths in the U.S. occurred in California.

Statement IV can't be inferred, because the table only gives information about the U.S. and there are other countries in North America.

So the correct answer is (C).

IV–2. Circle Graphs

CIRCLE GRAPHS are used to show how various sectors share in the whole. Circle graphs are sometimes called pie charts. Circle graphs usually give the percentage that each sector receives.

EXAMPLE: (Refer to the graph on page 219.)

4. Ⓐ Ⓑ Ⓒ Ⓓ Ⓔ   1. The amount spent on materials in 1960 was 120% of the amount spent on

    (A) research in 1960
    (B) compensation in 1960
    (C) advertising in 1970
    (D) materials in 1970
    (E) legal affairs in 1960

When using circle graphs to find ratios of various sectors, don't find the amounts each sector received and then the ratio of the amounts. Find the *ratio of the percentages,*

Expenditures of General Industries
By major categories

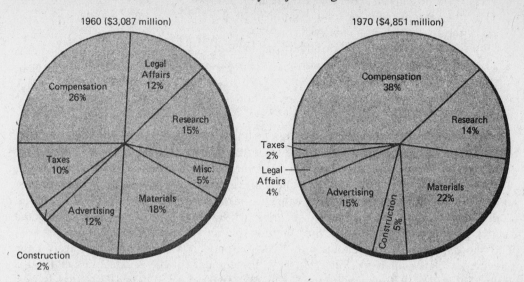

1960 ($3,087 million)   1970 ($4,851 million)

which is much quicker. In 1960, 18% of the expenditures were for materials. We want *x* where 120% of *x* = 18%; so *x* = 15%. Any category which received 15% of 1960 expenditures gives the correct answer, but only one of the five choices is correct. Here, the answer is (A) since research received 15% of the expenditure in 1960. Check the 1960 answers first since you need look only at the percentages, which can be done quickly. Notice that (C) is incorrect, since 15% of the expenditures for 1970 is different from 15% of the expenditures for 1960.

2. The fraction of the total expenditures for 1960 and 1970 spent on compensation was about
    2. Ⓐ Ⓑ Ⓒ Ⓓ Ⓔ

   (A) $\frac{1}{5}$ (D) $\frac{3}{7}$

   (B) $\frac{1}{4}$ (E) $\frac{1}{2}$

   (C) $\frac{1}{3}$

In 1960, 26% of $3,087 million was spent on compensation and in 1970 compensation received 38% of $4,851 million. The total expenditures for 1960 and 1970 are $(3,087 + 4,851) million. So the exact answer is $[(.26)(3,087) + (.38)(4,851)]/(3,087 + 4,851)$. Actually calculating the answer, you will waste a lot of time. Look at the answers and think for a second.

We are taking a weighted average of 26% and 38%. To find a weighted average, we multiply each value by a weight and divide by the total of all the weights. Here 26% is given a weight of 3,087 and 38% a weight of 4,851. The following general rule is often useful in average problems: The average or weighted average of a collection of values can *never* be:

  (1) less than the smallest value in the collection, or
  (2) greater than the largest value in the collection.

Therefore, the answer to the question must be greater than or equal to 26% and less than or equal to 38%.

Since $\frac{1}{5}$ = 20% and $\frac{1}{4}$ = 25%, which are both less than 26%, neither (A) nor (B) can be the correct answer. Since $\frac{3}{7} = 42\frac{6}{7}$% and $\frac{1}{2}$ = 50%, which are both greater than 38%, neither (D) nor (E) can be correct. Therefore, by elimination (C) is the correct answer.

3. Ⓐ Ⓑ Ⓒ Ⓓ Ⓔ   **3.** The amount spent in 1960 for materials, advertising, and taxes was about the same as

    (A) $\frac{5}{4}$ of the amount spent for compensation in 1960
    (B)   the amount spent for compensation in 1970
    (C)   the amount spent on materials in 1970
    (D) $\frac{5}{3}$ of the amount spent on advertising in 1970
    (E)   the amount spent on research and construction in 1970

First calculate the combined percentage for materials, advertising, and taxes in 1960. Since $18\% + 12\% + 10\% = 40\%$, these three categories accounted for 40% of the expenditures in 1960. You can check the one answer which involves 1960 now. Since $\frac{5}{4}$ of 26% = 32.5%, (A) is incorrect. To check the answers which involve 1970, you must know the amount spent on the three categories above in 1960. 40% of 3,087 is 1234.8; so the amount spent on the three categories in 1960 was $1,234.8 million. You could calculate the amount spent in each of the possible answers, but there is a quicker way. Find the *approximate* percentage that 1,234.8 is of 4,851, and check this against the percentages of the answers. Since $\frac{12}{48} = \frac{1}{4}$, the amount for the 3 categories in 1960 is about 25% of the 1970 expenditures. Compensation received 38% of 1970 expenditures, so (B) is incorrect. Materials received 22% and research and construction together received 19%; since advertising received 15%, $\frac{5}{3}$ of the amount for advertising yields 25%. So (D) is probably correct. You can check by calculating 22% of 4,851 which is 1,067.22, while 25% of $4,851 = 1,212.75$. Therefore, (D) is correct.

In inference questions involving circle graphs, *do not compare different percentages.* Note in question 3 that the percentage of expenditures in 1960 for the three categories (40%) is *not equal* to 40% of the expenditures in 1970.

IV–3.   Line Graphs

LINE GRAPHS are used to show how a quantity changes continuously. Very often the quantity is measured as time changes. If the line goes up, the quantity is increasing; if the line goes down, the quantity is decreasing; if the line is horizontal, the quantity is not changing. To measure the height of a point on the graph, use your pencil or a piece of paper (for example, the admission card to the exam) as a straight edge.

EXAMPLE: (Refer to the graph on page 221.)

1. Ⓐ Ⓑ Ⓒ Ⓓ Ⓔ   **1.** The ratio of productivity in 1967 to productivity in 1940 was about

    (A)   1:4   (D)   4:1
    (B)   1:3   (E)   9:1
    (C)   3:1

In 1967 productivity had an index number of 400, and the index numbers are based on 1940 = 100. So the ratio is 400:100 = 4:1. Therefore, the answer is (D). [If you used (incorrectly) output or employment (instead of productivity) you would get the wrong answer (E) or (C); if you confused the order of the ratio you would have incorrectly answered (A).]

TRENDS IN INDUSTRIAL INVESTMENT, LABOUR PRODUCTIVITY, EMPLOYMENT AND OUTPUT, 1940 TO 1967

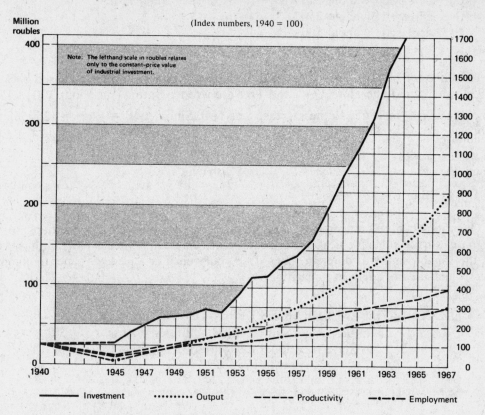

(Index numbers, 1940 = 100)

Note: The lefthand scale in roubles relates only to the constant-price value of industrial investment.

—— Investment   ·········· Output   ----- Productivity   —·—·— Employment

Source: United Nations Economics Bulletin for Europe

2. If 1 rouble = \$3, then the constant-price value of industrial investment in 1959 was about   2. Ⓐ Ⓑ Ⓒ Ⓓ Ⓔ

 (A) \$1.9 million
 (B) \$200 million
 (C) \$420,000,000
 (D) \$570,000,000
 (E) \$570,000 million

In 1959, the value was about 190 million roubles. (It was a little below 200 million.) The answers are all in dollars, so multiply 190 by 3 to get \$570 million or \$570,000,000 (D). If you are not careful about units, you may answer (B) or (E), which are incorrect.

3. Employment was at its minimum during the years shown in   3. Ⓐ Ⓑ Ⓒ Ⓓ Ⓔ

 (A) 1940
 (B) 1943
 (C) 1945

 (D) 1953
 (E) 1967

The minimum of a quantity displayed on a line graph is the lowest place on the line. Thus in 1945, (C), the minimum value of employment was reached.

4. Ⓐ Ⓑ Ⓒ Ⓓ Ⓔ   **4.**   Between 1954 and 1965, output

      (A)   decreased by about 10%
      (B)   stayed about the same
      (C)   increased by about 200%
      (D)   increased by about 250%
      (E)   increased by about 500%

The line for output goes up between 1954 and 1965, so output increased between 1954 and 1965. Therefore, (A) and (B) are wrong. Output was about 200 in 1954 and about 700 in 1965, so the increase was 500. Since $\frac{500}{200} = 2.5 = 250\%$, the correct answer is (D).

IV–4.   Bar Graphs

Quantities can be compared by the height or length of a bar in a bar graph. A bar graph can have either vertical or horizontal bars. You can compare different quantities or the same quantity at different times. Use your pencil or a piece of paper to compare bars which are not adjacent to each other.

DISABILITY BENEFICIARIES REPORTED AS REHABILITATED:
Number, as percent of all rehabilitated clients
of State vocational rehabilitation agencies,
Years 1955–1971

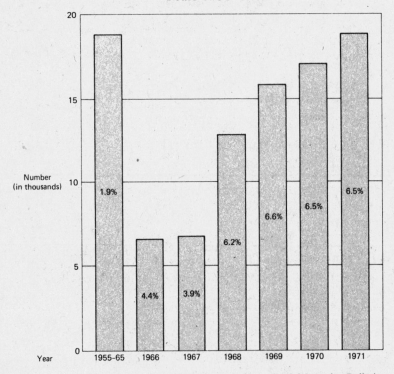

Source: Social Security Bulletin

EXAMPLE: (Refer to the graph on page 222.)

1. Between 1967 and 1971, the largest number of disability beneficiaries were reported as rehabilitated in the year   1. Ⓐ Ⓑ Ⓒ Ⓓ Ⓔ

   (A) 1967
   (B) 1968
   (C) 1969

   (D) 1970
   (E) 1971

The answer is (E) since the highest bar is the bar for 1971. The percentage of disability beneficiaries out of all rehabilitated clients was higher in 1969, but the *number* was lower.

2. Between 1955 and 1965, about how many clients were rehabilitated by State vocational rehabilitation agencies?   2. Ⓐ Ⓑ Ⓒ Ⓓ Ⓔ

   (A) 90,000
   (B) 400,000
   (C) 1,000,000

   (D) 1,900,000
   (E) 10,000,000

1.9% of those rehabilitated were disability beneficiaries, and there were about 19,000 disability beneficiaries rehabilitated. So if T is the total number rehabilitated, then 1.9% of $T = 19,000$ or $.019T = 19,000$. Thus, $T = 19,000/.019 = 1,000,000$ and the answer is (C).

IV-5. Cumulative Graphs

You can compare several categories by a graph of the cumulative type. These are usually bar or line graphs where the height of the bar or line is divided up proportionately among different quantities.

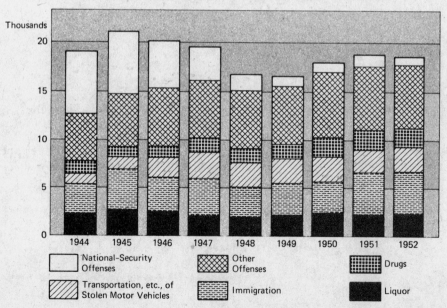

FEDERAL PRISONERS RECEIVED FROM THE COURTS, BY MAJOR OFFENSE GROUPS: Years 1944–1952

Source: Statistical Abstract of the U.S. 1953

1. Ⓐ Ⓑ Ⓒ Ⓓ Ⓔ **1.** In 1946, roughly what percent of the federal prisoners received from the courts were national-security offenders?

(A) 15
(B) 20
(C) 25

(D) 30
(E) 35

The total number of prisoners in 1946 was about 20,000, and national security offenders accounted for the part of the graph from just above 15,000 to just above 20,000. Therefore, there were about 20,000 − 15,000 = 5,000 prisoners convicted of national-security offenses. Since 5,000/20,000 = $\frac{1}{4}$ = 25%, the correct answer is (C).

2. Ⓐ Ⓑ Ⓒ Ⓓ Ⓔ **2.** Of the combined total for the four years 1947 through 1950, the largest number of offenders were in the category

(A) national-security offenses
(B) other offenses
(C) drugs

(D) immigration
(E) liquor

The correct answer is (B). Since other offenses had the most offenders in each year, that category must have the largest total number of offenders. [If you answered this question for the years 1944–1946, then (A) would be correct.]

3. Ⓐ Ⓑ Ⓒ Ⓓ Ⓔ **3.** Which of the following statements can be inferred from the graph?

I.   The number of federal prisoners received from the courts decreased each year from 1946 to 1948.
II. More than 40% of the prisoners between 1944 and 1952 came from the other offenses category.
III. 2% of the federal prisoners received in 1952 were convicted on heroin charges.

(A) I only
(B) III only
(C) I and II only

(D) I and III only
(E) I, II, and III

Statement I is true, since the height of the bar for each year was lower than the height of the bar for the previous year in 1946, 1947, and 1948.

Statement II is not true. For most of the years, other offenses accounted for about 25–30%, and it never was more than 40% in any year. Therefore, it could not account for more than 40% of the total.

Statement III can not be inferred. There is a category of drug offenders, but there is no information about specific drugs.

So, the correct answer is (A).

REVIEW OF FORMULAS

(Numbers next to the formulas refer to the section of the Math Review where the formula is discussed.)

Interest = Amount × Time × Rate	I–4
Discount = Cost × Rate of Discount	I–4
Price = Cost × (100% − Rate of Discount)	I–4
$x = \dfrac{1}{2a}\left[-b \pm \sqrt{b^2 - 4ac}\right]$ (quadratic formula)	II–2
Distance = Speed × Time	II–3
$a^2 + b^2 = c^2$ when a and b are the legs and c is the hypotenuse of a right triangle (Pythagorean Theorem)	III–4
Diameter of a circle = 2 × Radius	III–6
Area of a square = s^2	III–7
Area of a rectangle = LW	III–7
Area of a triangle = $\frac{1}{2} bh$	III–7
Area of a circle = πr^2	III–7
Area of a parallelogram = bh	III–7
Area of a trapezoid = $\frac{1}{2}(b_1 + b_2)h$	III–7
Circumference of a circle = πd	III–7
Perimeter of a square = $4s$	III–7
Perimeter of a rectangle = $2(L + W)$	III–7
Volume of a box = lwh	III–8
Volume of a cube = e^3	III–8
Volume of a cylinder = $\pi r^2 h$	III–8
Volume of a sphere = $\frac{4}{3} \pi r^3$	III–8
Surface area of a box = $2LW + 2LH + 2WH$	III–8
Surface area of a cube = $6e^2$	III–8
Surface area of a cylinder = $2\pi rh + 2\pi r^2$	III–8
Distance between points (x,y) and (a,b) is $\sqrt{(x - a)^2 + (y - b)^2}$	III–9

Hints for Answering Mathematics Questions

1. Make sure you answer the question you are asked to answer.

2. Look at the answers before you start to work out a problem; you can save a lot of time.

3. Don't waste time on superfluous computations.

4. *Estimate* whenever you can to save time.

5. Budget your time so you can try all the questions. (Bring a watch.)

6. You probably won't be able to answer all the questions; don't waste time worrying about it.

7. Do all the problems you know how to work *before* you start to think about those that you can't answer in a minute or two.

8. If you skip a question, make sure you skip that number on the answer sheet.

9. Don't make extra assumptions on inference questions (see the Logic Review section).

10. Work efficiently; don't waste time worrying during the test.

11. Make sure you express your answer in the units asked for.

12. On data sufficiency questions, don't do any more work than is necessary. (Don't solve the problem; you only have to know that the problem can be solved.)

Further Practice Exercises

The four exercises that follow will give you an indication of your ability to handle these mathematics questions. The time for each exercise is 30 minutes. Scoring for each of the exercises may be interpreted as follows:

> 20–25—SUPERIOR
> 16–19—ABOVE AVERAGE
> 11–15—AVERAGE
> 7–10—BELOW AVERAGE
> 0– 6—UNSATISFACTORY

Your score should be determined by counting the number of correct answers minus ¼ the number of incorrect answers.

MATHEMATICS
EXERCISE **A**

1. In 1955, it cost $12 to purchase one hundred pounds of potatoes. In 1975, it cost $34 to purchase one hundred pounds of potatoes. The price of one hundred pounds of potatoes increased X dollars between 1955 and 1975 with X equal to:

   (A) 1.20   (B) 2.20   (C) 3.40   (D) 22   (E) 34

2. A house cost Ms. Jones C dollars in 1965. Three years later she sold the house for 25% more than she paid for it. She has to pay a tax of 50% of the gain. (The gain is the selling price minus the cost.) How much tax must Ms. Jones pay?

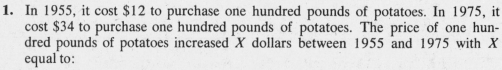

   (A) $\frac{1}{24}C$ (B) $\frac{C}{8}$ (C) $\frac{1}{4}C$ (D) $\frac{C}{2}$ (E) .6C

3. If the length of a rectangle is increased by 20%, and the width of the same rectangle is decreased by 20%, then the area of the rectangle

   (A) decreases by 20%   (B) decreases by 4%   (C) is unchanged   (D) increases by 20%   (E) increases by 40%

Use the following graph for questions 4-7.

Worldwide Military Expenditures

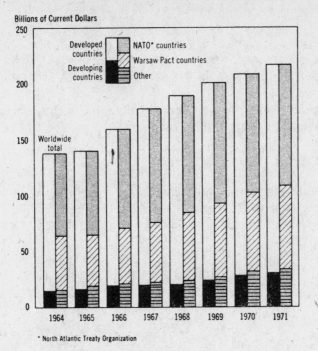

* North Atlantic Treaty Organization

Source: *Pocket Data Book U.S.A. 1973.*

4. Between 1964 and 1969, worldwide military expenditures

   (A) increased by about 50%   (B) roughly doubled   (C) increased by about 150%   (D) almost tripled   (E) increased by 10%

5. The average yearly military expenditure by the developing countries between 1964 and 1971 was approximately how many billions of current dollars?

   (A) 20   (B) 50   (C) 100   (D) 140   (E) 175

6. Which of the following statements can be inferred from the graph?
   I. The NATO countries have higher incomes than the Warsaw Pact countries.

   II. Worldwide military expenditures have increased each year between 1964 and 1971.

   III. In 1972 worldwide military expenditures were more than 230 billion current dollars.

   (A) I only   (B) II only   (C) I and II only   (D) II and III only   (E) I, II, and III

7. A speaker claims that the NATO countries customarily spend ⅓ of their combined incomes on military expenditures. According to the speaker, the combined incomes of the NATO countries (in billions of current dollars) in 1971 was about

   (A) 100   (B) 200   (C) 250   (D) 350   (E) 500

8. 8% of the people eligible to vote are between 18 and 21. In an election 85% of those eligible to vote who were between 18 and 21 actually voted. In that election, people between 18 and 21 who actually voted were what per cent of those people eligible to vote?
(A) 4.2   (B) 6.4   (C) 6.8   (D) 8   (E) 8.5

9. If n and p are both odd numbers, which of the following numbers *must* be an even number?
(A) $n + p$ (B) np (C) $np + 2$ (D) $n + p + 1$ (E) $2n + p$

10. It costs g cents a mile for gasoline and m cents a mile for all other costs to run a car. How many *dollars* will it cost to run the car for 100 miles?
(A) $\dfrac{g + m}{100}$ (B) $100g + 100m$ (C) $g + m$ (D) $g + .1m$ (E) g

11. What is the length of the line segment which connects A to B?
(A) $\sqrt{3}$ (B) 2   (C) $2\sqrt{2}$ (D) 4
(E) 8

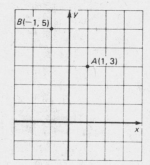

12. A cab driver's income consists of his salary and tips. His salary is $50 a week. During one week his tips were $\dfrac{5}{4}$ of his salary. What fraction of his income for the week came from tips?
(A) $\dfrac{4}{9}$ (B) $\dfrac{1}{2}$ (C) $\dfrac{5}{9}$ (D) $\dfrac{5}{8}$ (E) $\dfrac{5}{4}$

Use the table below for questions 13–17.

INCOME (IN DOLLARS)	TAX (IN DOLLARS)
0– 4,000	1% of income
4,000– 6,000	40 + 2 % of income over 4,000
6,000– 8,000	80 + 3% of income over 6,000
8,000–10,000	140 + 4% of income over 8,000
10,000–15,000	220 + 5% of income over 10,000
15,000–25,000	470 + 6% of income over 15,000
25,000–50,000	1,070 + 7% of income over 25,000

13. How much tax is due on an income of $7,500?
(A) $75   (B) $80   (C) $125   (D) $150   (E) $225

14. Your income for a year is $26,000. You receive a raise so that next year your income will be $29,000. How much *more* will you pay in taxes next year if the tax rate remains the same?
(A) $70   (B) $180   (C) $200   (D) $210   (E) $700

15. Joan paid $100 tax. If X was her income, which of the following statements is true?
(A) $0 < X < 4,000$ (B) $4,000 < X < 6,000$ (C) $6,000 < X < 8,000$
(D) $8,000 < X < 10,000$ (E) $10,000 < X < 15,000$

16. The town of Zenith has a population of 50,000. The average income of a person who lives in Zenith is $3,700 per year. What is the total amount paid in taxes by the people of Zenith? Assume each person pays tax on $3,700.
(A) $37 (B) $3700 (C) $50,000 (D) $185,000 (E) $1,850,000

17. A person who has an income of $10,000 pays what percent (to the nearest percent) of his or her income in taxes?
(A) 1 (B) 2 (C) 3 (D) 4 (E) 5

18. Given that x and y are real numbers, let $S(x,y) = x^2 - y^2$. Then $S(3, S(3,4)) =$
(A) -40 (B) -7 (C) 40 (D) 49 (E) 56

19. Eggs cost 90¢ a dozen. Peppers cost 20¢ each. An omelet consists of 3 eggs and ¼ of a pepper. How much will the ingredients for 8 omelets cost?
(A) $.90 (B) $1.30 (C) $1.80 (D) $2.20 (E) $2.70

20. It is 185 miles from Binghamton to New York City. If a bus takes 2 hours to travel the first 85 miles, how long must the bus take to travel the final 100 miles in order to average 50 miles an hour for the entire trip?
(A) 60 min. (B) 75 min. (C) 94 min. (D) 102 min. (E) 112 min.

21. What is the area of the figure below?
$ABDC$ is a rectangle and BDE is an isoceles right triangle.

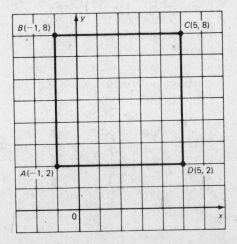

(A) ab (B) ab^2 (C) $b\left(a + \dfrac{b}{2}\right)$

(D) cab (E) $\dfrac{1}{2}bc$

22. If $2x + y = 5$ then $4x + 2y$ is equal to
(A) 5 (B) 8 (C) 9 (D) 10 (E) none of these

23. In 1967, a new sedan cost $2,500; in 1975, the same type of sedan cost $4,800. The cost of that type of sedan has increased by what percent between 1967 and 1975?
(A) 48 (B) 52 (C) 92 (D) 152 (E) 192

24. What is the area of the square $ABCD$?
(A) 10 (B) 18 (C) 24 (D) 36
(E) 48

25. If $x + y = 6$ and $3x - y = 4$, then $x - y$ is equal to
(A) −1   (B) 0   (C) 2   (D) 4   (E) 6

MATHEMATICS
EXERCISE **B**

Use the graphs below for questions 1–5.

Women in the Labor Force

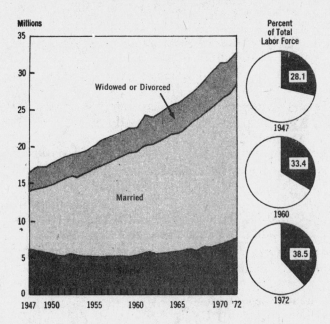

Source: *Pocket Data Book U.S.A. 1973. Bureau of the Census.*

1. The total labor force in 1960 was about y million with y equal to about
(A) 22   (B) 65   (C) 75   (D) 80   (E) 85

2. In 1947, the percentage of women in the labor force who were married was about
(A) 28   (B) 33   (C) 38   (D) 50   (E) 65

3. What was the first year when more than 20 million women were in the labor force?
(A) 1950   (B) 1953   (C) 1956   (D) 1958   (E) 1964

4. Between 1947 and 1972, the number of women in the labor force
(A) increased by about 50%   (B) increased by about 100%   (C) increased by about 150%   (D) increased by about 200%   (E) increased by about 250%

5. Which of the following statements about the labor force can be inferred from the graphs?
  I.   Between 1947 and 1957, there were no years when more than 5 million widowed or divorced women were in the labor force.
  II.   In every year between 1947 and 1972, the number of single women in the labor force has increased.
  III. In 1965, women made up more than ⅓ of the total labor force.
  (A) I only   (B) II only   (C) I and II only   (D) I and III only   (E) I, II, and III

6. If $\dfrac{x}{y} = \dfrac{2}{3}$ then $\dfrac{y^2}{x^2}$ is equal to

(A) $\dfrac{4}{9}$ (B) $\dfrac{2}{3}$ (C) $\dfrac{3}{2}$ (D) $\dfrac{9}{4}$ (E) $\dfrac{5}{2}$

7. In the figure, BD is perpendicular to AC. BA and BC have length a. What is the area of the triangle ABC?

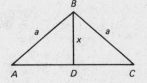

(A) $2x\sqrt{a^2 - x^2}$ (B) $x\sqrt{a^2 - x^2}$
(C) $a\sqrt{a^2 - x^2}$ (D) $2a\sqrt{x^2 - a^2}$
(E) $x\sqrt{x^2 - a^2}$

8. If two places are one inch apart on a map, then they are actually 160 miles apart. (The scale on the map is one inch equals 160 miles.) If Seton is 2⅞ inches from Monroe on the map, how many miles is it from Seton to Monroe?

(A) 3   (B) 27   (C) 300   (D) 360   (E) 460

9. In the accompanying diagram $ABCD$ is a rectangle. The area of isosceles right triangle $ABE = 7$, and $EC = 3(BE)$. The area of ABCD is

(A) 21   (B) 28
(C) 42   (D) 56
(E) 84

10. An automobile tire has two punctures. The first puncture by itself would make the tire flat in 9 minutes. The second puncture by itself would make the tire flat in 6 minutes. How long will it take for both punctures together to make the tire flat? (Assume the air leaks out at a constant rate.)

(A) $3\dfrac{3}{5}$ minutes   (B) 4 minutes   (C) $5\dfrac{1}{4}$ minutes   (D) $7\dfrac{1}{2}$ minutes

(E) 15 minutes

11. If n^3 is odd, which of the following statements are true?
    I. n is odd.
    II. n^2 is odd.
    III. n^2 is even.

(A) I only   (B) II only   (C) III only   (D) I and II only

(E) I and III only

Use the table below for questions 12–15.

Participation in National Elections

Persons in millions. Civilian noninstitutional population as of Nov. 1. Based on post-election surveys of persons reporting whether or not they voted; differs from table 103 data which are based on actual vote counts.

Characteristic	1964 Persons of voting age	1964 Percent voted	1968 Persons of voting age	1968 Percent voted	1972 Persons of voting age	1972 Percent voted
Total	111	69	117	68	136	63
Male	52	72	54	70	64	64
Female	58	67	62	66	72	62
White	99	71	105	69	121	64
Negro and other	11	57	12	56	15	51
Negro	10	58	11	58	13	52
Region:						
North and West	78	75	82	71	94	66
South	32	57	35	60	43	55
Age:						
18–24 years	10	51	12	50	25	50
25–44 years	45	69	46	67	49	63
45–64 years	38	76	40	75	42	71
65 years and over	17	66	18	66	20	63

Source: U.S. Bureau of the Census.

12. Which of the following groups had the highest percentage of voters in 1968?
(A) 18–24 years   (B) Female   (C) South   (D) 25–44 years   (E) Male

13. In 1972, what percent (to the nearest percent) of persons of voting age were female?
(A) 52   (B) 53   (C) 62   (D) 64   (E) 72

14. In 1968, how many males of voting age voted?
(A) 37,440,000   (B) 37,800,000   (C) 42,160,000   (D) 62,000,000
(E) 374,400,000

15. Let X be the number (in millions) of persons of voting age in the range 25–44 years who lived in the North and West in 1964. Which of the following includes all possible values and only possible values of X?
(A) $0 \leq X \leq 45$ (B) $13 \leq X \leq 45$ (C) $13 \leq X \leq 78$ (D) $45 \leq X \leq 78$ (E) $75 \leq X \leq 78$

16. There are 50 students enrolled in Business 100. Of the enrolled students, 90% took the final exam. Two-thirds of the students who took the final exam passed the final exam. How many students passed the final exam?
(A) 30   (B) 33   (C) 34   (D) 35   (E) 45

17. If a is less than b, which of the following numbers is greater than a and less than b?
(A) $(a+b)/2$ (B) $(ab)/2$ (C) $b^2 - a^2$ (D) ab (E) $b - a$

18. In the figure, OR and PR are radii of circles. The length of OP is 4. If $OR = 2$, what is PR? PR is tangent to the circle with center O.

(A) 2   (B) $\dfrac{5}{2}$ (C) 3   (D) $2\sqrt{3}$
(E) $3\sqrt{2}$

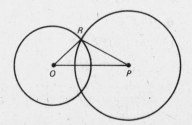

19. A bus uses one gallon of gasoline to travel 15 miles. After a tune-up, the bus travels 15% farther on one gallon. How many gallons of gasoline (to the nearest tenth) will it take for the bus to travel 150 miles after a tune-up?
(A) 8.5   (B) 8.7   (C) 8.9   (D) 9.0   (E) 10.0

20. If $x + 2y = 4$ and $x/y = 2$, then x is equal to
(A) 0   (B) $\dfrac{1}{2}$ (C) 1   (D) $\dfrac{3}{2}$ (E) 2

Use the following table for questions 21–23.

TIMED PERIOD (in minutes)	SPEED OF A TRAIN OVER A 3 HOUR PERIOD							
	0	30	45	60	90	120	150	180
SPEED AT TIME (in m.p.h.)	40	45	47.5	50	55	60	65	70

21. How fast was the train traveling 2½ hours after the beginning of the timed period?
(A) 50 m.p.h.   (B) 55 m.p.h.   (C) 60 m.p.h.   (D) 65 m.p.h.   (E) 70 m.p.h.

22. During the three hours shown on the table the speed of the train
(A) increased by 25%   (B) increased by 50%   (C) increased by 75%
(D) increased by 100%   (E) increased by 125%

23. At time t measured in minutes after the beginning of the time period, which of the following gives the speed of the train in accordance with the table?
(A) $\dfrac{1}{6}t$ (B) $10t$ (C) $40 + t$ (D) $40 + \dfrac{1}{6}t$ (E) $40 + 10t$

24. It costs $1,000 to make the first thousand copies of a book and x dollars to make each subsequent copy. If it costs a total of $7,230 to make the first 8,000 copies of a book, what is x?
(A) .89   (B) .90375   (C) 1.00   (D) 89   (E) 90.375

25. If 16 workers can finish a job in three hours, how long should it take 5 workers to finish the same job?
(A) $3\dfrac{1}{2}$ hours   (B) 4 hours   (C) 5 hours   (D) $7\dfrac{1}{16}$ hours   (E) $9\dfrac{3}{5}$ hours

MATHEMATICS
EXERCISE C

1. A box contains 12 poles and 7 pieces of net. Each piece of net weighs .2 pounds; each pole weighs 1.1 pounds. The box and its contents together weigh 16.25 pounds. How much does the empty box weigh?
(A) 1.2 pounds   (B) 1.65 pounds   (C) 2.75 pounds   (D) 6.15 pounds
(E) 16 pounds

2. If $a + b + c + d$ is a positive number, a minimum of x of the numbers a, b, c, and d must be positive where x is equal to
(A) 0   (B) 1   (C) 2   (D) 3   (E) 4

3. Consider the accompanying diagram. Which of the following statements is true?
(A) $KM < KL$ (B) $KM < LM$
(C) $KL + LM < KM$ (D) $KL < LM$ (E) $KL > LM$

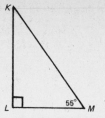

Use the graphs below for questions 4–6.

Population Characteristics

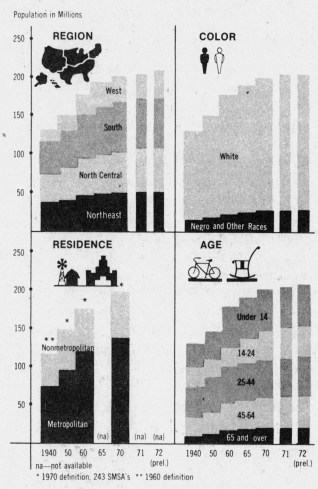

Source: *Pocket Data Book U.S.A. 1973. Bureau of the Census.*

4. In 1970, the ratio of the population living in metropolitan areas to the population living in nonmetropolitan areas was approximately
(A) 1 to 2 (B) 2 to 3 (C) 7 to 5 (D) 3 to 2 (E) 2 to 1

5. In 1950, the age group which had the fewest people was
(A) under 14 (B) 14–24 (C) 25–44 (D) 45–64 (E) 65 and over

6. How many of the regions shown had a population increase of less than 5% between 1940 and 1972?
(A) 0 (B) 1 (C) 2 (D) 3 (E) 4

7. Which of the following numbers is the largest?
   (A) $(2 + 2 + 2)^2$ (B) $[(2 + 2)^2]^2$ (C) $(2 \times 2 \times 2)^2$ (D) $2 + 2^2 + (2^2)^2$ (E) 4^3

8. In a survey of the town of Waso, it was found that 65% of the people surveyed watched the news on television, 40% read a newspaper, and 25% read a newspaper and watched the news on television. What percent of the people surveyed neither watched the news on television nor read a newspaper?
   (A) 0% (B) 5% (C) 10% (D) 15% (E) 20%

9. A worker is paid d dollars an hour for the first 8 hours she works in a day. For every hour after the first 8 hours, she is paid c dollars an hour. If she works 12 hours in one day, what is her average hourly wage for that day?
   (A) $(2d + c)/3$ (B) $8d + 4c$ (C) $(8d + 12c)/12$
   (D) $(4d + 8c)/12$ (E) $d + (\frac{1}{3})c$

10. A screwdriver and a hammer currently have the same price. If the price of a screwdriver rises by 5% and the price of a hammer goes up by 3%, how much more will it cost to buy 3 screwdrivers and 3 hammers?
    (A) 3% (B) 4% (C) 5% (D) 8% (E) 24%

11. If the radius of a circle is increased by 6%, then the area of the circle is increased by
    (A) .36% (B) 3.6% (C) 6% (D) 12.36% (E) 36%

12. Given that a and b are real numbers, let $f(a,b) = ab$ and let $g(a) = a^2 + 2$. Then $f[3, g(3)] =$
    (A) $3a^2 + 2$ (B) $3a^2 + 6$ (C) 27 (D) 29 (E) 33

13. A share of stock in Ace Enterprises cost D dollars on Jan. 1, 1975. One year later, a share increased to Q dollars. The fraction by which the cost of a share of stock has increased in the year is
    (A) $(Q - D)/D$ (B) $(D - Q)/Q$ (C) D/Q (D) Q/D (E) $(Q - D)/Q$

14. *ABCD* is a square, *EFGH* is a rectangle. $AB = 3$, $EF = 4$, $FG = 6$. The area of the region outside of *ABCD* and inside *EFGH* is
    (A) 6 (B) 9 (C) 12 (D) 15 (E) 24

Use the graphs below for questions 15–17.

	% OF PROTEIN	% OF CARBOHYDRATES	% OF FAT	COST PER 100 GRAMS
FOOD A	10	20	30	$1.80
FOOD B	20	15	10	$3.00
FOOD C	20	10	40	$2.75

15. If you purchase x grams of Food A, y grams of Food B, and z grams of Food C, the cost will be
    (A) $(\frac{9}{5}x + 3y + \frac{11}{4}z)$¢ (B) $\$(\frac{9}{5}x + 3y + \frac{11}{4}z)$ (C) $\$(1.8x + 3z + 2.75y)$
    (D) $(3x + 1.8y + 2.75z)$¢ (E) $\$(x + y + z)$

16. Which of the following diets would supply the most grams of protein?
   (A) 500 grams of A   (B) 250 grams of B   (C) 350 grams of C   (D) 150 grams of A and 200 grams of B   (E) 200 grams of B and 200 grams of C

17. All of the following diets would supply at least 75 grams of fat. Which of the diets costs the least?
   (A) 200 grams of A, 150 grams of B   (B) 500 grams of B, 100 grams of A
   (C) 200 grams of C   (D) 150 grams of A, 100 grams of C
   (E) 300 grams of A

18. CD is parallel to EF. $AD = DF$, CD = 4, and $DF = 3$. What is EF?
   (A) 4   (B) 5   (C) 6   (D) 7
   (E) 8

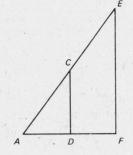

19. Which of the following fractions is the largest?
   (A) $\frac{5}{6}$ (B) $\frac{11}{14}$ (C) $\frac{12}{15}$ (D) $\frac{17}{21}$ (E) $\frac{29}{35}$

20. How much simple interest will $2,000 earn in 18 months at an annual rate of 6%?
   (A) $120   (B) $180   (C) $216   (D) $1,800   (E) $2,160

21. If $x + y > 5$ and $x - y > 3$, then which of the following gives all possible values of x and only possible values of x?
   (A) $x > 3$ (B) $x > 4$ (C) $x > 5$ (D) $x < 5$ (E) $x < 3$

22. If the average (or arithmetic mean) of 6 numbers is 4.5, what is the sum of the numbers?
   (A) 4.5   (B) 24   (C) 27   (D) 30   (E) can not be determined

23. A silo is filled to capacity with W pounds of wheat. Rats eat r pounds a day. After 25 days, what percent of the silo's capacity have the rats eaten?
   (A) $25r/W$ (B) $25r/100W$ (C) $2,500(r/W)$ (D) r/W (E) $r/25W$

24. If $x^2 + 2x - 8 = 0$, then x is either -4 or
   (A) -2 (B) -1 (C) 0   (D) 2   (E) 8

25. The interest charged on a loan is p dollars per 1,000 for the first month and q dollars per $1,000 for each month after the first month. How much interest will be charged during the first three months on a loan of $10,000?
   (A) $30p$ (B) $30q$ (C) $p + 2q$ (D) $20p + 10p$ (E) $10p + 20q$

MATHEMATICS
EXERCISE **D**

Use the graph below for questions 1–2.

Annual Percentage Change in Social Welfare Expenditures

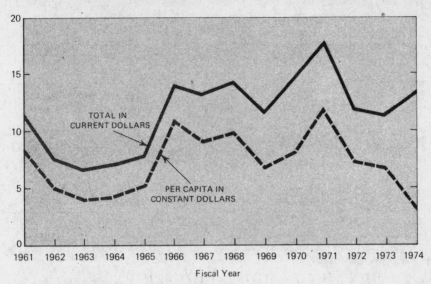

Source: *Social Security Bulletin.*

1. In which year between 1961 and 1974 were total social welfare expenditures in current dollars the highest?
   (A) 1961   (B) 1966   (C) 1970   (D) 1971   (E) 1974

2. If total social welfare expenditures were $10.8 billion in 1960, how many billion dollars were they in 1961?
   (A) .648   (B) 11.664   (C) 11.772   (D) 11.88   (E) 11.988

3. What is the area of the parallelogram *ABCD*?
   (A) 10   (B) 15   (C) 18
   (D) 20   (E) $4\sqrt{29}$

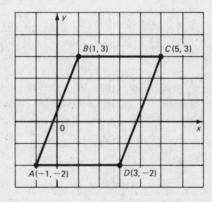

4. If k, m, and n are all integers which are divisible by 3, which of the following integers is divisible by 9?
   I. $k + m$
   II. km
   III. $k + m + n$
   (A) I only   (B) II only   (C) III only   (D) II and III only
   (E) I, II, and III

5. The Acme Company has 24 employees whose yearly salary is greater than $10,000. 15% of the employees of the Acme Company are paid yearly salaries which are greater than $10,000. How many employees does the Acme Company have?
(A) 24   (B) 100   (C) 120   (D) 150   (E) 160

Use the table below for questions 6–9.

PAYROLL OF L.T.D. INC.		
RANK	NUMBER IN RANK	WAGES PAID TO EMPLOYEES IN RANK
Manager	5	$110,000
Supervisor	25	$350,000
Assembly worker	500	$600,000
Total	530	$1,060,000

6. The wages paid to managers make up what percent (to the nearest per cent) of the total payroll?
(A) 5   (B) 9   (C) 10   (D) 11   (E) 42

7. The average wage for all employees is
(A) $1,200   (B) $2,000   (C) $18,000   (D) $20,000   (E) $22,000

8. The ratio of the average salary of a manager to the average salary of an assembly worker is
(A) 3 to 55   (B) 11 to 60   (C) 11 to 6   (D) 60 to 11   (E) 55 to 3

9. If 4 of the managers are paid wages of x dollars each, then the remaining manager is paid
(A) $22,000   (B) $(110,000 − x)   (C) $(110,000 − x)/4
(D) $(110,000 − 4x)   (E) $(22,000 − x)

10. A water tank has two drains. When only drain I is open, the tank will empty itself in 4 hours. When both drain I and II are open, the tank empties in $2\frac{1}{2}$ hours. How long does it take for the tank to empty if only drain II is open?
(A) $1\frac{1}{2}$ hours   (B) 2 hours   (C) 4 hours   (D) $5\frac{1}{2}$ hours   (E) $6\frac{2}{3}$ hours

11. A drawer contains 6 red socks and 4 blue socks. What is the probability that if 2 socks are picked (without looking) from the drawer, both of the socks will be red?
(A) $\frac{2}{15}$ (B) $\frac{4}{15}$ (C) $\frac{1}{3}$ (D) $\frac{2}{5}$ (E) $\frac{3}{5}$

12. A car originally was priced at $5,000. After one month, the price was discounted 10%. Two months later, the new price was discounted 20%, and the car was sold. How much did the buyer pay for the car?
(A) $1,400   (B) $1,500   (C) $3,500   (D) $3,600   (E) $3,750

13. The area of the isosceles triangle ABC is 48. $AD = DC$, and $AE = EB$. Let x be the area of the rectangle $DEFG$. Then x equals
(A) 6 (B) 12 (C) 18 (D) 24
(E) 36

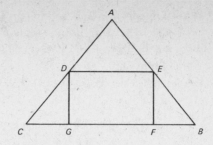

Use the graphs below for questions 14–17.

DISTRIBUTION OF U.S. LIFE INSURANCE COMPANIES BY REGION
MID-1972

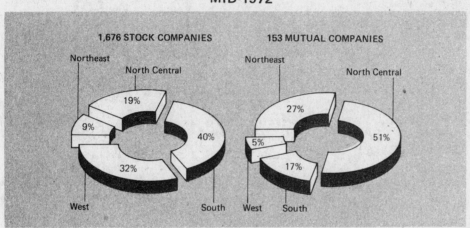

Source: Life Insurance Fact Book 1973, *Institute of Life Insurance.*

14. How many life insurance companies were there in the South in mid-1972?
(A) 26 (B) 670 (C) 696 (D) 732 (E) 1,043

15. Which region had the fewest life insurance companies in mid-1972?
(A) Northeast   (B) North Central   (C) South   (D) West
(E) can't determine

16. The ratio of stock companies in the South to stock companies in the West in mid-1972 was
(A) 1 to 2 (B) 4 to 5 (C) 5 to 4 (D) 4 to 1 (E) 2 to 1

17. Which of the following statements about life insurance companies in mid-1972 can be inferred from the graph?
 I. There are more mutual companies in the North Central region than there are stock companies in the North Central Region.
 II. There are three times as many mutual companies as stock companies in the Northeast.
 III. There are fewer than 10 mutual companies in the West.

(A) I only (B) II only (C) III only (D) I and II only (E) I, II, and III

18. What is $\dfrac{\frac{4}{7}}{\frac{2}{3}}$ divided by $\dfrac{5}{12}$?

(A) $\dfrac{10}{63}$ (B) $\dfrac{5}{14}$ (C) $\dfrac{14}{15}$ (D) $\dfrac{72}{35}$ (E) $\dfrac{63}{10}$

19. In order for the line segment AB to be parallel to the line segment CD, the coordinates of D must be $(3,x)$ with x equal to
    (A) 1   (B) 2   (C) 3   (D) 4   (E) 5

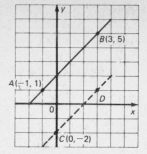

20. A farmer wishes to build a fence around a rectangular field. The field is 100 feet long and 60 feet wide. The fence will be of stone on one long side and of wire on the other three sides. Stone costs $5 a foot, and wire costs $2 a foot. How much will the fence cost?
    (A) $320   (B) $620   (C) $760   (D) $800   (E) $940

21. Which of the following integers is the square of an integer for every integer n?
    (A) $n^2 + 1$ (B) $n^2 + n$ (C) $n^2 + 2n$ (D) $n^2 + 2n + 1$ (E) $n^2 + 2n - 4$

22. A wheel with a diameter of 3 feet makes a revolution every 2 minutes. How many feet will the wheel travel in one hour?
    (A) 3π (B) 6π (C) 60π (D) 90π (E) 180π

Use the information below for questions 23–25.

Territorial Expansion

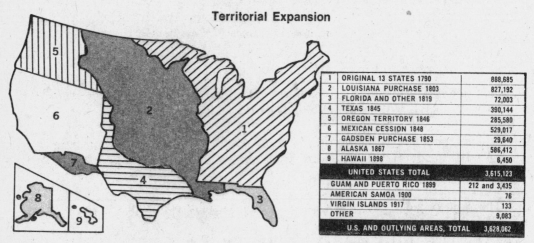

1	ORIGINAL 13 STATES 1790	888,685
2	LOUISIANA PURCHASE 1803	827,192
3	FLORIDA AND OTHER 1819	72,003
4	TEXAS 1845	390,144
5	OREGON TERRITORY 1846	285,580
6	MEXICAN CESSION 1848	529,017
7	GADSDEN PURCHASE 1853	29,640
8	ALASKA 1867	586,412
9	HAWAII 1898	6,450
	UNITED STATES TOTAL	**3,615,123**
	GUAM AND PUERTO RICO 1899	212 and 3,435
	AMERICAN SAMOA 1900	76
	VIRGIN ISLANDS 1917	133
	OTHER	9,083
	U.S. AND OUTLYING AREAS, TOTAL	**3,628,062**

GROSS AREA   Land and Water, square miles

Source: Pocket Data Book U.S.A. 1973. Bureau of the Census.

23. After the Louisiana Purchase the area of the United States had
    (A) roughly tripled   (B) roughly doubled   (C) increased slightly   (D) stayed the same   (E) decreased slightly

24. Which of the following percentages is closest to the percent of the United States total that is Alaska?
    (A) 10   (B) 15   (C) 20   (D) 25   (E) 30

25. The area of the United States in 1900 was about x times the area of the United States in 1800, where x is
    (A) ¼   (B) 3   (C) 4   (D) 5   (E) 6

Answers

The letter following each question number is the correct answer. The numbers in parenthesis refer to the sections of this chapter which explain the necessary mathematics principles. A more detailed explanation of all answers follows:

Mathematics Exercise A

1.	D	(I-1)
2.	B	(I-4)
3.	B	(III-7, I-4)
4.	A	(IV-4, IV-5, I-4)
5.	A	(IV-4, I-7)
6.	B	(IV-4)
7.	D	(IV-4, I-2)
8.	C	(I-4)
9.	A	(I-1)
10.	C	(II-1)
11.	C	(III-9, I-8)
12.	C	(I-2)
13.	C	(I-4)
14.	D	(I-4)
15.	C	(I-4)
16.	E	(I-7, I-4)
17.	B	(I-4, I-5)
18.	A	(II-1)
19.	D	(I-2)
20.	D	(II-3)
21.	C	(III-7, II-1, I-8)
22.	D	(II-2)
23.	C	(I-4)
24.	D	(III-9, III-7)
25.	A	(II-2)

Mathematics Exercise B

1.	B	(IV-2, IV-3)
2.	D	(IV-3)
3.	C	(IV-3)
4.	B	(IV-3)
5.	A	(IV-3)
6.	D	(I-8)
7.	B	(III-4, III-7)
8.	E	(II-5)
9.	D	(III-7)
10.	A	(II-3)
11.	D	(I-1)
12.	E	(IV-1)
13.	B	(IV-1)
14.	B	(IV-1)
15.	B	(IV-1, II-7)
16.	A	(I-4, I-2)
17.	A	(II-7)
18.	D	(III-6, III-4)
19.	B	(I-4)
20.	E	(II-2)
21.	D	(IV-1)
22.	C	(IV-1)
23.	D	(II-1)
24.	A	(II-2)
25.	E	(II-3)

Mathematics Exercise C

1.	B	(I-3)
2.	B	(II-7, I-6)
3.	E	(III-8)
4.	E	(IV-5, II-5)
5.	E	(IV-5)
6.	A	(IV-5)
7.	B	(I-8)
8.	E	(II-4)
9.	A	(I-7, II-1)
10.	B	(I-4)
11.	D	(III-7)
12.	E	(II-1)
13.	A	(I-2)
14.	D	(III-7)
15.	A	(II-1)
16.	E	(I-4)
17.	E	(IV-1)
18.	E	(III-4)
19.	A	(I-1, I-2, III-7)
20.	B	(I-4)
21.	B	(II-7)
22.	C	(I-7)
23.	C	(I-4)
24.	D	(II-1, II-2)
25.	E	(II-1)

Mathematics Exercise D

1.	E	(IV-3)
2.	E	(IV-3)
3.	D	(III-7, III-9)
4.	B	(I-1)
5.	E	(I-4)
6.	C	(I-4)
7.	B	(I-7)
8.	E	(II-5)
9.	D	(II-1)
10.	E	(II-3)
11.	C	(II-4)
12.	D	(I-4)
13.	D	(III-4, III-7)
14.	C	(IV-2)
15.	A	(IV-2)
16.	C	(IV-2)
17.	C	(IV-2)
18.	D	(I-2)
19.	A	(III-9, III-2)
20.	E	(III-7)
21.	D	(I-1, I-8, II-1)
22.	D	(III-7)
23.	B	(IV-1)
24.	B	(I-4)
25.	C	(IV-1)

Explanation of Answers

Mathematics Exercise A

1. **D**   The price increased by $34 - 12 = 22$ dollars.

2. **B**   She sold the house for 125% of C or $\frac{5}{4}C$. Thus, the gain is $\frac{5}{4}C - C = \frac{C}{4}$

    She must pay a tax of 50% of $\frac{C}{4}$ or $\frac{1}{2}$ of $\frac{C}{4}$. Therefore, the tax is $\frac{C}{8}$. Notice that the three years has nothing to do with the problem. Sometimes a question contains unnecessary information.

3. **B**   The area of a rectangle is length times width. Let L and W denote the original length and width. Then the new length is $1.2L$ and the new width is $.8W$. Therefore, the new area is $(1.2L)(.8W) = .96LW$ or 96% of the original area. So the area has decreased by 4%.

4. **A**   In 1964 military expenditures were about 140 billion and by 1969 they had increased to about 200 billion. $\frac{60}{140} = \frac{3}{7}$ which is almost 50%. By using a straight edge, you may see that the bar for 1969 is about half again as long as the bar for 1964.

5. **A**   Since the developing countries' military expenditures for every year were less than 30 billion, choice A is the only possible answer. Notice that by reading the possible answers first, you save time. You don't need the exact answer.

6. **B**   I can not be inferred since the graph indicates *only* the dollars spent on military expenditures, not the percent of income and not total income. II is true since each bar is higher than the previous bar to the left. III can not be inferred since the graph gives no information about 1972. So only statement II can be be inferred from the graph.

7. **D**   In 1971 the NATO countries spent over 100 billion and less than 150 billion on military expenditures. Since this was $\frac{1}{3}$ of their combined incomes the combined income is between 300 billion and 450 billion. Thus choice D must be the correct answer.

8. **C**   Voters between 18 and 21 who voted are 85% of the 8% of eligible voters. Thus, $(.08)(.85) = .068$, so 6.8% of the eligible voters were voters between 18 and 21 who voted.

9. **A**   Odd numbers are of the form $2x + 1$ where x is an integer. Thus if $n = 2x + 1$ and $p = 2k + 1$, then $n + p = 2x + 1 + 2k + 1 = 2x + 2k + 2$ which is even. Using $n = 3$ and $p = 5$, all the other choices give an odd number. In general, if a problem involves odd or even numbers, try using the fact that odd numbers are of the form $2x + 1$ and even numbers of the form $2y$ where x and y are integers.

10. **C**   To run a car 100 miles will cost $100 (g + m)$ cents. Divide by 100 to convert to dollars. The result is $g + m$.

11. **C**   Using the distance formula, the distance from A to B is $\sqrt{(1 - (-1))^2 + (3 - 5)^2} = \sqrt{4 + 4} = \sqrt{8} = \sqrt{4 \times 2} = \sqrt{4}\sqrt{2} = 2\sqrt{2}$. You have to be able to simplify $\sqrt{8}$ in order to obtain the correct answer.

12. **C**   Tips for the week were $\frac{5}{4} \cdot 50$ so his total income was $50 + \frac{5}{4}(50) = \frac{9}{4}(50)$. Therefore, tips made up $\frac{5/4(50)}{9/4(50)} = \frac{5/4}{9/4} = \frac{5}{9}$ of his income. *Don't* waste time figuring out the total income and the tip income. You can use the time to answer other questions.

13. **C** 7,500 is in the 6,000–8,000 bracket so the tax will be $80 + 3\%$ of the income over 6,000. Since $7,500 - 6,000 = 1,500$, the income over 6,000 is 1,500. 3% of 1500 $= (.03)(1500) = 45$, so the tax is $80 + 45 = 125$.

14. **D** The tax on 26,000 is $1,070 + 7\%$ of $(26,000 - 25,000)$. Thus, the tax is $1,070 + 70 = 1,140$. The tax on 29,000 is $1.070 + 7\%$ of $(29,000 - 25,000)$. Thus, the tax on 29,000 is $1,070 + 280 = 1,350$. Therefore, you will pay $1,350 - 1,140 = \$210$ more in taxes next year.
A faster method is to use the fact that the $3,000 raise is income over 25,000, so it will be taxed at 7%. Therefore, the tax on the extra $3,000 will be $(.07)(3,000) = 210$.

15. **C** If income is less than 6,000, then the tax is less than 80. If income is greater than 8,000, then the tax is greater than 140. Therefore, if the tax is 100, the income must be between 6,000 and 8,000. You *do not* have to calculate her exact income.

16. **E** Each person pays the tax on $3,700 which is 1% of 3700 or $37. Since there are 50,000 people in Zenith, the total taxes are $(37)(50,000) = \$1,850,000$.

17. **B** The tax on 10,000 is 220, so taxes are $\dfrac{220}{10,000} = .022 = 2.2\%$ of income. 2.2% is 2% after rounding to the nearest percent.

18. **A** $S(3,4) = 3^2 - 4^2 = 9 - 16 = -7$. Therefore, $S(3,S(3,4)) = S(3,-7) = 3^2 - (-7)^2 = 9 - 49 = -40$.

19. **D** 8 omelets will use $8 \cdot 3 = 24$ eggs and $8 \cdot \dfrac{1}{4} = 2$ peppers. Since 24 is two dozen, the cost will be $(2)(90¢) + (2)(20¢) = 220¢$ or $2.20.

20. **D** In order to average 50 m.p.h. for the trip, the bus must make the trip in $\dfrac{185}{50} = 3\dfrac{7}{10}$ hours which is 222 minutes. Since 2 hours or 120 minutes were needed for the first 85 miles, the final 100 miles must be completed in $222 - 120$ which is 102 minutes.

21. **C** The area of a rectangle is length times width so the area of *ABDC* is ab. The area of a triangle is one half of the height times the base. Since *BDE* is an isosceles right triangle, the base and height both are equal to b. Thus, the area of *BDE* is $\dfrac{1}{2}b^2$ Therefore, the area of the figure is $ab + \dfrac{1}{2}b^2$ which is equl to $b(a + \dfrac{b}{2})$. You have to express your answer as one of the possible answers, so you need to be able to simplify.

22. **D** Since $4x + 2y$ is equal to $2(2x + y)$ and $2x + y = 5$, $4x + 2y$ is equal to $2(5)$ or 10.

23. **C** The cost has increased by $4800 minus $2500 or $2300 between 1967 and 1975. So the cost has increased by $\dfrac{2300}{2500}$ which is .92 or 92%. Answer (E) is incorrect. The price in 1975 is 192% of the price in 1967, but the *increase* is 92%.

24. **D** The distance from $(-1, 2)$ to $(5, 2)$ is 6. (You can use the distance formula or just count the blocks in this case.) The area of a square is the length of a side squared, so the area is 6^2 or 36.

25. **A** Since $x + y = 6$ and $3x - y = 4$, we may add the two equations to obtain $4x = 10$, or $x = 2.5$. Then, because $x + y = 6$, y must be 3.5. Therefore, $x - y = -1$.

Mathematics Exercise B

1. **B** In 1960 women made up 33.4% or about ⅓ of the labor force. Using the line graph, there were about 22 million women in the labor force in 1960.

So the labor force was about 3(22) or 66 million. The closest answer among the choices is 65 million.

2. **D** In 1947, there were about 16 million women in the labor force, and about $14 - 6$ or 8 million of them were married. Therefore, the percentage of women in the labor force who were married is $\frac{8}{16}$ or 50%

3. **C** Look at the possible answers first. You can use your pencil and admission card as straight edges.

4. **B** In 1947, there were about 16 million women in the labor force. By 1972 there were about 32 million. Therefore, the number of women doubled which is an increase of 100%. (Not of 200%.)

5. **A** I is true since the width of the band for widowed or divorced women was never more than 5 million between 1947 and 1957. II is false since the number of single women in the labor force decreased from 1947 to 1948. III can not be inferred since there is no information about the total labor force or women as a percent of it in 1965. Thus, only I can be inferred.

6. **D** If $\frac{x}{y}$ is $\frac{2}{3}$, then $\frac{y}{x}$ is $\frac{3}{2}$. Since $\left(\frac{y}{x}\right)^2$ is equal to $\frac{y^2}{x^2}$, $\frac{y^2}{x^2}$ is $\left(\frac{3}{2}\right)^2$ or $\frac{9}{4}$.

7. **B** The area of a triangle is $\frac{1}{2}$ altitude times base. Since BD is perpendicular to AC, x is the altitude. Using the Pythagorean theorem, $x^2 + (AD)^2 = a^2$ and $x^2 + (DC)^2 = a^2$. Thus, $AD = DC$, and $AD = \sqrt{a^2 - x^2}$. So the base is $2\sqrt{a^2 - x^2}$. Therefore, the area is $\frac{1}{2}(x)(2\sqrt{a^2 - x^2})$ which is choice B.

8. **E** $1 : 160 :: 2\frac{7}{8} : x$. $x = 2\frac{7}{8}(160)$. $2\frac{7}{8}$ is $\frac{23}{8}$ so the distance from Seton to Monroe is $\frac{23}{8}(160) = 460$ miles.

9. **D** Let $EF = FG = GC$. Therefore, $BE = EF = FG = GC$. Draw perpendiculars EH, FI, GJ. Draw diagonals HF, IG, JC. The 8 triangles are equal in area since they each have the same altitude (AB or DC) and equal bases ($BE, EF, FG, GC, AH, HI, IJ, JD$). Since the area of $ABE = 7$, the area of $ABCD = (8)(7)$ or 56.

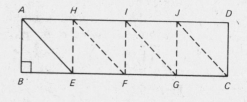

10. **A** In each minute the first puncture will leak $\frac{1}{9}$ of the air and the second puncture will leak $\frac{1}{6}$ of the air. Together $\frac{1}{9} + \frac{1}{6} = \frac{5}{18}$. So $\frac{5}{18}$ of the air will leak out in each minute. In $\frac{18}{5}$ or $3\frac{3}{5}$ minutes the tire will be flat.

11. **D** Since an even number times any number is even, and n times n^2 is odd, neither n or n^2 can be even. Therefore, n and n^2 must both be odd for n^3 to be odd. I and II are true, and III is false.

12. **E** Look in the fourth column.

13. **B** In 1972 there were 72 million females out of 136 million persons of voting age. $\frac{72}{136} = .529$ which is 53% to the nearest percent.

14. **B** In 1968, 70% of the 54 million males of voting age voted, and $(.7)(54,000,000) = 37,800,000$.

15. **B** Since 78 million persons of voting age lived in the North and West in 1964, and there were 65 million persons of voting age not in the 25–44 year range, there must be at least $78 - 65 = 13$ million people in the North and West in the 25–44 year range. X must be greater than or equal

to 13. Since there were 45 million people of voting age in the 25–44 year range, X must be less than or equal to 45.

16. **A** 90% of 50 is 45, so 45 students took the final. $\frac{2}{3}$ of 45 is 30. Therefore, 30 students passed the final.

17. **A** The average of two different numbers is always between the two. If $a = 2$ and $b = 3$, then $b^2 - a^2 = 5$, $ab = 6$, and $b - a = 1$ so C, D, and E must be false. If $a = \frac{1}{2}$ and $b = 1$, then $(ab)/2 = \frac{1}{4}$, so B is also false.

18. **D** Since the radius to the point of tangency is perpendicular to the tangent OR must be perpendicular to PR. Therefore, ORP is a right triangle, and $(PO)^2 = (OR)^2 + (PR)^2$. Then, $(PR)^2 = (PO)^2 - (OR)^2$. Thus, $(PR)^2 = 4^2 - 2^2$, and $PR = \sqrt{16 - 4} = \sqrt{12} = \sqrt{4}\sqrt{3} = 2\sqrt{3}$.

19. **B** After the tune-up, the bus will travel $(1.15)(15) = 17.25$ miles on a gallon of gas. Therefore, it will take $(150) \div (17.25) = 8.7$ (to the nearest tenth) gallons of gasoline to travel 150 miles.

20. **E** If $x/y = 2$, then $x = 2y$, so $x + 2y = 2y + 2y = 4y$. But $x + 2y = 4$, so $4y = 4$, or $y = 1$. Since $x = 2y$, x must be 2.

21. **D** 2½ hours is 150 minutes.

22. **C** The train's speed increased by $70 - 40$ which is 30 miles per hour. 30/40 is 75%.

23. **D** When $t = 0$, the speed is 40, so A and B are incorrect. When $t = 180$, the speed is 70, so C and E are incorrect. Choice D gives all the values which appear in the table.

24. **A** The cost of producing the first 8,000 copies is $1,000 + 7,000x$. $1,000 + 7,000x = \$7,230$. Therefore, $7,000x = 6230$ and $x = .89$.

25. **E** Assume all workers work at the same rate unless given different information. Since 16 workers take 3 hours, each worker does $\frac{1}{48}$ of the job an hour. Thus, the 5 workers will finish $\frac{5}{48}$ of the job each hour. $\frac{5}{48}x = \frac{48}{48}$ It will take $\frac{48}{5} = 9\frac{3}{5}$ hours for them to finish the job.

Mathematics Exercise C

1. **B** The 12 poles weigh $(12)(1.1) = 13.2$ pounds and the 7 pieces of net weigh $7(.2) = 1.4$ pounds, so the contents of the box weigh $13.2 + 1.4 = 14.6$ pounds. Therefore, the box by itself must weigh $16.25 - 14.6 = 1.65$ pounds.

2. **B** If all the numbers were not positive, then the sum could not be positive so A is incorrect. If a, b, and c were all -1 and d were 5, then $a + b + c + d$ would be positive so C, D, and E are incorrect.

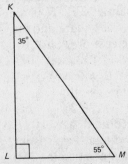

3. **E** Since the measure of angle M is 55°, the measure of angle K is 35°. Therefore, $KL > LM$ since the larger side is opposite the larger angle.

4. **E** The population in metropolitan areas in 1970 was about 140 million, and the population in nonmetropolitan areas was about $210 - 140$ or 70 million. Therefore, the ratio was about 140 to 70 or 2 to 1.

5. **E**   Compare the segments of the second bar under "age."

6. **A**   All regions increased by at least 10%. Compare the segments of the first bar with those of the last bar under "Region."

7. **B**   Choice A gives 6^2 or 36. Choice B gives 4^4 or 256. Choice C is 8^2 or 64. Choice D is $2 + 4 + 16$ or 22. Choice E is 4^3 or 64.

8. **E**   Since 25% read the newspaper and watched the news on television and 40% read the newspaper, $40\% - 25\%$ or 15% read the newspaper but did not watch the news on television. Thus $65\% + 15\%$ or 80% read the newspaper or watched the news on television, so $100\% - 80\%$ or 20% neither read the newspaper nor watched the news on television.

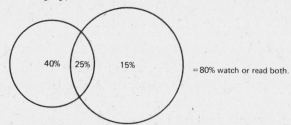

65% watch TV   40% read newspapers
$100\% - 80\% = 20\%$ neither watch nor read.

9. **A**   For the first 8 hours, she is paid a total of $8d$. For the final 4 hours $(12 - 8)$, she is paid $4c$. Therefore, her total pay is $8d + 4c$. To find the average hourly pay, divide by 12. To find the correct answer among the choices, you have to reduce the fraction. Divide the numerator by four and the denominator by four.

10. **B**   If the price of one screwdriver increases by 5%, then the price of three screwdrivers increases by 5% (not 15%). The percentage change is the same regardless of the number sold. Since a screwdriver and a hammer currently cost the same, the screwdrivers and the hammers each cost one half of the total price. So one half of the total is increased by 5%. The other half is increased by 3%. Therefore, the total price is increased by ½ (5%) + ½ (3%) =4%.

11. **D**   After the radius is increased by 6%, the radius will be 1.06 times the original radius. Since the area of a circle is πr^2, the new area will be $\pi(1.06r)^2 = \pi(1.1236r^2)$ or $1.1236\pi r^2$. Thus, the area has been increased by .1236 or by 12.36%.

12. **E**   Since $g(a) = a^2 + 2$, $g(3.)$ is $3^2 + 2$ or 11. So $f[3,g(3)]$ is $f(3,11) = 3 \times 11$ or 33.

13. **A**   The difference in the price is $Q - D$. So the fraction by which it has increased is $Q - D/D$. Note that the denominator is the *original* price.

14. **D**   Since *ABCD* is a square, the area of *ABCD* is 3^2 or 9. The area of the rectangle *EFGH* is *length* times *width* or $4 \times 6 = 24$. Thus, the area outside the square and inside the rectangle is $24 - 9$ or 15.

15. **A**   The cost of food A is $1.80 per hundred grams or 1.8¢ a gram, so *x* grams cost $(1.8x)$¢ or $(9/5)x$¢. Each gram of food B costs 3¢ so *y* grams of food B will cost $3y$¢. Each gram of food C costs 2.75¢ or $11/4$¢; thus, *z* grams of food C will cost $(11/4)z$¢. Therefore, the total cost is $[(9/5)x + 3y + (11/4)z]$¢.

16. **E**   Since food A is 10% protein, 500 grams of food A will supply 50 grams of protein. Food B is 20% protein so 250 grams of food B will supply 50 grams of protein. 350 grams of food C will supply 70 grams of protein. 150 grams of food A and 200 grams of food B will supply $15 + 40 = 55$ grams of protein. 200 grams of food B and 200 grams of food C will supply $40 + 40$ or 80 grams of protein. Choice E supplies the most protein.

17. **E** The diet of choice A will cost $2(\$1.80) + (3/2)(\$3) = \$3.60 + \$4.50 = \$8.10$. Choice B will cost $5(\$3) + \$1.80 = \$16.80$. Choice C costs $2(\$2.75) = \$5.50$. Choice D costs $(3/2)(\$1.80) + \$2.75 = \$2.70 + \$2.75 = \$5.45$. The diet of Choice E costs $3(\$1.80)$ or $\$5.40$ so Choice E costs the least.

18. **E** Since CD is parallel to EF, the triangles ACD and AEF are similar. Therefore, corresponding sides are proportional. So CD is to EF as AD is to AF. Since $AD = DF$, AD/AF is $\frac{1}{2}$. Therefore, EF is twice CD or 8.

19. **A** You need to find a common denominator for the fractions. One method is to multiply all the denominators. A quicker method is to find the least common multiple of the denominators. Since $6 = 3 \times 2$, $14 = 2 \times 7$, $15 = 3 \times 5$, $21 = 3 \times 7$, and $35 = 5 \times 7$, the least common multiple is $2 \times 3 \times 5 \times 7 = 210$. $5/6$ is $175/210$, $11/14$ is $165/210$, $12/15$ is $168/210$, $17/21$ is $170/210$, and $29/35$ is $174/210$. $5/6$ has the largest numerator.

20. **B** 18 months is $3/2$ of a year. Interest $=$ Amount $\times$ Time $\times$ Rate. $(\$2,000)(3/2)(.06) = \$180$.

21. **B** If $x + y > 5$ and $x - y > 3$, then, since both inequalities are of the same type, the corresponding sides can be added to obtain $2x > 8$ or $x > 4$.

22. **C** The average of 6 numbers is the sum of the numbers divided by 6. Thus, the sum of the numbers is the average multiplied by 6 or 4.5×6 which is 27.

23. **C** After 25 days the rats have eaten $25r$ pounds of wheat. So $(25r)/W$ is the fraction of the capacity eaten by the rats. To change this to percent, multiply by 100. $(25r)/W \times 100 = 2500(r/W)$.

24. **D** Factor $x^2 + 2x - 8$ into $(x + 4)(x - 2)$. If x is either -4 or 2, $x^2 + 2x - 8 = 0$, and D is the correct answer.

25. **E** The interest on the $\$10,000$ for the first month will be $10p$. For the next 2 months the interest will be $20q$. The total interest is $10p + 20q$.

Mathematics Exercise D

1. **E** Since the annual percentage change was positive in each year between 1961 and 1974, the total social welfare expenditures in current dollars increased in every year shown. Therefore, the expenditures were highest in the last year shown, 1974.

2. **E** In 1961, total social welfare expenditures increased by 11% from their value in 1960. Thus, in 1961, the total was 111% of $\$10.8$ billion or $(1.11)(10.8) = \$11.988$ billion.

3. **D** The area of a parallelogram is altitude $\times$ base. AD has length 4 so the base is 4. The altitude is perpendicular to the base, so the altitude to point B would be 5. Therefore, the area is 5×4 or 20.

4. **B** I and III are false as can be seen by letting $k = 12$, $m = 3$, and $n = 6$. II is true since, if k and m are divisible by 3, then $k = 3i$ and $m = 3j$ when i and j are integers. Therefore, $km = (3i)(3j)$ or $9ij$ which means km is divisible by 9.

5. **E** 15% of the total number of employees is 24. 15% is equal to $15/100$ or $3/20$, so $(3/20)x = 24$ when x is the number of employees. Therefore $x = (24)(20/3) = 160$.

6. **C** The total payroll is $\$1,060,000$, and the wages paid to managers $= \$110,000$. Since $110,000/1,060,000 = 11/106 = .10$ (rounding to the nearest hundredth) or 10%.

7. **B** The average wage is $\$1,060,000$ divided by 530 or $\$2,000$.

8. **E** The average salary of a manager is $\$110,000/5$ or $\$22,000$. The average

salary of an assembly worker is $600,000 divided by 500 or $1,200. So the ratio is 220 to 12 or 55 to 3.

9. **D** All 5 managers together earn $110,000. Since each one of the four makes x dollars, the remaining manager is paid $(110,000 − 4x).

10. **E** Drain I alone empties ¼ of the tank in an hour since it takes 4 hours to empty the tank. If Drain II takes x hours to empty the tank by itself, then it will empty $1/x$ of the tank per hour. Both drains together will empty the tank in 5/2 hours so both drains together empty 2/5 of the tank in one hour. Therefore, $1/4 + 1/x = 2/5$. $1/x = 3/20$. $x = 20/3$ or 6 2/3.

11. **C** Since there are 10 socks in the drawer and 6 of them are red, there are 10×9 different ways to pick 2 socks from the drawer, and 6×5 different ways to pick 2 red socks. Therefore, the probability of picking 2 red socks is $(6 \times 5)/(10 \times 9) = 30/90$ or 1/3.

12. **D** After the 10% discount, the price of the car was 90% of $5,000 or $4,500. After the second discount of 20% the selling price was 80% of $4,500 or $3,600.

13. **D** Because the triangle is isosceles, the angles DCG and EBF are equal. Drop a perpendicular from A to CB which will intersect DE at H. Then the triangles AHD, AHE, DGC, and EFB are all congruent. So DE must equal $CG + FB$ or half of BC. Also DG must be half of the altitude of ABC. Since 48 is ½ the altitude times BC, and the area of $DEFG$ is ¼ of BC times the altitude, the area of $DEFG$ is half of 48 or 24.

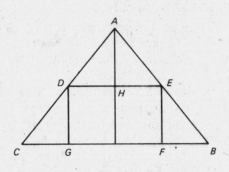

14. **C** The number of life insurance companies in the South is 40% of 1,676 + 17% of 153. $670 + 26 = 696$.

15. **A** Since most companies are stock companies, the Northeast is the most likely guess. The total in the Northeast is 9% (1,676) + 27% (153). Compare the result (191.8) with the nearest possibility which is the North Central. 19% of 1,676 is greater, even without adding mutual companies.

16. **C** The ratio is 40% to 32% or 5 to 4. Don't waste time figuring out the actual number of stock companies in the various regions.

17. **C** I is false since 51% of 153 is less than 19% of 1,676. II is false since 27% of 153 is less than 9% of 1,676. III is true since 5% of 153 is fewer than 10. Therefore, only III can be inferred from the graphs.

18. **D** 4/7 divided by 2/3 is $(4/7) \times (3/2)$ or 6/7. 6/7 divided by 5/12 is $6/7 \times 12/5$ or 72/35.

19. **A** If two lines are parallel, then the distance between the two lines along parallel lines must be equal. The easiest lines to use to calculate distances are lines parallel to the y axis. The distance along the y axis from C to AB is 4. AB intersects the y axis at the point (0,2). The distance from D to AB along the line parallel to the y axis must also be 4. D must have coordinates (3,1). $x = 1$.

20. **E** The fence will consist of 100 feet of stone and $100 + 60 + 60 = 220$ feet of wire. The cost will be $5(100) + $2(220) = $500 + $440 = $940.

21. **D** If $n = 1$ then Choice A is 2, Choice B is 2, Choice C is 3, Choice E is −1 so Choice D is the only possibility. Choice D is correct since $n^2 + 2n + 1 = (n + 1)^2$.

22. **D** The circumference of a circle is π times the diameter, so the circumference of the wheel is 3π feet. In one hour the wheel will make 30 revolutions, so it will travel $30(3\pi)$ or 90π feet in one hour.

23. **B** The Louisiana Purchase added about 830,000 square miles. The previous area was about 890,000 square miles, so the area almost doubled.

24. **B** Alaska is almost 600,000 square miles which is about 1/6 of 3,660,000 square miles. 1/6 is 16 2/3% so the correct answer is 15%. Save time by estimating; don't perform the calculations exactly.

25. **C** The area was about 3,600,000 square miles in 1900, and the area had been about 900,000 square miles in 1800. Since 4 times 900,000 is 3,600,000, x is about 4.

BASIC LOGIC REVIEW

A knowledge of the principles of elementary logic presented in this section can be helpful in many areas of the GMAT. Aside from the obvious benefits of having a sound reasoning ability to apply in solving Data Sufficiency and Mathematics problems, a capacity for logical thinking can also be extremely useful in the Verbal Aptitude area of the exam, where you are required to find logical relationships between words, and in the Reading Recall and Business Judgment sections where sound thinking is certain to increase your understanding of the passages you read. With this in mind, study the following material carefully.

Implications

Many types of questions on the exam ask you to determine if a statement can be inferred or deduced from certain given information. To say that a statement q can be inferred from a statement p means that whenever statement p is true, statement q must be true. This concept may also be expressed as *p implies q, q follows from p,* or *q can be deduced from p.* It is written $p \Rightarrow q$. Statement q is called the *conclusion* and statement p is called the *hypothesis* of the implication.

For an implication $p \Rightarrow q$ to be false, it is only necessary to find one case where the conclusion q is false and the hypothesis p is true.

EXAMPLE 1: Let p represent the statement *Tom owns a motorcycle.* Let q represent the statement *Tom owns a motor vehicle.* Can q be inferred from p?

Yes. All motorcycles are motor vehicles. Therefore, if Tom has a motorcycle he has a motor vehicle. (p is true, and q is true). Whenever p is true, so $p \Rightarrow q$.

Even though $p \Rightarrow q$ is true, $q \Rightarrow p$ is not necessarily true.

EXAMPLE 2: Let p and q represent the same statements used in **example** 1.

Does p follow from q?

No. Not all motor vehicles are motorcycles. Therefore, Tom could own a motor vehicle (q) without owning a motorcycle (p). Statement q is true but statement p is false. Since both statements must be true for the deduction to be true, $q \Rightarrow p$ is false.

EXAMPLE 3:

HOURS OF WORK NEEDED TO PURCHASE
(By Average Employee)

	1971	1972
One dozen eggs	10 min.	8 min.
Pair of shoes	3 hrs.	2 hrs. 45 min.
Suit	15 hrs.	15.5 hrs.
2 lbs. of potatoes	45 min.	42 min.
Automobile	600 hrs.	620 hrs.
Haircut	30 min.	30 min.
Bottle of milk	5 min.	4 min.
5 lbs. of meat	1 hr.	1 hr.

Which of the following conclusions can be inferred from the table?

I.   The employees were paid more in 1972 than they were in 1971.
II. The price of a haircut was the same in 1972 as it was in 1971.
III. In each year only two of the items shown on the table required more than 10 hours of work.

(A) I only
(B) II only
(C) III only
(D) II and III
(E) I, II, and III

This is an example of a type of inference problem found on the GMAT. The correct answer is C, statement III only. Statement I can not be inferred from the table since the table gives no information about the prices of the items in dollars. Statement II can not be inferred from the table since there is no information about the monetary wages of the average employee. Statement III can be inferred since only a suit and an automobile took more than ten hours of work in each year according to the table.

Do not make the mistake of assuming information which is not given. If you assumed that the price of eggs rose or stayed the same between 1971 and 1972 then you could infer statement I.

Connectives

If you connect two or more statements, you form a compound statement. The truth value of the statements which make up the compound statement and the connectives used in forming the compound statement will both affect the truth value of the compound statement.

Conjunction

The *conjunction* of two statements, p and q, may be expressed as *p and q*, or as *both p and q*. It is written $p \wedge q$. The conjunction $p \wedge q$ is true *only* when both of the statements p and q are true. If either one of the statements is false, then $p \wedge q$ is false. For example, let p represent the statement *Tom owns a boat*. Let q represent the statement *Tom owns a car*. The conjunction $p \wedge q$ is expressed verbally as *Tom owns a boat and Tom owns a car*, or as *Tom owns a boat and a car*. It is true *only* when Tom owns both a car and a boat. The statement would be false, for example, if Tom owned a car but did not own a boat.

The conjunction of more than two statements is true if each of the statements is true. If *any* of the statements are false, the conjunction is false. Verbal equivalents would be *p and q and r*, *each p, q, and r*, or *all of p, q, and r*. Consider the statement *Tom, Mary, and John each own a car*. This is the conjunction of the statements *Tom owns a car, Mary owns a car*, and *John owns a car*. The statement is true only if each of the three people own a car. The statement would be false if someone did not own a car. For example, the statement is false if Tom and Mary each own a car but John does not own a car.

EXAMPLE: Refer to the table given in Example 3 of the section on Implications. Let $p \land q$ represent the statement *An average employee had to work more than 2 hours and 50 minutes in each of the years 1971 and 1972 to purchase a pair of shoes*. Can $p \land q$ be inferred from the table?

No. This statement is the conjunction of two statements p and q where p is the statement *The average employee had to work more than 2 hours and 50 minutes in 1971 to purchase a pair of shoes*, and q is the statement *The average employee had to work more than 2 hours and 50 minutes in 1972 to purchase a pair of shoes*. Statement p is true but q is false so the statement *p and q* is false. Therefore, $p \land q$ can not be inferred from the table.

Disjunction

The disjunction of two statements, p and q, is expressed verbally as *either p or q*, or as *p or q*. The disjunction of p and q is written symbolically as $p \lor q$. Statement $p \lor q$ is false *only* when both p and q are false. It is true if at least one of the statements p and q is true. This can be shown in the following manner. Let p represent the statement *Tom owns a boat*. Let q represent the statement *Tom owns a car*. Disjunction $p \lor q$ is expressed verbally as *Tom owns a boat or a car*. Disjunction $p \lor q$ is true if Tom owns a boat, or if Tom owns a car, or if Tom owns both a boat and a car. It is false only if Tom owns neither a boat nor a car.

The disjunction of more than two statements is true if *any* of the statements is true. The disjunction is false *only* when *every* one of the statements is false. Verbal equivalents of $p \lor q \lor r$ would be *p or q or r*, or *at least one of p, q, and r is true*. Let $p \lor q \lor r$ represent the statement: *Tom or Mary or John owns a car*, the disjunction of the three statements, *Tom owns a car* (p), *Mary owns a car* (q), and *John owns a car* (r). The disjunction is false only if *none* of the three people (Tom, Mary, John) owns a car. The statement would be true if *any* one of the people (Tom, Mary, John) owns a car.

EXAMPLE: Refer to the table given in Example 3 of the section on Implications. Let $p \lor q \lor r$ represent the statement *In at least one of the years 1970, 1971, and 1972, the average employee had to work more than 2 hours and 50 minutes to purchase a pair of shoes*. Can $p \lor q \lor r$ be inferred from the table?

Yes. This statement is the disjunction of p, q, and r where p is the statement *An average employee had to work more than 2 hours and 50 minutes in 1970 to purchase a pair of shoes*, q the statement *An average employee had to work more than 2 hours and 50 minutes in 1971 to purchase a pair of shoes*, and r the statement *An average employee had to work more than 2 hours and 50 minutes in 1972 to purchase a pair of shoes*. Since q is true, the disjunction is true, even though r is false and there is no information about p on the table.

Compare the sections on Conjunctions and Disjunctions so that you clearly see the differences that exist between the two.

Venn Diagrams

A Venn Diagram is a picture representing a logical statement and is used to visualize logical relationships. The cases in which a given statement is true are represented in the diagram by shaded areas. The shaded area is called the *truth set* of the statement. Note the representation of statement p in the diagrams below.

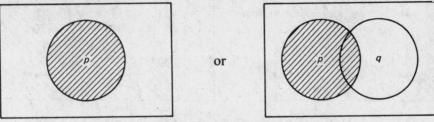

Consider the Venn Diagram for the conjunction $p \wedge q$.

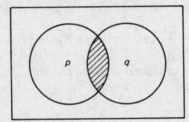

Since $p \wedge q$ is true only when both p and q are true, the truth set of $p \wedge q$ is the area that is common to both the truth set of p and the truth set of q. This is called the *intersection* of the two truth sets.

Now look at the Venn Diagram for the disjunction $p \vee q$.

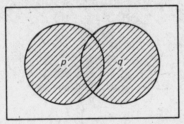

Since $p \vee q$ is true if either of the two statements p or q is true, the truth set of $p \vee q$ is the set of all cases in the truth set of p or in the truth set of q or in the truth set of both. This is called the *union* of the two truth sets.

For a discussion of the use of Venn Diagrams in simplifying counting problems, see section **II–14** of the Mathematics Review.

Negation

The negation of a statement p is expressed as *not p* and written $\sim p$. The statement $\sim p$ is false when p is true and true when p is false. Thus, the negation of p reverses the truth value of p. The Venn Diagram of the statement $\sim p$ is

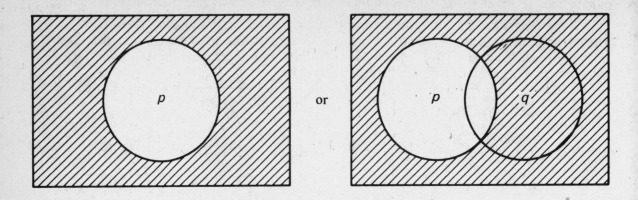

or

The truth set of $\sim p$ is called the complement of the truth set of p.

The shaded and unshaded areas in a Venn Diagram are interchanged by negation. This can be readily seen by drawing a diagram for $\sim(p \wedge q)$, the negation of $p \wedge q$. In this diagram only the area that represents p and q remains unshaded.

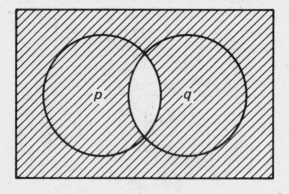

If you compare this diagram with the Venn Diagram that represents $p \wedge q$, you will see that the shaded areas are interchanged.

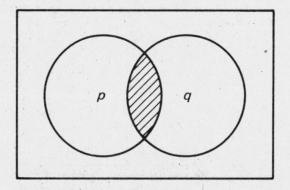

Carrying this idea a step further, it is possible to show that $\sim p \wedge \sim q$ is *not* a negation of $p \wedge q$. The truth set of $\sim p \wedge \sim q$ is the area common to the truth set of $\sim p$ and the truth set of $\sim q$.

The Venn Diagram for $\sim p$ is

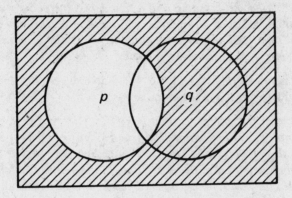

The Venn Diagram for $\sim q$ is

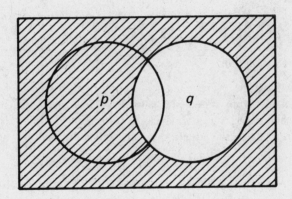

Therefore, taking the truth sets common to each statement and combining them, you can arrive at the Venn Diagram for $\sim p \wedge \sim q$, which is

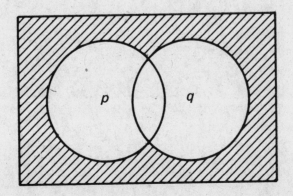

By comparing this diagram with the diagram for $p \wedge q$, you can see that the two are not interchanged. Thus, $\sim p \wedge \sim q$ is not the negation of $p \vee q$, and the two statements are not equivalent. This is an important fact to remember when solving counting problems.

As an illustration of this point, consider the following. Let p represent the statement *A car has a radio*. Let q represent the statement *A car has a heater*. Then, $p \wedge q$ represents the statement *A car has a radio and a heater*. In the same manner, $\sim(p \wedge q)$ represents the statement *A car does not have a radio and a heater*, but $\sim p \wedge \sim q$ is *A car does not have a radio and does not have a heater*. If a car had a radio but not a heater, $\sim(p \wedge q)$ would be true but $\sim p \wedge \sim q$ would be false.

The statements $\sim(p \vee q)$ and $\sim p \vee \sim q$ also differ. In fact, $\sim(p \vee q)$ is equivalent to $\sim p \wedge \sim q$ and $\sim p \vee \sim q$ is the same as $\sim(p \wedge q)$.

Statements of the form *everyone has . . . , all are . . . , each is . . . ,* are negated by *some have not . . . , all are not . . . , each is not . . . .* To negate the statement *All the members of the Smith family have red hair*, you would have to change it to *At least one of the members of the Smith family does not have red hair*. Notice that the statement *No member of the Smith family has red hair* is *not* the negation.

Statements of the form *some are . . . , at least one is . . . ,* have negations of the form *none are . . . , no one is . . . , everyone is not. . . .* The negation of the statement *Some children have been spoiled by their parents*, is *No children have been spoiled by their parents*.

EXPERIMENTAL QUESTION TYPES

Analysis of Explanations

This question type is designed to measure your ability to recognize logical relationships, draw conclusions from statements, and make inferences. Each set of questions consists of a short passage describing a situation, a statement of the result of this situation, and several statements relating to the situation which you must analyze using the procedure outlined below.

DIRECTIONS: For each set of questions, a fact situation and a result are presented. Several numbered statements follow the result. Each statement is to be evaluated in relation to the fact situation and result.

Consider each statement separately from the other statements. For each one, examine the following sequence of decisions, in the order A, B, C, D, E. Each decision results in selecting or eliminating a choice. *The first choice that cannot be eliminated* is the correct answer.

A   Is the statement *inconsistent* with, or contradictory to, something in the fact situation, the result, or both together? If so, choose A.
   If not,

B   Does the statement present a *possible adequate explanation* of the result? If so, choose B.
    If not,

C   Does the statement have to be true if the fact situation and the result are as stated? If so, the statement is *deducible* from something in the fact situation, the result, or both together; choose C.
    If not,

D   Does the statement either support or weaken a possible explanation of the result? If so, the statement is *relevant* to an explanation. Choose D.
    If not,

E   The statement is *irrelevant* to an explanation of the result. Choose E.

Use common sense to decide whether explanations are adequate and whether statements are inconsistent or deducible. No formal system of logic is presupposed. Do not consider extremely unlikely or remote possibilities.

Sample Analysis of Explanation Question Sets

Use the directions given above to answer the following sample Analysis of Explanations Question Sets. Check the answer explanations at the end of the chapter to see how you did. Study any questions you missed until you understand the reasoning involved.

Question Set 1

Situation: John Waters, an honor student at Reno City High School, has carefully considered the decision about which college he wishes to attend. Together with his parents, who are both practicing physicians, he has weighed the pros and cons of the large university versus the small college, the value of a degree from a prestigious Ivy League school in the East, in California, and in his home state of Nevada, and observed various attractive and comparable curricula. By the end of his senior year, he had been accepted by several schools, including Stanford University in California and Yale University in Connecticut. During the summer after his graduation from high school, he worked as a reservation clerk at a hotel in Lake Tahoe, Nevada.

Result: In September, John enrolled as a full-time student in the University of Nevada at Las Vegas School of Hotel Management.

1. John chose a state university because tuition is cheaper at a state school than at an Ivy League school.   1. Ⓐ Ⓑ Ⓒ Ⓓ Ⓔ

2. John did not do well on his SAT exam.   2. Ⓐ Ⓑ Ⓒ Ⓓ Ⓔ

3. John's parents did not approve of his choice of occupation.   3. Ⓐ Ⓑ Ⓒ Ⓓ Ⓔ

4. John found his work at Lake Tahoe limiting and boring.   4. Ⓐ Ⓑ Ⓒ Ⓓ Ⓔ

5. John did not want to follow in his parents' profession.   5. Ⓐ Ⓑ Ⓒ Ⓓ Ⓔ

6. John did not wish to be too far away from his home.   6. Ⓐ Ⓑ Ⓒ Ⓓ Ⓔ

7. John felt that thorough vocational preparation was more valuable than a liberal arts education.   7. Ⓐ Ⓑ Ⓒ Ⓓ Ⓔ

8. John had been considering a career in hotel management prior to his graduation from high school.   8. Ⓐ Ⓑ Ⓒ Ⓓ Ⓔ

Question Set 2

Situation: Mary and John Smith, the parents of Mark, age 15, and Sara, age 9, have been troubled for some time by the complaints of their children regarding allowances. Each claims that the other receives more money, and both claim that their friends receive greater allowances than they do. Mark and Sara have mentioned several times that their expenditures for school lunches and carfare leave little left over for entertainment.

Result: Mary and John Smith discussed the matter and decided that children should be given the experience of handling money and living within a budget. For a trial period from October 1 to Thanksgiving, they granted Mark an allowance of $15 per week and Sara $12 per week, under the stipulation that both children keep their spending within the weekly allotment. At the end of the trial period, Mark and Sara were to report what they had learned about living on a budget.

9. Ⓐ Ⓑ Ⓒ Ⓓ Ⓔ   9. During the third week of this period, Mark had to ask for an advance on his weekly allowance because of extra expenditures with a "date" at a school dance.

10. Ⓐ Ⓑ Ⓒ Ⓓ Ⓔ   10. At the end of November, both children presented written accounts of their various expenditures and savings.

11. Ⓐ Ⓑ Ⓒ Ⓓ Ⓔ   11. Lori Brown, a friend of Sara, told her parents of the Smith experiment but was turned down by her parents when she requested a regular weekly allowance. Lori's parents felt that young children should not be given the experience of handling money.

12. Ⓐ Ⓑ Ⓒ Ⓓ Ⓔ   12. At a school Parents Association meeting, Mrs. Smith introduced a resolution that budgeting be made part of the school curriculum, perhaps in the mathematics classes. She described the experiment in her family.

13. Ⓐ Ⓑ Ⓒ Ⓓ Ⓔ   13. On the average, Sara saved 50 cents a week from her allowance. She deposited these savings in her bank account.

14. Ⓐ Ⓑ Ⓒ Ⓓ Ⓔ   14. Mark requested that he be given extra family chores so that he could have more funds available for his expenditures. He was given extra money for taking care of the lawn and the family pets.

15. Ⓐ Ⓑ Ⓒ Ⓓ Ⓔ   15. Late in October Mark received a $10 check as a birthday gift from his grandparents. He purchased a football for $8.75.

16. Ⓐ Ⓑ Ⓒ Ⓓ Ⓔ   16. When Mr. and Mrs. Smith discussed the original problem, it was agreed that Mark would have to meet greater expenses because of his age and would have to have a larger allowance than his sister.

Question Set 3

Situation: At the bus station in Toonerville, Michael Bentley, a bus driver, told Florence Ford that her boyfriend, Joe Albertson, also a bus driver, had an important message for her and would like to meet her in the afternoon at the end of the bus route in Potterstown. Bentley told Neil Carson, who was at the ticket window, to sell her a one-half fare child's fare ticket, which he did. Bentley, who drove the bus to Potterstown, accepted Florence Ford's ticket as she entered the bus. On the return trip, Albertson was the driver and Florence rode free.

Result: After a company hearing, Joe Albertson was discharged, Michael Bentley was given a 30-day suspension without pay, and Neil Carson received a 10-day suspension without pay.

17. Ⓐ Ⓑ Ⓒ Ⓓ Ⓔ   17. The bus company spends large sums of money on surveillance of its employees for honesty and courtesy to riders.

EXPERIMENTAL QUESTION TYPES • 281

18. Ticket sellers are responsible for correct daily accounting of daily sales. 18. Ⓐ Ⓑ Ⓒ Ⓓ Ⓔ

19. Neil Carson had a good record with the bus company for more than 15 years. 19. Ⓐ Ⓑ Ⓒ Ⓓ Ⓔ

20. Michael Bentley claimed that while Joe Albertson is an old friend, he does not know Florence Ford. 20. Ⓐ Ⓑ Ⓒ Ⓓ Ⓔ

21. At the company hearing it was indicated that Bentley was guilty of not checking for a proper ticket given by an adult, even if there was no conspiracy to defraud the company. 21. Ⓐ Ⓑ Ⓒ Ⓓ Ⓔ

22. Wives of bus drivers are given bus passes which permit riding on company buses free. 22. Ⓐ Ⓑ Ⓒ Ⓓ Ⓔ

23. A supervisor testified that he overheard a conversation between Michael Bentley and Florence Ford in which he explained that it was dangerous for him to permit her to enter his bus without presenting some sort of bus ticket. 23. Ⓐ Ⓑ Ⓒ Ⓓ Ⓔ

24. A passenger on the bus testified that he was in the midst of asking Bentley some question about bus stops on the route when Florence Ford entered the bus and handed the driver a ticket which he accepted in a very casual fashion. 24. Ⓐ Ⓑ Ⓒ Ⓓ Ⓔ

25. Joe intends to marry Florence after he arranges a divorce from his present wife. 25. Ⓐ Ⓑ Ⓒ Ⓓ Ⓔ

26. The chief supervisor had received an anonymous letter from a rider who reported that Bentley was extending certain illegal courtesies to some steady riders. 26. Ⓐ Ⓑ Ⓒ Ⓓ Ⓔ

27. The union attorney claimed that most of the evidence presented was circumstantial evidence. He also stated that if there were some minor infractions the punishment was too severe. 27. Ⓐ Ⓑ Ⓒ Ⓓ Ⓔ

Question Set 4

Situation: In 1930 James Cronin received his doctorate in chemistry and urged his father to move his small dye plant from the heart of the city to an isolated bay area located miles from the nearest community. The difficulties with the water and air pollution authorities were thus solved. In 1935 the facilities were expanded and the number of employees increased from 20 to 100. A year later an additional building was added and the number of employees doubled. In 1950 small one-family houses began to spring up within a mile of the Cronin dye plant. As the population increased a bus route was established from the area of the dye plant to the heart of the city.

Result: Since 1960, community groups have been protesting the air pollution caused by the plant and clamoring for better sewage disposal of the chemical wastes.

28. A public school was built in the newly developed community in 1952. 28. Ⓐ Ⓑ Ⓒ Ⓓ Ⓔ

29. In 1970 the officers of the dye plant announced plans to move their establishment to another state. 29. Ⓐ Ⓑ Ⓒ Ⓓ Ⓔ

30. Wastes from a chemical plant pollute waters. 30. Ⓐ Ⓑ Ⓒ Ⓓ Ⓔ

31. Fishermen complained that the bay was no longer a good source of fish. 31. Ⓐ Ⓑ Ⓒ Ⓓ Ⓔ

32. Dr. Cronin claimed that the wastes from the plant were put through a dilution process before entering the main sewage pipes. 32. Ⓐ Ⓑ Ⓒ Ⓓ Ⓔ

33. Many of the employees of the Cronin dye plant purchased homes in the newly developed community. 33. Ⓐ Ⓑ Ⓒ Ⓓ Ⓔ

34. More than ever, the public is now becoming aware of industrial pollution. 34. Ⓐ Ⓑ Ⓒ Ⓓ Ⓔ

35. Ⓐ Ⓑ Ⓒ Ⓓ Ⓔ   **35.** A large grocery chain opened a supermarket in the shopping mall in the new community.

36. Ⓐ Ⓑ Ⓒ Ⓓ Ⓔ   **36.** Not until 1950 did the Cronin Dye Company find it necessary to build a parking lot for its employees.

Question Set 5

Situation: Eighteen years after he invented it, the U.S. Patent and Trademark Office granted R. Gordon Gould a patent for the technology responsible for solid-state lasers. These lasers account for about a third of all lasers. In 1959 a patent was awarded to Nobel Prize-winner Townes for his work on microwaves. Laser manufacturers accepted that patent as covering all lasers.

Result: Laser makers are objecting to the prospect of paying additional royalties to Gould.

37. Ⓐ Ⓑ Ⓒ Ⓓ Ⓔ   **37.** There is much confusion in regard to who is the actual inventor of lasers.

38. Ⓐ Ⓑ Ⓒ Ⓓ Ⓔ   **38.** The attorneys for a large manufacturer claim that the Townes patent was the basic patent for all lasers.

39. Ⓐ Ⓑ Ⓒ Ⓓ Ⓔ   **39.** Gould is confident that he will receive a similar patent covering lasers that use a gas such as a mixture of neon and helium as a lasing medium.

40. Ⓐ Ⓑ Ⓒ Ⓓ Ⓔ   **40.** A patent is good for 17 years after date of issue.

41. Ⓐ Ⓑ Ⓒ Ⓓ Ⓔ   **41.** After 1977 Gould may collect royalties from laser makers in spite of the fact that they have already paid royalties to Townes.

42. Ⓐ Ⓑ Ⓒ Ⓓ Ⓔ   **42.** Industry is expected to test Gould's patent in court.

43. Ⓐ Ⓑ Ⓒ Ⓓ Ⓔ   **43.** Inventions and discoveries that help mankind should be made available all over the world without payments of royalties.

44. Ⓐ Ⓑ Ⓒ Ⓓ Ⓔ   **44.** Industry may face payment of royalties for an additional patent on lasers in which energy is accumulated and then released in very powerful bursts by a technique called Q-switching.

45. Ⓐ Ⓑ Ⓒ Ⓓ Ⓔ   **45.** A notarized statement by Gould, dated November 13, 1957, gave the first description of a laser, as well as the first use of that word—an acronym for light amplification by stimulated emission of radiation.

46. Ⓐ Ⓑ Ⓒ Ⓓ Ⓔ   **46.** Laser manufacturers most probably will add the expenditures involved in the new royalties to the selling price.

Question Set 6

Situation: Sponsors of Saturday morning television programs have found a young captive audience to stimulate the sale of their breakfast cereals. Some nutritionists challenge the value of these sugary foods for growing children.

Result: Parent groups are urging governmental control over the sponsorship and presentation of these child-oriented Saturday morning television programs.

47. Ⓐ Ⓑ Ⓒ Ⓓ Ⓔ   **47.** Programs on noncommercial television channels are available on Saturday mornings.

48. Ⓐ Ⓑ Ⓒ Ⓓ Ⓔ   **48.** In our democracy the public has many avenues through which to make its views known.

49. The dental profession has warned parents of the dangers of excess sugar in the diet of children.

49. Ⓐ Ⓑ Ⓒ Ⓓ Ⓔ

50. The sugar content of breakfast cereals varies from 1% to 68%.

50. Ⓐ Ⓑ Ⓒ Ⓓ Ⓔ

51. It is the consumer's responsibility to read labels on breakfast cereals for its content and then buy wisely.

51. Ⓐ Ⓑ Ⓒ Ⓓ Ⓔ

52. In addition to sugar, one serving of most breakfast cereals provides about ¼ the daily needs of riboflavin, niacin, and iron.

52. Ⓐ Ⓑ Ⓒ Ⓓ Ⓔ

53. Some cereal-sponsored television programs on Saturday morning have educational value.

53. Ⓐ Ⓑ Ⓒ Ⓓ Ⓔ

54. Most breakfast cereals supply 300 calories when one ounce of cereal is added to ½ cup of Vitamin D fortified milk.

54. Ⓐ Ⓑ Ⓒ Ⓓ Ⓔ

55. Parents should control the television habits of their children.

55. Ⓐ Ⓑ Ⓒ Ⓓ Ⓔ

56. Liquor and cigarette advertising over the air has been banned.

56. Ⓐ Ⓑ Ⓒ Ⓓ Ⓔ

Question Set 7

Situation: The incidence of lateness to school had risen to the point where the principal of the school made it the chief part of the agenda of a faculty conference. Pointing out that pupils must take the matter of punctuality more seriously, he organized a committee to offer concrete suggestions on how to remedy this situation.

Result: After implementing some of the suggestions of this committee a marked improvement in punctuality was noted.

57. One of the rules imposed was that after three latenesses to school a student's parent be summoned to see the guidance counselor.

57. Ⓐ Ⓑ Ⓒ Ⓓ Ⓔ

58. A good number of students come to school on a school bus.

58. Ⓐ Ⓑ Ⓒ Ⓓ Ⓔ

59. The time of arrival to school was changed from 8:45 to 9:05.

59. Ⓐ Ⓑ Ⓒ Ⓓ Ⓔ

60. It was observed that some students, rather than being charged with a lateness, returned home to be considered absent rather than late.

60. Ⓐ Ⓑ Ⓒ Ⓓ Ⓔ

61. The school had a poor record for punctuality long before the appointment of the present principal.

61. Ⓐ Ⓑ Ⓒ Ⓓ Ⓔ

62. Most pupils live within walking distance of the school.

62. Ⓐ Ⓑ Ⓒ Ⓓ Ⓔ

63. It was announced that punctuality would be recorded on college transcripts.

63. Ⓐ Ⓑ Ⓒ Ⓓ Ⓔ

64. Incidence of lateness is greatest in bad weather.

64. Ⓐ Ⓑ Ⓒ Ⓓ Ⓔ

65. The Parents Association devoted an entire evening program to the problem of lateness to school.

65. Ⓐ Ⓑ Ⓒ Ⓓ Ⓔ

66. A school secretary was assigned to duty at the school entrance to issue late passes and make appropriate entries on the pupils' school records.

66. Ⓐ Ⓑ Ⓒ Ⓓ Ⓔ

Question Set 8

Situation: Because of a disappointing season in 1976—6 defeats and 1 victory—and poor attendance at football games, the coach resigned after 5 years of service at the A.B.C. High School.

Result: Varsity football was suspended in 1977.

67. Ⓐ Ⓑ Ⓒ Ⓓ Ⓔ **67.** It was the first season of football for the school that was defeated by A.B.C. High School in 1976.

68. Ⓐ Ⓑ Ⓒ Ⓓ Ⓔ **68.** The following is the record for the coach who resigned: 8 victories, 25 defeats, and 2 ties.

69. Ⓐ Ⓑ Ⓒ Ⓓ Ⓔ **69.** Many injuries, some very serious, were suffered by the football team in 1976.

70. Ⓐ Ⓑ Ⓒ Ⓓ Ⓔ **70.** The Alumni Association clamored for the resumption of varsity football, urging that a good coach be hired.

71. Ⓐ Ⓑ Ⓒ Ⓓ Ⓔ **71.** The editor of the school newspaper wrote an editorial claiming that pupils cannot be expected to support a team by attending games that seldom result in victory.

72. Ⓐ Ⓑ Ⓒ Ⓓ Ⓔ **72.** The profits made by the school basketball team have been used to subsidize the financial losses of the football team.

73. Ⓐ Ⓑ Ⓒ Ⓓ Ⓔ **73.** In 1974 the bleacher stands of the football field were rebuilt and a large electric scoreboard was erected.

74. Ⓐ Ⓑ Ⓒ Ⓓ Ⓔ **74.** Several parents clamored for the resumption of the sport. They made the claim that football had values other than winning games.

75. Ⓐ Ⓑ Ⓒ Ⓓ Ⓔ **75.** Some educators claim that high school football is generally poorly played and is a source of injuries to growing boys.

76. Ⓐ Ⓑ Ⓒ Ⓓ Ⓔ **76.** The price of admission to a football game was maintained at the same level from 1972 to 1976.

Question Set 9

Situation: The Environmental Epidemiology branch of the National Cancer Institute (NCI), in a study of 39 counties with a heavy concentration of petroleum refineries, found a very high incidence of cancer of the lung, the nasal cavity, and the skin.

Result: While industry has expressed a great concern for protecting its workers and neighbors from carcinogens, it considers this research badly conceived.

77. Ⓐ Ⓑ Ⓒ Ⓓ Ⓔ **77.** An official of the Occupational Safety and Health Administration has stated that it is almost impossible to do single, agent-oriented epidemiology studies.

78. Ⓐ Ⓑ Ⓒ Ⓓ Ⓔ **78.** Percival Pott, in the eighteenth century, observed that chimney sweeps had a high incidence of cancer of the scrotum.

79. Ⓐ Ⓑ Ⓒ Ⓓ Ⓔ **79.** In the NCI study a control group of counties which are not near petroleum refineries were studied for incidence of cancer of the lungs, the nasal cavity, and the skin.

80. Ⓐ Ⓑ Ⓒ Ⓓ Ⓔ **80.** Compounds such as anthracene escaping from refineries have been suggested to be cancer-causing agents.

81. Ⓐ Ⓑ Ⓒ Ⓓ Ⓔ **81.** Eastman Kodak, Dupont, and Shell Oil are just three of many corporations that have hired epidemiologists to make their own surveys of the health effects of oil refineries.

82. Ⓐ Ⓑ Ⓒ Ⓓ Ⓔ **82.** Twenty years before the bacterial cause of cholera was established, the British doctor John Snow mapped the cases of cholera and concluded that many of the victims were receiving their drinking water from a contaminated source.

83. Ⓐ Ⓑ Ⓒ Ⓓ Ⓔ **83.** Human cancer may take 20 years or more to develop and the human environment is so complex that pinpointing one specific factor as a cause is difficult.

84. Besides having petroleum refineries, many of the 39 counties also have petrochemical plants.

84. (A) (B) (C) (D) (E)

85. When animal tests showed that acrylonitrile is a potential carcinogen, one manufacturer of plastics drastically reduced exposure levels of its workers to this chemical.

85. (A) (B) (C) (D) (E)

86. Changing the location of refineries from densely populated areas would be a great financial loss to oil corporations.

86. (A) (B) (C) (D) (E)

87. A scientifically conducted research project should be tested with a large population. The number of people involved in the 39-county study is far short of that number.

87. (A) (B) (C) (D) (E)

88. Epidemiologists are medical detectives who track down and prevent communicable diseases. Where causative agents have not yet been established they examine patterns of incidence of disease.

88. (A) (B) (C) (D) (E)

Question Set 10

Situation: When Harry Hathaway applied for a $5000 loan for the purchase of a new car he was turned down as a bad credit risk. He discovered that his former wife ran up bills before their divorce.

Result: Mr. Hathaway borrowed $2000 from a friend and took an advance of salary to make up the difference. His employer agreed to deduct the advance of salary, without interest, in equal amounts over a period of ten months.

89. Under the separation agreement Harry's former wife promised to be legally responsible for all her debts. This agreement was signed one year before she ran up these unpaid bills.

89. (A) (B) (C) (D) (E)

90. The friend who made the $2000 loan was given as collateral a valuable painting that Harry's present wife had owned for many years.

90. (A) (B) (C) (D) (E)

91. The personnel manager of the firm in which Hr. Hathaway is employed offered to assist him in clearing his bad credit rating. He asked Mr. Hathaway to bring in the legal document which would be used to clear him of his former wife's debts.

91. (A) (B) (C) (D) (E)

92. The commercial bank that turned down the loan is one in which Mr. Hathaway was a depositor for at least ten years.

92. (A) (B) (C) (D) (E)

93. When the salesman who sold the car to Mr. Hathaway learned of the bank's denial of the loan, he made application for this loan at a credit union where he is a director. The credit union did not approve the loan because of the poor credit rating.

93. (A) (B) (C) (D) (E)

94. Mr. Hathaway's present car was in need of extensive and expensive repairs. He needs his car to get to his place of employment.

94. (A) (B) (C) (D) (E)

95. It was suggested that instead of purchasing a car, he lease a car on a long-term basis. In this case, his monthly charges would almost be equal to his monthly payroll deductions.

95. (A) (B) (C) (D) (E)

96. Mrs. Hathaway signed a contract to teach for one year in a nursery school to help the family finances during the period of payroll deductions.

96. (A) (B) (C) (D) (E)

Answers and Analysis

1. **A** This statement is inconsistent with the facts in the situation. We are told that both parents are practicing physicians. The problem of cost should not be a factor in John's decision.

2. **A** This is also inconsistent with the facts. John would probably not have been accepted by Stanford and Yale with poor SAT scores.

3. **E** Since John's parents could conceivably be disappointed with his choice of occupation, the statement is consistent and the correct answer is not (A). The statement, likewise, is not an adequate explanation of the result (B). There is nothing in the fact situation or the result to justify the deduction that John's parents opposed his choice of occupation (C). The statement does not support or weaken a possible explanation of the result (D). The answer, therefore, must be (E).

4. **A** Since John decided to enter a course of study in hotel management after his work at Lake Tahoe, he must have found the work enjoyable. The statement is inconsistent with the facts.

5. **C** The statement is not inconsistent with the fact situation or the result. The answer therefore is not (A). It does not present an explanation of the result (B). Since John chose a field of work other than that of his parents, we can deduce that he did not wish to become a physician.

6. **B** John's desire to be near his home is not inconsistent with the fact situation, the result, or both together. The answer is not (A). John's desire to be near his home is a possible explanation of his choice of school (B).

7. **B** Since John enrolled in a course preparing for a definite career, the statement is not inconsistent with the fact situation and the result. Therefore, (A) is incorrect. The statement does provide a possible adequate explanation of the result (B).

8. **C** The statement is not inconsistent with, nor does it contradict, the fact situation, the result, or both together. Thus, (A) is incorrect. The time when John first began to consider hotel management as a career does not provide an adequate explanation of the result (B). We may deduce that the statement is true because John must have filed an application for admission to the University of Nevada at Las Vegas at the time he filed the other applications, including the ones for Stanford and Yale.

9. **A** The result stipulates that both children are to keep their spending within their weekly allowances. The fact that Mark needed an advance on his allowance is inconsistent with the result. Mark did not manage to stay within his allotment. Had he put aside some money during the previous weeks for this unusual expense with his "date," he would have been practicing good budgeting.

10. **C** This is not inconsistent with the conditions of the result which states that the children are to report what they learned about living on a budget. Keeping records of expenditures and savings gives structure for discussions of this subject (A). Keeping records does not explain why the parents decided to experiment with the plan (B). However, we can deduce from the situation (in which the problem arose when the children requested larger allowances and the resulting experiment) that keeping written records will pinpoint the extent of the problem and the success of the plan devised by the parents.

11. **A** The parents of Lori Brown do not believe that children should be given the experience of handling money. This contradicts what Sara's parents believe, as evidenced by the facts of the result—the family experiment.

12. **C** Mrs. Smith's discussion of budgeting with other parents is consistent with the problem in her family (A). Her discussion at the meeting does not explain why her

family set up the experiment (B). However, it can be deduced from the fact situation (allowances) and the family experiment that Mrs. Smith would be anxious to make provision for an exchange of ideas, and to suggest ways of bringing the idea of budgeting into the classroom.

13. **D** The fact that Sara learned to live within her budget and actually put aside some savings is consistent with the facts of the result—to keep spending within the allotment (A). This does not explain why the Smiths put their children on a fixed weekly allowance (B). Sara's experience cannot be deduced from the problem or the devised plan, the solution (C), but it does support the idea that children can profit from an experience in budgeting.

14. **A** The fact that Mark sought ways of doing extra chores is a desirable trait. However, since he was planning to use the earnings to add to his regular weekly allowance, he is defeating the idea of living within the $15 per week budget. Thus, it is inconsistent with the result.

15. **E** Since the expenditure for the football was made during the experimental period, the statement is consistent with budgeting (A). The presentation of the gift and the expenditure of some of the money involved cannot explain why Mark was given a fixed allowance by his parents (B). The purchase of the football from the gift cannot be deduced from any phase of the Smith family project (C), nor does it explain why the parents decided to put Mark on a fixed allowance for the experimental period (D). The birthday gift and Mark's purchase of the football is irrelevant to the lesson on budgeting.

16. **B** The decision by the Smiths that Mark is entitled to a larger allowance than Sara is consistent with the facts of the result (A). It explains the fact that because of his age, he would have more expensive obligations than his younger sister.

17. **C** This is consistent with the facts since evidence of violations of company policy was detected by surveillance. Therefore (A) is incorrect. Because of this surveillance violations were detected, but this does not explain the disposition of the cases (B). The correct choice is (C) because the use of surveillance is deducible from the facts of the situation.

18. **D** If the ticket sellers are responsible only for correct cash, then it is consistent with the facts (A). Since it does not explain the result—why punishment resulted—(B) is not acceptable. It does not seem to be true according to the facts at the hearing. (C) is also incorrect. However, if this were the case it would weaken the result. Therefore (D) is correct.

19. **E** Neil's good record is not inconsistent with the allegations (A). It does explain why he was punished (B). His record is unrelated to the violations charged against him (C). The fact that his good previous record was not taken into account when the punishment was given makes (D) not acceptable. Therefore (E) is correct.

20. **A** If this statement is true, it would contradict the fact situation.
21. **B** This is consistent with charges made in the fact situation (A). Since this violation explains the result, (B) is correct.

22. **E** Since some passengers are permitted to ride free this statement is related to the fact situation (A). It does not explain the result (B). Since this privilege is not deducible from anything in the fact situation or the result, (C) is also incorrect. It neither supports nor weakens the result (D). The correct answer is (E) since it is irrelevant to an explanation of the result.

23. **B** The supervisor's testimony is related to the facts and the results (A). The evidence presented by the supervisor gives an explanation for the outcome of the hearing. Therefore (B) is correct.

24. **A** If this statement is true then it contradicts the charges against the driver and (A) is correct.

25. **E** This does not contradict anything in the fact situation or the result (A). Since it does not explain the result (B) is not acceptable. The forthcoming marriage cannot be deduced from the fact situation or the result (C). This fact neither weakens nor supports the result, so (D) is not acceptable and (E) is the correct answer.

26. **C** This is consistent with the behavior of the employees (A). Since it does not explain why the men were punished, (B) is not acceptable. However, it is deducible from the fact situation. Possibly, special surveillance was put on Bentley and this was responsible for the discoveries mentioned in the situation. Therefore (C) is correct.

27. **A** Since the attorney questioned the nature of evidence and challenged the punishment (the result), this statement is inconsistent with the fact situation and the result (A).

28. **C** It is reasonable to expect the need and the construction of a new school building in a new neighborhood. Therefore, it is consistent with the fact situation (A), but does not explain the result (B). Since it is deducible from the population growth mentioned in the fact situation, (C) is correct.

29. **E** It is conceivable that a company would plan to move its factory because of the protests (A). It does not explain the nature of the protests mentioned in the result (B). This cannot be deduced from anything in the fact situation or the result (C). Since this threat did not affect the attitude of the protesters, (D) is not acceptable and (E) is correct.

30. **B** This is consistent with the problem raised in the passage. One cannot deny that wastes from a chemical plant need special treatment to avoid pollution. This explains the result. Therefore (B) is correct.

31. **C** Since this is not inconsistent with the source of pollution mentioned in the fact situation, (A) is not acceptable. It does not give the reason for the reaction of the community (B). However, it can be deduced that pollution in the waters would kill most of the fish (C).

32. **D** This is consistent with the problem of pollution raised by the community (A). This statement does not explain the reason for the protest (B). The statement of the owner is not deducible from anything in the fact situation or the result (C) but the statement tends to weaken the charges made by the protesters (D).

33. **C** This is not inconsistent with anything in the fact situation or the result (A). It does not explain the result (B). Since one would be expected to seek residence near one's place of employment, this is deducible from the fact situation. Therefore (C) is correct.

34. **B** The fact that people are becoming aware of the dangers of pollution is consistent with the facts in the result (A). This gives an explanation for the action taken as described in the result. The correct answer is therefore (B).

35. **C** This explanation parallels the one given for statement 33. Executives of supermarkets are on the lookout for new, growing communities.

36. **A** This is not consistent with the facts mentioned. Before 1950 there was no public transportation available for the employees, who had to travel to an isolated area to go to the plant. By 1950 some employees lived close to the plant and, in addition, a bus line was established. Therefore (A) is correct.

37. **B** Confusion in regard to the actual inventor is consistent with the facts in the situation (A). Since it explains the result, the correct answer is (B).

38. **A** If this claim is upheld, it contradicts the claim by Gould. Therefore, (A) is correct.

39. **C** Since this is consistent with the patent already granted to Gould, (A) is incorrect. Since the laser makers are concerned with the recent patent, this statement does not explain the result (B). However, since the patent office has granted Gould a patent for his solid state lasers, it is reasonable to assume that the statement is correct and is deducible from the fact situation. Therefore (C) is correct.

40. **B** This statement is related to the problem of patents (A). The correct answer is (B) because it explains the result—the laser manufacturers are not anxious to pay royalties to Gould after having met the 17-year obligation to Townes.

41. **B** See the analysis for statement 40.

42. **C** This is not inconsistent with the fact situation or the result (A). It does not explain the result (B). Industry never hesitates to appeal unpopular court decisions. This is deducible from the result (C).

43. **A** This statement contradicts the entire principle of royalties discussed in this selection.

44. **B** See the analysis for statement 40.

45. **C** This helps justify the 1977 decision and is consistent with the fact situation (A). It does not explain the result (B). Since it is deducible from the fact that the patent was granted, (C) is correct.

46. **E** This is not inconsistent with the facts regarding Gould's patent (A). Since it is not related to the reaction of the laser makers, (B) is not acceptable. This statement may not be true (C). Since it does not support or weaken the result, (D) is not acceptable, and the correct answer is (E).

47. **A** Since noncommercial television channels offer Saturday morning programs, parents cannot claim that their children must be exposed to the cereal-sponsored programs. This contradicts the fact situation and the result.

48. **B** Since this mentions that the public can exert an influence, it is consistent with the fact situation and the result (A). Since it explains the result, (B) is correct.

49. **C** The concern for sugar in the diet is consistent with the problems expressed (A). Since concern about tooth decay is not the only reason for the result, (B) is not acceptable. Sugar intake in large quantities is associated with tooth decay. This statement is deducible from the reaction of parents who evidently must buy these products upon the requests of their children (C).

50. **A** This contradicts the great concern for the excess sugar content of breakfast cereals.

51. **E** This does not contradict the parents' concern (A). It neither explains the result (B) nor can this be deduced in anything in the fact situation or the result (C). Since this does not weaken or support the argument for controlling television programming, (D) is not acceptable and the correct answer is (E).

52. **A** Since most breakfast cereals supply essential nutritional elements in addition to sugar, this statement contradicts the charge made in the fact situation.

53. **D** Since parents object mainly to the commercials for these programs, the fact that some of these programs have educational value makes this consistent with the fact situation (A). This does not explain the result (B). Since this statement does not have to be true, (C) is not acceptable. However, this statement weakens the result. Therefore (D) is correct.

54. **E** This statement does not contradict anything in the fact situation or the result (A). Since it does not explain the result, (B) is not acceptable. This statement does not have any information that can be deduced from the fact situation or the result (C).

55. **A** This contradicts the concern of parents as to what is presented on the air. With parental guidance children will be watching programs that do not have any of the features mentioned in the selection.

56. **B** This statement is not inconsistent with anything in the fact situation or the result (A). This mentions a precedent for television censorship and therefore explains the result (B).

57. **B** The statement is consistent with the problem of lateness (A). Since pupils wanted to avoid this unpleasant visit, it probably motivated them to be punctual and thus it might be regarded as one of the reasons for the success of the program; therefore, (B) is correct.

58. **A** This contradicts the statement that excessive lateness was due to lack of concern for punctuality on the part of students. If a school bus is late, the occupants of the bus suffer. (A) is correct.

59. **B** This is not inconsistent with the problem in the passage (A). Moving up the time of arrival in the morning could offer some explanation for the success of the program. Therefore (B) is correct.

60. **A** This practice defeats the purpose of teaching the value of punctuality. Actually it contradicts the result that lateness decreased because of the program. Therefore (A) is correct.

61. **C** This is consistent with the fact situation (A). It does not explain the result of the program (B). This statement must be true since the selection suggests that it was a problem of long standing before the principal decided to take action. Since it is deducible from the fact situation, the correct answer is (C).

62. **E** This statement does not contradict anything in the selection (A). It gives no possible explanation for the improvement mentioned (B). Since it is not deducible from anything in the fact situation or the result, (C) is not acceptable. Because it neither supports nor weakens the outcome of the program, (D) is not correct. The answer is (E).

63. **B** This is not inconsistent with the fact situation or the result (A). The procedure mentioned could possibly explain the result, since pupils are concerned about their school record. Therefore (B) is correct.

64. **A** This is normal for all schools and is inconsistent with the problem of lateness in this school. Therefore the correct answer is (A).

65. **B** This is consistent with the fact situation and the result (A). The correct answer is (B) because parent cooperation was probably enlisted, and the result—the success of the program—was due at least in part to this influence.

66. **E** This is consistent with the problem of lateness (A). It does not explain the result (B) nor is it deducible from anything in the fact situation or the result (C). Since this routine practice does not motivate punctuality, (D) is not acceptable and the correct answer is (E).

67. **C** This statement is consistent with the fact that the school had a poor football record (A). This victory did not cause the suspension of football (B). The correct answer is (C) since this statement is deducible from the fact that the single victory came from a young, inexperienced team.

68. **A** This contradicts the statement that 1976 was a bad year and that the school was in the habit of enjoying good seasons. Evidently this coach had poor teams for five years. Therefore the correct answer is (A).

69. **B** This is consistent with the fact situation (A). Since this possibly explains why the sport was suspended, the correct answer is (B).

70. **D** The concern of the alumni is consistent with the problem (A). This is not an explanation for the result (B). This is not deducible from anything in the fact situation or the result (C). Since it weakens the result and actually offers an alternate suggestion, the correct answer is (D).

71. **C** This is consistent with the fact situation and the result (A). It does not explain the result but instead offers a reason for a statement in the fact situation (poor attendance). Therefore (B) is not acceptable. Since it is deducible from something in the fact situation, the correct answer is (C).

72. **B** This is consistent with the problems of the football team stated in the fact situation and the result (A). By showing that the football team could not maintain itself for many years, it suggests a possible reason for the result. The correct answer is (B).

73. **E** This statement is not contradictory to anything in the fact situation or the result (A). Since it does not justify the suspension of the sport, (B) is not acceptable. Since this is not deducible from anything in the passage, (C) is not correct. It neither supports nor weakens the result. Therefore (D) is not acceptable and (E) is the correct choice.

74. **A** Since this contradicts the result—the suspension of varsity football—the correct answer is (A).

75. **D** This statement is consistent with the facts of the passage (A). Since this is not the cause of the suspension of the sport, (B) is not acceptable. It is not deducible from anything in the fact situation or the result (C). Since it does support the action taken (the result), the correct answer is (D).

76. **E** This is not inconsistent with the fact situation or the result (A). Since it does not explain the result, (B) is not acceptable. The price of tickets is not deducible from anything in the fact situation or the result (C). Because it is not relevant to an explanation of the result, (D) is not acceptable and the correct choice is (E).

77. **A** This statement questions the validity of the result. Therefore the correct answer is (A).

78. **E** This statement is consistent with the discussion of the causes of cancer (A). Since it does not justify the conclusion in this case, (B) is not acceptable. It is not deducible from anything in this selection (C). Since it does not support or weaken an explanation in this particular case, (D) is incorrect and (E) is the correct choice.

79. **C** This is not inconsistent with the problem treated in this passage (A). Since it does not explain the criticism of industry, (B) is not acceptable. The correct answer is (C) because this statement is deducible from something in the fact situation. Evidently the NCI conducted its research with scientific procedure by setting up a control group.

80. **C** This statement is consistent with the problem studied (A). Since it does not explain the criticism of industry, (B) is also incorrect. Since it cites an example of what the refineries are producing, it is deducible from the fact situation and the correct answer is (C).

81. **B** The procedures mentioned are consistent with the problem discussed (A). Since this shows the concern of industry for its workers and its neighbors, it presents an explanation of the result. The correct answer is (B).

82. **E** Nothing in the statement is inconsistent with the facts in the selection (A). It does not explain the result (B). Since this early research is not deducible from anything in the fact situation or the result, (C) is not acceptable. It neither supports nor weakens the attitude of the petroleum industry (D). The correct answer is (E) because it is irrelevant to an explanation of the result.

83. **A** This statement questions the validity of the findings of the study by the NCI. Since it contradicts something in the fact situation, the correct answer is (A).

84. **D** This is consistent with the study to determine the relationship of cancer to the industrial environment (A). It does not explain the result (B). It does not have to be true and is not deducible from the fact situation or the result (C). However, it supports the contention of the petroleum industry that the research was badly conceived because the high incidence of cancer may be due to factors other than those from the refineries. The correct answer is (D).

85. **C** The concern for cancer-producing agents is the basis for the NCI study (A). This does not explain the criticism of the study (B). The correct answer is (C) because the statement is another illustration of possible industrial causes of cancer and this illustration is deducible from the fact situation.

86. **B** This is not inconsistent with the fact situation (A). The correct answer is (B) because it gives a reason for the result—the criticism by the petroleum industry.

87. **A** This statement proposes a criticism of the study that would invalidate the findings. Since it contradicts something in the fact situation, the correct answer is (A).

88. **E** The work of these scientists is consistent with the fact situation (A). It offers no explanation for the result (B) nor is it deducible from anything mentioned in the fact situation or the result (C). Since it does not affect an explanation of the result, (D) is not acceptable and the correct answer is (E).

89. **A** Since this contradicts the fact situation, the correct answer is (A). Harry Hathaway does not have a poor credit rating. His former wife is responsible for the dilemma.

90. **B** This is consistent with the result (A). Since it explains how Harry was able to obtain the $2000 loan, the correct answer is (B).

91. **B** The facts here are not inconsistent with Mr. Hathaway's problem (A). The correct answer is (B) because the presentation of proof of the facts no doubt influenced the company to cooperate by making the loan. It can be assumed that Harry had a good moral reputation and is a valuable employee but the company wanted to do some checking.

92. **C** This statement is not irrelevant to the fact situation. No doubt a central clearing agency gave the same report on his credit rating and his long standing as a depositor is irrelevant (A). This does not explain the result (B) but it is deducible from the fact situation so (C) is the correct answer.

93. **B** This is consistent with the problem facing Harry Hathaway (A). Since it explains that some other source was necessary in order to pay for the car, the correct answer is (B).

94. **C** This shows the necessity of getting a new car (A). It does not explain the result, so (B) is not acceptable. The correct answer is (C) since it is deducible from the fact situation. A new car was necessary.

95. **E** This statement suggests an alternate solution to the problem and is therefore consistent with the fact situation (A). It does not explain the result—the way in which the problem was solved (B). Since this suggestion is not deducible from anything in the fact situation or the result, (C) is not acceptable. It neither supports nor weakens the result (D). The correct answer is (E) because it is not relevant to the result.

96. **C** This is relevant to the result. The family budget will suffer in order to repay the loan (A). It does not explain the result (B). The correct answer is (C) since it can be deduced that additional income is necessary because of the result.

Logical Reasoning

This question type requires the application of logic to familiar situations and ideas. Thus, emphasis is placed on common sense, not legal precision or a formal training in logic.

DIRECTIONS: In this section you must judge the logic and reasoning employed in short sentences or paragraphs. You should choose the *best* answer to each question, that is, the one which most logically follows from the application of common sense. The best answer selection should not involve any logical inconsistency or any data not related to the logical issue presented. After making your choice, blacken your answer in the space provided.

1. Since rice serves the function in oriental cuisines that is served by bread in western cuisines, rice and bread must be very similar in taste.

   1. Ⓐ Ⓑ Ⓒ Ⓓ Ⓔ

   The writer's argument would be considerably weakened if attention were focused on the fact that

   (A) bread is made from wheat, not rice
   (B) bread and rice have differing nutritional value
   (C) oriental cuisines are based on foods and tastes not found in western cuisines
   (D) bread and rice are substantially different in shape
   (E) bread and rice come from related grains processed in the same manner

2. Ⓐ Ⓑ Ⓒ Ⓓ Ⓔ **2.** Since Phil always gets good marks in chemistry, he must be a good all-around student.

Which of the following statements most closely parallels the reasoning used in the above statement?

(A) Since all automobiles I have owned have four wheels, four must be the most economical number of wheels for an auto.

(B) Since all racing horses are fast, horses which never race must be slower.

(C) Since John always talks loudly, he must be hard of hearing.

(D) Since all mechanisms for social control that I know of are repressive, all forms of government are probably counterproductive.

(E) Since Tom is a good bowler, he probably excels at all sports.

Questions 3–4 are based on missing portions of the passage below. In completing each question, choose the answer which best fits the context of the passage.

Serum cholesterol levels in human blood have been linked to various physiological changes. These changes have ramifications both somatic and psychological, both desirable and dysfunctional. For example, it has been conclusively demonstrated that as the cholesterol level rises in the male bloodstream, hormonal output of pituitary and most other glandular organs increases proportionately. However, testosterone production increases geometrically with an arithmetic increase in serum level, thereby producing a sexual vitality inconsonant with other physiological impulses resulting from glandular product. Thus, increasing levels of serum cholesterol, especially in young males, can result in 3. Continuously high serum levels can also result in higher incidence of all forms of heart disease, especially in males aged 40 through 54. Chances of contracting any type of heart disease increase by a factor of four if serum levels are 50% above normal for a period of three or more consecutive years. If this high serum level is present in combination with other casual factors of heart disease, such as obesity, smoking, and lack of exercise, the chances of a heart attack during the given years can increase by as much as a factor of ten. Since high serum cholesterrol levels usually result from these other causal elements of heart disease, it follows that 4.

3. Ⓐ Ⓑ Ⓒ Ⓓ Ⓔ **3.** (A) disturbing discontinuities in physiological and psychological development
(B) lengthening of the prepubescent period
(C) a dangerous pattern of antisocial behavior
(D) severe psychological damage
(E) abnormal development of personality

4. Ⓐ Ⓑ Ⓒ Ⓓ Ⓔ **4.** (A) the actual increase in chances of heart attack cannot be calculated precisely
(B) the actual increase in chances of heart attack is much greater than either given factor
(C) the actual increase in chances of heart attack is much lower than either given factor
(D) high levels of serum cholesterol are as much a warning symptom as they are a cause of heart disease
(E) individuals exhibiting all such characteristics are especially susceptible

5. Ⓐ Ⓑ Ⓒ Ⓓ Ⓔ **5.** Since all people that I know are of the Protestant faith, Protestantism is probably the universal religion.

Which of the following statements most closely parallels the kind of reasoning used in the above statement?

(A) Since all Russian novels that I have read involve passion, Russians are probably very passionate people.

(B) Since all light bulbs I have seen operate electrically, all light probably results from electrical power.

(C) Since all carrots that I have seen are orange in color, carrots probably taste like oranges.

(D) Since all people that I know smile when they are happy, smiling is probably the universal way of expressing happiness.

(E) Since all clocks I have seen have hands, there is probably no better way to tell time.

6. If the cinema has replaced the theatre, technological advances have replaced spontaneous exhibitions as a source of entertainment.

6. Ⓐ Ⓑ Ⓒ Ⓓ Ⓔ

Which of the following statements most closely parallels the kind of reasoning used in the above statement?

(A) If lighters have replaced matches, butane has replaced sulfur as a source of light.

(B) If plastic has replaced glass, technology has replaced art.

(C) If Vitamin C pills have replaced oranges, synthetics have replaced natural foods as sources of essential nutrients.

(D) If pens have replaced pencils, science has replaced tradition.

(E) If soy has replaced wheat, the need for economy has surpassed the desire for flavor.

7. Since white is the amalgam of all colors, this paper is also blue.

7. Ⓐ Ⓑ Ⓒ Ⓓ Ⓔ

Which of the following statements most closely parallels the reasoning used in the above statement?

(A) Since I am holding up 4 fingers, I am also holding up 3 fingers.

(B) Since Portugal is on the Iberian Peninsula, it must be part of Spain.

(C) Since Alaska is part of the U.S., it must also be part of the North American continent.

(D) Since penguins are also birds, they must have wings.

(E) Since light is made up of rays, heat is a form of radiation.

8. New York City has a population of 8 million and spends $10 billion a year; the State of New Jersey has a population of 8 million, and spends $4 billion a year. New Jersey must be more efficient.

8. Ⓐ Ⓑ Ⓒ Ⓓ Ⓔ

The writer's argument would be considerably weakened if attention were focused on the fact that

(A) New Jersey is much larger geographically.

(B) New York is dissected by rivers.

(C) the cost of living is high in both states.

(D) New York City provides services that New Jersey does not.

(E) tax revenue in New York City is twice that of N.J.

9. Last year, inflation ran at 17% and the stock market dropped by 28%, but gold increased by almost 300%. Obviously, gold is the best investment there is.

9. Ⓐ Ⓑ Ⓒ Ⓓ Ⓔ

The writer's argument would be considerably weakened if attention were focused on the fact that

(A) silver appreciated by 150% last year.

(B) the U.S. dollar is not so strong in the world currency market as it once was.

(C) certain antiques nearly tripled in value last year.

(D) prior to last year and for a period of 40 years, gold appreciated in value by only 10%.

(E) the stock market has appreciated by nearly 40% since the first of the new year.

10. Ⓐ Ⓑ Ⓒ Ⓓ Ⓔ   10. I've smoked cigars from Jamaica, the Canary Islands, and Nicaragua. I say there are no cigars better than the Havanas I used to smoke 10 years ago. Unfortunately, Havanas are no longer imported here.

The writer's argument would be considerably weakened if attention were focused on the fact that

(A) Jamaican weather is identical to Havana weather.

(B) most of the former great Havana cigar growers are now located elsewhere.

(C) the soil in the Canary Islands is identical to Havana soil.

(D) the types of tobacco grown in Havana are identical to those grown in Nicaragua.

(E) ten years ago, Havana tobaccos were considerably inferior as compared with their present-day quality.

11. Ⓐ Ⓑ Ⓒ Ⓓ Ⓔ   11. Since amphibians predated all forms of life on land, intelligent life on this planet evolved from early sea creatures.

The writer's argument would be considerably strengthened if attention were focused on the fact that

(A) certain sea mammals exhibit great intelligence.

(B) landlocked reptiles eliminated all forms of amphibian life during the Paleozoic era.

(C) Darwin's theory of natural selection has never been conclusively proven.

(D) fossil remains indicate that the brains of amphibian creatures were very small.

(E) a human lung is qualitatively different from the gills of an amphibian.

12. Ⓐ Ⓑ Ⓒ Ⓓ Ⓔ   12. Since Napoleon was the best military strategist who ever lived, Patton's success in battle can be attributed to his emulation of Napoleon.

The writer's argument would be considerably weakened if attention were focused on the fact that

(A) Napoleon was beaten decisively at Waterloo.

(B) Patton's command was transferred to Omar Bradley.

(C) success in battle results from many factors in addition to strategies.

(D) Patton had modern missiles at his disposal.

(E) Napoleon fought against Britain and Russia; both of these countries were allies of Patton.

Questions 13–17 are based on missing portions of the passages below. In completing each question, choose the area which best fits the context of the respective passage.

"Conglomerate" is a term recently coined to describe a uniquely modern, uniquely American corporate phenomenon. The nomenclature refers to corporations whose primary tactic of expansion is diversification. That is, conglomerates are companies that grow by buying or somehow gaining control of other companies in unrelated fields of commerce. Conglomerates are uniquely modern because only an efficient large-scale system of capital funding could support such an acquisitive appetite on a regular basis. They are uniquely American, for only in this country is growth *per se* a legitimate corporate goal. The anti-trust law has limited certain kinds of "normal" growth in that corporations are often prohibited from controlling other corporations in the same or a related field of endeavor. Hence 13. This clearly reveals the American ambivalence to the corporate form since the industrial revolution—on the one hand, a blind faith in the ethos of growth, and on the other, an equally blind fear of "big business." This, in turn, explains the cyclical nature of America's trust-busting fervor.

The economic justification for conglomerates is at once simple and simplistic. It is argued that significant efficiency is to be found through the conglomerate form in terms of 14. Indeed, in his 1968 work *The American Challenge*, J. J. Servan-Schrieber argued that the threat of a global economy dominated by the U.S. is at bottom the result of American sophistication in, and monopoly of, modern, efficient management techniques. If all efficient managers are American, then all 15; if all efficient bureaucratic systems are American, then all of international business will adopt those systems. But an analysis of the first American conglomerate, the huge executive departments of government, can quickly dispel Mr. Servan-Schrieber's fear.

13. (A) the corporate lust for growth can be satiated only by expansion *across* industry lines
    (B) the problem is stated
    (C) American corporations are forced to try to circumvent the law
    (D) corporate entities strive for true monopoly
    (E) a schism has developed between different types of corporate managers

13. Ⓐ Ⓑ Ⓒ Ⓓ Ⓔ

14. (A) bureaucratic systems and high-level management services
    (B) one corporation owning others in the same field
    (C) the supply of raw materials
    (D) personnel selection
    (E) intra-industry consolidation

14. Ⓐ Ⓑ Ⓒ Ⓓ Ⓔ

15. (A) others are doomed to failure at the outset
    (B) Americans will manage all efficient foreign companies
    (C) international business will be effectively monopolized
    (D) foreign companies will seek to learn from America's management intelligentsia
    (E) domestic American business will achieve great success

15. Ⓐ Ⓑ Ⓒ Ⓓ Ⓔ

The dialectic was originally described by Hegel as a system which causes social movement. The process began with a thesis, the status quo, the extant system of distribution of social and economic power. The thesis is invariably attacked by the antithesis, the insurgent, the new solution to societal problems. Out of the conflict of these two emerges the synthesis, or that social structure or set of beliefs which combines elements of both the original thesis and the consequent antithesis. It is the synthesis that, in time, becomes the new thesis, and thus the dialectic process is 16. The notion of the dialectic in and of itself is merely an intellectually appealing way of describing that which is intuitively obvious. And since things obvious are rarely controversial, the dialectic 17. But Marx's interpretation of the dialectic cast it in the role of the metronome of history, guiding the inexorable rhythm of the human parade toward the best of all possible worlds—Communism.

16. Ⓐ Ⓑ Ⓒ Ⓓ Ⓔ   **16.** (A) perpetual
                              (B) redundant
                              (C) self-regenerative
                              (D) a circular process
                              (E) occasionally socially regressive

17. Ⓐ Ⓑ Ⓒ Ⓓ Ⓔ   **17.** (A) in its original form was merely descriptive
                              (B) passed permanently into the realm of obscurity
                              (C) was debated only in academic circles
                              (D) died the death of rhetoric
                              (E) became an analytic tool of conventional social theory

ANSWERS AND ANALYSIS

1. **C** It demonstrates that the two cuisines are essentially different, and thus function might be the only similarity between the two. Electricity does for some vehicles what gas does for others, but there is no similarity other than function between electricity and gas. (E) actually strengthens the author's argument. (A) is incorrect because the fact that the two come from different sources does not necessarily affect taste, e.g., sugar and saccharine. (B) does not relate to taste at all, yet taste is the obvious focus of the conclusion. (D) is equally irrelevant.

2. **E** The reasoning in this statement exactly parallels the reasoning in the given sentence, i.e., that what is true of someone in one context is true for that someone in all similar contexts. The logic of (A) is that what is true of some things predicates a different truth about all such things. The logic of (B) is that if a segment of a class of things exhibits a certain characteristic all members of the class not included in that segment do not exhibit that characteristic. (C) is obviously unrelated logically to the given sentence. (D) represents the same reasoning as (A).

3. **A** This relates to the focus of the first part of the passage. Since one gland's hormonal production outpaces the production of the others as the serum level rises, discontinuities in development are the likely result. (B) runs contrary to the author's logic, (C) is much too strong a statement relative to the author's previous tone, as is (D); (E) is unjustifiable because the author never mentions the effect of serum level on personality.

4. **D** Because high serum in combination with other factors results in a high risk of heart disease, and because high serum typically results from these other factors, cholesterol is both a warning and a cause of the disease. (A) is not at all justified by the text, and (B) and (C) contradict the sentence immediately preceding. (E) is just a rephrasing of the previous sentence.

5. **D** The reasoning in the given statement is a classic specific-to-general conclusion. (A) assumes that Russian novels accurately reflect Russian personality, mixing the metaphors in the specific-to-general process. If the first clause of (A) read "Since all Russians I have met are passionate," this might be the best answer. (B) also mixes metaphors in assuming that light bulbs are the sole source of light. (C) is ridiculous. (E) bears no relationship to the given statement whatsoever since it makes a value (qualitative) judgment, i.e., "no *better* way," rather than a purely quantitative conclusion, i.e., "no *other* way."

6. **C** The basic logic involved in the given statement is that X replaces Y, the basic nature of X has displaced the basic nature of Y in terms of a specific function. (C) parallels the given statement. (A) is defective in several ways, one of which being that not all lighters are butane, and thus the "function" described in the second clause of (A) is imprecise. (B)'s second clause contains no mention of function whatsoever; (D) and (E) are flawed in the same manner.

7. **A** The logic of the given statement is that the whole contains all and any of its constituent parts even though this may not be observable by merely usual scrutiny, i.e., salt contains both sodium and chloride. None of the answer selections parallels such reasoning except (A).

8. **D** This offers an explanation as to why New York City's budget might be larger and yet equally efficient. Therefore, the given statement is weakened. (A) is incorrect because there is no reason to assume a relationship between geographical size and higher spending. (B) has no reasonable relationship to budgetary spending. (C) is explicitly true for both states, and therefore could neither strengthen nor weaken the argument. (E) is flawed but seductive. Although higher tax revenues imply a revenue/expenditure efficiency in New York, the facts presented show New Jersey's tax revenue—one-half of New York City's—producing expenditures of less: For example, if revenue in New York equals $20B, then New Jersey revenue equals $10B. Efficiency ratio in New York City is thus 2/1, but in New Jersey, 2.5/1. Besides, unless it can be demonstrated that New York City gets more for its $10B than New Jersey gets for its $4B, the author's statement is not weakened.

9. **D** This shows that return on gold investments fluctuate widely, and thus, in some years, there were probably better investments than gold. (A) simply demonstrates that, at least last year, gold was a better investment relative to silver, thus *strengthening* the author's argument. (B) has no relevance to the statement, especially since the change in relative value is not specifically denominated in dollars (as opposed to francs or rubles). (C) has two flaws: first, only "certain antiques" tripled in value; secondly, they increased in value by only 200%. (E) has no relevance whatsoever.

10. **E** This demonstrates that present-day Havanas are superior to those the author used to smoke. (A), (B), (C) and (D) do not weaken the author's argument since they all relate solely to *one* component of cigar quality, no one of which can be evaluated against any other.

11. **A** This is the only selection which *strengthens* the author's statement; all others *weaken* his logic.

12. **C** If true, this weakens the writer's tautological consideration of "strategies" and "success." (A) and (B) merely state that both Patton and Napoleon were "defeated" in one way or another (on the battlefield or by the bureaucrats). Both choices are therefore neutral in terms of the writer's statement, particularly because he uses "best" instead of "perfect." (D) and (E) again state facts which do not relate to the logic of the writer's point.

13. **A** This follows logically since if *intra*-industry expansion is illegal, the only alternative is inter-industry expansion. (B), while not explicitly contrary to prior statements in the passage, in no way explains the sentence that it precedes. (C) is not

inferred in the passage, (D) contradicts the immediately foregoing sentence, and (E) has no basis anywhere in the passage.

14. **A** It is logical that all companies require roughly similar bureaucratic systems and high-level management services, since the higher the management the less need for day-to-day familiarity with the business of the various companies. (B) is stated earlier in the passage as being illegal. (C) assumes that companies operating in different industries, but under the "conglomorate" umbrella, have similar new materials requirements. This is not likely given the way "conglomerate" is earlier defined. (D) is completely irrelevant, since presumably different companies in unrelated fields need, for the most part, different personnel. (E) has no basis, since each company under the conglomerate superstructure retains a separate identity as well as a separate business.

15. **B** This follows logically, and is consistent with the author's tone. (A) states the converse of the first clause of the question sentence, and thus cannot logically flow from it. The fact that all efficient managers are American does not imply that all non-American managers are "doomed to failure at the outset." (C) is wrong because efficiency does not inevitably lead to monopoly. (D) is flawed because although true, it fits neither the content nor the tone of the rest of the passage; (E) suffers similarly.

16. **C** An accurate summation of the foregoing description. (A) is wrong because logically, no social system can be absolutely perpetual. (B) is wrong because earlier in the passage, the dialectic is called the source of social movement, and, as such could not be redundant. (D) and (E) are similarly contradictory.

17. **E** This both sums up the foregoing two sentences and provides excellent groundwork for the "But" of the next sentence. (A), while appealing, is too pejorative relative to the earlier parts of the passage. (*Note.* An incorrect answer to question 16 could easily cause another mistake here. This is often true in sections of this type.) (B) is contradicted by the rest of the passage, as is (D). (C) contradicts the previous sentence, since it indicates that the dialectic *was*, at some *level* (not frequency) controversial.

Case Evaluation

The objective of this question type is to test your ability to evaluate the validity of a conclusion that is based on facts given in a presented case, when new factors are introduced. The section consists of a reading passage (the case) which describes a situation and includes a principle or set of rules that apply to that situation. This is followed by a conclusion that may be drawn from the case. You are then given a set of statements that may change the nature of the case. Your job is to evaluate the effect that each statement has on the validity of the conclusion. You have to choose:

(A) if the statement clearly proves the conclusion.
(B) if the statement strengthens or reinforces the conclusion but does not clearly prove it.
(C) if the statement clearly disproves the conclusion.
(D) if the statement weakens the conclusion but does not clearly disprove it.
(E) if the statement has no relevance to the conclusion.

We have included several sample cases for practice. Before you begin you should bear in mind the following:

   a. Each case includes a principle of law or a set of rules upon which the conclusion is based. These principles or rules may be limited to one section of the text or may be scattered throughout the text. *Make sure you identify and understand ALL the principles involved.*

   b. The principles may be sound legal principles or they may be artificially constructed for the purpose of the particular case. In either case *you must accept them as valid and base your reasoning on them.*

   c. The *Conclusion* for each case may follow logically from what you have read in the text or may seem inappropriate according to your understanding of the case. This is because the statements which follow may change the nature of the case entirely. *Make sure you read the Conclusion carefully and understand its implications.*

   d. The *Statements* that come after the conclusion will either add facts to the case, change factual details quoted in the case, or in effect remove facts from the case. You should read each Statement and readapt the case accordingly. Each Statement must be taken individually. *Do not base your decision regarding one Statement on information presented in any other statement.*

   e. When *Evaluating* the effect of each statement on the conclusion you will choose one of the five *Criteria,* listed above. *Make sure you understand what each one of the Criteria implies.* Pay particular attention to (B) and (D) which tend to be tricky.

   f. When reading the *Case* pay particular attention to the way the facts are presented. *Distinguish between specific description of events and loose implications* which are designed to fool you into drawing false conclusions. Although the cases are written in very readable language you should pay attention to what seem like trivial details; *assume that every detail is important.*

   g. Finally, as the cases are drawn from real life situations that you may have experienced, you may tend to take sides or sympathize with certain characters. *Try to avoid letting your personal feelings influence your judgment.*

You can now begin to test yourself. Do each case separately and check the answers and analysis that appear after the third sample case.

DIRECTIONS: The following section contains three sample cases. Each case includes a principle of law or a set of rules relating to that particular case. Each case is followed by a conclusion concerning the nature of the case and a set of five statements which may affect the nature of the case. You must evaluate what effect each statement has on the validity of the conclusion and choose:

   (A) if the statement clearly proves the conclusion.
   (B) if the statement strengthens or reinforces the conclusion but does not clearly prove it.
   (C) if the statement clearly disproves the conclusion.
   (D) if the statement weakens the conclusion but does not clearly disprove it.
   (E) if the statement has no relevance to the conclusion.

Case 1

   Dagwood Bumble has been out of work five months and in final desperation begs Archie Plunkett to give him a job in his grocery store. Plunkett tells him that he can have a job as a packer in the back room on condition that he agrees to work for three-quarter pay and do anything he is told without question.

Thinking of his wife and five hungry children, Bumble agrees and begins packing sugar into five-pound bags, but according to his boss's instructions he short-weights each bag by a quarter pound. That day Plunkett's store gets raided by an inspector from the Department of Weights and Measures, and Bumble gets caught red-handed and is arrested.

Under the law a person is considered guilty of an illegal act which he commits under the direction of his superior unless it is committed under direct personal duress or compulsion, or under the immediate threat of death or serious bodily harm.

Conclusion: Dagwood Bumble is guilty of an illegal act.

Statements

1. Ⓐ Ⓑ Ⓒ Ⓓ Ⓔ   **1.** Bumble had not started packing the sugar when he was arrested.

2. Ⓐ Ⓑ Ⓒ Ⓓ Ⓔ   **2.** Bumble, who was afraid of losing his job, was prepared to carry out Plunkett's instructions.

3. Ⓐ Ⓑ Ⓒ Ⓓ Ⓔ   **3.** Plunkett was in the back room while Bumble was packing the short-weight sugar, to make sure that he was doing what he was told.

4. Ⓐ Ⓑ Ⓒ Ⓓ Ⓔ   **4.** Plunkett had been short-weighting his sugar for years.

5. Ⓐ Ⓑ Ⓒ Ⓓ Ⓔ   **5.** Plunkett was bigger and stronger than Bumble, and Bumble knew that he had a violent temper.

Case 2

Dr. Egon Lanolin, a brilliant industrial chemist, was employed by Tru-bute Soap Company in their research laboratories where he had been unsuccessfully working on a new formula synthetic soap for over a year. Roger Trube, owner-director of the company, impatient for results, confronted Dr. Lanolin and accused him of inefficiency and sheer laziness in his project. As a result Lanolin quit on the spot and found immediate employment with Fancilon Cosmetics, one of Tru-bute's major competitors.

Within a month Fancilon was on the market with a new synthetic soap called Synthilon. Tru-Bute sued Fancilon and Lanolin for the ownership and production rights for the new soap on the basis of an existing law.

A company or an individual shall have ownership rights to a product, invention or process that was initiated and developed wholly or partially by an employee during his period of employment by the said company or individual, provided that the product, invention or process is related to the employee's duties.

Conclusion: Tru-Bute should be awarded ownership of the synthetic soap formula.

Statements

6. Ⓐ Ⓑ Ⓒ Ⓓ Ⓔ   **6.** Fancilon had been working on a synthetic soap formula prior to Egon Lanolin's joining them.

7. Ⓐ Ⓑ Ⓒ Ⓓ Ⓔ   **7.** Dr. Lanolin did not quit Tru-bute, but was fired for not advancing on the formula.

8. Ⓐ Ⓑ Ⓒ Ⓓ Ⓔ   **8.** The process of setting up the production line and manufacturing the synthetic soap took three months.

9. Synthilon soap is based on Dr. Lanolin's formula which he completed only after the termination of his employment with Tru-Bute.

9. Ⓐ Ⓑ Ⓒ Ⓓ Ⓔ

10. Fancilon did not have its own research laboratories and operated chiefly by buying ready-made and proven formulas for its products.

10. Ⓐ Ⓑ Ⓒ Ⓓ Ⓔ

Case 3

George Funk buys his son, Bernie, a .22 caliber rifle for his thirteenth birthday. Funk gives Bernie careful instructions in gun care and maintenance and particularly in gun safety. Bernie is a bright and responsible youngster so his father assumes that he will not use the rifle in the house or environs, as they live in a crowded residential area.

One day when Funk is at work, Bernie takes the rifle into the back yard and starts shooting at birds. A stray bullet hits and injures Jock Bull, the Funks' neighbor, who was pruning his fruit trees in his own back yard. Jock sues Bernie's father for personal injury.

The law pertaining to this case states that a parent who has entrusted his child with a dangerous instrument is responsible for damages which the child causes with the instrument if the parent has not exercised sufficient care in letting the child use the instrument.

Conclusion: George Funk is responsible for Jock Bull's injury.

Statements

11. George Funk had locked the bullets in his safe and Bernie used bullets he had gotten from a friend.

11. Ⓐ Ⓑ Ⓒ Ⓓ Ⓔ

12. George Funk has no sons.

12. Ⓐ Ⓑ Ⓒ Ⓓ Ⓔ

13. It was Bernie's friend Manny who fired Bernie's rifle and injured Jock Bull that morning.

13. Ⓐ Ⓑ Ⓒ Ⓓ Ⓔ

14. The Funks did not live in a crowded residential area.

14. Ⓐ Ⓑ Ⓒ Ⓓ Ⓔ

15. George Funk knew that the key to the rifle cabinet where he kept Bernie's .22 rifle was identical to the key of Bernie's bicycle lock.

15. Ⓐ Ⓑ Ⓒ Ⓓ Ⓔ

ANSWERS AND ANALYSIS

1. **C** This statement *clearly disproves the conclusion* as Bumble had not yet carried out the illegal act of short-weighting the sugar.

2. **B** Although this does not clearly prove the conclusion, it certainly *strengthens* it as it shows Bumble's agreement to carry out an illegal act, while his fear of losing his job does not constitute *direct personal duress or compulsion*.

3. **C** Plunkett's presence in the room to supervise Bumble, who is desperate to keep his job, can be considered as *direct personal duress* and thus *clearly disproves* the conclusion that he is guilty.

4. **E** This fact has no bearing on the conclusion that Bumble is guilty.

5. **D** Although there is no evidence that Plunkett threatened Bumble physically, Bum-

ble's knowledge of Plunkett's violent temper may have been seen as a *threat of bodily harm* by Bumble and thus it *weakens the conclusion*.

6. **D** This statement *weakens the conclusion* as it allows for the possibility of Fancilon's independent development of the formula, but it does not *clearly disprove* it because the text does not say on whose formula the new soap is based.

7. **E** Whether Lanolin quit or was fired is totally *irrelevant to the conclusion*.

8. **C** This statement *clearly disproves* the conclusion as it dates the completion of the Synthilon formula two months before Lanolin joined Fancilon.

9. **A** The fact that the formula was Lanolin's *clearly proves* the conclusion as the text tells us that he had been working on it while employed by Tru-Bute. The time of completion of the formula does not affect the principle of ownership.

10. **B** This statement *strengthens the conclusion* by precluding Fancilon's independent development of the new soap, but as it does not establish that the formula for its soap is clearly Dr. Lanolin's, it does not prove the conclusion.

11. **D** This fact *weakens the conclusion* in that it shows that George Funk had exercised some care in his son's use of the rifle. But the key is *sufficient care,* and hiding the bullets was not sufficient in this case.

12. **C** Since George Funk has no sons, Bernie cannot be his son and so he is not responsible for any of Bernie's actions. This *clearly disproves* the conclusion.

13. **C** According to the cited law, George Funk is only responsible for damages caused by his child. This statement therefore *clearly disproves the conclusion*.

14. **E** Where the Funks lived *is not relevant to the conclusion,* which deals with George Funk's responsibility.

15. **A** This *clearly proves the conclusion* as it shows that George Funk had not exercised sufficient care in controlling his son's use of the rifle by knowingly allowing his automatic access to it.

FIVE
WORDS FREQUENTLY APPEARING ON THE GMAT

In your preparation for the GMAT it is important that you become familiar with the meanings of as many words as possible. This is specially true for success on the Verbal Aptitude sections of the test, but it also necessary for better comprehension of Reading Recall and Business Judgment passages where a few key words may hold the meaning of an entire paragraph.

The two vocabulary lists presented here contain words that frequently appear on the GMAT and many terms that you may encounter in the course of the exam. The General Vocabulary List includes definitions of words that could appear anywhere in the exam, although their main application is in the Verbal Aptitude sections. The Glossary of Business Terms is a special list of basic business vocabulary designed to enhance your understanding of Business Judgment passages.

Study each list carefully to familiarize yourself with these words. Refer to these listings to check the meaning of any difficult words you may encounter in other parts of this guide.

General Vocabulary List

Abase—to humiliate, degrade
Abash—to bewilder, confound
Abate—to remove, lessen
Abdicate—to forsake, give up
Aberration—deviation
Abeyance—inactivity
Abhor—to detest, hate
Abject—degraded, miserable
Abjure—to recant, revoke
Abnegate—to deny, denounce
Abominate—to dislike
Abort—to be unsuccessful, fail to develop

Abrade—to scrape out
Abrogate—to abolish
Abscond—to bolt, decamp, flee
Absolve—to pardon
Abstemious—eating or drinking sparingly
Abstract—summary
Abstruse—profound, hidden, hard to understand
Accede—to consent
Accessory—accomplice
Acclivity—incline, rising slope
Accolade—honor, award
Accord—to grant, allow

Accost—to greet aggressively
Accretion—adhesion, concretion
Accrue—to accumulate
Acerbity—sharpness, bitterness
Acme—summit, peak
Acolyte—attendant, helper
Acrimonious—sharp, acrid
Actuate—to put into action
Adamant—immovable
Adduce—to give as proof
Adjudicate—to decide (a case)
Adjunct—auxiliary, appendage
Adjure—to state on oath
Admonish—to caution, warn
Adroit—skillful, clever
Adulation—flattery
Adulterate—to corrupt, contaminate
Advent—coming
Adventitious—accidental
Advocate—counsel, defender
Aegis—protection
Aesthetic—pertaining to beauty
Affability—politeness, courtesy
Affinity—relation, alliance
Affluence—wealth
Aggrandize—to increase in power
Agnostic—one who doubts the existence of God
Agrarian—relating to farming
Alacrity—willingness, agility
Albeit—although
Alchemy—chemistry of the middle ages
Alimentary—supplying food
Allay—to soothe, calm
Allegory—parable, fable
Allocate—to distribute
Allude—to insinuate, refer
Altercation—quarrel
Alternation—recurrence, succession
Altruism—unselfish devotion
Amalgamate—to combine, unite
Ambidextrous—using both hands equally well
Ameliorate—to amend, improve
Amenable—responsible, liable
Amenity—pleasantness
Amiable—pleasing, loving
Amorphous—shapeless
Anachronism—something misplaced in time
Analgesic—pain-reducing drug
Analogy—similarity, affinity
Anarchy—absence of government
Anathema—ban, curse
Anchorite—hermit
Ancillary—subordinate
Anecdote—tale, story

Animate—to inspire, encourage
Animosity—enmity, hatred
Annals—historical accounts
Anneal—to heat glass, metals, etc.
Annotator—commentator
Anomaly—abnormality, deviation
Antagonist—opponent
Antecede—to come before (in time or place)
Antedate—to assign a date earlier than the actual one
Anterior—front
Antimacassar—cover used to protect furniture
Antipathy—aversion, dislike
Antithesis—contrast, direct opposite
Aperture—opening
Apex—highest point
Aphorism—saying, adage
Apiary—place where bees are kept
Aplomb—self-confidence
Apochryphal—of questionable authenticity
Apogee—farthest orbit point from the earth
Apoplexy—sudden loss of consciousness
Apostasy—abandoning of faith
Apothecary—druggist
Apothegm—short, pithy statement
Appall—to terrify, shock
Appellation—name, title
Apposite—suitable, appropriate
Apprise—to inform
Approbation—approval, consent
Arbiter—arbitrator, judge
Archaic—no longer used
Archipelago—chain of islands
Archives—place where records are kept
Arduous—difficult
Argot—slang
Array—rank, order, finery
Arrears—in debt
Articulate—to speak or write clearly
Artifice—mastery, trickery
Asperity—acrimony, harshness
Aspersion—slander, false accusation
Assay—to analyze chemically
Asseverate—to state positively
Assiduity—care, diligence
Assimilate—to absorb
Assuage—to pacify, calm
Astral—starry
Astringent—contracting (tissues), severe
Astute—shrewd
Atheist—one who denies the existence of God
Atrophy—to waste away, deteriorate
Attenuate—to weaken
Attrition—a wearing away, weakening
Audacious—bold

Augment — to increase
Augur — to predict
August — majestic, noble
Auspice — protection
Auspicious — fortunate, favorable
Austere — rigid, severe
Authoritative — powerful, commanding
Autocratic — arrogant, dictatorial
Autonomy — self-government
Auxiliary — assistant, helping
Avarice — greed, cupidity
Aver — assert
Averse — unwilling
Aviary — place where birds are kept
Avidity — eagerness
Avoirdupois — weight
Avow — declare
Awry — crooked, bent
Axiomatic — principle accepted as self-evident

Badger — to harass, nag
Badinage — banter
Baleful — harmful, evil
Balm — something that soothes
Banal — meaningless, commonplace
Bandy — to exchange (words)
Bane — cause of harm
Barrister — court lawyer
Bedizen — to dress in a gaudy, vulgar manner
Beguile — to deceive
Belabor — to attack verbally, drag out
Bellicose — warlike
Beneficient — liberal, kind
Benign — gentle, mild
Berate — to scold
Bereft — bereaved, deprived of
Bestial — savage
Bestride — to mount
Bicameral — having two legislative chambers
Biennial — every two years
Bilious — bad-tempered
Biped — two-footed animal
Bivouac — encampment
Bland — mild
Blasé — indifferent
Blasphemy — profane abuse of anything sacred
Blatant — noisy, vociferous
Blazon — to adorn, proclaim
Bluster — to swagger, boast
Bogus — counterfeit
Boisterous — violent, furious
Bombast — pompous speech
Botch — to ruin
Bounty — generosity

Bourgeois — middle class
Bovine — ox or cow
Brandish — to wave menacingly
Bravado — pretense of bravery
Breech — lower part of the body
Brigand — robber, bandit
Broach — to start a discussion
Browbeat — to intimidate
Brusque — abrupt in manner
Bucolic — rustic
Buffoon — clown
Buoyancy — lightness, animation
Bureaucracy — government of specialized functions and hierarchy of officials
Burgeon — bud, sprout
Burnish — to polish
Butte — hill
Buttress — prop, protuberance

Cabal — intrigue, faction
Cache — hiding place
Cacophony — harsh sound
Cadence — measured movement
Cajole — to coax, flatter
Caldron — kettle
Calligraphy — penmanship
Callous — hard, obdurate
Callow — unfledged
Calumny — slander, defamation
Canard — hoax
Canker — ulcer
Cant — tilt, whining speech
Cantilever — supporting bracket·
Canvass — to make a survey, solicit
Capacious — roomy, ample
Caper — frolic, mischievous act
Capitulate — to surrender
Caprice — whim, fancy
Captious — touchy, cross
Captivate — to charm, fascinate
Carnage — slaughter, massacre·
Carniverous — flesh-eating
Carom — rebound
Carp — to complain constantly
Carrion — decaying flesh
Castigate — to punish
Casuistry — false reasoning
Cataclysm — violent change or upheaval
Catalyst — agent of change
Cathartic — purifying
Catholic — universal
Caustic — sarcastic, corrosive
Cavil — to quibble
Celerity — rapidity, velocity

Censorious—fault-finding
Censure—to criticize sharply
Centrifugal—moving away from center
Cephalic—of the head
Cerebration—thought process
Chafe—fret, irritate
Chaff—worthless material
Chagrin—embarrassment
Charlatan—faker
Charnel—place where corpses are deposited
Chary—discretely cautious
Chastise—to castigate, correct
Chattel—slave
Chauvinism—fanatical patriotism
Chicanery—deception
Chimerical—imaginary
Choleric—irascible, easily angered
Chronic—always present
Churlish—ill-bred
Circuitous—roundabout, tortuous
Circumlocution—evasion in speech
Circumspect—watchful, cautious
Circumvent—to avoid
Citadel—fortress
Civility—politeness, affability
Clairvoyant—able to perceive something not readily apparent
Clandestine—secret, hidden
Cloy—to overindulge with an initially pleasing thing
Coagulate—to thicken, clot
Coalesce—to unite, join forces
Coda—ending section distinct from the main body of a work
Coerce—to force
Cogent—forcible, convincing
Cogitate—to think seriously
Cognate—related
Cognizant—aware
Cohesion—a sticking together
Collate—to put together in proper order
Colligate—to group together
Collocate—to arrange in position
Colloquy—conversation, dialogue
Collusion—secret agreement to defraud
Colophon—inscription in a book
Colorable—plausible, ostensible
Comestible—edible
Commensurate—proportionate
Commodious—spacious
Commute—alter, exchange
Compatible—consistent
Compendious—brief, short
Compendium—abridgement, abstract
Compunction—uneasiness, remorse

Conclave—secret meeting
Concomitant—accompanying
Concupiscence—strong desire
Condign—appropriate
Condone—to overlook as unimportant
Conduce—to lead toward a desired end
Configuration—shape, arrangement
Confiscatory—seized by authority
Conflagration—destructive fire
Confute—to disprove, refute
Congeal—to change to a solid state
Congenital—existing from birth
Congruous—appropriate, in agreement
Coniferous—cone-bearing
Conjecture—guess, conclusion
Conjure—to summon solemnly
Connive—cooperate secretly
Connoisseur—expert, critic
Connote—suggest, imply
Conscript—to force into service, draft
Consecrate—to sanctify, dedicate
Consonance—harmony
Consort—associate, companion
Constellation—group of stars
Consternation—sudden confusion, panic
Constituency—voters in a district
Constrain—to restrict movement, limit
Constrict—to shrink
Consummate—to complete
Contemn—to despise, scorn
Contemptuous—scornful, insolent
Contentious—argumentative
Contiguous—adjacent, touching
Contingency—casualty, occurrence
Contravene—to contradict
Contrition—remorse, repentance
Contrivance—plan, scheme
Controvert—to debate, dispute
Contumely—rudeness
Contusion—bruise
Conundrum—riddle
Conversant—familiar with
Convivial—joyous, festal
Convoke—to assemble
Convulse—to shake violently, agitate
Copious—abundant
Corollary—inference, result
Corona—crown, luminous circle
Corporeal—pertaining to the body
Corpulent—fat, stout
Correlate—to be in mutual relation
Corrigible—amenable, tractable
Corroborate—to strengthen, confirm
Coterie—group

Countenance—facial expression, composure
Countermand—to cancel with a contrary order
Covenant—contract
Covert—clandestine, secret
Covet—to desire, aspire to
Cower—to cringe in fear
Cozen—to trick
Crag—steep projecting rock
Crass—grossly stupid
Credence—belief, faith
Credible—believable
Credulity—simplicity, gullibility
Crimp—to bend into shape, pinch together
Cruciate—cross-shaped
Crux—vital point
Cryptic—mysterious
Cudgel—club
Culmination—highest point, climax
Culpable—deserving blame
Cumbrous—unwieldy
Cupidity—avarice, greed
Curry—to seek favor by flattery
Cursory—hasty, superficial
Cynical—sarcastic, sneering
Cynosure—center of attraction

Dalliance—dawdling
Dank—chilly and wet
Dastard—coward
Dauntless—valiant, intrepid
Dearth—scarcity
Debacle—complete failure, fiasco
Debase—to degrade, lower
Debauch—to corrupt
Debility—weakness
Debonair—affable, jaunty
Decamp—to break camp, depart suddenly
Decant—to pour
Deciduous—shedding (leaves) annually
Declaim—speak, debate
Declaration—announcement
Declivity—descent, slope
Decorous—proper, in good taste
Decrepit—run-down, worn-out
Decry—censure
Deference—honor, respect
Definitive—explicit, conclusive
Defunct—no longer existing
Deign—to condescend
Deleterious—harmful
Delineate—to describe
Demean—to behave properly
Denigrate—to defame, belittle
Denizen—inhabitant

Denote—to stand for, mean
Denude—to strip, divest
Deposition—removal (from office), testimony
Depraved—sinful
Deprecate—to disapprove of
Depreciate—to lessen the value of
Depute—to appoint, entrust
Derogatory—disparaging
Descry—to discover, make known
Desecrate—to profane, abuse
Desiccate—to dry up
Desist—to cease, stop
Despicable—contemptible
Desultory—loose, rambling
Deterrent—constraint, preventative
Detritus—product of disintegration
Devious—rambling, errant, tricky
Diametric—opposite
Diaphanous—extremely delicate, insubstantial
Dichotomy—division into two parts
Dictum—positive statement
Didactic—instructive
Diffident—lacking confidence, reserved
Diffuse—to spread without restraint
Dilate—to stretch, widen
Dilatory—tardy, lagging
Dilettante—one who dabbles superficially
Diligent—industrious, assiduous
Diluvial—pertaining to floods
Discern—to observe, perceive
Discompose—to upset the order of
Disconcert—to confound, disturb
Disconsolate—sad, forlorn
Discord—disagreement
Discountenance—disapproval
Discursive—rambling
Disdain—to scorn
Disingenuous—without candor
Disparage—to belittle
Disparate—distinct in quality
Disputation—debate
Disseminate—to spread widely
Dissident—disagreeing
Dissimulate—to put on a false appearance
Dissipate—to scatter or use wastefully
Dissolute—morally loose
Dissonant—lacking harmony
Dissuade—to advise against
Distend—to stretch out
Distrait—absentminded, distracted
Distraught—mentally upset
Diverge—to branch off, deviate
Divers—various
Divest—to deprive, strip off

Doctrinate — impractical theorist
Dogmatic — arrogant stating of opinion
Doldrums — low spirits
Dole — something given sparingly
Doleful — dismal
Dolorous — mournful
Dolt — stupid person
Dotage — senility
Dour — stern, gloomy
Dowdy — shabby, styleless
Dregs — undesirable leftovers
Drivel — silly talk
Droll — funny, amusing
Dross — refuse, waste
Dubious — uncertain
Dubitable — open to doubt
Dupe — to deceive
Duplicity — deception
Duress — restraint, force

Ebony — hard durable wood, black
Ebullient — enthusiastic
Ecclesiastical — pertaining to the church
Echelon — formation of units or troops
Eclectic — made up of elements from a variety of sources
Ecology — study of the relationships in an environment
Ecumenical — general, worldwide
Edict — public announcement, decree
Edifice — large building
Edify — to enlighten
Educe — to bring forth
Effable — capable of being expressed
Efface — to wipe out, erase
Efficacious — effective
Effigy — image, crude likeness
Effluence — flowing out
Effrontery — impudence
Effulgent — illuminated
Effusive — highly emotional
Egocentric — self-centered
Egregious — flagrant
Egression — emergence
Electorate — voting body
Elicit — to cause a response
Elision — omission
Eloquent — pleasingly expressive
Elucidate — to make clear
Elusive — hard to grasp
Emaciate — to make thin
Emanate — to come out from
Embellish — to ornament
Embody — to make perceptible, personify
Embroil — involve in an argument
Emend — to correct or alter (as in a literary work)

Emissary — messenger
Emollient — soothing substance
Emolument — salary, compensation
Emulate — to rival or try to equal
Enclave — distinct unit surrounded by foreign territory
Encomium — glowing praise
Encroach — trespass
Encyclopedia — compendium of knowledge
Endemic — restricted to a given locality
Endogenous — originating from within
Enervate — to lessen the vitality of
Enfranchise — to give the right to vote
Engender — to bring into being
Engross — to take the entire attention of
Engulf — to swallow up
Enigmatic — hard to understand, puzzling
Enjoin — to impose by order, prohibit
Enmesh — to entangle
Enmity — hostility
Enormity — outrageous act
Ensconce — to conceal, settle snugly
Entity — something that exists independently
Entomology — study of insects
Entreat — to implore
Enunciate — to announce, pronounce clearly
Ephemeral — short-lived
Epic — long, narrative poem
Epicure — one who has discriminating tastes for foods and liquors
Epigram — terse, witty saying
Epilogue — closing section of a literary work
Epistle — letter
Epitaph — inscription
Epithet — word or phrase characterizing a person or thing
Epitome — ideal example, embodiment
Epoch — event or time that marks the start of a new period
Equable — uniform, even
Equanimity — composure
Equivocal — purposely ambiguous
Equivocate — to purposely deceive
Era — period of time marked by certain events
Ergo — therefore
Ersatz — artificial, substitute
Erudite — learned
Escapement — notched device regulating movement in a mechanism
Escarpment — steep slope between level areas
Eschew — to shun
Esculent — edible
Escutcheon — shield containing a coat of arms
Esoteric — limited to a chosen few
Esthetic — beautiful

Estival – pertaining to summer
Ethereal – airy
Etude – musical composition used for practice
Eulogy – speech in praise of a dead person
Euphemism – substitution of a less offensive word
Euphony – agreeable sounds
Euphoria – feeling of well-being
Evanescent – fading from sight
Evasion – avoidance
Evince – to show plainly
Evoke – to call forth, produce
Evolve – to develop gradually
Exacerbate – to aggravate
Exacting – making severe demands
Exclude – to bar
Excoriate – to strip the skin of
Exculpate – to free from blame
Execrable – detestable
Execrate – to curse
Exemplary – serving as a model
Exempt – to excuse from responsibility others are subject to
Exhort – to entreat, appeal urgently
Exhume – to dig up
Exigency – situation making extremely urgent demands
Exigent – urgent
Exiguous – scanty, meager
Exogenous – originating from outside
Exonerate – to clear from blame
Exorcise – to expel (an evil spirit)
Expatiate – to speak or write at length, wander
Expedite – to speed up
Expeditious – prompt
Expiate – to make amends
Expound – to state in detail
Expunge – to erase
Expurgate – to remove passages (from a book)
Exquisite – very beautiful, perfected
Extant – still existing
Extemporary – impromptu
Extemporize – to improvise
Extenuate – to lessen the seriousness of
Extirpate – to destroy completely
Extol – to laud
Extraneous – not pertinent to the whole
Extricate – to set free
Extrinsic – not essential
Extrude – to force out
Exude – to discharge
Exult – to rejoice

Fabricate – to manufacture, invent
Fabulous – fictitious
Facade – front or main face of a building

Facetious – lightly joking
Facile – easily done
Facilitate – to make easier
Facsimile – reproduction
Factious – producing dissention
Factitious – artificially produced
Factotum – general worker
Fallacious – tending to mislead
Fallible – capable of erring
Fallow – cultivated land not in use
Fastidious – hard to please, meticulous
Fatuous – foolish
Fawn – to court favor, grovel
Fealty – intense faithfulness
Feasible – possible
Feculent – impure
Fecund – fertile
Feign – to simulate, pretend
Felicitous – appropriate, pleasant
Fell – dangerous, cruel
Ferret – to search out
Fervid – ardent
Fervor – ardor, zeal
Festoon – decorative chain
Fetid – stinking
Fetish – an object believed to have magical powers
Fettle – condition, state of fitness
Fiasco – complete failure
Fickle – capricious
Figment – fabrication
Filament – fine thread
Filch – to pilfer
Finesse – skill
Fissure – cleft or crack
Flaccid – soft and limp
Flagitious – wicked
Flagrant – outrageous
Flail – implement for threshing grain
Flair – aptitude, attractive quality
Flamboyant – showy
Flaunt – to show off
Flex – to bend
Flinch – to draw back
Flippant – lacking proper respect
Florescence – flowering
Floriculture – care of ornamental plants
Flout – to mock or scoff
Fluctuate – to vary
Foible – minor weakness
Foment – to stir up
Foray – to plunder
Forensic – relating to court or public debate
Forerunner – predecessor, sign warning of something to follow

Forlorn – miserable
Formidable – dreadful, awesome
Fortitude – courage
Fortnight – two weeks
Fortuitous – by chance
Fractious – unruly
Fraught – laden
Fray – fight
Frenetic – wildly excited
Frugal – thrifty
Fruition – accomplishment
Fulminate – to explode, denounce
Fulsome – disgusting
Furtive – stealthy

Gainsay – to contradict
Gambol – to frolic
Gamut – entire range
Garble – to distort
Garish – showy, gaudy
Garrulous – talkative
Gastronomy – art of good eating
Gauntlet – glove (medieval), ordeal
Gelid – frozen
Genial – cordial
Genre – sort or type, category
Genus – class, group with similar characteristics
Germane – fitting
Germinate – to develop, sprout
Gestation – development, pregnancy
Gibber – to speak rapidly, chatter
Gibe – to scoff, deride
Gird – to encircle
Glib – superficial, unconvincing
Glut – to oversupply
Glutton – one who overindulges
Goad – to spur
Gourmet – expert on good food and drink
Gradient – slope
Grandeur – splendor
Gratuitous – free of charge
Gratuity – tip
Gregarious – sociable
Grimace – expression of pain
Grommet – metal ring
Grueling – very tiring
Guild – organization of persons with common interests
Guile – deceitful behavior
Guise – false pretense
Gyrate – to move in a circular fashion

Hackneyed – overused, trite
Haphazard – not planned, random
Harangue – long speech

Harass – to torment
Harbinger – forerunner
Haughty – extremely proud
Hauteur – disdainful pride
Havoc – great destruction
Hawser – strong rope
Heady – impetuous
Hearth – fireplace floor
Hegemony – dominance of authority
Heinous – hateful, evil
Heptagon – seven-sided polygon
Heresy – anti-religious thought
Hermetic – airtight
Heterodox – differing from the accepted standard
Heterogeneous – differing in structure, mixed
Hexapod – something with six legs
Hiatus – gap
Hibernal – pertaining to winter
Hierarchy – an ordering by rank or grade
Hinder – to thwart, impede
Histrionic – theatrical
Hoax – practical joke, trick
Holocaust – complete destruction
Homily – sermon
Homogeneous – uniform in structure
Homologous – corresponding in structure
Horology – science of measuring time
Horrendous – horrible
Hortative – exhorting, pleading
Horticulture – the art of growing flowers, plants, fruits
Huddle – to crowd together
Humus – fertilizer, organic part of soil
Hurtle – to speed
Husbandry – cultivation and care of plants and animals
Hybrid – of mixed origin
Hydrophobia – fear of water
Hyperbole – exaggeration
Hypothesis – assumption

Idiosyncrasy – peculiar mannerism
Idyllic – pleasing, simple, pastoral
Ignoble – mean, base
Ignominious – shameful, degrading
Illicit – unlawful
Illimitable – boundless
Illusory – deceptive
Imbibe – to absorb or drink
Imbroglio – confused situation
Imbue – to permeate
Immolate – to offer in sacrifice
Immutable – unchangeable
Impale – to pierce through
Impalpable – not understood, vague
Impasse – deadlock

Impassioned – ardent, fervent
Impeach – to accuse
Impeccable – flawless
Impecunious – having no money, poor
Imperceptible – slight, subtle
Imperious – domineering
Impertinent – rude
Impervious – not influenced
Impetuous – impulsive
Impious – lacking reverence
Implicit – implied, not apparent
Imply – to indicate by indirect statement
Importune – to urge persistently
Impromptu – without preparation
Impudence – insolence
Impugn – to challenge as false
Impunity – freedom from harm
Impute – to attribute (something bad) to another
Inadvertence – negligence, oversight
Inalienable – unable to be taken away
Inane – lacking sense
Inarticulate – unable to speak clearly
Incendiary – one who excites or agitates
Inception – beginning
Incessant – never ceasing
Inchoative – just begun, initial
Incipient – beginning to appear
Inclement – stormy
Inclusive – taking all factors into account
Incognito – disguised
Incongruous – unconforming, inconsistent
Inconsiderable – trivial, small
Inconspicuous – not readily apparent
Incorrigible – not able to be corrected, delinquent
Incredulous – skeptical
Increment – increase, addition
Inculpate – to incriminate
Incumbent – officeholder, obligatory
Indefatigable – tireless
Indigenous – native to
Indigent – poor
Indolent – lazy
Indurate – hardened
Ineffable – unspeakable, indescribable
Ineluctable – inevitable
Ineptitude – awkwardness, incompetence
Inert – without power to move or resist
Inexorable – unrelenting
Infamy – bad reputation
Inference – conclusion
Infernal – hellish, fiendish
Infinitesimal – immeasurably small
Infrastructure – basic framework of an organization
Infringe – to encroach upon

Ingenious – resourceful, inventive
Ingenuous – frank, naive
Ingratiate – to seek someone's favor
Inherent – belonging by nature
Inimical – hostile
Iniquitous – unjust
Injunction – court order, command
Innate – natural, existing from birth
Innocuous – harmless
Innuendo – hint, allusion
Inscrutable – enigmatic, mysterious
Insidious – treacherous
Insinuate – to suggest, hint at artfully
Insipid – dull, tasteless
Insolvent – bankrupt
Instigator – one who incites action
Insular – narrow-minded, limited
Insurgent – one who revolts against established authority
Intangible – incorporeal, vague
Intemperance – excessive indulgence
Interdict – to prohibit
Interment – burial
Interminable – endless
Internment – confinement (of enemies)
Interpolate – to change by inserting new material
Interstice – space, interval
Intractable – unruly, stubborn
Intransigent – refusing to compromise
Intrepid – fearless
Intrinsic – inherent
Introvert – to turn inward
Intuition – insight
Inundate – to overflow, overwhelm
Inure – habituate
Invective – denunciation
Inveigh – to complain bitterly
Inveigle – to trick, entice
Investiture – installation in office
Inveterate – firmly established
Invidious – offensive
Invincible – unconquerable
Inviolate – sacred
Irascible – easily angered
Ironical – contrary to what was expected, sarcastic
Isthmus – narrow strip of land
Iterate – to repeat over and over
Itinerant – traveling from place to place

Jaundice – yellow pigmentation of the skin
Jaunty – lively
Jettison – to throw overboard, discard as superfluous
Jocose – humorous
Jocund – cheerful
Jocular – playful, jolly

Jostle — to elbow, agitate
Judicious — showing sound judgment
Juggernaut — massive destructive force
Juridical — pertaining to law
Juxtapose — to put side by side

Kaleidoscopic — changing
Kindred — family relationship
Kinetic — active
Kismet — fate
Kith — friends
Knave — dishonest person
Kudos — credit for an achievement, praise

Labyrinth — maze
Lacerate — to mangle, tear
Laconic — concise
Lambaste — to scold, censure
Lampoon — satirical attack
Languid — weak, dull
Languish — to become weak
Languor — lack of vitality
Larcenous — thievish
Largess — generous giving
Lascivious — lustful
Lassitude — fatigue
Latent — hidden
Laudatory — expressing praise
Lethal — deadly
Lethargic — sluggish
Levity — lightness, frivolity
Lexicon — dictionary
Libation — ceremonial drinking
Licentious — morally unrestrained
Limpid — clear, transparent
Lineament — a distinctive feature
Lissome — nimble
Litany — prayer, chant
Lithe — flexible
Litigation — lawsuit
Livid — discolored by a bruise, enraged
Locution — style of speech
Loquacious — talkative
Lucid — shining, readily understood
Ludicrous — absurd
Lugubrious — affectedly mournful
Luminary — outstanding person
Lurid — sensational

Macabre — gruesome
Machination — evil plot
Macrocosm — entity representing on a larger scale, one of its smaller units
Madrigal — song, ballad

Magistrate — official who administers laws
Magnanimous — generous
Maladroit — awkward
Malefactor — evildoer
Malevolent — arising from an evil will
Malfeasance — wrongdoing
Malign — to slander
Malinger — to feign illness
Malleable — flexible, adaptable
Martinet — very strict disciplinarian
Masticate — to chew up
Maudlin — foolishly sentimental
Megalomania — illusions of grandeur
Meliorate — to make or become better
Mellifluous — flowing sweetly, smoothly
Ménage — household
Mendacious — untruthful
Mendicant — beggar
Menial — servile
Mercurial — changeable, fickle
Meretricious — falsely alluring, gaudy
Meritorious — deserving honor
Mesmerize — hypnotize
Metamorphosis — change of form
Metaphor — figure of speech using one idea in place of another to denote a likeness between the two
Mete — to allot
Meticulous — careful with details
Mettle — spirit, courage
Miasma — pervading corruptive atmosphere
Microcosm — a small unit that is the epitome of a larger entity
Mien — manner, appearance
Militate — to work (for or against)
Millenium — 1000 years
Minion — favored person
Miscreant — villain
Misgiving — doubt
Misnomer — name wrongly applied
Missive — letter
Mitigate — to ease
Mnemonic — memory aid
Modicum — small portion
Modulate — to regulate
Mollify — to appease
Moot — debatable
Mordant — sarcastic
Mores — customs
Moribund — dying
Morose — gloomy
Motley — composed of many elements
Multifarious — diverse
Mundane — worldly
Munificent — generous, lavish

Myopia — nearsightedness
Myriad — very large number

Nadir — lowest point
Nape — back of the neck
Narcissism — self-love
Narrative — story, account
Nascent — coming into being
Nebulous — vague
Nefarious — very wicked
Nemesis — formidable rival, one who inflicts just punishment
Neology — use of an established word in a new way
Neophyte — beginner, convert
Nepotism — favoritism shown relatives
Nettle — irritate
Nexus — link, connection
Niggardly — stingy
Nocturnal — pertaining to night
Noisome — offensive, harmful to health
Nomenclature — system of names
Nonpareil — unequaled
Nonplussed — perplexed
Nostalgia — sentimental yearning for the past
Notorious — widely known
Noxious — harmful
Numismatic — monetary
Nuptial — pertaining to marriage
Nurture — train, rear

Obdurate — stubborn
Obeisance — gesture of respect
Obesity — stoutness, fatness
Obfuscate — to obscure
Objurgate — to denounce
Oblation — solemn offering
Oblique — evasive
Obloquy — widespread censure
Obsequious — servile
Obsolescent — falling into disuse
Obstreperous — noisy, unruly
Obstruct — to stop, close
Obtrude — to push out
Obtuse — stupid, blunt
Obviate — to prevent
Occidental — Western
Odious — disgusting
Odoriferous — giving off a smell
Officious — meddlesome
Olfactory — pertaining to smell
Oligarchy — government by a small group often for corrupt purposes
Ominous — threatening
Omnipotent — having unlimited power

Omnivorous — eating all sorts of food
Onerous — burdensome
Onus — burden
Opaque — not translucent
Opprobrious — disgraceful, infamous
Opulent — wealthy
Opus — work, composition
Orbit — revolving path
Ordinance — statute
Ordnance — artillery
Ordure — excrement
Ornate — showy
Ornery — obstinate
Ornithology — study of birds
Oscillate — to fluctuate between two points
Ossify — to change to bone
Ostensible — apparent
Ostentatious — showy
Ostracize — to banish
Overt — done openly
Overweening — arrogant

Palatable — agreeable to the senses
Pall — to lose effectiveness
Palliate — to reduce the intensity of
Pallid — pale
Palpable — obvious, easily perceived
Paltry — petty
Panacea — remedy for all maladies
Pandemic — widely spread
Parable — short story showing a moral
Paradigm — model, example
Paradox — a statement that seems contradictory but may be true in fact
Paragon — model of excellence
Paramount — highest in rank
Paraphernalia — personal belongings
Pariah — outcast
Parity — equality in value
Parody — farcical imitation
Paroxysm — sudden outburst
Parsimony — stinginess, thrift
Parsonage — pastor's dwelling
Pastoral — of shepherds, rural
Patent — evident
Pathos — something which arouses pity
Patrimony — property inherited from ancestors
Paucity — scarcity
Peculate — to embezzle
Pecuniary — involving money
Pedant — one who emphasizes trivial points of learning
Pejorative — worsening
Penchant — strong liking
Pendant — hanging object

Penitence — sorrow for sins
Penology — study of prisons and prison reform
Pensile — hanging
Penurious — stingy
Perambulate — to walk
Perdition — damnation
Perennial — enduring
Perfidy — treachery
Perforce — of necessity
Perfunctory — routine, superficial
Perigee — point of an orbit nearest the earth
Peripatetic — itinerant
Periphery — outside boundary
Periphrasis — using long phrasing instead of shorter expressions
Permeable — passable, penetrable
Permutation — change, alteration
Pernicious — destructive, fatal
Peroration — end of a speech
Perpetrate — carry out, commit
Perpetuate — cause to continue
Perquisite — something in addition to regular pay, tip, bonus
Personage — important person
Perspective — sense of proportion
Perspicacity — keen judgment
Perspicuous — easily understood
Pert — bold, cocky
Pertinent — relevant
Perturb — to upset, agitate
Peruse — to read carefully
Pervade — to spread throughout
Perverse — deviating from what is considered normal
Petulance — impatience
Phalanx — massed group of individuals
Philander — to court with no intention of marriage
Philistine — one governed by material rather than intellectual values
Philology — study of linguistics
Phlegmatic — sluggish
Phobia — persistent irrational fear
Picayune — of little value, petty
Piebald — marked with splotches of color, heterogeneous
Pillory — to scorn publicly
Piquant — agreeably stimulating, pungent
Pique — to offend, provoke
Piscatorial — pertaining to fish
Pithy — terse
Pixilated — amusingly eccentric
Placate — to appease
Placid — calm
Plaintive — melancholy
Plait — to braid, pleat
Platitude — trite remark

Plaudit — expression of approval
Plausible — seemingly reasonable
Plebiscite — popular vote
Plenary — full, complete
Plethora — overabundance
Plicate — folded lengthwise
Plumb — straight down, vertically
Ply — to use or practice diligently
Poach — to trespass
Poignant — pungent, touching the emotions
Polemic — involving dispute
Politic — prudent, expedient
Polity — political organization
Ponderous — unwieldy, dull
Pontificate — to orate, make dogmatic statements
Portend — to warn, foreshadow
Portentous — ominous
Posit — to postulate
Posterity — future generations
Postulate — hypothesis, axiom
Potable — suitable for drinking
Potpourri — mixture
Poultice — soft heated dressing applied to wounds
Pragmatic — practical, relating to fact
Prate — to chatter
Precarious — uncertain, risky
Precipitous — steep
Precipitate — hasty
Preclude — to shut out, prevent
Precursor — forerunner
Predacious — predatory
Predatory — tending to exploit others for one's own gain
Predicate — to affirm
Predilection — preconceived liking
Predispose — to make susceptible
Preeminent — outstanding, high-ranking
Preen — to dress up or adorn (oneself)
Premeditation — preplanning
Premise — statement forming the basis of an argument
Preponderate — to surpass in weight or power
Preposterous — absurd, ridiculous
Prerequisite — something needed for performing a function
Prescience — foreboding
Prescribe — to establish as a means of action
Presumptuous — too bold or forward
Pretentious — showy, making unjustified claims
Prevaricate — to evade the truth
Pristine — uncorrupted by society
Probity — integrity, honesty
Proclaim — to declare proudly
Proclivity — inclination
Prodigal — spendthrift
Prodigious — wonderous, enormous
Profane — irreligious

Proffer—to present for approval
Profligate—recklessly wasteful
Progeny—offspring
Prognosticate—to predict
Proliferate—to increase in number
Prolific—producing abundantly
Prolix—prolonged unduly
Prominent—noticeable, well-known
Promontory—high peak that overlooks lower land or water
Promulgate—to announce openly
Propensity—natural tendency
Propinquity—nearness
Propitiate—to appease
Propitious—favorable
Proponent—one in favor of
Propound—to present for discussion
Prorate—to divide proportionately
Prosaic—commonplace, dull
Proscribe—to outlaw, prohibit
Proselytize—to convert from one belief to another
Protagonist—main character in novel
Prototype—standard example
Provincial—having a limited outlook
Prurient—lustful, lewd
Puerile—childish, silly
Pulchritude—beauty
Punctilious—very exact
Pundit—learned person
Pungent—sharp sensation of taste and smell
Pugnacious—belligerent
Purloin—to steal
Purport—to give an appearance of, intend
Pusillanimous—lacking courage and resolve
Putative—assumed to exist
Putrefy—to rot
Pythonic—monstrous

Quadrant—one-quarter of a plane
Quaint—unusual, old-fashioned
Qualm—misgiving
Quandary—perplexed state
Querulous—complaining
Query—inquiry
Quiescent—quiet, still
Quintessence—perfect form
Quivering—shaking, trembling slightly
Quixotic—having highly romantic or chivalrous ideals

Raillery—playful teasing
Raiment—clothing
Rambunctious—boisterous
Ramification—offshoot, consequence
Rampant—widespread, without restraint

Ramshackle—loosely made, dilapidated
Rancor—ill will
Rankle—to cause resentment
Rapacious—greedy
Rapine—plunder
Ratification—formal approval
Raucous—rough sounding, boisterous
Ravenous—extremely eager for gratification
Recalcitrant—disobedient
Recant—to renounce
Recidivist—confirmed criminal
Reciprocal—complementary, mutually responsive
Recluse—hermit
Recondite—beyond ordinary understanding, concealed
Reconnoiter—to survey
Recreant—cowardly
Recrimination—countercharge
Rectitude—integrity
Recumbent—lying down
Redact—to edit
Redolent—fragrant
Redoubt—temporary fortification
Redress—to remedy, compensate
Redundant—superfluous, wordy
Refectory—dining hall
Referendum—popular vote on a measure submitted by a legislative body
Refractory—obstinate, unresponsive
Refute—to prove wrong
Refurbish—to renovate
Regale—to entertain
Regent—one who rules
Regicide—killing of a king
Regimen—system of diet, ruling system
Regressive—going backward
Relegate—to exile, to assign to a lower position
Reliquary—container for sacred objects
Remission—pardon, forgiveness, abatement
Remonstrate—to protest
Remunerate—to pay for work done, compensate
Renascent—reborn
Renegade—deserter, outcast
Renege—to go back on a promise
Renunciation—repudiation
Repast—meal
Repine—to long for
Replete—well filled
Reprehend—to criticize
Repression—stopping by force
Reprisal—act of retaliation
Reproach—disgrace, cause of blame
Reprobate—depraved, unprincipled
Reproof—rebuke, criticism
Repudiate—to refuse, reject, disown

Repugnant – distasteful, disliked
Requisite – requirement
Requital – suitable repayment
Rescind – to repeal, take back
Resilient – able to spring back into shape
Resplendent – dazzling
Restitution – restoration, refund
Restive – impatient
Resurgent – rising again
Resuscitate – revive
Retaliate – to get even
Reticence – silence, reserve
Retort – to make a witty reply
Retribution – just reward
Retroactive – extending to previous conditions
Retrograde – to go backward
Reverberate – to throw back, echo
Revile – to abuse verbally
Ribald – offensive, vulgar
Rife – widespread, abounding
Rift – opening, breach
Rigor – strictness
Risibility – laughter
Robust – healthy, strong
Rote – mechanical repetition or action
Rotund – rounded
Ruckus – noisy confusion
Rudiment – first principle, beginning of something
Ruminant – meditative
Ruminate – to meditate, ponder

Saccharine – overly sweet, affectedly agreeable
Sacrilege – desecration
Sagacious – shrewdly discerning
Salacious – lustful
Salient – conspicuous
Saline – salty
Sallow – dull greenish-yellow
Salubrious – wholesome
Salutary – curative
Salutatory – welcoming address
Sanctimony – pretended piety
Sanguine – confident, optimistic
Sapient – wise
Sardonic – scornful
Sartorial – pertaining to tailoring
Satiate – to satisfy, glut
Saturate – to soak, fill completely
Saturnine – sullen, sluggish
Savor – to relish, enjoy
Scabbard – sword sheath
Scathing – searing, blasting
Schematic – diagrammatic
Schism – split, difference of opinion

Scintilla – particle, trace
Scion – descendent
Scoff – derision
Scourge – whip, devastation
Scruple – small quantity, principle
Scrutinize – to examine closely
Scurrilous – coarse, vulgar
Secular – worldly, not religious
Sedition – rebellion
Sedulous – diligent
Semblance – appearance
Senescent – growing old
Sententious – given to moralistic expression
Sequester – to isolate
Serrate – having sawlike notches
Shallop – small, open boat
Shamble – to walk clumsily
Shunt – to turn to one side
Sibling – brother or sister
Sidle – move sidewise
Simile – figure of speech comparing two unlike things
Similitude – likeness
Simony – buying or selling of church pardons
Sinecure – easy job
Sinuous – bending, winding
Slothful – lazy
Sluice – artificial water channel
Sojourn – to remain somewhere temporarily
Solace – to comfort, console
Solicitous – showing care or concern
Soluble – able to be dissolved
Somatic – physical, of the body
Somnolent – sleepy, drowsy
Sonorous – full of sound, resonant
Sophistry – misleading but clever reasoning
Soporific – causing sleep
Sordid – dirty, ignoble
Spasmodic – intermittent
Spawn – to deposit eggs, bring forth
Specious – deceptively appealing
Specter – ghost
Sporadic – occasional
Spurious – false, not genuine
Staid – sedate
Stigma – mark of disgrace
Stilted – pompous
Stint – restriction
Stoicism – impassiveness, indifference
Stolid – showing little emotion
Stratagem – trick, device
Strategy – careful plan
Stricture – adverse criticism
Strident – harsh-sounding
Stultify – to appear foolish, impair

Stupor — loss of sensibility
Suave — polite, urbane
Subjoin — to append
Subjugate — to force to submit
Sublimate — to direct actions into more socially acceptable forms
Subservient — inferior, submissive
Subterfuge — deception used to evade something difficult or unpleasant
Subversive — destructive
Succinct — clearly and briefly stated
Succor — to help
Succulent — juicy
Suffuse — to overspread
Sully — to soil, stain
Sumptuous — lavish
Supercilious — haughty, contemptuous
Supernal — exalted, celestial
Supersede — to replace
Supervene — to happen additionally or unexpectedly
Supine — indolent, prone
Supple — flexible
Supplicate — to ask for humbly
Suppress — to keep from public knowledge
Surfeit — overindulgence
Surreptitious — acting in a secret and stealthy way
Surrogate — deputy, substitute
Sustenance — nourishment
Sycophant — self-serving flatterer
Syllogism — conclusion based on two premises
Synchronous — occurring simultaneously
Synopsis — summary
Synthesis — combining of elements to make a whole
Synthetic — man-made

Tacit — silent
Taciturn — tending toward silence
Tactic — means of accomplishing a purpose
Tactile — perceived by the sense of touch
Tantamount — equal in value
Tautology — needless repetition of an idea
Tawdry — gaudy, cheap
Taxonomy — classification (of plants and animals)
Temerity — foolish boldness
Temperate — moderate
Temporize — compromise
Tenacious — persistent, tough
Tenet — doctrine
Tenuous — unsubstantial, flimsy
Termagant — nagging woman
Terminus — end point
Terse — brief, to the point
Tertiary — third in order
Thespian — actor

Thrall — slave
Timorous — timid
Tirade — long, vehement speech or denunciation
Tithe — tenth part of something paid as a tax to a church
Titular — having a title without performing the functions involved
Tome — large book
Torpid — inactive, sluggish
Torrid — very hot
Toxic — pertaining to poison
Tractable — easily managed
Traduce — to slander
Tranquility — calmness, serenity
Transfuse — to transmit, imbue
Transgression — violation
Transitory — temporary
Translucent — permitting the passage of light
Transpire — to become known, happen
Transverse — placed crosswise
Travail — hard work
Travesty — ridiculous representation
Treble — to increase threefold
Tremulous — trembling
Trenchant — sharp, clear-cut
Trepidation — fear
Tribulation — misery, distress
Truculent — cruel, belligerent
Truncated — shortened, curtailed
Truncheon — club
Tumid — swollen, inflated
Tumultuous — violently turbulent
Turbid — muddy
Turgid — swollen
Turpitude — vileness
Tutelage — guardianship
Twit — to taunt

Ubiquitous — present everywhere simultaneously
Ulterior — lying beyond what is openly expressed
Umbrage — offense
Unctuous — oily, suave
Undaunted — determined in spite of adverse conditions
Undulate — to move in waves
Unerring — without fault
Ungainly — awkward, clumsy
Unmitigated — not lessened, absolute
Unobtrusive — not aggressive
Untenable — unable to be occupied or defended
Untoward — unfavorable
Upbraid — to scold, reproach
Uproarious — boisterous
Urbane — refined
Usurp — to take by force
Uxorial — pertaining to a wife

Vacillate — to show indecision
Vacuous — empty, stupid
Vagary — eccentric idea or action
Valorous — courageous
Vanguard — front part of a movement
Vapid — tasteless, flat
Variegated — marked with different colors
Vaunt — display boastfully
Vegetate — to lead an inactive life
Vehement — impassioned
Venal — open to corruption
Vendetta — extended bitter feud
Venerate — to show deep respect
Venial — excusable
Veracious — honest
Verbosity — wordiness
Verdant — green in color
Verisimilitude — truth
Verity — truth
Vermillion — bright red pigment
Vernacular — native language of a region
Versatile — able to change easily
Versification — metrical structure
Vertex — highest point
Vestige — trace
Viable — capable of living or functioning
Vicarious — experienced through the activity of another person
Vicissitude — changeability
Vilify — to defame
Vindicate — to clear from blame
Vindictive — wanting revenge
Virago — domineering woman
Viridity — greenness, naiveness
Virility — masculinity

Virulent — deadly, hateful
Viscous — sticky, lacking easy movement
Vitiate — to debase
Vitreous — pertaining to glass
Vituperate — to berate
Vivacious — spirited, lively
Vivid — vigorous, clear
Vixen — female fox
Vociferous — noisy
Volatile — quickly evaporating, explosive
Volition — act of determining
Voluble — talkative
Voracious — greedy
Votary — zealous follower
Votive — expressing a wish or vow
Vouchsafe — to grant

Waft — odor or sound carried through the air
Wan — pale
Wanton — reckless, immoral
Weal — well-being
Welter — confusion, turmoil
Wheedle — to coax
Whet — to arouse, stimulate
Windfall — unexpected gain
Wizened — dried up, withered
Wraith — ghost, apparition
Wrangle — to quarrel
Wroth — angry
Wry — twisted

Zany — fool, clown
Zealot — fanatic
Zenith — highest point
Zephyr — mild breeze

Glossary of Business Terms

Advertising — Any paid form of nonpersonal presentation and promotion of goods and services in such media as newspapers, magazines, television, radio, direct mail, and posters.

Amalgamation — The merger or consolidation of two corporations.

Amortization — A provision made in advance for the gradual liquidation of a future obligation by periodic charges against the capital account or by the creation of a money fund sufficient to meet the obligation when due.

Annuity — The payment or receipt of a fixed sum of money to a beneficiary at pre-determined, equal intervals of time.

Antitrust — Pertaining to legislation or procedures aimed at preventing or controlling monopoly power.

Arbitration — A procedure by which parties to a dispute allow a third party to mediate or decide the issue, the parties agreeing to abide by the decision.

Assets — The tangible or intangible properties of value owned by either a business or by an individual.

Balance of Payments — The "balance sheet" of a country's foreign transactions, basically reflecting the difference between payments made to and receipts from foreign nations over a given period of time.

Balance of Trade — A component of the balance of payments consisting of the residual between exports and imports.

Bankruptcy — A legal procedure used by one unable to meet his debts. After being declared bankrupt by a court, the bankrupt person surrenders his assets to the court for distribution to his creditors and is released from further liability on most debts.

Bear Market — A description of the stock market used when prices are generally going down.

Bond — A secured long-term obligation used to raise capital and promising to pay a specified sum at a set date(s) in the future.

Bond Market — A place to buy and sell bonds.

Bourgeoisie — The middle class.

Brand — A name, symbol, design, or term used to identify the product or service of a seller.

Broker — A selling agent who acts as intermediary between seller and buyer in negotiating a sale.

Bull Market — A description of the stock market used when the level of prices is generally rising.

Business — An economic unit that specializes in developing and distributing goods and/or services.

Capital — The money or other type of investments (goods, land, or equipment) used to produce other goods and/or services.

Capital Formation — The creation of capital goods. Capital formation comes from savings of individuals and businesses and may be used for business expansion, purchase of machinery and equipment, or on the labor force.

Capitalism — A term used synonymously with an economic system where the means of production and distribution are privately owned and where decisions as to what will be produced are made in the marketplace, with a high degree of consumer sovereignty.

Cartel — A contractual association of businesses where an agreement is made to divide markets, set prices, and determine promotion and other business activities.

Caveat Emptor — "Let the buyer beware."

Certificate — (see Notes and Certificates.)

Chain Store — A group of retail stores centrally owned and managed by one corporation.

Chattel — An article of tangible personal property.

Closed Shop — A company in which only union members are employed.

Collective Bargaining — The process by which representatives of labor and management seek to discuss, resolve, and settle their differences.

Commodity — An economic good that is the product of agriculture or mining.

Common Stock — A certificate of ownership in a corporation.

Communism — An economic system where the means of production are owned by the state. Decisions as to what to produce are made by a planning commission rather than directly by consumers.

Conglomerate — A corporation which has a wide diversification usually by acquiring other dissimilar industries or unrelated businesses through merger or purchase.

Consumer Cooperative — Goods produced by household consumers for consumption.

Consumers Group — A retail business owned and managed by consumers for their own use.

Consumer Sovereignty — The idea that consumers decide what goods and services will be produced.

Contract — A legally binding agreement between two or more parties which requires one party to perform a service in exchange for some form of consideration from the other party.

Corporation—A legal entity existing in law as if a single person with specific powers granted in a charter by a state or federal government. A major form of business organization made up of individuals to overcome the uncertain duration of a sole proprietorship or partnership.

Cost-of-Living Adjustment—An increase in wages according to provisions which are contained in some labor contracts or agreements and tied to increases in a cost-of-living index.

Currency—Something in circulation that has value and is used as a medium of exchange.

Current Assets—Assets of a short-term nature.

Debenture—An unsecured, long-term corporate obligation used to raise capital and promising to pay a specified sum at some future date.

Debt—Money, goods, or services owed to a creditor.

Deficit—The result of spending more than one's revenue, producing a loss in business operations.

Deflation—A decline of general price levels or a sharp decline in values.

Demand—The quantity of a good that will be bought at a given price.

Depreciation—The amount of capital lost by the wear and tear of equipment, buildings, and the like.

Devaluation—An official reduction in the exchange value of a currency by lowering its equivalency to some standard (e.g. gold) or some other medium of exchange.

Discount House—A retailing unit selling competitive goods below the "market" price.

Disposable Income—The income of an individual left after deducting taxes paid to federal, state, and local governments.

Duty—A tax on certain imports to prevent foreign products from having an advantage over domestic goods.

Economics—A system of abstract theories which attempts to explain the forces which govern the production, distribution, and consumption of goods and services.

Embargo—The governmental exclusion of certain foreign goods from entry into a country.

Entrepreneur—An individual who undertakes to assemble a business.

Equity—The money value of a property or interest in a property exclusive of claims against it.

Escrow—Property or money placed with a second person who holds it for a third person until the latter fulfills an obligation (as in a lease agreement).

Exports—Goods sold to another country or to businesses in other countries.

Expropriation—The take-over of individually-owned property by a government.

Fair Trade—The setting and maintaining of retail prices by the manufacturer or supplier of a product.

Fiscal Year—The year-long period used to delineate the administration of a business and its gains and losses. The beginning and end of the year correspond to the interests of the business, not the calendar.

Franchise—The licensing of retail establishments to operate according to an established pattern.

Free Trade—Trading between nations without tariffs or other trade barriers.

Goods and Services—The resources that businesses seek to develop and distribute, usually because the resources are scarce or in demand.

Gross National Product—The total value of all goods and services produced in a country during a given time period.

Gross Profit—The profit earned after deducting the cost of the goods sold, but before deducting other business expenditures.

Imports—Goods bought from a foreign country or from businesses in a foreign country.

Industrial Good—A good which is used primarily in the production of another good, e.g. electronic components as used in the manufacture of television sets.

Industrial Union—A labor union whose membership comprises workers from an entire industry.

Inflation—A chronic rise in the cost of living resulting from too much available money and credit in relation to the amount of goods and services existing.

Injunction—A court ruling that commands something to be done or restrains something from being done under penalty of law.

Inventory—A list of current assets such as property or goods.

Jobber—A term used synonymously with "wholesaler."

Laissez-Faire—"Let the people make or do what they choose." An attitude of governmental non-intervention in business affairs.

Liability—A debt owed by an individual to another or the equity of creditors in a business.

Lien—A charge upon real or personal property for the payment of a debt.

Management—The entrepreneurial function of a business enterprise; the coordination of the factors of production—land, labor, and capital.

Manufacturing—The process of adding value to basic materials by changing them into the form of goods.

Marginal Utility—An economic concept which relates the cost of a good to its degree of utility (or satisfaction) or availability (scarcity) at a given moment.

Market Area—The area over which goods and services are distributed.

Market Demand—The aggregate demand for a given good or service.

Marketing—The performance of business activities that direct the flow of goods and services from producer to consumer.

Marketing Research—The systematic gathering, recording, and analyzing of information pertaining to the marketing of a good or service.

Mediation—The introduction of a disinterested third party into the collective bargaining process for the purpose of offering non-binding suggestions for resolving the dispute.

Merchandising—The planning and supervision involved in the marketing of a good or service.

Merger—The combining of two independent businesses into one large business.

Middleman—A term used synonymously for "wholesaler."

Monopoly—A situation where there is only one supplier of a good or service.

Mortgage Bonds—A collateral bond on property which promises to pay by a lien on real property.

Net Income—The earnings of a business company after allowance for all expenses and taxes.

Notes and Certificates—Medium or short-term obligations which can be secured or unsecured.

Open Shop—A business enterprise where workers do not have to join a labor union.

Parity—The price at which agricultural goods would have to sell to give the farmer the same purchasing power as he possessed in a certain base year.

Partnership—A business of two or more persons that remains unincorporated.

Par Value—The stated (printed) value of a share of stock when issued.

Perquisite—A gift, bonus, or other benefit received in addition to a wage or salary.

Preferred Stock—A form of corporate ownership which has prior claims or assets over common stock; usually carries a fixed return.

Profit—The excess of revenue after all related expenses have been deducted.

Public Relations—The relations between a business enterprise and the public. Most large corporations have "public relations" departments that work to maintain a favorable public image distinct and separate from the company's advertising efforts.

Public Utility—An enterprise whose product or service is so important to the public that its operations, including the price it charges, are regulated by government.

Recession—A period of reduced economic activity, lack of economic growth, and high unemployment.

Resource—A natural source of material, wealth, or revenue.

Retailer—A business enterprise or individual who sells directly to the consumer.

Sales Forecast—An estimate of sales, in dollars or units, for a given period of time.

Short-Term—Refers to a time period usually of six months to a year.

Socialism—An economic system in which basic industries are owned and operated by the state.

Sole Proprietorship—A business with a single owner.

Specialty Goods—Goods purchased only occasionally; usually they are considered luxuries.

Speculative Buying—The purchasing of goods, commodities, or stock in the belief that the price or supply will change to one's economic advantage in the future.

Stagflation—Refers to a situation where the economy suffers from both inflation and recession (stagnation).

Standard of Living—A given level of wealth to which a person or group aspires.

Strike—A deliberate work stoppage by labor in an effort to force management to accede to union demands.

Subsidization—Aid or promotion of private industry with public funds.

Supply—The availability of a certain product and the changing quantities which will be available for sale as prices rise or fall.

Surety Bond—A bond which guarantees performance of a contract and protects against its nonperformance.

Surplus—The excess of a corporation's net worth over the par or stated value of its capital stock.

Tariff—A tax placed on imported goods.

Trademark—A name or mark pointing to the origin or ownership of goods to which it is applied. It is legally reserved for the exclusive use of the owner as maker or seller.

Ultimate Consumer—One who buys and/or uses goods for household consumption as distinguished from an industrial buyer.

Utility—The overall usefulness of a product to consumers. Utility together with scarcity determines the price of a product.

Utopia—An imaginative account of an ideal society.

Wholesaler—A business unit that buys goods in bulk from manufacturers for resale in smaller quantities to commercial, institutional, and government users.

Answer Sheet — Sample Test 1

Section I — Reading Recall

1. Ⓐ Ⓑ Ⓒ Ⓓ Ⓔ
2. Ⓐ Ⓑ Ⓒ Ⓓ Ⓔ
3. Ⓐ Ⓑ Ⓒ Ⓓ Ⓔ
4. Ⓐ Ⓑ Ⓒ Ⓓ Ⓔ
5. Ⓐ Ⓑ Ⓒ Ⓓ Ⓔ
6. Ⓐ Ⓑ Ⓒ Ⓓ Ⓔ
7. Ⓐ Ⓑ Ⓒ Ⓓ Ⓔ

8. Ⓐ Ⓑ Ⓒ Ⓓ Ⓔ
9. Ⓐ Ⓑ Ⓒ Ⓓ Ⓔ
10. Ⓐ Ⓑ Ⓒ Ⓓ Ⓔ
11. Ⓐ Ⓑ Ⓒ Ⓓ Ⓔ
12. Ⓐ Ⓑ Ⓒ Ⓓ Ⓔ
13. Ⓐ Ⓑ Ⓒ Ⓓ Ⓔ
14. Ⓐ Ⓑ Ⓒ Ⓓ Ⓔ

15. Ⓐ Ⓑ Ⓒ Ⓓ Ⓔ
16. Ⓐ Ⓑ Ⓒ Ⓓ Ⓔ
17. Ⓐ Ⓑ Ⓒ Ⓓ Ⓔ
18. Ⓐ Ⓑ Ⓒ Ⓓ Ⓔ
19. Ⓐ Ⓑ Ⓒ Ⓓ Ⓔ
20. Ⓐ Ⓑ Ⓒ Ⓓ Ⓔ
21. Ⓐ Ⓑ Ⓒ Ⓓ Ⓔ
22. Ⓐ Ⓑ Ⓒ Ⓓ Ⓔ

23. Ⓐ Ⓑ Ⓒ Ⓓ Ⓔ
24. Ⓐ Ⓑ Ⓒ Ⓓ Ⓔ
25. Ⓐ Ⓑ Ⓒ Ⓓ Ⓔ
26. Ⓐ Ⓑ Ⓒ Ⓓ Ⓔ
27. Ⓐ Ⓑ Ⓒ Ⓓ Ⓔ
28. Ⓐ Ⓑ Ⓒ Ⓓ Ⓔ
29. Ⓐ Ⓑ Ⓒ Ⓓ Ⓔ
30. Ⓐ Ⓑ Ⓒ Ⓓ Ⓔ

Section II — Mathematics

31. Ⓐ Ⓑ Ⓒ Ⓓ Ⓔ
32. Ⓐ Ⓑ Ⓒ Ⓓ Ⓔ
33. Ⓐ Ⓑ Ⓒ Ⓓ Ⓔ
34. Ⓐ Ⓑ Ⓒ Ⓓ Ⓔ
35. Ⓐ Ⓑ Ⓒ Ⓓ Ⓔ
36. Ⓐ Ⓑ Ⓒ Ⓓ Ⓔ
37. Ⓐ Ⓑ Ⓒ Ⓓ Ⓔ
38. Ⓐ Ⓑ Ⓒ Ⓓ Ⓔ
39. Ⓐ Ⓑ Ⓒ Ⓓ Ⓔ
40. Ⓐ Ⓑ Ⓒ Ⓓ Ⓔ
41. Ⓐ Ⓑ Ⓒ Ⓓ Ⓔ
42. Ⓐ Ⓑ Ⓒ Ⓓ Ⓔ
43. Ⓐ Ⓑ Ⓒ Ⓓ Ⓔ

44. Ⓐ Ⓑ Ⓒ Ⓓ Ⓔ
45. Ⓐ Ⓑ Ⓒ Ⓓ Ⓔ
46. Ⓐ Ⓑ Ⓒ Ⓓ Ⓔ
47. Ⓐ Ⓑ Ⓒ Ⓓ Ⓔ
48. Ⓐ Ⓑ Ⓒ Ⓓ Ⓔ
49. Ⓐ Ⓑ Ⓒ Ⓓ Ⓔ
50. Ⓐ Ⓑ Ⓒ Ⓓ Ⓔ
51. Ⓐ Ⓑ Ⓒ Ⓓ Ⓔ
52. Ⓐ Ⓑ Ⓒ Ⓓ Ⓔ
53. Ⓐ Ⓑ Ⓒ Ⓓ Ⓔ
54. Ⓐ Ⓑ Ⓒ Ⓓ Ⓔ
55. Ⓐ Ⓑ Ⓒ Ⓓ Ⓔ
56. Ⓐ Ⓑ Ⓒ Ⓓ Ⓔ
57. Ⓐ Ⓑ Ⓒ Ⓓ Ⓔ

58. Ⓐ Ⓑ Ⓒ Ⓓ Ⓔ
59. Ⓐ Ⓑ Ⓒ Ⓓ Ⓔ
60. Ⓐ Ⓑ Ⓒ Ⓓ Ⓔ
61. Ⓐ Ⓑ Ⓒ Ⓓ Ⓔ
62. Ⓐ Ⓑ Ⓒ Ⓓ Ⓔ
63. Ⓐ Ⓑ Ⓒ Ⓓ Ⓔ
64. Ⓐ Ⓑ Ⓒ Ⓓ Ⓔ
65. Ⓐ Ⓑ Ⓒ Ⓓ Ⓔ
66. Ⓐ Ⓑ Ⓒ Ⓓ Ⓔ
67. Ⓐ Ⓑ Ⓒ Ⓓ Ⓔ
68. Ⓐ Ⓑ Ⓒ Ⓓ Ⓔ
69. Ⓐ Ⓑ Ⓒ Ⓓ Ⓔ
70. Ⓐ Ⓑ Ⓒ Ⓓ Ⓔ
71. Ⓐ Ⓑ Ⓒ Ⓓ Ⓔ

72. Ⓐ Ⓑ Ⓒ Ⓓ Ⓔ
73. Ⓐ Ⓑ Ⓒ Ⓓ Ⓔ
74. Ⓐ Ⓑ Ⓒ Ⓓ Ⓔ
75. Ⓐ Ⓑ Ⓒ Ⓓ Ⓔ
76. Ⓐ Ⓑ Ⓒ Ⓓ Ⓔ
77. Ⓐ Ⓑ Ⓒ Ⓓ Ⓔ
78. Ⓐ Ⓑ Ⓒ Ⓓ Ⓔ
79. Ⓐ Ⓑ Ⓒ Ⓓ Ⓔ
80. Ⓐ Ⓑ Ⓒ Ⓓ Ⓔ
81. Ⓐ Ⓑ Ⓒ Ⓓ Ⓔ
82. Ⓐ Ⓑ Ⓒ Ⓓ Ⓔ
83. Ⓐ Ⓑ Ⓒ Ⓓ Ⓔ
84. Ⓐ Ⓑ Ⓒ Ⓓ Ⓔ
85. Ⓐ Ⓑ Ⓒ Ⓓ Ⓔ

Section III — Verbal Aptitude

86. Ⓐ Ⓑ Ⓒ Ⓓ Ⓔ
87. Ⓐ Ⓑ Ⓒ Ⓓ Ⓔ
88. Ⓐ Ⓑ Ⓒ Ⓓ Ⓔ
89. Ⓐ Ⓑ Ⓒ Ⓓ Ⓔ
90. Ⓐ Ⓑ Ⓒ Ⓓ Ⓔ
91. Ⓐ Ⓑ Ⓒ Ⓓ Ⓔ
92. Ⓐ Ⓑ Ⓒ Ⓓ Ⓔ
93. Ⓐ Ⓑ Ⓒ Ⓓ Ⓔ
94. Ⓐ Ⓑ Ⓒ Ⓓ Ⓔ
95. Ⓐ Ⓑ Ⓒ Ⓓ Ⓔ

96. Ⓐ Ⓑ Ⓒ Ⓓ Ⓔ
97. Ⓐ Ⓑ Ⓒ Ⓓ Ⓔ
98. Ⓐ Ⓑ Ⓒ Ⓓ Ⓔ
99. Ⓐ Ⓑ Ⓒ Ⓓ Ⓔ
100. Ⓐ Ⓑ Ⓒ Ⓓ Ⓔ
101. Ⓐ Ⓑ Ⓒ Ⓓ Ⓔ
102. Ⓐ Ⓑ Ⓒ Ⓓ Ⓔ
103. Ⓐ Ⓑ Ⓒ Ⓓ Ⓔ
104. Ⓐ Ⓑ Ⓒ Ⓓ Ⓔ
105. Ⓐ Ⓑ Ⓒ Ⓓ Ⓔ

106. Ⓐ Ⓑ Ⓒ Ⓓ Ⓔ
107. Ⓐ Ⓑ Ⓒ Ⓓ Ⓔ
108. Ⓐ Ⓑ Ⓒ Ⓓ Ⓔ
109. Ⓐ Ⓑ Ⓒ Ⓓ Ⓔ
110. Ⓐ Ⓑ Ⓒ Ⓓ Ⓔ
111. Ⓐ Ⓑ Ⓒ Ⓓ Ⓔ
112. Ⓐ Ⓑ Ⓒ Ⓓ Ⓔ
113. Ⓐ Ⓑ Ⓒ Ⓓ Ⓔ
114. Ⓐ Ⓑ Ⓒ Ⓓ Ⓔ
115. Ⓐ Ⓑ Ⓒ Ⓓ Ⓔ

116. Ⓐ Ⓑ Ⓒ Ⓓ Ⓔ
117. Ⓐ Ⓑ Ⓒ Ⓓ Ⓔ
118. Ⓐ Ⓑ Ⓒ Ⓓ Ⓔ
119. Ⓐ Ⓑ Ⓒ Ⓓ Ⓔ
120. Ⓐ Ⓑ Ⓒ Ⓓ Ⓔ
121. Ⓐ Ⓑ Ⓒ Ⓓ Ⓔ
122. Ⓐ Ⓑ Ⓒ Ⓓ Ⓔ
123. Ⓐ Ⓑ Ⓒ Ⓓ Ⓔ
124. Ⓐ Ⓑ Ⓒ Ⓓ Ⓔ
125. Ⓐ Ⓑ Ⓒ Ⓓ Ⓔ

Section IV — Data Sufficiency

126. Ⓐ Ⓑ Ⓒ Ⓓ Ⓔ   129. Ⓐ Ⓑ Ⓒ Ⓓ Ⓔ   133. Ⓐ Ⓑ Ⓒ Ⓓ Ⓔ   137. Ⓐ Ⓑ Ⓒ Ⓓ Ⓔ
127. Ⓐ Ⓑ Ⓒ Ⓓ Ⓔ   130. Ⓐ Ⓑ Ⓒ Ⓓ Ⓔ   134. Ⓐ Ⓑ Ⓒ Ⓓ Ⓔ   138. Ⓐ Ⓑ Ⓒ Ⓓ Ⓔ
128. Ⓐ Ⓑ Ⓒ Ⓓ Ⓔ   131. Ⓐ Ⓑ Ⓒ Ⓓ Ⓔ   135. Ⓐ Ⓑ Ⓒ Ⓓ Ⓔ   139. Ⓐ Ⓑ Ⓒ Ⓓ Ⓔ
                              132. Ⓐ Ⓑ Ⓒ Ⓓ Ⓔ   136. Ⓐ Ⓑ Ⓒ Ⓓ Ⓔ   140. Ⓐ Ⓑ Ⓒ Ⓓ Ⓔ

Section V — Business Judgment

141. Ⓐ Ⓑ Ⓒ Ⓓ Ⓔ   146. Ⓐ Ⓑ Ⓒ Ⓓ Ⓔ   151. Ⓐ Ⓑ Ⓒ Ⓓ Ⓔ   156. Ⓐ Ⓑ Ⓒ Ⓓ Ⓔ
142. Ⓐ Ⓑ Ⓒ Ⓓ Ⓔ   147. Ⓐ Ⓑ Ⓒ Ⓓ Ⓔ   152. Ⓐ Ⓑ Ⓒ Ⓓ Ⓔ   157. Ⓐ Ⓑ Ⓒ Ⓓ Ⓔ
143. Ⓐ Ⓑ Ⓒ Ⓓ Ⓔ   148. Ⓐ Ⓑ Ⓒ Ⓓ Ⓔ   153. Ⓐ Ⓑ Ⓒ Ⓓ Ⓔ   158. Ⓐ Ⓑ Ⓒ Ⓓ Ⓔ
144. Ⓐ Ⓑ Ⓒ Ⓓ Ⓔ   149. Ⓐ Ⓑ Ⓒ Ⓓ Ⓔ   154. Ⓐ Ⓑ Ⓒ Ⓓ Ⓔ   159. Ⓐ Ⓑ Ⓒ Ⓓ Ⓔ
145. Ⓐ Ⓑ Ⓒ Ⓓ Ⓔ   150. Ⓐ Ⓑ Ⓒ Ⓓ Ⓔ   155. Ⓐ Ⓑ Ⓒ Ⓓ Ⓔ   160. Ⓐ Ⓑ Ⓒ Ⓓ Ⓔ

Section VI — Data Sufficiency

161. Ⓐ Ⓑ Ⓒ Ⓓ Ⓔ   167. Ⓐ Ⓑ Ⓒ Ⓓ Ⓔ   173. Ⓐ Ⓑ Ⓒ Ⓓ Ⓔ   179. Ⓐ Ⓑ Ⓒ Ⓓ Ⓔ
162. Ⓐ Ⓑ Ⓒ Ⓓ Ⓔ   168. Ⓐ Ⓑ Ⓒ Ⓓ Ⓔ   174. Ⓐ Ⓑ Ⓒ Ⓓ Ⓔ   180. Ⓐ Ⓑ Ⓒ Ⓓ Ⓔ
163. Ⓐ Ⓑ Ⓒ Ⓓ Ⓔ   169. Ⓐ Ⓑ Ⓒ Ⓓ Ⓔ   175. Ⓐ Ⓑ Ⓒ Ⓓ Ⓔ   181. Ⓐ Ⓑ Ⓒ Ⓓ Ⓔ
164. Ⓐ Ⓑ Ⓒ Ⓓ Ⓔ   170. Ⓐ Ⓑ Ⓒ Ⓓ Ⓔ   176. Ⓐ Ⓑ Ⓒ Ⓓ Ⓔ   182. Ⓐ Ⓑ Ⓒ Ⓓ Ⓔ
165. Ⓐ Ⓑ Ⓒ Ⓓ Ⓔ   171. Ⓐ Ⓑ Ⓒ Ⓓ Ⓔ   177. Ⓐ Ⓑ Ⓒ Ⓓ Ⓔ   183. Ⓐ Ⓑ Ⓒ Ⓓ Ⓔ
166. Ⓐ Ⓑ Ⓒ Ⓓ Ⓔ   172. Ⓐ Ⓑ Ⓒ Ⓓ Ⓔ   178. Ⓐ Ⓑ Ⓒ Ⓓ Ⓔ   184. Ⓐ Ⓑ Ⓒ Ⓓ Ⓔ
                                                                                     185. Ⓐ Ⓑ Ⓒ Ⓓ Ⓔ

SIX
FIVE SAMPLE GMATs
WITH ANSWERS AND
ANALYSIS

Sample Test 1

Section I   Reading Recall

TOTAL TIME: 35 minutes

Part A: TIME—15 minutes

DIRECTIONS: This part contains three reading passages. You are to read each one carefully. You will have fifteen minutes to study the three passages and twenty minutes to answer questions based on them. When answering the questions, you will *not* be allowed to refer back to the passages.

Passage 1:

The United States economy made progress in reducing unemployment and moderating inflation. On the international side, this year was much calmer than last. Nevertheless, continuing imbalances in the pattern of world trade contributed to intermittent strains in the foreign exchange markets. These strains intensified to crisis proportions, precipitating a further devaluation of the dollar.

The domestic economy expanded in a remarkably vigorous and steady fashion. After a few lingering doubts about the strength of consumer demand in the opening weeks, the vitality of the expansion never came again into serious question. The resurgence in consumer confidence was reflected in the higher proportion of incomes spent for goods and services and the marked increase in consumer willingness to take on installment debt. A parallel strengthening in business psychology was manifested in a stepped-up rate of plant and equipment spending and a gradual pickup in outlays for inventory. Confidence in the economy was also reflected in the strength of the stock market and in the stability of the bond market, where rates showed little net change over the year as a whole despite the vigorous economic upturn. On several occasions during the year, the financial markets responded to shifting appraisals of the outlook for peace in Vietnam. For the year as a whole, consumer and business sentiment benefited from rising public expectations that a resolution of the conflict was in prospect and that East-West tensions were easing.

The underpinnings of the business expansion were to be found in part in the stimulative monetary and fiscal policies that had been pursued. Moreover, the restoration of sounder liquidity positions and tighter management control of production efficiency had also helped lay the groundwork for a strong expansion. In addition, the economic policy moves made by the President had served to renew optimism on the business outlook while boosting hopes that inflation would be brought under more effective control. Finally, of course, the economy was able to grow as vigorously as it did because sufficient leeway existed in terms of idle men and machines.

The United States balance of payments deficit declined sharply. Nevertheless, by any other test, the deficit remained very large, and there was actually a substantial deterioration in our trade account to a sizable deficit, almost two thirds of which was with Japan. It was to be expected that the immediate effect of devaluation would be a worsening in our trade accounts, with the benefits coming only later. While the overall trade performance proved disappointing, there are still good reasons for expecting the delayed impact of devaluation to produce in time a significant strengthening in our trade picture. Given the size of the Japanese component of our trade deficit, however, the outcome will depend importantly on the extent of the corrective measures undertaken by Japan. Also important will be our own efforts in the United States to fashion internal policies consistent with an improvement in our external balance.

The underlying task of public policy for the year ahead — and indeed for the longer run — remained a familiar one: to strike the right balance between encouraging healthy economic growth and avoiding inflationary pressures. With the economy showing sustained and vigorous growth, and with the currency crisis highlighting the need to improve our competitive posture internationally, the emphasis seemed to be shifting to the problem of inflation. The Phase Three program of wage and price restraint can contribute to dampening inflation. Unless productivity growth is unexpectedly large, however, the expansion of real output must eventually begin to slow down to the economy's larger run growth potential if generalized demand pressures on prices are to be avoided. Indeed, while the unemployment rates of a bit over five percent were still too high, it seems doubtful whether the much lower rates of four percent and below often cited as appropriate definitions of full employment do in fact represent feasible goals for the United States economy — unless there are improvements in the structure of labor and product markets and public policies influencing their operation. There is little doubt that overall unemployment rates can be brought down to four percent or less, for a time at least, by sufficient stimulation of aggregate demand. However, the resultant inflationary pressures have in the past proved exceedingly difficult to contain. After a point, moreover, it is questionable just how much, if any, additional reduction in unemployment can be permanently "bought" by accepting a stepped-up rate of inflation.

Passage 2:

These huge waves wreak terrific damage when they crash on the shores of distant lands or continents. Under a perfectly sunny sky and from an apparently calm sea, a wall of water may break twenty or thirty feet high over beaches and waterfronts, crushing houses and drowning unsuspecting residents and bathers in its path.

How are these waves formed? When a submarine earthquake occurs, it is likely to set up a tremendous amount of shock, disturbing the quiet waters of the deep ocean. This disturbance travels to the surface and forms a huge swell in the ocean many miles across. It rolls outward in all directions, and the water lowers in the center as another swell looms up. Thus, a series of concentric swells are formed similar to those made when a coin or small pebble is dropped into a basin of water. The big difference is in the size. Each of the concentric rings of basin water traveling out toward the edge is only about an inch across and less than a quarter of an inch high. The swells in the ocean are sometimes nearly a mile wide and rise to several multiples of ten feet in height.

Many of us have heard about these waves, often referred to by their Japanese name of "tsunami." For ages they have been dreaded in the Pacific, as no shore has been free from them. An underwater earthquake in the Aleutian Islands could start a swell that would break along the shores and cause severe damage in the southern part of Chile in South America. These waves travel hundreds of miles an hour, and one can understand how they would crash as violent breakers when caused to drag in the shallow waters of a coast.

Nothing was done about tsunamis until after World War II. In 1947 a particularly bad submarine earthquake took place south of the Aleutian Islands. A few hours later, people bathing in the sun along the quiet shores of Hawaii were dashed to death and shore-line property became a mass of shambles because a series of monstrous, breaking swells crashed along the shore and drove far inland. Hundreds of lives were lost in this catastrophe, and millions upon millions of dollars' worth of damage was done.

Hawaii (at that time a territory) and other Pacific areas then asked the U.S. Coast and Geodetic Survey to attempt to forecast these killer waves. With the blessing of the government, the Coast and Geodetic Survey initiated a program in 1948 known as the Seismic Seawave Warning System, using the earthquake-monitoring facilities of the agency, together with the world seismological data center, to locate submarine earthquakes as soon as they might occur. With this information they could then tell how severe a submarine earthquake was and could set up a tracking chart, with the center over the area of the earthquake, which would show by concentric time belts the rate of travel of the resulting wave. This system would indicate when and where, along the shores of the Pacific, the swells caused by the submarine earthquakes would strike.

Passage 3:

It is indisputable that in order to fulfill its many functions, water should be clean and biologically valuable. The costs connected with the provision of biologically valuable water for food production with the maintenance of sufficiently clean water, therefore, are primarily production costs. Purely "environmental" costs seem to be in this respect only costs connected with the safeguarding of cultural, recreational and sports functions which the water courses and reservoirs fulfill both in nature and in human settlements.

The problems of the atmosphere resemble those of water only partly. So far, the supply of air has not been deficient as was the case for water, and the dimensions of the air-shed are so vast that a number of people still hold the opinion that air need not be economized. However, scientific forecasts have shown that the time may be already approaching when clear and biologically valuable air will become problem No. 1.

Air being ubiquitous, people are particularly sensitive towards any reduction in the quality of the atmosphere, the increased contents of dust and gaseous exhalations, and particularly towards the presence of odors. The demand for purity of atmosphere, therefore, emanates much more from the population itself than from the specific sectors of the national economy affected by a polluted or even biologically aggressive atmosphere.

The households' share in atmospheric pollution is far bigger than that of industry which, in turn, further complicates the economic problems of atmospheric purity. Some countries have already collected positive experience with the reconstruction of whole urban sectors on the basis of new heating appliances based on the combustion of solid fossil fuels; estimates of the economic consequences of such measures have also been put forward.

In contrast to water where the maintenance of purity would seem primarily to be related to the costs of production and transport, a far higher proportion of the costs of maintaining the purity of the atmosphere derive from environmental considerations. Industrial sources of gaseous and dust emissions are well known and classified; their location can be accurately identified which makes them controllable. With the exception, perhaps, of the elimination of sulphur dioxide, technical means and technological processes exist which can be used for the elimination of all excessive impurities of the air from the various emissions.

Atmospheric pollution caused by the private property of individuals (their dwellings, automobiles, etc.) is difficult to control. Some sources such as motor vehicles are very mobile, and they are thus capable of polluting vast territories. In this particular case, the cost of anti-pollution measures will have to be borne, to a considerable extent, by individuals, whether in the form of direct costs or indirectly in the form of taxes, dues, surcharges, etc.

The problem of noise is a typical example of an environmental problem which cannot be solved passively, i.e., merely by protective measures, but will require the adoption of active measures, i.e., direct interventions at the source. The costs of a complete protection against noise are so prohibitive as to make it unthinkable even in the economically most developed countries. At the same time it would not seem feasible, either economically or politically, to force the population to carry the costs of individual protection against noise, for example, by reinforcing the sound insulation of their homes. A solution of this problem probably cannot be found in the near future.

If there is still time remaining, review the passages until all 15 minutes have elapsed.
Do not look at Part B until that time.

Part B: TIME—20 minutes

DIRECTIONS: Answer the following questions pertaining to information contained in the three passages you have just read. You may not turn back to those passages for assistance.

QUESTIONS TO

Passage 1:

1. The passage was most likely published in a

    (A) popular magazine   (D) financial journal
    (B) general newspaper   (E) textbook
    (C) science journal

2. The passage deals with the economy of

    (A) Japan   (D) the United States
    (B) Europe   (E) New York State
    (C) North America

3. Confidence in the economy was expressed by all of the following except

    (A) a strong stock market
    (B) a stable bond market
    (C) increased installment debt
    (D) increased plant and equipment expenditures
    (E) rising interest rates

4. Public confidence in the economy resulted in part from which of the following occurrences?

   I.   Possible peace in Vietnam
   II. Reduction in East-West tensions
  III. An entente with China

   (A) I only
   (B) III only
   (C) I and II only
   (D) II and III only
   (E) I, II, and III

5. Business expansion for the period under review was caused by

   (A) stimulative monetary and fiscal policies
   (B) rising interest rates
   (C) increased foreign trade
   (D) price and wage controls
   (E) Phase I

6. Most of the trade deficit in the balance of payments was attributed to which country?

   (A) United Kingdom   (D) France
   (B) Japan   (E) South America
   (C) Germany

7. Part of the public policy task—as outlined in the passage—is to

   (A) cut consumer spending
   (B) prevent balance of payments deficits
   (C) devalue the dollar
   (D) avoid inflationary pressures
   (E) increase the balance of trade

8. The Phase Three program contained

   (A) higher income taxes   (D) productivity measures
   (B) reduced government spending   (E) wage and price controls
   (C) devaluation of the dollar

9. The passage implies that the unemployment rate

   (A) cannot be reduced
   (B) can be reduced to below 4 percent
   (C) can be reduced to below 5 percent
   (D) can be reduced to below 6 percent
   (E) may or may not be reduced

10. The passage states that the unemployment rate at the time the article was written was

   (A) 6 percent   (D) a little over 4 percent
   (B) a little over 5 percent   (E) 4 percent
   (C) 5 percent

QUESTIONS TO

Passage 2:

11. The main subject of the passage is

    (A) the Japanese
    (B) Hawaii
    (C) waves
    (D) underwater earthquakes
    (E) early warning systems

12. The waves discussed in the passage usually occur during

    (A) stormy weather
    (B) clear weather
    (C) cold temperatures
    (D) deep swells
    (E) the night

13. The waves discussed in the passage are referred to as

    I. Tsunami
    II. Killer waves
    III. Submarines

    (A) I only
    (B) III only
    (C) I and II only
    (D) II and III only
    (E) I, II, and III

14. It is believed that the waves are caused by

    (A) seismatic conditions
    (B) concentric time belts
    (C) atmospheric conditions
    (D) underwater earthquakes
    (E) storms

15. The width of the waves is often

    (A) five feet
    (B) ten feet
    (C) one mile
    (D) 5 miles
    (E) more than thirty feet

16. The U.S. Coast and Geodetic Survey set up a program to

    I. Prevent submarine earthquakes
    II. Locate submarine earthquakes
    III. Determine the severity of submarine earthquakes

    (A) I only
    (B) III only
    (C) I and II only
    (D) II and III only
    (E) I, II, and III

17. Nothing was done about the waves until

    (A) death occurred
    (B) after World War I
    (C) a solution was found
    (D) millions of dollars worth of damage was incurred in Hawaii
    (E) 1937

18. The movement of the waves has been tracked at

    (A) 30 miles an hour
    (B) 40 miles an hour
    (C) 50 miles an hour
    (D) 100 miles an hour
    (E) more than a hundred miles an hour

19. According to the passage, the waves occurred in the area of the

    (A) Eastern U.S. seaboard   (D) Western Europe
    (B) Pacific   (E) Asia
    (C) Argentina

20. Given present wave-tracking systems, scientists can forecast all of the following except

    (A) the severity of underwater earthquakes
    (B) the wave's rate of travel
    (C) when a wave will strike
    (D) where a wave will strike
    (E) the height of the wave

QUESTIONS TO

Passage 3:

21. The passage discusses which of the following environmental areas?

    I. Noise
    II. Water
    III. Air

    (A) I only
    (B) III only
    (C) I and II only
    (D) II and III only
    (E) I, II, and III

22. According to the passage, problems of the atmosphere resemble those of water

    (A) completely
    (B) only partly
    (C) only in certain countries
    (D) only where pollution occurs
    (E) in developing countries

23. Scientific forecasts have shown that clear and biologically valuable air may soon become

    (A) extant
    (B) extinct
    (C) problem No. 1

    (D) cheaper to produce
    (E) economically feasible

24. According to the passage, which of the following contributes most to atmospheric pollution?

    (A) industry
    (B) production
    (C) households

    (D) mining
    (E) waste disposal

25. The maintenance of pure water is determined by

    I. Production costs
    II. Transport costs
    III. Research costs

    (A) I only
    (B) III only
    (C) I and II only
    (D) II and III only
    (E) I, II, and III

26. New heating appliances were developed to prevent damage to the

    (A) atmosphere
    (B) environment
    (C) water supply

    (D) power supply
    (E) economy

27. According to the passage, atmospheric pollution caused by private property is

    (A) easy to control
    (B) impossible to control
    (C) difficult to control

    (D) decreasing
    (E) negligible

28. The problem of noise can be solved through

    I. Active measures
    II. Passive measures
    III. Tax levies

    (A) I only
    (B) III only
    (C) I and II only
    (D) II and III only
    (E) I, II, and III

29. According to the passage, the costs of some anti-pollution measures will have to be borne by individuals because

    (A) individuals partly cause pollution
    (B) governments do not have adequate resources
    (C) industry is not willing to bear their share
    (D) individuals are more easily taxed than producers
    (E) individuals demand production which causes pollution

30. Complete protection against noise

    (A) may be forthcoming in the near future
    (B) is impossible to achieve
    (C) may have prohibitive costs
    (D) is possible only in developed countries
    (E) has been achieved in some countries

If there is still time remaining, you may review the questions in this section only.
You may not look at Part A or turn to any other section of the test.

Section II Mathematics

TIME: 75 minutes

DIRECTIONS: Solve each of the following problems; then indicate the correct answer on the answer sheet. [On the actual test you will be permitted to use any space available on the examination paper for scratch work.]

NOTE: A figure that appears with a problem is drawn as accurately as possible so as to provide information that may help in answering the question. Numbers in this test are real numbers.

31. A trip takes 6 hours to complete. After traveling $\frac{1}{4}$ of an hour, $1\frac{3}{8}$ hours, and $2\frac{1}{3}$ hours, how much time is necessary to complete the trip?

    (A) $2\frac{1}{12}$ hours   (D) $2\frac{1}{8}$ hours
    (B) 2 hours, $2\frac{1}{2}$ minutes   (E) 2 hours, $7\frac{1}{2}$ minutes
    (C) 2 hours, 5 minutes

32. If a stock average was 500 points at the beginning of a week and 400 points at the end of the same week, by what percent has it decreased during the week?

    (A) 20   (D) 27
    (B) 22   (E) 30
    (C) 25

Use the following graph for questions 33–36.

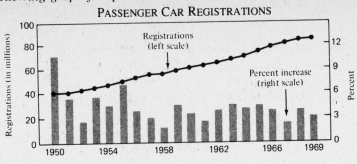

PASSENGER CAR REGISTRATIONS

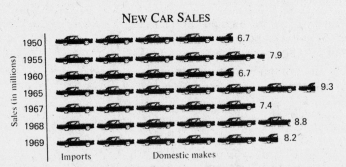

NEW CAR SALES

33. Of the years shown, the year which showed the greatest percent increase in passenger car registrations was

(A) 1950
(B) 1955
(C) 1965

(D) 1968
(E) 1969

34. In the pictograph representing new car sales, one car represents sales of about

(A) 1 million
(B) 1.5 million
(C) 2 million

(D) 2.5 million
(E) 3 million

35. In 1950, there were about x million passenger cars registered, where x equals

(A) 7
(B) 20
(C) 40

(D) 60
(E) 70

36. Which of the following statements about passenger car registrations and new car sales can be inferred from the graphs?

I. In 1955, the increase in passenger car registration was greater than 40%.
II. Between 1950 and 1969, the number of passenger cars registered roughly doubled.
III. In each year between 1950 and 1969, at least 5 million new cars were sold.

(A) I only
(B) II only
(C) III only
(D) I and II only
(E) I, II, and III

37. A car wash can wash 8 cars in 18 minutes. At this rate, how many cars can the car wash wash in 3 hours?

(A) 13
(B) 40.5
(C) 80
(D) 125
(E) 405

38. If the ratio of the areas of 2 squares is 2:1, then the ratio of the perimeters of the squares is

(A) 1:2
(B) 1:$\sqrt{2}$
(C) $\sqrt{2}$:1
(D) 2:1
(E) 4:1

Use the following table for questions 39–41.

Life insurance in force in the United States by type and geographic division

Division	Amount in 1972 (000,000 Omitted)				
	Ordinary	Group	Industrial	Credit	Total
New England	$ 53,174	$ 38,159	$ 1,309	$ 5,849	$ 98,491
Middle Atlantic......................	167,331	131,721	5,820	16,233	321,105
East North Central..................	175,636	139,388	7,274	21,453	343,751
West North Central................	71,614	43,087	1,489	8,859	125,049
South Atlantic	119,431	90,520	11,990	19,126	241,067
East South Central	41,552	30,940	5,166	7,913	85,571
West South Central	75,470	48,904	4,697	11,917	140,988
Mountain..............................	35,529	21,419	524	4,960	62,432
Pacific..................................	108,806	86,562	1,706	12,457	209,531
United States	$848,543	$630,700	$39,975	$108,767	$1,627,985

Division	Percent change 1962–1972				
	Ordinary	Group	Industrial	Credit	Total
New England ....,....................	+104.7%	+195.7%	−48.4%	+176.9%	+126.3%
Middle Atlantic......................	+ 82.8	+169.3	−25.7	+163.1	+107.9
East North Central..................	+110.9	+194.1	− 8.8	+202.0	+135.8
West North Central................	+118.6	+226.5	−15.7	+177.6	+145.6
South Atlantic	+158.6	+251.8	+29.1	+220.7	+176.6
East South Central	+151.9	+240.7	+31.7	+213.5	+167.2
West South Central	+141.6	+235.1	+22.9	+209.1	+163.5
Mountain..............................	+140.4	+235.9	− 0.8	+185.9	+166.6
Pacific..................................	+132.0	+179.3	−13.0	+132.6	+145.9
United States	+118.1%	+201.5%	+ 0.9%	+186.1%	+140.8%

Source: Institute of Life Insurance

39. The ratio of the amount of credit life insurance to the amount of ordinary life insurance in the Pacific region in 1972 was about

(A) 1 to 10
(B) 1 to 9
(C) 1 to 8
(D) 1 to 1
(E) 8 to 1

40. The region which had the largest amount of industrial life insurance in 1972 was

   (A) Middle Atlantic
   (B) East North Central
   (C) South Atlantic
   (D) East South Central
   (E) Pacific

41. How many of the types of life insurance shown had a greater percentage increase from 1962 to 1972 than the percent change in total life insurance from 1962 to 1972?

   (A) 0
   (B) 1
   (C) 2
   (D) 3
   (E) 4

42. In Leesville, 70% of the cars have whitewall tires and 25% of the cars are air-conditioned. If 20% of the cars are air-conditioned and have whitewall tires, what percentage of the cars have neither air-conditioning nor whitewall tires?

   (A) 5
   (B) 10
   (C) 15
   (D) 20
   (E) 25

43. A company issued 100,000 shares of stock. In 1970, each share of stock was worth $122.50. In 1973, each share of the stock was worth $111.10. How much less were the 100,000 shares worth in 1973 than in 1970?

   (A) $114,000
   (B) $1,100,040
   (C) $1,140,000
   (D) $114,000,000
   (E) $1,140,000,000

44. A worker's daily salary varies each day. In one week he worked five days. His daily salaries were $51.90, $52.20, $49.80, $51.50, and $50.60. What was his average daily wage for the week?

   (A) $50.80
   (B) $51.20
   (C) $51.50
   (D) $51.60
   (E) $255.00

Questions 45 and 46 refer to the graph on page 341.

45. The ratio of deaths from heart disease to deaths from cancer in 1969 was about

   (A) 2 to 3
   (B) 3 to 2
   (C) 2 to 1
   (D) 9 to 4
   (E) 3 to 1

46. The number of people who died in all accidents in 1969 was roughly

   (A) 56,000
   (B) 100,000
   (C) 112,000
   (D) 125,000
   (E) 560,000

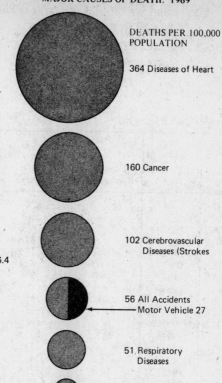

MAJOR CAUSES OF DEATH: 1969

DEATHS PER 100,000 POPULATION

364 Diseases of Heart

160 Cancer

102 Cerebrovascular Diseases (Strokes

56 All Accidents
Motor Vehicle 27

51 Respiratory Diseases

19 Diabetes

15 Cirrhosis of Liver

DEATHS FROM MOTOR VEHICLE ACCIDENTS

Thousands

1950   34.8

1960   38.1

1965   49.2

1969   56.4

47. A borrower pays 8% interest per year on the first $600 he borrows and 7% per year on the part of the loan in excess of $600. How much interest will the borrower pay on a loan of $6,000 for 1 year?

(A) $378
(B) $420
(C) $426
(D) $436
(E) $480

48. If $3x - 2y = 8$, then $4y - 6x$ is:

(A) -16
(B) -8
(C) 8
(D) 16
(E) none of these

Questions 49–51 refer to the table on page 342.

49. Which country among those shown had the third largest length of railroad?

(A) Argentina
(B) Brazil
(C) Canada
(D) Mexico
(E) United States

50. Which country had the most kilometers per area of railroad track?

(A) Argentina
(B) Canada
(C) Cuba
(D) Jamaica
(E) Peru

51. Between 1953 and 1965, passenger kilometers in Paraguay

(A) decreased by about 70%
(D) increased by about 20%
(B) decreased by about 40%
(E) increased by about 40%
(C) decreased by about 20%

Railroads: Length, Passengers, and Freight

	Year	Length (kilometers)	Length (miles)	Km. per area (1000 km.)	Km. per 1000 persons	Passenger kilometers (millions)	
						1953	1965
MEXICO	1968	19 749	12 271	10.04	0.42	2 987	3 882
COSTA RICA	1967	951	600	18.65	0.60	51	7—
EL SALVADOR	1966	513	318	24.43	0.17	"—	—
GUATEMALA	1965	958	595	8.79	0.22	—	—
HONDURAS	1967	1 005	624	8.10	0.43	—	—
NICARAGUA	1964	403	250	2.90	0.25	118	51
PANAMA	1966	650	403	8.55	0.51	—	—
Total, Central America		4 480	2 790	—	—	—	—
BARBADOS		—	—	—	—	—	—
CUBA	1963	5 122	3 233	44.54	0.71	—	822
DOMINICAN REPUBLIC	1966	560	347	11.67	0.15	—	—
HAITI	1964	254	157	9.07	0.06	—	—
JAMAICA	1967	330	205	30.00	0.18	43	54
TRINIDAD and TOBAGO	1967	13	8	2.54	0.01	—	—
Total, Caribbean		—	—	—	—	—	—
ARGENTINA	1965	40 180	24 966	14.47	1.78	13 564	12 829
BOLIVIA	1968	3 524	2 189	3.21	0.75	—	220
BRAZIL	1968	32 054	19 917	3.77	0.36	11 593	16 684
CHILE	1967	10 136	6 298	13.39	1.11	1 789	2 411
COLOMBIA	1966	3 435	2 134	3.02	0.18	668	513
ECUADOR	1964	1 154	717	4.26	0.23	106	52
GUYANA	1968	127	78	0.59	0.18	—	75
PARAGUAY	1969	441	274	1.08	0.19	60	35
PERU	1966	2 620	1 628	2.05	0.22	282	236
URUGUAY	1966	2 762	1 716	14.77	1.00	—	—
VENEZUELA	1964	484	300	0.54	0.06	21	44
Total, South America		96 917	60 217	—	—	—	—
Total, REPUBLICS		—	—	—	—	—	—
Comparison							
Canada	1967	69 472	43 168	7.53	3.40	4 805	4 287
UNITED STATES	1967	336 823	209 292	35.97	1.69	50 983	28 090

SOURCES:

PAU, IASI, *America en Cifras 1970*, Tables 333–01 and 333–03.
U.N., *Statistical Yearbook 1970*, Table 147.
University of California, *Cuba 1968: Supplement to the Statistical Abstract of Latin America*, Table 66.

Source: Statistical Abstract of Latin America 1970

52. It costs 10¢ a mile to fly and 12¢ a mile to drive. If you travel 200 miles, flying x miles of the distance and driving the rest, then the cost of the trip in dollars is

(A) 20
(D) $24 - .02x$
(B) 24
(E) $2400 - 2x$
(C) $24 - 2x$

53. If two identical rectangles R_1 and R_2 form a square when placed next to each other, and the length of R_1 is x times the width of R_1, then x is

(A) 1
(B) $3/2$
(C) $5/4$

(D) 2
(E) 3

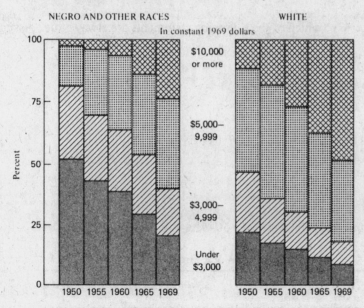

54. If the area of a square increases by 69%, then the side of the square increases by

(A) 13%
(B) 30%
(C) 39%

(D) 69%
(E) 130%

Use the following graph for questions 55–57.

Percent Distribution of Families by Income Group

NEGRO AND OTHER RACES   WHITE

In constant 1969 dollars

$10,000 or more

$5,000–9,999

$3,000–4,999

Under $3,000

1950 1955 1960 1965 1969   1950 1955 1960 1965 1969

55. Which of the following income groups contained the largest number of white families in 1950?

(A) under $3,000
(B) $3,000–4,999
(C) $5,000–9,999

(D) $10,000–19,999
(E) $20,000 or more

56. In 1969, the ratio of the number of white families with income of more than $5,000 to the number of white families with income of less than $5,000 was about

(A) 1 to 2
(B) 1 to 1
(C) 2 to 1

(D) 3 to 1
(E) 4 to 1

57. Which of the following statements can be inferred from the graphs?

 I. There were more white families than Negro families in 1965.
 II. Between 1950 and 1969, the percentage of families in the category "Negro and other races" with income under $3,000 decreased by more than 50%.
 III. The average income of a white family in 1969 was more than $3,000.

(A) only I
(B) only II
(C) only I and III
(D) only II and III
(E) I, II, and III

58. A used car dealer sells a car for $1,380 and makes a 20% profit. How much did the car cost the dealer?

(A) $1,100
(B) $1,120
(C) $1,150

(D) $1,180
(E) $1,560

59. If $x < z$ and $x < y$, which of the following statements are always true? Assume $x \geq 0$.

 I. $y < z$
 II. $x < yz$
 III. $2x < y + z$

(A) only I
(B) only II
(C) only III
(D) II and III only
(E) I, II, and III

Use the following table for questions 60–62.

Distribution of Work Hours in a Factory

Numbers of Workers		Number of Hours Worked
20		45–50
15		40–44
25		35–39
16		30–34
4		0–29
80	TOTAL	3100

60. What percentage worked 40 or more hours?

(A) 18.75

(B) 25

(C) 33⅓

(D) 40

(E) 43.75

61. The number of workers who worked from 40 to 44 hours is x times the number who worked up to 29 hours, where x is

(A) $^{15}/_{16}$

(B) $3^3/_4$

(C) 4

(D) 5

(E) $6^1/_4$

62. Which of the following statements can be inferred from the table?

  I. The average number of hours worked per worker is less than 40.

  II. At least 3 worked more than 48 hours.

  III. More than half of all the workers worked more than 40 hours.

(A) I only

(B) II only

(C) I and II only

(D) I and III only

(E) I, II, and III

63. A truck traveling at 70 miles per hour uses 30% more gasoline to travel a certain distance than it does when it travels at 50 miles per hour. If the truck can travel 19.5 miles on a gallon of gasoline at 50 miles per hour, how far can the truck travel on 10 gallons of gasoline at a speed of 70 miles per hour?

(A) 130

(B) 140

(C) 150

(D) 175

(E) 195

64. $\frac{2}{5} + \frac{1}{3} = \frac{x}{30}$, where x is

(A) 4

(B) 7

(C) 11

(D) 16

(E) 22

65. How many squares with sides ½ inch long are needed to cover a rectangle which is 4 feet long and 6 feet wide?

(A) 24

(B) 96

(C) 3,456

(D) 13,824

(E) 14,266

Use the following graph for questions 66–69.

AVERAGE ANNUAL RECEIPTS AND OUTLAYS OF U.S. GOVERNMENT 1967-1970

RECEIPTS

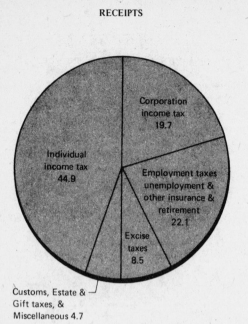

OUTLAYS

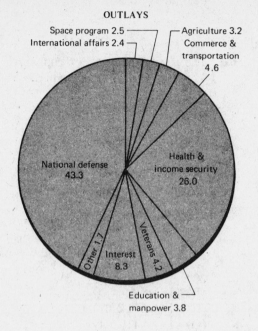

66. If the annual average receipts from the corporation income tax during the years 1967–1970 equal x, then the average annual receipts during this period were about

(A) $\dfrac{x}{4}$

(B) x^2

(C) $3x$

(D) $5x$

(E) x^5

67. The average annual combined outlay for veterans, education and manpower, and health and income security was roughly what fraction of the average annual outlays?

(A) $\frac{1}{4}$

(B) $\frac{1}{3}$

(C) $\frac{2}{5}$

(D) $\frac{1}{2}$

(E) $\frac{2}{3}$

68. What category received the second smallest average annual outlay during 1967–1970?

(A) excise taxes

(B) other

(C) veterans

(D) space program

(E) international affairs

69. If $\frac{5}{8}$ of the average annual outlays for agriculture was spent in the western U.S., what percentage of average annual outlays was spent on agriculture in the western U.S.?

(A) $\frac{5}{8}$ (D) 2

(B) 1   (E) 3.2

(C) $1\frac{1}{4}$

70. The next number in the geometric progression 5,10,20 . . . is

(A) 25   (D) 40

(B) 30   (E) 50

(C) 35

71. Eggs cost 8¢ each. If the price of eggs increases by $\frac{1}{8}$, how much will a dozen eggs cost?

(A) 90¢   (D) $1.12

(B) $1.08   (E) $1.18

(C) $1.10

72. A trapezoid $ABCD$ is formed by adding the isosceles right triangle BCE with base 5 inches to the rectangle $ABED$ where DE is t inches. What is the area of the trapezoid in square inches?

(A) $5t + 12.5$ (D) $(t + 5)^2$

(B) $5t + 25$ (E) $t^2 + 25$

(C) $2.5t + 12.5$

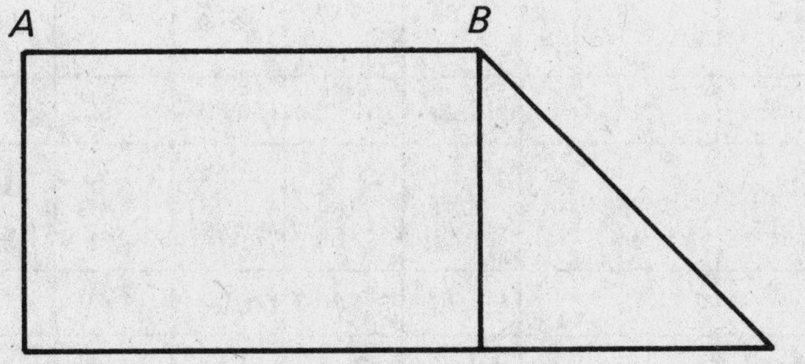

73. A manufacturer of jam wants to make a profit of $75 when he sells 300 jars of jam. It costs 65¢ each to make the first 100 jars of jam and 55¢ each to make each jar after the first 100. What price should he charge for the 300 jars of jam?

(A) $75   (D) $240

(B) $175   (E) $250

(C) $225

Use the following table for questions 74–77.

Prices of major trade commodities: 1962–1971

Commodity	Unit of measure	Country	Percent of world exports	1962	1966	1967	1968	1969	1970	1971
BEEF (Frozen)	100 pounds	Argentina	46	16.08	25.57	20.82	28.02	25.26	33.06	39.27
(Corned)	100 pounds	Argentina		32.86	38.90	40.17	41.42	39.75	39.27	39.99
(Frozen)	100 pounds	Uruguay	5	16.37	24.82	23.72	22.59	22.14	25.07	31.25M
(Preserved)	100 pounds	Uruguay		33.99	31.25	36.93	41.58	39.91	34.90	—
CACAO	100 pounds	Brazil	7	19.54	20.45	23.56	27.58	40.61	29.42	—
COFFEE	100 pounds	Brazil	40	29.67	34.31	31.83	31.72	31.47	42.97	—
	100 pounds	Colombia	16	38.22	44.58	39.99	40.41	38.41	50.09	47.33M
	100 pounds	Guatemala	4	37.05	41.63	38.14	36.10	—	47.96	44.52
	100 pounds	El Salvador	4	32.90	41.85	36.63	35.69	35.56	46.12	44.97
COPPER	100 pounds	Canada	12	29.31	46.91	46.16	48.42	50.63	63.07	47.05
	100 pounds	Chile	29	29.36	42.54	—	—	—	—	—
COTTON	100 pounds	Brazil	5	23.65	21.35	21.75	23.97	19.99	—	—
	100 pounds	Mexico	9	23.24	23.44	24.08	24.46	24.02	26.25	—
	100 pounds	United States	29	28.33	25.11	24.82	25.62	24.17	25.52	26.91M
HIDES	100 pounds	Argentina	16	—	—	—	—	—	—	—
LEAD	100 pounds	Canada	8	7.14	11.77	10.15	10.32	11.71	10.05	10.73M
	100 pounds	Mexico	16	9.06	10.97	11.34	10.65	12.25	13.60	13.47Sa
	100 pounds	Peru	9	5.14	10.30	9.25	8.68	10.03	13.21	—
LINSEED OIL	100 pounds	Argentina	—	10.09	7.83	7.53	8.47	9.30	9.21	8.90F
	100 pounds	Uruguay	—	11.41	7.58	6.82	8.51	8.96	8.58	8.10F
NEWSPRINT	Short ton	Canada	47	114.60	114.90	118.60	122.80	127.00	131.5	134.3M
PETROLEUM	Barrel	Colombia	1	2.49	2.01	1.96	1.97	1.96	1.88	2.09M
	Barrel	United States	15	—	—	—	—	—	—	—
QUEBRACHO	100 pounds	Argentina	82	5.74	7.51	7.44	7.88	8.71	9.75	10.12F
	100 pounds	Paraguay	18	6.21	7.17	7.22	7.46	7.94	9.08	9.69M
SISAL	100 pounds	Haiti	1	8.00	6.91	5.13	5.20	5.75	—	—
SUGAR	100 pounds	Dominican Republic	8	5.03	5.82	5.73	6.16	6.37	6.65	5.90
TIN	100 pounds	Bolivia	15	112.20	161.20	150.80	142.60	155.10	164.40	158.0M
WHEAT	Bushel	Argentina	4	1.67	1.51	1.61	1.56	1.61	1.49	1.60F
	Bushel	Canada	28	1.87	1.84	1.96	1.87	1.78	1.67	1.79M
	Bushel	United States	48	1.81	1.69	1.74	1.68	1.64	1.58	1.72M
WOOL	100 pounds	Argentina	9	37.70	34.80	36.00	34.61	35.90	34.50	30.2F
ZINC	100 pounds	Canada	36	9.05	12.11	11.13	10.98	11.26	11.97	11.76M
	100 pounds	Mexico	19	9.20	11.43	11.52	10.86	10.91	12.04	—

SOURCES:

IMF, *International Financial Statistics*, Vol. 23. No. 12. December 1970. and Vol. 24, August 1971.

NOTES:

1. Data given in current U.S. dollars. Unit values are derived from trade statistics of countries listed and are not wholesale prices of the commodity.

Source: Statistical Abstract of Latin America 1970

74. For how many different commodities did the countries shown account for more than 50% of the world's exports between 1962 and 1971?

(A) 1 (D) 4
(B) 2 (E) 5
(C) 3

75. The price per barrel of petroleum paid to Colombia in 1970 was about what percentage of the price per barrel in 1962?

(A) 70% (D) 81%
(B) 75% (E) 125%
(C) 79%

76. For how many of the commodities was the price received in 1970 less than that in 1962 in at least one country?

(A) 1 (D) 4
(B) 2 (E) 5
(C) 3

77. Which commodity yielded the most income for each unit of measure in 1970?

(A) Canadian copper (D) Colombian coffee
(B) Canadian newsprint (E) Mexican zinc
(C) Bolivian tin

78. A roofer can finish a roof in 7 hours by himself. If he hires two assistants who each work $\frac{2}{3}$ as fast as he does, how long will it take the three of them together to finish a roof?

(A) 2 hrs. (D) $3\frac{1}{2}$ hrs.
(B) $2\frac{1}{3}$ hrs. (E) $3\frac{2}{3}$ hrs.
(C) 3 hrs.

79. If a stock average was 1000 at the end of Monday's trading and it declined by 10% each day, what was the average at the end of Thursday's trading?

(A) 700 (D) 729
(B) 720 (E) 730
(C) 724

Questions 80–82 refer to the graph on page 350.

80. In 1970 the total amount of funds used for research and development was roughly x times the amount used in 1957, where x is

(A) 50% (D) 200%
(B) 100% (E) 250%
(C) 150%

81. The total amount of research and development funds used first exceeded $15 billion in

(A) 1958
(B) 1959
(C) 1960

(D) 1961
(E) 1963

82. Which of the following statements can be inferred from the graph?

    I. The amount of funds used for research and development increased every year between 1957 and 1970.

    II. The amount of funds used for research and development more than doubled between 1958 and 1968.

    III. Of the five categories shown, the most funds used have been for research and development performed by universities and funded by the federal government.

(A) I only
(B) II only
(C) I and II only
(D) II and III only
(E) I, II, and III

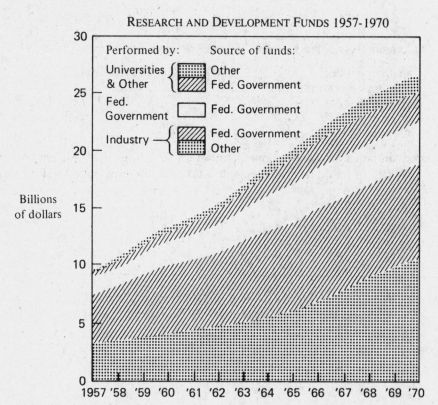

RESEARCH AND DEVELOPMENT FUNDS 1957-1970

83. A farmer walks around the outside of a rectangular field at a constant speed. It takes him twice as long to walk the length of the field as jt takes him to walk the width of the field. If he walked 300 yards when he walked around the field, what is the area of the field in square yards?

(A) 5,000
(B) 15,000
(C) 20,000

(D) 25,000
(E) 30,000

84. A company makes a profit of 7% selling goods which cost $2,000; it also makes a profit of 6% selling a machine which cost the company $5,000. How much total profit did the company make on both transactions?

(A) $300
(B) $400
(C) $420

(D) $440
(E) $490

85. If $\dfrac{x}{y} = \dfrac{3}{z}$, then $9y^2$ equals

(A) $\dfrac{x^2}{9}$

(B) x^3z

(C) x^2z^2

(D) $3x^2$

(E) $\left(\dfrac{1}{9}\right)x^2z^2$

If there is still time remaining, you may review the questions in this section only.
You may not turn to any other section of the test.

Section III   Verbal Aptitude

TIME: 20 minutes

Antonyms

DIRECTIONS: For each question below, select the lettered word or phrase that comes closest to being *opposite* in meaning to the word appearing in capital letters. Be sure to consider all meanings carefully.

86. SEDITIOUS: (A) incendiary (B) orderly (C) sedate (D) proper (E) quaint

87. REDOLENT: (A) enthusiastic (B) propitious (C) agreeable (D) fetid (E) unsure

88. PUERILE: (A) savory (B) aromatic (C) mature (D) sterile (E) weak

89. ABATE: (A) deter (B) proceed (C) deny (D) increase (E) animate

90. ACERBITY: (A) reluctance (B) weakness (C) lassitude (D) acidity (E) sweetness

91. ACTUATE: (A) dismiss (B) dissuade (C) demote (D) deny (E) denigrate

92. IRRESOLUTE: (A) resolved (B) determined (C) unsound (D) sensitive (E) defensible

93. FRACTIOUS: (A) delicate (B) solid (C) agreeable (D) liberal (E) wholesome

94. ADMONITION: (A) countenance (B) evasion (C) deposition (D) declaration (E) denial

95. ENMITY: (A) affection (B) security (C) approbation (D) ire (E) preponderance

96. ARTIFICE: (A) opening (B) skill (C) honesty (D) reality (E) cupidity

97. CONDUCE: (A) confide (B) direct (C) confirm (D) counteract (E) disprove

98. DEBILITY: (A) credibility (B) strength (C) waste (D) lucidity (E) simplicity

99. CONJURE: (A) propose (B) upset (C) deprecate (D) erect (E) consult

Word-Pair Relationships

DIRECTIONS: For each question below, determine the relationship between the pair of capitalized words and then select the lettered pair of words which have a similar relationship to the first pair.

100. AVIARY : ARBORETUM :: (A) animals : zoo (B) money : bank (C) letters : post office (D) dovecote : greenhouse (E) honey : beehive

101. CONVICT : PRISON :: (A) student : school (B) exile : banishment (C) juvenile delinquent : orphanage (D) prisoner : court (E) expectancy : closure

102. WATER : FLOOD :: (A) rain : river (B) wind : sleet (C) snow : blizzard (D) calm : severe (E) summer : winter

103. PENITENCE : OBDURACY :: (A) pensive : thoughtless (B) vacuous : empty (C) reward : award (D) happy : ecstatic (E) problem : solution

104. FORTITUDE : RESOLUTION :: (A) timidity : weakness (B) heroic : dastardly (C) medal : bravery (D) poem : poet (E) plan : execution

105. TAPE MEASURE : MEASUREMENT :: (A) scientist : observation (B) electricity : power (C) dictator : ruler (D) car : highway (E) hypothesis : theory

106. VOICE : AMPLIFIER :: (A) musician : instrument (B) wind : velocity (C) runner : distance (D) automobile : accelerator (E) shipment : expediter

107. PHLEGMATIC : ENERGETIC :: (A) perfidious : faithful (B) fissure : split (C) canvas : composition (D) forfeiture : confiscation (E) flagrant : atrocious

108. MURDER : GENOCIDE :: (A) accident : assault (B) attack : war (C) wind : tornado (D) stultify : invigorate (E) scanty : overdone

109. NEBULOUS : CLARIFICATION :: (A) trite : obscure (B) erroneous : emendation (C) abhor : hostile (D) accusation : investigation (E) break : accord

110. CLANDESTINE : SURREPTITIOUS :: (A) secret : subversive (B) annihilate : extirpate (C) plan : deviate (D) material : corporeal (E) subjugator : emancipator

111. AMALGAMATE : UNITED :: (A) conglomeration : assortment (B) organize : arranged (C) oscillate : display (D) dissipate : anticipated (E) trial : lawyer

112. EXORCISM : INCANTATION :: (A) confrontation : pandemonium (B) petition : candidate (C) devotion : prayer (D) neology : libation (E) incarcerate : cajole

Sentence Completions

DIRECTIONS: For each sentence below, select the lettered word or set of words which, when inserted in the sentence blanks, best completes the meaning of that sentence.

113. The _____ sources are so polluted that employees dare not _____ it.

(A) water . . . drink (B) air . . . imbibe (C) river . . . swim (D) energy . . . tap (E) atmospheric . . . test

114. The throbbing _____ of 20 _____ poured forth the music of Vivaldi, Mozart, and Bach.

    (A) soliloquy . . . voices (B) singing . . . musicians (C) sonority . . . stringed instruments (D) hum . . . recorders (E) motion . . . horns

115. More _____ would be seen as a step toward eventual resumption of diplomatic relations.

    (A) animosity (B) incentives (C) embargoes (D) trade (E) lobbying

116. That the _____ know their plight is clear from the way they dart in different _____ to find an exit.

    (A) participants . . . ways (B) victims . . . directions (C) birds . . . holes (D) animals . . . corners (E) rescuers . . . avenues

117. The theories of the two anthropologists look _____ opposed.

    (A) reliably (B) possibly (C) academically (D) diametrically (E) accedingly

118. The _____ received an emolument.

    (A) farmer (B) wife (C) employee (D) prisoner (E) invalid

119. The method of popular decision has been called a _____ or a(n) _____.

    (A) success . . . failure (B) mistake . . . affirmation (C) plebiscite . . . referendum (D) dictatorship . . . monarchy (E) myth . . . reality

120. Tax reduction will increase the _____ and _____ of consumers.

    (A) savings . . . returns (B) mobility . . . gregariousness (C) spending . . . inflation (D) income . . . purchasing power (E) leisure time . . . consumption

121. Muskrats are of the _____ food chain.

    (A) staple (B) forest (C) carnivorous (D) lemming (E) wild

122. It is the _____ attention to this dimension which makes the report so important.

    (A) unflinching (B) inceptive (C) fortuitous (D) dubious (E) redolent

123. The story itself is _____ simple.

    (A) incongruously (B) lugubriously (C) circuitously (D) abstrusely (E) inscrutably

124. He never stopped talking; he was _____.

    (A) silent (B) loquacious (C) pedantic (D) eccentric (E) restrained

125. For some people, their _____ state of mind prevents them from flying.

    (A) physiological (B) morbid (C) psychological (D) prodigious (E) perfidious

If there is still time remaining, you may review the questions in this section only.
You may not turn to any other section of the test.

Section IV   Data Sufficiency

TIME: 15 minutes

DIRECTIONS: Each of the following problems has a question and two statements which are labeled (1) and (2). Use the data given in (1) and (2) together with other available information (such as the number of hours in a day, the definition of *clockwise*, mathematical facts, etc.) to decide whether the statements are *sufficient* to answer the question. Then fill in space

  (A) if you can get the answer from (1) alone but not from (2) alone;

  (B) if you can get the answer from (2) alone but not from (1) alone;

  (C) if you can get the answer from (1) and (2) together, although neither statement by itself suffices;

  (D) if statement (1) alone suffices *and* statement (2) alone suffices;

  (E) if you cannot get the answer from statements (1) and (2) together, but need even more data.

All numbers used in this section are real numbers. A figure given for a problem is intended to provide information consistent with that in the question, but not necessarily with the additional information contained in the statements.

126. Are two triangles congruent?

  (1) Both triangles are right triangles.
  (2) Both triangles have the same perimeter.

127. Is x greater than zero?

  (1) $x^4 - 16 = 0$
  (2) $x^3 - 8 = 0$

128. If both conveyer belt A and conveyer belt B are used, they can fill a hopper with coal in one hour. How long will it take for conveyer belt A to fill the hopper without conveyer belt B?

  (1) Conveyer belt A moves twice as much coal as conveyer belt B.
  (2) Conveyer belt B would take 3 hours to fill the hopper without belt A.

129. A fly crawls around the outside of a circle once. A second fly crawls around the outside of a square once. Which fly travels further?

   (1) The diagonal of the square is equal to the diameter of the circle.
   (2) The fly crawling around the circle took more time to complete his journey than the fly crawling around the square.

130. How much did it cost the *XYZ* Corporation to insure its factory from fire in 1972?

   (1) It cost $5,000 for fire insurance in 1971.
   (2) The total amount the corporation spent for fire insurance in 1970, 1971, and 1972 was $18,000.

131. Is *y* larger than 1?

   (1) *y* is larger than 0.
   (2) $y^2 - 4 = 0$.

132. A worker is hired for 6 days. He is paid $2 more for each day of work than he was paid for the preceding day of work. How much was he paid for the first day of work?

   (1) His total wages for the 6 days were $150.
   (2) He was paid 150% of his first day's pay for the sixth day.

133. A car originally sold for $3,000. After a month, the car was discounted *x*%, and a month later the car's price was discounted *y*%. Is the car's price after the discounts less than $2,600?

   (1) $y = 10$
   (2) $x = 15$

134. What is the value of *a*?

   (1) $a = f$
   (2) $a = b$

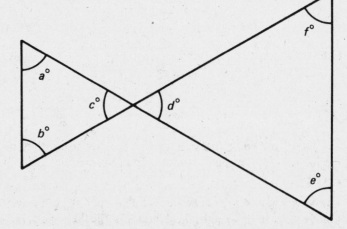

135. In triangle ABC, find z if $AB = 5$ and $y = 40$.

(1) $BC = 5$
(2) The bisector of angle B is perpendicular to AC.

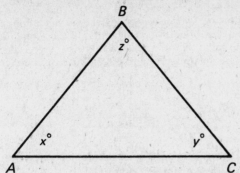

136. How much cardboard will it take to make an open cubical box with no top?

(1) The area of the bottom of the box is 4 square feet.
(2) The volume of the box is 8 cubic feet.

137. How many books are on a bookshelf?

(1) The total weight of all the books on the bookshelf is 40 pounds.
(2) The average weight of the books on the bookshelf is 2.5 pounds.

138. Is the figure $ABCD$ a rectangle?

(1) $x = 90$
(2) $AB = CD$

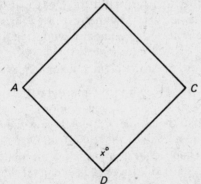

139. A sequence of numbers is given by the rule $a_n = (a_{n-1})^2$. What is a_5?

(1) $a_1 = -1$
(2) $a_3 = 1$

140. How much is John's weekly salary?

(1) John's weekly salary is twice as much as Fred's weekly salary.
(2) Fred's weekly salary is 40% of the total of Chuck's weekly salary and John's weekly salary.

If there is still time remaining, you may review the questions in this section only.
You may not turn to any other section of the test.

Section V   Business Judgment

TIME: 35 minutes

DIRECTIONS: Read the following two passages. After you have completed each of them you will be asked to answer two sets of questions. The first of these, data evaluation, involves determining the importance of specific factors included in the passage. The second, data application, consists of general questions relating to the passage. When answering questions, you may consult the passage.

Passage 1:

The success of the Abco Corporation in the investment-conscious country of Korea had recently been the subject of a government inquiry.

The Abco Corporation, along with a local leather merchant and a well-known American shoe machinery manufacturer constructed a shoe manufacturing plant in Korea. Government support for the enterprise was given because of high unemployment in the country, but despite the fact that there was at that time surplus shoe production—most factories having large excess capacities and underworked labor forces. It was known that Abco had promised the government, among others to (1) give employment to hundreds of workers, (2) to reduce the price of shoes by some 30 percent and (3) to export more than half their output.

In return for these promises, Abco received the following concessions from the government:

(1) Land was given the company on a lease basis for a period of 99 years rent free.
(2) A government owned contracting firm built the factory at low-subsidized prices.
(3) The company received loans at very low interest rates for an extended period of time. These loans could be renewed at company request at lower than the prevailing interest rate.
(4) The government trained workers at the plant at no expense to the company.

Within five years the company was thrown into bankruptcy hearings. The government was asked by both the company management and workers to grant the company an additional one million dollar loan so that some 300 employees would not lose their jobs during a time of high unemployment. Also, the Board of Directors stated that if the government would not agree to their request for a loan, the company should be purchased by the government for an "agreed" price, rather than let the hearings commence. Upon investigation, however, the government learned that the Abco Corporation had kept none of its original promises. For one, shoe prices at the factory were not lower than any of its competitors. As for exports, not only had the company failed to reach its promised goal of 50 percent, but as of the hearings, its exports for a five year period only amounted to 5 percent of total output. In light of these developments, the government established a special commercial committee to resolve this state of affairs.

Data Evaluation Questions

DIRECTIONS: Evaluate each of the following factors used in decision-making which relate to the passage you have just read by selecting

(A) for a *Major Objective*—the result desired by the executive;

(B) for a *Major Factor*—a primary consideration, spelled out in the passage, that influences the decision;

(C) for a *Minor Factor*—a less important consideration in the decision;

(D) for a *Major Assumption*—a conclusion reached by the executive not necessarily supported by the factors present;

(E) for an *Unimportant Issue*—a consideration not directly related to the problem.

141. Employment for shoe workers

142. High unemployment in the country

143. Excess shoe-manufacturing capacity

144. More loans for Abco

145. Investment incentives

Data Application Questions

DIRECTIONS: Answer each of the following questions using information contained in the passage.

146. Abco management desired that the company

I. Go into bankruptcy
II. Be purchased by its workers
III. Be purchased by the government

(A) I only
(B) III only
(C) I and II only
(D) II and III only
(E) I, II, and III

147. Although the government approved the Abco operation

I. Shoe manufacturers had excess capacity
II. World shoe prices had declined
III. Consumers were buying fewer shoes

(A) I only
(B) III only
(C) I and II only
(D) II and III only
(E) I, II, and III

148. Of all the promises given Abco by the government, which of the following were fulfilled?

    I. Exportation of 50 percent of output
    II. Lower shoe prices
    III. Employment of hundreds of workers

    (A) I only
    (B) III only
    (C) I and II only
    (D) II and III only
    (E) I, II, and III

149. It can be inferred from the passage that the failure of the company was due to

    I. Poor management
    II. Inflation
    III. Too many competitors in the shoe industry

    (A) I only
    (B) III only
    (C) I and II only
    (D) II and III only
    (E) I, II, and III

150. The government's decision to help establish Abco can be described as

    I. Optimistic
    II. Myopic
    III. Fortuitous

    (A) I only
    (B) III only
    (C) I and II only
    (D) II and III only
    (E) I, II, and III

Passage 2:

Norris Products Company, located in Pontiac, Michigan, produces small mechanical parts for the automobile industry. The firm sells both to automobile manufacturers and to individual car owners. It maintains an active research department and has always been a leader in product development. Mr. Joe Doran is director of product development and has five subordinates.

Management of the Norris Company believes that research has been worthwhile because several new products have been invented and patented by the laboratory and then put into regular production. Some of these products did not sell and were discontinued, but these failures were more than offset by the profits earned by those products which have been successful. Investigation discloses that 45 percent of the firm's present dollar volume of sales comes from products developed in its laboratory within the last ten years.

At a recent meeting of the Management Board (all top officials) Mr. Doran told about a new type of control for private airplanes, which he discovered quite by accident while working on an automobile steering problem. Mr. Doran is an avid aviation fan and owns his own plane; it was therefore natural for him to "find" this aircraft application as he worked on an automobile problem. He has applied for a Norris Company patent on the device. He feels that the device will be an overnight sales success and urges that it be produced immediately and placed on the market. The other officials, including Mr. Norris, even though they respect highly the ability of Mr. Doran, are of the opinion that the firm should manufacture only automobile parts and accessories. They argue that, even though they could produce the item, their marketing channels are keyed to automobile products and therefore it would take a great deal of added money to develop new and divergent sales contacts. It is their contention that the new idea should be either sold outright or an arrangement made by which they would collect royalties on sales for letting another concern (most likely a firm already in the aircraft business) use the idea.

Mr. Doran's retort is, "Remember the wagon manufacturers? They didn't want to enter the automobile business, and what happened to them!"

Data Evaluation Questions

DIRECTIONS: Evaluate each of the following factors used in decision-making which relate to the passage you have just read by selecting

(A) for a *Major Objective*—the result desired by the executive;

(B) for a *Major Factor*—a primary consideration, spelled out in the passage, that influences the decision;

(C) for a *Minor Factor*—a less important consideration in the decision;

(D) for a *Major Assumption*—a conclusion reached by the executive not necessarily supported by the factors present;

(E) for an *Unimportant Issue*—a consideration not directly related to the problem.

151. Channels of distribution

152. Expertise in the aircraft industry

153. A product discovered by accident

154. Mr. Doran applied for a Norris Co. patent

155. Production capability for the new product

Data Application Questions

DIRECTIONS: Answer each of the following questions using information contained in the passage.

156. According to the passage, the Norris Company sells

    I.   Laboratory equipment
   II.   Safety controls
  III. Small mechanical parts

  (A) I only
  (B) III only
  (C) I and II only
  (D) II and III only
  (E) I, II, and III

157. Joe Doran's product idea should be

    I.   Developed by his company
   II.   Sold to another company
  III. Licensed under a royalty agreement

  (A) I only
  (B) III only
  (C) I and II only
  (D) II and III only
  (E) I, II, and III

158. Joe Doran's new product idea was developed

    I.   By "accident"
   II.   In the Norris Company laboratory
  III. Over a ten year period

  (A) I only
  (B) III only
  (C) I and II only
  (D) II and III only
  (E) I, II, and III

159. Management of the Norris Company was reluctant to process Joe Doran's idea because the company lacked

    I.   Production facilities
   II.   Experience in the aircraft industry
  III. Distribution channels to reach the aircraft market

  (A) I only
  (B) III only
  (C) I and II only
  (D) II and III only
  (E) I, II, and III

160. Mr. Doran feels his product idea will be an "overnight sales success." On what basis does he hold to that belief?

I. A thorough research of the market
II. Past experience in the industry
III. Intuition

(A) I only
(B) III only
(C) I and II only
(D) II and III only
(E) I, II, and III

If there is still time remaining, you may review the questions in this section only.
You may not turn to any other section of the test.

Section VI Data Sufficiency

TIME: 25 minutes

DIRECTIONS: Each of the following problems has a question and two statements which are labeled (1) and (2). Use the data given in (1) and (2) together with other available information (such as the number of hours in a day, the definition of *clockwise*, mathematical facts, etc.) to decide whether the statements are *sufficient* to answer the question. Then fill in space

(A) if you can get the answer from (1) alone but not from (2) alone;

(B) if you can get the answer from (2) alone but not from (1) alone;

(C) if you can get the answer from (1) and (2) together, although neither statement by itself suffices;

(D) if statement (1) alone suffices *and* statement (2) alone suffices;

(E) if you cannot get the answer from statements (1) and (2) together, but need even more data.

All numbers used in this section are real numbers. A figure given for a problem is intended to provide information consistent with that in the question, but not necessarily with the additional information contained in the statements.

161. Find $x + 2y$.

   (1) $x + y = 4$
   (2) $2x + 4y = 12$

162. Is angle x a right angle?

   (1) $x = 2y$
   (2) $y = 1.5z$

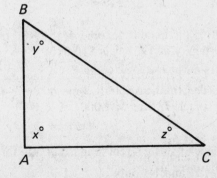

163. Is x greater than y?

   (1) $x = 2k$
   (2) $k = 2y$

164. How much profit did Toyland make selling 65 dolls if each doll costs $8?

(1) The amount the dolls sold for was $750.
(2) The dolls cost $7 each last year.

165. 50% of the people in Teetown have blue eyes and blond hair. What percent of the people in Teetown have blue eyes but do not have blond hair?

(1) 70% of the people in Teetown have blond hair.
(2) 60% of the people in Teetown have blue eyes.

166. The pentagon *ABCDE* is inscribed in the circle with center *O*. How many degrees is angle *ABC?*.

(1) The pentagon *ABCDE* is a regular pentagon.
(2) The radius of the circle is 5 inches.

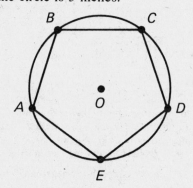

167. What is the area of the circle with center *O?* (*AB* and *DE* are straight lines)

(1) *DE* = 5 inches
(2) *AB* = 7 inches

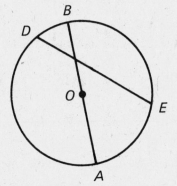

168. What is the taxable income of the Kell family in 1973? The taxable income of the Kell family in 1971 was $10,000.

(1) The Kell family had taxable income of $12,000 in 1972.
(2) The total taxable income of the Kell family for the three years 1971, 1972, and 1973 was $34,000.

169. A piece of string 6 feet long is cut into three smaller pieces. How long is the longest of the three pieces?

(1) Two pieces are the same length.
(2) One piece is 3 feet, 2 inches long.

170. If a group of 5 craftsmen take 3 hours to finish a job, how long will it take a group of 4 apprentices to do the same job?

    (1)   An apprentice does $\frac{2}{3}$ as much work as a craftsman.

    (2)   The 5 craftsmen and the 4 apprentices working together will take $1\frac{22}{23}$ hours to finish the job.

171. Is $\frac{1}{x}$ greater than $\frac{1}{y}$?

    (1) x is greater than 1.

    (2) x is less than y.

172. AB intersects CD at point O. Is AB perpendicular to CD? $AC = AD$.

    (1)   Angle CAD is bisected by AO.

    (2) $BC = AD$

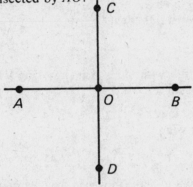

173. Plane X flies at r miles per hour from A to B. Plane Y flies at S miles per hour from B to A. Both planes take off at the same time. Which plane flies at a faster rate? Town C is between A and B.

    (1) C is closer to A than it is to B.

    (2)   Plane X flies over C before plane Y.

174. What is the value of $x + y$?

    (1) $2x + y = 4$

    (2) $x + 2y = 5$

175. What is the area of the circular section AOB? A and B are points on the circle which has O as its center.

    (1)   Angle $AOB = 36°$

    (2) $OB = OA$

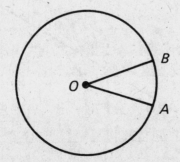

176. k is an integer. Is k divisible by 8?

    (1) k is divisible by 4.
    (2) k is divisible by 16.

177. How much is the average salary of the 30 assembly workers? The foreman is paid a salary of $12,000.

    (1) The total salary paid to the assembly workers and the foreman is $312,000.
    (2) The foreman's salary is 120% of the average salary of the assembly workers.

178. How far is it from town A to town B? Town C is 12 miles east of town A.

    (1) Town C is south of town B.
    (2) It is 9 miles from town B to town C.

179. How many vinyl squares with sides 5 inches long will be needed to cover the rectangular floor of a room?

    (1) The floor is 10 feet long.
    (2) The floor is 5 feet wide.

180. Mary must work 15 hours to make in wages the cost of a set of luggage. How many dollars does the set of luggage cost?

    (1) Jim must work 12 hours to make in wages the cost of the set of luggage.
    (2) Jim's hourly wage is 125% of Mary's hourly wage.

181. What is the value of x?

    (1) $\dfrac{x}{y} = 3$
    (2) $x - y = 9$

182. Is DE parallel to AB?

    (1) The triangles DEC and ABC are similar.
    (2) $CE = EB$

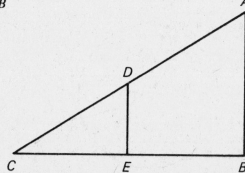

183. How many of the numbers x and y are positive? Both x and y are less than 20.

    (1) x is less than 5.
    (2) $x + y = 24$

184. What is the value of x? $PS = SR$.

    (1) $y = 30$
    (2) $PQ = QR$

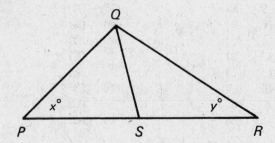

185. How much does the first volume of a 5 volume work weigh?

    (1) The first 3 volumes weigh 4 pounds.
    (2) The second, third and fourth volumes weigh a total of $3\frac{1}{2}$ pounds.

If there is still time remaining, you may review the questions in this section only.
You may not turn to any other section of the test.

Answers

Section I   Reading Recall

1. **(D)**	9. **(E)**	17. **(D)**	25. **(C)**
2. **(D)**	10. **(B)**	18. **(E)**	26. **(A)**
3. **(E)**	11. **(C)**	19. **(B)**	27. **(C)**
4. **(C)**	12. **(B)**	20. **(E)**	28. **(C)**
5. **(A)**	13. **(C)**	21. **(E)**	29. **(A)**
6. **(B)**	14. **(D)**	22. **(B)**	30. **(C)**
7. **(D)**	15. **(C)**	23. **(C)**	
8. **(E)**	16. **(D)**	24. **(C)**	

Section II   Mathematics

(Numbers in parentheses indicate the section in the Mathematics Review where material concerning the question is discussed.)

31. **(B)** (I–2)	50. **(C)** (IV–1)	68. **(E)** (IV–2)
32. **(A)** (I–4)	51. **(B)** (IV–1)	69. **(D)** (IV–2)
33. **(A)** (IV–4)	52. **(D)** (II–1)	70. **(D)** (II–6)
34. **(B)** (IV–4)	53. **(D)** (III–5)	71. **(B)** (I–2)
35. **(C)** (IV–3)	54. **(B)** (III–7, I–4)	72. **(A)** (III–7)
36. **(B)** (IV–3, IV–4)	55. **(C)** (IV–5)	73. **(E)** (II–3)
37. **(C)** (II–5)	56. **(E)** (IV–5)	74. **(E)** (IV–1)
38. **(C)** (II–5, III–7)	57. **(D)** (IV–5)	75. **(B)** (IV–1)
39. **(B)** (IV–1)	58. **(C)** (I–4)	76. **(E)** (IV–1)
40. **(C)** (IV–1)	59. **(C)** (II–7)	77. **(C)** (IV–1)
41. **(C)** (IV–1)	60. **(E)** (I–4)	78. **(C)** (II–3)
42. **(E)** (II–4)	61. **(B)** (II–2)	79. **(D)** (I–4)
43. **(C)** (I–3)	62. **(A)** (IV–1)	80. **(E)** (IV–5)
44. **(B)** (I–7)	63. **(C)** (I–4, II–3)	81. **(D)** (IV–5)
45. **(D)** (IV–1)	64. **(E)** (I–2)	82. **(C)** (IV–5)
46. **(C)** (IV–4)	65. **(D)** (III–7)	83. **(A)** (III–7)
47. **(C)** (I–4)	66. **(D)** (IV–2)	84. **(D)** (I–4)
48. **(A)** (II–2)	67. **(B)** (IV–2)	85. **(C)** (II–2)
49. **(A)** (IV–1)		

Section III   Verbal Aptitude

86. (B)	96. (C)	106. (E)	116. (B)
87. (D)	97. (D)	107. (A)	117. (D)
88. (C)	98. (B)	108. (C)	118. (C)
89. (D)	99. (C)	109. (B)	119. (C)
90. (E)	100. (D)	110. (B)	120. (D)
91. (B)	101. (B)	111. (B)	121. (C)
92. (B)	102. (C)	112. (C)	122. (A)
93. (C)	103. (A)	113. (A)	123. (B)
94. (A)	104. (A)	114. (C)	124. (B)
95. (A)	105. (B)	115. (D)	125. (C)

Section IV   Data Sufficiency

126. (E)	131. (C)	136. (D)
127. (B)	132. (D)	137. (C)
128. (D)	133. (B)	138. (E)
129. (A)	134. (E)	139. (D)
130. (E)	135. (D)	140. (E)

Section V   Business Judgment

141. (A)	146. (B)	151. (A)	156. (B)
142. (B)	147. (A)	152. (B)	157. (E)
143. (E)	148. (B)	153. (E)	158. (A)
144. (C)	149. (B)	154. (E)	159. (D)
145. (E)	150. (C)	155. (B)	160. (B)

Section VI   Data Sufficiency

161. (B)	168. (C)	174. (C)	180. (E)
162. (C)	169. (B)	175. (E)	181. (C)
163. (E)	170. (D)	176. (B)	182. (A)
164. (A)	171. (C)	177. (D)	183. (B)
165. (B)	172. (A)	178. (C)	184. (C)
166. (A)	173. (E)	179. (C)	185. (E)
167. (B)			

Analysis

Section I   Reading Recall

1. **(D)** This is clearly a subject dealing with the economy and economic policy. Note that **(E)** is too vague; an economic *policy* textbook might have been a correct answer.

2. **(D)** The United States is mentioned in paragraphs 1, 4, and 5.

3. **(E)** All of the others are given in paragraph 2.

4. **(C)** See paragraph 2: ". . . consumer and business sentiment benefited from rising public expectations that a resolution of the conflict [Vietnam] was in prospect and that East-West tensions were easing." The reference to the stock market response to possible peace in Vietnam is not an issue because of "shifting" appraisals, i.e., pessimism followed by downturns in the stock averages.

5. **(A)** See paragraph 3, line 1: "The underpinnings of the business expansion were to be found in part in the stimulative monetary and fiscal policies that had been pursued."

6. **(B)** See paragraph 4: ". . . there was actually a substantial deterioration in our trade account to a sizable deficit, almost two thirds of which was with Japan."

7. **(D)** See paragraph 5, line 1: Only **(D)** was mentioned.

8. **(E)** See paragraph 5, sentence 2: "The Phase Three program of wage and price restraint can contribute to dampening inflation."

9. **(E)** Paragraph 5 is obscure as to how much unemployment can be reduced. First, it states ". . . it seems doubtful whether the much lower rates of four percent and below often cited . . . do in part represent feasible goals. . . ." Further on the paragraph reads "There is little doubt that overall unemployment rates can be brought down to 4 percent or less, for a time at least. . . ."

10. **(B)** See paragraph 5: ". . . while the unemployment rates of a bit over 5 percent. . . ."

11. **(C)** The subject is about killer waves which are *caused* by underwater earthquakes **(D)**.

12. **(B)** See paragraph 1: "Under a perfectly sunny sky and from an apparently calm sea. . . ."

13. **(C)** Tsunami is the Japanese name (paragraph 3) and the term "killer" waves is mentioned in paragraph 5.

14. **(D)** See paragraph 2, line 1: "How are these waves formed? When a submarine earthquake occurs. . . ."

15. **(C)** See paragraph 2: "The swells in the ocean are sometimes nearly a mile wide. . . ."

16. **(D)** See paragraph 5: ". . . the Coast and Geodetic Survey initiated a program . . . to locate submarine earthquakes [and] tell how severe a submarine earthquake was. . . ."

17. **(D)** See paragraph 4.

18. **(E)** See paragraph 3: "These waves travel hundreds of miles an hour. . . ."

19. **(B)** See paragraph 3.

20. **(E)** All are mentioned in paragraph 5, except for the height of the wave.

21. **(E)** See paragraphs 1, 2, and 6: The passage deals with the problems of all three.

22. **(B)** See paragraph 2, line 1: "The problems of the atmosphere resemble those of water only partly."

23. **(C)** This is stated in paragraph 2.

24. **(C)** See paragraph 3: "The households' share in atmospheric pollution is far bigger than that of industry. . . ." The key word in the question is "most."

25. **(C)** Maintenance is determined by both production *and* transportation costs. Although paragraph 1 states that the maintenance of clean water is "primarily" one of production costs, paragraph 4 states that this problem is "related to the costs of production and transport. . . ."

26. **(A)** This is discussed in paragraph 3 in context with atmospheric pollution.

27. **(C)** See paragraph 5, line 1: "Atmospheric pollution caused by the private property of individuals . . . is difficult to control."

28. **(C)** See paragraph 6: Both active and passive resources. No mention is made of levying taxes.

29. **(A)** See paragraph 5: "*In this particular case,* the cost of anti-pollution measures will have to be borne to a considerable extent by individuals." "In this particular case" refers to the situation also described in the paragraph where pollution is caused by the private property of individuals.

30. **(C)** See paragraph 6: While noise abatement is not impossible to achieve, the "costs of a complete protection against noise are so prohibitive. . . ."

Section II   Mathematics

31. **(B)** The time needed to complete the trip is $\left(6 - \frac{1}{4} - 1\frac{3}{8} - 2\frac{1}{3}\right)$ hours. This equals $6 - (1+2) - \left(\frac{1}{4} + \frac{3}{8} + \frac{1}{3}\right) = 3 - \frac{6+9+8}{24} = 3 - \frac{23}{24} = 2\frac{1}{24} = 2$ hours $2\frac{1}{2}$ minutes.

32. **(A)** The average has decreased by $500 - 400$ or 100 points during the week, so the percentage of decrease is 100/500 or 20%.

33. **(A)** The bars in the upper figure give percent increase; the highest bar corresponds to the year 1950.

34. **(B)** The total sales of a year divided by the number of cars in the pictograph for any year will give the number of sales that a single car represents. In 1950, sales were 6.7 million, and there were about $4\frac{1}{2}$ cars in the pictograph. $6.7 \div \frac{9}{2} = 6.7 \times \frac{2}{9} \approx 6.3 \times \frac{2}{9} \approx 1.4$ (where $\approx$ denotes "approximately").

35. **(C)** The dots on the line graph and the left-hand scale give registrations. In 1950, there were about 40 million passenger cars registered.

36. **(B)**

    STATEMENT I is not true, since percentage is indicated by the right scale, not by the left scale.

    STATEMENT III cannot be inferred, since there are many years between 1950 and 1969 for which no sales figures are given.

    STATEMENT II is true, since registrations were about 40 million in 1950 and they increased to about 80 million by 1969.

    So only STATEMENT II can be inferred from the graphs.

37. **(C)** Since there are 180 minutes in 3 hours, then $\frac{x}{8} = \frac{180}{18}$, where x is the number of cars washed in 3 hours. Therefore, $x = 8 \times 10 = 80$.

38. **(C)** If s and t denote the sides of the two squares, then $s^2 : t^2 = 2 : 1$, or $\frac{s^2}{t^2} = \frac{2}{1}$. Thus $\left(\frac{s}{t}\right)^2 = \frac{2}{1}$ and $\frac{s}{t} = \frac{\sqrt{2}}{1}$.

39. **(B)** In the Pacific region, the amount of credit life insurance was $12,457,000,000 and the amount of ordinary life insurance $108,806,-000,000. Therefore, the ratio is about $\frac{12}{108}$ which equals $\frac{1}{9}$ or 1 to 9.

40. **(C)** Only the South Atlantic region had more than $10,000,000,000 in industrial life insurance in 1972.

41. **(C)** The percent change for total life insurance was 140.8%, so only group (201.5%) and credit (186.1%) had a greater percentage of increase from 1962 to 1972.

42. **(E)** The Venn diagram indicates the answer immediately. The region outside both circles denotes neither whitewall tires nor air-conditioning.

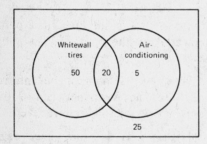

43. **(C)** Each share was worth $122.50 − $111.10 or $11.40 less in 1973 than it was in 1970. Therefore, the 100,000 shares were worth 100,000 × $11.40 or $1,140,000 less in 1973 than in 1970.

44. **(B)** Add up the daily wages to get the total wages for the week. $51.90 + 52.20 + 49.80 + 51.50 + 50.60 = $256.00. Divide $256.00 by 5 to get the average daily wage, $51.20.

45. **(D)** The exact ratio is $\frac{364}{160}$ or $\frac{91}{40}$, which is about 9 to 4.

46. **(C)** $\frac{27}{56}$ of all accident deaths occurred in motor vehicle accidents, and there were 56,400 motor vehicle deaths in 1969. So the number of accidental deaths is $56,400 \times \frac{56}{27}$. Since you need only an approximate answer and $\frac{56}{27}$ is about 2; 112,800 is a good approximation.

47. **(C)** The interest on the first $600 is (.08) ($600) or $48.00 for a year. There is $5,400 of the loan in excess of $600; so he must pay (.07)(5,400) or $378.00 interest for the year on the $5,400. Therefore, the interest for one year will be $48 + $378 or $426.

48. **(A)** $4y - 6x = -2(3x - 2y) = -2(8) = -16.$

49. **(A)** Argentina had 40,180 kilometers of railroad which is third after the United States and Canada.

50. **(C)** Check the column headed Km. per area. The largest entry in the column is 44.54, for Cuba.

51. **(B)** In 1953, there were 60 million passenger kilometers in Paraguay and in 1965 35 million, so passenger kilometers decreased by 25 million. $\frac{25}{60} = \frac{5}{12} = 41\frac{2}{3}\%$. Therefore, the decrease was about 40%.

52. **(D)** Since the total distance is 200 miles, of which you fly x miles, you drive $(200 - x)$ miles. Therefore, the cost is $10x + (200 - x)12$, which is $10x - 12x + 2400$ or $2400 - 2x$ cents. The answer in dollars is obtained by dividing by 100, which is $(24 - .02x)$ dollars.

53. **(D)** Since the sides of the square equal the length of the rectangles, which is twice the width, the length of R_1 is 2 times its width.

54. **(B)** If A_1 denotes the increased area and A the original area, then $A_1 = 1.69A$, since A_1 is A increased by 69%. Thus, $s_1^2 = A_1 = 1.69A = 1.69s^2$, where s_1 is the increased side and s the original side. Since the square root of 1.69 is 1.3, we have $s_1 = 1.3s$ so s is increased by .3 or 30%.

55. **(C)** The $5,000–9,999 income group is the only group which contained more than 30% of the white families in 1950.

56. **(E)** In 1969, about 80% of the white families had incomes of over $5,000, and about 20% of the white families had incomes of less than $5,000. Therefore, the ratio is about 80 to 20 or 4 to 1.

57. **(D)**

STATEMENT I can not be inferred since the graphs do not give any information about the number of white or Negro families.

STATEMENT II can be inferred since over 50% of the families in the category "Negro and other races" had an income of $3,000 or less, while in 1969 fewer than 25% of these families had an income of $3,000 or less; so the percentage decreased by more than $1/2$ or 50%.

STATEMENT III can be inferred, since about 50% of the white families had incomes of $10,000 or more in 1969. Therefore, the average income would be at least $5,000, even if the other 50% had no income.

Therefore, STATEMENTS II and III can be inferred from the graph, but STATEMENT I can not.

58. **(C)** Since the dealer made a profit of 20%, he sold the car for 120% of what the car cost. Thus, if C is the cost of the car, 120% of $C = $1,380$ or $(^6/_5)C = $1,380$. Therefore, $C = ^5/_6$ of $1,380, which is $1,150.

59. **(C)**

STATEMENT I is not always true. For example, 1 is less than 5 and 1 is less than 6, but 6 is not less than 5.

STATEMENT II is not always true, since $^3/_8 < ^1/_2$ and $^3/_8 < ^2/_3$ but $^3/_8$ is not less than $(^1/_2)(^2/_3) = ^1/_3$.

Since STATEMENT III is always true, (C) is the correct answer.

60. **(E)** The total number of workers is 80, and 35 of them work 40 or more hours. Therefore, $^{35}/_{80} = .4375 = 43.75\%$.

61. **(B)** 15 people worked 40 to 44 hours, and 4 worked up to 29 hours. So $4x = 15$, which means $x = ^{15}/_4 = 3^3/_4$.

62. **(A)**

STATEMENT I can be inferred, since the average number of hours worked is $\frac{3100}{80} = 38\frac{3}{4}$ which is less than 40.

STATEMENT II can not be inferred, since there is no information about the number of workers who worked over 48 hours.

STATEMENT III is not true, since there are only 35 workers who worked 40 or more hours.

63. **(C)** The truck uses 30% more gasoline to travel the same distance at 70 mph than it does at 50 mph. Therefore, the truck requires 130% of a gallon of gasoline, which is 1.3 gallons, to travel 19.5 miles at 70 mph. So the truck will travel $(10/1.3)(19.5)$ or 150 miles on 10 gallons of gas at 70 mph.

64. **(E)** Convert $^2/_5$ and $^1/_3$ into fractions with denominators of 30. Since $^2/_5 = ^{12}/_{30}$ and $^1/_3 = ^{10}/_{30}$, $^2/_5 + ^1/_3 = ^{12}/_{30} + ^{10}/_{30} = ^{22}/_{30}$, and x is equal to 22.

65. **(D)** The area of the rectangle is $4 \times 6 = 24$ square feet. Since 1 square foot is 144 square inches, the area of the rectangle is 3,456 square inches. Each square has an area of $(^1/_2)^2$ or $^1/_4$ square inches. Therefore, the number of squares needed $= 3,456 \div ^1/_4 = 3,456 \times 4 = 13,824$.

66. **(D)** The corporation income tax accounted for 19.7% of all average annual receipts for the years 1967–1970. Since 19.7% is about 20% or $^1/_5$, the average annual receipts were about 5 times the average annual receipts from the corporation income tax. Therefore, the answer is $5x$.

67. **(B)** Veterans received 4.2%, education and manpower 3.8%, and health and income security 26% of the average annual outlays; so together the three categories received $4.2\% + 3.8\% + 26\%$ or 34%. Since $^1/_3$ is $33^1/_3\%$, 34% is roughly $^1/_3$.

68. **(E)** International affairs received 2.4% which is more than "others" (1.7%) but less than every other category on the graph.

69. **(D)** Since $5/8$ of 3.2% = 5 × .4% = 2.0%, the correct answer is **(D)**.

70. **(D)** $\frac{10}{5} = 2 = \frac{20}{10}$, so the ratio of successive terms of the progression is 2. Therefore, the term which follows 20 is 2 times 20 or 40.

71. **(B)** Since $1/8$ of 8¢ is 1¢, each egg will cost 8¢ + 1¢ or 9¢ after the price has increased. The price of a dozen eggs will be 12 × 9¢ or $1.08.

72. **(A)** The area of trapezoid *ABCD* equals the area of rectangle *ABED*, which is $t \times 5$ (since $BE = BC = 5$), plus the area of triangle *BEC*, which is $\frac{(5 \times 5)}{2}$. The answers is thus $5t + 12.5$.

73. **(E)** The selling price of the jars should equal cost + $75. The cost of making 300 jars = $(100)65¢ + (200)55¢ = \$65 + \$110 = \$175$. So the selling price should be $175 + $75 or $250.

74. **(E)** The countries shown accounted for more than 50% of world exports in beef (51%), coffee (64%), quebracho (100%), wheat (80%), and zinc (55%).

75. **(B)** In 1962 the price was $2.49, and in 1970 the price was $1.88; so the percentage is $\frac{1.88}{2.49}$. We can divide 249 into 188, but it is faster to divide 250 into 188. $\frac{188}{250}$ is about 75%.

76. **(E)** The price dropped in linseed oil, cotton, petroleum, wheat and wool. Notice that for some commodities not all countries had prices which dropped but at least one country did.

77. **(C)** Bolivian tin received $164.40 per 100 pounds in 1970.

78. **(C)** Since each assistant does $2/3$ as much as the roofer, all 3 will accomplish $1 + 2(2/3)$ or $7/3$ as much as the roofer by himself. So they will finish the job in $7 \div 7/3$ or 3 hours.

79. **(D)** At the end of Tuesday it would be 1,000 − 100 or 900, since 10% of 1,000 = 100. At the end of Wednesday, it would be 810 or 900 − 90, and after Thursday's trading the stock average would be 810 − 81 or 729.

80. **(E)** In 1957, about $10 billion was spent on research and development; in 1970, more than $25 billion was spent. $\frac{25}{10} = 250\%$.

81. **(D)** The top of the graph is higher than 15 billion in 1961.

82. **(C)**

STATEMENT I can be inferred since the top of the graph is always rising.

STATEMENT II can also be inferred, since the amount of funds used in 1958 was less than $12 billion while the amount in 1968 was more than $24 billion.

STATEMENT III is not true, since the strip which denotes research and development performed by universities and others and funded by the federal government is narrower than many of the other categories so less was spent in that category.

83. **(A)** Since it takes twice as long to walk the length as the width, $l = 2w$ where l is the length and w the width. The perimeter equals $2l + 2w = 3l = 300$ yards, so the length is 100 yards and the width is 50 yards. Therefore, the area is 50 × 100 = 5,000 square yards.

84. **(D)** The company's profit = $(2,000)(.07) + (5,000)(.06) = \$140 + \$300 = \$440$.

85. **(C)** Since $\frac{x}{y} = \frac{3}{z}$, $xz = 3y$ and $9y^2 = (3y)^2$; so $9y^2 = (xz)^2 = x^2z^2$.

Section III   Verbal Aptitude

86. **(B)** SEDITIOUS: factious, rebellious. *Antonym:* orderly

87. **(D)** REDOLENT: odorous, fragrant. *Antonym:* fetid

88. **(C)** PUERILE: youthful, juvenile. *Antonym:* mature

89. **(D)** ABATE: lessen, reduce. *Antonym:* increase

90. **(E)** ACERBITY: sharpness, acrimony. *Antonym:* sweetness

91. **(B)** ACTUATE: move. instigate. *Antonym:* dissuade

92. **(B)** IRRESOLUTE: undetermined, vacillating. *Antonym:* determined

93. **(C)** FRACTIOUS: petulant, testy. *Antonym:* agreeable

94. **(A)** ADMONITION: warning, caution. *Antonym:* countenance

95. **(A)** ENMITY: animosity, hostility. *Antonym:* affection

96. **(C)** ARTIFICE: trick, delusion. *Antonym:* honesty

97. **(D)** CONDUCE: lead, contribute. *Antonym:* counteract

98. **(B)** DEBILITY: languor, weakness. *Antonym:* strength

99. **(C)** CONJURE: entreat, adjure. *Antonym:* deprecate

100. **(D)** An aviary is a place where birds are kept while an arboretum is a place for plants. Dovecote and greenhouse have the same relationship.

101. **(B)** A convict is sentenced to prison; an exile is sentenced to banishment.

102. **(C)** A flood is a compounded state (extreme form) of water. A blizzard and snow have the same relationship.

103. **(A)** The relationship is one of opposites. Penitence is an antonym of obduracy. The same relationship holds for pensive and thoughtless.

104. **(A)** The relationship is one of synonyms. Fortitude is a synonym of resolution as is timidity of weakness.

105. **(B)** A tape measure is an instrument used to provide measurement and electricity is the instrument used to provide power.

106. **(E)** An amplifier enlarges the voice as an expediter speeds a shipment.

107. **(A)** The relationship is one of antonyms. Perfidious is an antonym of faithful.

108. **(C)** Genocide is an extreme form of murder, as a tornado is an extreme form of wind.

109. **(B)** A clarification is the opposite of nebulous, while emendation is the opposite of erroneous.

110. **(B)** The relationship is one of antonyms. Annihilate is the opposite of extirpate.

111. **(B)** The relationship is one of synonyms. Amalgamate and united are the same, as are organize and arranged.

112. **(C)** An incantation is recited during exorcism while a prayer is recited during devotion.

113. **(A)** Air is not imbibed (B), neither do the other alternatives fit the meaning of the sentence.

114. **(C)** Recorders do not "hum" (D); a soliloquy is a rendering by one person, while musicians do not sing (B).

115. **(D)** While incentives (B) might be a logical alternative, trade (D) is more specific.

116. **(B)** Victims has the most meaning in the context of plight.

117. **(D)** Diametrically or "directly" opposed.

118. **(C)** Emolument means salary. A farmer who receives a salary is also an employee, but not vice-versa.

119. **(C)** A plebiscite calls on the "plebs" or common people for a vote of confidence. A referendum is the referring of questions,

e.g., "the right of 18 year olds to vote" to most or all of the citizens for a decision by vote.

120. **(D)** Tax reductions increase (real) income and raise purchasing power.

121. **(C)** Carnivorous or flesh-eating.

122. **(A)** It certainly is not fortuitous (accidental) nor dubious (unclear).

123. **(B)** Lugubriously or mournfully simple. It is not incongruously (incompatible), abstrusely (complex) nor inscrutably (latent).

124. **(B)** If he continued talking, he was loquacious (very talkative).

125. **(C)** Alternative (B) might seem plausible, but (C) is more inclusive; it covers those which fit in category (B).

Section IV   Data Sufficiency

126. **(E)**

A triangle with sides of lengths 3, 4, and 5 is a right triangle since $3^2 + 4^2 = 5^2$, and its perimeter is 12. A triangle with sides of lengths 2, $4\frac{4}{5}$, and $5\frac{1}{5}$ also has a perimeter of 12. And since $2^2 + (4\frac{4}{5})^2 = (5\frac{1}{5})^2$, it too is a right triangle. Therefore, two triangles can satisfy STATEMENTS (1) and (2) yet not be congruent. On the other hand, any pair of congruent right triangles satisfy STATEMENTS (1) and (2). Thus, STATEMENTS (1) and (2) together are not sufficient to answer the question.

127. **(B)**

$x^3 - 8 = 0$ has only $x = 2$ as a real solution. And 2 is greater than 0, so STATEMENT (2) alone is sufficient.

Since $x = 2$ and $x = -2$ are both solutions of $x^4 - 16 = 0$, STATEMENT (1) alone is not sufficient.

128. **(D)**

STATEMENT (1) is sufficient since it implies that conveyer belt A loads $\frac{2}{3}$ of the hopper while conveyer belt B loads only $\frac{1}{3}$ with both working. Since conveyer belt A loads $\frac{2}{3}$ of the hopper in a hour, it will take $1 \div \frac{2}{3}$ or $1\frac{1}{2}$ hours to fill the hopper by itself.

STATEMENT (2) is also sufficient since it implies that conveyer belt B fills $\frac{1}{3}$ of the hopper in 1 hour. Thus, conveyer belt A loads $\frac{2}{3}$ in one hour, and that means conveyer belt A will take $1\frac{1}{2}$ hours by itself.

129. **(A)** The first fly will travel a distance equal to the circumference of the circle which is π times the diameter. The second fly will travel $4s$ where s is the length of a side. Since the diagonal of a square has length $\sqrt{2}S$, the second fly will travel $4/\sqrt{2}$ times the diagonal of the square. Therefore, (1) alone is sufficient, since $4/\sqrt{2} = 4\sqrt{2}/2 = 2\sqrt{2}$ which is less than π. (2) alone is not sufficient, since one fly might have crawled faster than the other.

130. **(E)** Using (1) and (2) together, it is only possible to determine the total amount paid for fire insurance in 1970 and 1972. Since no relation is given between the amounts paid in 1970 and 1972, there is not enough information to determine the cost in 1972.

131. **(C)** (2) alone is not sufficient since both $y = 2$ and $y = -2$ satisfy $y^2 - 4 = 0$. (1) alone is not sufficient, since $\frac{1}{2}$ is larger than 0 but less than 1 while 3 is larger than 0 and larger than 1. The only solution of $y^2 - 4 = 0$ which is larger than 0 is 2 which is larger than 1. Therefore, (1) and (2) are sufficient.

132. **(D)** Let x be the amount he was paid the first day. Then he was paid $x + 2$, $x + 4$, $x + 6$, $x + 8$, and $x + 10$ dollars for the succeeding days. (1) alone is sufficient, since the total he was paid is $(6x + 30)$ dollars, and we can solve $6x + 30 = 150$ (to find that he was paid $20 for the first day). (2) alone is also sufficient. He was paid $(x + 10)$ on the sixth day, so (2) means that $(1.5)x = x + 10$ (which is the same as $x = 20$).

133. **(B)** Since 85% of $3,000 is $2,550, (2) alone is sufficient. (1) alone is not sufficient, since

if x were 5% (1) would tell us the price of the car is less than $2,600. But if x were 1%, (1) would imply that the price of the car is greater than $2,600.

134. **(E)** Vertical angles are equal, so $c = d$. Since the sum of the angles in a triangle is 180°, $a + b + c = d + e + f$ which means $a + b = e + f$. If we use (1) and (2), we have $a + a = e + a$ so $e = a$. And we know the triangles are similar. However this does not give any information about the value of a, since any two similar triangles can be made to satisfy conditions (1) and (2). Therefore, (1) and (2) together are not sufficient.

135. **(D)** (1) alone is sufficient since $BC = AB$ implies $x = y = 40$. Since the sum of the angles in a triangle is 180°, z must equal 100. (2) alone is sufficient. Let D be the point where the bisector of angle B meets AC. Then according to (2), triangle BDC is a right triangle. Since angle y is 40°, the remaining angle in triangle BDC is 50° and equals $\frac{1}{2}z$, so $z = 100$.

136. **(D)** Since there is a bottom and 4 sides, each a congruent square, the amount of cardboard needed will be $5e^2$ where e is the length of an edge of the box. So we need to find e. (1) alone is sufficient. Since the area of the bottom is e^2, (1) means $e^2 = 4$ with $e = 2$ feet. (2) alone is also sufficient. Since the volume of the box is e^3. (2) means $e^3 = 8$ and $e = 2$ feet.

137. **(C)** The average weight of the books is the total weight of all the books divided by the number of books on the shelf. Thus (1) and (2) together are sufficient. (Solve $2.5 = \frac{40}{x}$ for x, the number of books on the shelf.) (1) alone is not sufficient, nor is (2) alone sufficient.

138. **(E)** If $ABCD$ has the pairs of opposite sides equal and each angle is 90°, then it is a rectangle. But there are many quadrilaterals which have two opposite sides equal with one angle a right angle. For example, the figure has $AB = DC$ and $x = 90$, but it is not a rectangle. Therefore, (1) and (2) together are insufficient.

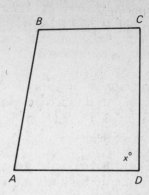

139. **(D)** (2) alone is sufficient, since if $a_3 = 1$ then $a_4 = (a_3)^2 = 1^2 = 1$; then $a_5 = (a_4)^2 = 1^2 = 1$. (1) alone is also sufficient. If $a_1 = -1$ then $a_2 = (a_1)^2 = 1$, and $a_3 = (a_2)^2 = 1$, but $a_3 = 1$ is given by (2) which we know is sufficient.

140. **(E)** Let J, F and C stand for the weekly salaries of John, Fred, and Chuck. (1) says $J = 2F$ and (2) says $F = .4(C + J)$. Since there is no information given about the values of C or F, we cannot deduce the value of J. Therefore, (1) and (2) together are insufficient.

Section V   Business Judgment

141. **(A)** Employment for workers (and shoe laborers in particular) was the *Major Objective* of the government in making a decision to encourage the establishment of Abco.

142. **(B)** See paragraph 2: High unemployment in the country was a *Major Factor* in approving the enterprise.

143. **(E)** Excess shoe manufacturing capacity *should* have been a major factor in making the decision, but according to the passage, apparently was considered to be an *Unimportant Issue*.

144. **(C)** That Abco needed more capital to continue in operation was a symptom of its

failure and not a cause; therefore, a *Minor Factor* in the government decision to help continue its operation.

145. **(E)** Investment incentives *were* a major factor in Abco's decision to establish in Korea, but do not figure in the government's current decision.

146. **(B)** See paragraph 4: Abco wanted the government to bail them out at an "agreed" price.

147. **(A)** Only the fact of excess capacity was mentioned.

148. **(B)** See paragraph 4: Abco did manage to employ some 300 workers.

149. **(B)** Whether the company suffered from poor management is unknown. However, since there was excess capacity in the industry, this is the same as too many competitors.

150. **(C)** Based on the facts, the government was optimistic in its assessment that Abco could succeed in such an industry and certainly myopic not to have realized the consequences of some obvious indicators, e.g., the over-supply of shoes.

151. **(A)** The major reason why management initially rejected Dorn's idea was because they lacked distribution channels to the aviation industry.

152. **(B)** Knowledge of the aircraft industry is a *Major Factor* and secondary to the lack of distribution channels.

153. **(E)** How the product idea was discovered is an *Unimportant Issue* in the decision of how to *exploit* it.

154. **(E)** Again, it is how to *exploit* the idea that is important.

155. **(B)** Production capability is as important as marketing ability. However, the passage states that the company has production capability (paragraph 3), so marketing ability still remains the number one concern.

156. **(B)** See paragraph 1: Small mechanical parts.

157. **(E)** All three alternatives are discussed in the passage.

158. **(A)** See paragraph 3: "he discovered quite by accident. . . ."

159. **(D)** Both reasons lead to management's cautious approach as discussed above.

160. **(B)** The passage makes no mention of any market research performed to test the marketability of the proposed product. Also we know the firm had no experience in the aviation industry.

Section VI   Data Sufficiency

161. **(B)**

STATEMENT (2) alone is sufficient. $2x + 4y = 2(x + 2y)$, so if $2x + 4y = 12$ then $2(x + 2y) = 12$ and $x + 2y = 6$.

STATEMENT (1) alone is insufficient. If you only use STATEMENT (1) then you can get $x + 2y = x + y + y = 4 + y$ but there is no information on the value of y.

162. **(C)**

Since the sum of the angles in a triangle is $180°$, $x + y + z = 180$. Using STATEMENT (1) alone we have $2y + y + z = 3y + z = 180$, which is insufficient to determine y or x.

Using STATEMENT (2) alone we have $x + 1.5z + z = x + 2.5z = 180$, which is not sufficient to determine x or z.

However, if we use both STATEMENTS (1) and (2) we obtain $3y + z = 4.5z + z = 5.5z = 180$, so $z = \frac{2}{11}$ of 180. Now $y = \frac{3}{2}$ of z, so $y = \frac{3}{11}$ of 180, and $x = \frac{6}{11}$ of 180. Therefore, x is not a right angle and STATEMENTS (1) and (2) are sufficient.

163. **(E)**

Since STATEMENT (1) only describes x and STATEMENT (2) only describes y both are needed to get an answer. Using STATEMENT (2), STATEMENT (1) becomes $x = 2k = 2 \cdot 2y = 4y$, so $x = 4y$. However, this is not sufficient, since if $y = -1$ then $x = -4$ and -4 is less than -1, but if $y = 1$ then $x = 4$ and x is greater than y.

164. **(A)**

If each doll costs $8, then 65 dolls will cost $8 \times \$65 = \$520$. Using STATEMENT (1), the profit is selling price minus cost = $750 - \$520 = \$230$, so STATEMENT (1) alone is sufficient.

STATEMENT (2) alone is not sufficient since you need to know what price the dolls sell for to find the profit.

165. **(B)**

STATEMENT (2) alone is sufficient. 60% of the people have blue eyes and 50% of the people have blue eyes and blond hair, so $60\% - 50\% = 10\%$ of the people have blue eyes but do not have blond hair.

STATEMENT (1) alone is not sufficient. Using STATEMENT (1) alone we can only find out how many people have blond hair and do not have blue eyes, in addition to what is given.

166. **(A)**

The sum of the angles of the pentagon are $540°$. (The sum of the angles of a polygon with n sides which is inscribed in a circle is $(n - 2)180°$.) STATEMENT (1) alone is sufficient. If the polygon is regular, all angles are equal and so angle ABC is $\frac{1}{5}$ of $540°$ or $108°$.

STATEMENT (2) alone is insufficient because the radius of the circle does not give any information about the angles of the pentagon.

167. **(B)**

The area of a circle is πr^2, where r is the radius of the circle. Since O is a point on the line AB, AB is a diameter of the circle. Therefore, since a radius is one half of a diameter, the radius of the circle is 3.5 inches. Thus, STATEMENT (2) alone is sufficient.

STATEMENT (1) alone is insufficient since there is no relation between DE and the radius.

168. **(C)**

Using STATEMENT (2) alone we have $\$10,000 + x + y = \$34,000$, where x is the taxable income for 1972 and y is the taxable income for 1973. So STATEMENT (2) alone is not sufficient.

STATEMENT (1) alone is not sufficient since no relation is given between taxable income in 1972 and 1973.

STATEMENTS (1) and (2) together give the equation $\$10,000 + \$12,000 + y = \$34,000$, which means $y = \$12,000$, where y is the taxable income for 1973.

169. **(B)**

STATEMENT (2) alone is sufficient. 3 feet, 2 inches is more than half of 6 feet so the piece of string 3 feet 2 inches long must be longer than the other 2 pieces put together.

STATEMENT (1) alone is insufficient. There is not enough information to find the length of *any* of the three pieces of string.

170. **(D)** Let r be the fraction of the job the 4 apprentices finish in 1 hour. Then $\frac{1}{r}$ is the amount of time in hours that it will take the 4 apprentices to finish the job. So it is sufficient to find r. The group of 5 craftsmen finishes $\frac{1}{3}$ of the job per hour, so each craftsman does $\frac{1}{15}$ of the job per hour.

STATEMENT (1) alone is sufficient. An apprentice will do $\frac{2}{3}$ of $\frac{1}{15} = \frac{2}{45}$ of the job per hour, so $r = \frac{8}{45}$.

STATEMENT (2) alone is sufficient. The craftsmen and the apprentices together will finish $\frac{1}{3} + r$ of the job per hour. Since it takes them $1\frac{22}{23}$ hours to finish the job, $(\frac{1}{3} + r)(\frac{45}{23}) = 1$ which can be solved for r.

171. **(C)**

STATEMENT (2) alone is not sufficient. -1 is less than 2 and $\frac{1}{-1}$ is less than $\frac{1}{2}$ but 1 is less than 2 and $\frac{1}{1}$ is greater than $\frac{1}{2}$.

STATEMENT (1) alone is insufficient since there is no information about y.

STATEMENTS (1) and (2) together imply that x and y are both greater than 1 and for two positive numbers x and y, if x is less than y then $\frac{1}{x}$ is greater than $\frac{1}{y}$.

172. **(A)**

STATEMENT (1) alone is sufficient. Since angle CAD is bisected by AO, the triangles AOD and AOC are congruent by side-angle-side (AO = AO). Therefore, angle AOD = angle AOC. Since the sum of the angles is 180° (CD is a straight line) the two angles are right angles and AB is ⊥ CD.

STATEMENT (2) alone is insufficient. We can choose B so that BC = AD whether or not AB ⊥ CD.

173. **(E)**

Since C is closer to A, if plane X is flying faster than plane Y it will certainly fly over C before plane Y. However, if plane X flys slower than plane Y, and C is very close to A, plane X would still fly over C before plane Y does. Thus, STATEMENTS (1) and (2) together are not sufficient.

174. **(C)**

STATEMENT (1) gives $x + y = 4 - x$ and since there is no further information about x, STATEMENT (1) alone is insufficient.

STATEMENT (2) alone is also insufficient because STATEMENT (2) only implies $x + y = 5 - y$. However, if you multiply STATEMENT (2) by −2 and add it to STATEMENT (1), the result is $-3y = -6$ or $y = 2$. So $x + y = 5 - 2 = 3$.

Therefore, STATEMENTS (1) and (2) together are sufficient and (C) is the answer.

175. **(E)**

Since the area of a circle is πr^2, the area of the circular section AOB is the fraction $\frac{x}{360}$ times πr^2, where angle AOB = x°. (There are 360° in the entire circle.) Using STATEMENT (1), we know x = 36 so $(\frac{x}{360})\pi r^2 = \frac{1}{10}\pi r^2$. However, STATEMENT (1) gives no information about the value of r, so STATEMENT (1) alone is insufficient.

STATEMENT (2) gives no information about the value of r, so STATEMENTS (1) and (2) together are insufficient.

176. **(B)**

An integer k is divisible by another integer m if k = mr, where r is an integer. So STATEMENT (1) implies k = 4r for some integer r. STATEMENT (1) alone is insufficient because 12 is divisible by 4 (4 · 3 = 12) but 12 is not divisible by 8.

STATEMENT (2) alone is sufficient. STATEMENT (2) implies that k = 16r for some integer r, but since 16 = 8 · 2 that means k = 8 · 2r and 2r is an integer, so k is divisible by 8.

177. **(D)**

STATEMENT (1) is sufficient. Since the foreman's salary is $12,000, the total of the assembly workers' salaries is $300,000. Therefore, the average salary is $300,000 ÷ 30 = $10,000.

STATEMENT (2) is sufficient. If A is the average salary of the assembly workers, then 120% of A is $12,000. Therefore, A = $12,000 ÷ $\frac{6}{5}$ = $10,000.

178. **(C)**

STATEMENT (2) alone is insufficient since you need to know what direction town B is from town C.

STATEMENT (1) alone is insufficient, since you need to know how far it is from town B to town C.

Using both STATEMENTS (1) and (2), A, B and C form a right triangle with legs of 9 miles and 12 miles. The distance from town A to town B is the hypotenuse of the triangle, so the distance from town A to town B is $\sqrt{9^2 + 12^2} = 15$ miles.

179. **(C)**

STATEMENTS (1) and (2) by themselves are insufficient since you need to know the area of the floor, and STATEMENT (1) only gives the length and STATEMENT (2) only gives the width. Using STATEMENTS (1) and (2) together, the area of the floor is 5 × 10 = 50 square feet. Since the area of each square is $5^2 = 25$ square inches, each square has area $^{25}/_{144}$ square feet. Therefore, the number of squares is $50 \div {}^{25}/_{144} = 288$.

180. **(E)**

STATEMENTS (1) and (2) only give relations between Mary's wages and Jim's wages and tell you the cost of the set of luggage in terms of hours of wages. Since there is no information about the value of the hourly wages in dollars, STATEMENTS (1) and (2) together are not sufficient.

181. **(C)**

STATEMENT (1) alone implies $x = 3y$. Since there is no more information about y, STATEMENT (1) alone is insufficient.

STATEMENT (2) alone gives $x = 9 + y$ but there is no information about y, so STATEMENT (2) alone is not sufficient.

STATEMENTS (1) and (2) together are sufficient. If $x = 9 + y$ and $x = 3y$, then $3y = 9 + y$ which gives $y = {}^9/_2$, so $x = (3)({}^9/_2) = {}^{27}/_2$.

182. **(A)**

Since in similar triangles corresponding angles are equal, angle CED = angle CBA. Therefore, DE is parallel to AB and STATEMENT (1) alone is sufficient.

STATEMENT (2) alone is insufficient since D could be *any* point on the line CA and there is at most one point on CA which will make DE parallel to AB.

183. **(B)**

If $x + y = 24$ then at least one of the numbers x or y is positive. If x is positive then $y =$

$24 - x$ and since x is less than 20, $24 - x = y$ is positive. The same argument shows that if y is positive so is x. Therefore, STATEMENT (2) alone is sufficient to show that both numbers are positive.

STATEMENT (1) alone is insufficient, since the fact that x is less than 5 does not tell whether x is positive and no information is given about y.

184. **(C)**

STATEMENT (2) alone implies $x = y$ since equal sides have equal angles in a triangle. Since there is no information about y, STATEMENT (2) alone is insufficient.

STATEMENT (1) alone is insufficient since there is no relation between x and y without STATEMENT (2).

STATEMENTS (1) and (2) together imply $x = y = 30$, so STATEMENTS (1) and (2) together are sufficient.

185. **(E)**

Denote by w_1 the weight of the first volume, by w_2 the weight of the second volume, by w_3 the weight of the third volume and by w_4 the weight of the fourth volume. STATEMENT (1) gives $w_1 + w_2 + w_3 = 4$ and STATEMENT (2) gives $w_2 + w_3 + w_4 = 3\frac{1}{2}$. Using STATEMENTS (1) and (2) you can obtain $w_1 - w_4 = \frac{1}{2}$ so $w_1 = w_4 + \frac{1}{2}$ but no other information is given about w_4. Therefore, STATEMENTS (1) and (2) together are insufficient.

Evaluating Your Score

Tabulate your score for each section of Sample Test 1 according to the directions on pages 4–5 and record the results in the Self-scoring Table below. Then find your rank for each score on the Self-scoring Scale and record it in the appropriate blank.

Self-scoring Table

PART	SCORE	RANK
1		
2		
3		
4		
5		
6		

Self-scoring Scale

PART	POOR	FAIR	GOOD	EXCELLENT
			ACHIEVEMENT	
1	0–15	16–21	22–25	26–30
2	0–29	30–40	41–47	48–55
3	0–20	21–28	29–34	35–40
4	0–7	8–10	11–12	13–15
5	0–10	11–14	15–16	17–20
6	0–12	13–17	18–21	22–25

Study again the Review sections covering material in Sample Test 1 for which you had a rank of FAIR or POOR. Then go on to Sample Test 2.

To obtain an approximation of your actual GMAT score see page 5.

Answer Sheet — Sample Test 2

Section I — Reading Recall

1. (A) (B) (C) (D) (E)
2. (A) (B) (C) (D) (E)
3. (A) (B) (C) (D) (E)
4. (A) (B) (C) (D) (E)
5. (A) (B) (C) (D) (E)
6. (A) (B) (C) (D) (E)
7. (A) (B) (C) (D) (E)

8. (A) (B) (C) (D) (E)
9. (A) (B) (C) (D) (E)
10. (A) (B) (C) (D) (E)
11. (A) (B) (C) (D) (E)
12. (A) (B) (C) (D) (E)
13. (A) (B) (C) (D) (E)
14. (A) (B) (C) (D) (E)

15. (A) (B) (C) (D) (E)
16. (A) (B) (C) (D) (E)
17. (A) (B) (C) (D) (E)
18. (A) (B) (C) (D) (E)
19. (A) (B) (C) (D) (E)
20. (A) (B) (C) (D) (E)
21. (A) (B) (C) (D) (E)
22. (A) (B) (C) (D) (E)

23. (A) (B) (C) (D) (E)
24. (A) (B) (C) (D) (E)
25. (A) (B) (C) (D) (E)
26. (A) (B) (C) (D) (E)
27. (A) (B) (C) (D) (E)
28. (A) (B) (C) (D) (E)
29. (A) (B) (C) (D) (E)
30. (A) (B) (C) (D) (E)

Section II — Mathematics

31. (A) (B) (C) (D) (E)
32. (A) (B) (C) (D) (E)
33. (A) (B) (C) (D) (E)
34. (A) (B) (C) (D) (E)
35. (A) (B) (C) (D) (E)
36. (A) (B) (C) (D) (E)
37. (A) (B) (C) (D) (E)
38. (A) (B) (C) (D) (E)
39. (A) (B) (C) (D) (E)
40. (A) (B) (C) (D) (E)
41. (A) (B) (C) (D) (E)
42. (A) (B) (C) (D) (E)
43. (A) (B) (C) (D) (E)

44. (A) (B) (C) (D) (E)
45. (A) (B) (C) (D) (E)
46. (A) (B) (C) (D) (E)
47. (A) (B) (C) (D) (E)
48. (A) (B) (C) (D) (E)
49. (A) (B) (C) (D) (E)
50. (A) (B) (C) (D) (E)
51. (A) (B) (C) (D) (E)
52. (A) (B) (C) (D) (E)
53. (A) (B) (C) (D) (E)
54. (A) (B) (C) (D) (E)
55. (A) (B) (C) (D) (E)
56. (A) (B) (C) (D) (E)
57. (A) (B) (C) (D) (E)

58. (A) (B) (C) (D) (E)
59. (A) (B) (C) (D) (E)
60. (A) (B) (C) (D) (E)
61. (A) (B) (C) (D) (E)
62. (A) (B) (C) (D) (E)
63. (A) (B) (C) (D) (E)
64. (A) (B) (C) (D) (E)
65. (A) (B) (C) (D) (E)
66. (A) (B) (C) (D) (E)
67. (A) (B) (C) (D) (E)
68. (A) (B) (C) (D) (E)
69. (A) (B) (C) (D) (E)
70. (A) (B) (C) (D) (E)
71. (A) (B) (C) (D) (E)

72. (A) (B) (C) (D) (E)
73. (A) (B) (C) (D) (E)
74. (A) (B) (C) (D) (E)
75. (A) (B) (C) (D) (E)
76. (A) (B) (C) (D) (E)
77. (A) (B) (C) (D) (E)
78. (A) (B) (C) (D) (E)
79. (A) (B) (C) (D) (E)
80. (A) (B) (C) (D) (E)
81. (A) (B) (C) (D) (E)
82. (A) (B) (C) (D) (E)
83. (A) (B) (C) (D) (E)
84. (A) (B) (C) (D) (E)
85. (A) (B) (C) (D) (E)

Section III — Verbal Aptitude

86. (A) (B) (C) (D) (E)
87. (A) (B) (C) (D) (E)
88. (A) (B) (C) (D) (E)
89. (A) (B) (C) (D) (E)
90. (A) (B) (C) (D) (E)
91. (A) (B) (C) (D) (E)
92. (A) (B) (C) (D) (E)
93. (A) (B) (C) (D) (E)
94. (A) (B) (C) (D) (E)
95. (A) (B) (C) (D) (E)

96. (A) (B) (C) (D) (E)
97. (A) (B) (C) (D) (E)
98. (A) (B) (C) (D) (E)
99. (A) (B) (C) (D) (E)
100. (A) (B) (C) (D) (E)
101. (A) (B) (C) (D) (E)
102. (A) (B) (C) (D) (E)
103. (A) (B) (C) (D) (E)
104. (A) (B) (C) (D) (E)
105. (A) (B) (C) (D) (E)

106. (A) (B) (C) (D) (E)
107. (A) (B) (C) (D) (E)
108. (A) (B) (C) (D) (E)
109. (A) (B) (C) (D) (E)
110. (A) (B) (C) (D) (E)
111. (A) (B) (C) (D) (E)
112. (A) (B) (C) (D) (E)
113. (A) (B) (C) (D) (E)
114. (A) (B) (C) (D) (E)
115. (A) (B) (C) (D) (E)

116. (A) (B) (C) (D) (E)
117. (A) (B) (C) (D) (E)
118. (A) (B) (C) (D) (E)
119. (A) (B) (C) (D) (E)
120. (A) (B) (C) (D) (E)
121. (A) (B) (C) (D) (E)
122. (A) (B) (C) (D) (E)
123. (A) (B) (C) (D) (E)
124. (A) (B) (C) (D) (E)
125. (A) (B) (C) (D) (E)

Section IV — Data Sufficiency

126. Ⓐ Ⓑ Ⓒ Ⓓ Ⓔ   129. Ⓐ Ⓑ Ⓒ Ⓓ Ⓔ   133. Ⓐ Ⓑ Ⓒ Ⓓ Ⓔ   137. Ⓐ Ⓑ Ⓒ Ⓓ Ⓔ
127. Ⓐ Ⓑ Ⓒ Ⓓ Ⓔ   130. Ⓐ Ⓑ Ⓒ Ⓓ Ⓔ   134. Ⓐ Ⓑ Ⓒ Ⓓ Ⓔ   138. Ⓐ Ⓑ Ⓒ Ⓓ Ⓔ
128. Ⓐ Ⓑ Ⓒ Ⓓ Ⓔ   131. Ⓐ Ⓑ Ⓒ Ⓓ Ⓔ   135. Ⓐ Ⓑ Ⓒ Ⓓ Ⓔ   139. Ⓐ Ⓑ Ⓒ Ⓓ Ⓔ
                   132. Ⓐ Ⓑ Ⓒ Ⓓ Ⓔ   136. Ⓐ Ⓑ Ⓒ Ⓓ Ⓔ   140. Ⓐ Ⓑ Ⓒ Ⓓ Ⓔ

Section V — Business Judgment

141. Ⓐ Ⓑ Ⓒ Ⓓ Ⓔ   146. Ⓐ Ⓑ Ⓒ Ⓓ Ⓔ   151. Ⓐ Ⓑ Ⓒ Ⓓ Ⓔ   156. Ⓐ Ⓑ Ⓒ Ⓓ Ⓔ
142. Ⓐ Ⓑ Ⓒ Ⓓ Ⓔ   147. Ⓐ Ⓑ Ⓒ Ⓓ Ⓔ   152. Ⓐ Ⓑ Ⓒ Ⓓ Ⓔ   157. Ⓐ Ⓑ Ⓒ Ⓓ Ⓔ
143. Ⓐ Ⓑ Ⓒ Ⓓ Ⓔ   148. Ⓐ Ⓑ Ⓒ Ⓓ Ⓔ   153. Ⓐ Ⓑ Ⓒ Ⓓ Ⓔ   158. Ⓐ Ⓑ Ⓒ Ⓓ Ⓔ
144. Ⓐ Ⓑ Ⓒ Ⓓ Ⓔ   149. Ⓐ Ⓑ Ⓒ Ⓓ Ⓔ   154. Ⓐ Ⓑ Ⓒ Ⓓ Ⓔ   159. Ⓐ Ⓑ Ⓒ Ⓓ Ⓔ
145. Ⓐ Ⓑ Ⓒ Ⓓ Ⓔ   150. Ⓐ Ⓑ Ⓒ Ⓓ Ⓔ   155. Ⓐ Ⓑ Ⓒ Ⓓ Ⓔ   160. Ⓐ Ⓑ Ⓒ Ⓓ Ⓔ

Section VI   Analysis of Explanations

161. Ⓐ Ⓑ Ⓒ Ⓓ Ⓔ   171. Ⓐ Ⓑ Ⓒ Ⓓ Ⓔ   181. Ⓐ Ⓑ Ⓒ Ⓓ Ⓔ   191. Ⓐ Ⓑ Ⓒ Ⓓ Ⓔ
162. Ⓐ Ⓑ Ⓒ Ⓓ Ⓔ   172. Ⓐ Ⓑ Ⓒ Ⓓ Ⓔ   182. Ⓐ Ⓑ Ⓒ Ⓓ Ⓔ   192. Ⓐ Ⓑ Ⓒ Ⓓ Ⓔ
163. Ⓐ Ⓑ Ⓒ Ⓓ Ⓔ   173. Ⓐ Ⓑ Ⓒ Ⓓ Ⓔ   183. Ⓐ Ⓑ Ⓒ Ⓓ Ⓔ   193. Ⓐ Ⓑ Ⓒ Ⓓ Ⓔ
164. Ⓐ Ⓑ Ⓒ Ⓓ Ⓔ   174. Ⓐ Ⓑ Ⓒ Ⓓ Ⓔ   184. Ⓐ Ⓑ Ⓒ Ⓓ Ⓔ   194. Ⓐ Ⓑ Ⓒ Ⓓ Ⓔ
165. Ⓐ Ⓑ Ⓒ Ⓓ Ⓔ   175. Ⓐ Ⓑ Ⓒ Ⓓ Ⓔ   185. Ⓐ Ⓑ Ⓒ Ⓓ Ⓔ   195. Ⓐ Ⓑ Ⓒ Ⓓ Ⓔ
166. Ⓐ Ⓑ Ⓒ Ⓓ Ⓔ   176. Ⓐ Ⓑ Ⓒ Ⓓ Ⓔ   186. Ⓐ Ⓑ Ⓒ Ⓓ Ⓔ   196. Ⓐ Ⓑ Ⓒ Ⓓ Ⓔ
167. Ⓐ Ⓑ Ⓒ Ⓓ Ⓔ   177. Ⓐ Ⓑ Ⓒ Ⓓ Ⓔ   187. Ⓐ Ⓑ Ⓒ Ⓓ Ⓔ   197. Ⓐ Ⓑ Ⓒ Ⓓ Ⓔ
168. Ⓐ Ⓑ Ⓒ Ⓓ Ⓔ   178. Ⓐ Ⓑ Ⓒ Ⓓ Ⓔ   188. Ⓐ Ⓑ Ⓒ Ⓓ Ⓔ   198. Ⓐ Ⓑ Ⓒ Ⓓ Ⓔ
169. Ⓐ Ⓑ Ⓒ Ⓓ Ⓔ   179. Ⓐ Ⓑ Ⓒ Ⓓ Ⓔ   189. Ⓐ Ⓑ Ⓒ Ⓓ Ⓔ   199. Ⓐ Ⓑ Ⓒ Ⓓ Ⓔ
170. Ⓐ Ⓑ Ⓒ Ⓓ Ⓔ   180. Ⓐ Ⓑ Ⓒ Ⓓ Ⓔ   190. Ⓐ Ⓑ Ⓒ Ⓓ Ⓔ   200. Ⓐ Ⓑ Ⓒ Ⓓ Ⓔ

Sample Test 2

Reading Recall

TOTAL TIME: 35 minutes

Part A: TIME—15 minutes

DIRECTIONS: This part contains three reading passages. You are to read each one carefully. You will have fifteen minutes to study the three passages and twenty minutes to answer questions based on them. When answering the questions, you will *not* be allowed to refer back to the passages.

Passage 1:

With Friedrich Engels, Karl Marx in 1848 published the *Communist Manifesto,* calling upon the masses to rise and throw off their economic chains. His maturer theories of society were later elaborated in his large and abstruse work *Das Capital.* Starting as a non-violent revolutionist, he ended life as a major social theorist more or less sympathetic with violent revolution, if such became necessary in order to change the social system which he believed to be frankly predatory upon the masses.

On the theoretical side, Marx set up the doctrine of surplus value as the chief element in capitalistic exploitation. According to this theory, the ruling classes no longer employed military force primarily as a means to plundering the people. Instead, they used their control over employment and working conditions under the bourgeois capitalistic system for this purpose, paying only a bare subsistence wage to the worker while they appropriated all surplus values in the productive process. He further taught that the strategic disadvantage of the worker in industry prevented him from obtaining a fairer share of the earnings by bargaining methods and drove him to revolutionary procedures as a means to establishing his economic and social rights. This revolution might be peacefully consummated by parliamentary procedures if the people prepared themselves for political action by mastering the materialistic interpretation of history and by organizing politically for the final event. It was his belief that the aggressions of the capitalist class would eventually destroy the middle class and take over all their sources of income by a process of capitalistic absorption of industry—a process which has failed to occur in most countries.

With minor exceptions, Marx's social philosophy is now generally accepted by left-wing labor movements in many countries, but rejected by centrist labor groups, especially those in the United States. In Russia and other Eastern European countries, however, Socialist leaders adopted the methods of violent revolution because of the opposition of the ruling classes. Yet, many now hold that the present Communist regime in Russia and her satellite countries is no longer a proletarian movement based on Marxist social and political theory, but a camouflaged imperialistic effort to dominate the world in the interest of a new ruling class.

It is important, however, that those who wish to approach Marx as a teacher should not be "buffaloed" by his philosophic approach. They are very likely to in these days, because those most interested in propogating the ideas of Marx, the Russian Bolsheviks, have swallowed down his Hegelian philosophy along with his science of revolutionary engineering, and they look upon us irreverent peoples who presume to meditate social and even revolutionary problems without making our obeisance to the mysteries of Dialectic Materialism, as a species of unredeemed and well-nigh unredeemable barbarians. They are right in scorning our ignorance of the scientific ideas of Karl Marx and our indifference to them. They are wrong in scorning our distaste for having practical programs presented in the form of systems of philosophy. In that we simply represent a more progressive intellectual culture than that in which Marx received his education—a culture farther emerged from the dominance of religious attitudes.

Passage 2:

The basic character of our governmental and political institutions conditions the federal budgetary system. The working relationships between branches, and between the elements within each branch, are intricate, subtle, and in continuous change—affected by partisan politics, personalities, social forces, and public opinion. A few landmark stages in the evolution of the present system provide perspective.

In 1789 Alexander Hamilton, as the first Secretary of the Treasury, affirmed and successfully established a position of strong executive leadership in matters of public finance. His proposals on revenues, banking, and the assumption of prior debts of both national and state governments were based on his philosophy that federal fiscal policies should be designed to encourage economic growth. However, Hamilton's successors, and the Presidents under whom they served, did not follow his concept of executive responsibility for "plans of finance."

Partly through default, Congress took charge of all phases of fiscal policy. At the outset, each chamber was so small that coherent initiative was possible. (The first House had some 60 members—about the number of its present Appropriations Committee.) Spending estimates, considered in Committee of the Whole in 1789, were later referred to the Committee on Ways and Means. In 1865 expenditures were assigned to a new Appropriations Committee while revenues remained with the Ways and Means Committee. In 1885 most spending proposals were subdivided among the legislative committees so that appropriation bills came to be handled by numerous committees (14 in the House and 15 in the Senate), each dealing directly with the departments. The presidential role was minimal.

By the turn of the century there was a clear need for reform in financial management. At all levels of government, officials spent money on activities "as authorized by law" and in line with "appropriations" made by legislative bodies—usually after committee consideration. Other officials collected taxes and fees under various unrelated statutes. Such a system—or lack-of-system—worked within reason as long as governments had little to do. But as government activities grew, becoming more technical and closely interrelated, this lack-of-system bogged down.

Several factors played a part in the eventual breakthrough. In the first decade of the twentieth century, an "executive budget" came into successful use by some cities and states. President Taft's Commission on Efficiency and Economy prepared an illustrative federal budget which—while rejected by Congress—commanded broad public support. The more advanced methods developed by European governments came to American attention. World War I precipitated accounting chaos, with an aftermath of scandal. The need for new and better methods was established beyond dispute.

The Budget and Accounting Act of 1921 placed direct responsibility for preparation and execution of the federal budget upon the President, making a unified federal budget possible for the first time. The Act set up two new organizational units, the General Accounting Office (GAO) and the Bureau of the Budget. GAO is headed by the Comptroller General, appointed by the President *with* senate approval for a 15-year term, and is regarded as primarily a congressional rather than an executive resource. The Bureau, under a Director appointed by the President *without* senate confirmation and serving at his pleasure, has from its inception been the President's chief reliance in budgetary and related matters.

Passage 3:

In describing the Indians of the various sections of the United States at different stages in their history, some of the factors which account for their similarity amid difference can be readily accounted for, others are difficult to discern.

The basic physical similarity of the Indians from Alaska to Patagonia is explained by the fact that they all came originally from Asia by way of the Bering Strait and the Aleutian Islands into Alaska and then southward. They came in different waves, the earliest around 25,000 years ago, the latest probably not long before America was discovered by Europeans. Because these people all came from Asia and were therefore drawn from the same pool of Asiatic people, they tended to look alike. But since the various waves of migration crossed into Alaska at widely separated times, there were differences among them in their physical characteristics.

There were also differences in cultural equipment. The earliest arrivals are known to science only through their simple tools of chipped stone and bone. Despite their limited technical equipment, some of the New Mexico Indians were very successful big game hunters. Twenty-five thousand years ago they were hunting the wooly mammoth, the giant bison, the ground sloth and the camel, all characteristic animals of the closing phases of the last ice age.

After their arrival from Asia in various waves across the Bering Strait, the early peoples in the Americas slowly spread southward into the vast empty spaces of the two continents. A group of people moving slowly down the Mackenzie River valley east of the Rockies into the general region of Southern Alberta, then eastward across the northern prairies reaching the wooded country around the upper Mississippi and the Western Great Lakes, then in a southeastward movement following the Mississippi valley until some final settlement was reached in the Gulf states, would encounter a wide variety of physical environments. At various stages of such wanderings they would have to evolve methods of coping with the cold, barren, tundra country of northern Canada; the prairies, cold, treeless but well stocked with large game; then later the completely different flora and fauna of the Minnesota-Wisconsin-Illinois area, thickly forested and well watered and providing an abundance of small game and wild vegetable foods; then the semi-tropical character of the lower Mississippi country as they neared the Gulf of Mexico. Since such a migration would be spread over many centuries, the modification of whatever basic culture they had on their arrival from Asia would be very slow. Yet the end result would be completely different from their original culture. It would also be different from the final culture of a closely allied group who became separated from them early in their wanderings and whose movements led them into different types of country. In its final form, the culture of this second group would have little in common with that of the first except perhaps a continuing resemblance in language and in physical type.

If there is still time remaining, review the passages until all 15 minutes have elapsed.
Do not look at Part B until that time.

Part B: TIME—20 minutes

DIRECTIONS: Answer the following questions pertaining to information contained in the three passages you have just read. You may not turn back to those passages for assistance.

QUESTIONS TO

Passage 1:

1. According to Marx, the chief element in capitalist exploitation was the doctrine of

   (A) just wages
   (B) the price system
   (C) surplus value
   (D) predatory production
   (E) subsistence work

2. Which of the following books did Marx author or co-author?

   I. *Communist Manifesto*
   II. *Das Capital*
   III. *Political Taxation*

   (A) I only
   (B) III only
   (C) I and II only
   (D) II and III only
   (E) I, II, and III

3. According to the passage, Marx started his philosophical life as a

   (A) social theorist
   (B) believer in non-violent revolution
   (C) believer in violent revolution
   (D) follower of Hegel
   (E) follower of Engels

4. According to the passage, Marx ended his life as

   I. A believer in non-violent revolution
   II. Accepting violent revolution
   III. A social theorist

   (A) I only
   (B) III only
   (C) I and II only
   (D) II and III only
   (E) I, II, and III

5. The author holds that the present Communist regime in Russia can best be categorized as a(n)

   (A) proletarian movement
   (B) socialist government
   (C) imperialistic state
   (D) revolutionary government
   (E) social democracy

SAMPLE TEST 2 • 389

6. One of Marx's theories mentioned in the passage is called

(A) Dialectic Materialism   (D) Materialistic Value
(B) Hegelian Socialism   (E) Countervailing Power
(C) Social Engineering

7. Marx's social philosophy is now generally accepted by

(A) centrist labor groups
(B) most labor unions
(C) left-wing labor unions
(D) only those in Communist countries
(E) only those in Russia

8. It can be concluded that the author of the passage is

(A) sympathetic to Marx's ideas
(B) unsympathetic to Marx's ideas
(C) uncritical of Marx's interpretation of history
(D) a believer in Hegelian philosophy
(E) a Lenenist-Marxist

9. Which of the following classes did Marx believe should control the economy?

(A) working class   (D) lower class
(B) upper class   (E) capitalist class
(C) middle class

10. According to Marx, a social and economic revolution could take place through

    I. Parliamentary procedures
   II. Political action
  III. Violent revolution

(A) I only
(B) III only
(C) I and II only
(D) II and III only
(E) I, II, and III

QUESTIONS TO

Passage 2:

11. Alexander Hamilton's philosophy was that federal fiscal policies should

(A) be expansionary
(B) encourage economic growth
(C) be determined by Congress
(D) encourage a balanced budget
(E) be determined by the President

12. Hamilton's successors

    I.   Followed his economic philosophy of "plans of finance"
    II. Followed his social philosophy
    III. Did not follow his philosophy of strong executive leadership

    (A) I only
    (B) III only
    (C) I and II only
    (D) II and III only
    (E) I, II, and III

13. Looking at the history of U.S. fiscal management, spending estimates were *first* considered by the

    I.   Committee of the Whole
    II. Appropriations Committee
    III. Ways and Means Committee

    (A) I only
    (B) III only
    (C) I and II only
    (D) II and III only
    (E) I, II, and III

14. At the turn of the century, there was need for

    (A) strong executive leadership
    (B) a new finance committee
    (C) more Congressional interest in finance
    (D) overall reform of financial management
    (E) more financial legislation

15. The "executive budget" was first used

    (A) by Alexander Hamilton
    (B) in the 19th century
    (C) in the first decade of the 20th century
    (D) by President Eisenhower
    (E) by President Truman

16. President Taft's federal budget was

    (A) based on procedures used by some European governments
    (B) enthusiastically accepted by Congress
    (C) a failure
    (D) rejected by Congress
    (E) vilified by the public

17. In 1921, the responsibility for preparation and execution of the federal budget fell upon the

(A) President
(B) Congress
(C) Bureau of Accounts
(D) House of Representatives
(E) Senate

18. In the General Accounting Office, the Comptroller General is

(A) appointed by the President
·(B) appointed by the President without Senate approval
(C) appointed by the President with Senate approval
(D) a civil service employee
(E) an elected official

19. The Director of the Budget is

(A) appointed by the President
(B) appointed by the President with Senate approval
(C) appointed by the President without Senate approval
(D) a civil service employee
(E) an elected official

20. The working relationships between government branches are affected by all of the following except

(A) partisan politics
(B) personalities
(C) social forces
(D) public opinion
(E) the military

QUESTIONS TO

Passage 3:

21. According to the passage, Indians who migrated to what is now the United States originated in

(A) Asia
(B) Africa
(C) South America
(D) Alaska
(E) Patagonia

22. Physical differences among Indians who migrated to Alaska can be accounted for by the fact that they came

(A) from different places
(B) from different tribes
(C) at different times
(D) from different races
(E) to different places

23. It is estimated that Indians first came to what is now the United States about

(A) 5,000 years ago
(B) 10,000 years ago
(C) 15,000 years ago
(D) 25,000 years ago
(E) 50,000 years ago

24. The intent of the author is to expound on the Indians'

    (A) cultural background   (D) migration patterns
    (B) eating habits   (E) physical characteristics
    (C) technical abilities

25. According to the passage, the southernmost area reached by the Indians was the

    (A) northern prairies   (D) Mackenzie River valley
    (B) upper Mississippi   (E) Gulf States
    (C) Great Lakes

26. Which of the following Indians were noted for their hunting prowess?

    (A) Mississippi   (D) New Mexico
    (B) Bering   (E) Patagonia
    (C) Mackenzie

27. Although the Indians' culture underwent change, what characteristics remained fairly stable?

    I. Language
   II. Physical type
  III. Technical abilities

    (A) I only
    (B) III only
    (C) I and II only
    (D) II and III only
    (E) I, II, and III

28. Which animals were hunted by the Indians when they first migrated to the Americas?

    I. Bison
   II. Wooly mammoth
  III. Camel

    (A) I only
    (B) III only
    (C) I and II only
    (D) II and III only
    (E) I, II, and III

29. According to the author, some of the Indians were

    (A) extremely intelligent
    (B) bi-lingual
    (C) slow to adjust to new environments
    (D) largely a farming people
    (E) successful big game hunters

30. The passage most likely was written by a(n)

(A) economist
(B) historian
(C) educator

(D) social scientist
(E) anthropologist

If there is still time remaining, you may review the questions in this section only.
You may not look at Part A or turn to any other section of the test.

Section II   Mathematics

TIME: 75 minutes

DIRECTIONS: Solve each of the following problems; then indicate the correct answer on the answer sheet. [On the actual test you will be permitted to use any space available on the examination paper for scratch work.]

NOTE: A figure that appears with a problem is drawn as accurately as possible so as to provide information that may help in answering the question. Numbers in this test are real numbers.

31. A borrower pays 6% interest on the first $500 he borrows and $5\frac{1}{2}$% on the part of the loan in excess of $500. How much interest will the borrower have to pay on a loan of $5,500?

(A) $275
(B) $280
(C) $302.50

(D) $305
(E) $330

32. If $2x - y = 4$, then $6x - 3y$ is

(A) 4
(B) 6
(C) 8

(D) 10
(E) 12

33. The next number in the arithmetical progression 5, 11, 17, . . . is

(A) 18
(B) 22
(C) 23

(D) 28
(E) 33

Use the following graph for questions 34–36.

INSTALLED CAPACITY OF ELECTRIC UTILITY GENERATING PLANTS 1920-1952

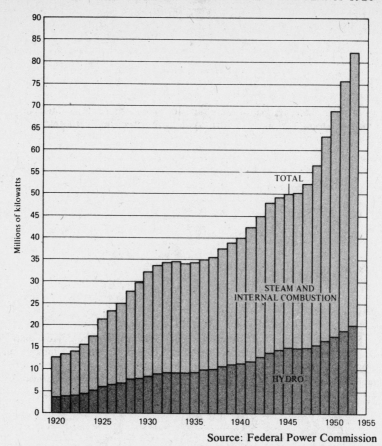

Source: Federal Power Commission

34. In what year did the installed capacity first reach 50 million kilowatts?

(A) 1939
(B) 1944
(C) 1945

(D) 1947
(E) 1950

35. In 1952, the installed capacity of steam and internal combustion plants was about *x* times the installed capacity of the hydro plants where *x* is

(A) $\frac{1}{2}$
(B) 1
(C) 2

(D) 3
(E) 4

36. Which of the following statements about the installed capacity of electric utility generating plants between 1920 and 1952 can be inferred from the graph?

I. In the period 1930–39, there was less of an increase in capacity than in either of the periods 1920–1929 or 1940–1949.
II. More than $\frac{1}{5}$ of the capacity in 1925 was produced by hydro plants.
III. The increase in capacity in kilowatts between 1945 and 1952 was greater than the increase between 1925 and 1945.

(A) I only
(B) II only
(C) I and III only

(D) II and III only
(E) I, II, and III

37. A warehouse has 20 packers. Each packer can load $\frac{1}{8}$ of a box in 9 minutes. How many boxes can be loaded in $1\frac{1}{2}$ hours by all 20 packers?

(A) $1\frac{1}{4}$
(B) $10\frac{1}{4}$
(C) $12\frac{1}{2}$
(D) 20
(E) 25

38. In Motor City 90% of the population owns a car, 15% owns a motorcycle, and everybody owns a car or motorcycle or both. What percent of the population owns a motorcycle but not a car?

(A) 5
(B) 8
(C) 9
(D) 10
(E) 15

Use the following table for questions 39–40.

TABLE 2.—Children under 18 years old, by age group, type of family, labor force status of mother, and race, March 1972

Type of family, labor force status of mother, and race	Number of children (thousands)		
	Under 18 years	Under 6 years	6 to 17 years
Total children	65,255	19,235	46,020
Mother in labor force	25,762	5,607	20,155
Husband-wife family	56,625	17,173	39,452
Mother in labor force	21,722	4,838	16,884
Mother not in labor force	34,903	12,335	22,568
Female family head	7,924	1,977	5,947
Mother in labor force	4,040	769	3,271
Mother not in labor force	3,884	1,208	2,676
Other male family head	706	85	621
White children, total	56,303	16,603	39,700
Mother in labor force	21,539	4,495	17,044
Husband-wife family	50,796	15,409	35,387
Mother in labor force	18,799	4,031	14,768
Mother not in labor force	31,997	11,378	20,619
Female family head	4,967	1,130	3,837
Mother in labor force	2,740	464	2,276
Mother not in labor force	2,227	666	1,561
Other male family head	540	64	476
Negro children, total	8,093	2,345	5,748
Mother in labor force	3,855	999	2,856
Husband-wife family	5,078	1,504	3,574
Mother in labor force	2,609	707	1,902
Mother not in labor force	2,469	797	1,672
Female family head	2,855	821	2,034
Mother in labor force	1,246	292	954
Mother not in labor force	1,609	529	1,080
Other male family head	160	20	140

Source: Social Security Bulletin

39. Approximately how many children between the ages of 6 to 17 did not have mothers in the labor force in 1972?

(A) 20,000,000
(B) 26,000,000
(C) 28,000,000

(D) 30,000,000
(E) 46,000,000

40. Roughly x percent of the Negro children under 6 years of age had mothers in the labor force, where x is

(A) 30
(B) 35
(C) 40

(D) 50
(E) 55

41. A chair originally cost $50.00. The chair was offered for sale at 108% of its cost. After a week the price was discounted 10% and the chair was sold. The chair was sold for

(A) $45.00
(B) $48.60
(C) $49.00

(D) $49.40
(E) $54.00

42. A worker is paid x dollars for the first 8 hours he works each day. He is paid y dollars per hour for each hour he works in excess of 8 hours. During one week he works 8 hours on Monday, 11 hours on Tuesday, 9 hours on Wednesday, 10 hours on Thursday, and 9 hours on Friday. What is his average daily wage in dollars for the five day week?

(A) $x + \dfrac{7}{5}y$

(B) $2x + y$

(C) $\dfrac{5x + 8y}{5}$

(D) $x + 2y$

(E) $5x + 7y$

43. What is the area of a rectangular field which is 25 yards wide and 50 yards long?

(A) 625 square yards
(B) 1,000 square yards
(C) 1,250 square yards

(D) 1600 square yards
(E) 2,500 square yards

Use the chart below for questions 44–47.

CHANGE IN POPULATION OF THE UNITED STATES BETWEEN 1940 AND 1950

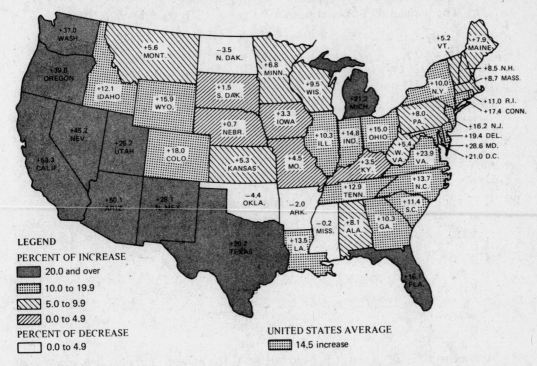

LEGEND

PERCENT OF INCREASE

- 20.0 and over
- 10.0 to 19.9
- 5.0 to 9.9
- 0.0 to 4.9

PERCENT OF DECREASE

- 0.0 to 4.9

UNITED STATES AVERAGE

14.5 increase

Source: Department of Commerce. Bureau of the Census

44. Which state had the largest percentage of increase in population between 1940 and 1950?

(A) Arizona
(B) Arkansas
(C) California
(D) Florida
(E) Maine

45. How many states had population decreases between 1940 and 1950?

(A) 1
(B) 2
(C) 3
(D) 4
(E) 5

46. If the population of the United States in 1940 was 100 million, then the population of the United States in 1950 was approximately

(A) 100 million
(B) 105 million
(C) 110 million
(D) 115 million
(E) 120 million

47. Which of the following statements about population changes between 1940 and 1950 can be inferred from the graph?

    I.   Less than 6 states had population increases of ⅓ or more.

    II. The number of people living in Oregon in 1950 was larger than the number of people living in Washington.

    III. The population of Nebraska was larger in 1950 than it was in 1940.

    (A) I only
    (B) III only
    (C) I and III only
    (D) II and III only
    (E) I, II and III

48. If 12 apples cost 63¢, how much should 4 apples cost?

    (A) 19¢   (D) 31¢
    (B) 21¢   (E) 32¢
    (C) 25¢

49. A car costs $2,500 when it is brand new. At the end of each year it is worth ⅘ of what it was at the beginning of the year. What is the car worth when it is 3 years old?

    (A) $1,000   (D) $1,340
    (B) $1,200   (E) $1,430
    (C) $1,280

Use the following table for questions 50–52.

Type of vehicle	Cost of fuel for 500-mile trip
Automobile	$15
Motorcycle	$ 5
Bus	$20
Truck	$50
Airplane	$70

50. What is the cost of fuel for a 300-mile trip by automobile?

    (A) $5   (D) $15
    (B) $9   (E) $30
    (C) $12

51. If the wages of a bus driver for a 500-mile trip are $70, and the only costs for a bus are the fuel and the driver's wages, how much should a bus company charge to charter a bus and driver for a 500-mile trip in order to obtain 120% of the cost?

(A) $24
(B) $90
(C) $94
(D) $104
(E) $108

52. If 3 buses, 4 automobiles, 2 motorcycles, and one truck each make a 500-mile trip, what is the average fuel cost per vehicle?

(A) $5
(B) $15
(C) $18
(D) $20
(E) $24

53. If $x + 2y = 2x + y$, then $x - y$ is equal to

(A) 0
(B) 2
(C) 4
(D) 5
(E) none of the preceding

54. 15% of the families in state x have an income of $25,000 or more. $^2/_3$ of the families with income of $25,000 or more in state x own a boat. What fraction of the families own a boat and have an income of $25,000 or more in state x?

(A) $^1/_{15}$
(B) $^1/_{12}$
(C) $^1/_{10}$
(D) $^4/_{21}$
(E) $^9/_{40}$

55. If the angles of a triangle are in the ratio 1:2:2, then the triangle

(A) is isosceles
(B) is obtuse
(C) is a right triangle
(D) is equilateral
(E) has one angle greater than 80°

Use the following graphs for questions 56–60.

U.S. DEFENSE EXPENDITURES ABROAD

BY MAJOR CATEGORIES

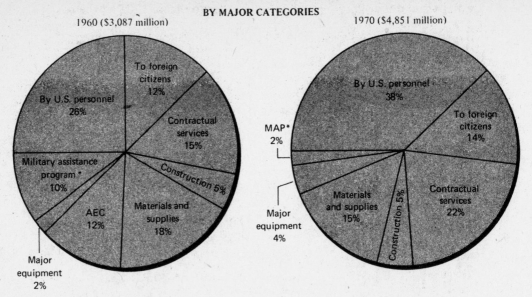

1960 ($3,087 million)

1970 ($4,851 million)

BY MAJOR COUNTRIES AND AREAS

1960 ($3,087 million)

1970 ($4,851 million)

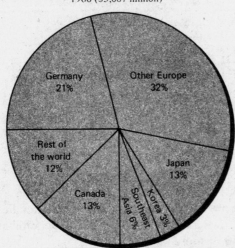
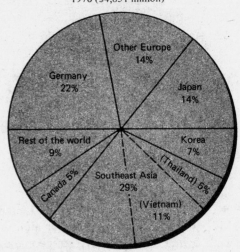

* Includes NATO Infrastructure

Source: U.S. Department of Commerce, Bureau of Economic Analysis

56. In 1970, x was spent in Canada for defense where x is about

   (A) 200 million   (D) 250 million
   (B) 230 million   (E) 260 million
   (C) 240 million

57. In 1960, what fraction of defense expenditures was used in all for the Military Assistance Program, AEC, and materials and supplies?

   (A) $3/10$ (D) $2/5$
   (B) $7/20$ (E) $11/25$
   (C) $39/100$

58. Which of the following countries received the least amount of defense expenditures in 1970?

    (A) Germany
    (B) Japan
    (C) Vietnam
    (D) Korea
    (E) Thailand

59. If $\frac{5}{7}$ of the defense expenditures in Europe other than Germany was spent in Spain, about how much was spent in Spain in 1970?

    (A) $308 million
    (B) $485 million
    (C) $550 million
    (D) $750 million
    (E) $1,200 million

60. Which of the following statements about direct expenditures abroad for goods and services can be inferred from the graphs?

    I.   In both 1960 and 1970, more than $\frac{1}{5}$ of the expenditures was spent in Germany.
    II. The total amount of expenditures increased by more than $\frac{1}{3}$ between 1960 and 1970.
    III. More than $\frac{2}{5}$ of the total expenditures for 1960 and 1970 together was spent by U.S. personnel.

    (A) I only
    (B) II only
    (C) I and II only
    (D) II and III only
    (E) I, II, and III

61. If a car travels at a constant rate of 60 miles per hour, how long will it take to travel 255 miles?

    (A) $3\frac{3}{4}$ hours
    (B) 4 hours
    (C) $4\frac{1}{8}$ hours
    (D) $4\frac{1}{4}$ hours
    (E) $4\frac{1}{2}$ hours

62. A car travels 15 miles on a gallon of gas but after a tune-up the car uses only $\frac{3}{4}$ as much gas as before. How many miles will the car travel on a gallon of gas after the tune-up?

    (A) 15
    (B) $16\frac{1}{2}$
    (C) $17\frac{1}{2}$
    (D) $18\frac{2}{3}$
    (E) 20

63. Successive discounts of 20% and 15% are equal to a single discount of

    (A) 30%
    (B) 32%
    (C) 34%
    (D) 35%
    (E) 36%

Use the following graphs for questions 64–67.

PER CAPITA PERSONAL HEALTH CARE EXPENDITURES

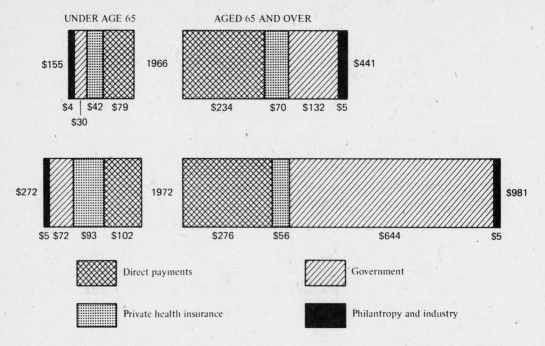

Source: Social Security Bulletin

64. If there were about 20 million people 65 and over in 1966, how much did the government spend on personal health care for people aged 65 and over in 1966?

(A) $26 million
(B) $264 million
(C) $2 billion

(D) $2.640 billion
(E) $3.6 billion

65. Between 1966 and 1972, the per capita amount spent by the government on personal health care for those under age 65 increased by x% where x is

(A) 100
(B) 120
(C) 140

(D) 220
(E) 240

66. In 1972, the fraction contributed by philanthropy and industry towards expenditures for personal health care for those aged 65 and over was about

(A) $1/500$
(B) $1/196$
(C) $1/99$

(D) $1/88$
(E) $2/101$

67. Which of the following statements about expenditures for personal health care between 1966 and 1972 can be inferred from the graphs?

    I.   The total amount spent for those aged 65 and over in 1972 was more than 3 times as much as the total amount spent on those under 65.

    II. Between 1966 and 1972, the amount spent per capita by those aged 65 and over increased in each of the four categories (direct payments, government, private health insurance, philanthropy).

    III. The government paid more than $\frac{1}{2}$ of the amount of expenditures for those aged 65 and over in 1972.

    (A) I only
    (B) II only
    (C) III only
    (D) I and III only
    (E) II and III only

68. Oranges cost $1.00 for a crate containing 20 oranges. If oranges are sold for 6¢ each, what percent of the selling price is the profit?

    (A) 5%   (D) 20%
    (B) 10%   (E) 25%
    (C) $16\frac{2}{3}$%

69. A hen lays $7\frac{1}{2}$ dozen eggs during the summer. There are 93 days in the summer and it costs $10 to feed the hen for the summer. How much does it cost in food for each egg produced?

    (A) 10¢   (D) $13\frac{1}{13}$¢
    (B) $11\frac{1}{9}$¢   (E) 15¢
    (C) $12\frac{9}{13}$¢

70. If the diameter of a circle has length d, the radius length r, and the area equals a, then which of the following statements are true?

    I. $a = \pi d^2$
    II. $d = 2r$
    III. $\dfrac{a}{d} = \pi\dfrac{r}{2}$

    (A) only II
    (B) I and II only
    (C) I and III only
    (D) II and III only
    (E) I, II, and III

Use the following graph for questions 71–74.

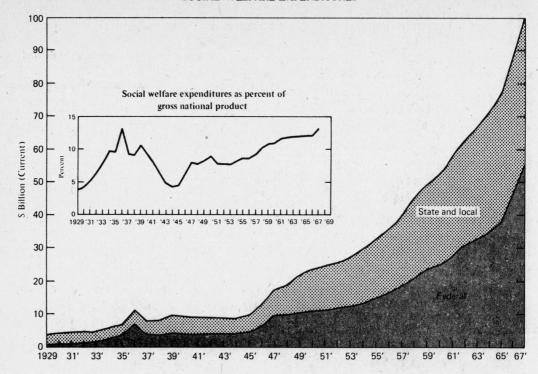

SOCIAL WELFARE EXPENDITURES

Source: Social Security Bulletin

71. During the period from 1929 to 1944 in what year were social welfare expenditures the highest?

(A) 1933
(B) 1935
(C) 1936
(D) 1939
(E) 1944

72. The Gross National Product in 1958 was about

(A) $100 billion
(B) $200 billion
(C) $300 billion
(D) $450 billion
(E) $600 billion

73. In 1957, the federal government spent about *x* times as much as state and local governments on social welfare, where *x* is

(A) $1/4$
(B) $1/2$
(C) 1
(D) 2
(E) 3

74. Which of the following statements about social welfare expenditures can be inferred from the graph?

    I. The percentage of Gross National Product spent on social welfare decreased between 1939 and 1943.

   II. The state and local governments never spent more than $60 billion on social welfare in any of the years between 1929 and 1967.

  III. Between 1929 and 1933, the state and local government spent more on social welfare than did the federal government.

    (A) I only
    (B) II only
    (C) I and III only
    (D) II and III only
    (E) I, II, and III

75. If hose A can fill up a tank in 20 minutes, and hose B can fill up the same tank in 15 minutes, how long will it take for the hoses together to fill up the tank?

    (A) 5 minutes
    (B) $7\frac{1}{2}$ minutes
    (C) $8\frac{4}{7}$ minutes
    (D) $9\frac{2}{7}$ minutes
    (E) 12 minutes

76. If 5 men take 2 hours to dig a ditch, how long will it take 12 men to dig the ditch?

    (A) 45 minutes
    (B) 50 minutes
    (C) 54 minutes
    (D) 60 minutes
    (E) 84 minutes

Use the following table for questions 77–79.

Car Production at Plant T for One Week

	Number of cars produced	Total daily wages
MONDAY	900	$30,000
TUESDAY	1200	$40,000
WEDNESDAY	1500	$52,000
THURSDAY	1400	$50,000
FRIDAY	1000	$32,000

77. What was the average number of cars produced per day for the week shown?

    (A) 1,000
    (B) 1,140
    (C) 1,180
    (D) 1,200
    (E) 1,220

78. What was the average cost in wages per car produced for the week?

    (A) $25
    (B) $26
    (C) $29
    (D) $32
    (E) $34

79. Which of the following statements about the production of cars and the wages paid for the week can be inferred from the table?

    I.   ¼ of the cars were produced on Wednesday.
    II. More employees came to the plant on Friday than on Monday.
    III. ²/₅ of the days accounted for ½ the wages paid for the week.

    (A) I only
    (B) II only
    (C) I and II only
    (D) I and III only
    (E) I, II, and III

80. How many rectangular plots 40 yards long by 30 yards wide can be obtained from a field which is a square with sides 1200 yards long?

    (A) 100   (D) 1200
    (B) 120   (E) 14000
    (C) 1000

81. A train travels from Cleveland to Toledo in 2 hours and 10 minutes. If the distance from Cleveland to Toledo is 150 miles, then the average speed of the train is about

    (A) 60 mph   (D) 72 mph
    (B) 66 mph   (E) 75 mph
    (C) 70 mph

82. If $x > 2$ and $y > -1$, then

    (A) $xy > -2$ (D) $-x > 2y$
    (B) $-x < 2y$ (E) $x < 2y$
    (C) $xy < -2$

83. What is the area of the rectangle $ABCD$, if the length of AC is 5 and the length of AD is 4?

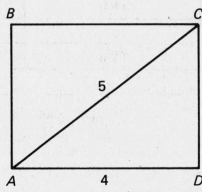

    (A) 3   (D) 15
    (B) 6   (E) 20
    (C) 12

84. If electricity costs k¢ an hour, heat $\$d$ an hour, and water w¢ an hour, how much will all three cost for 12 hours?

(A) $12(k + d + w)$¢

(D) $\$\left(12k + \dfrac{12d}{100} + 12w\right)$

(B) $\$(12k + 12d + 12w)$

(E) $\$(.12k + 12d + .12w)$

(C) $\$(k + 100d + w)$

85. If $x = y = 2z$ and $x \cdot y \cdot z = 256$, then x equals

(A) 2

(D) $4\sqrt[3]{2}$

(B) $2\sqrt[3]{2}$

(E) 8

(C) 4

If there is still time remaining, you may review the questions in this section only.
You may not turn to any other section of the test.

Section III   Verbal Aptitude

TIME: 20 minutes

Antonyms

DIRECTIONS: For each question below, select the lettered word or phrase that comes closest to being *opposite* in meaning to the word appearing in capital letters. Be sure to consider all meanings carefully.

86. ABSTRUSE: (A) detested (B) detained (C) obvious (D) tight (E) rebuilt

87. COAGULATE: (A) strengthen (B) release (C) plunge (D) dissipate (E) prepare

88. PROCLIVITY: (A) proposition (B) propensity (C) aversion (D) activity (E) delay

89. TACIT: (A) late (B) open (C) implied (D) skilled (E) indiscreet

90. VORACIOUS: (A) bellicose (B) powerful (C) generous (D) inclined (E) stoic

91. SAGACIOUS: (A) fat (B) stupid (C) happy (D) unwelcome (E) irrational

92. RETICENT: (A) repellent (B) related (C) communicative (D) truthful (E) repetitious

93. FECUND: (A) barren (B) timid (C) sinister (D) determined (E) awful

94. FURTIVE: (A) active (B) expected (C) open (D) abetting (E) fearful

95. INCLEMENT: (A) incipient (B) inevitable (C) new (D) kind (E) contrary

96. NOTORIOUS: (A) wicked (B) enigmatic (C) respected (D) open (E) political

97. DILATE: (A) expand (B) contract (C) remedy (D) include (E) concentrate

98. BOISTEROUS: (A) peaceful (B) undaunted (C) covert (D) auspicious (E) fatal

99. ECLECTIC: (A) agnostic (B) dogmatic (C) habitual (D) incisive (E) impulsive

Word-Pair Relationships

DIRECTIONS: For each question below, determine the relationship between the pair of capitalized words and then select the lettered pair of words which have a similar relationship to the first pair.

100. SAMPLE : UNIVERSE :: (A) plan : research (B) individual : population (C) mathematics : statistics (D) element : electron (E) tactic : strategy

101. CARBOHYDRATES : OBESITY :: (A) aversion : regression (B) sugar : cavities (C) pressure : burst (D) hostility : war (E) sick : hospital

102. PROMISE : FULFILL :: (A) pawn : redeem (B) pledge : surfeit (C) plan : action (D) commit : hedge (E) abrogate : release

103. ADDICTED : DEDICATED :: (A) infected : supporter (B) fanatic : enthusiast (C) disease : chronic (D) injected : permanent (E) habit : continuous

104. RECALL : REMEMBER :: (A) falsification : forgery (B) behave : action (C) construct : terminate (D) cigarette : tobacco (E) pipe : stem

105. ABUNDANCE : LUXURY :: (A) developed : growing (B) humble : unpretentious (C) poverty : indigence (D) pilot : plane (E) reserved : suppressed

106. STAMP : LETTER :: (A) words : telegram (B) coin : telephone (C) gasoline : automobile (D) road : toll (E) profession : license

107. FUEL : PIPES :: (A) air : lungs (B) food : stomach (C) wood : trees (D) cars : freeway (E) power : generator

108. EXEMPTION : EXCLUSION :: (A) debarment : prevention (B) immunity : isolation (C) forgive : condone (D) discharge : elimination (E) enclosure : open

109. INDIGENOUS : FOREIGN :: (A) indifferent : interested (B) resident : visitor (C) native : extraneous (D) part : whole (E) outsider : inhabitant

110. EFFICACIOUS : LACKING :: (A) efficient : incompetent (B) effective : effortless (C) missing : missive (D) trial : failure (E) attempt : error

111. EIGHT : OCTAVE :: (A) top : bottom (B) centimeter : meter (C) fifth : quart (D) thousand : millenium (E) foot : yard

112. THROW : TARGET :: (A) aim : hit (B) dive : water (C) tactic : objective (D) movement : destination (E) laughter : joy

Sentence Completions

DIRECTIONS: For each sentence below, select the lettered word or set of words which, when inserted in the sentence blanks, best completes the meaning of that sentence.

113. We strongly favor fair _____ to victims of manufacturing defects.

(A) play (B) compensation (C) probity (D) consultations (E) instructions

114. The _____ of a man might well be measured by his _____ of himself.

(A) worth . . . opinion (B) weight . . . estimation (C) education . . . value (D) value . . . picture (E) ability . . . judgment

115. It was the practice in a certain country for the President to offer a full _____ to some prisoners on the national holiday.

(A) restitution (B) amnesty (C) acquittal (D) pardon (E) clemency

116. Police, prepared for a long _____, held a(n) _____ on the street.

(A) discussion . . . council (B) seige . . . meeting (C) time . . . gathering (D) intercession . . . suspect (E) strike . . . assembly

117. The meeting between the two was _____ with _____ significance.

(A) begun . . . extraneous (B) complicated . . . no (C) fraught . . . historical (D) ended . . . reciprocal (E) broken off . . . little

118. It was not a(n) _____ beginning for the railroad as two trains _____.

(A) early . . . were late (B) bad . . . were on time (C) auspicious . . . collided (D) inadequate . . . stalled (E) plausible . . . failed

119. Some _____ of why he does not think that to be their _____ came in the subject he discussed.

(A) indication . . . intention (B) example . . . inversion (C) part . . . machine (D) mention . . . conversation (E) foreboding . . . posture

120. The best _____ is that he thinks he has _____ of time.

(A) story . . . plenty (B) explanation . . . run out (C) part . . . lost control (D) solution . . . arrived (E) estimate . . . want

121. It was the first time since the _____ effort to _____ an accord last year.

(A) prohibitory . . . announce (B) reciprocal . . . purchase (C) abortive . . . reach (D) last . . . convey (E) pessimistic . . . abrogate

122. Like the United States, England was forced by economic events to embrace a program of _____ restraints despite past pronouncements espousing less _____.

(A) financial . . . interference (B) voluntary . . . optimism (C) compulsory . . . intervention (D) literary . . . control (E) temporary . . . freedom

123. To say that a study is synthetic and _____ is to say that it is _____.

(A) general . . . theoretical (B) timely . . . insipid (C) biased . . . reliable (D) absolute . . . accurate (E) dated . . . extemporary

124. People who are loquacious are also called _____.

(A) lazy (B) independent (C) talkative (D) eloquent (E) tormented

125. The development of agriculture and that of industry act and react on each other; they are complementary and not _____.

(A) redundant   (B) concentrated   (C) associated   (D) competitive   (E) organized

If there is still time remaining, you may review the questions in this section only.
You may not turn to any other section of the test.

Section IV   Data Sufficiency

TIME: 15 minutes

DIRECTIONS: Each of the following problems has a question and two statements which are labeled (1) and (2). Use the data given in (1) and (2) together with other available information (such as the number of hours in a day, the definition of *clockwise*, mathematical facts, etc.) to decide whether the statements are *sufficient* to answer the question. Then fill in space

(A)   if you can get the answer from (1) alone but not from (2) alone;

(B)   if you can get the answer from (2) alone but not from (1) alone;

(C)   if you can get the answer from (1) and (2) together, although neither statement by itself suffices;

(D)   if statement (1) alone suffices *and* statement (2) alone suffices;

(E)   if you cannot get the answer from statements (1) and (2) together, but need even more data.

All numbers used in this section are real numbers. A figure given for a problem is intended to provide information consistent with that in the question, but not necessarily with the additional information contained in the statements.

126.   Is x greater than y?

(1) $3x = 2k$
(2) $k = y^2$

127.   Is $ABCD$ a parallelogram?

(1) $AB = CD$
(2) AB is parallel to CD.

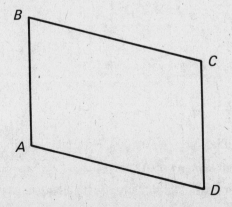

128. What was Mr. Smith's combined income for the years 1965–1970? In 1965 he made $10,000.

   (1) His average yearly income for the years 1965–1970 was $12,000.
   (2) In 1970, his income was $20,000.

129. How much profit did Walker's Emporium make selling dresses?

   (1) Each dress cost $10.
   (2) 600 dresses were sold.

130. k is a positive integer. Is k a prime number?

   (1) No integer between 2 and $\sqrt{k}$ inclusive divides k evenly.

   (2) No integer between 2 and $\dfrac{k}{2}$ inclusive divides k evenly, and k is greater than 5.

131. The towns A, B, and C lie on a straight line. C is between A and B. The distance from A to B is 100 miles. How far is it from A to C?

   (1) The distance from A to B is 25% more than the distance from C to B.
   (2) The distance from A to C is $\frac{1}{4}$ of the distance from C to B.

132. Is AB perpendicular to CD?

   (1) $AC = BD$
   (2) $x = y$

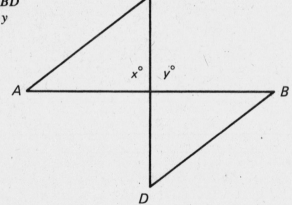

133. What is the value of $x - y$?

   (1) $x + 2y = 6$
   (2) $x = y$

134. The number of eligible voters is 100,000. How many eligible voters voted?

   (1) 63% of the eligible men voted.
   (2) 67% of the eligible women voted.

135. If $z = 50$, find the value of x.

    (1) $RS \neq ST$
    (2) $x + y = 60$

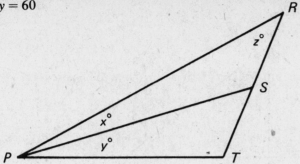

136. How much was the original cost of a car which sold for $2300?

    (1)   The car was sold for a discount of 10% from its original cost.
    (2)   The sales tax was $150.

137. The hexagon *ABCDEF* is inscribed in the circle with center *O*. What is the length of *AB?*

    (1)   The radius of the circle is 4 inches.
    (2)   The hexagon is a regular hexagon.

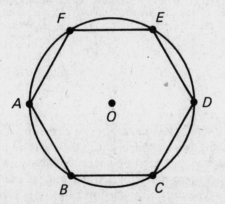

138. How many rolls of wallpaper are necessary to cover the walls of a room whose floor and ceiling are rectangles 12 feet wide and 15 feet long?

    (1)   A roll of wallpaper covers 20 square feet.
    (2)   There are no windows in the walls.

139. What is the average daily wage of a worker who works five days? He made $80 the first day.

    (1)   The worker made a total of $400 for the first four days of work.
    (2)   The worker made 20% more each day then he did on the previous day.

140. Is *ABC* a right triangle? *AB* = 5; *AC* = 4.

    (1) *BC* = 3

    (2) *AC* = *CD*

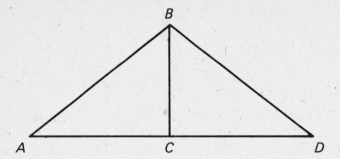

If there is still time remaining, you may review the questions in this section only.
You may not turn to any other section of the test.

Section V   Business Judgment

TIME: 35 minutes

DIRECTIONS: Read the following two passages. After you have completed each of them you will be asked to answer two sets of questions. The first of these, data evaluation, involves determining the importance of specific factors included in the passage. The second, data application, consists of general questions relating to the passage. When answering questions, you may consult the passage.

Passage 1:

In 1967 Mr. Ed Sim, a chemical engineer, began experimenting in his spare time with a new formula for processing fresh orange juice. By 1970 he had perfected the process to such an extent that he was ready to begin production in a small way. His process enabled him to extract 18 percent more juice from oranges than was typically extracted by a pressure juicer of the type currently used in cafes. His process also removed some of the bitterness which got into the juice from the peelings when oranges were squeezed without peeling them.

Since many of the better quality restaurants preferred to serve fresh orange juice instead of canned or frozen juice, Mr. Sim believed he could find a ready market for his product. Another appeal of his product would be that he could maintain more consistent juice flavor than haphazard restaurant juicing usually produced.

Mr. Sim patented the process and then started production. Since his capital was limited, he began production in a small building which previously had been a woodworking shop. Mr. Sim, with the help of his brother, marketed the juice through local restaurants. The juice was distributed in glass jugs which proved to be rather expensive because of high breakage. The new product was favorably accepted by the public, and the business proved to be a success.

Mr. Sim began to receive larger and more frequent orders from his customers and their business associates. In 1972 he quit his regular job in order to devote full time to his juice business. He soon reached his capacity because of his inability to cover personally a larger area with his pickup truck. Advertising was on a small scale because of limited funds. Faced with these problems of glass jug breakage, advertising and limited distribution, Mr. Sim approached a regional food distributor for a solution. Mr. Sim was offered a plan whereby the distributor would advertise and distribute the product on the basis of 25 percent of gross sales. The distributor would assist Mr. Sim in securing a loan from the local bank to expand production.

Before he had an opportunity to contact the bank to borrow money, Mr. Sim was introduced to Mr. Bernie Lubo, a plastics engineer, who produced plastic containers. Mr. Sim mentioned his own problems in the expansion of his business. Mr. Lubo wanted to finance expanded juice production with the understanding that plastic containers would be used for marketing the orange juice. He would lend the money interest free, but he was to receive 40 percent of the net profits for the next ten years. Distribution and advertising were to be done through a local broker for 25 percent of gross sales. The principal on Mr. Lubo's invested money was to be repaid by Mr. Sim on a basis of 10 percent of his share of the profits. Mr. Lubo was to retain an interest in the profits of the firm until the loan was repaid, or at least for ten years.

Data Evaluation Questions

DIRECTIONS: Evaluate each of the following factors used in decision-making which relate to the passage you have just read by selecting

(A) for a *Major Objective*—the result desired by the executive;

(B) for a *Major Factor*—a primary consideration, spelled out in the passage, that influences the decision;

(C) for a *Minor Factor*—a less important consideration in the decision;

(D) for a *Major Assumption*—a conclusion reached by the executive not necessarily supported by the factors present;

(E) for an *Unimportant Issue*—a consideration not directly related to the problem.

141. Cost of securing a loan

142. High breakage of glass jugs

143. Business expansion

144. Public acceptance of the product

145. General economic trends

Data Application Questions

DIRECTIONS: Answer each of the following questions using information contained in the passage.

146. A major appeal of Mr. Sim's product was its

    I.   Ability to extract more juice
   II.   Removing the bitterness of juice
  III.   Utilization of orange peels

  (A) I only
  (B) III only
  (C) I and II only
  (D) II and III only
  (E) I, II, and III

147. Which of the following reasons were given for the need to expand Mr. Sim's business?

    I.   High breakage of glass jugs
   II.   Production reached capacity
  III.   Larger and more frequent orders received

  (A) I only
  (B) III only
  (C) I and II only
  (D) II and III only
  (E) I, II, and III

148. According to the expansion plan suggested by the food distributor, the distributor would

    I.   Advertise the product
   II.   Loan money to Mr. Sim
  III.   Receive 50 percent of gross sales

  (A) I only
  (B) III only
  (C) I and II only
  (D) II and II only
  (E) I, II, and III

149. According to Mr. Lubo's plan, he offered Mr. Sim a(n)

    I.   Interest free loan
   II.   Distribution channel
  III.   Free use of plastic containers

  (A) I only
  (B) III only
  (C) I and II only
  (D) II and III only
  (E) I, II, and III

150. Which of the following prevented immediate expansion of Mr. Sim's business?

    I.   He could not acquire a patent
   II.   His product was more expensive than frozen orange juice
 III.   He lacked expansion capital

    (A) I only
    (B) III only
    (C) I and II only
    (D) II and III only
    (E) I, II, and III

Passage 2:

Speculations and prophecies are not the sort of thing Mr. Gage deals in. "I deal in facts," he said, "and one of the outstanding facts of the Congo's relationship with the United States is that the Congo is an old and good client of the U.S. This can be substantiated by another fact," he noted, "which is that in the first 20 years or so of our existence we have exceeded a deficit trading account with America of some $1 billion.

Despite the fact that the Congo's exports to the United States will no doubt increase, Mr. Gage believes that his country's trade deficit will also increase. "The U.S. is a tough market, in which the Congo has to face stiff competition both in the area of prices from such low wage countries as Taiwan and Korea, and in quality from such distinguished competitors as Italy, France and, of course, America itself. We have to compete with the quality suppliers by offering more sophisticated goods."

Another problem which must be faced is the business recession in the United States and the demand by some labor unions and Congressmen for legislation restricting the import of goods. Although such legislation is not given much chance of passage, some increase in protectionist sentiment might develop, effectively reducing exports to the United States. With these facts in mind, Mr. Gage, the Congo's Trade Minister, seriously began considering alternative strategies for his country's export efforts.

The first strategy was expanding the Congo's promotional effort in the United States. At present, the Congo spends about $50,000 in all sorts of promotional activities, mainly in leaflets and brochures sent to importers and large retail chains. While it is known that the advertising appropriation figure is a moderate one for a country of the Congo's size, it is not known what the effect of the promotion has been. Since it is difficult to judge the effectiveness of promotion of this kind, some have suggested to the Minister that the Congo open a trade center in the United States where its goods could be exhibited on a permanent basis. Such a center could also be the focal point for the preparation and dissemination of promotional material. Opponents of such a measure claim that such a center would be prohibitive in cost and offer no guarantee that the investment will produce a satisfactory return. Moreover, the critics state that until the Congo produces more sophisticated goods of better quality, it is useless to try and compete with domestic U.S. producers. The Congo should concentrate on the sale of specialized goods which are not produced in large quantities in the U.S. As to what goods should be sold in the U.S., a survey of the market was suggested.

Data Evaluation Questions

DIRECTIONS: Evaluate each of the following factors used in decision-making which relate to the passage you have just read by selecting

    (A) for a *Major Objective*—the result desired by the executive;

    (B) for a *Major Factor*—a primary consideration, spelled out in the passage, that influences the decision;

(C) for a *Minor Factor*—a less important consideration in the decision;

(D) for a *Major Assumption*—a conclusion reached by the executive not necessarily supported by the factors present;

(E) for an *Unimportant Issue*—a consideration not directly related to the problem.

151. Reducing the Congo's trade deficit

152. The business recession in the U.S.

153. The Congo is an old client of the U.S.

154. Competition from Italy and France

155. Impending trade legislation in the U.S.

Data Application Questions

DIRECTIONS: Answer each of the following questions using information contained in the passage.

156. Protectionist legislation in the United States

   I.   Would reduce U.S. imports
   II. Is not given much chance of passage
   III. Would restrict U.S. exports

   (A) I only
   (B) III only
   (C) I and II only
   (D) II and III only
   (E) I, II, and III

157. With regard to the Congo's promotional campaign in the United States, the Trade Minister

   I.   Praised its success
   II. Suggested increasing the budget
   III. Was not sure how effective the promotion really was

   (A) I only
   (B) III only
   (C) I and II only
   (D) II and III only
   (E) I, II, and III

158. To increase the Congo's exports to the United States, it was suggested that

    I.   Product prices be increased
   II.   A trade center be opened in the United States
  III.   Only specialized goods be sold in the United States

  (A) I only
  (B) III only
  (C) I and II only
  (D) II and III only
  (E) I, II, and III

159. Those demanding passage of restrictionist trade legislation in the United States include

    I.   Congressmen
   II.   Labor unions
  III.   Business groups

  (A) I only
  (B) III only
  (C) I and II only
  (D) II and III only
  (E) I, II, and III

160. Which trade strategy did the Congo's Trade Minister consider?

    I.   Increasing the promotional effort in the United States
   II.   Opening a trade center in the United States
  III.   Increasing the quality of goods sold in the United States

  (A) I only
  (B) III only
  (C) I and II only
  (D) II and III only
  (E) I, II, and III

If there is still time remaining, you may review the questions in this section only.
You may not turn to any other section of the test.

Section VI   Analysis of Explanations

TIME: 30 minutes

DIRECTIONS: You will be given a fact situation and a result, followed by a series of statements. You are to evaluate each statement in relation to the fact situation and the result. Each statement is to be considered separately from the other statements. Examine each statement as follows:

1. Is the statement inconsistent with or contrary to the fact situation, the result, or both? If your answer is *yes*, choose (A) as your answer. If your answer is no, continue to the next possibility.

2. Does the statement present an adequate explanation of the result? If your answer is *yes*, choose (B) as your answer. If your answer is no, examine the third possibility.

3. Is the statement deducible from the fact situation, the result, or both? If your answer is *yes*, choose (C) as your answer. If your answer is no, examine the fourth possibility.

4. Is the statement relevant to the result by either supporting or weakening a possible explanation of the result? If your answer is *yes*, choose (D) as your answer. If your answer is no, continue to the last possibility.

5. Is the statement irrelevant to an explanation of the result? If so, choose (E) as your answer.

You should consider and eliminate your choices in the order given above. The first question you can answer *yes* should be the one you choose. Remote or unlikely possibilities should be ignored. Use common sense.

QUESTION SET 1

Situation: According to a recent report by the Bureau of Labor Statistics some 2.2 million men of prime-working age in the labor force neither hold nor seek jobs.

Result: A new breed of males in the 25–45 age group, who question the work ethic, has appeared.

161. In California a young man has given up looking for a new job. He is busy caring for the two children of his widowed sister who holds a position at the local high school. While he enjoys seeing the children off to school, cooking, cleaning, and shopping, he often compares his former 40-hour a week job with his 24-hour responsibility of household chores.

162. Many fear that legislation moving the statutory retirement age from 65 to 70 would cause greater unemployment for younger workers.

163. A poorly written job résumé often costs a young man a good position.

164. J.J.A. gave up a well-paying supervisory job when he found that his blood pressure was affected by the responsibilities of his job. He now finds his family demands are less and his health is good as he manages the family budget on his wife's income.

165. In one area of Florida there is an entire community of boat dwellers who spend most of their time sailing and fishing. Only seldom are they involved in doing odd jobs.

166. After Mr. J. inherited a substantial sum of money, he left his $30,000 position and now spends most of his time traveling around the world, always on the alert for attractive investment situations.

167. Self-employed individuals who leave the labor market are not included in the figures of the Bureau of Labor Statistics.

168. A job counseling and career management service states that at least 80% of all good executive, administrative, and professional jobs available in New York are not advertised or listed.

169. Some individuals regard welfare benefits as "begging" and prefer to live on their savings. They lower their standards of living and seek odd jobs for some form of income.

170. A man disabled from birth can be deprived of his Social Security benefits if he marries a disabled woman who was not eligible for the same kind of federal payments.

171. For older workers, the combination of early retirement and disability pay can actually exceed salary.

QUESTION SET 2

Situation: In an attempt to end cheating on term papers, Professor Johnson set down some definite rules and regulations regarding the required term paper. The project is to be at least 24 double-spaced, typewritten pages. The subject of the report is to be one from a list of 20 given by the teacher. A bibliography must be included. Under no circumstance should a direct quotation be more than 10 typewritten lines. No outside help is to be sought.

Result: After careful scrutiny the term papers of Lori Brown, Michael Liebow, Ann Lehman, Philip Marks, and Sara Jones were returned with unsatisfactory ratings. All others were acceptable.

172. Professor Johnson engaged a group of graduate students to read the term papers and check references and bibliographies. He himself then read each paper along with the comments made by the graduate students.

173. The college librarian reported that several students in this class had photocopied the same series of pages from one particular reference book.

174. Lori and Michael cooperatively prepared one term paper and submitted two slightly altered manuscripts.

175. A local agency with offices close to the college campus supplies term papers at reasonable fees. Professor Johnson had discovered in previous semesters that students make use of this service.

176. Herbert Martin received some glowing comments on his 20-page, double-spaced report.

177. Philip Marks was reported to the dean for submitting a paper used several years earlier by a fraternity brother.

178. Samuel Baruch submitted a term paper practically copied from an obscure reference book.

179. One student received special permission to use a topic closely related to one on Professor Johnson's original list.

180. Sara Jones admitted that her family had purchased an encyclopedia that provides, upon request, a number of prepared reports on any subject. She admitted that her term paper was mainly the report furnished by this service.

Question Set 3

Situation: Joan Brown purchased a cashmere sweater for $45.00 at the Gacy Department Store. Weeks later she decided she did not like it. Because she had removed the price tag, she was asked to see the department supervisor, who inspected it for possible wear. Joan resented the fact that she was then asked to complete a form to explain why she was returning the article. After a long wait she finally reached a clerk in the Credit Department who told her that $40.50 would be credited to her charge account since the price of the article had been reduced by 10% since her purchase date.

Result: Joan canceled her credit card with the Gacy Department Store with a letter stating that she was dissatisfied with the way she was treated when she returned the sweater.

181. Each cash register in the Gacy store bears the following notice: Merchandise returned within 7 days of purchase will receive cash refund if (1) price tag has not been removed and (2) cash receipt accompanies the returned merchandise.

182. Joan had a good credit rating with the Gacy store.

183. Joan came home tired, exhausted and upset after returning the sweater.

184. Mr. Brown plans to apply for a new credit card. He told Joan that the store usually has good values and that the employees were following store regulations when she returned the sweater.

185. A storewide sale was conducted a few days after Joan purchased the sweater.

186. The department supervisor who inspected the sweater was recently promoted to this position.

187. The charge of $45.00 had already been paid by the Browns.

188. Joan spent almost two hours in the store when she returned the sweater. When she complained to one of the salespeople, she was scolded for having kept the merchandise so long before deciding to return it.

189. The cuffs of the sleeves of the sweater were carefully examined before the merchandise was accepted by the store.

190. Joan claimed that the workmanship on the cashmere sweater was substandard.

Question Set 4

Situation: Meprobamate is a carbamate derivative which has been shown in various studies to have effects at multiple sites in the central nervous system. Physicians prescribe this for relief of anxiety and tension, and to promote sleep in anxious, tense patients. Various pharmaceutical firms market this substance, sometimes with slight variations, with its own trade name. Some examples are Miltown, Bamadex, Deprol and Kesso-Bamate tablets. Consumer advocates claim that if pharmacists were permitted to substitute generic drugs for trade name products the public would pay less for the same prescribed drugs.

Result: Various state legislators have introduced bills that would permit substitution of generic drugs for brand names.

191. Wyeth Laboratories markets meprobamate under the trade name Equanil.

192. Less than 15% of all prescriptions call for generic names.

193. Large doses of meprobamate may cause chronic intoxication.

194. Some physicians report that patients ask them about the advisability of filling the prescriptions with generic products rather than brand name drugs.

195. Some major drug concerns were accused of using "scare" tactics to influence public opinion in favor of the more expensive trade name drugs.

196. Evidence has been presented to show that some drug companies purchased generic drugs made by small companies and sold them under their own label.

197. Medical societies have opposed the substitution of trade name products for less expensive drugs.

198. The Food and Drug Administration conducts drug testing programs to prevent substandard generic drugs from appearing on the market.

199. Drug concerns make a higher profit on trade name products than they do on generic drugs.

200. The addition of a chemical to a basic formula of meprobamate may alter its efficacy.

If there is still time remaining, you may review the questions in this section only.
You may not turn to any other section of the test.

Answers

Section I   Reading Recall

1. **(C)**	9. **(A)**	17. **(A)**	25. **(E)**
2. **(C)**	10. **(E)**	18. **(C)**	26. **(D)**
3. **(B)**	11. **(B)**	19. **(C)**	27. **(C)**
4. **(D)**	12. **(B)**	20. **(E)**	28. **(E)**
5. **(C)**	13. **(A)**	21. **(A)**	29. **(E)**
6. **(A)**	14. **(D)**	22. **(C)**	30. **(E)**
7. **(C)**	15. **(C)**	23. **(D)**	
8. **(B)**	16. **(D)**	24. **(D)**	

Section II   Mathematics

(Numbers in parentheses indicate the section in the Mathematics Review where material concerning the question is discussed.)

31. **(D)** (I–4)	50. **(B)** (II–7)	69. **(B)** (I–2)
32. **(E)** (II–2)	51. **(E)** (I–4)	70. **(D)** (III–6, III–7)
33. **(C)** (II–6)	52. **(C)** (I–7)	71. **(C)** (IV–3)
34. **(C)** (IV–4)	53. **(A)** (II–2)	72. **(D)** (IV–3)
35. **(D)** (IV–4)	54. **(C)** (I–2)	73. **(C)** (IV–3)
36. **(E)** (IV–4)	55. **(A)** (III–4)	74. **(E)** (IV–3)
37. **(E)** (II–5)	56. **(C)** (IV–2)	75. **(C)** (II–3)
38. **(D)** (II–4)	57. **(D)** (IV–2)	76. **(B)** (II–3)
39. **(B)** (IV–1)	58. **(E)** (IV–2)	77. **(D)** (IV–1, I–7)
40. **(C)** (IV–1)	59. **(B)** (IV–2)	78. **(E)** (IV–1, I–7)
41. **(B)** (I–4)	60. **(C)** (IV–2)	79. **(D)** (IV–1)
42. **(A)** (II–3)	61. **(D)** (II–3)	80. **(D)** (III–7)
43. **(C)** (III–7)	62. **(E)** (I–2)	81. **(C)** (II–3)
44. **(C)** (IV–1)	63. **(B)** (I–4)	82. **(B)** (II–7)
45. **(D)** (IV–1)	64. **(D)** (IV–5)	83. **(C)** (III–4, III–7)
46. **(D)** (IV–1, I–4)	65. **(C)** (IV–5)	84. **(E)** (II–3)
47. **(C)** (IV–1)	66. **(B)** (IV–5)	85. **(E)** (II–2)
48. **(B)** (II–5)	67. **(C)** (IV–5)	
49. **(C)** (II–6)	68. **(C)** (I–4)	

Section III   Verbal Aptitude

86. (C)	96. (C)	106. (B)	116. (B)
87. (D)	97. (B)	107. (A)	117. (C)
88. (C)	98. (A)	108. (B)	118. (C)
89. (B)	99. (B)	109. (C)	119. (A)
90. (C)	100. (B)	110. (A)	120. (B)
91. (B)	101. (B)	111. (D)	121. (C)
92. (C)	102. (C)	112. (B)	122. (C)
93. (A)	103. (B)	113. (B)	123. (A)
94. (C)	104. (A)	114. (A)	124. (C)
95. (D)	105. (C)	115. (D)	125. (D)

Section IV   Data Sufficiency

126. (E)	130. (D)	134. (E)	138. (E)
127. (C)	131. (D)	135. (E)	139. (B)
128. (A)	132. (B)	136. (A)	140. (A)
129. (E)	133. (B)	137. (C)	

Section V   Business Judgment

141. (B)	146. (C)	151. (A)	156. (C)
142. (C)	147. (D)	152. (B)	157. (B)
143. (A)	148. (A)	153. (C)	158. (D)
144. (D)	149. (A)	154. (C)	159. (C)
145. (E)	150. (B)	155. (D)	160. (E)

Section VI   Analysis of Explanations

161. (B)	171. (E)	181. (C)	191. (C)
162. (E)	172. (D)	182. (E)	192. (C)
163. (E)	173. (E)	183. (B)	193. (E)
164. (B)	174. (B)	184. (A)	194. (B)
165. (C)	175. (C)	185. (C)	195. (D)
166. (B)	176. (A)	186. (E)	196. (B)
167. (A)	177. (B)	187. (E)	197. (D)
168. (E)	178. (A)	188. (B)	198. (E)
169. (B)	179. (E)	189. (C)	199. (C)
170. (E)	180. (B)	190. (A)	200. (A)

Analysis

Section I   Reading Recall

1. **(C)** See paragraph 2, line 1.

2. **(C)** See paragraph 1.

3. **(B)** See paragraph 1: "Starting as a non-violent revolutionist. . . ."

4. **(D)** See paragraph 1: ". . . he ended life as a major social theorist . . . sympathetic with violent revolution. . . ."

5. **(C)** See paragraph 3: ". . . Russia . . . is no longer a proletarian movement . . . but a camouflaged imperialistic effort. . . ."

6. **(A)** See paragraph 4.

7. **(C)** See paragraph 3: Of course it is accepted by those in **(D)** and **(E)**, but also by those in **(C)**.

8. **(B)** This can be deduced from the last paragraph.

9. **(A)** See paragraph 2.

10. **(E)** All these are mentioned in paragraph 1.

11. **(B)** See paragraph 2: ". . . fiscal policies should be designed to encourage economic growth."

12. **(B)** See paragraph 2: They did not.

13. **(A)** See paragraph 3: The Committee of the Whole.

14. **(D)** See paragraph 4, line 1.

15. **(C)** See paragraph 5: "In the first decade of the twentieth century, an 'executive budget' came into successful use. . . ."

16. **(D)** See paragraph 5: It was rejected.

17. **(A)** See paragraph 6, line 1: The responsibility was given by the Budget and Accounting Act of 1921.

18. **(C)** See paragraph 6.

19. **(C)** See paragraph 6.

20. **(E)** See paragraph 1: All factors but **(E)** are relevant.

21. **(A)** See paragraph 2.

22. **(C)** See paragraph 2: They came at different times.

23. **(D)** See paragraph 2.

24. **(D)** Paragraphs 2 and 4 especially mention the various points of migration which the Indians reached.

25. **(E)** See paragraph 4.

26. **(D)** See paragraph 3: ". . . the New Mexico Indians were very successful big game hunters."

27. **(C)** See the last line of paragraph 4.

28. **(E)** All these are given in paragraph 3.

29. **(E)** See paragraph 3.

30. **(E)** Certainly, alternatives **(A)** and **(C)** do not correspond to the contents of the passage, while **(B)** and **(D)** are too general. The main point in the passage is the migration of Indians, their cultures, and their acclimation to new surroundings. These subjects are in the domain of the anthropologist.

Section II   Mathematics

31. **(D)** Since he pays 6% on the first $500, this equals (.06)(500) or $30 interest on the first $500. He is borrowing $5,500 which is $5,000 in excess of the first $500. Thus, he also pays $5\frac{1}{2}$% of $5,000, which is (.055) (5,000) or $275.00. Therefore, the total interest is $305.

32. **(E)** $6x - 3y$ is $3(2x - y)$. Since $2x - y = 4$, $6x - 3y = 3 \cdot 4$ or 12.

33. **(C)** The progression is arithmetic and $11 - 5 = 6 = 17 - 11$, so every term is 6 more than the previous term. Therefore, the next term after 17 is $17 + 6$ or 23.

34. **(C)** The bar first touched 50 in 1945.

35. **(D)** In 1952, hydro plants had about 21 million kilowatts, while the total capacity was about 84 million kilowatts. Therefore, the capacity of the steam and internal combustion plants in 1952 was about $(84 - 21)$ or 63 million kilowatts. Since $\frac{63}{21} = 3$, x is 3.

36. **(E)**

    STATEMENT I is true since the graph is almost horizontal between 1930 and 1939, whereas it rises between 1920 and 1929 and between 1940 and 1949.

    Since the total capacity in 1952 was less than 25 million kilowatts and the capacity of the hydro plants in 1925 was more than 5 million kilowatts, STATEMENT II can be inferred.

    STATEMENT III is also true. Between 1925 and 1945, the capacity went from about 22 million to about 50 million kilowatts, which is an increase of about 28 million kilowatts. However, the capacity in 1952 was about 84 million kilowatts, so the increase between 1945 and 1952 was about 34 million kilowatts.

    Therefore, STATEMENTS I, II, and III can all be inferred from the graph.

37. **(E)** Since each packer loads $\frac{1}{8}$ of a box in 9 minutes, the 20 packers will load $\frac{20}{8}$ or $2\frac{1}{2}$ boxes in 9 minutes. There are 90 minutes in $1\frac{1}{2}$ hours; so the 20 packers will load $10 \times 2\frac{1}{2}$ or 25 boxes in $1\frac{1}{2}$ hours.

38. **(D)** The entire population can be divided into three nonoverlapping parts: owns both a car and a motorcycle, owns a car but not a motorcycle, and owns a motorcycle but not a car. If we denote these categories by A, B, and C respectively, we know that $A + B + C = 100\%$. Also, since $A + B$ consists of all the people who own a car, we have $A + B = 90\%$. Therefore, C must be 10%. But C is the category of people who own a motorcycle but do not own a car.

39. **(B)** The total number of children between 6 and 17 in 1972 was about 46,000,000 and of these 20,155,000 had mothers in the labor force. Therefore, about 46,000,000 minus 20,000,000, or 26,000,000, did not have mothers in the labor force.

40. **(C)** There were 2,345,000 Negro children under 6, of whom 999,000 had mothers in the labor force. $\frac{999,000}{2,345,000}$ is about $\frac{1,000,000}{2,350,000}$ or $\frac{100}{235}$, which is roughly $\frac{5}{12} \cdot \frac{5}{12} = 5 \times 8\frac{1}{3}\% = 41\frac{2}{3}\%$.

41. **(B)** Since 108% of $50 = (1.08)(50) = $54, the chair was offered for sale at $54.00. It was sold for 90% of $54 since there was a 10% discount. Therefore, the chair was sold for $(.9)(\$54)$ or $48.60.

42. **(A)** Here's a table of the hours worked:

	Mon.	Tues.	Wed.	Thurs.	Fri.	Wages for week
	8	8	8	8	8	$5x$
excess over 8 hrs	0	3	1	2	1	$(0 + 3 + 1 + 2 + 1)y = 7y$.

    The average daily wage equals

    $\frac{(5x + 7y)}{5}$, or $x + \frac{7}{5}y$.

43. **(C)** The area of a rectangle is length times width; so the area of the field is 50×25 square yards or 1,250 square yards.

44. **(C)** California's population increased by 53.3%.

45. **(D)** Arkansas, Mississippi, North Dakota, and Oklahoma had decreases in population.

46. **(D)** The population of the United States increased by 14.5% between 1940 and 1950. So if the population was 100 million in 1940, it would have been 114.5 million in 1950. Therefore, the correct answer is 115 million.

47. **(C)**

STATEMENT I is true. $\frac{1}{3}$ is $33\frac{1}{3}$% and only California, Arizona, Florida, Nevada, Oregon, and Washington had population increases of more than $33\frac{1}{3}$%.

STATEMENT II cannot be inferred since the graph tells us only that the *percentage* increase in Oregon's population was larger than the *percentage* increase in Washington's population. There is no information about the number of people living in each state.

STATEMENT III is true because Nebraska's population increased by .7%.

Therefore, only STATEMENTS I and III can be inferred from the graph.

48. **(B)** Since 4 is $\frac{1}{3}$ of 12, 4 apples cost $\frac{1}{3}$ of 63¢, which is 21¢.

49. **(C)** Let x_n be what the car is worth after n years. Then we know $x_0 = \$2,500$ and $x_{n+1} = \frac{4}{5} x_n$. So $x_1 = \frac{4}{5} \times 2,500$, which is $2,000$, x_2 is $\frac{4}{5} \times 2,000$, which is $1,600$, and finally x_3 is $\frac{4}{5} \times 1,600$, which is $1,280$. Therefore, the car is worth \$1,280 at the end of three years.
OR
$x_3 = \frac{4}{5} x_2 = \frac{4}{5} (\frac{4}{5} x_1) = (\frac{4}{5})(\frac{4}{5})(\frac{4}{5} x_0) = \frac{64}{125} x_0$. $(\frac{64}{125})2500 = 1280$.

50. **(B)** Since 300 miles is $\frac{3}{5}$ of 500 miles, it should cost $\frac{3}{5}$ of \$15 to travel 300 miles by automobile. Therefore, the cost is \$9.

51. **(E)** Since the only costs are \$20 for fuel and \$70 for the drivers wages, the total cost is \$90. Therefore, the company should charge 120% of \$90, which is (1.2)(\$90) or \$108.00.

52. **(C)** The total fuel cost will be $3 \cdot 20 + 4 \cdot 15 + 2 \cdot 5 + 1 \cdot 50$, which is \$180. Since there are 10 vehicles, the average fuel cost is 180/10 or \$18 per vehicle.

53. **(A)** Since $x + 2y = 2x + y$, we can subtract $x + 2y$ from each side of the equation and the result is $0 = x - y$.

54. **(C)** $\frac{2}{3}$ of the 15% of the families with income over \$25,000 own boats. Since $\frac{2}{3}$ of 15% = 10%, $\frac{1}{10}$ of the families own boats and have an income of \$25,000 or more.

55. **(A)** The angles are in the ratio of 1:2:2, so 2 angles are equal to each other, and both are twice as large as the third angle of the triangle. Since a triangle with two equal angles must have the sides opposite equal, the triangle is isosceles. (Using the fact that the sum of the angles of a triangle is 180°, you can see that the angles of the triangle are 72°, 72° and 36°, so only (A) is true.)

56. **(C)** In 1970, total expenditures were \$4,851 million, of which 5% was spent in Canada; so x is 5% of \$4,851 million, or \$242.55 million. Therefore, the correct answer is about 240 million.

57. **(D)** In 1960, the military assistance program used 10%, the AEC 12%, and materials and supplies 18%. So all together the three programs received $(10 + 12 + 18)$% or 40% of defense expenditures; 40% = $\frac{2}{5}$.

58. **(E)** Thailand received 5% of defense expenditures in 1970.

59. **(B)** Since 14% was spent in "other Europe" in 1970, $\frac{5}{7}$ of 14% or 10% was spent in Spain in 1970. Thus, 10% of \$4,851 million, or about \$485 million, was spent in Spain in 1970.

60. **(C)**

STATEMENT I can be inferred since $\frac{1}{5} = 20$% and in both years more than 20% was spent in Germany.

The expenditures for 1970 were \$4,851 million and for 1960 \$3,087 million; so the expenditures increased by $\$(4,851 - 3,087)$ million or \$1,764 million. Since \$1,764 million is more than $\frac{1}{3}$ of \$3,087 million, STATEMENT II can be inferred from the graph.

STATEMENT III is false. $\frac{2}{5} = 40$%; U.S. personnel spent 26% in 1960 and 38% in 1970, so it is impossible for U.S. personnel to have spent 40% of the total for 1960 and 1970.

Therefore, only STATEMENTS I and II can be inferred from the graphs.

61. **(D)** The car travels at 60 mph; so the time to travel 255 miles is $\frac{255}{60}$ hours. Since $\frac{255}{60} = 4\frac{15}{60} = 4\frac{1}{4}$, it takes $4\frac{1}{4}$ hours.

62. **(E)** After the tune-up, the car will travel 15 miles on $\frac{3}{4}$ of a gallon of gas. So it will travel $\frac{15}{3/4}$ or $\frac{4}{3} \times 15$ or 20 miles on one gallon of gas.

63. **(B)** The price after a discount of 20% is 80% of P, the original price. After another 15% discount, the price is 85% of 80% of P or $(.85)(.80)P$, which equals $.68P$. Therefore, after the successive discounts, the price is 68% of what it was originally, which is the same as a single discount of 32%.

64. **(D)** Since the government spent $132 per capita on personal health care for people aged 65 and over in 1966, the total expenditure by the government was $(20)(132)$ million, which is $2,640 million, or $2.640 billion.

65. **(C)** In 1966, the government spent $30 per capita on people under 65; by 1972 the per capita amount for those under 65 was $72. Therefore, the increase was $42. Since $\frac{42}{30} = 1.4 = 140\%$, the correct answer is (C).

66. **(B)** In 1972, philanthropy and industry contributed $5 out of the $981 per capita spent on personal health care for those aged 65 and over. Therefore, the fraction is $\frac{5}{981}$, which is about $\frac{5}{980} = \frac{1}{196}$.

67. **(C)**

STATEMENT I cannot be inferred since the graph gives only per capita amounts. The total amount will also depend on the number of people in each group.

STATEMENT II is false since private health insurance decreased from $70 to $56 per capita.

STATEMENT III is true since $644 is more than $\frac{1}{2}$ of $981.

Therefore, only STATEMENT III can be inferred from the graphs.

68. **(C)** Since there are 20 oranges in a crate, a crate of oranges is sold for $20 \times 6\cent$ or $1.20. A crate of oranges costs $1.00; so the profit on a crate is $1.20 - $1.00 or $.20. Therefore, the rate of profit $= \frac{.20}{1.20} = \frac{1}{6} = 16\frac{2}{3}\%$.

69. **(B)** $7\frac{1}{2}$ dozen is $\frac{15}{2} \times 12 = 90$, so during the summer the hen lays 90 eggs. The food for the summer costs $10, so the cost in food per egg is $\frac{\$10}{90} = \frac{\$1}{9} = 11\frac{1}{9}\cent$.

70. **(D)**

STATEMENT I is not true since the diameter is not equal to the radius and the area of the circle is πr^2.

STATEMENT II is true since the length of a diameter is twice the length of a radius.

STATEMENT III is true since $a = \pi r^2 = \pi r(d/2) = \pi(r/2)d$. Therefore, $a/d = \pi(r/2)$.

Therefore, only STATEMENTS II and III are true.

71. **(C)** The graph was highest in 1935.

72. **(D)** In 1958 about 10% of the Gross National Product was spent on social welfare and about $45 billion on social welfare. Therefore, the Gross National Product was about $450 billion.

73. **(C)** The federal government spent about $20 billion in 1957, and the total was about $40 billion. Therefore, the state and local governments spent about $20 billion. So the federal government and state and local governments spent about the same amount.

74. **(E)**

STATEMENT I is true since the graph giving the percentage of Gross National Product falls from 1939 to 1943.

STATEMENT II is true since the state and local expenditures have never reached $50 billion ($\frac{1}{2}$ of the height of the whole scale).

STATEMENT III is true because the state and local portion is greater than the federal government portion between 1929 and 1933.

Therefore, STATEMENTS I, II and III can all be inferred from the graph.

75. **(C)** Since hose A takes 20 minutes to fill the tank, it fills up $\frac{1}{20}$ of the tank each minute. Since hose B fills up the tank in 15 minutes, it fills up $\frac{1}{15}$ of the tank each minute. Therefore, hose A and hose B together will fill up $\frac{1}{20} + \frac{1}{15}$ or $\frac{3+4}{60}$ or $\frac{7}{60}$ of the tank each minute. Thus, it will take $\frac{60}{7}$ or $8\frac{4}{7}$ minutes to fill the tank.

76. **(B)** If T is the amount of time it takes for 12 men to dig the ditch, then $T = \frac{5}{12}$ of $2 = \frac{5}{6}$ of an hour. Therefore, the 12 men will take 50 minutes.

77. **(D)** The total number of cars produced was $900 + 1200 + 1500 + 1400 + 1000$ or $6,000$. So the average per day is $\frac{6,000}{5}$ or 1,200 cars per day.

78. **(E)** There were 6,000 cars produced and the total wages paid for the week was ($30,000 + $40,000 + $52,000 + $50,000 + $32,000) or $204,000. Therefore, the average cost in wages per car $= \frac{\$204,000}{6,000} = \$34$.

79. **(D)**

STATEMENT I is true since the total number of cars produced was 6,000 and $\frac{1}{4}$ of 6,000 is 1,500.

STATEMENT II cannot be inferred since there is no data about the number of employees. If some employees are paid more than others, there may be fewer employees present who receive higher wages.

STATEMENT III is true since $102,000 was paid on Wednesday and Thursday and $102,000 is $\frac{1}{2}$ of the weekly total of $204,000.

Therefore, only STATEMENTS I and III can be inferred from the graph.

80. **(D)** The area of the field is $(1200)^2$ or 1,440,000 square yards. The area of each plot is 40×30 or 1200 square yards. Therefore, the number of plots $= \frac{1,440,000}{1,200} = 1,200$.

81. **(C)** The train travels 150 miles in 2 hours and 10 minutes which is $2\frac{1}{6}$ hours. Therefore, the average speed is $\frac{150}{2\frac{1}{6}} = 150 \times \frac{6}{13} = \frac{900}{13} = 69\frac{3}{13}$ or about 70 miles per hour.

82. **(B)** Since $x > 2$, then $-x < -2$; but $y > -1$ implies $2y > -2$. Therefore, $-x < -2 < 2y$ so $-x < 2y$. None of the other statements is always true. (A) is false if x is 5 and $y = -\frac{1}{2}$; (C) is false if $x = 3$ and $y = -\frac{1}{2}$; (D) is false if $x = 3$ and $y = 3$, and (E) is false if $x = 3$ and $y = -\frac{1}{2}$.

83. **(C)** Since $ABCD$ is a rectangle, all angles are right angles. The area of a rectangle is length times width; and the length of AD is 4. Using the Pythagorean theorem we have $4^2 + (\text{width})^2 = 5^2$, so the $(\text{width})^2$ is $25 - 16 = 9$. Therefore, the width is 3, and the area is $4 \times 3 = 12$.

84. **(E)** The electricity costs $12k¢$ for 12 hours, the heat costs $12d$ for 12 hours, and the water costs $12w¢$ for 12 hours. So the total is $12k¢ + \$12d + 12w¢$ or $\$.12k + \$12d + \$.12w$ which is $\$(.12k + 12d + .12w)$.

85. **(E)** Since $x = 2z$ and $y = 2z$, $x \cdot y \cdot z = (2z)(2z)(z) = 4z^3$; but $x \cdot y \cdot z = 256$ so $4z^3 = 256$. Therefore, $z^3 = 64$ and z is 4; so $x = 8$.

Section III   Verbal Aptitude

86. **(C)** ABSTRUSE: profound, enigmatic. *Antonym:* obvious

87. **(D)** COAGULATE: mix, thicken. *Antonym:* dissipate

88. **(C)** PROCLIVITY: tendency, propensity. *Antonym:* aversion

89. **(B)** TACIT: implied, silent. *Antonym:* open

90. **(C)** VORACIOUS: greedy, ravenous. *Antonym:* generous

91. **(B)** SAGACIOUS: discerning, wise. *Antonym:* stupid

92. **(C)** RETICENT: reserved, secretive. *Antonym:* communicative

93. **(A)** FECUND: fertile, productive. *Antonym:* barren

94. **(C)** FURTIVE: sly, stealthy. *Antonym:* open

95. **(D)** INCLEMENT: severe, cruel. *Antonym:* kind

96. **(C)** NOTORIOUS: infamous, well-known. *Antonym:* respected

97. **(B)** DILATE: expand, stretch. *Antonym:* contract

98. **(A)** BOISTEROUS: violent, loud. *Antonym:* peaceful

99. **(B)** ECLECTIC: selecting what appears best from various doctrines. *Antonym:* dogmatic

100. **(B)** A sample (as in a survey) is part of the universe. An individual is part of a population.

101. **(B)** Carbohydrates may cause obesity. Sugar may cause cavities.

102. **(C)** One fulfills a promise, whereas action carries out a plan.

103. **(B)** One who is addicted gives himself up habitually, e.g. for food, for a cause, etc.; dedicated is a milder form of the same behavior. A similar relationship is held between a fanatic and an enthusiast.

104. **(A)** Recall and remember are synonyms as are falsification and forgery. Behave and action are related in the same manner, but grammatically different. The correct grammatical form would be: behave : act.

105. **(C)** Again, the relationship is one of synonyms. Abundance : luxury :: poverty : indigence.

106. **(B)** A stamp is payment for sending a letter (using the mails), while a coin is payment for using a pay telephone.

107. **(A)** Fuel flows through pipes as air flows through lungs.

108. **(B)** Exemption and immunity both mean to free someone from an obligation, while exclusion and isolation mean a refusal to admit someone.

109. **(C)** Indigenous is an antonym of foreign, as native is an antonym of extraneous. While other alternatives are also antonyms, e.g., outsider : inhabitant, only (C) has the same meaning as indigenous : foreign. Note that (E) might have been acceptable if it were written inhabitant : outsider.

110. **(A)** Efficacious (adequate) is the opposite of lacking as efficient is an antonym of incompetent.

111. **(D)** An octave consists of eight notes; a millenium is a thousand years.

112. **(B)** As one throws to "hit" a target, one dives to "hit" a certain spot in the water.

113. **(B)** Alternative (B) clearly has the most substance and meaning.

114. **(A)** Alternatives (C) and (E) can be ruled out, because one does not judge ability by subjective factors. Alternatives (D) and (B) do not make sense in the context.

115. **(D)** Alternatives (A) and (C) are incorrect because their meaning is not clear, and prisoners are not "acquitted" once they have been sentenced to a prison term. Alternative (E), clemency (leniency), is also unclear; i.e., what form does clemency take? Amnesty (B) is usually only granted to political prisoners, but in any case, it also means pardon, which is alternative (D).

116. **(B)** The police would hardly hold a council or assembly on the street for purposes of a

strike or a discussion, but they would more likely meet to discuss a seige.

117. **(C)** All the first word fill-ins are acceptable, but (C) has the most meaning when both words are used.

118. **(C)** Alternative (D) might be acceptable, but (C) has more meaning.

119. **(A)** In alternatives (B) through (D), only the first word fill-ins have meaning.

120. **(B)** has the most meaning.

121. **(C)** An effort is not pessimistic (or optimistic) as in (E), nor prohibitory (A). Alternative (B) hardly makes sense; and one does not convey an accord (D).

122. **(C)** The term "financial" restraints is too implicit; (B) and (E) are unclear; and (D) has little meaning.

123. **(A)** Terms such as "insipid" and "absolute" are not used to refer to studies. In (E), if a study is dated (old), it cannot be extemporary (timely).

124. **(C)** Loquacious means talkative.

125. **(D)** If they are complementary, they are *not* competitive.

Section IV   Data Sufficiency

126. **(E)**

Since STATEMENT (1) describes only x and STATEMENT (2) describes only y, both are needed to get an answer. Using STATEMENT (2), STATEMENT (1) becomes $3x = 2k = 2y^2$, so $x = \dfrac{2y^2}{3}$. However, this is not sufficient, since if $y = -1$ then $x = \frac{2}{3}$ and x is greater than y, but if $y = 1$ then again $x = \frac{2}{3}$ but now x is less than y.

Therefore, STATEMENTS (1) and (2) together are not sufficient.

127. **(C)**

$ABCD$ is a parallelogram if AB is parallel to CD and BC is parallel to AD. STATEMENT (2) tells you that AB is parallel to CD, but this is not sufficient since a trapezoid has only one pair of opposite sides parallel. Thus, STATEMENT (2) alone is not sufficient.

STATEMENT (1) alone is not sufficient since a trapezoid can have the two nonparallel sides equal.

However, using STATEMENTS (1) and (2) together we can deduce that BC is parallel to AD, since the distance from BC to AD is equal along two different parallel lines.

128. **(A)**

STATEMENT (1) alone is sufficient. The average is the combined income for 1965–1970 divided by 6 (the number of years). Therefore, the combined income is 6 times the average yearly income.

STATEMENT (2) alone is not sufficient since there is no information about his income for the years 1966–1969.

129. **(E)**

To find the profit, we must know the selling price of the dress as well as its cost. STATEMENTS (1) and (2) together are not sufficient, since there is no information about the selling price of the dresses.

130. **(D)**

k is a prime if none of the integers 2, 3, 4, . . . up to $k - 1$ divide k evenly. STATEMENT (1) alone is sufficient since if k is not a prime then $k = (m)(n)$ where m and n must be integers less than k. But this means either m or n must be less than or equal to $\sqrt{k}$, since if m and n are both larger than $\sqrt{k}$, $(m)(n)$ is larger than $(\sqrt{k})(\sqrt{k})$ or k. So STATEMENT (1) implies k is a prime.

STATEMENT (2) alone is also sufficient, since if $k = (m)(n)$ and m and n are both larger than $\dfrac{k}{2}$, then $(m)(n)$ is greater than $\dfrac{k^2}{4}$; but $\dfrac{k^2}{4}$ is greater than k when k is larger than 5. Therefore, if no integer between 2 and $\dfrac{k}{2}$ inclusive divides k evenly, then k is a prime.

131. (D)

Since we are given the fact that 100 miles is the distance from A to B, it is sufficient to find the distance from C to B. This is because 100 minus the distance from C to B is the distance from A to C. STATEMENT (1) says that 125% of the distance from C to B is 100 miles. Thus, we can find the distance from C to B, which is sufficient. Since the distance from A to C plus the distance from C to B is the distance from A to B, we can use STATEMENT (2) to set up the equation 5 times the distance from A to C equals 100 miles.

Therefore, STATEMENTS (1) and (2) are each sufficient.

132. (B)

STATEMENT (1) alone is not sufficient. If the segment AC is moved further away from the segment BD, then the angles x and y will change. So STATEMENT (1) does not ensure that CD and AB are perpendicular.

STATEMENT (2) alone is sufficient. Since AB is a straight line, $x + y$ equals 180. Thus, if $x = y$, x and y both equal 90 and AB is perpendicular to CD. So the correct answer is (B).

133. (B)

STATEMENT (2) alone is sufficient, since $x = y$ implies $x - y = 0$.

STATEMENT (1) alone is not sufficient. An infinite number of pairs satisfy STATEMENT (1), for example, $x = 2$, $y = 2$, for which $x - y = 0$, or $x = 4$, $y = 1$, for which $x - y = 3$.

134. (E)

Since there is no information on how many of the eligible voters are men or how many are women, STATEMENTS (1) and (2) together are not sufficient.

135. (E)

We need to find the measure of angle PSR or of angle PST. Using STATEMENT (2), we can find angle PTR, but STATEMENT (1) does not give any information about either of the angles needed.

136. (A)

STATEMENT (1) is sufficient since it means 90% of the original cost is $2300. Thus, we can solve the equation for the original cost.

STATEMENT (2) alone is insufficient, since it gives no information about the cost.

137. (C)

Draw the radii from O to each of the vertices. These lines divide the hexagon into six triangles. STATEMENT (2) says that all the triangles are congruent since each of their pairs of corresponding sides is equal. Since there are 360° in a circle, the central angle of each triangle is 60°. And, since all radii are equal, each angle of the triangle equals 60°. Therefore, the triangles are equilateral, and AB is equal to the radius of the circle. Thus, if we assume STATEMENT (1), we know the length of AB. Without STATEMENT (1), we can't find the length of AB.

Also, STATEMENT (1) alone is not sufficient, since AB need not equal the radius unless the hexagon is regular.

138. (E)

We need to know the area of the walls. To find the area of the walls, we need the distance from the floor to the ceiling. Since neither STATEMENT (1) nor (2) gives any information about the height of the room, together they are not sufficient.

139. (B)

STATEMENT (2) alone is sufficient, since we know $80 was the amount the worker made the first day. We can use STATEMENT (2) to find his pay for each day thereafter and then find the average daily wage.

STATEMENT (1) alone is not sufficient, since there is no way to find out how much the worker made on the fifth day.

140. (A)

STATEMENT (1) alone is sufficient. Since $3^2 + 4^2 = 5^2$, ABC is a right triangle by the Pythagorean theorem.

STATEMENT (2) alone is not sufficient since you can choose a point D so that $AC = CD$ for any triangle ABC.

Section V   Business Judgment

141. **(B)** The cost of securing a loan is a *Major Factor* in making the decision; that is, the expansion of his business.

142. **(C)** The high breakage of glass jugs is a *Minor Factor* relating to which company to use in securing a loan.

143. **(A)** The issue of business expansion is clearly the *Major Objective* of Mr. Sim.

144. **(D)** Public acceptance of the product is a *Major Assumption* which has led Mr. Sim to expand his business.

145. **(E)** General economic conditions were an *Unimportant Issue* bearing upon Mr. Sim's decision to expand, and were not mentioned in the passage. Whether Mr. Sim considered such factors in his decision is an unknown.

146. **(C)** See paragraph 1: Among the major appeals of Mr. Sim's product were its ability to extract 18 percent more juice than conventional means, and the removal of bitterness from the peelings.

147. **(D)** See paragraph 4: Mr. Sim needed to expand his business because he had reached production capacity and could not fill the growing demand for his product.

148. **(A)** See paragraph 4: Among the alternatives listed in this question, only the first, the promise to advertise the product, was given by the distributor.

149. **(A)** See paragraph 5: Among the alternatives listed in the question, only the first, an interest free loan, was offered by Mr. Lubo.

150. **(B)** See paragraph 3: Mr. Sim had a patent; whether his product was more expensive than the use of frozen orange juice was not an issue. Of most importance, he lacked expansion capital.

151. **(A)** See paragraph 1: The *Major Objective* of the Congo was to provide a viable means by which its $1 billion trade deficit with the United States could be reduced.

152. **(B)** A *Major Factor* considered by Mr. Gage, the Congo's Trade Minister, in determining alternative trade strategies was the business recession in the United States at the time. This, of course, would affect the sale of Congo goods.

153. **(C)** That the Congo is an old client of the United States only means that reciprocal trade relations have been good. As such, it has led to a large trade deficit which the Congo is trying—unsuccessfully to date—to correct. However, it is a *Minor Factor*, related solely to the problem.

154. **(C)** Competition from Italy and France is a *Minor Factor*, relating to the problem of how to penetrate the United States market.

155. **(D)** Impending trade legislation in the United States is a *Major Assumption* which might be weighed by the decision maker, in this case Mr. Gage, when considering the alternative trade strategies suggested for the Congo.

156. **(C)** See paragraph 3: Protectionist trade legislation, the objective of which would be to restrict U.S. imports, was not given much chance of passage.

157. **(B)** Paragraph 4 states that it is difficult to measure the effectiveness of such promotion, ergo, the Trade Minister could not really make an evaluation.

158. **(D)** Both alternatives II and III are given in paragraph 4.

159. **(C)** See paragraph 3: Business groups were not mentioned.

160. **(E)** See paragraph 4: All three alternatives were considered by the Trade Minister.

Section VI — Analysis of Explanations

161. **(B)** This is a good illustration of the result. Therefore it is consistent with the fact situation (A) and the correct answer is (B).

162. **(E)** This is not inconsistent with the problem of unemployment of young people (A). It does not explain the present condition (B). Since this information is not deducible from anything in the fact situation or the result, (C) is not acceptable. It does not support or weaken the present situation (result) so we cannot accept (D). The correct answer is (E) since it is irrelevant to an explanation of the result.

163. **(E)** This does not deny that the statistics are valid (A). It does not explain the result (B). Since this does not have to be true, (C) is incorrect. It does not give evidence to support or weaken the result so (D) is not acceptable and (E) is the correct choice.

164. **(B)** This is another illustration. See the analysis for question **161**.

165. **(C)** This is not inconsistent with the fact situation or the result (A). It does not explain the result since the community may be represented by all age groups (B). The correct answer is (C) because it is true and deducible from the statements made in the selection. This would indicate that people from all age groups question the work ethic.

166. **(B)** This is consistent with the result (A). It gives evidence supportive of the result (B).

167. **(A)** The correct answer is (A) because this questions the validity of the statistics given in the fact situation.

168. **(E)** This is not contradictory to anything in the selection (A). It does not explain the result (B). It is not deducible from anything in the fact situation or the result (C) and neither supports nor weakens the result (D). Therefore the correct answer is (E).

169. **(B)** This is consistent with the facts of the result (A). It is an illustration of the appearance of a new breed that questions the work ethic as well as our welfare system. Therefore the correct answer is (B).

170. **(E)** This Supreme Court decision does not contradict the fact situation or the result (A). Since it does not explain the result, (B) is not acceptable. It is not deducible from anything in the selection (C) and does not support or weaken the result (D). Therefore the correct answer is (E).

171. **(E)** The analysis of this question is similar to that of statement 162. The difference between these two is that statement 162 offers more competition for jobs while this question provides openings of employment. However, as the selection states, the new breed of males would not be affected greatly by the supply and demand of the labor market.

172. **(D)** This is not inconsistent with the fact situation or the result (A). Since it does not mention that the graduate students detected the student violations, (B) is not acceptable. This is not deducible from anything in the fact situation (C). The correct answer is (D) because it helps explain the care with which the term papers were scrutinized.

173. **(E)** The work in the library might have been proper so that it is consistent with the fact situation (A). Since the photocopying may have nothing to do with the papers returned with unsatisfactory ratings, (B) is not acceptable. This is not deducible from anything in the selection (C). Since it neither supports nor weakens the result, (D) is incorrect and (E) is the correct choice.

174. **(B)** This is consistent with the result (A). It does give an adequate explanation for the professor's action (result). Therefore (B) is correct.

175. **(C)** This is not in contradiction to the professor's concern about honesty (A). It does not explain the result because it is possible that the students did not use this service (B). It is deducible from the fact situation. Evidently, the professor was aware of this service and he hoped to prevent his students from using it.

176. **(A)** This contradicts the fact that a term paper was to be at least 24 pages in length. Therefore (A) is correct.

177. **(B)** This is not inconsistent with the result (A). The correct answer is (B) because it gives a reason for the unsatisfactory rating of Philip's paper (the result).

178. **(A)** This contradicts the fact that the professor and his assistants detected all cases of cheating. Since it contradicts the results, the correct answer is (A).

179. **(E)** With special permission this did not violate the rules set down (A). Since it does not explain the result, (B) is not acceptable. It is not deducible from anything in the fact situation or the result (C). Since it neither supports nor weakens the result, (D) is not acceptable and (E) is the correct answer.

180. **(B)** See the analysis for statement 177.

181. **(C)** This is consistent with the fact situation (A). Since it does not explain why Joan reacted as she did (B) is not correct. The correct answer is (C) because the action of the employees of the department store was in accordance with the policy of the store. It is deducible from the fact situation.

182. **(E)** This does not contradict anything in the fact situation or the result (A). Since it does not explain Joan's reaction, (B) is not acceptable. This is not deducible from anything in the selection (C). Since it neither supports nor weakens an explanation of the result, (D) is incorrect and (E) is the correct answer.

183. **(B)** This is consistent with the result (A). The correct answer is (B) because it gives an explanation for Joan's decision, though the employees did everything in accordance with store policy.

184. **(A)** Mr. Brown's decision is contrary to the reaction of his wife. Therefore the correct answer is (A).

185. **(C)** This is in accordance with the fact situation. The store policy was followed by making an allowance for the returned article at the current reduced price (A). It does not explain the result (B). It can be deduced from the fact situation. Therefore (C) is correct.

186. **(E)** This does not contradict anything in the fact situation or the result (A). It does not explain the result (B). It cannot be deduced from anything that happened (C). Since it does not weaken or support an explanation of the result, (D) is not acceptable and (E) is the correct choice.

187. **(E)** This is not inconsistent with the fact situation or the result (A). It does not explain the result (B). This fact cannot be deduced from anything in the selection (C). Since this neither supports nor weakens the explanation of the result, (D) is not acceptable and (E) is the correct choice.

188. **(B)** This is consistent with the fact situation (A). It does give a clue to the inconvenience that Joan experienced and presents a possible reason for her reaction (the result). Therefore (B) is the correct choice.

189. **(C)** This does not contradict anything in the selection (A). It does not explain the result (B) but it can be assumed that the store would want to check to see whether the returned merchandise had been worn. Therefore it is deducible from the fact situation and the correct choice is (C).

190. **(A)** This is contrary to the fact situation. There is no mention of the fact that Joan was returning the sweater because of poor workmanship.

191. **(C)** This is consistent with the facts of the selection (A). Since it does not explain the action of the law makers, (B) is not acceptable. It is deducible from the facts since it presents an illustration of the practice. Therefore (C) is the correct answer.

192. **(C)** This does not deny anything in the fact situation (A). Since it does not explain the reason for the legislation, (B) is also incorrect. Since it presents a reason for concern by consumers, it is deducible from the fact situation and (C) is correct.

193. **(E)** This is not denied in the fact situation (A). It does not explain the reason for the result (B). Since the statement need not be true, (C) is not acceptable. The effect of this drug neither weakens nor strengthens the result since this factor is not relevant. Therefore (D) is incorrect and the correct choice is (E).

194. **(B)** This does not deny any facts in the selection (A). Since it shows consumer concern for solving the problem, it presents a possible explanation for the introduction of legislation by their elected representatives (result). Therefore (B) is correct.

195. **(D)** This is in line with the fact situation and the result (B). It does not explain the result (B) nor can it be deduced from anything in the selection (C). However it tends to weaken the action of state legislators by using "scare" tactics. Therefore (D) is correct.

196. **(B)** This is consistent with the fact situation (A). The correct answer is (B) because it shows the need for legislation to protect the consumer.

197. **(D)** The analysis of this question is similar to that for statement 195.

198. **(E)** This statement explains safety precautions taken by this government agency but the selection deals with economy. Since it does not contradict anything, (A) is incorrect. Since it does not explain the need for legislation, (B) is not acceptable. Since it is not deducible from anything in the fact situation or the result, (C) is incorrect. It does not support or weaken the result. Therefore, (D) is not acceptable and (E) is the correct choice.

199. **(C)** This does not deny any statement in the selection (A). It does not explain the result (B). The correct answer is (C) since it can be assumed that the profit motive is behind the present situation in the drug industry.

200. **(A)** This contradicts what the fact situation states. According to this statement not all products containing meprobamate have the same efficacy.

Evaluating Your Score

Tabulate your score for each section of Sample Test 2 according to the directions on pages 4–5 and record the results in the Self-scoring Table below. Then find your rank for each score on the Self-scoring Scale and record it in the appropriate blank.

Self-scoring Table

PART	SCORE	RANK
1		
2		
3		
4		
5		
6		

Self-scoring Scale

PART	ACHIEVEMENT			
	POOR	FAIR	GOOD	EXCELLENT
1	0–15	16–21	22–25	26–30
2	0–29	30–40	41–47	48–55
3	0–20	21–28	29–34	35–40
4	0– 7	8–10	11–12	13–15
5	0–10	11–14	15–16	17–20
6	0–20	21–28	29–34	35–40

Study again the Review sections covering material in Sample Test 2 for which you had a rank of FAIR or POOR. Then go on to Sample Test 3.

To obtain an approximation of your actual GMAT score see page 5.

Answer Sheet — Sample Test 3

Section I — Reading Recall

1. Ⓐ Ⓑ Ⓒ Ⓓ Ⓔ
2. Ⓐ Ⓑ Ⓒ Ⓓ Ⓔ
3. Ⓐ Ⓑ Ⓒ Ⓓ Ⓔ
4. Ⓐ Ⓑ Ⓒ Ⓓ Ⓔ
5. Ⓐ Ⓑ Ⓒ Ⓓ Ⓔ
6. Ⓐ Ⓑ Ⓒ Ⓓ Ⓔ
7. Ⓐ Ⓑ Ⓒ Ⓓ Ⓔ

8. Ⓐ Ⓑ Ⓒ Ⓓ Ⓔ
9. Ⓐ Ⓑ Ⓒ Ⓓ Ⓔ
10. Ⓐ Ⓑ Ⓒ Ⓓ Ⓔ
11. Ⓐ Ⓑ Ⓒ Ⓓ Ⓔ
12. Ⓐ Ⓑ Ⓒ Ⓓ Ⓔ
13. Ⓐ Ⓑ Ⓒ Ⓓ Ⓔ
14. Ⓐ Ⓑ Ⓒ Ⓓ Ⓔ

15. Ⓐ Ⓑ Ⓒ Ⓓ Ⓔ
16. Ⓐ Ⓑ Ⓒ Ⓓ Ⓔ
17. Ⓐ Ⓑ Ⓒ Ⓓ Ⓔ
18. Ⓐ Ⓑ Ⓒ Ⓓ Ⓔ
19. Ⓐ Ⓑ Ⓒ Ⓓ Ⓔ
20. Ⓐ Ⓑ Ⓒ Ⓓ Ⓔ
21. Ⓐ Ⓑ Ⓒ Ⓓ Ⓔ
22. Ⓐ Ⓑ Ⓒ Ⓓ Ⓔ

23. Ⓐ Ⓑ Ⓒ Ⓓ Ⓔ
24. Ⓐ Ⓑ Ⓒ Ⓓ Ⓔ
25. Ⓐ Ⓑ Ⓒ Ⓓ Ⓔ
26. Ⓐ Ⓑ Ⓒ Ⓓ Ⓔ
27. Ⓐ Ⓑ Ⓒ Ⓓ Ⓔ
28. Ⓐ Ⓑ Ⓒ Ⓓ Ⓔ
29. Ⓐ Ⓑ Ⓒ Ⓓ Ⓔ
30. Ⓐ Ⓑ Ⓒ Ⓓ Ⓔ

Section II — Mathematics

31. Ⓐ Ⓑ Ⓒ Ⓓ Ⓔ
32. Ⓐ Ⓑ Ⓒ Ⓓ Ⓔ
33. Ⓐ Ⓑ Ⓒ Ⓓ Ⓔ
34. Ⓐ Ⓑ Ⓒ Ⓓ Ⓔ
35. Ⓐ Ⓑ Ⓒ Ⓓ Ⓔ
36. Ⓐ Ⓑ Ⓒ Ⓓ Ⓔ
37. Ⓐ Ⓑ Ⓒ Ⓓ Ⓔ
38. Ⓐ Ⓑ Ⓒ Ⓓ Ⓔ
39. Ⓐ Ⓑ Ⓒ Ⓓ Ⓔ
40. Ⓐ Ⓑ Ⓒ Ⓓ Ⓔ
41. Ⓐ Ⓑ Ⓒ Ⓓ Ⓔ
42. Ⓐ Ⓑ Ⓒ Ⓓ Ⓔ
43. Ⓐ Ⓑ Ⓒ Ⓓ Ⓔ

44. Ⓐ Ⓑ Ⓒ Ⓓ Ⓔ
45. Ⓐ Ⓑ Ⓒ Ⓓ Ⓔ
46. Ⓐ Ⓑ Ⓒ Ⓓ Ⓔ
47. Ⓐ Ⓑ Ⓒ Ⓓ Ⓔ
48. Ⓐ Ⓑ Ⓒ Ⓓ Ⓔ
49. Ⓐ Ⓑ Ⓒ Ⓓ Ⓔ
50. Ⓐ Ⓑ Ⓒ Ⓓ Ⓔ
51. Ⓐ Ⓑ Ⓒ Ⓓ Ⓔ
52. Ⓐ Ⓑ Ⓒ Ⓓ Ⓔ
53. Ⓐ Ⓑ Ⓒ Ⓓ Ⓔ
54. Ⓐ Ⓑ Ⓒ Ⓓ Ⓔ
55. Ⓐ Ⓑ Ⓒ Ⓓ Ⓔ
56. Ⓐ Ⓑ Ⓒ Ⓓ Ⓔ
57. Ⓐ Ⓑ Ⓒ Ⓓ Ⓔ

58. Ⓐ Ⓑ Ⓒ Ⓓ Ⓔ
59. Ⓐ Ⓑ Ⓒ Ⓓ Ⓔ
60. Ⓐ Ⓑ Ⓒ Ⓓ Ⓔ
61. Ⓐ Ⓑ Ⓒ Ⓓ Ⓔ
62. Ⓐ Ⓑ Ⓒ Ⓓ Ⓔ
63. Ⓐ Ⓑ Ⓒ Ⓓ Ⓔ
64. Ⓐ Ⓑ Ⓒ Ⓓ Ⓔ
65. Ⓐ Ⓑ Ⓒ Ⓓ Ⓔ
66. Ⓐ Ⓑ Ⓒ Ⓓ Ⓔ
67. Ⓐ Ⓑ Ⓒ Ⓓ Ⓔ
68. Ⓐ Ⓑ Ⓒ Ⓓ Ⓔ
69. Ⓐ Ⓑ Ⓒ Ⓓ Ⓔ
70. Ⓐ Ⓑ Ⓒ Ⓓ Ⓔ
71. Ⓐ Ⓑ Ⓒ Ⓓ Ⓔ

72. Ⓐ Ⓑ Ⓒ Ⓓ Ⓔ
73. Ⓐ Ⓑ Ⓒ Ⓓ Ⓔ
74. Ⓐ Ⓑ Ⓒ Ⓓ Ⓔ
75. Ⓐ Ⓑ Ⓒ Ⓓ Ⓔ
76. Ⓐ Ⓑ Ⓒ Ⓓ Ⓔ
77. Ⓐ Ⓑ Ⓒ Ⓓ Ⓔ
78. Ⓐ Ⓑ Ⓒ Ⓓ Ⓔ
79. Ⓐ Ⓑ Ⓒ Ⓓ Ⓔ
80. Ⓐ Ⓑ Ⓒ Ⓓ Ⓔ
81. Ⓐ Ⓑ Ⓒ Ⓓ Ⓔ
82. Ⓐ Ⓑ Ⓒ Ⓓ Ⓔ
83. Ⓐ Ⓑ Ⓒ Ⓓ Ⓔ
84. Ⓐ Ⓑ Ⓒ Ⓓ Ⓔ
85. Ⓐ Ⓑ Ⓒ Ⓓ Ⓔ

Section III — Verbal Aptitude

86. Ⓐ Ⓑ Ⓒ Ⓓ Ⓔ
87. Ⓐ Ⓑ Ⓒ Ⓓ Ⓔ
88. Ⓐ Ⓑ Ⓒ Ⓓ Ⓔ
89. Ⓐ Ⓑ Ⓒ Ⓓ Ⓔ
90. Ⓐ Ⓑ Ⓒ Ⓓ Ⓔ
91. Ⓐ Ⓑ Ⓒ Ⓓ Ⓔ
92. Ⓐ Ⓑ Ⓒ Ⓓ Ⓔ
93. Ⓐ Ⓑ Ⓒ Ⓓ Ⓔ
94. Ⓐ Ⓑ Ⓒ Ⓓ Ⓔ
95. Ⓐ Ⓑ Ⓒ Ⓓ Ⓔ

96. Ⓐ Ⓑ Ⓒ Ⓓ Ⓔ
97. Ⓐ Ⓑ Ⓒ Ⓓ Ⓔ
98. Ⓐ Ⓑ Ⓒ Ⓓ Ⓔ
99. Ⓐ Ⓑ Ⓒ Ⓓ Ⓔ
100. Ⓐ Ⓑ Ⓒ Ⓓ Ⓔ
101. Ⓐ Ⓑ Ⓒ Ⓓ Ⓔ
102. Ⓐ Ⓑ Ⓒ Ⓓ Ⓔ
103. Ⓐ Ⓑ Ⓒ Ⓓ Ⓔ
104. Ⓐ Ⓑ Ⓒ Ⓓ Ⓔ
105. Ⓐ Ⓑ Ⓒ Ⓓ Ⓔ

106. Ⓐ Ⓑ Ⓒ Ⓓ Ⓔ
107. Ⓐ Ⓑ Ⓒ Ⓓ Ⓔ
108. Ⓐ Ⓑ Ⓒ Ⓓ Ⓔ
109. Ⓐ Ⓑ Ⓒ Ⓓ Ⓔ
110. Ⓐ Ⓑ Ⓒ Ⓓ Ⓔ
111. Ⓐ Ⓑ Ⓒ Ⓓ Ⓔ
112. Ⓐ Ⓑ Ⓒ Ⓓ Ⓔ
113. Ⓐ Ⓑ Ⓒ Ⓓ Ⓔ
114. Ⓐ Ⓑ Ⓒ Ⓓ Ⓔ
115. Ⓐ Ⓑ Ⓒ Ⓓ Ⓔ

116. Ⓐ Ⓑ Ⓒ Ⓓ Ⓔ
117. Ⓐ Ⓑ Ⓒ Ⓓ Ⓔ
118. Ⓐ Ⓑ Ⓒ Ⓓ Ⓔ
119. Ⓐ Ⓑ Ⓒ Ⓓ Ⓔ
120. Ⓐ Ⓑ Ⓒ Ⓓ Ⓔ
121. Ⓐ Ⓑ Ⓒ Ⓓ Ⓔ
122. Ⓐ Ⓑ Ⓒ Ⓓ Ⓔ
123. Ⓐ Ⓑ Ⓒ Ⓓ Ⓔ
124. Ⓐ Ⓑ Ⓒ Ⓓ Ⓔ
125. Ⓐ Ⓑ Ⓒ Ⓓ Ⓔ

Section IV — Data Sufficiency

126. Ⓐ Ⓑ Ⓒ Ⓓ Ⓔ 129. Ⓐ Ⓑ Ⓒ Ⓓ Ⓔ 133. Ⓐ Ⓑ Ⓒ Ⓓ Ⓔ 137. Ⓐ Ⓑ Ⓒ Ⓓ Ⓔ
127. Ⓐ Ⓑ Ⓒ Ⓓ Ⓔ 130. Ⓐ Ⓑ Ⓒ Ⓓ Ⓔ 134. Ⓐ Ⓑ Ⓒ Ⓓ Ⓔ 138. Ⓐ Ⓑ Ⓒ Ⓓ Ⓔ
128. Ⓐ Ⓑ Ⓒ Ⓓ Ⓔ 131. Ⓐ Ⓑ Ⓒ Ⓓ Ⓔ 135. Ⓐ Ⓑ Ⓒ Ⓓ Ⓔ 139. Ⓐ Ⓑ Ⓒ Ⓓ Ⓔ
                    132. Ⓐ Ⓑ Ⓒ Ⓓ Ⓔ 136. Ⓐ Ⓑ Ⓒ Ⓓ Ⓔ 140. Ⓐ Ⓑ Ⓒ Ⓓ Ⓔ

Section V — Business Judgment

141. Ⓐ Ⓑ Ⓒ Ⓓ Ⓔ 147. Ⓐ Ⓑ Ⓒ Ⓓ Ⓔ 153. Ⓐ Ⓑ Ⓒ Ⓓ Ⓔ 159. Ⓐ Ⓑ Ⓒ Ⓓ Ⓔ
142. Ⓐ Ⓑ Ⓒ Ⓓ Ⓔ 148. Ⓐ Ⓑ Ⓒ Ⓓ Ⓔ 154. Ⓐ Ⓑ Ⓒ Ⓓ Ⓔ 160. Ⓐ Ⓑ Ⓒ Ⓓ Ⓔ
143. Ⓐ Ⓑ Ⓒ Ⓓ Ⓔ 149. Ⓐ Ⓑ Ⓒ Ⓓ Ⓔ 155. Ⓐ Ⓑ Ⓒ Ⓓ Ⓔ 161. Ⓐ Ⓑ Ⓒ Ⓓ Ⓔ
144. Ⓐ Ⓑ Ⓒ Ⓓ Ⓔ 150. Ⓐ Ⓑ Ⓒ Ⓓ Ⓔ 156. Ⓐ Ⓑ Ⓒ Ⓓ Ⓔ 162. Ⓐ Ⓑ Ⓒ Ⓓ Ⓔ
145. Ⓐ Ⓑ Ⓒ Ⓓ Ⓔ 151. Ⓐ Ⓑ Ⓒ Ⓓ Ⓔ 157. Ⓐ Ⓑ Ⓒ Ⓓ Ⓔ 163. Ⓐ Ⓑ Ⓒ Ⓓ Ⓔ
146. Ⓐ Ⓑ Ⓒ Ⓓ Ⓔ 152. Ⓐ Ⓑ Ⓒ Ⓓ Ⓔ 158. Ⓐ Ⓑ Ⓒ Ⓓ Ⓔ 164. Ⓐ Ⓑ Ⓒ Ⓓ Ⓔ
                                                        165. Ⓐ Ⓑ Ⓒ Ⓓ Ⓔ

Section VI — Mathematics

166. Ⓐ Ⓑ Ⓒ Ⓓ Ⓔ 176. Ⓐ Ⓑ Ⓒ Ⓓ Ⓔ 186. Ⓐ Ⓑ Ⓒ Ⓓ Ⓔ 196. Ⓐ Ⓑ Ⓒ Ⓓ Ⓔ
167. Ⓐ Ⓑ Ⓒ Ⓓ Ⓔ 177. Ⓐ Ⓑ Ⓒ Ⓓ Ⓔ 187. Ⓐ Ⓑ Ⓒ Ⓓ Ⓔ 197. Ⓐ Ⓑ Ⓒ Ⓓ Ⓔ
168. Ⓐ Ⓑ Ⓒ Ⓓ Ⓔ 178. Ⓐ Ⓑ Ⓒ Ⓓ Ⓔ 188. Ⓐ Ⓑ Ⓒ Ⓓ Ⓔ 198. Ⓐ Ⓑ Ⓒ Ⓓ Ⓔ
169. Ⓐ Ⓑ Ⓒ Ⓓ Ⓔ 179. Ⓐ Ⓑ Ⓒ Ⓓ Ⓔ 189. Ⓐ Ⓑ Ⓒ Ⓓ Ⓔ 199. Ⓐ Ⓑ Ⓒ Ⓓ Ⓔ
170. Ⓐ Ⓑ Ⓒ Ⓓ Ⓔ 180. Ⓐ Ⓑ Ⓒ Ⓓ Ⓔ 190. Ⓐ Ⓑ Ⓒ Ⓓ Ⓔ 200. Ⓐ Ⓑ Ⓒ Ⓓ Ⓔ
171. Ⓐ Ⓑ Ⓒ Ⓓ Ⓔ 181. Ⓐ Ⓑ Ⓒ Ⓓ Ⓔ 191. Ⓐ Ⓑ Ⓒ Ⓓ Ⓔ 201. Ⓐ Ⓑ Ⓒ Ⓓ Ⓔ
172. Ⓐ Ⓑ Ⓒ Ⓓ Ⓔ 182. Ⓐ Ⓑ Ⓒ Ⓓ Ⓔ 192. Ⓐ Ⓑ Ⓒ Ⓓ Ⓔ 202. Ⓐ Ⓑ Ⓒ Ⓓ Ⓔ
173. Ⓐ Ⓑ Ⓒ Ⓓ Ⓔ 183. Ⓐ Ⓑ Ⓒ Ⓓ Ⓔ 193. Ⓐ Ⓑ Ⓒ Ⓓ Ⓔ 203. Ⓐ Ⓑ Ⓒ Ⓓ Ⓔ
174. Ⓐ Ⓑ Ⓒ Ⓓ Ⓔ 184. Ⓐ Ⓑ Ⓒ Ⓓ Ⓔ 194. Ⓐ Ⓑ Ⓒ Ⓓ Ⓔ 204. Ⓐ Ⓑ Ⓒ Ⓓ Ⓔ
175. Ⓐ Ⓑ Ⓒ Ⓓ Ⓔ 185. Ⓐ Ⓑ Ⓒ Ⓓ Ⓔ 195. Ⓐ Ⓑ Ⓒ Ⓓ Ⓔ 205. Ⓐ Ⓑ Ⓒ Ⓓ Ⓔ

Sample Test 3

Section I   Reading Recall

TOTAL TIME: 35 minutes

Part A: TIME—15 minutes

DIRECTIONS: This part contains three reading passages. You are to read each one carefully. You will have fifteen minutes to study the three passages and twenty minutes to answer questions based on them. When answering the questions, you will *not* be allowed to refer back to the passages.

Passage 1:

. The main burden, of assuring that the resources of the federal government are well managed falls on relatively few of the five million men and women whom it employs. Under the department and agency heads there are 8,600 political, career, military, and foreign service executives—the top managers and professionals—who exert major influence on the manner in which the rest are directed and utilized. Below their level there are other thousands with assignments of some managerial significance, but we believe that the line of demarcation selected is the best available for our purposes in this attainment.

In addition to Presidential appointees in responsible posts, the 8,600 include the three highest grades under the Classification Act; the three highest grades in the postal field service; comparable grades in the foreign service; general officers in the military service; and similar classes in other special services and in agencies or positions excepted from the Classification Act.

There is no complete inventory of positions or people in federal service at this level. The lack may be explained by separate agency statutes and personnel systems, diffusion among so many special services, and absence of any central point (short of the President himself) with jurisdiction over all upper-level personnel of the government.

This Committee considers establishment and maintenance of a central inventory of these key people and positions to be an elementary necessity, a first step in improved management throughout the Executive Branch.

Top Presidential appointees, about 500 of them, bear the brunt of translating the philosophy and aims of the current administration into practical programs. This group includes the secretaries and assistant secretaries of cabinet departments, agency heads and their deputies, heads and members of boards and commissions with fixed terms, and chiefs and directors of major bureaus, divisions, and services. Appointments to many of these politically sensitive positions are made on recommendation by department or agency heads, but all are presumably responsible to Presidential leadership.

One qualification for office at this level is that there be no basic disagreement with Presidential political philosophy, at least so far as administrative judgments and actions are concerned. Apart from the bi-partisan boards and commissions, these men are normally identified with the political party of the President, or are sympathetic to it, although there are exceptions.

There are four distinguishable kinds of top Presidential appointees, including:

— Those whom the President selects at the outset to establish immediate and effective control over the government (e.g., Cabinet secretaries, agency heads, his own White House staff and Executive Office Personnel).

— Those selected by department and agency heads in order to establish control within their respective organizations (e.g.— assistant secretaries, deputies, assistants to, and major line posts in some bureaus and divisions).

— High-level appointees who— though often requiring clearance through political or interest group channels, or both— must have known scientific or technical competence (e.g.— the Surgeon General, the Commissioner of Education).

— Those named to residual positions traditionally filled on a partisan patronage basis.

These appointees are primarily regarded as policy makers and overseers of policy execution. In practice, however, they usually have substantial responsibilities in line management, often requiring a thorough knowledge of substantive agency programs.

Passage 2:

Under state fair trade acts, a producer or distributor of a good bearing his brand, trademark, or name can prescribe by contract either a minimum or stipulated resale price of that good, depending upon the particular state law. Prior to the passage of the fair trade laws, resale price maintenance agreements were considered illegal because such agreements by a producer with more than one distributor prevent price competition among those distributors. The effect is the same as if the distributors had combined and agreed to fix price.

In late 1963, forty states had fair trade laws; of these, twenty-three had "nonsigner" clauses. According to the nonsigner provision, all resellers are bound by the terms of the resale price maintenance contract signed by any *one* reseller. To be truly effective, a state fair trade law must contain a nonsigner provision; for unless the manufacturer has some control over the noncontracting price-cutter, there can be little effective control by the manufacturer over resale prices. In addition, in late 1963 special legislation in nine states made resale price maintenance with respect to alcoholic beverages either mandatory or subject to control by state liquor control agencies.

Not all branded goods are covered by the fair trade laws. Closeout sales are excepted. Exceptions are made in some of these laws on sales to colleges and libraries. Some make provisions to except damaged goods or those from which the brand or trade names have been removed or obliterated.

An obstacle to the success of fair trade is the fact that cut-price mail-order shipments of goods out of an area which has no fair trade law into a fair trade state cannot be prevented by an enforcement action under the fair trade law of the state into which the goods are shipped. For the buyer takes title to the goods in the location from which the goods are shipped. The mail-order business can thus be used to evade a state fair trade act. Likewise, an advertisement within a fair-trade state of cut prices of goods available in a non-fair-trade area has been judged not to be within the jurisdiction of the state fair trade law. Sales from within a fair-trade state to customers outside the state in a non-fair-trade area cannot, however, be made at cut prices.

Maintaining a fair-trade program is fraught with several legal problems. Responsibility for enforcement falls upon the producer or distributor, who must monitor and take legal action against the price-cutters. Legal enforcement must be continuous, vigorous, and effective; it cannot be selective. An assortment of marketing devices contrived by retailers to evade fair-trade prices, such as the granting of trading stamps in abnormally high volume or the placing of excessive value on the trade-in of durable consumer items, must be dealt with by court action. Further, utilization of fair trade prevents a manufacturer from itself selling in competition with those distributors, either wholesalers or retailers, who are governed by its fair-trade contracts, for the effect of such an arrangement is a horizontal agreement.

Passage 3:

U.S. trade with Eastern Europe has been small basically because of a determination, which was reflected in both government and business, that we did not want to engage in this kind of trade, that it was not in the national interest, not only for security reasons, but because of the whole antagonistic atmosphere that has prevailed over the last twenty-five years.

Many businessmen feel that this basic antagonism has very substantially disappeared. The Nixon Administration has been rather cautious in moving to any liberalization in terms of our legislative posture toward this area of the world. Surprisingly, Congress, particularly the Senate, has been pressing the Administration to do more.

The House has been tranquil on the subject, being content to follow the lead of the Senate and the Administration. In the Executive Branch, there is no question that in 1969 there was very sharp, very deep, and sometimes very bitter division as to what our policy should be. The President had said, rather ambivalently, that he favored liberalization of trade "at the appropriate time," thus allowing considerable room to maneuver. The issue first arose when the Export Control Act came up for renewal during 1969. The basic division was, of course, obvious within the Administration.

It is surprising that so many businessmen, when inquiring about license applications, are totally unaware of what happens when a major project is presented to the government —what steps it goes through before a decision is reached. It might be worthwhile to touch very briefly on this matter.

In the Executive Branch of government there are three basic interest groups, all of whom are deeply concerned with any major issue of economic activity in this area.

First, our defense establishment, which has responsibility for security and which interprets this responsibility very narrowly. It is not interested in any offsets or any balancing of trade. It considers itself a highly professional organization. In considering a project, it asks only whether our national security is jeopardized—there are no peripheral arguments. When the project has any real magnitude, when it makes a major contribution to the economic base of the host country, the answer from the defense establishment is that there is a security consideration and it therefore opposes the project.

On the other hand, the political group, which is centered in the State Department, is interested primarily in foreign relations. Here there is deep commitment to build east-west bridges and traditionally to support any activity that will facilitate or encourage broader trade.

Third, the Commerce Department has the responsibility both for expanding exports and for administering the Export Control Act. The Commerce Department feels that it factors these various elements and has a responsibility to the entire business community. It has a deep awareness that even if we in the United States do not authorize these transactions there is almost always comparable technology in other parts of the world. Further, the department feels that it is self-defeating to deny export license applications out of a transcendent concern for national security.

Usually, then, both the Commerce and the State Departments are in favor of approving such applications. When there is any division (there is a very strange rule of unanimity in government—that nothing can happen unless everybody is in agreement), the case moves to the White House where it often becomes involved in political byplay—whether concerned with oil in the Near East, prisoners of war in North Vietnam, or the SALT talks. However, major progress has been made in this area, particularly now that the National Security Council has advocated economic interests to a large degree and such interests in the White House have been transferred to the Council on International Economic Policy, whence it takes a separate route to the President.

If there is still time remaining, review the passages until all 15 minutes have elapsed.
Do not look at Part B until that time.

Part B: TIME—20 minutes

DIRECTIONS: Answer the following questions referring to information contained in the three passages you have just read. You may not turn back to those passages for assistance.

QUESTIONS TO

Passage 1:

1. According to the passage, about how many top managerial professionals work for the federal government?

    (A) five million
    (B) two million
    (C) twenty thousand
    (D) ten thousand
    (E) five thousand

2. No complete inventory exists of positions in the three highest levels of government service because

    (A) no one bothered to count them
    (B) computers cannot handle all the data
    (C) separate agency personnel systems are used
    (D) the President never requested such information
    (E) the Classification Act prohibits a census

3. Top Presidential appointees translate the aims of the administration into

    (A) action
    (B) political decisions
    (C) practical programs
    (D) legislation
    (E) fruition

4. Top Presidential appointees must be in agreement with the President's political philosophy in which of the following areas?

    I.   Administrative judgments
    II. Administrative actions
    III. Administrative policies

    (A) I only
    (B) III only
    (C) I and II only
    (D) II and III only
    (E) I, II, and III

5. Applicants for Presidential appointments are usually identified with or are members of

    (A) large corporations
    (B) the foreign service
    (C) government bureaus
    (D) academic circles
    (E) the President's political party

6. Appointees that are selected by the President include

    (A) U.S. marshalls and attorneys
    (B) military officers
    (C) agency heads
    (D) commissioners
    (E) congressional committee members

7. Appointees usually have to possess expertise in

    (A) line management
    (B) military affairs
    (C) foreign affairs
    (D) strategic planning
    (E) constitutional law

8. According to the passage, Presidential appointees are regarded primarily as

    (A) highly competent individuals
    (B) policy makers
    (C) staff managers
    (D) decision-makers
    (E) career executives

9. Appointees selected by department and agency heads include

    (A) military men
    (B) cabinet secretaries
    (C) assistant secretaries
    (D) diplomats
    (E) residual position holders

10. This passage might have been extracted from a book about all of the following subjects except

    (A) public administration
    (B) political science
    (C) management
    (D) government
    (E) marketing

QUESTIONS TO

Passage 2:

11. Essentially fair trade legislation

    (A) allows manufacturers to stipulate the resale price of a good
    (B) allows manufacturers to bypass distributors in sales to retailers

    (C)   provides that manufacturers engage in fair and equal trade with distributors

    (D)   allows manufacturers to maintain a fair markup on their goods

    (E)   exempts resale items from anti-trust legislation

12. A "nonsigner clause" stipulates that

    (A)   all resellers who do not sign fair trade contracts are not bound by them

    (B)   all resellers are bound by the terms of the fair trade contract signed by one reseller

    (C)   resellers are not bound by law to sign fair trade contracts

    (D)   all branded goods are covered by the fair trade legislation

    (E)   "nonsigners" are exempt from the provisions of fair trade legislation

13. It can be inferred from the passage that fair trade laws would be most welcomed by

    (A)   discount stores   (D)   supermarkets

    (B)   wholesale distributors   (E)   gasoline stations

    (C)   small-volume retailers

14. An obstacle to the success of fair trade is that

    (A)   not all states have these laws

    (B)   not all resellers are bound by the laws

    (C)   cut-rate goods can be mailed from a non-fair-trade state

    (D)   manufacturers may not avail themselves of all privileges given by the legislation

    (E)   loss-leader selling is prohibited

15. Responsibility for enforcing fair trade falls on the

    (A)   state   (D)   manufacturer

    (B)   federal government   (E)   retailer

    (C)   courts

16. Some categories of goods are exempted from fair trade laws, such as

    (A)   pharmaceutical products   (D)   closeout sales

    (B)   alcoholic beverages   (E)   private label goods

    (C)   imports

17. At the time the passage was written, how many states had fair trade laws?

    (A)   all states   (D)   about thirty

    (B)   about ten   (E)   about forty

    (C)   about twenty

18. Retailers have used various methods to evade fair trade prices, such as

    (A)   refusing to comply with the law

    (B)   dealing with more than one supplier

    (C)   giving extra trading stamps

    (D)   giving extra discounts

    (E)   refusal to deal with the manufacturer

19. It is stated in the passage that fair trade laws are enacted by

   (A) states
   (B) the federal government
   (C) local municipalities
   (D) both states and the federal government
   (E) both states and local municipalities

20. It can be inferred from the passage that fair trade

   (A) stimulates competition among retailers
   (B) stifles competition among retailers
   (C) makes retailing less profitable
   (D) exempts many goods from legislation
   (E) is inexpensive to maintain and police

QUESTIONS TO

Passage 3:

21. U.S. trade with Eastern Europe has been small because

   (A) the terms of trade were unfavorable to the U.S.
   (B) the U.S. is anti-communist
   (C) such trade was not in the national interest of the U.S.
   (D) Eastern European goods are inferior
   (E) Eastern European countries did not want U.S. goods

22. According to the passage, U.S.–Eastern European trade prospects seem

   (A) favorable, because of Congressional approval
   (B) favorable, because of Presidential approval
   (C) doubtful, because of Congressional opposition
   (D) doubtful, because of Administration opposition
   (E) immediately possible

23. In matters of trade policy with Eastern Europe, the Executive Branch (in 1969) could be characterized as

   (A) unanimously in favor   (D) divided
   (B) favorably disposed   (E) against
   (C) uncertain

24. The author states that the Defense Department considers trade prospects only in light of

   (A) U.S. defense security   (D) their magnitude
   (B) their potential profitability   (E) their cost
   (C) their contribution to the host country

25. It is stated in the passage that the Export Control Act is administered by the

   (A) State Department   (D) National Security Council
   (B) Defense Department   (E) Executive Branch
   (C) Commerce Department

26. With respect to U.S.–East European trade, it is inferred that the State Department

 (A) favors more trade
 (B) takes a cautious approach
 (C) has a "wait-and-see" attitude
 (D) is not in favor of more trade at this time
 (E) will follow the lead of Congress

27. The positions of the Defense and Commerce Departments with respect to more U.S.–East European trade are

 (A) similar to each other
 (B) outdated
 (C) opposed to each other
 (D) self-defeating
 (E) in agreement with the State Department

28. The positions of the State and Commerce Departments with respect to more U.S.–East European trade are

 (A) similar to each other
 (B) outdated
 (C) opposed to each other
 (D) self-defeating
 (E) in agreement with the Defense Department

29. The Commerce Department feels that if the U.S. does not trade with Eastern European countries

 (A) our foreign relations will be affected
 (B) other countries will get this business
 (C) our balance of payments will deteriorate
 (D) our dollar reserves will shrink
 (E) our technology lead with the rest of the world will deteriorate

30. When there is divided opinion in the Executive Branch as to the approval of export licenses, the case goes to the

 (A) State Department
 (B) Council on International Economic Policy
 (C) National Security Council
 (D) White House
 (E) Commerce Department

If there is still time remaining, you may review the questions in this section only.
You may not look at Part A or turn to any other section of the test.

Section II   Mathematics

TIME: 75 minutes

DIRECTIONS: Solve each of the following problems; then indicate the correct answer on the answer sheet. [On the actual test you will be permitted to use any space available on the examination paper for scratch work.]

NOTE: A figure that appears with a problem is drawn as accurately as possible so as to provide information that may help in answering the question. Numbers in this test are real numbers.

31. If 64% of the students in a class got a grade of C and there are 200 students in the class, how many students in the class received a grade of C?

(A) 64
(B) 118
(C) 124

(D) 128
(E) 164

32. If $2x + y = 10$ and $x = 3$, what is $x - y$?

(A) −4
(B) −1
(C) 0

(D) 1
(E) 7

33. If a worker can pack $1/6$ of a carton of canned food in 15 minutes and there are 40 workers in a factory, how many cartons should be packed in the factory in $1\frac{2}{3}$ hours?

(A) 33
(B) $40\frac{2}{9}$
(C) $43\frac{4}{9}$

(D) $44\frac{4}{9}$
(E) $45\frac{2}{3}$

34. Potatoes cost 15¢ a pound. If the price of potatoes rises by 10%, how much will 10 pounds of potatoes cost?

(A) 17¢
(B) $1.50
(C) $1.60

(D) $1.65
(E) $1.75

35. A truck driver must complete a 180-mile trip in 4 hours. If he averages 50 miles an hour for the first three hours of his trip, how fast must he travel in the final hour?

(A) 30 mph
(B) 35 mph
(C) 40 mph

(D) 45 mph
(E) 50 mph

36. If a triangle has base B and the altitude of the triangle is twice the base, then the area of the triangle is

(A) $\frac{1}{2}AB$
(B) AB
(C) $\frac{1}{2}B^2$

(D) B^2
(E) $2B$

37. If the product of two numbers is 10 and the sum of the two numbers is 7, then the larger of the two numbers is

(A) −2
(B) 2
(C) 3

(D) 4¼
(E) 5

38. Oranges cost $x a bag for the first 100 bags a store buys from a wholesaler. All bags bought in addition to the first 100 get a discount of 10%. How much does it cost to buy 150 bags of oranges from the wholesaler?

(A) $100
(B) $140x
(C) $145x

(D) $150x
(E) $100x + $50

39. If the lengths of the two sides of a right triangle adjacent to the right angle are 8 and 15 respectively, then the length of the side opposite the right angle is.

(A) $\sqrt{258}$
(B) 15.8
(C) 16

(D) 17
(E) 17.9

40. A store sells a baseball glove for $10.20 and makes a profit of 20%. How much did the baseball glove cost the store?

(A) $8.30
(B) $8.50
(C) $8.92

(D) $9.15
(E) $9.65

41. It costs x¢ each to print the first 600 copies of a newspaper. It costs $\left(x - \dfrac{y}{10}\right)$¢ for every copy after the first 600. How much does it cost to print 1,500 copies of the newspaper?

(A) 1500x¢
(B) 150y¢
(C) (1500x − 90y)¢

(D) $(150x − 9y)
(E) $15x

42. If the side of a square increases by 40%, then the area of the square increases by

(A) 16%
(B) 40%
(C) 96%

(D) 116%
(E) 140%

43. If 28 cartons of soda cost $21.00, then 7 cartons of soda should cost

(A) $5.25
(B) $5.50
(C) $6.40

(D) $7.00
(E) $10.50

44. Plane P takes off at 2 A.M. and flies at an average speed of x mph. Plane Q takes off at 3:30 A.M. and flies the same route as P but travels at an average speed of y mph. Assuming that y is greater than x, how many hours after 3:30 A.M. will plane Q overtake plane P?

(A) $\frac{3}{2}x$ hrs.

(B) $\frac{3}{2}$ hrs.

(C) $\frac{3}{2y}$ hrs.

(D) $\frac{3}{2(y-x)}$ hrs.

(E) $\frac{3x}{2(y-x)}$ hrs.

45. A worker is paid $20 for each day he works, and he is paid proportionately for any fraction of a day he works. If during one week he works $\frac{1}{8}, \frac{2}{3}, \frac{3}{4}, \frac{1}{3}$, and 1 full day, what are his total earnings for the week?

(A) $40.75

(B) $52.50

(C) $54

(D) $57.50

(E) $58.25

Use the following table for questions 46–47.

DISTRIBUTION OF TEST SCORES IN A CLASS

Number of Students	Number of Correct Answers
10	36 to 40
16	32 to 35
12	28 to 31
14	26 to 27
8	0 to 25

46. What percent of the class answered 32 or more questions correctly?

(A) 20

(B) 26

(C) $32\frac{1}{2}$

(D) $43\frac{1}{3}$

(E) 52

47. The number of students who answered 28 to 31 questions correctly is x times the number who answered 25 or fewer correctly, where x is

(A) $\frac{2}{3}$

(B) 1

(C) $\frac{3}{2}$

(D) $\frac{7}{4}$

(E) 2

48. If the product of 3 consecutive integers is 210, then the sum of the two smaller integers is

(A) 5

(B) 11

(C) 12

(D) 13

(E) 18

49. Cereal costs $\frac{1}{3}$ as much as bacon. Bacon costs $\frac{5}{4}$ as much as eggs. Eggs cost what fraction of the cost of cereal?

(A) $\frac{5}{12}$ (D) $\frac{12}{5}$

(B) $\frac{5}{4}$ (E) $\frac{4}{5}$

(C) $\frac{5}{3}$

50. A truck gets 15 miles per gallon of gas when it is empty. When the truck is full, it travels only 80% as far on a gallon of gas as when empty. How many gallons will the loaded truck use to travel 80 miles?

(A) $5\frac{1}{3}$ (D) $6\frac{2}{3}$

(B) 6   (E) $6\frac{3}{4}$

(C) $6\frac{1}{3}$

51. If x and y are negative numbers, which of the following statements are always true?

I. $x - y$ is negative.   II. $-x$ is positive   III. $(-x)(-y)$ is positive.

(A) I only   (D) II and III only

(B) II only   (E) I and III only

(C) I and II only

52. A car travels at 70 miles an hour for the first hour and a half of a trip. After the first $1\frac{1}{2}$ hours the car travels at 50 miles an hour. How long will the car take to drive 200 miles?

(A) $1\frac{1}{2}$ hours   (D) $3\frac{1}{5}$ hours

(B) 2 hours   (E) $3\frac{2}{5}$ hours

(C) $2\frac{3}{5}$ hours

53. A manufacturer makes books at a cost of $\$x$ each for the first 1,000 copies. The second thousand copies cost $\$(x - 2y)$ each. How much will it cost to make 1,600 copies of a book?

(A) $\$1600x$ (D) $\$1600x - \$1200y$

(B) $\$160x + \$120y$ (E) $\$16,000x - \$1200y$

(C) $\$1600x + \$1200y$

54. If $\frac{1}{3} < x$, then

(A) x is greater than 1

(B) x is greater than 3

(C) $\frac{1}{x}$ is greater than 3

(D) $\frac{1}{x}$ is less than 3

(E) all of the above statements are true

55. $\frac{1}{3} + \frac{2}{7} = \frac{x}{42}$ where x is

(A) $\frac{13}{21}$

(B) 13

(C) 21

(D) 24.5

(E) 26

56. If $r + x + y + z = 12$ and x is less than 6, then at least k of the numbers $r, x, y,$ and z must be positive, where k is

(A) 0

(B) 1

(C) 2

(D) 3

(E) 4

57. If the radius of a sphere is increased by a factor of 2, then the volume of the sphere is increased by a factor of

(A) 1

(B) 2

(C) 4

(D) 6

(E) 8

58. Successive discounts of 10% and 15% are equivalent to a simple discount of

(A) 11.5%

(B) 16.5%

(C) 20%

(D) 23.5%

(E) 25%

59. How many rectangular tiles 4 inches wide and 6 inches long are necessary to cover the floor of a square room with sides 12 feet long?

(A) 6

(B) 60

(C) 144

(D) 576

(E) 864

60. If the two sides of a right triangle adjacent to the right angle have lengths $n - 1$ and $2\sqrt{n}$, then the length of the side of the triangle opposite the right angle is

(A) $n - 1$

(B) $4\sqrt{n}$

(C) $4n$

(D) $\sqrt{n^2 + 2n}$

(E) $n + 1$

61. Which of the following triangles has the largest area?

(A) an equilateral triangle whose sides have length 3, 3, 3

(B) an isosceles triangle whose sides have length 4, 4, 3½

(C) an equilateral triangle whose sides have length 4, 4, 4

(D) an isosceles triangle whose sides are 3, 3, 4

(E) all of the above

62. How much bigger is the area of a triangle with sides of length 3, 4, and 5 miles, than the area of a square whose sides are 2 miles long?

(A) 1 square mile
(B) 2 square miles
(C) 4 square miles
(D) 6 square miles
(E) 8 square miles

63. A worker is paid $2.50 an hour for the first 8 hours he works each day. He is paid one and a half of the regular rate for any time he works over 8 hours in a day. How long does he have to work to make $27.50 in a day?

(A) 8 hours
(B) 9 hours
(C) 9½ hours
(D) 10 hours
(E) 11 hours

64. How much simple interest will you have to pay if you borrow $650 for 6 months at an annual interest rate of 8%?

(A) $26.00
(B) $26.50
(C) $34.00
(D) $40.00
(E) $52.00

65. At 1 A.M. a car is traveling at 50 miles per hour. The driver accelerates so that at the end of each hour he is traveling 10% faster than he was at the beginning of the hour. How many miles per hour is the car traveling by 3 A.M.?

(A) 55
(B) 60
(C) 60.5
(D) 61.5
(E) 120

66. A function is given by the rule $f(x) = x^2 + 2$. What is $f(a + 2)$?

(A) $a^2 + 2$
(B) $a^2 + 4$
(C) $a^2 + 6$
(D) $a^2 + 2a + 4$
(E) $a^2 + 4a + 6$

67. If a car travels at a constant rate of 50 mph, how long will it take to travel 222½ miles?

(A) 3 hrs. 44 min.
(B) 4 hrs.
(C) 4 hrs. 22 min.
(D) 4 hrs. 27 min.
(E) 4 hrs. 44 min.

68. What is the length of *AB*?
Angle *ACB* is 90°; *AC* = 5; *CB* = 6.

(A) 7 (B) 7.5 (C) 7.67 (D) $\sqrt{61}$ (E) 8

69. If $x < 2$ and $y > 2$ then $x < y$

(A) always
(B) only if $y > 0$
(C) only if $x > 0$

(D) never
(E) sometimes

70. To increase the cross sectional area of a circular pipe by 44%, the diameter of the pipe should be increased by

(A) 4%
(B) 12%
(C) 16%

(D) 20%
(E) 44%

71. A car has 10 gallons of gas in its tank. The car gets $15 - x/10$ miles to the gallon when it travels at the rate of x mph. How many miles will the car travel at 45 mph before it runs out of gas?

(A) 105
(B) 110
(C) 115

(D) 120
(E) 150

72. If 3 men working independently and at the same rate turn out 210 boxes an hour, how many employees working at the same rate are necessary to produce 490 boxes an hour?

(A) 5
(B) 6
(C) 7

(D) 8
(E) 9

73. If one conveyer belt moves 4 tons of coal in 36 minutes and another conveyer moves 5 tons of coal in 40 minutes, how long should it take both conveyers working independently to move 3 tons of coal?

(A) $11\,^2/_5$ min
(B) $12\,^{12}/_{17}$ min
(C) $13\,^4/_{13}$ min

(D) 24 min
(E) 27 min

74. A company's profit rate is 5% on its first $1,000 of sales each day and $4\,^1/_4$% on all sales in excess of $1,000 for that day. How many dollars profit will the company make in a day when its sales are $5,235?

(A) $205.40
(B) $222.48
(C) $229.99
(D) $272.49
(E) $285.37

75. If $x + y = 3$ then $2x + 2y$ is equal to

(A) 3
(B) 6
(C) 8

(D) 10
(E) none of these

76. If $x > 3$ then $1/x$ is

(A) $> 1/3$
(B) $< 1/3$
(C) < 0

(D) negative
(E) > 3

77. If a bank charges interest at a rate of 5% on the first 1,000 dollars of a loan and 4% on the balance of the loan over the first thousand dollars, then what percent of 5,000 will it charge on a loan of $5,000?

(A) 4.1
(B) 4.2
(C) 4.25.

(D) 4.33
(E) 5

78. A toy was originally priced at $13.00 and then was discounted 10%. After a month the toy was sold at another 10% discount. How much was the toy sold for?

(A) $10.05
(B) $10.40
(C) $10.53

(D) $10.62
(E) $10.73

79. How much interest will $5,500 earn in a year at a rate of 6%?

(A) $30
(B) $33
(C) $300

(D) $330
(E) $333

80. If the price of a stock doubles every six months and it is currently selling at $1.00 a share, how long will it take before the stock is selling for more than $63 a share?

(A) 3 years
(B) 3.5 years
(C) 4 years

(D) 4.5 years
(E) 8 years

81. If a ton of coal and 500 gallons of oil together cost $1,000 and 3 tons of coal and 300 gallons of oil cost $1,200, how much does a gallon of oil cost?

(A) $1.00
(B) $1.25
(C) $1.45

(D) $1.50
(E) $10.00

82. If a diameter of a circle is doubled, then the area of the circle is

(A) the same
(B) doubled
(C) tripled

(D) quadrupled
(E) quintupled

83. If $\frac{x}{y} = 2$, then $\frac{y^2}{x^2}$ is equal to

(A) $\frac{1}{4}$

(B) $\frac{1}{2}$

(C) 1

(D) 2

(E) 4

84. An employer pays two workers X and Y a total of $550 a week. X is paid 120% of the amount that Y is paid. How much is Y paid each week?

(A) $200

(B) $235

(C) $250

(D) $260

(E) $300

85. A worker can work overtime a maximum of 2 days a week. If he makes x dollars a day when he works no overtime and he makes $x + y$ when he works overtime, what is the maximum amount he can make in a 5 day week?

(A) $5x$

(B) $3x + 3y$

(C) $3x + 2y$

(D) $5x + 2y$

(E) $5x + 5y$

If there is still time remaining, you may review the questions in this section only.
You may not turn to any other section of the test.

Section III Verbal Aptitude

TIME: 20 minutes

Antonyms

DIRECTIONS: For each question below, select the lettered word or phrase that comes closest to being *opposite* in meaning to the word appearing in capital letters. Be sure to consider all meanings carefully.

86. ABJURE: (A) injure (B) pledge (C) abdicate (D) realize (E) conjure

87. MITIGATE: (A) lose (B) transfer (C) intensify (D) abstain (E) extract

88. SPURIOUS: (A) soft (B) harmful (C) new (D) authentic (E) contradictory

89. TORRID: (A) wet (B) animated (C) cold (D) closed (E) even

90. CIRCUMSPECTION: (A) regret (B) humility (C) generosity (D) joy (E) recklessness

91. DESULTORY: (A) sad (B) methodical (C) rough (D) pleasant (E) contented

92. DISSONANCE: (A) heat (B) loudness (C) harmony (D) noise (E) disparity

93. INCREDULOUS: (A) irreligious (B) creditable (C) indifferent (D) believing (E) confused

94. OBDURATE: (A) unsusceptible (B) tender (C) right (D) intelligent (E) meager

95. UNGAINLY: (A) graceful (B) exceptional (C) winning (D) sensible (E) average

96. DISCERN: (A) observe (B) overlook (C) separate (D) include (E) disorganize

97. CONVIVIAL: (A) encouraging (B) unsociable (C) ignorant (D) tranquil (E) folksy

98. ALACRITY: (A) slowness (B) clarity (C) attractiveness (D) unfriendliness (E) culpability

99. PERFIDIOUS: (A) awkward (B) homely (C) faithful (D) comprehensible (E) ignorant

Word-Pair Relationships

DIRECTIONS: For each question below, determine the relationship between the pair of capitalized words and then select the lettered pair of words which have a similar relationship to the first pair.

100. COMPUTER : SLIDE RULE :: (A) car : driver (B) quadrant : teacher (C) reader : book (D) clock : sundial (E) solution : problem

101. BATTERY : FLASHLIGHT :: (A) sun : warmth (B) mercury : vapor (C) fertilizer : grass (D) tires : automobile (E) coal : furnace

102. MUFF : HANDS :: (A) helmet : head (B) polish : nails (C) glasses : eyes (D) anklet : legs (E) earring : ears

103. PHILATELIST : STAMPS :: (A) philanthropist : charity (B) entomologist : words (C) numismatist : medals (D) ornithologist : horticulture (E) government : taxes

104. PLACID : TRANQUILIZER :: (A) action : reaction (B) somnolent : sedative (C) cold : pill (D) run : frightened (E) traffic light : obey

105. MATURITY : INFANCY :: (A) culmination : inception (B) work : burden (C) applause : performance (D) seed : grass (E) foundation : building

106. FLORICULTURE : FLOWERS :: (A) gold : ore (B) bushel : grain (C) horticulture : raisins (D) cultivation : vegetables (E) arboriculture : trees

107. AVIARY : BIRDS :: (A) animals : zoo (B) money : bank (C) letters : post office (D) aquarium : fish (E) honey : bee-hive

108. MUSLIN : PLAIN :: (A) inlaid : tile (B) brocade : ornate (C) montage : colored (D) wool : decorated (E) linen : fragile

109. DISCOURSE : EPILOGUE :: (A) music : coda (B) speech : applause (C) stanza : poetry (D) sunset : dark (E) beginning : end

110. PLANE : PILOT :: (A) election : politician (B) conduct : police (C) radar : repairman (D) arms : captain (E) store : manager

111. DECADE : CENTURY :: (A) decibel : unit (B) decimeter : meter (C) decimal : equation (D) delineate : boundary (E) deuce : ace

112. MODEL : REALITY :: (A) blueprint : house (B) design : prototype (C) formula : chemical (D) hypothesis : theory (E) prognosis : diagnosis

Sentence Completions

DIRECTIONS: For each sentence below, select the lettered word or set of words which, when inserted in the sentence blanks, best completes the meaning of that sentence.

113. A _____ system depends upon the willingness of management to accept _____.

(A) business . . . payment (B) competitive . . . risks (C) socialist . . . dictatorship (D) communist . . . failures (E) patronage . . . bribes

114. With some exceptions, _____ generally have criticized advertising as _____.
(A) marketers . . . innocuous (B) consumers . . . helpful (C) economists . . . wasteful (D) businessmen . . . misleading (E) producers . . . ineffective

115. Attitudes are _____ to respond in an evaluative way toward objects.

(A) ways (B) bound (C) predispositions (D) believed (E) conditioned

116. The relationship between _____ and _____ has been closely studied.

(A) commodities . . . prices (B) research . . . development (C) advertising . . . sales (D) statistics . . . forecasting (E) commerce . . . inflation

117. The voters gave the winner a _____ without a _____.

(A) parade . . . permit (B) majority . . . plurality (C) victory . . . mandate
(D) plebiscite . . . referendum (E) majority . . . election

118. Caveat emptor, let the _____ beware!

(A) traitor (B) populace (C) assembly (D) buyer (E) trespasser

119. The _____ received an emolument.

(A) farmer (B) wife (C) employee (D) prisoner (E) lawyer

120. In spite of heavy bombing, the bridge was _____.

(A) extant (B) palliated (C) tumified (D) collapsed (E) promulgated

121. The malingerer thought he could escape the _____.

(A) voyage (B) ballgame (C) work (D) party (E) election

122. Wars usually result from _____ among the parties involved.

(A) dissonance (B) doubt (C) prudence (D) disagreement (E) frustration

123. The _____ action of the participants led the referee to _____ the fight.

(A) belligerent . . . cancel (B) enthusiastic . . . begin (C) unwarranted . . . stop
(D) inert . . . postpone (E) wild . . . enter

124. At the scene of the crime, the _____ was apprehended.

(A) victim (B) assailant (C) malefactor (D) observer (E) delinquent

125. Smoothness in the flow of _____ is an essential part of good _____ writing.

(A) supposition . . . newspaper (B) words . . . order (C) information . . . report
(D) facts . . . novel (E) fiction . . . chronicle

If there is still time remaining, you may review the questions in this section only.
You may not turn to any other section of the test.

Section IV   ·Data Sufficiency

TIME: 15 minutes

DIRECTIONS: Each of the following problems has a question and two statements which are labeled (1) and (2). Use the data given in (1) and (2) together with other available information (such as the number of hours in a day, the definition of *clockwise*, mathematical facts, etc.) to decide whether the statements are *sufficient* to answer the question. Then fill in space

(A) if you can get the answer from (1) alone but not from (2) alone;

(B) if you can get the answer from (2) alone but not from (1) alone;

(C) if you can get the answer from (1) and (2) together, although neither statement by itself suffices;

(D) if statement (1) alone suffices *and* statement (2) alone suffices;

(E) if you cannot get the answer from statements (1) and (2) together, but need even more data.

All numbers used in this section are real numbers. A figure given for a problem is intended to provide information consistent with that in the question, but not necessarily with the additional information contained in the statements.

126.   In triangle *ABC*, find *x* if *y* = 40.

   (1)   *AB* = *BC*
   (2)   *z* = 100

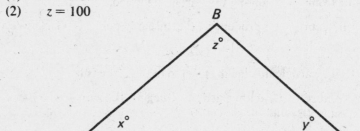

127.   What is the area of the shaded part of the circle? *O* is the center of the circle.

   (1)   The radius of the circle is 4.
   (2)   *x* is 60.

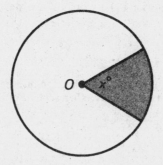

128.   What was Mr. Kliman's income in 1970?

   (1)   His total income for 1968, 1969, and 1970 was $41,000.
   (2)   He made 20% more in 1969 than he did in 1968.

129. If l and l' are straight lines, find y.

   (1) $x = 100$
   (2) $z = 80$

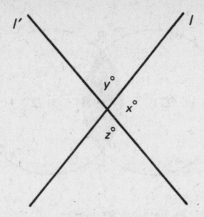

130. Fifty students have signed up for at least one of the courses German I and English I. How many of the 50 students are taking German I but not English I?

   (1) 16 students are taking German I and English I.
   (2) The number of students taking English I but not German I is the same as the number taking German I but not English I.

131. Is $ABCD$ a square?

   (1) $AD = AB$
   (2) $x = 90$

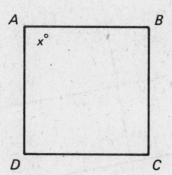

132. The XYZ Corporation has 7,000 employees. What is the average yearly wage of an employee of the XYZ Corporation?

   (1) 4,000 of the employees are executives.
   (2) The total amount the company pays in wages each year is $77,000,000.

133. Is $x > y$?

   (1) $(x + y)^2 > 0$
   (2) x is positive

134. What is the area of the shaded region if both circles have radius 4 and O and O' are the centers of the circles?

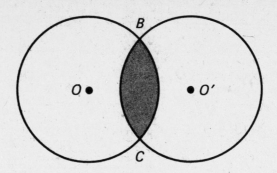

(1) The area enclosed by both circles is 29π.
(2) The line connecting O and O' is perpendicular to the line connecting B and C (B and C are the points where the two circles intersect).

135. How long will it take to travel from A to B? It takes 4 hours to travel from A to B and back to A.

(1) It takes 25% more time to travel from A to B than it does to travel from B to A.
(2) C is midway between A and B, and it takes 2 hours to travel from A to C and back to A.

136. l, l', and k are straight lines. Are l and l' parallel?

(1) $x = y$
(2) $y = z$

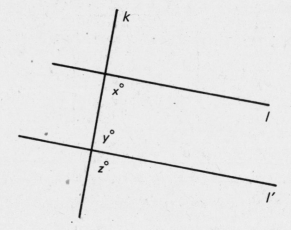

137. What is $x + y + z$?

(1) $x + y = 3$
(2) $x + z = 2$

138. How much cardboard will it take to make a rectangular box with a lid the length of whose base is 7 inches?

(1) The width of the box will be 5 inches.
(2) The height of the box will be 4 inches.

139. What is the profit on 15 boxes of detergent?

    (1) The cost of a crate of boxes of detergent is $50.

    (2) Each crate contains 100 boxes of detergent.

140. Which of the two figures, *ABCD* or *EFGH*, has the largest area?

    (1) The perimeter of *ABCD* is longer than the perimeter of *EFGH*.

    (2) *AC* is longer than *EG*.

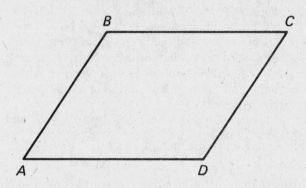 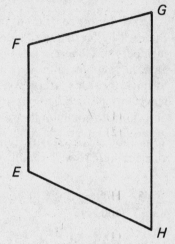

If there is still time remaining, you may review the questions in this section only.
You may not turn to any other section of the test.

Section V   Business Judgment

TIME: 35 minutes

DIRECTIONS: Read the following two passages. After you have completed each of them you will be asked to answer two sets of questions. The first of these, data evaluation, involves determining the importance of specific factors included in the passage. The second, data application, consists of general questions relating to the passage. When answering questions, you may consult the passage.

Passage 1:

Mr. Hesh came to Zaire this year straight from a four year assignment as Commercial Attaché in his country's embassy in Liberia. One of the first questions asked him came from executives of Zaire's small but growing textile industry and was about the possibility of expanding sales to the American market. They felt that if this were possible, many more people could be employed in this sector of industry, having a favorable effect on the country's economy.

"While I have been here only a short time," began Mr. Hesh, "I would certainly be prepared to say that everything I've seen indicates a tremendous future, particularly in the textile and small parts industries. Zaire has gone beyond the stage of manufacturing simple items, and is now moving into the more sophisticated goods."

Mr. Hesh has a great deal of confidence in Zaire inventiveness and offers as an example the pre-fab diner. "We sold you the manufacturing capability for this diner, and you are now producing a much better version and selling it back to us." He considers this legitimate and beneficial for an active trading relationship. Other Zaire goods and services that he feels are of particular interest for the American market are clothing and other textiles. Out of this line, but also in the area of creativity, is fashions for which he foresees an ever brighter future in America. Such unique services as those provided by the Institute for Literary Translations, which works largely on U.S. assignments, are another important Zaire export item.

Investments by American firms is another avenue of commercial relations that Mr. Hesh believes is going to increase.

Asked for his reaction to the proposed legislation to limit textile imports into the United States, Mr. Hesh said, "it looks as if the bill has a good chance of passing. Numerous members of Congress have spoken in support of the bill, and the Secretary of Commerce gave his support after a prolonged effort to solve the problem in other ways. It is unfortunate that his efforts were not successful. It is always preferable to solve such problems through negotiations rather than by unilateral actions, but certain countries were not willing to commit themselves to adequate restraints."

In light of Mr. Hesh's remarks, Zaire's textile executives were considering what the chances were to successfully penetrate the American textile market.

Data Evaluation Questions

DIRECTIONS: Evaluate each of the following factors used in decision-making which relate to the passage you have just read by selecting

- (A) for a *Major Objective*—the result desired by the executive;
- (B) for a *Major Factor*—a primary consideration, spelled out in the passage, that influences the decision;
- (C) for a *Minor Factor*—a less important consideration in the decision;
- (D) for a *Major Assumption*—a conclusion reached by the executive not necessarily supported by the factors present;
- (E) for an *Unimportant Issue*—a consideration not directly related to the problem.

141.   Expanding textile sales to the U.S.

142.   Confidence in Zaire inventiveness

143.   American investment in Zaire

144.   Zaire is an African country

145.   American trade protection

Data Application Questions

DIRECTIONS: Answer each of the following questions using information contained in the passage.

146. Expanding textile sales to the U.S. would

    I.   Decrease world textile prices
   II.   Increase profits in the textile industry
  III.   Increase employment in Zaire

  (A) I only
  (B) III only
  (C) I and II only
  (D) II and III only
  (E) I, II, and III

147. According to the Commercial Attaché, Zaire manufactures

    I.   Mainly simple goods
   II.   Mostly cheap products
  III.   Some sophisticated goods

  (A) I only
  (B) III only
  (C) I and II only
  (D) II and III only
  (E) I, II, and III

148. Mr. Hesh suggested that some products could be sold in the American market, such as

    I.   Heavy machinery
   II.   Clothing
  III.   Fashion design

  (A) I only
  (B) III only
  (C) I and II only
  (D) II and III only
  (E) I, II, and III

149. According to the passage, the protectionist trade bill before the U.S. Congress would limit the importation of

    I.   Textiles
   II.   Machinery
  III.   Agricultural products

  (A) I only
  (B) III only
  (C) I and II only
  (D) II and III only
  (E) I, II, and III

150. Goods other than textiles that Zaire might successfully sell in the U.S. market include

    I.   Small parts
    II. Translations
    III. Pre-fab diners

  (A) I only
  (B) III only
  (C) I and II only
  (D) II and III only
  (E) I, II, and III

151. According to Mr. Hesh, trade disagreements can be best resolved through

    I.   Legislation
    II. Unilateral action
    III. Negotiation

  (A) I only
  (B) III only
  (C) I and II only
  (D) II and III only
  (E) I, II, and III

152. According to Mr. Hesh's comments about trade relations, he would be considered to favor

    I.   Protectionism
    II. Trade barriers
    III. Liberalized trade

  (A) I only
  (B) III only
  (C) I and II only
  (D) II and III only
  (E) I, II, and III

Passage 2:

For the past two years, Bennett Joseph, head of the regional firm R and S Packing Company, had been seriously considering the use of U.S. government grade labeling for its high-quality canned fruits and vegetables. Having enjoyed an excellent reputation for more than 30 years with the public, these canned goods under the trademark "Delish" were known throughout the area by distributors and consumers alike as some of the best.

The grade-labeling problem had come to the fore as the result of a new food supermarket chain called *Gaynes*. The new chain, a national organization, was making a depth penetration in the region by spending a sizeable portion of its large advertising and promotion budget for pushing its own private brands of frozen and canned fruits and vegetables. Its advertising emphasized that the public could find both grade and descriptive labeling on each package and can. The descriptive labels listed the type of food, the can size, the number of servings per can, the net contents, and the name and address of the chain.

Joseph had always paid careful attention to the descriptive labeling on R and S products but had been most reluctant to commit the company to the use of grade labeling. Joseph's reluctance was supported by the company's advertising and promotion manager and the production boss, who believed with him that grade labeling could hardly bring out the fresh flavor and taste upon which the company prided itself and had been able to capture through its own special heating, processing, and canning techniques.

A factor that seriously concerned Joseph in the use of grade labels on canned fruits and vegetables was the possible use of a high grade on one of the grading characteristics to offset a low score on another. This method could hardly help R and S, whose pack was known by distributors and consumers alike to be much better even than the highest grades of its competitors.

While Joseph was pondering this problem, he mulled over what he had read about grade labeling. In the first place, grading and labeling of canned foods had been developed to protect and help the consumer. Through the Department of Agriculture, federal standards had been set up for standardization, grading, and inspection work. To encourage voluntary use of these standards, the Department of Agriculture hired inspectors who carried out the federal inspection program at production periods. For canned fruits and vegetables, the grades were A, B, and C, which were based on such criteria as uniformity, succulence, and color—not flavor or food value.

Joseph certainly agreed that grade labeling could provide additional information for the consumer. R and S could also use it in company advertisements to supplement its own descriptive labels. But didn't everyone know about the taste and quality of R and S products? He also wondered what happened when a company using grade labeling saw the qualities of fruits and vegetables change from year to year. At one period, that quality might be high for most growers; it might also be low during another. Too, some factors that were very important in their effect on consumer choice could not be subjected to a grading discipline. For example, the range of individual tastes was impossible to standardize. Certainly taste, Joseph felt, should be just as important—perhaps more so—than the other, more tangible criteria used to grade canned goods.

Data Evaluation Questions

DIRECTIONS: Evaluate each of the following factors used in decision-making which relate to the passage you have just read by selecting

(A) for a *Major Objective*—the result desired by the executive;

(B) for a *Major Factor*—a primary consideration, spelled out in the passage, that influences the decision;

(C) for a *Minor Factor*—a less important consideration in the decision;

(D) for a *Major Assumption*—a conclusion reached by the executive not necessarily supported by the factors present;

(E) for an *Unimportant Issue*—a consideration not directly related to the problem.

153. Establishment of a new supermarket chain

154. Standardization of food products

155. Grade labeling of food products

156. Federal food standards

157. Continuing the R & S brand image

Data Application Questions

DIRECTIONS: Answer each of the following questions using information contained in the passage.

158. According to the passage, grade labeling was intended to

    I. Increase the cost of canning
    II. Increase competition
    III. Protect and inform the consumer

    (A) I only   (D) II and III only
    (B) III only   (E) I, II, and III
    (C) I and II only

159. R & S did not adopt grade labeling because

    I. It had little reason to do so
    II. The government did not require it
    III. It was too expensive

    (A) I only
    (B) III only
    (C) I and II only
    (D) II and III only
    (E) I, II, and III

160. Which of the following R & S employees had doubts about the efficacy of adopting grade labeling?

    I. Bennett Joseph
    II. The advertising manager
    III. The production manager

    (A) I only
    (B) III only
    (C) I and II only
    (D) II and III only
    (E) I, II, and III

161. Which government agency supervises the labeling program?

    I.   Department of Commerce
   II.   Department of Health
 III.   Department of Agriculture

  (A) I only
  (B) III only
  (C) I and II only
  (D) II and III only
  (E) I, II, and III

162. Grading of fruits and vegetables was based on

    I.   Taste
   II.   Color
 III.   Uniformity

  (A) I only
  (B) III only
  (C) I and II only
  (D) II and III only
  (E) I, II, and III

163. *Gaynes* labels include

    I.   food content
   II.   net contents
 III.   price per unit

  (A) I only
  (B) III only
  (C) I and II only
  (D) II and III only
  (E) I, II, and III

164. R & S management had doubts about grade labeling because

    I.   Grading could not adequately describe the quality of the contents
   II.   A high grade on one characteristic might be used to offset a low grade on another
 III.   Consumers would be confused

  (A) I only
  (B) III only
  (C) I and II only
  (D) II and III only
  (E) I, II, and III

165. According to Mr. Bennett Joseph, one of the most important criteria to grade canned goods should be

    I.   A,B,C values
   II.   Price
  III.   Consumer tastes

   (A) I only
   (B) III only
   (C) I and II only
   (D) II and III only
   (E) I, II, and III

If there is still time remaining, you may review the questions in this section only. You may not turn to any other section of the test.

Section VI   Mathematics

TIME: 35 minutes

DIRECTIONS: Solve each of the following problems; then indicate the correct answer in the space provided. [On the actual test you will be permitted to use any space available on the examination paper for scratch work.]

NOTE: A figure that appears with a problem is drawn as accurately as possible so as to provide information that may help in answering the question. Numbers in this test are real numbers.

166. $^{15}/_{16} = x\%$ where x is

(A)   87.75   (D)   94.65
(B)   90   (E)   95
(C)   93.75

167.   If it takes worker F 15 minutes to load a truck by himself and it takes worker S 20 minutes to load the same truck by himself, how long should it take worker F and worker S together to load the truck?

(A) $8\frac{2}{3}$ min.   (D)   10 min.
(B) $8\frac{4}{7}$ min.   (E) $10\frac{3}{4}$ min.
(C) $9\frac{1}{2}$ min.

168.   A car traveling at 50 miles per hour increases its speed at the rate of 5 miles per hour each hour. How long will it take before the car reaches 65 miles per hour?

(A)   1 hr.   (D)   3 hr.
(B)   2 hr.   (E)   13 hr.
(C) $2\frac{1}{2}$ hr.

169.   The Tarrytown factory produces 75 cars an hour when it is operating at 50% of its capacity. The Mahwah factory produces 100 cars an hour when it is operating at 80% of its capacity. What is the ratio of the production of the Tarrytown factory to the production of the Mahwah factory when they are both operating at full (100%) capacity?

(A)   3 to 4   (D)   6 to 5
(B)   5 to 6   (E)   4 to 3
(C)   7 to 8

170.   If the average (arithmetic mean) of 5 integers is 7, what is the sum of the integers?

(A)   7   (D)   40
(B)   30   (E)   15,120
(C)   35

Use the following graphs for questions 171–174.

LABOR COSTS IN INDUSTRY

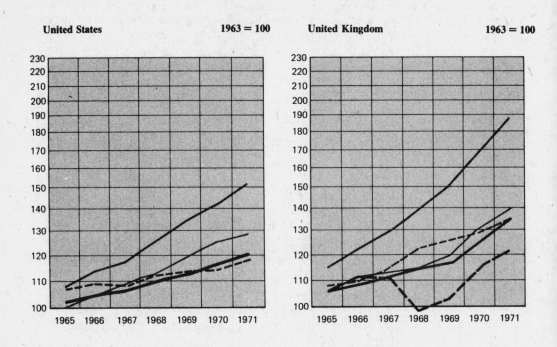

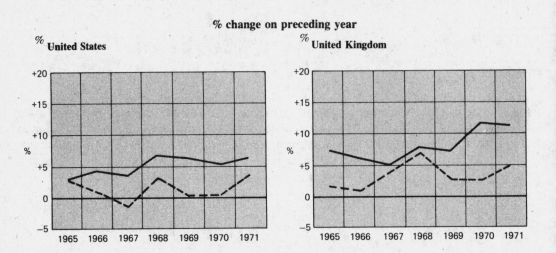

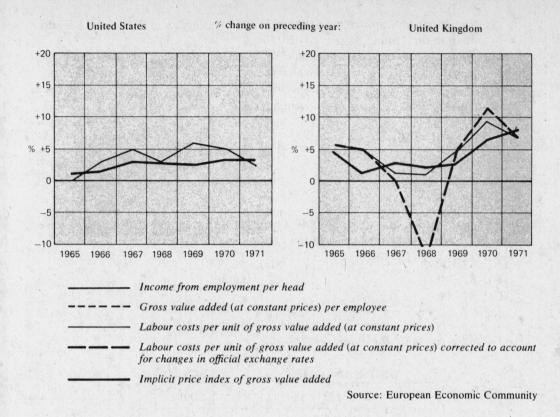

United States   % change on preceding year: United Kingdom

——————— Income from employment per head

- - - - - - Gross value added (at constant prices) per employee

——————— Labour costs per unit of gross value added (at constant prices)

━━ ━━ ━━ Labour costs per unit of gross value added (at constant prices) corrected to account
for changes in official exchange rates

━━━━━━━ Implicit price index of gross value added

Source: European Economic Community

171. According to the graphs, the one indicator that has increased at least 5% every
year is

(A) income from employment per head in the United States
(B) income from employment per head in the United Kingdom
(C) gross value added per employee in the United States
(D) gross value added per employee in the United Kingdom
(E) implicit price index of gross value added in the United Kingdom

172. If income from employment per head in the United States had been 250 instead of
100 in 1963, then at the beginning of 1971 it would have been approximately

(A) 147   (D) 330
(B) 150   (E) 365
(C) 250

173. The difference between income from employment per head and labor costs per unit
of gross value added (at constant prices) in the United States between 1965 and
1971 has

(A) decreased by 50%
(B) stayed about the same
(C) increased by about 90%
(D) more than doubled
(E) more than quadrupled

174. Which of the following statements about labor costs in industry between 1965 and 1971 can be inferred from the graphs?

   I. Income from employment per head in 1965 was higher in the United Kingdom than in the United States.
   II. The rate of increase of income from employment per head in the United Kingdom from 1963 to 1971 was greater than any other indicator shown.
   III. Gross value added (at constant prices) per employee in the United States in 1970 was less than ⁹/₅ of its value in 1963.

   (A) II only
   (B) III only
   (C) I and II only
   (D) II and III only
   (E) I, II, and III

175. The original price of a car is $3,000. The price is discounted 20% and then raised by 10%. What is the new price of the car?

   (A) $2,400
   (B) $2,640
   (C) $2,700
   (D) $2,760
   (E) $2,800

Use the following table for questions 176–178.

GROSS INCOME	TAX
$10,000	$2,000
$12,000	$2,700
$14,000	$3,600
$16,000	$4,600
$18,000	$5,800
$20,000	$7,200

176. At what rate is a gross income of $10,000 taxed?

   (A) 2%
   (B) 10%
   (C) 18%
   (D) 20%
   (E) 22%

177. If a person with a gross income of $10,000 receives $10,000 more in gross income, how much tax does he pay on the extra $10,000?

   (A) $2,000
   (B) $4,600
   (C) $5,200
   (D) $5,800
   (E) $7,200

178. The taxes paid by 2 people, each with a gross income of $10,000, are what fraction of the tax paid by a person with a gross income of 20,000?

   (A) $5/18$
   (B) $23/72$
   (C) $5/9$
   (D) $27/12$
   (E) $10/9$

179. If one pump can pump u cubic feet of water a minute and another pump can pump v cubic feet of water a minute, how many minutes will it take both pumps together to pump 50 cubic feet of water?

(A) $u + v$

(B) $50u + v$

(C) $50u + 50v$

(D) $\dfrac{50}{u} + v$

(E) $\dfrac{50}{u + v}$

180. The interior angles of a trapezoid are in the ratio $2 : 4 : 5 : 7$. How many degrees is the smallest interior angle of the trapezoid?

(A) 10

(B) 20

(C) 30

(D) 40

(E) 45

181. What is $\frac{9}{7}$ divided by $\frac{5}{6}$?

(A) $\frac{5}{6}$

(B) $\frac{15}{14}$

(C) $\frac{27}{24}$

(D) $\frac{10}{7}$

(E) $\frac{54}{35}$

Use the graph and table below for questions 182–185.

UNDER 19
$11.5 Billion

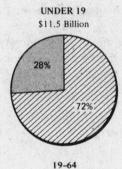

28%

72%

19-64
$40.7 Billion

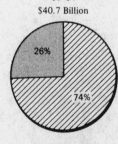

26%

74%

65 AND OVER
$19.8 Billion

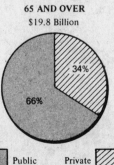

34%

66%

Public   Private

Distribution of public funds for Personal Health Care

Age	Percentage distribution		
	Total	Federal funds	State and local funds
All ages	100.0	66.3	33.7
Under 19	100.0	57.9	42.1
19–64	100.0	51.2	48.8
65 and over	100.0	80.8	19.2

Source: Social Security Bulletin

182. Which of the following categories accounts for the largest amount of personal health care expenditures?

(A) private, under 19
(B) public, under 19
(C) private, 19 to 64
(D) public, 65 and over
(E) private, 65 and over

183. Approximately how much is spent from federal funds for health care of people 65 and over?

(A) $9 billion
(B) $10.5 billion
(C) $12 billion
(D) $13.2 billion
(E) $19.8 billion

184. The ratio of the amount of money taken from public sources for health care for those between 19 and 64 and those 65 and over is about

(A) $\frac{1}{2}$
(B) $\frac{3}{4}$
(C) $\frac{7}{8}$
(D) $\frac{4}{3}$
(E) $\frac{2}{1}$

185. Which of the following statements about expenditures for personal health care during the fiscal year 1972 can be inferred from the graphs and table?

I. More than $\frac{1}{7}$ of the total expenditures for personal health care were spent for the under 19 group.
II. The expenditures from private sources for the under 19 group were higher than the expenditures from private sources for the 65 and over group.
III. The group which accounted for the largest expenditure of state and local funds was the 19 to 64 group.

(A) I only
(B) II only
(C) I and II only
(D) II and III only
(E) I, II, and III

Use the graph below for questions 186–187.

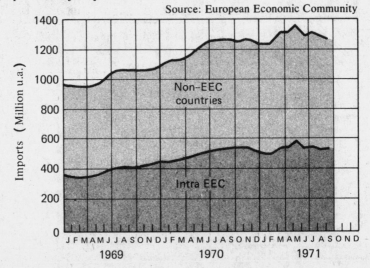

Source: European Economic Community

186. The maximum value of imports from non-EEC countries during the time shown on the graph was about

(A) 590
(B) 600
(C) 700
(D) 750
(E) 1350

187. During the time shown, imports from non-EEC countries divided by total imports have been roughly

(A) ¼
(B) ½
(C) 1
(D) 3/2
(E) 2

188. The total weekly wages paid to 15 workers was $1,800. Five of the workers earned $180 each that week. What was the average weekly wage for the remaining 10 workers?

(A) $50
(B) $90
(C) $100
(D) $105
(E) $110

189. If the two sides of a right triangle adjacent to the right angle have lengths of 5 and 12 respectively, then the length of the side opposite the right angle is

(A) 5
(B) 10
(C) 13
(D) 15
(E) 17

Use the table below for questions 190–192.

SPEED of a car over a 3 hour period

Time since start (in minutes)	30	60	90	105	120	150	180
Speed at time (in mph)	50	55	60	62.5	67.5	65	60

190. How fast was the car traveling 2½ hours after the start?

(A) 60 mph
(B) 62.5 mph
(C) 65 mph
(D) 67.5 mph
(E) 70 mph

191. During the last hour of the time period shown on the table, the speed of the car

(A) decreased by 10 mph
(B) decreased by 7.5 mph
(C) decreased by 5 mph
(D) decreased by 2.5 mph
(E) stayed the same

192. Which of the following statements about the speed of the car during the 3 hour period can be inferred from the table?

    I.   The average speed was 60 mph.
    II. The car slowed down during the fifth half-hour of the time period.
    III. The slowest speed the car traveled at was 50 mph.

(A) II only   (C) I and III only   (E) I, II, and III
(B) III only   (D) II and III only

193. If John makes 4 baskets in an hour and Allison makes 6 baskets in an hour and ten minutes, how many baskets will they make together in two hours?

(A) 8   (C) $12\frac{3}{7}$ (E) $18\frac{2}{7}$
(B) $10\frac{1}{4}$ (D) $15\frac{6}{11}$

194. If the sum of four consecutive integers is 26, what is their product?

(A) 210   (C) 840   (E) 2,964
(B) 336   (D) 1,680

195. If $x^2 + 3x - 4 = 0$, then x is either 1 or

(A) -4 (C) 0   (E) 4
(B) -1 (D) 3

Use the graph below for questions 196–198.

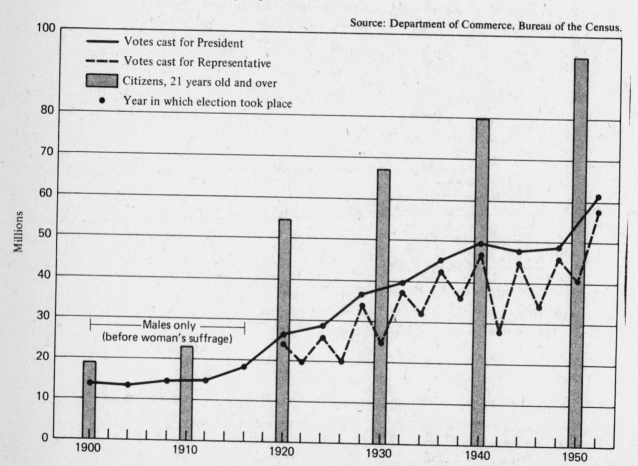

Source: Department of Commerce, Bureau of the Census.

196. About how many million votes were cast for president in the 1948 election?

(A) 45

(B) 49

(C) 51

(D) 58

(E) 62

197. In the 1940 election, the fraction of citizens 21 years old and over who voted for president was

(A) $\frac{3}{8}$

(B) $\frac{1}{2}$

(C) $\frac{5}{8}$

(D) $\frac{7}{8}$

(E) $\frac{9}{8}$

198. The election with the smallest number of voters for representatives between 1931 and 1951 was

(A) 1932

(B) 1938

(C) 1942

(D) 1944

(E) 1946

199. If $x + y = 2$ and $y > 3$, then

(A) $x < -1$

(B) $x > -1$

(C) $x < 0$

(D) $x > 0$

(E) $x = 3$

200. How much is $\frac{2}{3}$ of $\frac{5/2}{3/4}$?

(A) $\frac{2}{3}$

(B) $\frac{5}{4}$

(C) $\frac{9}{5}$

(D) $\frac{20}{9}$

(E) 5

Use the following charts for questions 201–204.

ENROLLEES IN THE HOSPITAL INSURANCE PROGRAM JULY 1, 1966.

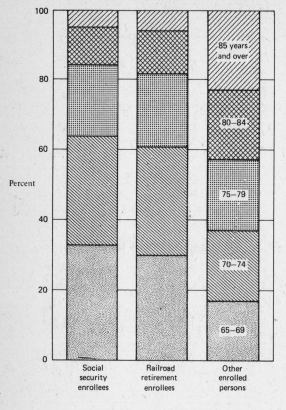

Characteristic	All enrolled persons	Persons entitled to social security benefits	Persons entitled to railroad retirement benefits	Other enrolled persons
Total number (in thousands)........	18,859	15,856	821	2,446
Age:				
Percent.................	100.0	100.0	100.0	100.0
65–69.................	31.2	33.4	30.4	17.3
70–74.................	29.5	31.0	30.3	20.1
75–79.................	20.6	20.6	21.6	20.3
80–84.................	11.9	10.6	12.1	20.2
85 and over........	6.8	4.5	5.6	22.0
Sex:				
Percent.................	100.0	100.0	100.0	100.0
Men...................	42.8	45.3	48.4	24.2
Women..............	57.2	54.7	51.6	75.8
Race:				
Number reporting (in thousands)...	18,227	15,848	795	1,848
Percent.................	100.0	100.0	100.0	100.0
White.................	92.3	93.2	92.2	84.4
Nonwhite...........	7.7	6.8	7.8	15.6

Source: Social Security Bulletin

201. Approximately how many people who are entitled to social security benefits are in the age group 65–69?

(A) 5,000,000
(B) 5,300,000
(C) 5,600,000
(D) 6,000,000
(E) 6,500,000

202. The ratio of men to women in the category of other enrolled persons is about

(A) 1 to 3
(B) 1 to 2
(C) 2 to 3
(D) 3 to 1
(E) 4 to 1

203. Which of the following statements about enrollees in the hospital insurance program can be inferred from the charts?

I. There are more enrollees 85 and over entitled to social security benefits than enrollees aged 85 and over in the other enrolled persons category.

II. More than 9 times as many whites are enrolled as nonwhites of those reporting race.

III. More than $\frac{1}{3}$ of all enrollees are in the age category 65–69.

(A) II only
(B) III only
(C) I and II only
(D) II and III only
(E) I, II, and III

204. If 50% of all retired people were enrolled in the hospital insurance program on July 1, 1966, how many retired people were there on July 1, 1966?

(A) 36,000
(B) 37,718
(C) 37,634,000

(D) 37,718,000
(E) 38,518,000

205. A truck originally was priced at $6,800. It was discounted 10% and a month later was discounted 15% more, and sold. How much was the truck sold for?

(A) $5,100
(B) $5,152
(C) $5,198

(D) $5,202
(E) $5,248

If there is still time remaining, you may review the questions in this section only.
You may not turn to any other section of the test.

Answers

Section I   Reading Recall

1. **(D)**	9. **(C)**	17. **(E)**	25. **(C)**
2. **(C)**	10. **(E)**	18. **(C)**	26. **(A)**
3. **(C)**	11. **(A)**	19. **(A)**	27. **(C)**
4. **(C)**	12. **(B)**	20. **(B)**	28. **(A)**
5. **(E)**	13. **(C)**	21. **(C)**	29. **(B)**
6. **(C)**	14. **(C)**	22. **(A)**	30. **(D)**
7. **(A)**	15. **(D)**	23. **(D)**	
8. **(B)**	16. **(D)**	24. **(A)**	

Section II   Mathematics

(Numbers in parentheses indicate the section in the Mathematics Review where material concerning the question is discussed.)

31. **(D)** (I-4)	50. **(D)** (I-4)	69. **(A)** (II-7)
32. **(B)** (II-2)	51. **(D)** (I-6)	70. **(D)** (III-7, I-4)
33. **(D)** (II-3)	52. **(E)** (II-3)	71. **(A)** (II-3)
34. **(D)** (I-4)	53. **(D)** (II-3)	72. **(C)** (II-3)
35. **(A)** (I-7)	54. **(D)** (II-7)	73. **(B)** (II-3)
36. **(D)** (III-7)	55. **(E)** (I-2)	74. **(C)** (I-4)
37. **(E)** (II-2)	56. **(B)** (I-6, II-7)	75. **(B)** (II-2)
38. **(C)** (I-4)	57. **(E)** (III-8)	76. **(B)** (II-7)
39. **(D)** (III-4)	58. **(D)** (I-4)	77. **(B)** (I-4)
40. **(B)** (I-4)	59. **(E)** (III-7)	78. **(C)** (I-4)
41. **(C)** (II-3)	60. **(E)** (III-4)	79. **(D)** (I-4)
42. **(C)** (I-4, III-7)	61. **(C)** (III-4, III-7)	80. **(A)** (II-6)
43. **(A)** (II-6)	62. **(B)** (III-7)	81. **(D)** (II-2)
44. **(E)** (II-3)	63. **(D)** (I-2)	82. **(D)** (III-6)
45. **(D)** (I-2)	64. **(A)** (I-4)	83. **(A)** (II-2)
46. **(D)** (I-4)	65. **(C)** (I-4)	84. **(C)** (II-2)
47. **(C)** (II-3)	66. **(E)** (II-1)	85. **(D)** (II-1)
48. **(B)** (I-1)	67. **(D)** (II-3)	
49. **(D)** (I-2)	68. **(D)** (III-4)	

Section III — Verbal Aptitude

86. (B)	96. (B)	106. (E)	116. (C)
87. (C)	97. (B)	107. (D)	117. (C)
88. (D)	98. (A)	108. (B)	118. (D)
89. (C)	99. (C)	109. (A)	119. (C)
90. (E)	100. (D)	110. (E)	120. (A)
91. (B)	101. (E)	111. (B)	121. (C)
92. (C)	102. (A)	112. (A)	122. (D)
93. (D)	103. (C)	113. (B)	123. (C)
94. (B)	104. (B)	114. (C)	124. (B)
95. (A)	105. (A)	115. (C)	125. (C)

Section IV — Data Sufficiency

126. (D)	130. (C)	134. (A)	138. (C)
127. (C)	131. (E)	135. (A)	139. (E)
128. (E)	132. (B)	136. (C)	140. (E)
129. (D)	133. (E)	137. (E)	

Section V — Business Judgment

141. (A)	146. (B)	151. (B)	156. (B)	161. (B)
142. (C)	147. (B)	152. (B)	157. (A)	162. (D)
143. (E)	148. (D)	153. (B)	158. (B)	163. (C)
144. (E)	149. (A)	154. (C)	159. (A)	164. (C)
145. (D)	150. (A)	155. (B)	160. (E)	165. (B)

Section VI — Mathematics

(Numbers in parentheses indicate the section in the Mathetmatics Review where material concerning the question is discussed.)

166. (C) (I-4)	180. (D) (III-5, II-5)	194. (D) (I-7)
167. (B) (II-3)	181. (E) (I-2)	195. (A) (II-2)
168. (D) (II-3)	182. (C) (IV-2)	196. (B) (IV-3)
169. (D) (II-5, 1-4)	183. (B) (IV-2)	197. (C) (IV-3, IV-4)
170. (C) (I-7)	184. (B) (IV-2, I-5)	198. (C) (IV-4)
171. (B) (IV-3)	185. (E) (IV-2)	199. (A) (II-7)
172. (E) (IV-3)	186. (D) (IV-5)	200. (D) (I-2)
173. (D) (IV-3)	187. (B) (IV-5)	201. (B) (IV-1)
174. (D) (IV-3)	188. (B) (I-7)	202. (A) (II-5, I-5)
175. (B) (I-4)	189. (C) (III-4)	203. (C) (IV-1)
176. (D) (I-4)	190. (C) (IV-1)	204. (D) (I-4)
177. (C) (IV-1)	191. (B) (IV-1)	205. (D) (I-4)
178. (C) (I-2)	192. (A) (IV-1)	
179. (E) (II-3)	193. (E) (I-2)	

Analysis

Section I   Reading Recall

1. **(D)** Note that the question asks "about how many" which requires an approximate figure. Of all the alternative answers, **(D)** comes closest to the 8,600 employees given in paragraph 1.

2. **(C)** See paragraph 3, lines 1 and 2.

3. **(C)** See paragraph 5, line 1: "Top Presidential appointees, . . . bear the brunt of translating the philosophy and aims of the current administration into practical programs."

4. **(C)** See paragraph 6, line 1: ". . . there be no basic disagreement with Presidential political philosophy, at least so far as administrative judgments and actions are concerned."

5. **(E)** See paragraph 6, last line.

6. **(C)** See paragraph 7: "Those whom the President selects. . . ." and following.

7. **(A)** See paragraph 8: ". . . they usually have substantial responsibilities in basic management."

8. **(B)** Paragraph 8, line 1: "These appointees are primarily regarded as policy makers. . . ."

9. **(C)** See paragraph 7: "Those selected by department and agency heads . . ." and following.

10. **(E)** Alternatives (B) through (D) are definitely acceptable, leaving (E) as the only possible answer.

11. **(A)** See paragraph 1.

12. **(B)** See paragraph 2: ". . . all resellers are bound by the terms of the . . . contract. . . ."

13. **(C)** This is inferred throughout the passage.

14. **(C)** See paragraph 4, line 1.

15. **(D)** Paragraph 5: "Responsibility for enforcement falls upon the producer or distributor. . . ."

16. **(D)** See paragraph 3: "Closeout sales are excepted."

17. **(E)** This is found in paragraph 2, line 1.

18. **(C)** See paragraph 5: ". . . granting of trading stamps in abnormally high volume. . . ."

19. **(A)** See paragraph 2, line 1.

20. **(B)** These laws stifle competition because retailers cannot compete on a price basis.

21. **(C)** See paragraph 1, line 1.

22. **(A)** See paragraph 2: "Congress, particularly the Senate, has been pressing the Administration to do more" to liberalize East-West trade.

23. **(D)** See paragraph 3: ". . . there is no question that in 1969 there was very sharp, very deep, and sometimes very bitter division. . . ."

24. **(A)** See paragraph 6: ". . . it asks only whether our national security is jeopardized. . . ."

25. **(C)** See paragraph 8, line 1.

26. **(A)** This is found in paragraph 7.

27. **(C)** The Defense Department (in paragraph 6) takes a dim view toward such trade expansion, while the Commerce Department favors it (in paragraphs 8 and 9).

28. **(A)** Both are in favor. See paragraph 9, line 1: ". . . both the Commerce and State Departments are in favor. . . ."

29. **(B)** See paragraph 8: ". . . if we in the United States do not authorize these transactions there is almost always comparable technology in other parts of the world," i.e., other nations will obtain this trade.

30. **(D)** See paragraph 9: "When there is any division . . . the case moves to the White House. . . ."

Section II   Mathematics

31. **(D)** 64% of 200 is $(.64)(200)$, which equals 128. Therefore, 128 students received a grade of C.

32. **(B)** Since $x = 3$, $2x + y = 6 + y$; so $6 + y = 10$ and $y = 4$. Therefore, $x - y = 3 - 4 = -1$.

33. **(D)** Since 15 minutes is $\frac{1}{4}$ of an hour, each worker can pack $4 \times \frac{1}{6}$ or $\frac{2}{3}$ of a case an hour. The factory has 40 workers, so they should pack $40 \times \frac{2}{3}$ or $\frac{80}{3}$ cases each hour. Therefore, in $1\frac{2}{3}$ or $\frac{5}{3}$ hours the factory should pack $\left(\frac{5}{3} \times \frac{80}{3}\right)$, which equals $\frac{400}{9}$ or $44\frac{4}{9}$ cases.

34. **(D)** If potatoes cost 15¢ a pound, then 10 pounds will cost $1.50. If the price increases by 10%, then 10 pounds of potatoes will cost 110% of $1.50, which is $1.65.

35. **(A)** Since the truck driver averaged 50 miles per hour for the first three hours, he traveled 3×50 or 150 miles during the first three hours. Since he needs to travel $180 - 150$ miles in the final hour, he should drive at 30 mph.

36. **(D)** The area of a triangle is $\frac{1}{2}$ the base times the altitude. The altitude is $2B$, so the area is $(\frac{1}{2})(B)(2B)$ or B^2.

37. **(E)** If we denote the two numbers by x and y, then $xy = 10$ and $x + y = 7$. Then x is $7 - y$ and $(7 - y)y = 7y - y^2 = 10$ or $y^2 - 7y + 10 = 0$. But $y^2 - 7y + 10$ equals $(y - 5)(y - 2)$; so the two numbers are 5 and 2. The correct answer can be selected quickly by inspection of the choices.

38. **(C)** Since the first 100 bags cost $x each, the total cost of the first 100 bags is $100x$. Since the remaining 50 bags are discounted 10%, each bag costs 90% of $x or $(.90)x$ and the 50 bags cost $45x$. Thus, the total cost is $145x$.

39. **(D)** According to the Pythagorean theorem, the length squared equals $8^2 + 15^2$, which is 289. So the length of the side opposite the right angle is 17.

40. **(B)** The store made a profit of 20%; so the store sold the glove for 120% of what the glove cost. If C is the cost of the glove, 120% of $C = \$10.20$, or $\frac{6}{5}C = \$10.20$. Therefore, $C = \frac{5}{6}$ of $10.20, which is $8.50.

41. **(C)** The first 600 copies cost a total of $600x$¢. There are $1,500 - 600$ or 900 copies after the first 600, each of which costs $\left(x - \frac{y}{10}\right)$¢; so the 900 copies cost $900\left(x - \frac{y}{y}\right)$¢, which equals $(900x - 90y)$¢. Therefore, the total cost is $(1500x - 90y)$¢.

42. **(C)** If s is the original side of the square, then s^2 is the area of the original square. The side of the increased square is 140% of s or $(1.4)s$. Therefore, the area of the increased square is $(1.4s)^2$ or $1.96s^2$, which is 196% of the original area. Thus, the area has increased by 96%.

43. **(A)** If P is the price of 7 cartons, then $\frac{7}{28} = \frac{P}{21}$, so $P = \frac{1}{4}$ of $21, which is $5.25.

44. **(E)** Plane P will travel $\frac{3}{2}$ of an hour before Q takes off, so it will be $\frac{3x}{2}$ miles away at 3:30 A.M. Let t denote the number of hours after 3:30 A.M. it takes Q to overtake P. By then P has flown $tx + \frac{3x}{2}$ miles and Q has flown ty miles. We want the value of t, where $ty = tx + \frac{3x}{2}$, or $t(y - x) = \frac{3x}{2}$. Therefore, $t = \frac{3x}{2(y - x)}$.

45. **(D)** Note that $\left(\frac{2}{3} + \frac{1}{3}\right)$ equals 1 full day, and that $\left(\frac{1}{8} + \frac{3}{4}\right)$ is shy $\frac{1}{8}$ of being 1 full day. So he works $2\frac{7}{8}$ days altogether.

$$\left(2\frac{7}{8}\right)(20) = \left(\frac{23}{8}\right)(20) = \frac{460}{8} = \$57.50.$$

46. **(D)** There were 26 (16 + 10) students who answered 32 or more questions correctly. Since the total number of students is 60, and $\frac{26}{60} = .43\frac{1}{3}$, $43\frac{1}{3}\%$ of the class answered 32 or more questions correctly.

47. **(C)** 12 students had scores of 28 to 31, and 8 scores of 25 or less; so $8x = 12$ and $x = \frac{12}{8} = \frac{3}{2}$.

48. **(B)** The product of 3 consecutive integers is of the form $(x-1)(x)(x+1)$ and a good approximation to this is x^3. Since $6^3 = 216$, a good guess for x is 6, 6 is correct since $5 \times 6 \times 7 = 210$. Therefore, the sum of the two smaller integers is $5 + 6$ or 11.

49. **(D)** Let C, B, and E denote the cost of cereal, bacon, and eggs respectively. Then $C = \frac{1B}{3}$ and $B = \frac{5E}{4}$, or $E = \frac{4B}{5}$. Therefore, $E = \frac{4B}{5}$ and $B = 3C$; so we conclude that $E = \left(\frac{4}{5}\right)3C = \frac{12C}{5}$.

50. **(D)** Since 80% of 15 is 12, the loaded truck travels 12 miles on a gallon of gas. Therefore, it will use $\frac{80}{12}$ or $6\frac{8}{12}$ or $6\frac{2}{3}$ gallons of gas to travel 80 miles.

51. **(D)**

STATEMENT I is true, since the band which denotes corporation income taxes is wider in 1946 than in 1947.

STATEMENT II is false, since the top line on the receipts graph falls between 1945 and 1950.

STATEMENT III is true, since the top line on the expenditures graph is lower in 1948 than at any other time between 1945 and 1952.

Therefore, only STATEMENTS I and III can be inferred from the graph.

52. **(E)** In the first $1\frac{1}{2}$ hours, the car will travel $\frac{3}{2} \times 70$ or 105 miles. In order to travel a total of 200 miles the car has 95 miles left. At a speed of 50 miles per hour it will take $\frac{95}{50}$ or $1\frac{9}{10}$ hours to travel 95 miles. Therefore, the total traveling time necessary to travel 200 miles is $1\frac{1}{2} + 1\frac{9}{10}$, which equals $3\frac{4}{10}$ or $3\frac{2}{5}$ hours.

53. **(D)** The first 1,000 copies will cost $\$1,000x$. There are 600 copies after the first thousand, each costing $\$(x - 2y)$, so all 600 cost $\$600x - \$1200y$. Therefore, the cost of 1,600 copies is $\$1600x - \$1200y$.

54. **(D)** If $\frac{1}{3} < x$, then since inverting positive numbers reverses inequalities, $\frac{1}{1/3} > \frac{1}{x}$. Since $\frac{1}{1/3} = 3$, 3 is greater than $\frac{1}{x}$ or $\frac{1}{x}$ is less than 3. (x is positive since it is greater than $\frac{1}{3}$.)

55. **(E)** $\frac{1}{3} = \frac{14}{42}$ and $\frac{2}{7} = \frac{12}{42}$, so $\frac{1}{3} + \frac{2}{7} = \frac{26}{42}$. Therefore, $x = 26$.

56. **(B)** Since 12 is positive, one of the numbers must be positive because the sum of negative numbers is negative. If r is 13, then $x = 0$, $y = -1$, and $z = 0$ satisfy $r + x + y + w = 12$ and $x < 6$.

57. **(E)** The volume of a sphere of radius r is $\frac{4}{3}\pi r^3$. If r is replaced by $2r$, the volume $= \frac{4}{3}\pi(2r)^3 = \frac{4}{3}\pi 8r^3 = 8\left(\frac{4}{3}\pi r^3\right)$, so the volume has increased by a factor of 8.

58. **(D)** The price of an object which costs C is $C(1 - d)$, where d is the discount. Therefore, the price of something after successive discounts of 10% and 15% $= C(1 - 10\%)(1-15\%)=C(90\%)(85\%)$, which is $C(76.5\%)$. So $1 - d = 76.5\%$ and the successive discount is equivalent to a single discount of $100\% - 76.5\%$, which equals 23.5%.

Another method for solving the problem would be to calculate the discount on an item which costs $100. After the 10% discount the item would cost $100(.90) = \$90$ and the second discount would be $\$(90)(.15)=\$13.50$. The final cost would be $\$90 - \$13.50 = \$76.50$. Therefore, the discount was $23.50, so the rate of discount is $\frac{23.50}{100} = 23.5\%$.

59. **(E)** The area of the room is 12^2 or 144 square feet. The area of a tile $= \frac{1}{3} \times \frac{1}{2} = \frac{1}{6}$ of a square foot since the area of a rectangle is length times width. The number of tiles necessary $= 144 \div \frac{1}{6} = 6 \times 144 = 864$ tiles.

Notice that we changed all the measurements into feet. We can also do the problem by changing all measurements into inches, but the multiplication and division would take more time.

60. **(E)** According to the Pythagorean theorem, the length of the hypotenuse, the side opposite the right angle, is the square root of $(n - 1)^2 + (2\sqrt{n})^2$, which is $n^2 - 2n + 1 + 4n$ or $n^2 + 2n + 1$. This equals $(n + 1)^2$. Therefore, the answer is $\sqrt{(n + 1)^2}$, which is $n + 1$.

61. **(C)** The area in (A) is clearly less than that in (C). So (A) and (E) are eliminated. Since each of the other triangles has a side of length 4, use that side as the base in the area formula. Whichever triangle has the largest altitude will have the largest area. (C) will have a larger altitude than either (B) or (D) since the sides of (C) beside the base are longer.

62. **(B)** The area of the triangle is $\frac{1}{2}(a \cdot b)$ where the base is a and the altitude b. Since $3^2 + 4^2 = 5^2$, the triangle is a right triangle. So if 4 is the length of the base, 3 is the length of the altitude. Thus, the area of the triangle is $\frac{1}{2} \cdot$

$3 \cdot 4$ or 6 square miles. The area of the square is 2^2 or 4 square miles. The area of the triangle is thus 2 square miles larger than the area of the square.

63. **(D)** If he works 8 hours, he makes $(8)(\$2.50)$ or $20.00. For any time worked over 8 hours he makes $(1.5)(\$2.50)$ or $3.75 an hour. So find x, the number of hours, such that $(\$3.75)x = \$27.50 - \$20.00$ or $7.50. Therefore, $x = 2$, and the total number of hours is $8 + 2$ or 10.

64. **(A)** Interest $=$ principal $\times$ annual rate $\times$ time. The principal is $650.00; the annual rate is 8%; the time is 6 months or $\frac{1}{2}$ year. Thus, the interest $= (\$650)(.08)(\frac{1}{2}) = (\$650)(.04) = \$26.00$.

65. **(C)** At 2 A.M. the car is traveling $(.10)50$ or 5.0 mph faster than at 1 A.M. So at 2 A.M. the car is traveling at 55 mph. At 3 A.M. the car is traveling $(.10)55$ or 5.5 mph faster than at 2 A.M. Therefore, the car is traveling 60.5 mph at 3 A.M.

66. **(E)** According to the rule given $f(a + 2)$ is $(a + 2)^2 + 2$ which is $(a^2 + 4a + 4) + 2$ or $a^2 + 4a + 6$.

67. **(D)** The time needed to travel 222.5 miles when traveling at a constant rate of 50 mph is $\frac{222.5}{50}$ or 4.45 hrs. Since $.45$ hrs. $= (.45)(60)$ min. $= 27$ min., the correct answer is 4 hrs. 27 min.

68. **(D)** Because angle ACB is a right angle, $(AC)^2 + (CB)^2 = (AB)^2$. Thus $(AB)^2 = 25 + 36 = 61$. Therefore, $AB = \sqrt{61}$.

69. **(A)** Since any number less than 2 is less than any number greater than 2, x is always less than y.

70. **(D)** Area $= \pi r^2$ and $2r = d$; thus, Area $= \pi\left(\frac{d}{2}\right)^2 = \frac{\pi}{4}d^2$. So to increase the area by 44%, d^2 must be increased by 44%. Hence, if d_1 is the increased diameter, $(d_1)^2 = (1.44) \ d^2$ which means $d_1 = 1.2d$ (since $\sqrt{1.44} = 1.2$). Therefore, the diameter must be increased by 20%.

71. **(A)** When the car travels at 45 mph, it will get $15 - \frac{45}{10}$ or 10.5 miles per gallon. The car has 10 gallons of gas so it will travel $(10)(10.5)$ or 105 miles before it runs out of gas.

72. **(C)** If 3 men produce 210 boxes, then each man produces 70 boxes. Therefore $\frac{490}{70}$ or 7 men will produce 490 boxes.

73. **(B)** Conveyer 1 moves 4 tons in 36 minutes or $\frac{4}{36} = \frac{1}{9}$ tons per minute. Conveyer 2 moves 5 tons in 40 minutes or $\frac{5}{40} = \frac{1}{8}$ tons per minute. Working together the conveyers will move $\left(\frac{1}{8} + \frac{1}{9}\right)$ or $\frac{17}{72}$ tons per minute. Thus if x is the amount of time it takes to move 3 tons of coal, then $\left(\frac{17}{72}\right)x = 3$. Therefore, $x = (3)\left(\frac{72}{17}\right) = \frac{216}{17} = 12\frac{12}{17}$ minutes.

72. **(C)** The company makes 5% on the first $1,000, so it makes $(.05)(\$1,000)$ or $50 on the first $1,000 of sales. On the remaining $4,235 of sales, the company makes $4\frac{1}{4}\%$; so it makes $(.0425)(\$4,235)$ or $179.99. Therefore, the total profit is $229.99.

75. **(B)** $2x + 2y = 2(x + y) = (2)(3)$, since $x + y = 3$. Therefore, 6 is the correct answer.

76. **(B)** If $x > 3$, then both numbers are positive. Therefore, $\frac{1}{x} < \frac{1}{3}$.

77. **(B)** The total interest on the loan will be $(.05)(\$1,000) + (.04)(\$4,000) = \$50 + \$160 = \$210$. The percentage will be $210/5,000 = .042$ or 4.2%.

78. **(C)** The toy was priced at $(\$13)(.90)$ after the first discount and was finally sold at another 10% discount. Therefore, it was sold for $(\$13)(.90)(.90) = (\$13)(.81) = \$10.53$.

79. **(D)** $(.06)(\$5,500) = \$330.00$.

80. **(A)** The stock will be selling at $2.00 after 6 months, $4.00 after a year, etc. Therefore, after k 6-month periods, the stock will be selling at $(\$2.00)^k$. Since $2^5 = 32$ and $2^6 = 64$, the stock will be selling at less than $63 after $2\frac{1}{2}$ years but at more than $63 after 3 years.

81. **(D)** Let C be the cost of a ton of coal, and let G be the cost of a gallon of oil. Translating the statements into equations, we have

$$C + 500G = \$1,000$$
$$3C + 300G = \$1,200.$$

Subtract the second equation from three times the first equation and the result is $1,200\,G = \$1,800$. Therefore, $G = \$1.50$.

82. **(D)** The area of a circle is πr^2 where r is the radius of the circle. The diameter of a circle is $2r$; so if the diameter is doubled the radius is doubled. If the radius is doubled, then the square of the radius is quadrupled $[(2r)^2 = 4r^2]$. So the area of the circle is quadrupled.

83. **(A)** Since $\frac{x}{y}$ is not zero, $\frac{y}{x} = 1/\frac{x}{y} = \frac{1}{2}$. But

$$\frac{y^2}{x^2} = \left(\frac{y}{x}\right)^2 = \left(\frac{1}{2}\right)^2 = \frac{1}{4}.$$

84. **(C)** Let x be the amount X is paid and y be the amount Y is paid. Since $x = (1.2)y$, $x + y = (2.2)y$. But we know $x + y = \$550$; so $(2.2)y = \$550$. Dividing each side, we have $y = \$250$.

85. **(D)** There are only 2 days he can work overtime, so there are at most 2 days he can make $x + y$ per day. On the other 3 days the most he can make is x per day. So his maximum salary for the 5 days is $2(x + y) + 3x = 5x + 2y$.

Section III Verbal Aptitude

86. **(B)** ABJURE: recant, revoke. *Antonym:* pledge

87. **(C)** MITIGATE: alleviate, abate. *Antonym:* intensify

88. **(D)** SPURIOUS: counterfeit, false. *Antonym:* authentic

89. **(C)** TORRID: hot, scorching. *Antonym:* cold

90. **(E)** CIRCUMSPECTION: watchfulness, caution. *Antonym:* recklessness

91. **(B)** DESULTORY: rambling, superficial. *Antonym:* methodical

92. **(C)** DISSONANCE: discord, lack of agreement. *Antonym:* harmony

93. **(D)** INCREDULOUS: skeptical, doubtful. *Antonym:* believing

94. **(B)** OBDURATE: callous, insensible. *Antonym:* tender

95. **(A)** UNGAINLY: clumsy, awkward. *Antonym:* graceful

96. **(B)** DISCERN: observe, perceive. *Antonym:* overlook

97. **(B)** CONVIVIAL: sociable, hospitable. *Antonym:* unsociable

98. **(A)** ALACRITY: willingness, quickness. *Antonym:* slowness

99. **(C)** PERFIDIOUS: faithless, insidious. *Antonym:* faithful

100. **(D)** A slide rule is a kind of computer. A sundial is a kind of clock.

101. **(E)** A battery powers a flashlight. Coal powers a furnace.

102. **(A)** A muff covers the hands. A helmet covers the head.

103. **(C)** Both are hobbyists. A philatelist collects stamps. A numismatist collects medals. Note that a government **(E)** collects taxes, but not as a hobby!

104. **(B)** A tranquilizer makes one placid. A sedative makes one somnolent.

105. **(A)** Maturity is the opposite of infancy. Culmination is the opposite of inception.

106. **(E)** Floriculture is the raising of flowers. Arboriculture is the raising of trees.

107. **(D)** An aviary is a bird haven or large cage. An aquarium is a fish tank or tanks.

108. **(B)** Muslin is a plain cloth. Brocade is an ornate cloth.

109. **(A)** An epilogue is at the end of a discourse. A coda is a final passage of a music piece.

110. **(E)** A pilot has responsibility for running a plane. A manager is responsible for running a store.

111. **(B)** A decade is a tenth part of a century. A decimeter is a tenth part of a meter.

112. **(A)** A model is a framework of reality or a real situation. A blueprint is a model of a house.

113. **(B)** Risks necessarily go along with competition.

114. **(C)** The word criticized implies a negative such as wasteful. Neither businessmen nor producers are apt to be critical as they continue to use advertising.

115. **(C)** Predispositions, or inclinations.

116. **(C)** Economists and marketers are interested in determining the effect that advertising has on sales.

117. **(C)** A winner can gain a victory without a mandate, interpreted as a majority of all the voters. The other alternatives have little or no meaning in context.

118. **(D)** Caveat Emptor, Latin for let the buyer beware.

119. **(C)** Emolument means a salary.

120. **(A)** Still standing; existing.

121. **(C)** malingerer means someone who shirks work.

122. **(D)** contains the best *meaning*.

123. **(C)** Alternatives (A), (B), and (E) have no meaning in context; a referee would not postpone a scheduled fight owing to the participants' ineptness, but he might stop the fight if the participants' behavior was unwarranted, e.g., fighting in an unsportsmanlike manner.

124. **(B)** has the most *meaning*.

125. **(C)** Alternatives (A), (B), (D), and (E) are illogical.

Section IV   Data Sufficiency

126. **(D)** (1) alone is sufficient, since if two sides of a triangle are equal, the angles opposite the equal sides are equal. Since $AB = BC$ then $x = y$, so $x = 40$. (2) alone is sufficient since the sum of the angles of a triangle is 180°. Therefore, if $z = 100$ and $y = 40$, x must equal $180 - 100 - 40 = 40$. Therefore, each statement alone is sufficient.

127. **(C)** (1) tells us the area of the circle is $\pi 4^2 = 16\pi$. Since there are 360° in the whole circle, (2) tells us that the shaded area is $^{60}/_{360}$ or $\frac{1}{6}$ of the area of the circle. Thus, using both (1) and (2), we can answer the question, but since we need both the radius of the circle and the value of x, neither of them alone is sufficient. Therefore, the answer is (C).

128. **(E)** Using (1) we can find the income for 1970 if we know the income for 1968 and 1969, but (1) gives no more information about the income for 1968 and 1969. If we also use (2) we can get the income in 1969 if we know the income for 1968, but we still can't determine the income for 1968. Therefore, both together are not sufficient.

129. **(D)** Since a straight line forms an angle of 180° and l' is a straight line, we know $x + y = 180$. If we use (1) we get $y = 80$, so (1) alone is sufficient. When two straight lines intersect, the vertical angles are equal. So $y = z$; thus if we use (2) we have that $y = 80$. Therefore, (2) alone is sufficient. Thus, each statement alone is sufficient.

130. **(C)** In the figure, x denotes the number taking German I but not English I, and y the number taking English I but not German I. From (1) we know that $x + 16 + y = 50$; from (2), $x = y$. Neither statement alone can be solved for x, but both together are sufficient (and yield $x = 17$).

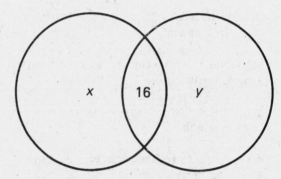

131. **(E)** (1) alone is not sufficient because it only says two sides are equal; in a square all four sides are equal. Even if we use (2) we don't know if $ABCD$ is a square since *all* angles have to be right angles in a square. Therefore, both statements together are insufficient.

132. **(B)** The average yearly wage per employee is the total amount of wages divided by the number of employees. So (2) alone is sufficient since it gives the total amount of wages and we are given the number of employees. (1) alone is not sufficient, since (1) by itself does not tell us the total wages. Therefore, the answer is (B).

133. **(E)** Since the square of any nonzero number is positive, (1) says $x + y \neq 0$ or $x \neq -y$. So (1) alone is not sufficient. If we also assume (2), we know only that x is positive and unequal to $-y$, not whether x is greater than or less than y. Thus (1) and (2) together are insufficient.

134. **(A)** Since the circles both have radius 4, the figure $OBO'C$ is a rhombus (each side is a radius) and the diagonals BC and OO' (of a rhombus) are perpendicular. So (2) does not give any new information, and is thus not sufficient alone. (1) alone is sufficient. The area of each circle is 16π since the radius of each circle is 4. If there were no shaded area, the area enclosed by both circles would be $16\pi + 16\pi = 32\pi$. Since the area enclosed by both circles is 29π, the shaded area is $32\pi - 29\pi$ or 3π. So (1) alone is sufficient but (2) alone is insufficient.

135. **(A)** Let x be the time it takes to travel from A to B and let y be the time it takes to travel from B to A. We know $x + y = 4$. (1) says x is 125% of y or $x = \frac{5}{4}y$. So using (1) we have $x + \frac{5}{4}x = 4$ which we can solve for x. Thus, (1) alone is sufficient. (2) alone is not sufficient since we need information about the relation of x to y to solve the problem and (2) says nothing about the relation between x and y. Therefore, (1) alone is sufficient but (2) alone is insufficient.

136. **(C)** (1) alone is insufficient. If x and y were right angles, (1) would imply that l and l' are parallel, but if x and y are not right angles, (1) would imply that l and l' are not parallel. (2) alone is not sufficient since it gives information only about l' and says nothing about the relation of l and l'. (1) and (2) together give $x = z$ which means that l and l' are parallel. Therefore, (1) and (2) together are sufficient but neither alone is sufficient.

137. **(E)** If we use (1), we have $x + y + z = 3 + z$, but we have no information about z, so (1) alone is insufficient. If we use (2) alone, we have $x + y + z = y + 2$, but since we have no information about y, (2) alone is insufficient. If we use both (1) and (2), we obtain $x + y + z = y + 2 = 3 + z$. We can also add (1) and (2) to obtain $2x + y + z = 5$, but we can't find the value of $x + y + z$ without more information. So the answer is **(E)**.

138. **(C)** We need to know the surface area of the box. Since each side is a rectangle, we know the surface area will be $2LW + 2LH + 2HW$ where H is the height of the box, L is the length, and W is the width. We are given that $L = 7$, so to answer the question we need H and W. Since (1) gives only the value of W and (2) gives only the value of H, neither alone is sufficient. But both (1) and (2) together are sufficient.

139. **(E)** The profit is the selling price minus the cost, so to answer the question we need to know both the selling price and the cost of 15 boxes of detergent. Since (1) and (2) give information only about the cost but no information about the selling price, both statements together are insufficient.

140. **(E)** (1) alone is not sufficient. A four-sided figure can have both larger perimeter and smaller area than another four-sided figure, or it could have larger perimeter and larger area. (2) alone is also insufficient since the length of one diagonal does not determine the area of a four-sided figure. (1) and (2) together are also insufficient, as shown by the figure.

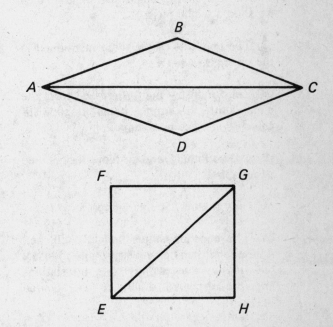

(1) and (2) are both satisfied and the area of *EFGH* is larger than *ABCD*. But (1) and (2) could still be satisfied and the area of *ABCD* be larger than the area of *EFGH*; so the answer is (E).

Section V   Business Judgment

141. **(A)** Expanding sales to the U.S. is the objective of Zaire's textile executives.

142. **(C)** Confidence in Zaire's inventiveness, while potentially beneficial, was a minor factor in the executive's immediate search for ways to penetrate the American market.

143. **(E)** That American companies might invest in Zaire was of no immediate concern to the textile executives, although conceivably it might benefit them in the future.

144. **(E)** That Zaire is an African country had no influence on the decision or the decision makers.

145. **(D)** The consequences of and probability that restrictive legislation might be passed by the American Congress was considered by Mr. Hesh and the textile executives. The assumption seemed to be that such legislation would pass.

146. **(B)** The only one of the three mentioned in the passage was III.

147. **(B)** Zaire industry had progressed from the manufacture of simple items to sophisticated goods. See paragraph 2.

148. **(D)** Both clothing and fashion design. See paragraph 3.

149. **(A)** Only textiles. See paragraph 5.

150. **(A)** The question states "might" sell, i.e., it is a conditional possibility. Zaire industry has *already* successfully sold translations and pre-fabricated diners to the United States.

151. **(B)** His attitude is given in the next to last paragraph, lines 5 and 6.

152. **(B)** Throughout the passage, Mr. Hesh advocates more trade between Zaire and the United States. Moreover, in the next to last paragraph, his opinion is that pending legislation to limit imports (protectionism) is undesirable. Thus, Mr. Hesh can be classified as in favor of liberalized trade.

153. **(B)** The establishment of a new supermarket chain in the R & S market area and its use of grade labeling was a major factor considered by Joseph in his decision to adopt (or not) the practice.

154. **(C)** The fact that the government's program would standardize grading was a minor factor related to the consideration of whether or not to adopt the practice.

155. **(B)** Grade labeling was a major factor considered by R & S in determining the consequences of their adoption on the future sale of their products.

156. **(B)** Federal food standards were also a major factor in the decision.

157. **(A)** In deciding whether to adopt grade labeling, Mr. Joseph's major consideration was what effect it would have on consumer acceptance of his products. Since R & S already enjoyed a high reputation, Joseph did not want to take any action that would jeopardize it.

158. **(B)** See the last paragraph. It is clear that grade labeling was intended to help the consumer identify brands by level of quality.

159. **(A)** R & S management felt that it enjoyed a good reputation as canners of high quality canned fruits and vegetables. Already having this favorable brand image, there was little reason to adopt grade labeling.

160. **(E)** All three. See the third paragraph.

161. **(B)** The Department of Agriculture. See paragraph 5.

162. **(D)** Taste was not a consideration in the Department of Agriculture's labeling procedure. See paragraph 5.

163. **(C)** The labels include type of food; can size; number of servings per can; net contents; and name and address of the chain. See paragraph 2, lines 6–8.

164. **(C)** See paragraph 3, lines 4–6 and paragraph 4, lines 1–3.

165. **(B)** See the last paragraph, lines 9–10.

Section VI   Mathematics

166. **(C)** $\frac{15}{16} = .9375$ which is 93.75%.

167. **(B)** Worker F loads $\frac{1}{15}$ of the truck in a minute and worker S loads $\frac{1}{20}$ of the truck in a minute. Therefore, working together they load $\frac{1}{15} + \frac{1}{20} = \frac{7}{60}$ of the truck in a minute. So it will take them $\frac{60}{7} = 8\frac{4}{7}$ minutes to load the truck.

168. **(D)** Since the car accelerates its speed 5 mph, at the end of each hour it will be traveling 5 mph faster than it was at the beginning of the hour. The car was traveling 50 mph to begin with so it has to be traveling 15 mph faster to go 65 mph. Therefore, it will take $\frac{15}{5} = 3$ hours to reach a speed of 65 mph.

169. **(D)** Since 75 cars an hour is 50% $= \frac{1}{2}$ of its capacity, the Tarrytown factory will produce $75 \times 2 = 150$ cars an hour at full capacity. 100 cars an hour is 80% $= \frac{4}{5}$ of the capacity of the Mahwah factory, so at full

capacity it will produce $100 \times \frac{5}{4} = 125$ cars an hour. Therefore, the Tarrytown production at full capacity divided by the Mahwah production at full capacity is $\frac{150}{125} = \frac{6}{5}$ or a ratio of 6 to 5.

170. **(C)** The average is the sum of the 5 integers divided by 5. Since the average is 7, the sum of the 5 integers is $5 \times 7 = 35$.

171. **(B)** The solid black line which represents income from employment per head in the United Kingdom is the only line which never drops below 5%. Therefore, it is the only indicator which has increased by at least 5% every year.

172. **(E)** When income from employment per head in the United States was 100 in 1963, it was about 146 at the beginning of 1971. If it was 250 in 1963 and x at the beginning of 1971, then $\frac{146}{100} = \frac{x}{250}$ so $x = 365$.

173. **(D)** The difference between the solid black line (income from employment) and the solid red line (labor cost per unit of gross value) in the United States was about 8 in 1965. By 1971 it was more than 20 but less than 30. Therefore, it more than doubled, but it did not quadruple.

174. **(D)**

STATEMENT I cannot be inferred since the graphs only compare the later values in the U.S. to earlier values in the U.S. There is no information which compares the value of any of the indicators in the U.S. and U.K. (For example, if the value of income from employment per head in 1963 was twice as high in the U.S. as in the U.K., then the value would still be higher in the U.S. in 1971 although it increased at a higher *rate* between 1963 and 1971 in the U.K.)

STATEMENT II can be inferred since in 1963 *all* indicators were at 100 and only income from employment per head in the U.K. had gone over 160 by 1971.

STATEMENT III can be inferred since $\frac{6}{5}$ of 100 = 120 and the black dotted line never went over 120 in 1970.

Therefore, only STATEMENTS II and III can be inferred from the graph.

175. **(B)** After the 20% discount, the price of the car is 80%, which is .8 of $3,000, or $2,400. If the price is now raised by 10%, then the price is raised by .1 of $2,400, or $240. Therefore, the final price is $2,400 + $240 = $2,640.

176. **(D)** The tax on a gross income of $10,000 is $2,000. Since $\frac{2,000}{10,000} = .2 = 20\%$, the rate of taxation is 20%.

177. **(C)** The tax on $20,000 is $7,200 and the tax on $10,000 is 2,000. Therefore, he will pay $7,200 − $2,000 or $5,200 tax on the extra $10,000.

178. **(C)** Each person with an income of $10,000 pays $2,000 in taxes, so together they pay $4,000 in taxes. The tax on $20,000 is $7,200, so the fraction is $\frac{\$4,000}{\$7,200} = \frac{40}{72} = \frac{10}{18} = \frac{5}{9}$.

179. **(E)** Working together both pumps pump $(u + v)$ cubic feet of water per minute, so it will take $\frac{50}{u + v}$ minutes to pump 50 cubic feet of water.

180. **(D)** A trapezoid can be divided into 2 triangles by connecting any two opposite vertices, so the sum of the interior angles is 360°. Since $2 + 4 + 5 + 7 = 18$ and $\frac{360}{18} = 20$, the angles are 40°, 80°, 100°, and 140°. Therefore, the smallest angle is 40°.

181. **(E)** $\frac{9/7}{5/6}$ is equal to $\frac{9}{7} \times \frac{6}{5} = \frac{54}{35}$.

182. **(C)** Since the largest percentage is 74%, and the largest amount spent is by the 19 to 64 age group, the amount spent by the 19 to 64 age group from private sources is larger than the amount spent in any of the other categories.

183. **(B)** $19.8 billion is spent on health care for those 65 and over, and 66% of that comes from public sources. The table tells us that for people 65 and over, 80.8% of the public sources are federal funds. So (.66) (.808) (19.8) billion is spent from federal funds on health care for those 65 and over. To save time notice that .66 is about $\frac{2}{3}$ and .808 is about $\frac{4}{5}$, so the answer is about $\frac{2}{3} \times \frac{4}{5} \times$ (19.8 billion) which is $\frac{8 \times 6.6}{5}$ billion $= \frac{52.8}{5} = 10.56 billion.

184. **(B)** 26% is about $\frac{1}{4}$, so about $\frac{1}{4}$ of the $40.7 billion of the 19 to 64 group comes from public funds. This is about $10.2 billion. 66% is about $\frac{2}{3}$, so about $\frac{2}{3}$ of the $19.8 billion of the 65 and over group comes from public sources. Therefore, about $13.2 billion comes from public sources, so the ratio is $\frac{10.2}{13.2}$, or about $\frac{3}{4}$.

185. **(E)**

The total expenditure for health care is (11.5 + 40.7 + 19.8) billion = $72 billion. $11.5 billion was spent for the under 19 group. Since 11.5 is more than $\frac{1}{7}$ of 72, STATEMENT I is true.

STATEMENT II is true since 72% of 11.5 is more than 34% of 19.8.

STATEMENT III is also true. The under 19 group gets 42.1% of 28% of 11.5 billion from state and local funds, the 19 to 64 group gets 19.2% of 66% of 19.8 billion from state and local groups, and the 65 and over group gets 19.2% of 6% of 19.8 billion from state and local group. It is obvious that the under 19 groups gets less than the 19 to 64 group. Since $\frac{1}{2}$ of $\frac{1}{4}$ of 40.7 is much larger than $\frac{1}{5}$ of $\frac{2}{3}$ of 20, we can see that the 19 to 64 group gets the most from state and local funds.

Therefore, STATEMENTS I, II, and III all can be inferred.

186. **(D)** Imports from non-EEC countries are denoted by the grey area which is the *difference* between the two lines. This difference was the largest in **M** (the fifth month) of 1971 when total imports were about 1350 and imports from the EEC were about 600. So the maximum was about $1350 - 600$ or 750.

187. **(B)** Since the grey area represents about one half the total import area of the graph, the answer is $\frac{1}{2}$.

188. **(B)** Since 5 of the workers earned $180 each, those 5 workers earned a total of $900. The total for all 15 workers was $1,800, so the remaining 10 workers earned a total of $1,800 - $900 = $900. Therefore, the average weekly wage of the 10 remaining workers is $\frac{1}{10}$ of $900 which is $90.

189. **(C)** Using the Pythagorean theorem, we can determine that the square of the length of the side opposite the right angle is equal to $5^2 + 12^2$ which equals 169. Since the square root of 169 is 13, the side has length 13.

190. **(C)** Since $2\frac{1}{2}$ hours is equal to 150 minutes, you must look in the column with time equal to 150. $2\frac{1}{2}$ hours after it started, the car was traveling at 65 mph.

191. **(B)** At the end of 2 hours (120 minutes) the speed was 67.5 mph and at the end of 3 hours (180 minutes) the speed of the car was 60 mph. Therefore, the speed decreased by 7.5 mph during the last hour of the 3-hour period shown on the table.

192. **(A)**

STATEMENT I cannot be inferred since we need to know how far the car traveled in the three hours to find its average speed.

STATEMENT II is true because at the beginning of the fifth half hour (120 minutes) the car was going 67.5 mph but at the end of the fifth half hour (150 minutes) the car was going 65 mph. Since 65 mph is slower than 67.5 mph, the car must have slowed down during the fifth half hour.

STATEMENT III cannot be inferred because the table only gives the speed of the car at certain times during the 3 hours. The car may have started out going 0 miles per hour.

Therefore, only STATEMENT II can be inferred from the table.

193. **(E)** Since John makes 4 baskets in 1 hour, he will make 8 in 2 hours. Since Allison makes 6 baskets in 1 hr. 10 min. $\left(\frac{7}{6}\text{ of an hour}\right)$, she makes 1 basket in $\frac{7}{36}$ of an hour, and she will make $\frac{2}{7/36} = 2 \times \frac{36}{7} = \frac{72}{7} = 10\frac{2}{7}$ in 2 hours. Therefore, together they will make $18\frac{2}{7}$ baskets in 2 hours.

194. **(D)** The average of the four integers is $\frac{1}{4}$ of 26 which is $6\frac{1}{2}$, so the integers should include 6 and 7. If you add 5, 6, 7, and 8, the result is 26, so the four integers are 5, 6, 7, and 8. The product of $5 \times 6 \times 7 \times 8 = 30 \times 56 = 1,680$.

195. **(A)** Factor $x^2 + 3x - 4$ into $(x - 1)(x + 4)$. $x^2 + 3x - 4$ is equal to 0 only if $x - 1$ or $x + 4$ is equal to 0. Therefore, $x^2 + 3x - 4 = 0$ only when $x = 1$ or $x = -4$.

196. **(B)** The solid line denoting presidential votes was just below the 50 million mark in 1948.

197. **(C)** About 50 million of the 80 million citizens 21 years old or over voted for president in 1940. Therefore, the proportion is about $\frac{50 \text{ million}}{80 \text{ million}}$ which is $\frac{5}{8}$.

198. **(C)** Between 1931 and 1951 the only election in which the dotted line (representatives) was below 30 was in 1942.

199. **(A)** Since $x + y = 2$, this implies that $x = 2 - y$. If $y > 3$, then $2 - y$ is < -1, so $x < -1$.

200. **(D)** $\frac{5/2}{3/4} = \frac{5}{2} \times \frac{4}{3} = \frac{10}{3}$, so $\frac{2}{3}$ of $\frac{10}{3}$ is $\frac{2}{3} \times \frac{10}{3} = \frac{20}{9}$.

201. **(B)** There are 15,856 thousand people entitled to social security benefits and 33.4% are in the age group. Since 33.4% is approximately $\frac{1}{3}$, approximately 5,300,000 are in the 65–69 age group.

202. **(A)** 24.2% of the people in the category of other enrolled persons are men and 75.8% are women. The ratio of 24.2 to 75.8 is about 1 to 3 since $3 \cdot 25 = 75$.

203. **(C)**

STATEMENT I is true since 4.5% of 15,856,-000 is more than 22% of 2,446,000.

STATEMENT II is true. 92.3% of the people are white and 7.7% are nonwhite and 92.3 is more than 9 times 7.7.

STATEMENT III is not true because only 31.2% of all enrollees are in the 65–69 age group and $\frac{1}{3}$ is $33\frac{1}{3}$%.

Therefore, only STATEMENTS I and II can be inferred.

204. **(D)** There were 18,859 thousand people enrolled. Since 50% = $\frac{1}{2}$, 18,859 thousand people is $\frac{1}{2}$ the number of retired people. Therefore, there were 37,718,000 retired people on July 1, 1966.

205. **(D)** After the first discount the truck was selling for 90% of $6,800, which is $6,120. The selling price of the truck was 85% of $6,120, which is $5,202.

Evaluating Your Score

Tabulate your score for each section of Sample Test 3 according to the directions on pages 4–5 and record the results in the Self-scoring Table below. Then find your rank for each score on the Self-scoring Scale and record it in the appropriate blank.

Self-scoring Table

PART	SCORE	RANK
1		
2		
3		
4		
5		
6		

Self-scoring Scale

Achievement

PART	POOR	FAIR	GOOD	EXCELLENT
1	0–15	16–21	22–25	26–30
2	0–29	30–40	41–47	48–55
3	0–20	21–28	29–34	35–40
4	0–7	8–10	11–12	13–15
5	0–12	13–17	18–20	21–25
6	0–20	21–28	29–34	35–40

Study again the Review sections covering material in Sample Test 3 for which you had a rank of FAIR or POOR. Then go on to Sample Test 4.

To obtain an approximation of your actual GMAT score see page 5.

Sample Test 4

Section I   Reading Recall

TOTAL TIME: 35 minutes

Part A: TIME — 15 minutes

DIRECTIONS: This part contains three reading passages. You are to read each one carefully. You will have fifteen minutes to study the three passages and twenty minutes to answer questions based on them. When answering the questions, you will *not* be allowed to refer back to the passages.

Passage 1:

The economic condition of the low-income regions of the world is one of the great problems of our time. Their progress is important to the high-income countries, not only for humanitarian and political reasons but also because rapid economic growth in the low-income countries could make a substantial contribution to the expansion and prosperity of the world economy as a whole.

The governments of most high-income countries have in recent years undertaken important aid programs, both bilaterally and multilaterally, and have thus demonstrated their interest in the development of low-income countries. They have also worked within the General Agreement on Tariffs and Trade (GATT) for greater freedom of trade and, recognizing the special problems of low-income countries, have made special trading arrangements to meet their needs. But a faster expansion of trade with high-income countries is necessary if the low-income countries are to enjoy a satisfactory rate of growth.

This statement is therefore concerned with the policies of high-income countries toward their trade with low-income countries. Our recommendations are based on the conviction that a better distribution of world resources and a more rational utilization of labor are in the general interest. A liberal policy on the part of high-income countries with respect to their trade with low-income countries will not only be helpful to the low-income countries but, when transitional adjustments have taken place, beneficial to the high-income countries as well.

It is necessary to recognize however, that in furthering the development of low-income countries, the high-income countries can play only a supporting role. If development is to be successful, the main effort must necessarily be made by the people of the low-income countries. The high-income countries are, moreover, likely to provide aid and facilitate trade more readily and extensively where the low-income countries are seen to be making sound and determined efforts to help themselves, and thus to be making effective use of their aid and trade opportunities.

It is, then, necessary that the low-income countries take full account of the lessons that have been learned from the experience of recent years, if they wish to achieve successful development and benefit from support from high-income countries. Among the most important of these lessons are the following:

Answer Sheet — Sample Test 4

Section I — Reading Recall

1. Ⓐ Ⓑ Ⓒ Ⓓ Ⓔ
2. Ⓐ Ⓑ Ⓒ Ⓓ Ⓔ
3. Ⓐ Ⓑ Ⓒ Ⓓ Ⓔ
4. Ⓐ Ⓑ Ⓒ Ⓓ Ⓔ
5. Ⓐ Ⓑ Ⓒ Ⓓ Ⓔ
6. Ⓐ Ⓑ Ⓒ Ⓓ Ⓔ
7. Ⓐ Ⓑ Ⓒ Ⓓ Ⓔ

8. Ⓐ Ⓑ Ⓒ Ⓓ Ⓔ
9. Ⓐ Ⓑ Ⓒ Ⓓ Ⓔ
10. Ⓐ Ⓑ Ⓒ Ⓓ Ⓔ
11. Ⓐ Ⓑ Ⓒ Ⓓ Ⓔ
12. Ⓐ Ⓑ Ⓒ Ⓓ Ⓔ
13. Ⓐ Ⓑ Ⓒ Ⓓ Ⓔ
14. Ⓐ Ⓑ Ⓒ Ⓓ Ⓔ

15. Ⓐ Ⓑ Ⓒ Ⓓ Ⓔ
16. Ⓐ Ⓑ Ⓒ Ⓓ Ⓔ
17. Ⓐ Ⓑ Ⓒ Ⓓ Ⓔ
18. Ⓐ Ⓑ Ⓒ Ⓓ Ⓔ
19. Ⓐ Ⓑ Ⓒ Ⓓ Ⓔ
20. Ⓐ Ⓑ Ⓒ Ⓓ Ⓔ
21. Ⓐ Ⓑ Ⓒ Ⓓ Ⓔ
22. Ⓐ Ⓑ Ⓒ Ⓓ Ⓔ

23. Ⓐ Ⓑ Ⓒ Ⓓ Ⓔ
24. Ⓐ Ⓑ Ⓒ Ⓓ Ⓔ
25. Ⓐ Ⓑ Ⓒ Ⓓ Ⓔ
26. Ⓐ Ⓑ Ⓒ Ⓓ Ⓔ
27. Ⓐ Ⓑ Ⓒ Ⓓ Ⓔ
28. Ⓐ Ⓑ Ⓒ Ⓓ Ⓔ
29. Ⓐ Ⓑ Ⓒ Ⓓ Ⓔ
30. Ⓐ Ⓑ Ⓒ Ⓓ Ⓔ

Section II — Mathematics

31. Ⓐ Ⓑ Ⓒ Ⓓ Ⓔ
32. Ⓐ Ⓑ Ⓒ Ⓓ Ⓔ
33. Ⓐ Ⓑ Ⓒ Ⓓ Ⓔ
34. Ⓐ Ⓑ Ⓒ Ⓓ Ⓔ
35. Ⓐ Ⓑ Ⓒ Ⓓ Ⓔ
36. Ⓐ Ⓑ Ⓒ Ⓓ Ⓔ
37. Ⓐ Ⓑ Ⓒ Ⓓ Ⓔ
38. Ⓐ Ⓑ Ⓒ Ⓓ Ⓔ
39. Ⓐ Ⓑ Ⓒ Ⓓ Ⓔ
40. Ⓐ Ⓑ Ⓒ Ⓓ Ⓔ
41. Ⓐ Ⓑ Ⓒ Ⓓ Ⓔ
42. Ⓐ Ⓑ Ⓒ Ⓓ Ⓔ
43. Ⓐ Ⓑ Ⓒ Ⓓ Ⓔ

44. Ⓐ Ⓑ Ⓒ Ⓓ Ⓔ
45. Ⓐ Ⓑ Ⓒ Ⓓ Ⓔ
46. Ⓐ Ⓑ Ⓒ Ⓓ Ⓔ
47. Ⓐ Ⓑ Ⓒ Ⓓ Ⓔ
48. Ⓐ Ⓑ Ⓒ Ⓓ Ⓔ
49. Ⓐ Ⓑ Ⓒ Ⓓ Ⓔ
50. Ⓐ Ⓑ Ⓒ Ⓓ Ⓔ
51. Ⓐ Ⓑ Ⓒ Ⓓ Ⓔ
52. Ⓐ Ⓑ Ⓒ Ⓓ Ⓔ
53. Ⓐ Ⓑ Ⓒ Ⓓ Ⓔ
54. Ⓐ Ⓑ Ⓒ Ⓓ Ⓔ
55. Ⓐ Ⓑ Ⓒ Ⓓ Ⓔ
56. Ⓐ Ⓑ Ⓒ Ⓓ Ⓔ
57. Ⓐ Ⓑ Ⓒ Ⓓ Ⓔ

58. Ⓐ Ⓑ Ⓒ Ⓓ Ⓔ
59. Ⓐ Ⓑ Ⓒ Ⓓ Ⓔ
60. Ⓐ Ⓑ Ⓒ Ⓓ Ⓔ
61. Ⓐ Ⓑ Ⓒ Ⓓ Ⓔ
62. Ⓐ Ⓑ Ⓒ Ⓓ Ⓔ
63. Ⓐ Ⓑ Ⓒ Ⓓ Ⓔ
64. Ⓐ Ⓑ Ⓒ Ⓓ Ⓔ
65. Ⓐ Ⓑ Ⓒ Ⓓ Ⓔ
66. Ⓐ Ⓑ Ⓒ Ⓓ Ⓔ
67. Ⓐ Ⓑ Ⓒ Ⓓ Ⓔ
68. Ⓐ Ⓑ Ⓒ Ⓓ Ⓔ
69. Ⓐ Ⓑ Ⓒ Ⓓ Ⓔ
70. Ⓐ Ⓑ Ⓒ Ⓓ Ⓔ
71. Ⓐ Ⓑ Ⓒ Ⓓ Ⓔ

72. Ⓐ Ⓑ Ⓒ Ⓓ Ⓔ
73. Ⓐ Ⓑ Ⓒ Ⓓ Ⓔ
74. Ⓐ Ⓑ Ⓒ Ⓓ Ⓔ
75. Ⓐ Ⓑ Ⓒ Ⓓ Ⓔ
76. Ⓐ Ⓑ Ⓒ Ⓓ Ⓔ
77. Ⓐ Ⓑ Ⓒ Ⓓ Ⓔ
78. Ⓐ Ⓑ Ⓒ Ⓓ Ⓔ
79. Ⓐ Ⓑ Ⓒ Ⓓ Ⓔ
80. Ⓐ Ⓑ Ⓒ Ⓓ Ⓔ
81. Ⓐ Ⓑ Ⓒ Ⓓ Ⓔ
82. Ⓐ Ⓑ Ⓒ Ⓓ Ⓔ
83. Ⓐ Ⓑ Ⓒ Ⓓ Ⓔ
84. Ⓐ Ⓑ Ⓒ Ⓓ Ⓔ
85. Ⓐ Ⓑ Ⓒ Ⓓ Ⓔ

Section III — Business Judgment

86. Ⓐ Ⓑ Ⓒ Ⓓ Ⓔ
87. Ⓐ Ⓑ Ⓒ Ⓓ Ⓔ
88. Ⓐ Ⓑ Ⓒ Ⓓ Ⓔ
89. Ⓐ Ⓑ Ⓒ Ⓓ Ⓔ
90. Ⓐ Ⓑ Ⓒ Ⓓ Ⓔ

91. Ⓐ Ⓑ Ⓒ Ⓓ Ⓔ
92. Ⓐ Ⓑ Ⓒ Ⓓ Ⓔ
93. Ⓐ Ⓑ Ⓒ Ⓓ Ⓔ
94. Ⓐ Ⓑ Ⓒ Ⓓ Ⓔ
95. Ⓐ Ⓑ Ⓒ Ⓓ Ⓔ

96. Ⓐ Ⓑ Ⓒ Ⓓ Ⓔ
97. Ⓐ Ⓑ Ⓒ Ⓓ Ⓔ
98. Ⓐ Ⓑ Ⓒ Ⓓ Ⓔ
99. Ⓐ Ⓑ Ⓒ Ⓓ Ⓔ
100. Ⓐ Ⓑ Ⓒ Ⓓ Ⓔ

101. Ⓐ Ⓑ Ⓒ Ⓓ Ⓔ
102. Ⓐ Ⓑ Ⓒ Ⓓ Ⓔ
103. Ⓐ Ⓑ Ⓒ Ⓓ Ⓔ
104. Ⓐ Ⓑ Ⓒ Ⓓ Ⓔ
105. Ⓐ Ⓑ Ⓒ Ⓓ Ⓔ

Section IV — Data Sufficiency

106. Ⓐ Ⓑ Ⓒ Ⓓ Ⓔ   109. Ⓐ Ⓑ Ⓒ Ⓓ Ⓔ   113. Ⓐ Ⓑ Ⓒ Ⓓ Ⓔ   117 Ⓐ Ⓑ Ⓒ Ⓓ Ⓔ
107. Ⓐ Ⓑ Ⓒ Ⓓ Ⓔ   110. Ⓐ Ⓑ Ⓒ Ⓓ Ⓔ   114. Ⓐ Ⓑ Ⓒ Ⓓ Ⓔ   118. Ⓐ Ⓑ Ⓒ Ⓓ Ⓔ
108. Ⓐ Ⓑ Ⓒ Ⓓ Ⓔ   111. Ⓐ Ⓑ Ⓒ Ⓓ Ⓔ   115. Ⓐ Ⓑ Ⓒ Ⓓ Ⓔ   119. Ⓐ Ⓑ Ⓒ Ⓓ Ⓔ
   112. Ⓐ Ⓑ Ⓒ Ⓓ Ⓔ   116. Ⓐ Ⓑ Ⓒ Ⓓ Ⓔ   120. Ⓐ Ⓑ Ⓒ Ⓓ Ⓔ

Section V — Verbal Aptitude

121. Ⓐ Ⓑ Ⓒ Ⓓ Ⓔ   127. Ⓐ Ⓑ Ⓒ Ⓓ Ⓔ   133. Ⓐ Ⓑ Ⓒ Ⓓ Ⓔ   139. Ⓐ Ⓑ Ⓒ Ⓓ Ⓔ
122. Ⓐ Ⓑ Ⓒ Ⓓ Ⓔ   128. Ⓐ Ⓑ Ⓒ Ⓓ Ⓔ   134. Ⓐ Ⓑ Ⓒ Ⓓ Ⓔ   140. Ⓐ Ⓑ Ⓒ Ⓓ Ⓔ
123. Ⓐ Ⓑ Ⓒ Ⓓ Ⓔ   129. Ⓐ Ⓑ Ⓒ Ⓓ Ⓔ   135. Ⓐ Ⓑ Ⓒ Ⓓ Ⓔ   141. Ⓐ Ⓑ Ⓒ Ⓓ Ⓔ
124. Ⓐ Ⓑ Ⓒ Ⓓ Ⓔ   130. Ⓐ Ⓑ Ⓒ Ⓓ Ⓔ   136. Ⓐ Ⓑ Ⓒ Ⓓ Ⓔ   142. Ⓐ Ⓑ Ⓒ Ⓓ Ⓔ
125. Ⓐ Ⓑ Ⓒ Ⓓ Ⓔ   131. Ⓐ Ⓑ Ⓒ Ⓓ Ⓔ   137. Ⓐ Ⓑ Ⓒ Ⓓ Ⓔ   143. Ⓐ Ⓑ Ⓒ Ⓓ Ⓔ
126. Ⓐ Ⓑ Ⓒ Ⓓ Ⓔ   132. Ⓐ Ⓑ Ⓒ Ⓓ Ⓔ   138. Ⓐ Ⓑ Ⓒ Ⓓ Ⓔ   144. Ⓐ Ⓑ Ⓒ Ⓓ Ⓔ
   145. Ⓐ Ⓑ Ⓒ Ⓓ Ⓔ

Section VI — Business Judgment

146. Ⓐ Ⓑ Ⓒ Ⓓ Ⓔ   151. Ⓐ Ⓑ Ⓒ Ⓓ Ⓔ   156. Ⓐ Ⓑ Ⓒ Ⓓ Ⓔ   161. Ⓐ Ⓑ Ⓒ Ⓓ Ⓔ
147. Ⓐ Ⓑ Ⓒ Ⓓ Ⓔ   152. Ⓐ Ⓑ Ⓒ Ⓓ Ⓔ   157. Ⓐ Ⓑ Ⓒ Ⓓ Ⓔ   162. Ⓐ Ⓑ Ⓒ Ⓓ Ⓔ
148. Ⓐ Ⓑ Ⓒ Ⓓ Ⓔ   153. Ⓐ Ⓑ Ⓒ Ⓓ Ⓔ   158. Ⓐ Ⓑ Ⓒ Ⓓ Ⓔ   163. Ⓐ Ⓑ Ⓒ Ⓓ Ⓔ
149. Ⓐ Ⓑ Ⓒ Ⓓ Ⓔ   154. Ⓐ Ⓑ Ⓒ Ⓓ Ⓔ   159. Ⓐ Ⓑ Ⓒ Ⓓ Ⓔ   164. Ⓐ Ⓑ Ⓒ Ⓓ Ⓔ
150. Ⓐ Ⓑ Ⓒ Ⓓ Ⓔ   155. Ⓐ Ⓑ Ⓒ Ⓓ Ⓔ   160. Ⓐ Ⓑ Ⓒ Ⓓ Ⓔ   165. Ⓐ Ⓑ Ⓒ Ⓓ Ⓔ

Section VII — Writing Ability

166. Ⓐ Ⓑ Ⓒ Ⓓ Ⓔ   172. Ⓐ Ⓑ Ⓒ Ⓓ Ⓔ   178. Ⓐ Ⓑ Ⓒ Ⓓ Ⓔ   184. Ⓐ Ⓑ Ⓒ Ⓓ Ⓔ
167. Ⓐ Ⓑ Ⓒ Ⓓ Ⓔ   173. Ⓐ Ⓑ Ⓒ Ⓓ Ⓔ   179. Ⓐ Ⓑ Ⓒ Ⓓ Ⓔ   185. Ⓐ Ⓑ Ⓒ Ⓓ Ⓔ
168. Ⓐ Ⓑ Ⓒ Ⓓ Ⓔ   174. Ⓐ Ⓑ Ⓒ Ⓓ Ⓔ   180. Ⓐ Ⓑ Ⓒ Ⓓ Ⓔ   186. Ⓐ Ⓑ Ⓒ Ⓓ Ⓔ
169. Ⓐ Ⓑ Ⓒ Ⓓ Ⓔ   175. Ⓐ Ⓑ Ⓒ Ⓓ Ⓔ   181. Ⓐ Ⓑ Ⓒ Ⓓ Ⓔ   187. Ⓐ Ⓑ Ⓒ Ⓓ Ⓔ
170. Ⓐ Ⓑ Ⓒ Ⓓ Ⓔ   176. Ⓐ Ⓑ Ⓒ Ⓓ Ⓔ   182. Ⓐ Ⓑ Ⓒ Ⓓ Ⓔ   188. Ⓐ Ⓑ Ⓒ Ⓓ Ⓔ
171. Ⓐ Ⓑ Ⓒ Ⓓ Ⓔ   177. Ⓐ Ⓑ Ⓒ Ⓓ Ⓔ   183. Ⓐ Ⓑ Ⓒ Ⓓ Ⓔ   189. Ⓐ Ⓑ Ⓒ Ⓓ Ⓔ
   190. Ⓐ Ⓑ Ⓒ Ⓓ Ⓔ

Severe damage has been done by inflation. A sound financial framework evokes higher domestic savings and investment as well as more aid and investment from abroad. Budgetary and monetary discipline and a more efficient financial and fiscal system help greatly to mobilize funds for investment and thereby decisively influence the rate of growth. Foreign aid should also be efficiently applied to this end.

The energies of the people of low-income countries are more likely to be harnessed to the task of economic development where the policies of their governments aim to offer economic opportunity for all and to reduce excessive social inequalities.

Development plans have tended to concentrate on industrial investment. The growth of industry depends, however, on concomitant development in agriculture. A steady rise in productivity on the farms, where in almost all low-income countries a majority of the labor force works, is an essential condition of rapid over-all growth. Satisfactory development of agriculture is also necessary to provide an adequate market for an expanding industrial sector and to feed the growing urban population without burdening the balance of payments with heavy food imports. Diminishing surpluses in the high-income countries underline the need for a faster growth of agricultural productivity in low-income countries. Success in this should, moreover, lead to greater trade in agricultural products among the low-income countries themselves as well as to increased exports of some agricultural products to the high-income countries.

There can be no doubt about the urgency of the world food problem. Adequate nourishment and a balanced diet are not only necessary for working adults but are crucial for the mental and physical development of growing children. Yet, in a number of low-income countries where the diet is already insufficient the production of food has fallen behind the increase in population. A continuation of this trend must lead to endemic famine. The situation demands strenuous efforts in the low-income countries to improve the production, preservation, and distribution of food so that these countries are better able to feed themselves.

Passage 2:

The concept of "standard of living" is a wide and multifaceted one. In the absence of comprehensive measurement, it is commonly expressed empirically in terms of consumption or in terms of income.

One of the most comprehensive expressions of standard of living is total consumption over an extended period, where consumption is defined not only as family purchases but also as (1) consumption of goods and services produced by the family; (2) consumption of public services provided without payment; and (3) consumption of goods and services received as compensation for labor, over and above wages and salary. It may be assumed that total consumption is less subject to incidental fluctuations than income. Moreover, it reflects not only current income but also past income and savings, windfalls, and expectations regarding future income.

Current monetary income constitutes the main indicator for the standard of living; however, standard of living is not determined solely by current income, but also by past income, accumulated assets and expectations for future income. Moreover, the standard of living of a family is influenced by the value of the public services from which it benefits and the rate of taxes which it has to pay.

Between 1964 and 1970 the standard of living of the urban population rose. During this period, average real income increased by approximately 5% per annum. During the economic recession (1966–67), the income of all strata was adversely affected, particularly that of lower income groups. Since the end of the recession, a trend of decreasing inequality in income distribution has occurred, most noticeably among the lower income brackets. In 1970, the degree of income inequality was similar to that of the year 1964, despite the fact that during the latter period two external factors—an increase in welfare payments and the aging of the population—acted towards increasing the degree of inequality.

In the period under review, the standard of living of families originating from Asia and Africa improved relative to that of all families. This improvement found expression in higher income levels, better housing, a higher ownership rate of consumer durables and an increase in the proportion of families in higher income brackets. However, even after the improvement in their relative position during the past decade, their average income is still only 70% of the overall average for all families.

One of the important factors behind the income differential between families of African and Asian origins and the rest of the population is the level of education. In recent years the gap between these two groups has narrowed among the younger generation, but it is still substantial. Unless the education gap is significantly reduced between these two groups, other means employed in an attempt to produce more income equality will be thwarted. More resources must be immediately put to the task of improving educational opportunities for families of African and Asian origin, without of course, reducing the educational facilities and opportunities open to the rest of the population.

Passage 3:

Much has been written about the need for increasing our knowledge of marketing in other countries and how different marketing systems operate in delivering goods and services to consumers. American businessmen have long been interested in foreign markets for the purpose of stimulating trade. Analysis of the mechanisms of a given country's internal trade and the structural and environmental factors of its marketing system are necessary to the success of an American firm's marketing efforts abroad.

Knowledge of a country's marketing system is of equal importance to the potential investor. Information pertaining to channels of distribution, promotional facilities, and the marketing experience of management should have weight in the investment decision equal to factors such as financing, the possibility of expropriation, and plant location. Moreover, American businessmen are certainly not limited to investment in manufacturing industry abroad; there may be profitable opportunities for the introduction of American marketing institutions and techniques in other countries. The extent to which American dollars should be channeled into the introduction of American marketing innovations depends upon the answers to the following questions: (1) to what extent is it possible to "transplant" American marketing operations or institutions to foreign countries, and (2) would such transplantations, if successful, contribute to the economic development of the recipient country?

In light of the above, research is needed to determine the factors responsible for the acceptance and growth of marketing innovations so that an understanding of the adoption process can aid American businessmen contemplating the introduction of similar marketing techniques in other developing countries.

Take the case of an American marketing innovation: self-service. Whether self-service shops can be successful outside the United States depends upon sufficient population density, consumer income and the availability of suitable store locations and manpower. But even when these environmental forces are positive, cultural constraints may still serve as a barrier to the development of self-service. For example, a packaged foods industry cannot develop unless culturally developed habits of buying only "fresh" foods and produce can be overcome. Moreover, consumers must be sufficiently literate to select products from store shelves without the help of sales clerks.

The traditional pattern of shopping (in many countries) at different locations for each category of goods—e.g. dairy products, vegetables, meat, etc.—is a custom that has been learned and reinforced over many years. It does not break down easily. Daily shopping trips may be more of a social endeavor, providing the housewife contact with her friends at the local market or grocery, although hand-to-mouth buying may also result from low incomes and lack of refrigeration and storage facilities.

In Israel, the first supermarket was successful in changing the shopping patterns of many housewives who traditionally shopped at different stores for meat, dairy products, vegetables and fruit, and baked goods. Housewives preferred the self-service shop because it reduced total shopping time and offered quality food at lower prices. Working women switched to the self-service shop because it is open during their lunch hour, unlike the small shops that close at midday for several hours. Besides introducing a wider assortment of products at lower prices, standardized packaging, pricing, and quality was afforded the Israeli consumer. Although prepackaged meats and produce were not accepted by many consumers at first, there are indications that buying habits have changed. For example, packaged meat now accounts for about 25 percent of total sales of Israel's two major self-service food chains. In addition, the rate of increase of packaged meat sales at one chain (Consumer Union) is now greater than that of other commodities.

If there is still time remaining, review the passages until all 15 minutes have elapsed. Do not look at Part B until that time.

Part B: TIME — 20 minutes

QUESTIONS TO

Passage 1:

DIRECTIONS: Answer the following questions pertaining to information contained in the three passages you have just read. You may not turn back to these passages for assistance.

1. The economic conditions of low-income countries are important to high-income countries because of

    I. Humanitarian reasons
    II. Political reasons
    III. Cultural reasons

  (A) I only
  (B) III only
  (C) I and II only
  (D) II and III only
  (E) I, II, and III

2. According to the passage, governments of most high-income countries have

  (A) not worked for freer trade with low-income countries
  (B) undertaken important aid programs for low-income countries
  (C) injected massive doses of capital into low-income countries
  (D) provided training programs for low-income country entrepreneurs
  (E) helped improve the educational systems of low-income countries

3. The major subject of the passage is concerned with

  (A) trade relations of high-income countries towards low-income countries
  (B) foreign trade problems of low-income countries
  (C) fiscal and monetary problems of low-income countries
  (D) trade arrangements under the GATT organization
  (E) general economic problems of low-income countries

4. If low-income countries expect aid from high-income countries, they must

  (A) spend the aid wisely
  (B) put their own house in order first
  (C) learn from the experience of developed countries
  (D) curb inflation
  (E) all the above

5. Which of the following policies is mentioned for its influence upon the rate of economic growth?

  (A) an efficient financial and fiscal system
  (B) a trade surplus
  (C) a democratic government
  (D) little reliance upon foreign aid
  (E) a budgetary surplus

6. Industrial growth depends upon a parallel growth of the

(A) labor force
(B) agricultural system
(C) balance of payments
(D) urban population
(E) monetary system

7. The passage states that participation of high-income countries is limited to

(A) ten percent of their GNP
(B) a supporting role
(C) regulations stipulated by GATT
(D) what low-income countries can absorb
(E) monetary aid only

8. In order to better use foreign aid, low-income countries should

(A) not take more than they can use
(B) budget the capital wisely
(C) reduce excessive social inequalities
(D) concentrate on commercial development
(E) establish agricultural communes

9. Which of the following statements represents a major problem in the agricultural systems of low-income countries?

I. The increase in food production is less than population growth.
II. Food distribution is inefficient.
III. Food prices are too high.

(A) I only
(B) III only
(C) I and II only
(D) II and III only
(E) I, II, and III

10. If low-income countries could develop economically at a faster rate, the result would be

(A) less inflation
(B) lower deficits in their balance of trade
(C) liberal trade policies
(D) better distribution of world resources
(E) more equitable fiscal policies

QUESTIONS TO

Passage 2:

11. The author expresses "standard of living" in terms of

    (A) total goods and services produced
    (B) consumption of goods and services
    (C) real income
    (D) per-capita income
    (E) discretionary income

12. Which income period best expresses "standard of living"?

    (A) past income
    (B) current income
    (C) future income
    (D) all of the above
    (E) none of the above

13. Consumption is defined as

    (A) total family purchases
    (B) total family purchases plus goods and services produced by the family
    (C) public services provided by the state
    (D) income minus expenditures on necessities
    (E) goods and services actually consumed

14. Between 1964 and 1970, average real income

    (A) remained stable
    (B) increased by about 5 percent annually
    (C) decreased slightly
    (D) decreased during the recession
    (E) decreased by 5 percent annually

15. According to the passage, income inequality (during 1970)

    (A) declined among all strata
    (B) declined most significantly among lower income groups
    (C) widened between the rich and the poor strata
    (D) did not change appreciably
    (E) declined among older groups in the population

16. The author believes that inequality of income might be narrowed if

    (A) the tax structure is reformed
    (B) the educational gap between different population groups is reduced
    (C) more jobs could be found for people of Asian-African origin
    (D) real incomes increased
    (E) a system of price controls were implemented

17. The standard of living of Asian-African immigrants improved as measured by all of the following factors *except*

   (A) higher income levels
   (B) better housing
   (C) increased ownership of consumer durables
   (D) a shift in population centers
   (E) an increased proportion of these families in higher income brackets

18. It may be inferred that the author of the passage is a(n)

   (A) engineer
   (B) food specialist
   (C) economist
   (D) bank president
   (E) efficiency expert

19. Even though the income level of families of Asian-African origin increased relatively, their average income is still

   (A) only about equal to that of other groups
   (B) about 70 percent of the overall national average
   (C) close to the national average, but slightly below
   (D) about 50 percent of the national average
   (E) about 25 percent of the national average

20. Between 1964 and 1970, the standard of living of the urban population

   (A) declined
   (B) increased
   (C) stagnated
   (D) remained about constant
   (E) doubled

QUESTIONS TO

Passage 3:

21. According to the author, knowledge of foreign marketing systems is essential because it

   (A) cements relations between countries
   (B) helps us to know about other people
   (C) stimulates foreign trade
   (D) improves channels of distribution
   (E) teaches us something about our own marketing system

22. The passage implies that marketing can contribute to

   (A) improving goods and services
   (B) economic development
   (C) more efficient promotion and advertising
   (D) full employment
   (E) growth of economic institutions

23. The introduction of American marketing techniques abroad depends upon the

   (A) educational level in the host country
   (B) amount of investment capital available
   (C) efficient channels of distribution
   (D) extent to which the technique(s) can be "transplanted"
   (E) none of the above

24. A most important constraint to the introduction of self-service shops seems to be

   (A) cultural barriers
   (B) income
   (C) education
   (D) capital formation
   (E) population dispersion

25. In Israel, daily shopping trips to the food market occur because of

   (A) a lack of supermarkets
   (B) social reasons as much as economic ones
   (C) low per-capita incomes
   (D) poor transportation facilities
   (E) fluctuating food supplies

26. Working women prefer self-service shops owing to

   (A) lower food prices
   (B) better quality food products
   (C) more convenient shopping hours
   (D) wider choice of commodities
   (E) pre-packaged meats and vegetables

27. Concerning the transfer of American marketing techniques abroad, the author concludes that

   (A) most countries can accept these techniques
   (B) they are not operable in most countries
   (C) more research is needed into this subject
   (D) the transfer depends upon capital availability
   (E) only developed countries can use American marketing techniques

28. The author states that adoption of self-service is a function of

   I. Household income
   II. Cultural and structural constraints
   III. Population density

   (A) I only   (C) I and II only   (E) I, II and III
   (B) III only   (D) II and III only

29. The article from which this passage was extracted probably appeared in a(n)

   (A) academic journal
   (B) accounting journal
   (C) management textbook
   (D) popular magazine
   (E) newspaper editorial

30. Based on the Israeli experience, we can conclude that the adoption of self-service by developing countries

   (A) is hopeless
   (B) shows some promise
   (C) no conclusion can be made
   (D) the authors are extremely optimistic
   (E) none of the above

If there is still time remaining, you may review the questions in this section only. You may not look at Part A or turn to any other section of the test.

Section II   Mathematics

TIME: 75 minutes

DIRECTIONS: Solve each of the following problems; then indicate the correct answer on the answer sheet. [On the actual test you will be permitted to use any space available on the examination paper for scratch work.]

NOTE: A figure that appears with a problem is drawn as accurately as possible so as to provide information that may help in answering the question. Numbers in this test are real numbers.

31. If 32 students in a class are female and there are 18 male students in the class, what percentage of the class is female?

   (A) 32%   (D) 64%
   (B) 36%   (E) 72%
   (C) 56.25%

32. If $x + y = 2$ and $y = 5$ what is $x - y$?

   (A) −8   (D) 2
   (B) −5   (E) 8
   (C) −3

Use the following graph for questions 33–35.

SHARE OF COMPUTER MARKET
(Percentage of machines in domestic use)

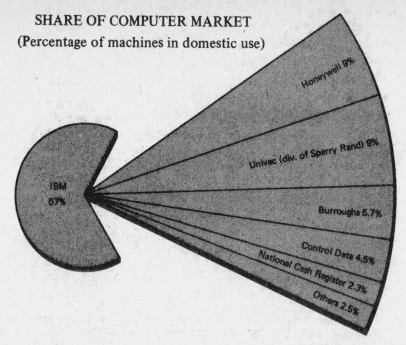

33. IBM's share of the computer market is roughly *x* times the total of all other companies; *x* equals

(A) $\frac{1}{10}$ (D) 2
(B) $\frac{1}{2}$ (E) 3
(C) $1\frac{1}{2}$

34. If Control Data and National Cash Register merged, the merged firm's new rank in share of the market would be

(A) 2   (D) 5
(B) 3   (E) 6
(C) 4

35. Consider the following statements

  I. Univac's share of the market is greater than those of Burroughs and Control Data combined.
 II. Honeywell and Univac togetner have less than a third of IBM's share of the market.
III. IBM's share of the market is 30 times larger than that of National Cash Register.

Which of the above statements are true?

(A) II only
(B) III only
(C) I and II
(D) I and III
(E) I, II and III

36. If a job takes 12 men 4 hours to complete, how long should it take 15 men to complete the job?

(A) 2 hrs. 40 min.
(B) 3 hrs.
(C) 3 hrs. 12 min.
(D) 3 hrs. 24 min.
(E) 3 hrs. 30 min.

37. Apples cost 10¢ each. If the price of apples rises by 12%, how much will a dozen apples cost?

(A) 12¢
(B) $1.20
(C) $1.32
(D) $1.34
(E) $1.36

38. How long must a driver take to drive the final 70 miles of a trip if he wants to average 50 miles an hour for the entire trip and during the first part of the trip he drove 50 miles in 1½ hours?

(A) 54 min
(B) 1 hr
(C) 66 min
(D) 70 min
(E) 75 min

Use the following table for questions 39–41.

MAJOR WAGE NEGOTIATIONS IN 1973

Month	Employer	Unions	Workers Covered
January	Popular Price Dresses	Ladies Garment Workers	59,950
February	N.J. Apparel Contractors	Ladies Garment Workers	27,050
March	Con Edison	Utility Workers	16,800
April	Goodyear	Rubber Workers	23,000
May	General Electric Co.	Electrical Workers (I.U.E.)	90,000
	Int. Paper Kraft Division	United Paperworkers, Electrical Brotherhood	11,500
	Nat. Skirt and Sportswear Assn. N.Y. Coat and Suit Assn.	Ladies Garment Workers	51,500
June	Westinghouse Electric	Electrical Workers (I.U.E.)	36,300
	Calif. Processors	Teamsters	56,550
	Nat. Master Freight	Teamsters	450,000
	Railroads	United Transportation Union	135,000
July	U.S. Postal Service	Postal Workers	600,000
September	Major Automobile Makers	Auto Workers	670,250
October	Mack Truck	Auto Workers	13,900
December	Budd	Auto Workers	19,200

Source: U.S. Dept. of Labor.

39. For how many months in 1973 are there major wage negotiations which involve fewer than 150,000 workers?

(A) 4   (D) 7
(B) 5   (E) 8
(C) 6

40. How many workers will have wage negotiations handled by the Ladies Garment Workers Union in 1973?

(A) 51,500
(B) 87,000
(C) 102,000
(D) 130,000
(E) 138,500

41. Of those workers whose wages will be negotiated in 1973, which union represents the largest number?

(A) Ladies Garment Workers
(B) Meat Cutters
(C) Teamsters
(D) Postal Workers
(E) Auto Workers

42. If a rectangle has length L and the width is one half of the length, then the area of the rectangle is

(A) L (D) $\frac{1}{4}L^2$
(B) L^2 (E) $2L$
(C) $\frac{1}{2}L^2$

43. Eggs cost 50¢ a dozen for the first 100 dozen a store buys from a wholesaler and 47¢ a dozen for all those bought in addition to the first 100 dozen. How much does it cost to buy 150 dozen eggs from the wholesaler?

(A) $70.50   (D) $123.50
(B) $72.00   (E) $150.00
(C) $73.50

44. If the product of two numbers is 5 and one of the numbers is $\frac{3}{2}$, then the sum of the two numbers is

(A) $4\frac{1}{3}$ (D) $5\frac{1}{6}$
(B) $4\frac{2}{3}$ (E) $6\frac{1}{2}$
(C) $4\frac{5}{6}$

45. Which of the following sets of numbers can be used as the lengths of the sides of a triangle?

I. [5,7,12]
II. [2,4,10]
III. [5,7,9]

(A) I only
(B) III only
(C) I and II only
(D) I and III only
(E) II and III only

46. What is the next number in the sequence 2,5,8 ... ?

(A) 7
(B) 9
(C) 10
(D) 11
(E) 12

47. A dealer owns a group of station wagons and motorcycles. If the number of tires (excluding spare tires) on the vehicles is 30 more than twice the number of vehicles, then the number of station wagons the dealer owns is

(A) 10
(B) 15
(C) 20
(D) 30
(E) 45

Use this graph for questions 48–51.

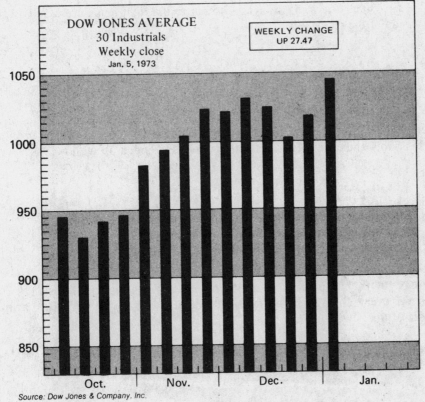

Source: Dow Jones & Company, Inc.

48. In which week during the last three months of 1972 was the average close at the highest value?

(A) first week in Nov.
(B) fourth week in Nov.
(C) second week in Dec.
(D) third week in Dec.
(E) fifth week in Dec.

49. Between which two successive weeks (of those shown) did the average drop the most?

    (A) first and second weeks in Oct.
    (B) fourth week in Oct. and first week in Nov.
    (C) third and fourth weeks in Nov.
    (D) first and second weeks in Dec.
    (E) third and fourth weeks in Dec.

50. What was the lowest value of the average during the time shown?

    (A) 910   (D) 939
    (B) 922   (E) 970
    (C) 931

51. During how many weeks (of those shown) was the average close between 960 and 1000?

    (A) 2   (D) 5
    (B) 3   (E) 6
    (C) 4

52. If the two sides of a right triangle adjacent to the right angle are 5 and 12, then the third side of the triangle is

    (A) 7   (D) 13
    (B) 9   (E) 15
    (C) 11

53. Rich sold his skis for $160.00 and his ski boots for $96.00. He made a profit of 20% on his boots and took a 10% loss on his skis. He ended up with a

    (A) loss of $1.78
    (B) loss of $1.50
    (C) gain of $3.20
    (D) gain of $7.53
    (E) gain of $17.06

54. It costs 10¢ each to print the first 500 copies of a newspaper. It costs $(10 - x/50)$¢ each for every copy after the first 500. What is x if it cost $75.00 to print 1,000 copies of the newspaper?

    (A) 2.5   (D) 250
    (B) 100   (E) 300
    (C) 25

55. The amount of coal necessary to heat a home cost $53.00 in 1972 and will increase at the rate of 15% a year. The amount of oil necessary to heat the same home cost $45.00 in 1972 but will increase at the rate of 20% a year. In 1974 which of the following methods would heat the home for the cheapest price?

(A) Use of only coal
(B) Use of only oil
(C) Use of coal or oil since they cost the same amount
(D) Use of oil for 8 months and coal for 4 months
(E) Use of coal for 8 months and oil for 4 months

56. If the side of a square increases by 30%, then its area increases by

(A) 9%
(B) 30%
(C) 60%
(D) 69%
(E) 130%

57. Train Y leaves New York at 1 A.M. and travels east at an average speed of x mph. If train Z leaves New York at 2 A.M. and travels east, at what average rate of speed will train Z have to travel in order to catch train Y by 5:30 A.M.?

(A) $\frac{5}{6}x$
(B) $\frac{9}{8}x$
(C) $\frac{6}{5}x$
(D) $\frac{9}{7}x$
(E) $\frac{3}{2}x$

Use this graph for question 58.

ANTIPOLLUTION FUNDING DURING THE 70s
(Cost in billions of dollars for 1971–1980)

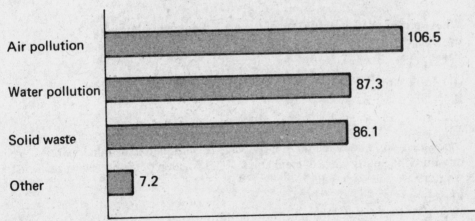

58. The ratio of air pollution funding to water pollution funding is about

(A) 2 to 1
(B) 3 to 2
(C) 6 to 5
(D) 5 to 6
(E) 2 to 3

59. If 30 boxes of pencils cost a total of $5.10, then 4 boxes of pencils should cost

(A) 52¢
(B) 68¢
(C) 78¢
(D) 85¢
(E) 93¢

60. A worker is paid r dollars for each hour he works up to 8 hours a day. For any time worked over 8 hours he is paid at the rate of $(1.5)r$ dollars an hour. The total amount of dollars the worker will earn if he works 11 hours in a day is

(A) $(4.5)r$
(B) $(5.5)r$
(C) $(9.25)r$
(D) $(11)r$
(E) $(12.5)r$

61. If the product of 3 consecutive integers is 120, then the sum of the integers is

(A) 9
(B) 12
(C) 14
(D) 15
(E) 17

Use the table below for questions 62 and 63.

Grants from the XYZ Foundation	1971	1972
Colleges	5.2	4.9
Medical research	3.1	3.5
Other	1.7	1.8
Total	10.0	10.2

62. Medical research grants between 1971 and 1972

(A) decreased by 4%
(B) stayed about the same
(C) increased by about 10%
(D) increased by about 13%
(E) increased by about 21%

63. What percent of the total grants of the *XYZ* Foundation for both years was received by colleges?

(A) 49.8
(B) 50
(C) 50.2
(D) 50.5
(E) 51

64. Mechanics are paid twice the hourly wage of salesmen. Custodial workers are paid one-third the hourly wage of mechanics. What fraction of the hourly wage of custodial workers are salesmen paid?

(A) $\frac{1}{3}$
(B) $\frac{1}{2}$
(C) $\frac{2}{3}$
(D) $\frac{4}{3}$
(E) $\frac{3}{2}$

65. If x and y are negative, then which of the following statements are always true?

 I. $x + y$ is positive
 II. xy is positive
III. $x - y$ is positive

(A) I only
(B) II only
(C) III only
(D) I and III only
(E) II and III only

66. An unloaded truck travels 10 miles on a gallon of gas. When the same truck is loaded it travels only 85% as far on a gallon of gas. How many gallons of gas will the loaded truck use to travel 50 miles?

(A) 5
(B) 5.67
(C) 5.88

(D) 6.02
(E) 6.3

67. If $8a = 6b$ and $3a = 0$ then

(A) a and b are equal
(B) $a = 6$
(C) $\dfrac{b}{a} = \dfrac{4}{3}$

(D) $a = 6$ and $b = 8$
(E) $\dfrac{a}{b} = \dfrac{3}{4}$

68. A horse can travel at the rate of 5 miles per hour for the first two hours of a trip. After the first two hours the horse's speed drops to 3 miles per hour. How many hours will it take the horse to travel 20 miles?

(A) 4
(B) 5
(C) $5\frac{1}{3}$

(D) $5\frac{1}{2}$
(E) $5\frac{2}{3}$

Use the following table for questions 69–72

THE BUDGET DOLLAR

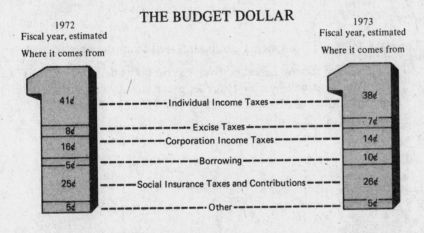

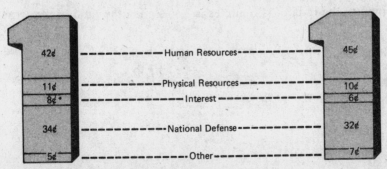

*Excludes interest paid to trust funds

69. In each year the category which provided the most income was

    (A) borrowing
    (B) individual income taxes
    (C) human resources
    (D) social insurance taxes
    (E) national defense

70. The change in the percentage of the budget allocated to human resources between 1972 and 1973 is expected to be

    (A) −3%
    (B) −2%
    (C) 0%
    (D) +2%
    (E) +3%

71. In 1973 which one of the following categories was estimated to require the largest amount of the budget?

    (A) human resources
    (B) national defense
    (C) physical resources
    (D) interest and national defense
    (E) physical resources and national defense

72. Which of the following statements can be inferred from the graph?

    I. The amount of money collected from excise taxes declined from 1972 to 1973.
    II. The government will borrow twice as much money in 1973 as it did in 1972.
    III. Of the total amount of income in 1972 and 1973, 15% came from Corporation Income Taxes.

    (A) None
    (B) III only
    (C) I and II only
    (D) II and III only
    (E) I, II, and III

73. If the ratio of the radii of two circles is 3 to 2, then the ratio of the areas of the two circles is

    (A) 2 to 3   (D) 9 to 4
    (B) 3 to 4   (E) 3 to 2
    (C) 4 to 9

74. −5 times (− 4) is

    (A) −20   (D) −54
    (B) 54   (E) −5
    (C) 20

75. If $\dfrac{1}{x} < \dfrac{1}{y}$ then

(A) $x > y$
(B) x and y are negative
(C) x and y are positive
(D) $x < y$
(E) none of the preceding statements follows

76. A manufacturer of boxes wants to make a profit of x dollars. When he sells 5,000 boxes it costs 5¢ a box to make the first 1,000 boxes and then it costs y¢ a box to make the remaining 4,000 boxes. What price in dollars should he charge for the 5,000 boxes?

(A) $5,000 + 1,000y$
(B) $5,000 + 1,000y + 100x$
(C) $50 + 10y + x$
(D) $5,000 + 4,000y + x$
(E) $50 + 40y + x$

Use the following graph for questions 77–80.

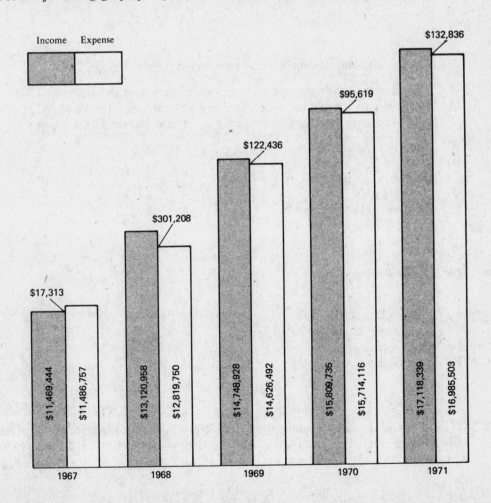

77. In what year was the profit (income minus expenses) the greatest?

(A) 1967
(B) 1968
(C) 1969

(D) 1970
(E) 1971

78. In how many of the years was the profit larger than in the preceding year?

(A) 0
(B) 1
(C) 2

(D) 3
(E) 4

79. Between which two successive years was the rise (in dollars) in income the greatest?

(A) 1967 and 1968
(B) 1968 and 1969
(C) 1969 and 1970
(D) 1970 and 1971
(E) insufficient information to determine

80. Which of the following statements can be inferred from the graph?

I. The company made a profit in all the years shown on the graph.
II. The company's profit increased in every year between 1969 and 1971.
III. The company's expenses increased in each year shown on the graph.

(A) I only
(B) II only
(C) III only
(D) I and III only
(E) I, II, and III

81. If $x - 2$ is less than y then

(A) x and y are positive
(B) y is less than $x + 2$
(C) y is greater than x
(D) $y + 2$ is greater than x
(E) none of the preceding

82. Wheat costs $2.00 a bushel and corn costs $3.00 a bushel. If the price of wheat rises 10% a month and the price of corn is unchanged, how many months will it take before a bushel of corn costs less than a bushel of wheat?

(A) 2
(B) 3
(C) 4

(D) 5
(E) 6

83. If $\frac{1}{2} + \frac{1}{4} = \frac{x}{15}$, then x is

(A) 10
(B) 11.25
(C) 12
(D) 13.75
(E) 14

84. If $x + y + z + w = 15$, then at least k of the numbers x, y, z, w must be positive where k is

(A) 0
(B) 1
(C) 2
(D) 3
(E) 4

85. If the length of a rectangle is increased by 11%, then the area of the rectangle is increased by

(A) 11%
(B) 21%
(C) 110%
(D) 111%
(E) 121%

If there is still time remaining, you may review the questions in this section only.
You may not turn to any other section of the test.

Section III   Business Judgment

TIME: 35 minutes

DIRECTIONS: Read the following two passages. After you have completed each of them you will be asked to answer two sets of questions. The first of these, data evaluation, involves determining the importance of specific factors included in the passage. The second, data application, consists of general questions relating to the passage. When answering questions, you may consult the passage.

Passage 1:

The problems of marketing citrus, like any other product, vary from area to area within Western Europe. There are however, two major problems which face citrus growers. One, which is a regional problem, concerns the restrictive and protective practices of the Common Market. The other, which is an overall problem, is the generally static level of citrus consumption.

In the early 1960's when the Common Market set out its agricultural policies, it included citrus under the general heading of "fruit and vegetables." Citrus was, therefore, treated in the same way as commodities grown within the EEC area; the purpose of the policies was and is to protect home-grown produce, although, in fact, the only Citrus growing area in the group is Italy which produces oranges only in sufficient quantities to meet between 4% and 6% of the total EEC consumption of this fruit. Whereas duties on most other fruit and vegetables entering the Common Market area from outside have been replaced by "variable prices," citrus entering the area is burdened with a duty which has gradually increased in size. Conversely, the home grown Italian oranges are now marketed among members of the EEC free of duty.

The quality standards adopted by the EEC are the International (Geneva) standards, originally intended to be applied at the point of shipping. The EEC is however, applying them at point of docking, thereby penalizing those countries whose crops have to travel long distances.

Most exporting citrus countries—including the USA, Brazil, Israel, Italy and South Africa—have been accustomed to using the chemical "diphenyl" as an external preservative. The World Health Organization has confirmed that the quantities applied (100–110 p.p.m.) offer no danger to the consumer.

The EEC however, will not accept more than 70 p.p.m. of diphenyl. This makes it difficult for exporters whose goods have to travel long distances, to maintain high standards at the point of arrival.

Under EEC regulations, all fruit treated with diphenyl must have marking to this effect on the container and the shops marketing the goods must be advised of the use of the chemical. Yet harmful chemicals are used on fruit and vegetables grown within the EEC, without any requirement that their use be declared.

In considering his country's coming program for the export of citrus fruit to EEC countries, Mr. Limon had to assess the effect that the above constraints would have on the development of a strong marketing strategy. With this in mind, he set out to prepare his report for his government's export authority.

Data Evaluation Questions

DIRECTIONS: Evaluate each of the following factors used in decision-making which relate to the passage you have just read by selecting

(A) for a *Major Objective* — the result desired by the executive;

(B) for a *Major Factor* — a primary consideration, spelled out in the passage, that influences the decision;

(C) for a *Minor Factor* — a less important consideration in the decision;

(D) for a *Major Assumption* — a conclusion reached by the executive not necessarily supported by the factors present;

(E) for an *Unimportant Issue* — a consideration not directly related to the problem.

86. Static level of citrus consumption.

87. EEC citrus quality standards.

88. Development of a citrus export strategy.

89. Harmful chemicals are used on fruit grown in EEC countries.

90. Italy is a member of the Common Market.

Data Application Questions

DIRECTIONS: Answer each of the following questions using information contained in the passage.

91. It can be inferred from the passage that diphenyl

   I. can be used in large quantities
  II. is used by citrus exporters
 III. preserves the quality of citrus

(A) I only
(B) III only
(C) I and II only
(D) II and III only
(E) I, II and III

92. Trade barriers or restrictions to the export of citrus to EEC countries include

    I. discriminatory quality standards
   II. tariffs
  III. stable citrus consumption

   (A) I only
   (B) III only
   (C) I and II only
   (D) II and III only
   (E) I, II and III

93. Citrus producing countries that are members of the EEC include

    I. South Africa
   II. Israel
  III. Italy

   (A) I only
   (B) III only
   (C) I and II only
   (D) II and III only
   (E) I, II and III

94. The EEC quality standards are

    I. the International (Geneva) standards
   II. discriminatory
  III. complicated

   (A) I only
   (B) III only
   (C) I and II only
   (D) II and III only
   (E) I, II and III

95. It may be inferred from the passage that some goods sold among EEC member countries

    I. are exempt from duty
   II. travel long distances
  III. have strong demand

   (A) I only
   (B) III only
   (C) I and II only
   (D) II and III only
   (E) I, II and III

Passage 2:

The Parks Company, located in New York City, has engaged exclusively in the manufacture of baking powder since it was founded seventy-five years ago. Current sales are approximately $800,000 annually. The sales volume, measured in commodity units instead of dollars, shows a decline of about 11 percent over the past decade. The company has a small office force and employs approximately 50 people in the production process, which is divided into (1) the mixing department, (2) the assembly department, and (3) the final inspection and packing department.

In 1935, distribution was foreign as well as national. Today the sale of the product is confined to New England and the Middle Atlantic states. Mr. Andrew H. Pendler, the president, attributes this significant decrease in both market area and sales volume to high tariff rates, sterner competition, and trade dislocations caused by World War II.

Mr. Gordon Janis, the sales manager, after studying the market closely, arrived at a different set of reasons why sales have been dropping. In the first place, according to Janis, sales to commercial consumers have diminished to practically nothing. Many modern bakeries buy the necessary chemicals and manufacture their own baking powder. Secondly, the population has become urbanized. Formerly, when a larger portion of the citizenry was suburban, many housewives did their own baking. Today people in cities are close to bakeries and other outlets where they can buy the finished product, and improved transportation has enabled fresh bakery products to be readily available at retail outlets. The third reason which Mr. Janis considers significant is the growing popularity of ready-mixes. The natural tendency of practically all human beings is to get as much as they can for a minimum of effort. Since ready-mixes do save housewives a good deal of labor, this type of product has been well received.

Mr. Janis believes that the company "cannot cope with the first two factors," and therefore his suggestion for increasing sales is to branch out and manufacture ready-mix baking products which will compare favorably with nationally known brands. Management was particularly receptive to Janis' idea because production of ready-mixes would require only minor changes in personnel and the cost of additional machinery would be relatively small.

Without further investigation, the manufacture of Parks' ready-mixes was started. After several months, ready-mix sales still amounted to less than 10 per cent of gross sales, and 85 per cent of ready-mix sales were in New York City. The entire position of the company was in jeopardy. Both Mr. Pendler and Mr. Janis were worried about the business, but neither seemed to know what to do.

Data Evaluation Questions

DIRECTIONS: Evaluate each of the following factors used in decision-making which relate to the passage you have just read by selecting

(A) for a *Major Objective* — the result desired by the executive;

(B) for a *Major Factor* — a primary consideration, spelled out in the passage, that influences the decision;

(C) for a *Minor Factor* — a less important consideration in the decision;

(D) for a *Major Assumption* — a conclusion reached by the executive not necessarily supported by the factors present;

(E) for an *Unimportant Issue* — a consideration not directly related to the problem.

96. Declining sales volume

97. The company is located in New York

98. Production of a ready-mix baking product

99. Urbanization of the population

100. Increased world trade

Data Application Questions

DIRECTIONS: Answer each of the following questions using information contained in the passage.

101. According to company management, sales volume declined owing to

    I. High tariff rates
    II. Increased competition
    III. World War II

    (A) I only
    (B) III only
    (C) I and II only
    (D) II and III only
    (E) I, II and III

102. Parks sales volume had declined by about

    (A) 1 percent
    (B) 5 percent
    (C) 10 percent
    (D) 15 percent
    (E) 25 percent

103. Baking powder sales declined because

    I. Bakeries made their own powder
    II. Housewives switched to ready-mixes
    III. Manufacturing costs increased

    (A) I only
    (B) III only
    (C) I and II only
    (D) II and III only
    (E) I, II and III

SAMPLE TEST 4 • 529

104. The Parks Company management can be characterized as

    I. Good decision makers
   II. Good market researchers
  III. Poor businessmen

(A) I only   (D) II and III only
(B) III only   (E) I, II and III
(C) I and II only

105. According to the passage, the decision to make ready-mixes was based on the following consideration(s)

    I. Management was worried about the business
   II. Ready-mixes were growing in popularity
  III. Production of ready-mixes was possible without incurring major additional capital and labor costs

(A) I only   (D) II and III only
(B) III only   (E) I, II and III
(C) I and II only

If there is still time remaining, you may review the questions in this section only.
You may not turn to any other section of the test.

Section IV   Data Sufficiency

TIME: 15 minutes

DIRECTIONS: Each of the following problems has a question and two statements which are labeled (1) and (2). Use the data given in (1) and (2) together with other available information (such as the number of hours in a day, the definition of *clockwise*, mathematical facts, etc.) to decide whether the statements are *sufficient* to answer the question. Then fill in space

(A) if you can get the answer from (1) alone but not from (2) alone;

(B) if you can get the answer from (2) alone but not from (1) alone;

(C) if you can get the answer from (1) and (2) together, although neither statement by itself suffices;

(D) if statement (1) alone suffices *and* statement (2) alone suffices;

(E) if you cannot get the answer from statements (1) and (2) together, but need even more data.

All numbers used in this section are real numbers. A figure given for a problem is intended to provide information consistent with that in the question, but not necessarily with the additional information contained in the statements.

106. A rectangular field is 40 yards long. Find the area of the field.

(1) A fence around the outside of the field is 140 yards long.
(2) The distance from one corner of the field to the opposite corner is 50 yards.

107. Is x greater than 0?

(1) $x^3 + 1 = 0$
(2) $x^2 - \frac{1}{2} = 0$

108. There are 450 boxes to load on a truck. A and B working independently but at the same time take 30 minutes to load the truck. How long should it take B working by himself to load the truck?

(1) A loads twice as many boxes as B.
(2) A would take 45 minutes by himself.

109.

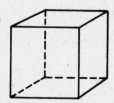

Is the figure above a cube?

(1) The lengths of all edges are equal.
(2) The angle between any two edges that meet is a right angle.

110. A car drives around a circular track once. A second car drives from point *A* to point *B* in a straight line. Which car travels farther?

   (1) The car driving around the circular track takes a longer time to complete its trip than the car traveling in a straight line.
   (2) The straight line from *A* to *B* is $1\frac{1}{2}$ times as long as the diameter of the circular track.

111. Find $x + y$

   (1) $x - y = 6$
   (2) $2x + 3y = 7$

112. Find the length of *AC* if *AB* has length 3 and *x* is 45.

   (1) $z = 45$
   (2) $y = 90$

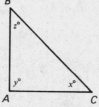

113. How much did it cost Mr. Jones to insure his car for the year 1971?

   (1) He spent $300.00 for car insurance in 1970.
   (2) The total amount he spent for car insurance in 1969, 1970, and 1971 was $905.00

114. It costs 50 cents in tolls, 2 dollars in gas, and at least 1 dollar for parking to drive (round trip) from Utopia to Green Acres each day. The train offers a weekly ticket. Which is the cheaper way to travel per week?

   (1) The weekly train ticket costs 15 dollars.
   (2) Parking costs a total of 6 dollars.

115. Is *ABDC* a rectangle?

   (1) *AD* and *BC* bisect each other at *E*.
   (2) Angle *ACD* is 90°.

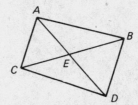

116. A worker is hired for five days. He is paid $5.00 more for each day of work than he was paid for the preceding day of work. What was the total amount he was paid for the five days of work?

   (1) He had made 50% of the total by the end of the third day.
   (2) He was paid twice as much for the last day as he was for the first day.

117. Is *y* larger than *x*?

   (1) $x + y = 2$
   (2) $\dfrac{x}{y} = 2$

118. Does a circle with diameter *d* have greater area than a square of side *s*?

   (1) $d < (\sqrt{2})s$
   (2) $d < s$

119. 5 apples cost 80 cents. How much will it cost to buy 10 apples and 3 oranges?

(1) Oranges cost 6 for 50 cents.
(2) 10 apples and 6 oranges cost $2.10.

120. A pair of skis originally sold for $160.00. After a discount of $x\%$, the skis were discounted $y\%$. Do the skis cost less than $130.00 after the discounts?

(1) $x = 20$ (2) $y = 15$

If there is still time remaining, you may review the questions in this section only.
You may not turn to any other section of the test.

Section V   Verbal Aptitude

TIME: 15 minutes

Antonyms

DIRECTIONS: For each question below, select the lettered word or phrase that comes closest to being *opposite* in meaning to the word appearing in capital letters. Be sure to consider all meanings carefully.

121. ABANDONMENT: (A) desertion (B) renunciation (C) maintenance (D) profligation (E) abjuration

122. ADROIT: (A) prim (B) unskillful (C) correct (D) strong (E) apt

123. PRESCRIBE: (A) soothe (B) impose (C) enjoin (D) prohibit (E) describe

124. SPECIOUS: (A) genuinely logical (B) sometimes funny (C) constricted (D) inadmissible (E) avoidable

125. HAUGHTY: (A) intelligent (B) mature (C) chilly (D) meek (E) arrogant

126. INSOLENT: (A) solvent (B) outrageous (C) polite (D) lazy (E) indigent

127. ASSIDUOUS: (A) courteous (B) inactive (C) careless (D) stylish (E) sensual

128. DISCRETE: (A) wet (B) joined (C) large (D) soft (E) near

129. INTREPID: (A) vulgar (B) intrusive (C) chronic (D) cowardly (E) jealous

Word-Pair Relationships

DIRECTIONS: For each question below, determine the relationship between the pair of capitalized words and then select the lettered pair of words which have a similar relationship to the first pair.

130. ARTIST : PAINT :: (A) doctor : patient (B) mechanic : car (C) physics : formula (D) chemist : discovery (E) sculptor : clay

131. TIMIDITY : COWARDICE :: (A) honor : weakness (B) virtue : dishonesty (C) economy : parsimony (D) shirker : valor (E) protected : silent

132. NEUROSIS : PSYCHOSIS :: (A) sickness : doctor (B) cold : influenza (C) nervousness : reaction (D) remedy : treatment (E) flood : rain

133. SPHERE : HEMISPHERE :: (A) circle : quadrant (B) polygon : hexagon (C) angle : square (D) triangle : rectangle (E) linear : curvilinear

134. VESTMENT : ECCLESIASTICAL :: (A) mountain : clouds (B) uniform : military (C) scientific : alchemy (D) forecast : reality (E) light : spiritual

135. INAUGURATION : PRESIDENT :: (A) promotion : executive (B) nomination : officer (C) elected : politician (D) ordination : priest (E) lottery : winner

136. RULE : NATION :: (A) command : army (B) prevent : irregularity (C) anarchy : chaos (D) tension : motivation (E) solve : problem

137. HARMONY : MUSIC :: (A) agreement : mathematics (B) electrons : physics (C) eclipse : astronomy (D) abjure : sociology (E) politics : history

Sentence Completions

DIRECTIONS: For each sentence below, select the lettered word or set of words which, when inserted in the sentence blanks, best completes the meaning of that sentence.

138. Economic development is likely to be _____ if stock market conditions are not _____.

   (A) speeded . . . constrained
   (B) hampered . . . favorable
   (C) forthcoming . . . propitious
   (D) justified . . . deleterious
   (E) maintained . . . honored

139. Leibnitz considered his law of historical continuity to be _____.

   (A) dogmatic
   (B) descriptive
   (C) axiomatic
   (D) absurd
   (E) evoked

140. In a surprising number of cases, the _____ from automobile to farm-implement manufacturing was relatively easy.

(A) transition
(B) conformity
(C) success
(D) strategy
(E) business

141. The immediate _____ of _____ change in any period are births, deaths, and the net number of migrants.

(A) producers . . . economic
(B) result . . . social
(C) consequence . . . rapid
(D) determinants . . . population
(E) effect . . . social

142. The measurement of _____ has long been a central problem in applied economics.

(A) energy
(B) productivity
(C) sales
(D) land
(E) currency

143. The more frequently persons _____ with one another, the more alike their _____ tend to become.

(A) interact . . . activities
(B) eat . . . speech
(C) travel . . . income
(D) disagree . . . schisms
(E) study . . . economics

144. The theories of the two anthropologists look _____ opposed.

(A) reliably
(B) possibly
(C) academically
(D) diametrically
(E) accedingly

145. Brazil is the largest and most _____ Latin country in the world.

(A) aggressive
(B) populous
(C) prodigious
(D) alluring
(E) flourishing

If there is still time remaining, you may review the questions in this section only.
You may not turn to any other section of the test.

Section VI Business Judgment

TIME: 35 minutes

DIRECTIONS: Read the following two passages. After you have completed each of them you will be asked to answer two sets of questions. The first of these, data evaluation, involves determining the importance of specific factors included in the passage. The second, data application, consists of general questions relating to the passage. When answering questions, you may consult the passage.

Passage 1:

The second day of Vespucci SpA's annual sales conference in Milan threatened to end in uproar. The business equipment manufacturer's 28 salesmen had received sales manager Guido Tulli's proposals to re-assign them to new territories with angry condemnation.

Explaining the reasons behind the drastic measures, Tulli had reminded the salesmen that the company was suffering from declining sales and had a serious cash flow problem. This was mainly due to slow payments by customers. Accounts receivable were increasing at an alarming rate, he had told them.

Under Tulli's plan, the company's top salesmen were to be switched from the areas with high sales to areas that currently yielded low sales. He had explained that this would mean the more experienced salesmen could concentrate on building up sales in the less productive regions. The less experienced salesmen could easily handle the well-developed territories.

Some of the firm's leading salesmen immediately started to object. "I have spent years building up my territory," one of them protested. "I do not see why I should have to start all over again in a new region."

Tulli pointed out that he felt that the firm's best salesmen were being wasted in these well-developed sales regions. "You are simply going to well-established customers and taking orders," he argued.

An experienced salesman contested this view, observing he had greatly increased sales in his territory the previous year by persuading existing customers to expand their amount of orders in business stationery.

This supported his view, retorted Tulli, that the salesmen in the well-established territories were becoming stale, and were failing to uncover new customers. "This is only natural," he added. "When I was promoted to sales manager, I was amazed how successful my successor was in getting new orders in my old territory. The company badly needs your experience to develop the weaker regions."

Another experienced salesman asked if the new plan would mean salesmen would get an extra bonus or higher commission rates for establishing new accounts. Tulli began to explain why he thought this was impractical, when he was interrupted by one of the younger salesmen who had been sitting at the back of the room quietly fuming. He told

Tulli that he felt completely demotivated by the proposal to remove them from the undeveloped territories.

Tulli tried to reassure the young salesman that the company did not regard them as failures. The changes were being made simply because the company was having difficulties, and needed to boost sales quickly, he pointed out.

Tulli swallowed hard before announcing another new policy he knew was likely to upset the gathered salesmen. "The management board has also decided that in future sales commissions will be paid quarterly and only on those orders for which payments have been received from customers," he announced nervously. "As from today it will be your responsibility to raise the subject of slow payments with customers. Moreover, no new orders will be accepted from customers until all overdue payments are received."

This was too much for the salesmen to take and the meeting erupted into a noisy uproar. "Why shouldn't we be paid for orders we have succeeded in getting?" demanded one salesman furiously. "It is not our job to collect debts," protested another.

"This contravenes our employment contract," shouted yet another.

The salesmen were all talking agitatedly at once when Tulli decided to close the proceedings for that day. He rushed to a nearby hotel where group managing director Leon Cavello was staying overnight. He was due to address the conference the following morning.

"Our proposals have met with even more hostility than we expected," Tulli told Cavello, relating how the meeting had broken up in disorder. "I'm afraid you will have a hard time of it tomorrow convincing them that the proposals are in everybody's interest. But I don't think we can dodge the issue now. We have to tackle it while we have them all together."

Cavello nodded gravely. His first inclination was to proceed with the proposals whether or not the salesmen approved. On the other hand, he reflected, salesmen are the key to a company's success. It might be unwise to impose a new system on them without their consent.

Data Evaluation Questions

DIRECTIONS: Evaluate each of the following factors used in decision-making which relate to the passage you have just read by selecting

(A) for a *Major Objective*—the result desired by the executive;

(B) for a *Major Factor*—a primary consideration, spelled out in the passage, that influences the decision;

(C) for a *Minor Factor*—a less important consideration in the decision;

(D) for a *Major Assumption*—a conclusion reached by the executive not necessarily supported by the factors present;

(E) for an *Unimportant Issue*—a consideration not directly related to the problem.

146. Vespucci SpA's declining sales

147. Vespucci's accounts receivable problem

148. Vespucci is an Italian company

149. Improved cash flow

150. Higher commission rates paid to salesmen will not lead to the establishment of new accounts

Data Application Questions

DIRECTIONS: Answer each of the following questions using information contained in the passage.

151. According to the passage, Tulli proposed that Vespucci salesmen cannot accept new orders from customers unless

    I.   The sales manager approves
    II. The new orders are profitable
    III. Customer payments are up to date

  (A) I only
  (B) III only
  (C) I and II only
  (D) II and III only
  (E) I, II, and III

152. Vespucci's cash flow problem was caused by

    I.   Poor salesmanship
    II. Declining sales
    III. Slow payments by customers

  (A) I only
  (B) III only
  (C) I and II only
  (D) II and III only
  (E) I, II, and III

153. According to Tulli, sales could be increased if salesmen would be

    I.   Reassigned territories
   II. Responsible for collecting overdue accounts
  III. Spending more time in the field

  (A) I only
  (B) III only
  (C) I and II only
  (D) II and III only
  (E) I, II, and III

154. Tulli gave the following reason(s) in support of his reorganization plan

    I.   Declining salesmen's morale
   II. Sales territories were too large
  III. Too few new customers were obtained

  (A) I only
  (B) III only
  (C) I and II only
  (D) II and III only
  (E) I, II, and III

155. Reducing credit to customers will likely lead to a

    I.   Reduction in accounts receivable
   II. Increased cash flow
  III. More sales

  (A) I only
  (B) III only
  (C) I and II only
  (D) II and III only
  (E) I, II, and III

Passage 2:

There was panic in the marketing department of Stimmung AG, just outside Düsseldorf, Germany. The computer bureau had just telephoned to say that the statistical sample had been done incorrectly and the address labels for the survey were wrong. The printers had to be contacted urgently to stop the mail survey from being sent out.

The man in charge of the survey, Robert Klein, a market researcher with the company for the past three years, was nowhere to be found.

The marketing manager, Jorg Mitte, was away at an exhibition of do-it-yourself products manufactured by the company.

Dieter Gross, the commercial director, who got the telephone call and had to handle the problem, was furious. The following Monday he demanded to know why Klein had not been available during office hours. Klein was not prepared to make false excuses.

"I promised to meet my wife. So I left half an hour earlier," Klein told Gross. Gross's face expressed his anger.

"I put in a lot of extra hours," Klein went on to explain. "Just last week I gave up two evenings to fly to England and back on business. Tomorrow night I am expected to attend an important conference and exhibition. Would you prefer that I should not go?"

"That is up to you," said Gross. "If you wish to go, by all means do so. But I still expect you to be in your office during normal office hours, so that you are here when we need you."

Following his meeting with Gross, Klein made a telephone call to cancel his reservation at the conference.

When Mitte returned from his business trip, Klein informed him that henceforth he intended to work normal office hours, and no more.

Mitte was appalled. "But I don't know why you are complaining," he told Klein. "You know you can always take time off when you have been away on business."

Klein shook his head. "I am not willing to sneak out of here like a child, and make sure I am not seen, or tell you I am somewhere when I am not," he said. "I am not complaining. I am quite happy to work normal office hours, as the company asks."

Mitte reluctantly decided to take up the matter with Gross. He was reluctant because he and Gross had a somewhat strained relationship. Yet they had to work together.

"It is important — essential, in fact — that my market researchers work evenings and on weekends," he said. "They cannot make our telephone surveys to men at home during the working day. Also, they often have to work after hours to finish analyses and get reports out on time."

Gross was unimpressed. "Other people, including other market researchers, do not mind working overtime when needed," he said. "Why should Klein?"

Mitte had to draw up courage to argue further with his superior. "Look, the days when my employees are willing to work overtime for nothing, for the sake of the company, are fast coming to an end," he said. "If they see Klein enjoying his free evenings, while they have to work overtime, they will soon become demotivated. They will start wanting to work normal office hours too. But it will not suit me. I am the one who will feel the pressure of getting reports out on time."

Gross was suspicious of Mitte's motives. He felt that a simple issue of discipline was now being blown up out of all proportion. Anyway, he was under instructions from the chief executive to tighten up.

"I am sorry," Gross said, "but I cannot start changing company working conditions or policy for one department."

Mitte did not know what to do. Should he speak out once and for all against Gross's inflexible attitude on company policy, and risk a showdown? Should he go direct to the company president? Or should he accept Gross's policy and adopt Klein's attitude, with all its consequences?

Data Evaluation Questions

DIRECTIONS: Evaluate each of the following factors used in decision-making which relate to the passage you have just read by selecting

(A) for a *Major Objective*—the result desired by the executive;

(B) for a *Major Factor*—a primary consideration, spelled out in the passage, that influences the decision;

(C) for a *Minor Factor*—a less important consideration in the decision;

(D) for a *Major Assumption*—a conclusion reached by the executive not necessarily supported by the factors present;

(E) for an *Unimportant Issue*—a consideration not directly related to the problem.

156. Stimmung AG's office discipline

157. The company's product line

158. Gross's inflexible attitude

159. Robert Klein's personality

160. Klein was employed three years with Stimmung

Data Application Questions

DIRECTIONS: Answer each of the following questions using information contained in the passage.

161. According to the marketing manager, Klein's behavior was

   I. Fully justified
  II. Motivated by a desire for more compensation
 III. Damaging to departmental morale

  (A) I only
  (B) III only
  (C) I and II only
  (D) II and III only
  (E) I, II, and III

162. According to the passage, among the alternatives that Mitte must weigh are

  I. Seek relaxation of company work rules
 II. Accept Klein's stand of no work after normal office hours
 III. Resign from the company

 (A) I only
 (B) III only
 (C) I and II only
 (D) II and III only
 (E) I, II, and III

163. Mitte hesitated to discuss the overtime problem with Gross because

  I. There was lack of company precedent
 II. He knew Gross would not change his mind
 III. He did not get along with Gross

 (A) I only
 (B) III only
 (C) I and II only
 (D) II and III only
 (E) I, II, and III

164. According to the company's organization structure as given in the passage, Gross should have discussed the problem directly with

  I. Klein
 II. The company president
 III. Mitte

 (A) I only
 (B) III only
 (C) I and II only
 (D) II and III only
 (E) I, II, and III

165. If market researchers must work overtime, a possible solution to Klein's problem might be to

  I. Introduce a system of overtime compensation
 II. Have one employee stand in for another in case of absence
 III. Reschedule market research projects during normal office hours

 (A) I only
 (B) III only
 (C) I and II only
 (D) II and III only
 (E) I, II, and III

If there is still time remaining, you may review the questions in this section only.
You may not turn to any other section of the test.

Section VII Writing Ability

TIME: 30 minutes

DIRECTIONS: Each of the sentences in this section is either correct or contains one error in grammar, usage, diction (choice of words), idiom or punctuation. If there is an error it will be found in one of the underlined parts of the sentence, labeled (A), (B), (C), or (D). If you identify an error mark the appropriate letter on your answer sheet. If there is no error in the sentence mark (E)—no error.

Note: Assume that all parts of the sentence that are not underlined are correct and cannot be changed.

166. The wear and tear on the body is a medical problem. No error
    A   B   C   D   E

167. The team are assembling behind the main grandstand next to the playing field.
    A   B   C   D
    No error
    E

168. I can't go there now, but I plan to go there tomorrow. No error
    A   B   C   D   E

169. The First World War changed the major international financial relationships. No
    A   B   C   D
    error
    E

170. A shot was fired in the dark but a policeman seen where the bullet came from.
    A   B   C   D
    No error
    E

171. He plays his violin every day so that he would become concertmaster of the
    A   B   C
    orchestra. No error
    D   E

172. Man's greatest source of enlightenment lies in the printed word. No error
    A   B   C   D   E

173. The workers were enthused over the prospects for a wage increase. No error
    A   B   C   D   E

174. The museum which we visited in center city was beautiful. No error
    A   B   C   D   E

175. We were determined to arrive on time, irregardless of the inclement weather. No
     A   B   C   D
     error
     E

176. After the battle was over, the soldiers will advance to the front lines. No error
     A   B   C   D   E

177. I read in the newspaper that in Nigeria they grow large tomatoes. No error
     A   B   C   D   E

178. To master the proper backstroke, the breathing must be carefully controlled. No error
                  A   B   C   D   E

179. The key to the persistence of the family farm, is the difficulty of routinizing agri-
         A   B   C
     cultural operations. No error
          D   E

180. While one part of the TV program carried the football game, the other part shows
                A   B   C
     the training of the teams. No error
           D   E

181. Prior to the exam the instructor had told us to keep an eye on the time , to write
     A   B   C
     clearly, and no cheating. No error
                 D   E

182. The rainy season had already began by the time they arrived in Burma that year.
                      A   B   C   D
     No error
     E

183. How could you even dream of doing such a thing without me standing next to
         A   B   C   D
     you to make sure it was safe? No error
                                   E

184. Neither Arthur nor Mary has the slightest idea to whom this letter should be ad-
                          A   B
     dressed to because the original envelope has been lost. No error
          C   D   E

185. Did Fred say , "I'm really interested in buying a larger share of the company" ?
              A B   C   D
     No error
     E

186. In this series of television programs, they want to show us the corruption and
              A   B   C
     graft that lies beneath the surface even in the most progressive societies. No error
               D   E

187. Having <u>been delayed</u> by <u>unfavorable</u> weather, it <u>was</u> not possible for our plane to
        $\quad\quad$ A $\quad\quad\quad\quad$ B $\quad\quad\quad\quad\quad$ C

arrive <u>in time</u> for the connecting flight. <u>No error</u>
        $\quad$ D $\quad\quad\quad\quad\quad\quad\quad\quad\quad$ E

188. Despite what we <u>had heard</u> about Dr. Plunkett, <u>we found</u> <u>him</u> to be a <u>considerable</u>
        $\quad\quad\quad\quad\quad$ A $\quad\quad\quad\quad\quad\quad\quad\quad$ B $\quad\quad$ C $\quad\quad\quad\quad$ D

and kind man. <u>No error</u>
        $\quad\quad\quad\quad\quad$ E

189. Whenever these three <u>eminent</u> scientists spoke to <u>each other</u> an argument <u>was bound</u>
        $\quad\quad\quad\quad\quad\quad\quad$ A $\quad\quad\quad\quad\quad\quad\quad\quad$ B $\quad\quad\quad\quad\quad\quad$ C

<u>to ensue.</u> <u>No error</u>
        D $\quad\quad$ E

190. The <u>less</u> chances you take, the greater your peace of mind <u>will be</u> but, <u>then again,</u>
        $\quad$ A $\quad\quad\quad\quad\quad\quad\quad\quad\quad\quad\quad\quad\quad\quad\quad$ B $\quad\quad\quad$ C

the high profits that you hope for may never <u>eventuate.</u> <u>No error</u>
        $\quad\quad\quad\quad\quad\quad\quad\quad\quad\quad\quad\quad\quad\quad$ D $\quad\quad\quad$ E

If there is still time remaining, you may review the questions in this section only.
You may not turn to any other section of the test.

Answers

Section I   Reading Recall

1. (C)	9. (C)	17. (D)	25. (B)
2. (B)	10. (D)	18. (C)	26. (C)
3. (A)	11. (B)	19. (B)	27. (C)
4. (E)	12. (D)	20. (B)	28. (E)
5. (A)	13. (E)	21. (C)	29. (A)
6. (B)	14. (B)	22. (B)	30. (B)
7. (B)	15. (B)	23. (D)	
8. (C)	16. (B)	24. (A)	

Section II   Mathematics

(Numbers in parentheses indicate the section in the Mathematics Review where material concerning the question is discussed.)

31. (D) (I–4)	50. (C) (IV–3)	69. (B) (IV–2)
32. (A) (II–2)	51. (A) (IV–3)	70. (E) (IV–2)
33. (D) (IV–2)	52. (D) (III–4)	71. (A) (IV–2)
34. (C) (IV–2)	53. (A) (I–4)	72. (A) (IV–2)
35. (A) (IV–2)	54. (D) (II–3)	73. (D) (III–7, II–5)
36. (C) (II–3)	55. (B) (I–4)	74. (C) (I–6)
37. (D) (I–4)	56. (D) (III–7)	75. (E) (II–7)
38. (A) (II–3)	57. (D) (II–3)	76. (E) (I–4, II–3)
39. (E) (IV–1)	58. (C) (IV–3, II–5)	77. (B) (IV–4)
40. (E) (IV–1)	59. (B) (II–5)	78. (C) (IV–4)
41. (E) (IV–1)	60. (E) (II–3)	79. (A) (IV–4)
42. (C) (III–7)	61. (D) (I–1)	80. (C) (IV–4)
43. (C) (II–3, II–2)	62. (D) (IV–1)	81. (D) (II–7)
44. (C) (II–2)	63. (B) (IV–2)	82. (D) (I–8)
45. (B) (III–4)	64. (E) (II–3)	83. (B) (I–2)
46. (D) (II–6)	65. (B) (II–7)	84. (B) (I–6)
47. (B) (II–2, II–3)	66. (C) (I–2)	85. (A) (III–7, I–4)
48. (C) (IV–3)	67. (A) (I–2, II–2)	
49. (E) (IV–4)	68. (C) (II–3)	

Section III — Business Judgment

86. (B)	91. (D)	96. (B)	101. (E)
87. (B)	92. (C)	97. (E)	102. (C)
88. (A)	93. (B)	98. (A)	103. (C)
89. (E)	94. (C)	99. (B)	104. (B)
90. (C)	95. (A)	100. (E)	105. (D)

Section IV — Data Sufficiency

106. (D)	110. (B)	114. (A)	118. (B)
107. (A)	111. (C)	115. (C)	119. (D)
108. (D)	112. (D)	116. (D)	120. (A)
109. (C)	113. (E)	117. (C)	

Section V — Verbal Aptitude

121. (C)	128. (B)	135. (D)	142. (B)
122. (B)	129. (D)	136. (A)	143. (A)
123. (D)	130. (E)	137. (A)	144. (D)
124. (A)	131. (C)	138. (B)	145. (B)
125. (D)	132. (B)	139. (C)	
126. (C)	133. (A)	140. (A)	
127. (C)	134. (B)	141. (D)	

Section VI — Business Judgment

146. (B)	152. (D)	158. (B)	164. (B)
147. (B)	153. (C)	159. (B)	165. (C)
148. (E)	154. (B)	160. (C)	
149. (A)	155. (A)	161. (B)	
150. (D)	156. (A)	162. (C)	
151. (B)	157. (E)	163. (B)	

Section VII — Writing Ability

166. (E)	173. (B)	180. (C)	187. (C)
167. (A)	174. (A)	181. (D)	188. (D)
168. (D)	175. (C)	182. (A)	189. (B)
169. (E)	176. (C)	183. (D)	190. (A)
170. (C)	177. (C)	184. (C)	
171. (A)	178. (B)	185. (E)	
172. (E)	179. (E)	186. (B)	

Analysis

Section I   Reading Recall

1. **(C)** See paragraph 1: "Their progress is important to the high-income countries, not only for humanitarian and political reasons. . . ."

2. **(B)** Paragraph 2: "governments of most high-income countries have in recent years undertaken important aid programs. . . ."

3. **(A)** See paragraphs 3 and 4 especially.

4. **(E)** All are mentioned. See paragraphs 4, 6, 7 and 8.

5. **(A)** Paragraph 6: "a more efficient financial and fiscal system help greatly to mobilize funds for investment" and following.

6. **(B)** See paragraph 8; the section which states that industrial growth depends upon agricultural productivity.

7. **(B)** See paragraphs 2 and especially 4: "high-income countries can play only a supporting role."

8. **(C)** See paragraph 7: "governments aim . . . to reduce excessive social inequalities."

9. **(C)** Only the first two are mentioned. I is mentioned in paragraph 9, II is implied in paragraphs 8 and 9.

10. **(D)** See paragraph 3: If low income countries could speed their economic growth, then "a better distribution of world resources" would occur.

11. **(B)** In paragraph 2, this definition is given: "it is commonly expressed empirically in terms of consumption or in terms of income."

12. **(D)** See the last sentence of paragraph 2.

13. **(E)** See paragraph 2, item 3.

14. **(B)** This is given in paragraph 4.

15. **(B)** In paragraph 4 it is stated that the degree of income inequality in 1970 was the same as that in 1964, when "a trend of decreasing inequality . . . among the lower income brackets" had occurred.

16. **(B)** See paragraph 6: "Unless the education gap is significantly reduced . . . more income equality will be thwarted."

17. **(D)** See paragraph 5: The standard of living improvement was expressed in "high income levels, better housing, a higher ownership rate of consumer durables and an increase in the proportion of families in higher income brackets."

18. **(C)** The entire passage deals with standards of living and income levels of population groups, an important subject of economics.

19. **(B)** See paragraph 5: "their average income is still only 70% of the overall average for all families."

20. **(B)** See the first sentence of paragraph 4: "Between 1964 and 1970 the standard of living of the urban population rose."

21. **(C)** See paragraph 1: "American businessmen have long been interested in foreign markets for the purpose of stimulating trade."

22. **(B)** See the statement that such "transplantations" could aid economic development as given in paragraph 2.

23. **(D)** Paragraphs 2 and 3 deal with this issue.

24. **(A)** See paragraph 4 ff, e.g., the resistance to packaged foods, new shopping behavior, etc.

25. **(B)** See paragraph 5: "Daily shopping trips may be more of a social endeavor."

26. **(C)** See paragraph 6: "it reduced total shopping time . . . working women switched . . . because it is open during their lunch hour."

27. **(C)** See paragraph 3: "research is needed to determine the factors responsible for the acceptance and growth of marketing innovations."

28. **(E)** All three. The first two are specifically stated in paragraph 4, the last is inferred from the passage.

29. **(A)** is most appropriate. Alternatives (B), (D) and (E) can be immediately excluded. (C) is excluded because "Management" is not the *major* topic discussed.

30. **(B)** The Israeli experience shows that there is hope that similar countries might successfully adopt self-service.

Section II   Mathematics

31. **(D)** There are 50 students in the class. Since $\frac{32}{50} = .64$, females make up 64% of the class.

32. **(A)** Since y is 5 and $x + y = 2$, $x + 5 = 2$. Add -5 to each side of the equation to obtain $x = -3$. Therefore, $x - y = -3 -(5) = -8$.

33. **(D)** IBM's share of the market is 67% and the total share of the other companies is 33%. Since $2(33)\% = 66\%$, the answer is roughly 2.

34. **(C)** If the two firms merge, their share would would be $(4.5 + 2.3)\%$. The merged firm would have a 6.8% market share which would make it fourth behind IBM, Honeywell, and Univac.

35. **(A)** Statement I is false since Univac has 9% of the market which is less than 5.7% + 4.5% or 10.2%. Statement II is true since together Univac and Honeywell have a share amounting to 18% of the market which is less than one third of the 67% which

IBM controls. Statement III is false since $30(2.3)\% = 69\%$ which is larger than 67%.

36. **(C)** Since 15 is $\frac{5}{4}$ of 12, it takes 15 men only $\frac{4}{5}$ as long as 12 men to do the job. $\frac{4}{5}$ of 4 = $3\frac{1}{5}$ hours, or 3 hrs. 12 min.

37. **(D)** The new price of apples is $(1.12)10¢ = 11.2¢$ each. Therefore, $12(11.2)¢ = 134.4¢ = \$1.34$.

38. **(A)** The total length of the trip will be 120 miles. Hence to average 50 mph for the trip, he must take 2.4 hrs. total traveling time. Since he has already traveled for 1.5 hrs., he must complete the trip in 2.4–1.5 or .9 hrs. or 54 min.

39. **(E)** Jan., Feb., March, April, Aug., Oct., Nov., and Dec.

40. **(E)** The wage negotiations will involve 87,000 in Jan. and Feb., and 51,500 in May. So the total is 138,500.

41. **(E)** The Auto Workers have one agreement involving 670,250. This agreement by itself makes their coverage the largest.

42. **(C)** Area = length times width = $(L)(\frac{1}{2}L) = \frac{1}{2}L^2$.

43. **(C)** The first 100 dozen cost $(100)(50¢) = \$50.00$ Since the total purchase is 150 dozen, the last 50 dozen cost 47¢ each. So the total cost is $\$50.00 + 50(47¢) = \$50.00 + \$23.50 = \$73.50$.

44. **(C)** Let x be the unknown number. Then $\left(\frac{3}{2}\right)x = 5$; so $x = (5)\left(\frac{2}{3}\right) = \frac{10}{3}$. The sum of the two numbers is $x + \frac{3}{2} = \frac{10}{3} + \frac{3}{2} = \frac{29}{6} = 4\frac{5}{6}$.

45. **(B)** The length of any side of a triangle must be less than the sum of the lengths of the other two sides. Since $5 + 7 = 12$ and 10 is greater than $2 + 4$, I and II cannot be the sides of a triangle. $5 + 7$ is greater than 9, $5 + 9$ is greater than 7, and $7 + 9$ is greater than 5. Therefore, there is a triangle whose sides have lengths of 5, 7, and 9.

46. **(D)** $2+3=5$ and $5+3=8$, so the next number is $8+3$ or 11.

47. **(B)** Each station wagon has 4 tires and each motorcycle has 2 tires. Let x be the number of station wagons and let y be the number of motorcycles. Then $4x + 2y$ is the total number of tires which must equal $2(x+y)+30$. Thus, $4x + 2y = 2x + 2y + 30$ yielding $4x = 2x + 30$ with $2x = 30$ or $x = 15$.

48. **(C)** Use your pencil to compare the height of the columns.

49. **(E)** (B), (C), (D), are wrong since the average rose. The drop was roughly 35 pts. between the first and second weeks in October compared to about 25 pts. between the third and fourth weeks in December.

50. **(C)** The week with lowest value was the second week in October. (Each notch between 900 and 950 indicates 5 pts.)

51. **(A)** The average closed between 960 and 1,000 only at the end of the first and second weeks of November.

52. **(D)** The square of the hypotenuse, the side opposite the right angle, equals $(5)^2 + (12)^2$ or $25 + 144$ or 169. So the length of the side opposite the right angle is $\sqrt{169}$ or 13.

53. **(A)** Price = (cost)(rate). Let x be the original cost of the skis. Then $\$160 = x(.9)$, so $x = \$177.78$. Let y be the original cost of the boots then $\$96 = y(1.2)$, so $y = \$80$. So he made $\$96 - \$80 = \$16$ on the boots and lost $\$177.78 - \$160 = \$17.78$ on the skis. Therefore, he lost $1.78.

54. **(D)** The cost in cents of printing 1000 copies equals $500(10) + (1000 - 500)\left(10 - \dfrac{x}{50}\right) = 5000 + 500\left(10 - \dfrac{x}{50}\right)$. Therefore, $7500 = 5000 + 5000 - 10x$, $10x = 2500$, and $x = 250$.

55. **(B)** The increase in cost between 1972 and 1973 is the product (cost in 1972) · (rate of increase). The cost in 1973 will be the cost in 1972 (1 + rate of increase). Also, the cost in 1974 will equal (cost in 1973) (1 + rate of increase) or (cost in 1972) (1 + rate of increase)². So the cost of coal for 1974 = $\$(53)(1.15)^2 = \$(53)(1.32225) = \$70.09$, and the cost of oil for 1974 = $\$(45)(1.2)^2 = \$(45)(1.44) = \$64.80$. Since oil is cheaper than coal, (D) and (E) are incorrect because replacing oil by coal for any amount of time raises the cost.

56. **(D)** Let s be the side of the original square. Since the side of the increased square is $1.3s$, the area of the increased square is $1.69(s^2)$. Therefore, the area has increased by $1.69(s^2) - s^2$ or by $.69(s^2)$ or 69%.

57. **(D)** By 5:30 A.M. train Y will have traveled $(4\frac{1}{2})x$ miles. So train Z must travel $(4\frac{1}{2})x$ miles in $3\frac{1}{2}$ hours. The average rate of speed necessary is $\dfrac{4\frac{1}{2}x}{3\frac{1}{2}}$ which equals $\dfrac{\frac{9}{2}x}{\frac{7}{2}}$ or $\dfrac{9}{7}x$.

58. **(C)** $(6)(18) = 108$ and $(5)(18) = 90$. To make quick estimates, check the amount funded for water pollution if air pollution received 100. For example, if the ratio were 3 to 2, water pollution would get only 66.7 billion dollars.

59. **(B)** Let x be the cost in cents of 4 boxes of pencils. $\dfrac{4}{30} = \dfrac{x}{5.10}$, which means $x = \$\left(\dfrac{4}{30}\right)(5.10) = \$.68 = 68\cent$.

60. **(E)** The amount the worker is paid for working T hours if T is larger than 8 is $8r + (T - 8)(1.5)r$. When $T = 11$, the worker will be paid $8r + 3(1.5)r = (12.5)r$.

61. **(D)** The product of three consecutive integers is of the form $x(x + 1)(x + 2)$. A good approximation to this is $(x + 1)^3$. Since $5^3 = 125$, a good guess is 4, 5, 6. This is correct because $(4)(5)(6) = 120$. The sum of these three numbers is 15.

62. **(D)** Medical research grants increased by .4 between 1971 and 1972. The fractional increase is $\dfrac{.4}{3.1}$. Since $\dfrac{.4}{3.2} = \dfrac{1}{8} = 12.5\%$, 13% is the best estimate.

63. **(B)** Total amount was 20.2 and the total amount the colleges received was 10.1. The colleges received $\dfrac{10.1}{20.2}$ or $\dfrac{1}{2}$ or 50%.

64. **(E)** Let M be the mechanic's hourly wage, C the custodial worker's hourly wage, and S the salesman's hourly wage. Then $M = 2S$, and $C = \frac{1}{3}M$ or $M = 3C$, hence $3C = 2S$, $S = \frac{3}{2}C$.

65. **(B)** Statement I is false since $(-1) + (-2) = -3$, and III is false since $(-1) - (-2) = 1$. But II is true since $(-x)(-y) = xy$, for all x and y.

66. **(C)** The loaded truck gets $(.85)10$ miles or 8.5 miles per gallon. The loaded truck will require $\frac{50}{8.5}$ or 5.88 gallons to travel 50 miles.

67. **(A)** Since $3a = 0$, a must equal 0, which implies that $b = 0$. Note that $\frac{b}{a}$ and $\frac{a}{b}$ are not defined.

68. **(C)** The horse will travel 10 miles in the first two hours. The horse will take $\frac{10}{3}$ or $3\frac{1}{3}$ hours to travel the final 10 miles. So the total time is $5\frac{1}{3}$ hours.

69. **(B)** Income is part of "Where it comes from."

70. **(E)** In 1972 human resources received 42% of each budget dollar and in 1973 it received 45% of each budget dollar. So this budget allocation was estimated to rise by 3%, thus the difference is +3%.

71. **(A)** Note that the question refers to 1973.

72. **(A)** Statement I is false since the graph indicates only that the percentage of the total collected was less. (If the total in 1973 was much larger, the amount collected from excise taxes could have increased.) II is false since, again, the graph gives only percentages not amounts. III is false for the same reason.

73. **(D)** Let r_1 be the radius of the first circle and r_2 the radius of the second circle. Then $\frac{r_1}{r_2} = \frac{3}{2}$, so $r_1 = \left(\frac{3}{2}\right)r_2$, and $\pi(r_1)^2 = \pi\frac{9}{4}(r_2)^2$. Since the area of a circle is π (radius)^2, then the ratio of the areas is 9 to 4.

74. **(C)** $(-5)(-4) = (5)(4)$.

75. **(E)** Let $x = -3$ and $y = 2$, then $\frac{1}{-3} < \frac{1}{2}$, so (A), (B), and (C) are false. Let $x = 3$ and $y = 2$; then $\frac{1}{3} < \frac{1}{2}$ so (D) is false. (E) is the only correct answer.

76. **(E)** The selling price of the boxes should equal x plus the cost. The cost in cents of making 5,000 boxes is $(1,000)5\cancel{c} + (4,000)y$ which equals $50 + 40y$ in dollars. So the selling price should be $50 + 40y + x$.

77. **(B)** The profit is indicated by the arrow.

78. **(C)** 1968 and 1971.

79. **(A)** The rise in income was greater than $1,600,000 only between 1967 and 1968, and between 1968 and 1969. The gain was greater in the former.

80. **(C)** Statement I is false since there was a loss in 1967. II is false since the profits decreased from 1968 to 1969.

81. **(D)** If $x - 2 < y$, then $x < y + 2$.

82. **(D)** The price of wheat in dollars will be $2(1.10)^n$ a bushel after n months, and this will be greater than 3 when $(1.10)^n$ is greater than 1.5. $(1.1)^2 = 1.21$, $(1.1)^3 = 1.331$, $(1.1)^4 = 1.4641$, $(1.1)^5 = 1.61051$; therefore, after 5 months the price of wheat will be higher.

83. **(B)** If $\frac{1}{2} + \frac{1}{4} = \frac{x}{15}$, then since $\frac{1}{2} + \frac{1}{4} = \frac{3}{4}$, we have that $\frac{3}{4} = \frac{x}{15}$. So $x = \frac{45}{4} = 11\frac{1}{4} = 11.25$.

84. **(B)** If three of the numbers were negative, then as long as the fourth is greater than the absolute value of the sum of the other three, the sum of all four will be positive. For example, $(-50) + (-35) + (-55) + 155 = 15$.

85. **(A)** Area $= LW$. The increased length is $1.11L$ and W is unchanged; so the increased area is $(1.11L)W = (1.11)(LW) = (1.11)A$. Therefore, the increase in area is $1.11A - A = .11A$; and the area is increased by 11%.

Section III   Business Judgment

86. **(B)** The static level of demand for citrus is a major factor in the development of a marketing strategy. Given this level, the question is whether marketing strategy, such as advertising, can increase the demand for the products.

87. **(B)** The EEC's citrus quality standards are a major factor influencing export strategy since they are intended to make it difficult for non-EEC producers to sell to Common Market countries.

88. **(A)** The development of a marketing strategy for the export of citrus to the Common Market is the decision maker's major objective.

89. **(E)** That harmful chemicals are used on fruit grown in the Common Market does not influence the marketing strategy of the decision maker.

90. **(C)** That Italy is a member of the EEC is a minor factor; that Italy grows citrus *is* a major factor, however.

91. **(D)** Diphenyl is a preservative agent used to protect citrus shipped long distances. See paragraphs 4 and 5.

92. **(C)** Tariffs (import taxes) and discriminatory quality standards (see the discussion on diphenyl) were used by EEC countries to restrain the exports of non-EEC countries.

93. **(B)** Italy. See paragraph 2.

94. **(C)** See paragraph 3.

95. **(A)** The passage states, in paragraph 2, that oranges were sold to other EEC countries duty free. It may be inferred that other products are so treated.

96. **(B)** Declining sales volume was a symptom rather than a cause of the company's problem; therefore, it is a major factor requiring a decision as to how the decline can be corrected.

97. **(E)** Company location had no direct bearing on the issues discussed in the passage.

98. **(A)** The production of ready-mixes is the major objective of management. Whether the decision was a correct one can be discerned by the reader; nevertheless, this is the direction in which management decided to go.

99. **(B)** The urbanization of the population leading to the consumption of commercially-baked food products was a major factor in management's consideration to manufacture a home-baking product.

100. **(E)** The increase in world trade had no direct bearing on the company's problem. As management saw it, an increase in *tariff rates* abroad caused a decline in their overseas sales.

101. **(E)** See paragraph 2: high tariff rates, sterner competition, and trade distortions caused by World War II.

102. **(C)** It was 11 percent. See paragraph 1.

103. **(C)** Manufacturing costs were not a factor. See paragraph 3.

104. **(B)** To have let sales decline for so long without taking any action and then finally reacting in a superficial way—making decisions without adequate research and consideration—is poor managerial action.

105. **(D)** Management was certainly worried about the business, but this apprehension did not directly lead to *specific* action as factors I and II did.

Section IV   Data Sufficiency

106. **(D)** Area = (length)(width) = 40(width). So to find the area we must know the width. The perimeter of a rectangle is twice (length + width). (1) tells us the perimeter equals 140 yds. Since the length is 40 yds, the width is 30 yds, so (1) is sufficient. If we connect 2 opposite corners of the field, then it is divided into 2 right triangles where the

side opposite the right angle has length 50 and one of the other sides has length 40. Since $(40)^2 + (width)^2 = (50)^2$ the width is 30, and (2) is sufficient by itself.

107. **(A)** Statement (1) is $x^3 + 1 = 0$, which means $x^3 = -1$; the only solution to this equation is -1. So x is not greater than 0. Therefore, (1) alone is sufficient. Statement (2) says $x^2 - \frac{1}{2} = 0$ or $x^2 = \frac{1}{2}$. There are two possible solutions to this equation, one positive and the other negative. So (2) by itself is not sufficient.

108. **(D)** Statement (1) is sufficient since it implies that A loaded 300 boxes in 30 minutes and B loaded 150 boxes. So B should take 90 minutes to load the 450 boxes by himself. (2) is also sufficient since it implies A loads 10 boxes per minute; hence A loads 300 boxes in 30 minutes, and by the above argument we can deduce that B will take 90 minutes.

109. **(C)** A cube is a solid with 6 faces, all of which are congruent squares. Statement (1) is not sufficient since a solid with 2 of the faces as diamonds (rhombus) is not a cube but does satisfy (1). ⬭ . Statement (2) is not sufficient since a solid with 2 or 4 of the faces congruent rectangles is not a cube ▭ But (1) and (2) together mean that each face is a congruent square.

110. **(B)** The first car will travel a distance equal to the circumference of the circle, which is π times the diameter. Since π is greater than $1\frac{1}{2}$, (2) is sufficient. (1) is not sufficient since one car might have traveled at a faster rate than the other.

111. **(C)** Statement (1) tells us only that $x = 6 + y$, so it is not sufficient. In the same way (2) alone will give only one of the unknowns in terms of the other. However, if we use both (1) and (2), we obtain a system of two equations which can be solved for x and y.

112. **(D)** Since we know that the sum of the angles in a triangle is 180° and that $x = 45$, (1) implies (2) and (2) implies (1). Either one is sufficient, since if $z = 45$, then $x = z$ and the sides opposite the equal angles are equal. Hence $AC = AB = 3$.

113. **(E)** Using (1) and (2) together it is possible to determine only the total paid in 1969 and 1971. No relation is given between the amounts paid in 1969 and 1971; thus there is not enough information to determine the cost in 1971.

114. **(A)** It costs $10 in gas, $2.50 in the tolls, and at least $5 in parking to drive each week. So driving costs at least $17.50 a week. (1) is sufficient. Without information on the price of the train ticket we can not compare the two methods, so (2) is not sufficient.

115. **(C)** Statement (1) is not sufficient since the diagonals of *any* parallelogram bisect each other. Statement (2) is not sufficient since the other angles of the figure do not have to be right angles. However, (1) and (2) together are sufficient. Statement (1) implies the figure is a parallelogram. In a parallelogram, opposite angles are equal and the sum of all four angles must be 360°. Thus, if one of the angles in a parallelogram is 90°, all of the angles are right angles and the parallelogram is a rectangle.

116. **(D)** Let x be the amount he was paid on the first day; then he was paid $x + 5$, $x + 10$, $x + 15$, and $x + 20$ for the remaining days of work. The total amount he was paid is $5x + 50$. Thus if we can find x, we can find the total amount he was paid. Statement (1) is sufficient since after 3 days his total pay was $x + x + 5 + x + 10$ or $3x + 15$; this is equal to $\frac{1}{2}(5x + 50)$. So $3x + 15 = 2.5(x) + 25$ which implies $x = 20$. Statement (2) is sufficient since he was paid $x + 20$ on the last day and so $x + 20 = 2x$ which implies $x = 20$.

Remember that to answer the question it is not necessary to actually *solve* the equations given in statements 1 and 2. You only have to know that they will give you an equation which can be solved for x. Don't bother to actually solve the problem since you only have a limited amount of time to work all the questions in this section.

117. **(C)** Statement (1) alone is not sufficient since $x = 3$, $y = -1$, and $x = -1$, $y = 3$ satisfy $x + y = 2$. Statement (2) alone is not sufficient since $x = 2$, $y = 1$ and $x = -2$, $y = -1$ satisfy (2) However, since (2) says $x = 2y$, using (1) $x + y = 2y + y = 2$ we see that $y = \frac{2}{3}$ and $x = \frac{4}{3}$. So (1) and (2) together are sufficient.

118. **(B)** Area of the circle is $\pi r^2 = \pi\left(\dfrac{d}{2}\right)^2 = \dfrac{\pi}{4}d^2$ and the area of the square is s^2. Statement (2) is sufficient. $d < s$ implies $d^2 < s^2$ and $\dfrac{\pi}{4}$ is less than 1. So $\dfrac{\pi}{4}d^2 < d^2 < s^2$. (Note that since d and s are both positive $d < s$ does imply $d^2 < s^2$.) However, if $d < \sqrt{2}s$ then $d^2 < 2s^2$ so $\dfrac{\pi}{4}d^2 < \dfrac{\pi}{2}s^2$. But $\dfrac{\pi}{2}$ is larger than 1, so the area of the circle could be larger or smaller than s^2. Thus (1) alone is not sufficient.

119. **(D)** 10 apples will cost $1.60. Hence if we can discover the cost of three oranges we can solve the problem. Statement (1) is sufficient since (1) implies 3 oranges will cost 25¢. Statement (2) is also sufficient since we know 10 apples cost $1.60, thus (2) implies (1) which we know to be sufficient.

120. **(A)** Since 80% of $160 = $128, we know that after the first discount the skis cost less than $130. Any further discount will only lower the price. So (1) alone is sufficient. Statement (2) alone is not sufficient since if x were 10%, (2) would tell us the price was less than $130; but if x were 1%, (2) would imply that the price was greater than $130.

Section V   Verbal Aptitude

121. **(C)** ABANDONMENT: desertion, dereliction. *Antonym:* maintenance

122. **(B)** ADROIT: skillful, clever. *Antonym:* unskillful

123. **(D)** PRESCRIBE: appoint, ordain. *Antonym:* prohibit

124. **(A)** SPECIOUS: plausible, showy. *Antonym:* genuinely logical

125. **(D)** HAUGHTY: arrogant, disdainful. *Antonym:* meek

126. **(C)** INSOLENT: rude, impertinent. *Antonym:* polite

127. **(C)** ASSIDUOUS: diligent, careful. *Antonym:* careless

128. **(B)** DISCRETE: separate. *Antonym:* joined

129. **(D)** INTREPID: brave, fearless. *Antonym:* cowardly

130. **(E)** An artist creates by using paint. A sculptor uses clay.

131. **(C)** Cowardice is an extreme and negative degree of timidity. Parsimony is a negative degree of economy.

132. **(B)** Neurosis is a milder form of mental disease than psychosis. A cold is a milder form of physical disease than influenza.

133. **(A)** A hemisphere is half (or part of) a sphere. A quadrant is one-third (or part of) a circle.

134. **(B)** Vestment is clothing worn in ecclesiastical circles. A uniform is clothing worn in military circles.

135. **(D)** A president is inaugurated. A priest is ordained.

136. **(A)** The leader rules a nation. The leader commands an army.

137. **A)** Harmony is the pleasing combination of tones in a musical chord. Agreement is the pleasing combination of numbers in a mathematical equation.

138. **(B)** Another possibility is (A), but "conditions are not constrained" has an unclear meaning.

139. **(C)** Axiomatic, or an established principle is implied since Liebnitz' "historical continuity" is a law.

140. **(A)** From automobile to farm-implement implies a transition.

141. **(D)** The most meaningful in this sentence; births, deaths, and the net number of migrants are the determinants of population change.

142. **(B)** is the only logical answer.

143. **(A)** As people in given societies or groups *interact* with one another, their *activities* or behavior tends to be alike.

144. **(D)** *Diametrically*, or directly opposed.

145. **(B)** Another possibility is (C) prodigious, or *enormous*, but that is already mentioned: "Brazil is the *largest* country."

Section VI — Business Judgment

146. **(B)** The company has two major problems. The first mentioned in the passage is declining sales. The only explanation found in the passage is that salesmen have not developed enough new customers. Declining sales was a major factor in Tulli's decision to reassign salesmen, although one can argue if his decision is correct. The second problem is the factor of increasing accounts receivables, because of slow customer payments. This problem, in turn, is a symptom of declining sales.

147. **(B)** As pointed out above, increasing accounts receivables was a major company problem and was a *Major Factor* in Tulli's decision to reassign salesmen and to change the company's compensation policy.

148. **(E)** The nationality of the company is an *Unimportant Issue*.

149. **(A)** The cash shortage is the problem uppermost in management's considerations. This condition was the primary issue which led to the change in compensation policy and the reassignment of salesmen.

150. **(D)** Tulli concluded that higher commission rates would not motivate salesmen to estab-

lish new accounts, even though there is indication that this is what salesmen would want. Moreover, no facts were given to support Tulli's view that such a policy would not work.

151. **(D)** the only reason given was III. See paragraph 10.

152. **(D)** whether poor salesmanship was a cause or not cannot be determined from the information contained in the passage.

153. **(C)** Spending more time in the field was not mentioned.

154. **(B)** Only III was mentioned in the passage. Salesmen's morale will certainly be affected if the reassignment plan is adopted by management.

155. **(A)** Reducing credit to customers will cause a decline in sales. It is likely that customers will switch to other companies whose credit policies are more liberal.

156. **(A)** The *Major Objective* of top management is whether office discipline—exemplified by the Klein case—can be tightened. The decision involves establishing firm guidelines for work conditions including, of course, the question of overtime.

157. **(E)** The company's product line is an *Unimportant Issue*.

158. **(B)** Gross's inflexible attitude and approach to the problem was a *Major Factor* leading to Klein's reaction and to the need for a policy decision.

159. **(B)** Klein's reacting like an injured person rather than taking a more "professional" attitude to the problem is a *Major Factor* determining the way Mitte will have to formulate a solution.

160. **(C)** Klein's three years with the company is a *Minor Factor*. The relationships involved are more important than the time factor.

161. **(B)** Mitte was concerned that if Klein ceased to work after normal office hours, other employees would follow his action.

162. **(C)** Mitte can either relax company work rules to accommodate Klein or accept Klein's statement that he will work only during normal office hours. No mention was made of resigning as an alternative course of action.

163. **(B)** See paragraph 12.

164. **(B)** Since Mitte is Klein's supervisor, Gross should have waited until his (Mitte's) return and discussed the problem directly with him. This may have avoided Klein's angry reaction as Gross and Mitte may have worked out a solution together.

165. **(C)** Only III is feasible, since many research projects have to be continued into the evenings in order to meet deadlines. Also, as mentioned in the passage, telephone surveys among men at home had to be done in the evenings, necessitating overtime work.

Section VII   Writing Ability

166. **(E)** Since both subjects are joined by the word *and*, they are considered as a single thing. Hence we use the single form *is* and not *and*.

167. **(A)** The word *team* is a collective noun and is considered singular when the group is regarded as a unit. Therefore, the singular form *is* should be used.

168. **(D)** One should avoid repetitions in sentences. The correct form is: "I can't go there now, but I plan to go tomorrow."

169. **(E)** No error.

170. **(C)** *Seen* is the wrong tense. *Saw* is the correct form.

171. **(A)** *Plays* is an illogical time form. The verb tense should be *played*.

172. **(E)** No error.

173. **(B)** Enthused is the colloquial expression for enthusiastic, the preferred word usage.

174. **(A)** *Which* is redundant and is not needed as a connecting word between the two clauses of the sentence.

175. **(C)** An error in diction, or improper word usage. Irregardless is a substandard form of regardless.

176. **(C)** *After the battle* indicates the past, while the rest of the sentence is in the future tense. Part C should read *advanced*.

177. **(C)** The use of a personal pronoun (they) in an impersonal sense (as in the sentence) should be avoided. The sentence should read: "I read in the newspaper that large tomatoes are grown in Nigeria."

178. **(B)** In this sentence, it seems as if *the breathing* is doing the swimming. The problem here is the dangling phrase which must be given a word to modify. The sentence should read: To master the proper backstroke, *the swimmer must carefully control his breathing*.

179. **(E)** No error.

180. **(C)** This is a complex sentence with one main clause (the TV program) and one subordinate clause (the training sequence). However, the error is in tense. The main clause is in the past tense, while the subordinate clause is in the present. It should also be in the past tense, i.e., "the other part showed. . . ."

181. **(D)** The series of instructions requires parallel structures and so *no cheating* should be *not to cheat*.

182. **(A)** *Had . . . begun*; the past participle is required in the past perfect form and not *began*, which is the past simple form of the verb.

183. **(D)** The subject of the gerund *standing* should be in the possessive form; *my* and not *me*.

184. **(C)** The preposition *to* is redundant in this case as it appears earlier attached to the pronoun *whom*.

185. **(E)** No error.

186. **(B)** The pronoun *they* has no antecedent.

187. **(C)** The subject of the modifying phrase *Having been delayed by unfavorable weather* is obviously *our plane*, which should follow directly after the phrase.

188. **(D)** The correct word is *considerate*, meaning *thoughtful of the needs of others* and not *considerable*, meaning *great in size or importance*.

189. **(B)** The expression *each other* is confined to relationships between two; in this case *one another* is required.

190. **(A)** The adjective *less* refers to quantity; *fewer*, which refers to countable units, i.e., *chances* is required here.

Evaluating Your Score

Tabulate your score for each section of Sample Test 4 according to the directions on pages 4–5 and record the results in the Self-scoring Table below. Then find your rank for each score on the Self-scoring Scale and record it in the appropriate blank.

Self-scoring Table

PART	SCORE	RANK
1		
2		
3		
4		
5		
6		
7		

Self-scoring Scale

			ACHIEVEMENT	
PART	POOR	FAIR	GOOD	EXCELLENT
1	0–15	16–21	22–25	26–30
2	0–29	30–40	41–47	48–55
3	0–10	11–14	15–16	17–20
4	0–7	8–10	11–12	13–15
5	0–12	13–17	18–20	21–25
6	0–10	11–14	15–16	17–20
7	0–12	13–17	18–20	21–25

Study again the Review sections covering material in Sample Test 4 for which you had a rank of FAIR or POOR. Then go on to Sample Test 5.

To obtain an approximation of your actual GMAT score see page 5.

Answer Sheet — Sample Test 5

Section I — Reading Comprehension

1. (A) (B) (C) (D) (E)
2. (A) (B) (C) (D) (E)
3. (A) (B) (C) (D) (E)
4. (A) (B) (C) (D) (E)
5. (A) (B) (C) (D) (E)
6. (A) (B) (C) (D) (E)

7. (A) (B) (C) (D) (E)
8. (A) (B) (C) (D) (E)
9. (A) (B) (C) (D) (E)
10. (A) (B) (C) (D) (E)
11. (A) (B) (C) (D) (E)
12. (A) (B) (C) (D) (E)

13. (A) (B) (C) (D) (E)
14. (A) (B) (C) (D) (E)
15. (A) (B) (C) (D) (E)
16. (A) (B) (C) (D) (E)
17. (A) (B) (C) (D) (E)
18. (A) (B) (C) (D) (E)

19. (A) (B) (C) (D) (E)
20. (A) (B) (C) (D) (E)
21. (A) (B) (C) (D) (E)
22. (A) (B) (C) (D) (E)
23. (A) (B) (C) (D) (E)
24. (A) (B) (C) (D) (E)
25. (A) (B) (C) (D) (E)

Section II — Mathematics

26. (A) (B) (C) (D) (E)
27. (A) (B) (C) (D) (E)
28. (A) (B) (C) (D) (E)
29. (A) (B) (C) (D) (E)
30. (A) (B) (C) (D) (E)
31. (A) (B) (C) (D) (E)
32. (A) (B) (C) (D) (E)

33. (A) (B) (C) (D) (E)
34. (A) (B) (C) (D) (E)
35. (A) (B) (C) (D) (E)
36. (A) (B) (C) (D) (E)
37. (A) (B) (C) (D) (E)
38. (A) (B) (C) (D) (E)
39. (A) (B) (C) (D) (E)

40. (A) (B) (C) (D) (E)
41. (A) (B) (C) (D) (E)
42. (A) (B) (C) (D) (E)
43. (A) (B) (C) (D) (E)
44. (A) (B) (C) (D) (E)
45. (A) (B) (C) (D) (E)
46. (A) (B) (C) (D) (E)
47. (A) (B) (C) (D) (E)

48. (A) (B) (C) (D) (E)
49. (A) (B) (C) (D) (E)
50. (A) (B) (C) (D) (E)
51. (A) (B) (C) (D) (E)
52. (A) (B) (C) (D) (E)
53. (A) (B) (C) (D) (E)
54. (A) (B) (C) (D) (E)
55. (A) (B) (C) (D) (E)

Section III — Business Judgment

56. (A) (B) (C) (D) (E)
57. (A) (B) (C) (D) (E)
58. (A) (B) (C) (D) (E)
59. (A) (B) (C) (D) (E)
60. (A) (B) (C) (D) (E)
61. (A) (B) (C) (D) (E)

62. (A) (B) (C) (D) (E)
63. (A) (B) (C) (D) (E)
64. (A) (B) (C) (D) (E)
65. (A) (B) (C) (D) (E)
66. (A) (B) (C) (D) (E)
67. (A) (B) (C) (D) (E)

68. (A) (B) (C) (D) (E)
69. (A) (B) (C) (D) (E)
70. (A) (B) (C) (D) (E)
71. (A) (B) (C) (D) (E)
72. (A) (B) (C) (D) (E)
73. (A) (B) (C) (D) (E)

74. (A) (B) (C) (D) (E)
75. (A) (B) (C) (D) (E)
76. (A) (B) (C) (D) (E)
77. (A) (B) (C) (D) (E)
78. (A) (B) (C) (D) (E)
79. (A) (B) (C) (D) (E)
80. (A) (B) (C) (D) (E)

Section IV — Data Sufficiency

81. (A) (B) (C) (D) (E)
82. (A) (B) (C) (D) (E)
83. (A) (B) (C) (D) (E)

84. (A) (B) (C) (D) (E)
85. (A) (B) (C) (D) (E)
86. (A) (B) (C) (D) (E)
87. (A) (B) (C) (D) (E)

88. (A) (B) (C) (D) (E)
89. (A) (B) (C) (D) (E)
90. (A) (B) (C) (D) (E)
91. (A) (B) (C) (D) (E)

92. (A) (B) (C) (D) (E)
93. (A) (B) (C) (D) (E)
94. (A) (B) (C) (D) (E)
95. (A) (B) (C) (D) (E)

Section V — Writing Ability

96. Ⓐ Ⓑ Ⓒ Ⓓ Ⓔ
97. Ⓐ Ⓑ Ⓒ Ⓓ Ⓔ
98. Ⓐ Ⓑ Ⓒ Ⓓ Ⓔ
99. Ⓐ Ⓑ Ⓒ Ⓓ Ⓔ
100. Ⓐ Ⓑ Ⓒ Ⓓ Ⓔ
101. Ⓐ Ⓑ Ⓒ Ⓓ Ⓔ
102. Ⓐ Ⓑ Ⓒ Ⓓ Ⓔ
103. Ⓐ Ⓑ Ⓒ Ⓓ Ⓔ

104. Ⓐ Ⓑ Ⓒ Ⓓ Ⓔ
105. Ⓐ Ⓑ Ⓒ Ⓓ Ⓔ
106. Ⓐ Ⓑ Ⓒ Ⓓ Ⓔ
107. Ⓐ Ⓑ Ⓒ Ⓓ Ⓔ
108. Ⓐ Ⓑ Ⓒ Ⓓ Ⓔ
109. Ⓐ Ⓑ Ⓒ Ⓓ Ⓔ
110. Ⓐ Ⓑ Ⓒ Ⓓ Ⓔ
111. Ⓐ Ⓑ Ⓒ Ⓓ Ⓔ
112. Ⓐ Ⓑ Ⓒ Ⓓ Ⓔ

113. Ⓐ Ⓑ Ⓒ Ⓓ Ⓔ
114. Ⓐ Ⓑ Ⓒ Ⓓ Ⓔ
115. Ⓐ Ⓑ Ⓒ Ⓓ Ⓔ
116. Ⓐ Ⓑ Ⓒ Ⓓ Ⓔ
117. Ⓐ Ⓑ Ⓒ Ⓓ Ⓔ
118. Ⓐ Ⓑ Ⓒ Ⓓ Ⓔ
119. Ⓐ Ⓑ Ⓒ Ⓓ Ⓔ
120. Ⓐ Ⓑ Ⓒ Ⓓ Ⓔ
121. Ⓐ Ⓑ Ⓒ Ⓓ Ⓔ

122. Ⓐ Ⓑ Ⓒ Ⓓ Ⓔ
123. Ⓐ Ⓑ Ⓒ Ⓓ Ⓔ
124. Ⓐ Ⓑ Ⓒ Ⓓ Ⓔ
125. Ⓐ Ⓑ Ⓒ Ⓓ Ⓔ
126. Ⓐ Ⓑ Ⓒ Ⓓ Ⓔ
127. Ⓐ Ⓑ Ⓒ Ⓓ Ⓔ
128. Ⓐ Ⓑ Ⓒ Ⓓ Ⓔ
129. Ⓐ Ⓑ Ⓒ Ⓓ Ⓔ
130. Ⓐ Ⓑ Ⓒ Ⓓ Ⓔ

Section VI — Business Judgment

131. Ⓐ Ⓑ Ⓒ Ⓓ Ⓔ
132. Ⓐ Ⓑ Ⓒ Ⓓ Ⓔ
133. Ⓐ Ⓑ Ⓒ Ⓓ Ⓔ
134. Ⓐ Ⓑ Ⓒ Ⓓ Ⓔ
135. Ⓐ Ⓑ Ⓒ Ⓓ Ⓔ

136. Ⓐ Ⓑ Ⓒ Ⓓ Ⓔ
137. Ⓐ Ⓑ Ⓒ Ⓓ Ⓔ
138. Ⓐ Ⓑ Ⓒ Ⓓ Ⓔ
139. Ⓐ Ⓑ Ⓒ Ⓓ Ⓔ
140. Ⓐ Ⓑ Ⓒ Ⓓ Ⓔ

141. Ⓐ Ⓑ Ⓒ Ⓓ Ⓔ
142. Ⓐ Ⓑ Ⓒ Ⓓ Ⓔ
143. Ⓐ Ⓑ Ⓒ Ⓓ Ⓔ
144. Ⓐ Ⓑ Ⓒ Ⓓ Ⓔ
145. Ⓐ Ⓑ Ⓒ Ⓓ Ⓔ

146. Ⓐ Ⓑ Ⓒ Ⓓ Ⓔ
147. Ⓐ Ⓑ Ⓒ Ⓓ Ⓔ
148. Ⓐ Ⓑ Ⓒ Ⓓ Ⓔ
149. Ⓐ Ⓑ Ⓒ Ⓓ Ⓔ
150. Ⓐ Ⓑ Ⓒ Ⓓ Ⓔ

Section VII — Case Evaluation

151. Ⓐ Ⓑ Ⓒ Ⓓ Ⓔ
152. Ⓐ Ⓑ Ⓒ Ⓓ Ⓔ
153. Ⓐ Ⓑ Ⓒ Ⓓ Ⓔ
154. Ⓐ Ⓑ Ⓒ Ⓓ Ⓔ
155. Ⓐ Ⓑ Ⓒ Ⓓ Ⓔ
156. Ⓐ Ⓑ Ⓒ Ⓓ Ⓔ
157. Ⓐ Ⓑ Ⓒ Ⓓ Ⓔ
158. Ⓐ Ⓑ Ⓒ Ⓓ Ⓔ
159. Ⓐ Ⓑ Ⓒ Ⓓ Ⓔ
160. Ⓐ Ⓑ Ⓒ Ⓓ Ⓔ

161. Ⓐ Ⓑ Ⓒ Ⓓ Ⓔ
162. Ⓐ Ⓑ Ⓒ Ⓓ Ⓔ
163. Ⓐ Ⓑ Ⓒ Ⓓ Ⓔ
164. Ⓐ Ⓑ Ⓒ Ⓓ Ⓔ
165. Ⓐ Ⓑ Ⓒ Ⓓ Ⓔ
166. Ⓐ Ⓑ Ⓒ Ⓓ Ⓔ
167. Ⓐ Ⓑ Ⓒ Ⓓ Ⓔ
168. Ⓐ Ⓑ Ⓒ Ⓓ Ⓔ
169. Ⓐ Ⓑ Ⓒ Ⓓ Ⓔ
170. Ⓐ Ⓑ Ⓒ Ⓓ Ⓔ

171. Ⓐ Ⓑ Ⓒ Ⓓ Ⓔ
172. Ⓐ Ⓑ Ⓒ Ⓓ Ⓔ
173. Ⓐ Ⓑ Ⓒ Ⓓ Ⓔ
174. Ⓐ Ⓑ Ⓒ Ⓓ Ⓔ
175. Ⓐ Ⓑ Ⓒ Ⓓ Ⓔ
176. Ⓐ Ⓑ Ⓒ Ⓓ Ⓔ
177. Ⓐ Ⓑ Ⓒ Ⓓ Ⓔ
178. Ⓐ Ⓑ Ⓒ Ⓓ Ⓔ
179. Ⓐ Ⓑ Ⓒ Ⓓ Ⓔ
180. Ⓐ Ⓑ Ⓒ Ⓓ Ⓔ

181. Ⓐ Ⓑ Ⓒ Ⓓ Ⓔ
182. Ⓐ Ⓑ Ⓒ Ⓓ Ⓔ
183. Ⓐ Ⓑ Ⓒ Ⓓ Ⓔ
184. Ⓐ Ⓑ Ⓒ Ⓓ Ⓔ
185. Ⓐ Ⓑ Ⓒ Ⓓ Ⓔ
186. Ⓐ Ⓑ Ⓒ Ⓓ Ⓔ
187. Ⓐ Ⓑ Ⓒ Ⓓ Ⓔ
188. Ⓐ Ⓑ Ⓒ Ⓓ Ⓔ
189. Ⓐ Ⓑ Ⓒ Ⓓ Ⓔ
190. Ⓐ Ⓑ Ⓒ Ⓓ Ⓔ

Sample Test 5

Section I Reading Comprehension

TIME: 30 minutes

DIRECTIONS: This part contains four reading passages. You are to read each one carefully. When answering the questions, you *will* be able to refer to the passages. The questions are based on what is *stated* or *implied* in each passage. You have thirty minutes to complete this section.

Passage 1:

A report reveals in facts and figures what should have been known in principle, that quite a lot of business companies are going to go under during the coming decade, as tariff walls are progressively dismantled. Labor and capital valued at $12 billion are to be made idle through the impact of duty-free imports. As a result, 35,000 workers will be
(5) displaced. Some will move to other jobs and other departments within the same firm. Around 15,000 will have to leave the firm now employing them and work elsewhere.

The report is measuring exclusively the influence of free trade with Europe. The authors do not take into account the expected expansion of production over the coming years. On the other hand, they are not sure that even the export predictions they make
(10) will be achieved. For this presupposes that a suitable business climate lets the pressure to increase productivity materialize.

There are two reasons why this scenario may not happen. The first one is that industry on the whole is not taking the initiatives necessary to adapt fully to the new price situation it will be facing as time goes by.

(15) This is another way of saying that the manufacturers do not realize what lies ahead. The government is to blame for not making the position absolutely clear. It should be saying that in ten years time tariffs on all industrial goods imported from Europe will be eliminated. There will be no adjustment assistance for manufacturers who cannot adapt to this situation.

(20) The second obstacle to adjustment is not stressed in the same way in the report; it is the attitude of the service sector. Not only are they unaware that the Common Market treaty concerns them too, they are artificially insulated from the physical pressures of international competition. The manufacturing sector has to be forced to apply its nose to the grindstone for some time now, by the increasingly stringent import-liberalization pro-
(25) gram.

The ancillary services on which the factories depend show a growing indifference to their work obligations. They seem unaware that overmanned ships, and underutilized container equipment in the ports, and repeated work stoppages slow the country's attempts to narrow the trade gap. The remedy is to cut the fees charged by these services so as to
(30) reduce their earnings—in exactly the same way as earnings in industrial undertakings are reduced by the tariff reduction program embodied in the treaty with the European Community.

There is no point in dismissing 15,000 industrial workers from their present jobs during the coming ten years if all the gain in productivity is wasted by costly harbor, transport,

(35) financial, administrative and other services. The free trade treaty is their concern as we[ll]
Surplus staff should be removed if need be, from all workplaces, not just from the fa[c]
tories. Efficiency is everybody's business.

1. The attitude of the report can be best expressed as

   (A) vindictive because industry is not more responsive to the business climate
   (B) optimistic that government will induce industry to make needed changes
   (C) critical of labor unions
   (D) pessimistic that anything can be done to reduce the trade gap
   (E) objective in assessing the influence of free trade on employment

2. What is the meaning of *free trade* in line 7?

   (A) unlimited sale of goods in Europe
   (B) trade on a barter basis
   (C) the elimination of tariffs
   (D) price-discounted goods sold to European countries
   (E) trade with only the so-called "free countries," i.e., Western Europe

3. What meaning can be inferred from the term *adjustment assistance* in line 18?

   (A) unemployment compensation
   (B) some sort of financial assistance to manufacturers hurt by free trade
   (C) help in relocating plants to Europe
   (D) aid in reducing work stoppages
   (E) subsidy payments to increase exports

4. The author's recommendation seems to be that

   (A) unemployment should be avoided at all costs
   (B) redundant labor should be removed in all sectors
   (C) government should control the service sector
   (D) tariffs should not be lowered
   (E) workers should be retrained

5. Which of the following titles best describes the content of the passage?

   (A) *The Prospects of Free Trade*
   (B) *Government Intervention in World Trade*
   (C) *Trade With the Common Market*
   (D) *What Lies Ahead?*
   (E) *Unemployment and Adjustment Assistance*

Passage 2:

The fundamental objectives of sociology are the same as those of science generally—
discovery and explanation. To *discover* the essential data of social behavior and the co[n]
nections among the data is the first objective of sociology. To *explain* the data and t[he]
connections is the second and larger objective. Science makes its advances in terms [of]
(5) both of these objectives. Sometimes it is the discovery of a new element or set of e[le]
ments that marks a major breakthrough in the history of a scientific discipline. Closely r[e]
lated to such discovery is the discovery of relationships of data that had never been note[d]

before. All of this is, as we know, of immense importance in science. But the drama of
discovery, in this sense, can sometimes lead us to overlook the greater importance of ex-
(10) planation of what is revealed by the data. Sometimes decades, even centuries, pass before
known connections and relationships are actually explained. Discovery and explanation are
the two great interpenetrating, interacting realms of science.

The order of reality that interests the scientists is the *empirical* order, that is, the order
of data and phenomena revealed to us through observation or experience. To be precise
(15) or explicit about what is, and is not, revealed by observation is not always easy, to be sure.
And often it is necessary for our natural powers of observation to be supplemented by the
most intricate of mechanical aids for a given object to become "empirical" in the sense
just used. That the electron is not as immediately visible as is the mountain range does
not mean, obviously, that it is any less empirical. That social behavior does not lend itself
(20) to as quick and accurate description as, say, chemical behavior of gases and compounds
does not mean that social roles, statuses, and attitudes are any less empirical than mole-
cules and tissues. What is empirical and observable today may have been nonexistent in
scientific consciousness a decade ago. Moreover, the empirical is often data *inferred* from
direct observation. All of this is clear enough, and we should make no pretense that
(25) there are not often shadow areas between the empirical and the nonempirical. Nevertheless, the first point to make about any science, physical or social, is that its world of data
is the empirical world. A very large amount of scientific energy goes merely into the
work of expanding the frontiers, through discovery, of the known, observable, empirical
world.

(30) From observation or discovery we move to *explanation*. The explanation sought by the
scientist is, of course, not at all like the explanation sought by the theologian or meta-
physician. The scientist is not interested—not, that is, in his role of scientist—in ultimate, transcendental, or divine causes of what he sets himself to explain. He is interested
in explanations that are as empirical as the data themselves. If it is the high incidence of
(35) crime in a certain part of a large city that requires explanation, the scientist is obliged to
offer his explanation in terms of factors which are empirically real as the phenomenon of
crime itself. He does not explain the problem, for example, in terms of references to the
will of God, demons, or original sin. A satisfactory explanation is one that is not only
empirical, however, but one that can be stated in the terms of a *causal proposition*. De-
(40) scription is an indispensable point of beginning, but description is not explanation. It is
well to stress this point, for there are all too many scientists, or would-be scientists, who
are primarily concerned with data gathering, data counting, and data describing, and who
seem to forget that such operations, however useful, are but the first step. Until we have
accounted for the problem at hand, explained it causally by referring the data to some
(45) principle or generalization already established, or to some new principle or generalization,
we have not explained anything.

6. According to the passage, scientists are not interested in theological explanations
because

    (A) scientists tend to be atheists
    (B) theology cannot explain change
    (C) theological explanations are not empirical
    (D) theology cannot explain social behavior
    (E) scientists are concerned with data gathering

7. The major objective of the passage is to

   (A) show that explanation is more important than discovery
   (B) prove that sociology is a science
   (C) explain the objectives of sociology
   (D) discuss scientific method
   (E) describe social behavior

8. Which of the following statements agrees with the author's position?

   (A) science is the formulation of unverified hypotheses
   (B) explanation is inferred from data
   (C) causation is a basis for explanation
   (D) generalization is a prerequisite for explanation
   (E) empiricism is the science of discovery

9. Judging from the contents of the passage, the final step in a study of social behavior would be to

   (A) discover the problem
   (B) establish principles
   (C) offer an explanation of the data by determining causation
   (D) collect data
   (E) establish generalizations

10. According to the passage, which of the following activities aid the advance of science?

    I. Finding data relationships
    II. Building a taxonomy
    III. Laboratory experiments
    (A) I only   (B) only   (C) I and II only
    (D) I and III only   (E) I, II, and III

11. The author's main point in the first paragraph may be best described by which of the following statements?

    (A) science and sociology are interdisciplinary
    (B) the first objective of sociology is discovery
    (C) discovery without explanation has little use
    (D) discovery and explanation are fundamental to building a science
    (E) It takes a long time before relationships of data are discovered

Passage 3:

A polytheist always has favorites among the gods, determined by his own temperament, age and condition, as well as his own interest, temporary or permanent. If it is true that everybody loves a lover, then Venus will be a popular deity with all. But from lovers she will elicit special devotion. In ancient Rome, when a young couple went out together to
(5)   see a procession or other show, they would of course pay great respect to Venus, when her image appeared on the screen. Instead of saying, "Isn't love wonderful?" they would say, "Great art thou, O Venus." In a polytheistic society you could tell a good deal about a person's frame of mind by the gods he favored, so that to tell a girl you were trying to woo that you thought Venus overrated was hardly the way to win her heart. But in any
(10) case, a lovesick youth or maiden would be spontaneously supplicating Venus.

The Greeks liked to present their deities in human form; it was natural to them to symbolize the gods as human beings glorified, idealized. But this fact is also capable of misleading us. We might suppose that the ancients were really worshipping only themselves; that they were, like Narcissus, beholding their own image in a pool, so that their worship
(15) was *anthropocentric* (man-centered) rather than *theocentric* (god-centered). We are in danger of assuming that they were simply constructing the god in their own image. This is not necessarily so. The gods must always be symbolized in one form or another. To give them a human form is one way of doing this, technically called *anthropomorphism* (from the Greek *anthropos*, a man, and *morphé*, form). People of certain temperaments and with-
(20) in certain types of culture seem to be more inclined to it than are others. It is, however, more noticeable in others than in oneself, and those who affect to despise it are sometimes conspicuous for their addiction to it. A German once said an Englishman's idea of God is an Englishman twelve feet tall. Such disparagement of anthropomorphism occurred in the ancient world, too. The Celts, for instance, despised Greek practice in this
(25) matter, preferring to use animals and other such symbols. The Egyptians favored more abstract and stylized symbols, among which a well-known example is the solar disk, a symbol of Rà, the sun-god.

Professor C. S. Lewis tells of an Oxford undergraduate he knew who, priggishly despising the conventional images of God, thought he was overcoming anthropomorphism by
(30) thinking of the Deity as infinite vapor or smoke. Of course even the bearded-old-man image can be a better symbol of Deity than ever could be the image, even if this were psychologically possible, of an unlimited smog.

What is really characteristic of all polytheism, however, is not the worship of idols or humanity or forests or stars; it is, rather, the worship of innumerable *powers* that confront
(35) and affect us. The powers are held to be valuable in themselves; that is why they are to be worshipped. But the values conflict. The gods do not cooperate, so you have to play them off against each other. Suppose you want rain. You know of two gods, the dry-god who sends drought and the wet-god who sends rain. You do not suppose that you can just pray to the wet-god to get busy, and simply ignore the dry-god. If you do so, the lat-
(40) ter may be offended, so that no matter how hard the wet-god tries to oblige you, the dry-god will do his best to wither everything. Because both gods are powerful you must take both into consideration, begging the wet-god to be generous and beseeching the dry-god to stay his hand.

12. It can be inferred from the passage that polytheism means a belief in

    (A) Greek gods
    (B) more than one god
    (C) a god-centered world
    (D) powerful deities
    (E) infinite gods

13. The author's statement in lines 7–8 that "you could tell a good deal about a person's frame of mind by the gods he favored" means that

    (A) those who believed in gods were superstitious
    (B) worship was either anthropocentric or theocentric
    (C) gods were chosen to represent a given way of life
    (D) the way a person thinks depends on the power of deities
    (E) some cultures devised gods as representations of what the people thought of themselves

14. According to the passage, the author would most likely agree that ancient cultures

    I. symbolized their deities only in human form
   II. symbolized the gods in many forms
  III. were mainly self worshippers
(A) I only   (B) II only   (C) I and II only
(D) I and III only   (E) I, II, and III

15. The main point the author makes about anthropomorphism in lines 19–27 is that

(A) certain cultures are inclined to anthropomorphism
(B) those who demean anthropomorphism may actually refer to it
(C) the disparagement of anthropomorphism is common to both ancient and modern cultures
(D) Germans tend to be more theocentric than the English
(E) anthropomorphism is a practice common to all cultures

16. It may be inferred from the last paragraph that polytheism entails

(A) a commonality of interests among the deities
(B) predictable consequences
(C) incoherence and conflict among the "powers"
(D) an orderly universe
(E) worshipping one god at a time

Passage 4:
(This passage was written in 1970.)

It appears that the easiest kind of occupation is that of the forecaster. If a dismal future is forecasted, and remedial actions are taken, and the future turns out better than predicted—the forecaster can claim disaster was avoided because he was listened to. If, however, his pessimism was well founded, the forecaster can take credit for being an able

(5)   predictor of future events. In this last case, if corrective action was taken—but failed—the forecaster can claim the amount of action was insufficient, too late, or of the wrong kind.

One reason that the forecasting business has, in itself, become a growth industry is that every institution must plan ahead to stay ahead. Everyone today seems to be interested in

(10) gaining whatever insights they can as to what the trends of the near future will be like. Unfortunately, many of the people that are telling us about the nature of expected changes are basing their predictions on an irrational interpretation of recent past events, and not on factual data. Most of these popular forecasts are inspirational but not very actionable.

(15)   If we flash back to the early 1960s we can quickly retrace the course of events which are the basis for many popular predictions. John Gardner, in his then recently published book, *Self Renewal*, commented that many Americans were operating on a principal of "whatever is—is right doctrine." However, within a few years this mood drastically changed. Radical student movements, Vietnam peace marches, Civil Rights demonstra-

(20) tions, Women's Liberation, Consumerism, Ecology and other events tended to make Gardner's doctrine no longer descriptive of these events. Within a period of less than five years the rapidity of change in attitudes and values was overwhelming. From a no questioning era we suddenly began to question everything and anything—from the institution of marriage to the government's right to engage in war.

(25) The key question is not what happened but why it happened. To answer this question we must take account of the important factors which induced change, and attach to each its due weight. Also, we must attempt to specify how these factors interrelated and interacted with each other. This, of course, is very difficult because of the number of factors involved, and their far reaching impact. If we just analyze one factor at a time, we would be guilty

(30) of fuzzy or erroneous conclusions. For example, let us illustrate the advantage of structuring the interconnections between interrelated factors. Suppose that you are in charge of a program to build low-income housing. You are working diligently to provide decent homes for poverty-stricken people. You are praised for your far-sighted genuine concern, having been quoted as saying that your housing projects will help eliminate poverty. You

(35) finally succeed but your success has the unintended result of increasing poverty. Why? Low-income housing merely draws more poor people into an area where very few jobs existed—this creates an even worse supply and demand situation for jobs—and the city's poverty problems are worsened.

(40) In essence, we are saying that to arrive at any meaningful conclusion when studying a problem, we must first list all the factors which influence the final result or outcome, and the interrelation between these factors. The housing case demonstrated that a series of short run answers to a problem might create worse problems in the long run.

17. Which of the following statements best exemplifies the author's viewpoint?

(A) Forecasting is a dismal business.
(B) Forecasters are generally pessimistic.
(C) There is a growing demand for forecasters.
(D) Forecasting is inspirational.
(E) Forecasters are always right.

18. Which of the following statements may be inferred from the first paragraph of the passage?

 I. Forecasters are never wrong.
 II. Forecasters are adept at hedging.
 III. Forecasting should be improved.
(A) I only (B) II only (C) I and II only
(D) I and III only (E) I, II, and III

19. Which of the following statements best describes the point the author is trying to make in the housing case?

(A) Housing projects cannot eliminate poverty.
(B) Poor people resent low-income housing.
(C) The project was not a long-run solution to the poverty problem.
(D) The project director was guilty of "fuzzy" thinking.
(E) The project suffered from cost overruns.

20. The author's main purpose in the passage is to

(A) introduce new hypotheses
(B) describe his experiences
(C) discuss the early 1960s
(D) explain the housing case
(E) improve the art of forecasting

21. According to the passage, Gardner's thesis

    (A) is no longer operative
    (B) is operative today
    (C) was operative in the early 1960s
    (D) was never operative
    (E) is completely false

22. It can be inferred from the passage that the antithesis of the "whatever is—is right" doctrine would be

    (A) "whatever is—is always wrong"
    (B) "whatever is—should be questioned"
    (C) "whatever is—should be opposed"
    (D) "whatever is—should be improved"
    (E) "whatever is—should remain"

23. It is the author's opinion that to improve forecasting there must be better

    (A) interpretation of causal factors
    (B) description of events
    (C) insights of trends
    (D) interpretation of facts
    (E) statistical analysis of data

24. The author exhorts forecasters to

    (A) analyze one fact at a time
    (B) plan ahead to stay ahead
    (C) base predictions on past events
    (D) quickly retrace the course of events
    (E) analyze all interrelated causal factors

25. According to the passage, the author's attitude to the environmental changes given in lines 18–24 is one of

    (A) ambivalence
    (B) disapproval
    (C) approval
    (D) consternation
    (E) surprise

If there is still time remaining, you may review the questions in this section only.
You may not turn to any other section of the test.

Section II   Mathematics

DIRECTIONS: Solve each of the following problems; then indicate the correct answer on the answer sheet. [On the actual test you will be permitted to use any space available on the examination paper for scratch work.]

NOTE: A figure that appears with a problem is drawn as accurately as possible so as to provide information that may help in answering the questions. Numbers in this test are real numbers.

26. What is the next number in the geometric progression 4, 12, 36?

    (A) 44
    (B) 60
    (C) 72

    (D) 108
    (E) 144

27. An angle of x degrees has the property that its complement is equal to ⅙ of its supplement where x is

    (A) 30
    (B) 45
    (C) 60

    (D) 63
    (E) 72

28. If a company makes a profit of $250 on sales of $1,900, the profit was approximately what percentage of sales?

    (A) 10%
    (B) 12%
    (C) 13%

    (D) 15%
    (E) 17%

29. Which of the following numbers is the least common multiple of the numbers 2, 3, 4, and 5?

    (A) 12
    (B) 24
    (C) 30

    (D) 40
    (E) 60

30. In a certain town 40% of the people have brown hair, 25% have brown eyes, and 10% have both brown hair and brown eyes. What percentage of the people in the town have neither brown hair nor brown eyes?

    (A) 35
    (B) 40
    (C) 45

    (D) 50
    (E) 55

31. If the altitude of a triangle increases by 5% and the base of the triangle increases by 7%, by what percent will the area of the triangle increase?

    (A) 3.33%
    (B) 5%
    (C) 6%

    (D) 12%
    (E) 12.35%

32. A shipping firm charges 2¢ a pound for the first 20 pounds of package weight and 1.5¢ for each pound or fraction of a pound over 20 pounds of package weight. How much will it charge to ship a package which weighs 23½ pounds?

   (A) 6¢
   (B) 40¢
   (C) 45¢
   (D) 46¢
   (E) 52¢

33. If paper costs 1¢ a sheet, and a buyer gets a 2% discount on all the paper he buys after the first 1,000 sheets, how much will it cost to buy 5,000 sheets of paper?

   (A) $49.20
   (B) $50.00
   (C) $3,920.00
   (D) $4,920.00
   (E) $5,000.00

34. Tom's salary is 150% of John's salary. John's salary is 80% of Steve's salary. What is the ratio of Steve's salary to Tom's salary?

   (A) 1 to 2
   (B) 2 to 3
   (C) 5 to 6
   (D) 6 to 5
   (E) 5 to 4

35. A driver is taking a 5 hour trip. If he travels 135 miles in the first 3 hours, how far will he have to drive in the final 2 hours in order to average 50 miles an hour for the entire trip?

   (A) 50 miles
   (B) 55 miles
   (C) 110 miles
   (D) 115 miles
   (E) 165 miles

36. If it takes 50 workers 4 hours to dig a sewer, how long should it take 30 workers to dig the same sewer?

   (A) 2 hrs., 24 min.
   (B) 5 hrs., 12 min.
   (C) 6 hrs., 12 min.
   (D) 6 hrs., 20 min.
   (E) 6 hrs., 40 min.

37. Dictionaries weigh 6 pounds each and a set of encyclopedias weighs 75 pounds. 20 dictionaries are shipped in each box. 2 sets of encyclopedias are shipped in each box. A truck is loaded with 98 boxes of dictionaries and 50 boxes of encyclopedias. How much does the truck's load weigh?

   (A) 588 pounds
   (B) 7,500 pounds
   (C) 11,750 pounds
   (D) 19,260 pounds
   (E) 22,840 pounds

38. Mary is paid $600 a month on her regular job. During July in addition to her regular job, she makes $400 from a second job. Approximately what percentage of her annual income does Mary make in July?

   (A) 8
   (B) 8⅓
   (C) 12½
   (D) 13
   (E) 14

39. If the area of a triangle with base S is equal to the area of a square with side S, then the altitude of the triangle is

(A) $\frac{1}{2}S$

(B) S

(C) $2S$

(D) $3S$

(E) $4S$

40. A train travels at an average speed of 20 mph through urban areas, 50 mph through suburban areas, and 75 mph through rural areas. If a trip consists of traveling half an hour through urban areas, $3\frac{1}{2}$ hours through suburban areas, and 3 hours through rural areas, what is the train's average speed for the entire trip?

(A) 50 mph

(B) $53\frac{2}{7}$ mph

(C) $54\frac{3}{7}$ mph

(D) $58\frac{4}{7}$ mph

(E) $59\frac{2}{7}$ mph

41. $(x - y)(y + 3)$ is equal to

(A) $x^2 - 3y + 3$

(B) $xy - 3y + y^2$

(C) $xy - y^2 - 3y + 3x$

(D) $xy - 3y + y^2 + 3x$

(E) $y^2 - 3y + 3x - xy$

42. If $x < y$, $y < z$, and $z > w$, which of the following statements is always true?

(A) $x > w$

(B) $x < z$

(C) $y = w$

(D) $y > w$

(E) $x < w$

43. What is the ratio of $\frac{2}{3}$ to $\frac{5}{4}$?

(A) $\frac{1}{4}$

(B) $\frac{10}{12}$

(C) $\frac{8}{15}$

(D) $\frac{20}{6}$

(E) $\frac{2}{7}$

44. Of the numbers 7, 9, 11, 13, 29, 33, how many are prime numbers?

(A) none

(B) 3

(C) 4

(D) 5

(E) all

45. A company issues 100,000 shares of stock. In 1960 each of the shares was worth $9.50. In 1970 each share was worth $13.21. How much more were the 100,000 shares worth in 1970 than in 1960?

(A) $37,000

(B) $37,010

(C) $37,100

(D) $371,000

(E) $371,100

46. A worker's daily salary varies each day. In one week he worked five days. His daily salaries were $40.62, $41.35, $42.00, $42.50, and $39.53. What was his average daily salary for the week?

(A) $40.04

(B) $40.89

(C) $41.04

(D) $41.20

(E) $206.00

47. One dozen eggs and ten pounds of apples are currently the same price. If the price of a dozen eggs rises by 10% and the price of apples goes up by 2%, how much more will it cost to buy a dozen eggs and ten pounds of apples?

(A) 6%   (D) 20%
(B) 10%   (E) 30%
(C) 12%

48. Find x when $x + y = 4$, and $2y = 6$

(A) 1   (D) -3
(B) $\dfrac{3}{2}$ (E) -1
(C) -2

49. If 25 men an unload a truck in 1 hour and 30 minutes, how long should it take 15 men to unload the truck?

(A) 2 hours   (D) 2½ hours
(B) 2¼ hours   (E) 3 hours
(C) 2⅓ hours

50. A car gets 20 miles per gallon of gas when it travels at 50 miles per hour. The car gets 12% fewer miles to the gallon at 60 miles per hour. How far can the car travel at 60 miles per hour on 11 gallons of gas?

(A) 193.6 miles   (D) 204.3 miles
(B) 195.1 miles   (E) 220 miles
(C) 200 miles

51. Feathers cost $500 a ton for the first 12 tons and $(500 − x)$ a ton for any tons over 12. What is x, if it costs $10,000 for 30 tons of feathers?

(A) 270.00   (D) 277.78
(B) 277.00   (E) 280.00
(C) 277.70

52. The angles of a triangle are in the ratio 2:3:4. The largest angle in the triangle is

(A) 30°   (D) 75°
(B) 50°   (E) 80°
(C) 70°

53. Find the area of the trapezoid $ABCD$. $AB = CD = 5$, $BC = 10$, $AD = 16$, and BE is an altitude of the trapezoid.

(A) 50   (D) 80
(B) 52   (E) 160
(C) 64

54. If x is greater than 2, which of the following statements are true?

    I. x is negative.
    II. x is positive.
    III. $2x$ is greater than or equal to x.
    IV. x^2 is greater than or equal to x.
    (A) III only
    (B) IV only
    (C) I and III only
    (D) I, III, and IV only
    (E) II, III, and IV only

55. A worker is digging a ditch. He gets 2 assistants who work ⅔ as fast as he does. If all 3 work on a ditch they should finish it in what fraction of the time that the worker takes working alone?

    (A) ³⁄₇   (D) ⁴⁄₃
    (B) ½   (E) ⁷⁄₃
    (C) ¾

If there is still time remaining, you may review the questions in this section only.
You may not turn to any other section of the test.

Section III   Business Judgment

TIME: 35 minutes

DIRECTIONS: Read the following two passages. After you have completed each of them you will be asked to answer two sets of questions. The first of these, data evaluation, involves determining the importance of specific factors included in the passage. The second, data application, consists of general questions relating to the passage. When answering questions, you may consult the passage.

Passage 1:

The Climax Corporation manufactures a line of major electrical appliances distributed through sixty wholesalers, many of whom are company owned. Retailers carry competitive lines, but wholesalers do not; portable appliances move to market through nonexclusive distributors.

The company presently depends on wholesalers to provide service either directly or through supervision of retailers' service departments. When the warranty is involved, the manufacturer furnishes the parts and the wholesaler the labor. Retailers who perform the service function are given a larger discount than are those who return the goods to the wholesaler to fulfill the guarantee.

Home office officials are currently questioning the adequacy of the service thus rendered either under the terms of the warranty or independently. Typical retailers carry several brands and, in general, do not have competent service personnel. The result is that the blame for the defect is passed back to the manufacturer. This, said the sales manager, is a major consideration. Others believed that reduction of service costs would follow centralizing the entire operation in the hands of a relatively few factory service branches or in carefully trained service personnel employed by a relatively few widely distributed wholesalers. Costs would be thus reduced, and, at the same time, the quality of service rendered would be enhanced, it was claimed.

The product service manager argued that more money should be spent on training retail sales service personnel. Retailers like to render service, he claimed, since it helps to bring traffic into their stores and thus is profitable. A third possibility explored was the promotion of good service by concerns who service but do not sell appliances.

During the conference, the rise of the discount house was discussed. It was thought to be a phenomenon partly based on the realization that good independent service can be secured in most markets and for most appliances. There may be an exception in the case of TV sets, it was admitted, since it is common to find great resentment as to quality of service and delay in meeting calls.

The subsequent discussion raised questions as to the validity of the policy of requiring the retailer to give free service time under the terms of the guarantee. Often owners expect to receive this service free, even though they bought the appliance elsewhere. Some company officials believed that the company should pay dealers for their time costs when they enable the company to make good on its guarantee. One executive pointed out, during a heated discussion on this point, that at least one major automobile company now pays its dealers for making repairs under the warranty.

About this time the sales manager read about a consumer survey that found that the average owner gave little thought to service availability when buying an appliance, except perhaps in the case of TV sets. But when trouble arises, the owner expected the maker to "stand behind his product" and not fall back on any excuse as to costs or time involved, limitations which are found in the normal warranty.

Data Evaluation Questions

DIRECTIONS: Evaluate each of the following factors used in decision-making which relate to the passage you have just read by selecting

(A) for a *Major Objective*—the result desired by the executive;

(B) for a *Major Factor*—a primary consideration, spelled out in the passage, that influences the decision;

(C) for a *Minor Factor*—a less important consideration in the decision;

(D) for a *Major Assumption*—a conclusion reached by the executive not necessarily supported by the factors present;

(E) for an *Unimportant Issue*—a consideration not directly related to the problem.

56. Training retail service personnel

57. The rise of the discount house

58. Typical retailers do not have competent service personnel

59. Adequacy of service demanded by consumers

60. Centralizing the service operation

61. Climax Corporation distributes through 60 wholesalers

Data Application Questions

DIRECTIONS: Answer each of the following questions using information contained in the passage.

62. Under Climax Corporation's current warranty, which agency repairs defective appliances?

    I. Wholesaler
  II. Retailer
 III. Manufacturer

  (A) I only
  (B) III only
  (C) I and II only
  (D) II and III only
  (E) I, II, and III

63. Which of the following reasons are given by executives of Climax Corporation to reconsider their service system?

    I.   Retailers do not have competent service personnel
    II.   Climax's service system is revised annually
    III.   The customers were not utilizing the service

    (A) I only
    (B) III only
    (C) I and II only
    (D) II and III only
    (E) I, II, and III

64. Some executives believed that if service were centralized

    I.   Quality of service would be improved
    II.   Service costs would decrease
    III.   Fewer call-backs would occur

    (A) I only
    (B) III only
    (C) I and II only
    (D) II and III only
    (E) I, II, and III

65. According to the passage, buyers of appliances at the time of purchase regard service availability

    I.   As an important factor
    II.   As a minor factor
    III.   As an unimportant issue

    (A) I only
    (B) III only
    (C) I and II only
    (D) II and III only
    (E) I, II, and III

66. According to the passage, retailers like to service appliances because it

    I.   Brings traffic to the store
    II.   Is profitable
    III.   Keeps them busy

    (A) I only
    (B) III only
    (C) I and II only
    (D) II and III only
    (E) I, II, and III

67. Increased purchases of appliances through discount stores would mean that

    I.   Retailer service availability is not a strong motive in the buying decision

    II.   Discount stores must increase their service ability

    III.   Climax Corporation's sales will decline

    (A) I only
    (B) III only
    (C) I and II only
    (D) I and III only
    (E) I, II, and III

Passage 2:

Sam Hoe's small furniture factory was doing more business than ever before and had a solid backlog of orders that ensured continuous production. Its profits, however, had not kept pace with production. Rising machinery, lumber, and hardware costs, higher wages, and higher operating expenses all combined to eat into profits. Mr. Hoe was concerned about this situation and had thought about raising prices on many of his products. This was not practical at the present, however, because the prices of most items had been increased within the last six months. Among various alternatives, he had considered opening an outlet to retail his own products.

The Hoe Company had been established when Sam's father had started a small woodworking shop in his garage twenty years before. When Sam had come into the business about five years later, the shop had been moved to a warehouse on the outskirts of town. At that time, much of the space was used for storage of materials and finished goods. Through the next ten years more and more of the storage area had been taken over for equipment and work space; therefore an additional storage building had been constructed next to the original building. The payroll had grown to twenty craftsmen, who were supervised by a production manager. Mr. Hoe and one bookkeeper did the purchasing, accounting and sales work.

The shop, located in a city of 25,000 people, had begun on a special order custom basis, selling mainly to local residents. Through the years a standard line of tables and chairs had been developed, which now accounted for 78 percent of sales. Most of the standard line furniture was sold through four wholesalers to retail furniture stores in a five state area. Two outlets in the city, a department store and a large furniture showroom, bought directly from the factory. Although most orders for custom made items came from within the state, a few came from states from all areas of the country.

In examining his sales and profit records for the past two years, Mr. Hoe found that while sales had increased steadily, profits showed only a very slight increase over the preceding year. Further study showed that while the sale of custom made merchandise netted a consistently good profit, standard items, sold on a slimmer margin, lost money in some cases. Rising material costs and more rigid specifications and demands from large retail purchasers had both contributed to the problem. Unfortunately, the number of orders for custom work had to be limited, for top craftsmen were in short supply and much of this work demanded highly skilled cabinetmakers.

Discussing the situation with his production manager, Mr. Hoe commented, "Sam, what would you think about opening a retail showroom here? The way I see it, our standard items are popular and almost sell themselves. There's plenty of room since we added the new building, and fixing up a nice-looking showroom shouldn't be too difficult or expensive. If we cut out the retailer's margin and split it between the customer and ourselves, we can cut prices—or hold them steady, anyway—and still make a decent profit. What do you say?"

Data Evaluation Questions

DIRECTIONS: Evaluate each of the following factors used in decision-making which relate to the passage you have just read by selecting

(A) for a *Major Objective*—the result desired by the executive;

(B) for a *Major Factor*—a primary consideration, spelled out in the passage, that influences the decision;

(C) for a *Minor Factor*—a less important consideration in the decision;

(D) for a *Major Assumption*—a conclusion reached by the executive not necessarily supported by the factors present;

(E) for an *Unimportant Issue*—a consideration not directly related to the problem.

68. Higher operating expenses

69. Increased demand for furniture

70. Storage space

71. Employs 20 craftsmen

72. A retail showroom

73. Availability of cabinetmakers

Data Application Questions

DIRECTIONS: Answer each of the following questions using information contained in the passage.

74. Although production at Sam Hoe's factory was increasing steadily

    I. Employee morale was low
    II. Prices were fluctuating
    III. Profits increased only slightly

(A) I only
(B) III only
(C) I and II only
(D) II and III only
(E) I, II, and III

75. Sam Hoe considered a price increase for his goods, but decided against it because

    I.   Competition was too intense
   II.   His father was against it
 III.   He had had a general price increase within the past six months

   (A) I only
   (B) III only
   (C) I and II only
   (D) II and III only
   (E) I, II, and III

76. Most of Sam Hoe's furniture sales were generated by

    I.   Standard line items
   II.   American colonial lines
 III.   Custom pieces

   (A) I only
   (B) III only
   (C) I and II only
   (D) II and III only
   (E) I, II, and III

77. Sam Hoe wanted to increase his output of custom items and

    I.   Was constrained from doing so because of a labor shortage
   II.   Scheduled an expansion of his factory space
 III.   Received encouragement from his production manager

   (A) I only
   (B) III only
   (C) I and II only
   (D) II and III only
   (E) I, II, and III

78. Mr. Hoe's furniture was sold mainly to

    I.   Areas throughout the United States
   II.   Local residents
 III.   A five state area

   (A) I only
   (B) III only
   (C) I and II only
   (D) II and III only
   (E) I, II, and III

79. Mr. Hoe wanted to open a retail showroom to

   I. Increase his profitability
   II. Sell excess stock
   III. Cut down on advertising expenses

   (A) I only
   (B) III only
   (C) I and II only
   (D) II and III only
   (E) I, II, and III

80. Mr. Hoe's profits eroded because

   I. Large retailers demanded higher quality control
   II. Raw materials increased in price
   III. Wholesale margins had increased

   (A) I only
   (B) III only
   (C) I and II only
   (D) II and III only
   (E) I, II, and III

If there is still time remaining, you may review the questions in this section only.
You may not turn to any other section of the test.

Section IV   Data Sufficiency

TIME: 15 minutes

DIRECTIONS: Each of the following problems has a question and two statements which are labeled (1) and (2). Use the data given in (1) and (2) together with other available information (such as the number of hours in a day, the definition of *clockwise*, mathematical facts, etc.) to decide whether the statements are *sufficient* to answer the question. Then fill in space

(A) if you can get the answer from (1) alone but not from (2) alone;

(B) if you can get the answer from (2) alone but not from (1) alone;

(C) if you can get the answer from (1) and (2) together, although neither statement by itself suffices;

(D) if statement (1) alone suffices *and* statement (2) alone suffices;

(E) if you cannot get the answer from statements (1) and (2) together, but need even more data.

All numbers used in this section are real numbers. A figure given for a problem is intended to provide information consistent with that in the question, but not necessarily with the additional information contained in the statements.

81. *ABC* is a triangle inscribed in circle *AOCB*. Is *AC* a diameter of the circle *AOCB*?

   (1) Angle *x* is a right angle.
   (2) The length of *AB* is ¾ the length of *BC*.

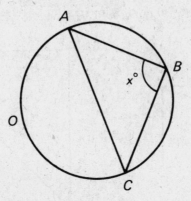

82. A cylindrical tank has a radius of 10 feet and its height is 20 feet. How many gallons of a liquid can be stored in the tank?

   (1) A gallon of the liquid occupies about .13 cubic feet of space.
   (2) The diameter of the tank is 20 feet.

83. How many books are on the bookshelf?

   (1) The average weight of each book is 1.2 pounds.
   (2) The books and the bookshelf together weigh 34 pounds.

84. Is the triangle *ABC* congruent to the triangle *DEF*? Angle *x* is equal to angle *y*.

   (1) *AB* is equal to *DE*.
   (2) *BC* is equal to *EF*.

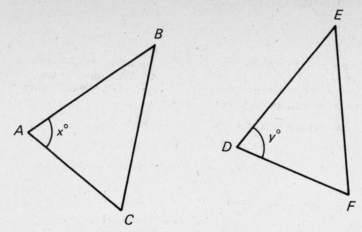

85. A plane flies over New York City. What is its speed in miles per hour?

(1) The plane is flying in a circle.
(2) The plane is flying at the speed of $\frac{1}{9}$ mile per second.

86. Mr. Carpenter wants to build a room in the shape of a rectangle. The area of the floor will be 32 square feet. What is the length of the floor?

(1) The length of the floor will be twice the width of the floor.
(2) The width of the floor will be 4 feet less than the length of the floor.

87. Do the rectangle *ABCD* and the square *EFGH* have the same area?

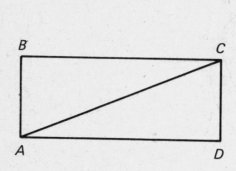
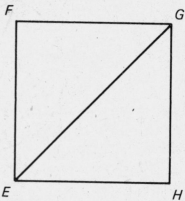

(1) $AC = EG$, $AB = \frac{1}{2}\, EH$
(2) The area of triangle *ABC* is not equal to the area of triangle *EFG*.

88. How much does Susan weigh?

(1) Susan and Joan together weigh 250 pounds.
(2) Joan weighs twice as much as Susan.

89. Two different holes, hole *A* and hole *B*, are put in the bottom of a full water tank. If the water drains out through the holes, how long before the tank is empty?

(1) If only hole *A* is put in the bottom, the tank will be empty in 24 minutes.
(2) If only hole *B* is put in the bottom, the tank will be empty in 42 minutes.

90. Find $x + y$

    (1) $x - \ y = \ 6$
    (2) $2x - 2y = 12$

91. C is a circle with center D and radius 2. E is a circle with center F and radius R. Are there any points which are on both E and C?

    (1) The distance from D to F is $1 + R$.
    (2) $R = 3$.

92. Mr. Parker made \$20,000 in 1967. What is Mr. Parker's average yearly income for the three years 1967 to 1969?

    (1) He made 10% more in each year than he did in the previous year.
    (2) His total combined income for 1968 and 1969 was \$46,200.

93. Is angle x a right angle?

    (1) $y = z$
    (2) $(AC)^2 + (CB)^2 = (AB)^2$

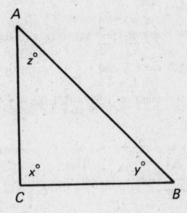

94. John and Paul are standing together on a sunny day. John's shadow is 10 feet long. Paul's shadow is 9 feet long. How tall is Paul?

    (1) John is 6 feet tall.
    (2) John is standing 2 feet away from Paul.

95. Is x greater than y?

    (1) x^2 is greater than y^2
    (2) $x + 3$ is greater than $y + 2$

If there is still time remaining, you may review the questions in this section only.
You may not turn to any other section of the test.

Section V Writing Ability

TIME: 20 minutes

DIRECTIONS: Each of the sentences in this section is either correct or contains one error in grammar, usage, diction (choice of words), idiom or punctuation. If there is an error it will be found in one of the underlined parts of the sentence, labeled (A), (B), (C), or (D). If you identify an error mark the appropriate letter on your answer sheet. If there is no error in the sentence mark E—no error.

Note: Assume that all parts of the sentence that are not underlined are correct and cannot be changed.

96. Everyone in the family looks well in this family portrait   except Uncle Robert
                           (A) (B)   (C)
    and me. No error
    (D)   (E)

97. Neither Bob nor I am satisfied with the terms of the agreement we made. No error
                   (A) (B)   (C)   (D)   (E)

98. Although Eunice and I were seriously worried about the matter ,   the amount of
                        (A)   (B)   (C)   (D)
    hours we spent on it was ridiculously small. No error
                                                  (E)

99. They met Simpson two or three months before they decided to open their im-
         (A)   (B)   (C)
    port-export business last summer. No error
    (D)   (E)

100. Realizing how much had been expected of me , my confidence rocketed until
                        (A)   (B)   (C)
     I was able to face my adversaries boldly. No error
                                        (D)   (E)

101. May I have a loan of your pump for a while because my front tire is flat. No error
              (A)   (B)   (C)   (D)   (E)

102. I read in the newspaper that the governor together with his wife and three daughters
         (A)   (B)
     are returning from New York by plane. No error
     (C)   (D)   (E)

103. The study concerned itself mainly with the affects of anxiety on decision making in
                         (A)   (B)   (C)
     high-risk situations. No error
     (D)   (E)

104. The queue of angry investors had by now grown until it ran the length of the block;
           _____(A)_____   _____(B)_____
Wentworth , acting as spokesman , rapped violently on the plate glass doors
___(C)___   (D)
of the bank. No error
           (E)

105. I am sure that it would be all right if no one but him was allowed to tender their
                      ____(A)____   __(B)_ (C)   (D)
resignation. No error
            (E)

106. Neither of my parents, who were born in Eastern Europe, understand the full im-
         _(A)_   __(B)__   _(C)_
plications of a democratic electoral system. No error
                          ____(D)____   (E)

107. If you would have come earlier, as I had advised, you would never have been
              ___(A)___   ___(B)___   __(C)__
misled by that crude trick. No error
_(D)_   (E)

108. Thomas stated , moreover, that Benson had not made an effort, which annoyed
                       _(A)_   _____(B)_____   __(C)__
Benson even more. No error
      __(D)__   (E)

109. This new model travels faster then last year's model which it supercedes. No error
         _(A)_   _(B)_ __(C)__   ___(D)___   (E)

110. Send it back to whomever it really belongs ; I no longer care whose it is.
                       ___(A)___   (B)   _(C)_   __(D)__
No error
(E)

111. When the fog descended on us, visibility became so bad that I could not hardly see
                        __(A)__   __(B)__   _(C)_
the man who was walking one yard in front of me. No error
         ____(D)____   (E)

112. The set of texts required for this assignment is to be found in the library so that
                                                 __(A)__
everyone of the students is able to refer to it at all times. No error
_(B)_   (C)   (D)   (E)

113. The situation would have been far different than it is today, had Carlo listened to
                  ____(A)____   ____(B)____   __(C)__
the good advice given him by his tutor. No error
              __(D)__   (E)

114. The data has been updated to include the latest readings. No error
         __(A)_ (B) __(C)__   _(D)_   (E)

115. We <u>strongly</u> recommend that Parker <u>is told</u> about his physical condition as soon
   (A)   (B)
as possible <u>in order</u> to <u>allow</u> him to make the necessary arrangements. <u>No error</u>
    (C)   (D)   (E)

116. Roberta is the one <u>who</u> seems convinced that we <u>are</u> trying to harm her, <u>irregard-</u>
        (A)   (B)   (C)
less <u>of how much</u> we have done for her benefit. <u>No error</u>
   (D)   (E)

117. <u>Providing</u> you <u>have studied</u> hard, you <u>will</u> be able to do this assignment as well as
  (A)   (B)   (C)
we without any help from them. <u>No error</u>
(D)   (E)

118. Three people came into the study— his former wife , his best friend , and
             (A)   (B)   (C)
his <u>mother-in-law</u>. <u>No error</u>
  (D)   (E)

119. The <u>advise</u> we had <u>gotten</u>, had come <u>just</u> at the right time in our dealings <u>in this</u>
   (A)   (B)   (C)   (D)
most unfortunate matter. <u>No error</u>
        (E)

120. Margaret <u>hung</u> <u>up</u> all the clothes that <u>had</u> been <u>laying</u> around the room. <u>No error</u>
    (A) (B)   (C)   (D)   (E)

121. His conclusions are so different <u>from</u> the <u>ones</u> that you and I <u>am</u> prepared to ac-
           (A)   (B)   (C)
cept , even under the present circumstances. <u>No error</u>
 (D)   (E)

122. George , the foreman of the production line, told Mr. Crosby that <u>he</u> had
   (A)   (B)
<u>inadvertently</u> shipped out a defective batch. <u>No error</u>
  (C)   (D)   (E)

123. The <u>assistant-in-chief</u> <u>immediately</u> noticed the <u>tapes'</u> color <u>;</u> and called for his
   (A)   (B)   (C)   (D)
superior. <u>No error</u>
   (E)

124. Let us now take account of <u>these data</u> <u>that</u> we have been given and use <u>them</u> as
         (A)   (B)   (C)
<u>the bases</u> for our further research. <u>No error</u>
 (D)   (E)

125. They <u>had sent</u> all their friends, <u>except</u> for Laura and I, a letter of greeting. <u>No error</u>
   (A)   (B)   (C) (D)   (E)

126. Joan felt badly about losing the earrings which her husband had sent her for their
     ‾‾‾‾‾(A)‾‾‾‾‾   ‾‾(B)‾ ‾(C)‾   ‾(D)‾

     anniversary. No error
                  ‾‾(E)‾

127. The three advantages of his plan are : its simplicity, the fact that it can be ap-
                                          ‾(A)‾   ‾(B)‾

     plied immediately , and its probable popularity among the local population. No
                       ‾(C)‾   ‾‾(D)‾

     error
     ‾(E)‾

128. After visiting the doctor, she decided to follow his instructions, and made plans to
                                             ‾‾‾(A)‾‾‾

     move without delay to Salt Springs where she could be sure of a healthy climate.
     ‾‾‾‾‾(B)‾‾‾‾‾   ‾(C)‾   ‾‾(D)‾

     No error
     ‾(E)‾

129. There was scarcely no time given to think about the problem before the bell for the
              ‾(A)‾   ‾(B)‾ ‾(C)‾   ‾‾(D)‾

     end of class. No error
                   ‾‾(E)‾

130. You will have to intervene in this fight between Sandra and me. No error
         ‾(A)‾   ‾(B)‾   ‾‾(C)‾‾   ‾(D)‾ ‾(E)‾

If there is still time remaining, you may review the questions in this section only.
You may not turn to any other section of the test.

Section VI Business Judgment

TIME: 35 minutes

DIRECTIONS: Read the following two passages. After you have completed each of them you will be asked to answer two sets of questions. The first of these, data evaluation, involves determining the importance of specific factors included in the passage. The second, data application, consists of general questions relating to the passage. When answering questions, you may consult the passage.

Passage 1:

For some months retail and consumer audits had indicated a lower market share for Pandora Specialty Products in the U.K. than Charles Smith, the marketing director in Britain, was willing to believe.

Pandora's ex-factory sales were some 20% over the retail sales figures indicated by research. Meanwhile the international company's young U.S. subsidiary, Pandora Inc., which had some 12 months earlier opened a plant in upper New York State, was having a rough time. Sales had declined sharply, a month ago, and showed no sign of recovery.

Jack Haldane, managing director of the U.K. company and a director of the international board, did not connect the two circumstances. The U.K. was doing well, so clearly the market research initiated by Smith was wrong.

Smith was concerned by the U.K. situation, although he would not admit it to Haldane. There had to be a reason for the difference between factory output in the U.K. and what was sold after passing through the independent wholesalers.

Smith now ran parallel samples and conducted further research in the U.K. All the figures tended to bear out the audit data.

A close examination of individual accounts revealed that much of the discrepancy could be traced to several large and medium-sized wholesalers. Visits to these companies revealed nothing untoward, however; their levels of stock had not appreciably increased.

A month or two later, Haldane received a confidential memo from the president of the U.S. company. It stated that, quite by accident, some U.K. manufactured Pandora products had been found in a U.S. wholesaler. The man had been reticent about their source.

Haldane immediately called Smith in to his office. Without comment he passed across the memo.

Smith grimaced. "I had my suspicions," he said, handing the memo back. "After all, the sales volume unaccounted for in the U.K. almost exactly matches the sales lost in the U.S."

"So what has been going on?" Haldane demanded.

"I have examined the price structure in the U.S. in detail," Smith replied, "and I have found that even allowing for freight and duty it would be possible for an efficient single distributor to undercut our U.S. company's distributors by some 15% or even 20%."

Haldane frowned. "So the evidence points strongly to heavy unofficial exports to the ,," he said.

Smith nodded.

"Which no doubt has been made possible," Haldane continued, "by the fact that the . company's pricing strategy placed their leading brand at the top end of the market."

"As you will recall," Smith said drily, "I voiced my objections to that policy at the time. thought the product was overpriced. But in the end the accountants and the agency con- ced me that, with the heavy cost of distribution and advertising, it was the only hope a quick return on the plant."

"Well, it seems to have backfired," Haldane observed.

He got up from behind his desk and started pacing his office. "As managing director of U.K. company I'm more than happy to see our plant here running to capacity," he d. "But as a member of the international board I'm also acutely aware of the growing blems of Pandora Inc. So what do we do? Any ideas?"

"Well, one thing is certain," Smith replied, "I don't see how we can stop our indepen- nt wholesalers exporting to the U.S. if they want to. And you can't really blame any olesaler taking advantage of the exchange rates."

"That may be true but it is not much help to our U.S. company," Haldane said.

Smith felt like saying: "It's all very well saying that, but you ought to have sorted out whole pricing strategy, at international board level, long ago."

Instead, he gave Haldane another unpalatable truth. "If the U.S. company alters its cing strategy now," he said, "it's going to make nonsense of a very expensive advertis- , and promotion campaign. But if they don't do anything, can *we* do anything to hten things up at this end?"

Data Evaluation Questions

DIRECTIONS: Evaluate each of the following factors used in decision-making which relate to the passage you have just read by selecting

(A) for a *Major Objective*—the result desired by the executive;
(B) for a *Major Factor*—a primary consideration, spelled out in the passage, that influ- ences the decision;
(C) for a *Minor Factor*—a less important consideration in the decision;
(D) for a *Major Assumption*—a conclusion reached by the executive not necessarily sup- ported by the factors present;
(E) for an *Unimportant Issue*—a consideration not directly related to the problem.

31. Sales of Pandora's U.S. subsidiary declined

32. Pricing strategy of the U.S. subsidiary

33. The U.S. plant was located in New York State

34. The U.S. product was priced well above that produced in the U.K.

35. The U.K. plant was producing near capacity

DIRECTIONS: Answer each of the following questions using information contained in the passage.

136. According to the passage, in order to stop exports of Pandora products from the U.K. to the U.S., management can

    I.   Close the U.S. plant
    II.   Apply sanctions to U.K. wholesalers
    III.   Alter the pricing strategy of the U.S. product

    (A) I only
    (B) III only
    (C) I and II only
    (D) II and III only
    (E) I, II, and III

137. The reason why U.K. wholesalers could export and still compete with a U.S.-made product was because of

    I.   The higher quality of the U.K.-made product
    II.   Low U.S. tariffs on U.K. imports
    III.   A relatively high price structure for the U.S.-made product

    (A) I only
    (B) III only
    (C) I and II only
    (D) II and III only
    (E) I, II, and III

138. According to the passage, Smith blamed the U.S. subsidiary's troubles partly on bad advice from the company's

    I.   Advertising agency
    II.   Managing director
    III.   Board of directors

    (A) I only
    (B) III only
    (C) I and II only
    (D) II and III only
    (E) I, II, and III

139. Smith had received evidence to explain the U.S. subsidiary's problem from

    I.   Audits of U.K. factory shipments
    II.   The U.S. subsidiary's president
    III.   A confidential letter from a U.K. wholesaler

    (A) I only
    (B) III only
    (C) I and II only
    (D) II and III only
    (E) I, II, and III

140. Smith was reluctant to alter the U.S. subsidiary's pricing strategy because

    I.   U.S. management would claim "interference" in its affairs

    II. It was too late to do anything

    III. The advertising campaign in the U.S. would be wasted

    (A) I only

    (B) III only

    (C) I and II only

    (D) II and III only

    (E) I, II, and III

Passage 2:

Luigi Cappa was beginning to wonder what had made him give up a smoothly running job in New York to tackle what had turned out to be a baffling problem in southern Italy.

He was a U.S. citizen, and if he had stayed with his company he might have had a seat on the board within two years.

Then an uncle in Turin, in northern Italy, had written to Cappa, imploring him to come and run his printing plant near Palermo in Sicily, which produced transfer designs and other specialized printing, some of it for export.

Cappa was 28 years old, unmarried and ambitious. The offer had appealed to him in several ways.

First, there was the chance to be his own boss immediately. Second, there was the challenge, as Cappa saw it, of bringing U.S. know-how to the Italian family firm. Third, there was the satisfaction of returning as a man of some authority to the country where his own father had been born.

He was a believer in scientific management. He also believed that people everywhere are basically alike and will respond in about the same way to the carrot of cash rewards and the stick of firm leadership.

After only a few months in Palermo, he knew differently. Cappa's uncle had set up the plant five years previously with the active encouragement of the Italian government. But the 300-strong labor force still had no loyalty to the company from the north. The workers still dreamed of orange groves rather than production targets.

Indeed, on one occasion Cappa had found a worker blissfully cleaning equipment from one of the printing machines in an orange grove near the plant. When he had ordered him back into the plant the man had looked astonished and replied: "Why should I work inside when I can do my job here?"

Productivity was very low. When Cappa had visited a local barber, who knew that he worked in the printing plant but did not know he was the boss, the man had said: "Sir, can you get me a job with the printing company so that I no longer have to work?"

As Cappa walked round the plant he saw plenty of modern machines. He also saw a workforce that yearned to be out in the sun, and wondered how he could get his employees to change their attitudes.

First, he tried using his personal appeal as an American-Italian. That did not work. He would have been more successful, he ruefully admitted to himself, had he been born in Palermo.

He instituted production committees, which were supposed to generate their own ideas of improving productivity. He worked at them very hard but they too were a dismal failure.

When managers sat on the committees the workers seemed struck dumb, failing to produce constructive ideas. Then, when Cappa gave the committee more autonomy to run their own affairs, their members used the time allocated for their meetings to leave the factory and take a siesta outside.

Cappa decided that a bonus system relating pay directly to output was the only solution. At first the union opposed this, saying it was the kind of piecework they had been fighting against. Then, to Cappa's surprise, they gave in. He thought he had won a victory.

If so, it was a hollow one. The workers began demanding the bonus as a right, whether or not they had worked extra hours or produced more. When Cappa refused to pay, the workers went on strike.

Cappa felt that he was dealing with forces beyond his control, with people who, although Italian, he could not fully understand.

"They just don't seem to want to participate," he wrote to a friend in New York. "If you give them the chance to run their own affairs, they take advantage of it. If you offer them a carrot, they eat half your arm as well. And if you wave a stick, they strike."

He could advise his uncle to concentrate production in Turin and get rid of the Palermo plant. But then he would have to return to the U.S. without a job and with a feeling of defeat.

Alternatively, Cappa could find a way of motivating his workers. But *how*, he asked himself for the thousandth time.

Data Evaluation Questions

DIRECTIONS: Evaluate each of the following factors used in decision-making which relate to the passage you have just read by

(A)   for a *Major Objective*—the result desired by the executive;
(B)   for a *Major Factor*—a primary consideration, spelled out in the passage, that influences the decision;
(C)   for a *Minor Factor*—a less important consideration in the decision;
(D)   for a *Major Assumption*—a conclusion reached by the executive not necessarily supported by the factors present;
(E)   for an *Unimportant Issue*—a consideration not directly related to the problem.

141.   Company headquarters were in northern Italy

142.   People everywhere are basically alike

143.   How to motivate the Sicilian worker

144.   Low worker productivity

145.   Higher pay would improve output

Data Application Questions

DIRECTIONS: Answer each of the following questions using information contained in the passage.

146. According to the passage, low productivity was the result of

    I.   Improper worker training
   II.   Low pay
  III.   Lack of worker commitment to the firm

   (A) I only
   (B) III only
   (C) I and II only
   (D) II and III only
   (E) I, II, and III

147. A major conclusion of the passage is that

    I.   Sicilian workers cannot be motivated by methods appropriate elsewhere
   II.   Expatriate managers are unsuitable in Italy
  III.   Scientific management is unworkable in Italy

   (A) I only
   (B) III only
   (C) I and II only
   (D) II and III only
   (E) I, II, and III

148. Cappa used which of the following means to motivate workers?

    I.   Participative management
   II.   Payment related to productivity
  III.   His ethnic relation to the workers

   (A) I only
   (B) III only
   (C) I and II only
   (D) II and III only
   (E) I, II, and III

149. Cappa was induced to take the job at his uncle's plant because of

    I.   Monetary considerations
   II.   His belief in scientific management
  III.   Self-esteem

   (A) I only
   (B) III only
   (C) I and II only
   (D) II and III only
   (E) I, II, and III

150. It can be concluded from the passage that Sicilian workers are

    I.   Individualists
    II. Self-motivated
    III. Responsive to firm leadership

    (A) I only
    (B) III only
    (C) I and II only
    (D) II and III only
    (E) I, II, and III

If there is still time remaining, you may review the questions in this section only.
You may not turn to any other section of the test.

Section VII Case Evaluation

TIME: 30 minutes

DIRECTIONS: In this section you will be presented with a short case including a principle of law or a set of rules, relating to the case. This is followed by a short conclusion concerning the nature of the case. The conclusion is followed by ten statements that may affect the nature of the case. You are to determine what effect each statement has on the validity of the conclusion and choose:

(A) if the statement clearly proves the conclusion.
(B) if the statement strengthens or reinforces the conclusion but does not clearly prove it.
(C) if the statement clearly disproves the conclusion.
(D) if the statement weakens the conclusion but does not clearly disprove it.
(E) if the statement has no relevance to the conclusion.

NOTE: Each statement will add information that may change the nature of the case considerably. You are to treat each statement individually and not base your decision on information presented in any other statement. For the purposes of this test you are to assume that the legal principles mentioned are correct.

Case 1

Murchison is the owner of an abandoned bakery which has been condemned for demolition as an "unsafe edifice." The property on which the bakery stands is fenced off by an 8-foot fence upon which there are prominent signs with the words "No Trespassing—Private Property." Vandals constantly break the fence and school children have been using the property as a short cut for years.

One night John Sheparton, returning home from a party, remembers the short cut of his school days and decides to use it. While crossing the property, Sheparton sees a rat scampering up the wall of the old bakery and instinctively throws a stone at it. His stone smashes a window of the bakery and hits an old electrical fuse box, causing a fire which spreads rapidly through the old building.

Murchison has been using the old building as a temporary warehouse for a large shipment of fireworks. The fire ignites the whole lot in a massive series of explosions.

Sheparton is found still on the property, dazed but unhurt, by Murchison who lives nearby.

Murchison sues Sheparton for the full value of the goods destroyed by the fire.

Under the law, any trespasser who causes through his own negligence or lack of care, any damage to property or goods is liable for the damage if the said trespasser was aware that he was on private property and if reasonable actions had been taken by the owner to prevent trespassing and to adequately protect his goods.

Conclusion: Sheparton is liable for damage.

Statements

151. Sheparton had entered the property through a relatively large break in the fence near which there were no "No Trespassing" signs.

152. Murchison made a point of repairing the fence as soon as each breach was discovered.

153. The fireworks were stored in the same room as inflammable materials.

154. After climbing the fence in order to enter the property, Sheparton had thrown stones to see how many windows he could break.

155. Sheparton was injured seriously by the explosion.

156. As a precaution against fire, Murchison had ordered the electricity to the bakery cut more than one month prior to the fire.

157. Murchison caught Sheparton running away outside of the property.

158. Under a separate law, all flammable materials under storage may only be stored in suitably registered premises in order to qualify for insurance or damages.

159. Murchison employed a night watchman who was on duty on the night of the fire and who had told Sheparton to leave the grounds immediately.

160. Sheparton, who entered the property through an open side gate, was illiterate.

Case 2

Since their independence in 1966 the two bordering states of Pimpang and Dimpang have maintained a strained peace. Whereas Pimpang has a duly elected democratic government, Dimpang is ruled ruthlessly by Colonel Bong who has named himself Life President and is called "Bongo"—Big Uncle, by the terrified population. In the last two years Colonel Bong has stepped up his military training program and has been making loud statements about "the unity of the Pang Peninsula," the territory that is now divided by his border with Pimpang.

In one of the border villages of Pimpang, the men discover that half their herd of cattle has disappeared. Arming themselves with sticks, they set out following the hoofprints which lead them across the border right into the middle of a military maneuver of the Dimpang 12th Regiment. The 12th Regiment opens fire on them, killing all but one of the villagers. The survivor gets back across the border and reports the incident.

As this is the tenth incident within a very short time, the prime minister of Pimpang, apprehensive of Dimpang's motives, orders military action. A small unit of Pimpang commandos crosses into Dimpang but Colonel Bong's mercenary trained forces are waiting and launch a full-scale invasion against the unprepared Pimpang. They take over the entire Pang Peninsula—a full third of Pimpang's territory. Claiming provocation, Colonel Bong parades the captured Pimpang commando officer in front of the television cameras and the commando confesses.

According to international law, a state that first crosses into the territory of another state by armed military force with intention to harm or gain control of the population or property of the latter state is deemed "the aggressor" unless responding to provocation. An act of provocation is defined as any military action taken against a state or any direct threat of military action or any direct interference with a state's lanes of international transport. A state retaliating to provocation is not deemed an aggressor.

Conclusion: Dimpang is not the aggressor in this case.

Statements

161. Dimpang had been carrying out extensive military maneuvers in the border region prior to the invasion.

162. The villagers were armed with rifles and not sticks.

163. The cattle had been stolen by a raiding party of the Dimpang army acting under orders.

164. Colonel Bong had planned to invade Pimpang with or without provocation and had carried out devious activities to justify his invasion.

165. The Pimpang commandos were intercepted by the Dimpang forces before the former had managed to cross into Dimpang territory.

166. Dimpang had no intentions of invading Pimpang prior to the incident.

167. The Pimpang force did in fact enter Dimpang but was two fully armored divisions and not a small commando unit.

168. It is the prime minister of Pimpang and not Colonel Bong, who has been making public pronouncements about "the unity of the Pang Peninsula."

169. The facts presented in the text are all true and no other facts apply.

170. The unit that crossed into Dimpang territory was actually a guerrilla force from a third country and not a Pimpang military unit.

Case 3

Moss has been admiring Sterling's imported Italian sports car for quite a while and has expressed his desire to buy it on a number of occasions. Imagine his surprise when one day Sterling tells him that he is prepared to sell him the car because he needs the money urgently for a business venture. Sterling also says that the market value of the car is $6,000 but as they are neighbors he is prepared to take only $5,000 cash from Moss.

Moss asks about the car's condition and is told by Sterling that it is "in perfect shape" and that he has had no major mechanical problems whatsoever. Moss says he is happy to hear that because he would only be prepared to buy the car if it were mechanically sound, knowing the expense of imported parts.

They go for a spin in the car but only Sterling does the driving, as he claims that his insurance does not cover any other driver.

Satisfied by the performance, Moss agrees to buy the car and they return to Sterling's apartment, where the deal is completed.

The happy new owner, Moss, takes the car out onto the open road to put it through its paces. When he pushes the gear into overdrive there is a deafening crashing noise as the gear box tears away, causing damage to the engine and the drive shaft. The cost of repair would come to over $3,000.

Moss, claiming that he was "taken for a ride," demands the cancellation of the sale and his money back.

Under the law a sale agreement may be considered invalid if the property or goods under mention, prior to the act of sale, do not meet the specification or description expressed by the seller to the best of his knowledge, or if the seller knowingly concealed any fault or defect of the said goods, or made any misstatement of facts relating to the sale which would tend to deceive or mislead the buyer.

Conclusion: The sale agreement between Sterling and Moss is valid.

Statements

171. Sterling had only a few minor mechanical problems with the car and these had been repaired prior to the sale.

172. Sterling knew that that particular model was notorious for its gear problems.

173. Sterling had insurance coverage for any driver driving his car.

174. Moss and Sterling live in different parts of town.

175. Sterling knew that the gear was on the verge of breakdown before he offered his car for sale.

176. Sterling actually needs money to pay his gambling debts and not as he had told Moss.

177. Sterling, who had no real mechanical skill or knowledge, had taken the car into the dealer a day before and had had it checked thoroughly.

178. Sterling had heard a clicking noise coming from the gear but had been told by his garage mechanic that it was not a serious matter.

179. Up to the moment of sale, Sterling had no indication whatsoever that there was anything wrong with his car.

180. Moss had no problems at all with the gear after the sale.

Case 4

Berkley Burke buys an old, run-down house which he wants to renovate and convert into his family home. He must vacate his present rented apartment by September 30 of that year. Burke contracts Harry Jospe, a local builder, to carry out the renovation according to plans drawn by Jospe. The contract, which they both sign, stipulates the extent, quality, and price as well as the commencement date of the work. Jospe informs Burke that as the owner he has to apply for a building permit.

The work is to begin on July 1, when Jospe comes back from vacation. Burke is a bit worried about the timing but Jospe assures him that he will do his best to finish before the lease on Burke's apartment runs out.

One month before the work is due to start, Burke comes to Jospe and tells him that he wishes to cancel the contract due to certain circumstances. Jospe, who has already committed himself to the job by canceling other work, is very angry and tells Burke that the contract is binding and refuses to release him. Moreover, Jospe threatens to sue Burke if he prevents him from fulfilling the contract.

In law, the *relief from performance* principle states that a party may be relieved from a required performance of a contractual obligation when the performance becomes impossible. Impossibility of performance may occur when, in a contract to render personal services, the actor dies, or is shown to be incompetent in carrying out the contracted services, or when the subject of the agreement is destroyed, or when the law changes rendering performance illegal.

All the above hold unless it can be shown that the party requesting relief from performance has knowingly contrived the circumstances in order to rescind the contractual agreement or had knowledge in advance of signing such agreement, that performance would be impossible, in which case that party is liable for damages equivalent to the value of the contractual agreement.

Conclusion: If Jospe sues Burke, Burke, claiming the relief from performance principle, will win the case.

Statements

181. Burke wishes to cancel the contract because he claims that in their contract Jospe has overcharged him considerably.

182. Jospe lied when he said that he was coming back from vacation on July 1.

183. The old house on Burke's plot was burned to the ground in a freak fire.

184. Due to financial difficulties Burke will be forced to sell the property on which the old house stands—his only real asset.

185. Up until the day Burke came to cancel the contract, he had not applied for a building permit, which normally takes 3 months to process. (Building without a permit is illegal.)

186. New municipal by-laws passed in June have rezoned the area to industrial, and no residential building will be allowed after September 1.

187. Burke's wife has sued for divorce and Burke, who is not contesting the divorce, will not need the house.

188. Jospe, who is a local man, knew in advance of signing the contract that the zoning laws for the area might be changed.

189. Burke, deciding that renovating an old house was going to be more expensive than building a new one, had the old house demolished.

190. Burke has discovered that Jospe does not hold a builder's license and has no experience in renovations.

If there is still time remaining, you may review the questions in this section only.
You may not turn to any other section of the test.

Answers

Section I   Reading Comprehension

1. **(E)**	8. **(C)**	15. **(B)**	22. **(B)**
2. **(C)**	9. **(C)**	16. **(C)**	23. **(A)**
3. **(B)**	10. **(A)**	17. **(C)**	24. **(E)**
4. **(B)**	11. **(D)**	18. **(B)**	25. **(A)**
5. **(A)**	12. **(B)**	19. **(C)**	
6. **(C)**	13. **(E)**	20. **(E)**	
7. **(C)**	14. **(B)**	21. **(C)**	

Section II   Mathematics

(Numbers in parentheses indicate the section in the Mathematics Review where material concerning the question is discussed.)

26. **(D)** (II–6)	36. **(E)** (II–3)	46. **(D)** (I–7)
27. **(E)** (III–1, II–2)	37. **(D)** (II–3)	47. **(A)** (I–4)
28. **(C)** (I–4)	38. **(D)** (I–4)	48. **(A)** (II–2)
29. **(E)** (I–1)	39. **(C)** (III–7)	49. **(D)** (II–3)
30. **(C)** (II–4)	40. **(D)** (I–7)	50. **(A)** (I–4, II–3)
31. **(E)** (III–7,I–4)	41. **(C)** (II–1)	51. **(D)** (II–3)
32. **(D)** (II–3)	42. **(B)** (II–7)	52. **(E)** (II–5, III–4)
33. **(A)** (I–4)	43. **(C)** (I–2, II–5)	53. **(B)** (III–7)
34. **(C)** (II–3,II–5)	44. **(C)** (I–1)	54. **(E)** (II–7)
35. **(D)** (II–3)	45. **(D)** (II–3)	55. **(A)** (II–3)

Section III   Business Judgment

56. **(B)**	63. **(A)**	70. **(C)**	77. **(A)**
57. **(C)**	64. **(C)**	71. **(E)**	78. **(D)**
58. **(B)**	65. **(B)**	72. **(A)**	79. **(A)**
59. **(D)**	66. **(C)**	73. **(B)**	80. **(C)**
60. **(B)**	67. **(A)**	74. **(B)**	
61. **(E)**	68. **(B)**	75. **(B)**	
62. **(C)**	69. **(B)**	76. **(A)**	

Section IV   Data Sufficiency

81. **(A)**	85. **(B)**	89. **(C)**	93. **(B)**
82. **(A)**	86. **(D)**	90. **(E)**	94. **(A)**
83. **(E)**	87. **(D)**	91. **(A)**	95. **(E)**
84. **(E)**	88. **(C)**	92. **(D)**	

Section V   Writing Ability

96.	(B)	105.	(D)	114.	(A)	123.	(D)
97.	(E)	106.	(B)	115.	(B)	124.	(E)
98.	(D)	107.	(A)	116.	(C)	125.	(C)
99.	(A)	108.	(C)	117.	(A)	126.	(A)
100.	(C)	109.	(B)	118.	(E)	127.	(A)
101.	(A)	110.	(E)	119.	(A)	128.	(D)
102.	(C)	111.	(C)	120.	(D)	129.	(B)
103.	(B)	112.	(E)	121.	(C)	130.	(E)
104.	(E)	113.	(B)	122.	(B)		

Section VI   Business Judgment

131.	(B)	136.	(B)	141.	(B)	146.	(B)
132.	(A)	137.	(B)	142.	(D)	147.	(A)
133.	(E)	138.	(A)	143.	(A)	148.	(E)
134.	(B)	139.	(C)	144.	(B)	149.	(B)
135.	(C)	140.	(B)	145.	(D)	150.	(A)

Section VII   Case Evaluation

151.	(D)	161.	(D)	171.	(B)	181.	(C)
152.	(B)	162.	(E)	172.	(D)	182.	(E)
153.	(C)	163.	(C)	173.	(D)	183.	(A)
154.	(A)	164.	(D)	174.	(E)	184.	(B)
155.	(E)	165.	(C)	175.	(C)	185.	(D)
156.	(B)	166.	(B)	176.	(E)	186.	(B)
157.	(E)	167.	(A)	177.	(E)	187.	(E)
158.	(C)	168.	(E)	178.	(C)	188.	(E)
159.	(A)	169.	(A)	179.	(A)	189.	(C)
160.	(C)	170.	(C)	180.	(E)	190.	(A)

Analysis

1. **(E)** The report (on which the passage is based) is certainly not optimistic (B), but rather pessimistic in its assessment, although not specifically about the trade gap (D). Nor can the report be characterized as vindictive (A) or critical of labor unions (C). After all, as pointed out in the passage, it is labor that will suffer. The answer is (E). This is specifically expressed in the first and second paragraphs.

2. **(C)** Free trade is the reduction or elimination of tariffs and duties on exports. See lines 3 and 16–18.

3. **(B)** Manufacturers that cannot increase productivity in order to lower prices will not be able to compete with duty free imports. Manufacturers who cannot adapt to this situation will not receive adjustment assistance, i.e., subsidies or some other financial payments to buttress them in the face of foreign competition.

4. **(B)** The author's recommendation is that redundant labor should be removed. See lines 36–37.

5. **(A)** Even though the subject of trade with the Common Market (C) is discussed, the major thrust of the passage is on the consequences of free trade—in this case, with the Common Market.

6. **(C)** This is stated in paragraph 3 of the passage.

7. **(C)** The major objective is to explain the objectives of sociology which are the same as those of science. See line 1.

8. **(C)** A discussion of this point is given in paragraph 3. The other answers are either factually incorrect or incomplete.

9. **(C)** The final step or objective of science—according to the passage—is explanation (line 3), or better stated as a causal proposition. See lines 38–39.

10. **(A)** Only I is mentioned in the passage, although all are useful in building a science.

11. **(D)** Answers (B) and (E) are mentioned in the passage, but are secondary in importance to (D). Answer (C) is not correct, and answer (A) is not mentioned in the passage.

12. **(B)** This is mentioned in the first and the final paragraphs. In any case, the prefix *poly* means many and the suffix *theist* means one who believes in a god or gods.

13. **(E)** Answers (A), (B) and (D) cannot be inferred from the passage. Answer (C) is consonant with what the author has to say, but (E) is a stronger example of the question statement.

14. **(B)** I is incorrect since they worshipped gods in both human and other forms. See lines 24ff.

15. **(B)** Although the author states that certain cultures are more inclined to anthropocentric worship (A), he mentions it while making the point that there are those who attribute it to others, even though practicing it themselves.

16. **(C)** The paragraph indicates that if the universe is partly controlled by the "wet-god" (it rains), then the "dry-god" lacks control. This is an example of incoherence. If you pray for rain, you must also pray to prevent the "dry-god" from exercising his powers, an example of potential conflict. Hence there is hardly a commonality of interests or order in a polytheistic system.

17. **(C)** This statement is made in line 8. While it would seem that (E) is implied in the first paragraph, this thought is negated in line 13.

18. **(B)** The first paragraph illustrates the author's belief that if a forecaster predicts a dismal future, no matter what the outcome, he can claim credit for action taken (if it worked), or disassociate himself from a wrong decision.

19. **(C)** While the project director might be guilty of "fuzzy" thinking (D), the main point the author is trying to make is that the housing project was a short-term solution to what was essentially a long-run problem. This point is also stated in lines 42–43.

20. **(E)** Clearly, the author's primary purpose is to point out some of the problems in forecasting and how they might be eliminated.

21. **(C)** Gardner's thesis is discussed in lines 16–18. His thesis was that in the early 1960s (when his book was written), Americans were operating on the basis of a no-questioning value system. According to the passage, this value system changed after several years, but we cannot infer that it is no longer operative (A) for it may have changed again since the passage was written (in 1970 as stated). For the same reason we cannot infer that the thesis applies today.

22. **(B)** Answer (B) can be inferred from the examples given in lines 19–21 and also the statement contained in lines 22–24. Answer (A) is unacceptable because of the word always—this does not appear in the passage.

23. **(A)** This opinion is explicitly stated in lines 26 and 27.

24. **(E)** This exhortation is stated in lines 40–42.

25. **(A)** The author makes no comment about these environmental changes, except that they represent a change in attitudes and values of the population. The author makes no value judgment of his own, so we can say that his attitude was one of ambivalence.

Section II   Mathematics

26. **(D)** Since $\dfrac{12}{4} = 3 = \dfrac{36}{12}$ the ratio of one term to the previous term is 3. So if x is the next term, $\dfrac{x}{36} = 3$ and $x = 3(36) = 108$.

27. **(E)** The complement of x is an angle of $90 - x$ degrees, and the supplement of x is an angle of $180 - x$ degrees. Thus, we have $90 - x = \dfrac{1}{6}$ $(180 - x) = 30 - \dfrac{1}{6}x$, so $60 = \dfrac{5}{6}x$ or $x = 72$.

28. **(C)** The profit was $250 on sales of $1,900, so the ratio of profit to sales is $\dfrac{250}{1,900} = \dfrac{25}{190}$ which is approximately .132 or about 13%.

29. **(E)** Since 4 is a multiple of 2, the least common multiple of 3, 4, and 5 will be the least common multiple of 2, 3, 4, and 5. 3, 4, and 5 have no common factors so the least common multiple is $3 \cdot 4 \cdot 5 = 60$.

30. **(C)** Since 10% have both brown eyes and brown hair, and 25% have brown eyes, 15% of the people have brown eyes but do not have brown hair. Thus, 40% + 15% or 55% of the people have brown eyes or brown hair or both. Therefore, 100% − 55% or 45% of the people have neither brown eyes nor brown hair.

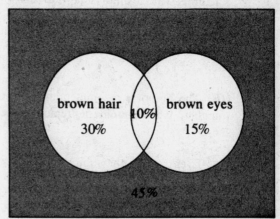

31. **(E)** Area = ½ (altitude) (base). The increased altitude is (1.05) altitude and the increased base is (1.07) base. Therefore, the increased area is ½ (1.05) (1.07) (altitude) (base). So the increased area is (1.1235) area. Thus, the area has increased by 12.35%.

32. **(D)** The first 20 pounds cost $20 \cdot 2\cent = 40\cent$. The package weighs 3½ pounds more than 20 pounds, so there are 3 pounds and one fraction of a pound over 20 pounds. The weight over 20 pounds will cost. $4 \cdot (1.5)\cent = 6\cent$. Therefore, the total cost will be 46¢.

33. **(A)** Since $5{,}000 - 1{,}000 = 4{,}000$, there are 4,000 sheets which will be discounted. The 4,000 sheets cost 4,000¢ or $40.00 before the discount, so they will cost $(.98)(\$40.00)$ or $39.20 after the 2% discount. The first 1,000 sheets cost 1¢ each so they cost 1,000¢ or $10.00. Therefore, the total cost of the 5,000 sheets will be $49.20.

34. **(C)** Let T be Tom's salary, J be John's salary, and S be Steve's salary, then the given information is $T = (1.5)J$ and $J = (.8)S$. Changing to fractions we get $T = \dfrac{3}{2}J$ and $J = \dfrac{4}{5}S$ so $S = \dfrac{5}{4}J$. Therefore, $\dfrac{S}{T} = \dfrac{5}{4}J / \dfrac{3}{2}J = \dfrac{5}{4} / \dfrac{3}{2} = \dfrac{5}{4}\cdot\dfrac{2}{3} = \dfrac{5}{6}$. The ratio is 5 to 6.

35. **(D)** If the average speed is 50 mph, then in 5 hours the driver will travel $5 \cdot 50$ miles or 250 miles. He traveled 135 miles in the first 3 hours, so he needs to travel $250 - 135 = 115$ miles in the final 2 hours.

36. **(E)** 30 workers are $\dfrac{3}{5}$ of 50 workers, so it should take the 30 workers $\dfrac{5}{3}$ as long as the 50 workers. Therefore, the 30 workers should take $\dfrac{5}{3}\cdot 4 = \dfrac{20}{3} = 6\dfrac{2}{3}$ hours = 6 hours and 40 minutes.

37. **(D)** Each box of dictionaries weighs $6 \times 20 = 120$ pounds. Each box of encyclopedias weighs $2 \times 75 = 150$ pounds. So the load weighs $98 \times 120 + 50 \times 150 = 19{,}260$ pounds.

38. **(D)** Mary makes $600 a month on her regular job. Therefore, she receives $600 \cdot 12 = \$7{,}200$ a year from her regular job. Her only other income is $400. So her total yearly income is $7,600. She makes $600 + \$400 = \$1{,}000$ during July, so she makes $1{,}000/7{,}600 = {}^5\!/_{38}$ which is about .13 of her annual income during July. Therefore, Mary makes about 13% of her annual income in July.

39. **(C)** The area of the triangle is ½(altitude) (base) = ½ (altitude)S. The area of the square is S^2. Therefore, ½S(altitude) = S^2, so the altitude must be $2S$.

40. **(D)** The train will average 50 mph for 3½ hours, 75 mph for 3 hours and 20 mph for half an hour. So the distance of the trip is $(3½)(50) + (3)(75) + (½)(20) = 175 + 225 + 10 = 410$ miles. The trip takes 7 hours. Therefore, the average speed is $410/7 = 58\,{}^4\!/_7$ mph.

41. **(C)**
$$(x - y)(y + 3) = x(y + 3) - y(y + 3)$$
$$= xy + 3x - y^2 - 3y$$
$$= xy - y^2 - 3y + 3x$$

42. **(B)** If $x < y$ and $y < z$, then $x < z$. All the other statements may be true but are not always true.

43. **(C)** The ratio is $\dfrac{2}{3} \Big/ \dfrac{5}{4}$ which is equal to $\dfrac{2}{3}\cdot\dfrac{4}{5} = \dfrac{8}{15}$

44. **(C)** 3 divides 9 evenly and 3 divides 33 evenly, so 9 and 33 are not primes. 7, 11, 13, and 29 have no divisors except 1 and themselves, so they are all primes. Thus, the set of numbers contain 4 prime numbers.

45. **(D)** Each share is worth $13.21 - \$9.50$ or $3.71 more in 1970 than it was in 1960. So 100,000 shares are worth $(\$3.71)(100{,}000)$ or $371,000.00 more in 1970 than they were in 1960.

46. **(D)** Add up all the daily wages for the week: $\$40.62 + 41.35 + 42.00 + 42.50 + 39.53 = \$206.00$. Divide $206.00 by 5 to get the average daily wage, $41.20.

47. **(A)** If the price of a pound of apples rises 2%, then the price of ten pounds of apples rises 2%. This is because the percentage change is the same for any amount sold. Since a dozen eggs and ten pounds of apples currently cost the same, each costs one half of the total price. Therefore, one half of the total is increased by 10% and the other half is increased by 2%, so the total price is increased by $½(10\%) + ½(2\%) = 6\%$.

48. **(A)** $2y = 6$, so $y = 3$. Therefore, $x + 3 = 4$; so $x = 1$.

49. **(D)** Each man does $\frac{1}{25}$ of the job in $1\frac{1}{2}$ hours. Thus, 15 men will do $\frac{15}{25}$ or $\frac{3}{5}$ of the job in $1\frac{1}{2}$ hours. So 15 men will complete the job in $\frac{5}{3}\cdot\frac{3}{2}=\frac{5}{2}=2\frac{1}{2}$ hours. Another method gives $\frac{15}{25}=\frac{3/2}{x}$ where x is the time 15 men will take to complete the job. Therefore, $15x=\frac{3}{2}\cdot 25=\frac{75}{2}$ so $x=\frac{5}{2}=2\frac{1}{2}$.

50. **(A)** The car gets $100\% - 12\%$ or 88% of 20 miles to the gallon at 60 miles per hour. Thus, the car gets $(.88)(20)$ or 17.6 miles to the gallon at 60 mph. Therefore, it can travel $(11)(17.6)$ or 193.6 miles.

51. **(D)** The first 12 tons cost $(12)(\$500)$ or $\$6,000$. When you purchase 30 tons, you are buying 18 tons in addition to the first 12 tons costing additionally $\$(500 - x)(18)$. Since $\$10,000 - \$6,000 = \$4,000$, we get $\$9,000 - 18x = \$4,000$, and $18x = \$5,000$. So $x = 277.78$.

52. **(E)** The sum of the angles of a triangle is $180°$. Let x be the number of degrees in the largest angle; then the other angles are $\frac{1}{2}x$ and $\frac{3}{4}x$ degrees. Therefore, $\frac{1}{2}x + \frac{3}{4}x + x = \frac{9}{4}x = 180°$, so $x = 80°$.

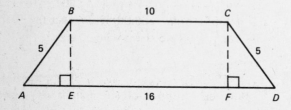

53. **(B)** If we draw $CF \perp AD$, then $\triangle ABE \cong \triangle DCF$ and $AE = FD = 3$. Then $BE = 4$. Thus the area of the trapezoid, which equals the product of the altitude and the average of the bases, equals $(4)(\frac{1}{2})(10 + 16) = 52$.

54. **(E)** Since x is greater than 2 and 2 is greater than 0, x is greater than 0. Therefore, STATEMENT I is false but STATEMENT II is true.

If we add x to each side of the inequality $x > 0$ we obtain $x + x > x + 0$, so $2x > x$. Therefore, STATEMENT III is true.

Since x is greater than 2 which is greater than 1, we know $x > 1$. Multiply the inequality by x (x is positive so the inequality is preserved); the result is $x^2 > x$, so STATEMENT IV is true. Therefore, STATEMENTS II, III, and IV are true.

55. **(A)** Since each assistant does $\frac{2}{3}$ as much as the worker, all 3 will accomplish $1 + 2(\frac{2}{3})$ or $\frac{7}{3}$ as much as the worker by himself. So they will finish the job in $1 \div \frac{7}{3}$ or $\frac{3}{7}$ as much time as it would take the worker by himself.

Section III   Business Judgment

56. **(B)** The major decision to be made by the executives of Climax Corporation is whether to maintain their present service operation, or if not, what alternative would be best. In this question, the training of retail service personnel is a *Major Factor* in making that decision; it was suggested by the product service manager that more money be spent on such training. It is not a *Major Objective* because no decision has been made that more training is the answer to their problem. It is obviously not the only answer.

57. **(C)** The rise of the discount house is a *Minor Factor* to be considered only because consumers who buy appliances at such stores do so under the realization that discount houses do not have service facilities. The question, of course, is why consumers do buy appliances at discount stores when they know the dealers do not provide service.

58. **(B)** The fact that typical (i.e., the average) retailers do not have competent service personnel is a, if not *the, Major Factor* in making a decision about Climax's service system. The other important factor, of course, is whether consumers really expect service facilities in each retail store.

59. **(D)** The adequacy of service demanded by consumers is a *Major Assumption* that must be examined before a decision about service

can be made. In simple terms, how much service do consumers really want? Where do they want this service—from retailers, wholesalers, the manufacturer? In several places in the passage, some concern about this problem is expressed. See the discussion about discount stores and TV sets.

60. **(B)** Centralizing the service operation is a *Major Factor* or consideration. It is not an objective because no decision as to the final form of the operation has been made.

61. **(E)** The number of wholesalers is unimportant; the fact that they are company owned (and controlled) is an important issue.

62. **(C)** In paragraph two, it is stated that repairs are made either by retailers or wholesalers. In the case of wholesalers, the manufacturer supplies the parts, the wholesaler the labor.

63. **(A)** The adequacy of service rendered by retailers was given as the major reason for the review of Climax's service operation. It was felt that present service was inadequate owing to the lack of competent service personnel among retailers.

64. **(C)** See paragraph 3. The sales manager and others believed that if the service operation were centralized, its quality would increase while its costs would decrease.

65. **(B)** According to the results of the consumer survey quoted in paragraph 7, consumers did not pay much attention to the availability of service at the *time of purchase*.

66. **(C)** See paragraph 4. Retailers like to service appliances because of the profit and store traffic generated.

67. **(A)** Discount stores are able to cut prices because they do not bear the cost of service departments. Therefore, if consumer purchases increase through these outlets, it means that they do not regard service availability when making a decision to purchase. Moreover, it is mentioned in the passage that a consumer survey found the "average owner gave little thought to service availability when buying an appliance."

68. **(B)** The major decision to be made by Sam Hoe is whether to open a retail showroom for the sale of his custom line. He felt that this strategy might be a solution to his major problem of a declining profit position. If he could retail his own products, he felt that his profit margin would be improved. Therefore, the fact of higher operating expenses was a *Major Factor* in making his decision.

69. **(B)** The increased demand for furniture which Sam Hoe had experienced was a *Major Factor* leading him to consider opening a retail showroom.

70. **(C)** Storage space is an *Unimportant Issue* in making the decision; it bears no direct relation to the manufacture and sale of furniture in this problem.

71. **(E)** Mr. Hoe's workshop employed 20 craftsmen but this fact wouldn't affect the opening of a showroom. It is an *Unimportant Issue*.

72. **(A)** Sam's major decision is whether to open a retail showroom or not. This is the *Major Objective*. See the explanation in answer 68 above.

73. **(B)** The scarcity of cabinetmakers limited Mr. Hoe's output of custom built furniture and therefore was a *Major Factor* in his contemplation of how to increase the profitability of his standard furniture line.

74. **(B)** See paragraphs 1 and 4. Profits were not increasing at the same rate as production. The other factors were not mentioned.

75. **(B)** See paragraph 1. Sam did consider a price increase, but did not take any action of the sort since he had recently raised prices of most items during the past six months.

76. **(A)** See paragraph 3. Custom furniture accounted for 78 percent of sales.

77. **(A)** See paragraph 4. Demand for Sam's custom line of furniture was increasing, but he had to limit his output owing to a shortage of skilled craftsmen.

78. **(D)** See paragraph 3. Most of Mr. Hoe's standard line was sold in a five-state area, while most of his custom made items were sold within the state. Only a few items of the latter category were sold throughout the country.

79. **(A)** By selling at a factory location, Mr. Hoe could reduce his distribution costs.

80. **(C)** No mention was made of wholesalers' margins. Answers I and II are given in paragraphs 1 and 4.

Section IV   Data Sufficiency

81. **(A)**
STATEMENT (1) alone is sufficient. If angle x is a right angle, then AOC is a semi-circle. Therefore, AC is a diameter.
STATEMENT (2) alone is insufficient. There are many (an infinite number) triangles we can inscribe in the circle such that $AB = \frac{3}{4}BC$. Not all of these will have AC as a diameter.
Therefore, STATEMENT (1) alone is sufficient, but STATEMENT (2) alone is not sufficient.

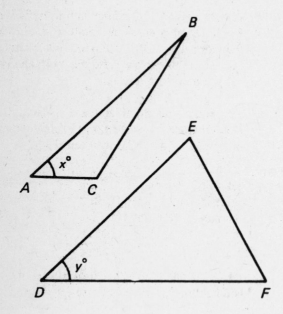

82. **(A)**
To find how many gallons the tank will hold, we need to calculate the volume of the tank and then divide this by the volume of one gallon of the liquid. Therefore, STATEMENT (1) alone is sufficient.
STATEMENT (2) alone is not sufficient (note that it gives no further information about the tank). We need to know how much space a gallon of the liquid occupies.
Therefore, STATEMENT (1) alone is sufficient, but STATEMENT (2) alone is not.

83. **(E)**
STATEMENT (1) alone is not sufficient. We still need the total weight of the books; then we can divide by the average weight to obtain the number of books.
STATEMENT (2) tells us how much the books and the bookshelf together weigh, but we don't know how much the books weigh.
So STATEMENTS (1) and (2) together are not sufficient.

84. **(E)**
STATEMENT (1) alone is not sufficient, since many noncongruent triangles can have a side and an angle which are equal.
By the same reasoning, STATEMENT (2) alone is not sufficient.
STATEMENTS (1) and (2) together are not sufficient. For two triangles to be congruent, they must have two pairs of corresponding sides and the *included* angles equal. For example, the following two triangles satisfy STATEMENTS (1) and (2) and angle $x =$ angle y but they are not congruent.
Therefore, STATEMENTS (1) and (2) together are not sufficient.

85. **(B)**
STATEMENT (2) alone is sufficient, since we can multiply $\frac{1}{9}$ by (60×60) to obtain the speed in mph.
STATEMENT (1) alone is not sufficient, because the plane's flying in a circle gives us no information about the exact speed of the plane.
So STATEMENT (2) alone is sufficient, but STATEMENT (1) alone is not.

86. (D)

STATEMENT (1) alone is sufficient. If $L =$ the length of the floor, then STATEMENT (1) says the width is $\frac{1}{2}L$. The area of the floor is length times width or $(L)(\frac{1}{2}L)$ or $\frac{1}{2}L^2$. Since the area is equal to 32 square feet, we have $\frac{1}{2}L^2 = 32$ so $L^2 = 64$ and $L = 8$ feet.

STATEMENT (2) alone is sufficient. Let $W =$ the width of the floor. Then STATEMENT (2) says $W = L - 4$. So the area is $L(L - 4)$ or $L^2 - 4L$ which equals 32. Therefore, L satisfies $L^2 - 4L - 32 = 0$, and since $L^2 - 4L - 32 = (L - 8)(L + 4)$, $L^2 - 4L - 32 = 0$ if and only if $L = 8$ or $L = -4$. Since $L = -4$ has no meaning for the problem, $L = 8$.

So STATEMENT (1) alone is sufficient, and STATEMENT (2) alone is sufficient.

87. (D) We have to determine whether $(AB)(BC)$ which is the area of the rectangle $ABCD$ is equal to $(EH)^2$ which is the area of the square $EFGH$.

STATEMENT (1) alone is sufficient. Since ABC is a right triangle, $BC = \sqrt{(AC)^2 - (AB)^2}$, and using STATEMENT (1) we have $BC = \sqrt{(EG)^2 - \frac{1}{4}(EH)^2}$. Using the fact that $EFGH$ is a square, we know $(EG)^2 = 2(EH)^2$, so we can express BC in terms of EH. Using STATEMENT (1) we can express AB as $\frac{1}{2}EH$, so $(AB)(BC)$ can be expressed as a multiple of $(EH)^2$. Notice that to answer the question you don't have to actually set up the equation. If you work it out you will find that the area of $ABCD$ is $\frac{\sqrt{7}}{4}(EH)^2$, so the areas are not equal. *Don't* waste time carrying out the extra work on the test.

STATEMENT (2) alone is sufficient since the diagonal of a rectangle divides the rectangle into two congruent triangles. Therefore, the area of $ABCD$ is equal to the area of $EFGH$ if and only if the area of ABC is equal to the area of EFG.

88. (C)

STATEMENT (2) says $J = 2S$, where $J =$ Joan's weight and $S =$ Susan's weight. But since we don't know Joan's weight, STATEMENT (2) alone is not sufficient.

STATEMENT (1) says $J + S = 250$; so if we use STATEMENT (2) we have $2S + S = 250$

or $S = \frac{250}{3} = 83\frac{1}{3}$. But STATEMENT (1) alone is not sufficient. If we use only STATEMENT (1), we don't know how much Joan weighs. Therefore, STATEMENTS (1) and (2) together are sufficient, but neither statement alone is sufficient.

89. (C)

In each minute, hole A drains $\frac{1}{24}$ of the tank according to STATEMENT (1). Since we have no information about B, STATEMENT (1) alone is not sufficient.

In each minute, hole B drains $\frac{1}{42}$ of the tank according to STATEMENT (2), but STATEMENT (2) gives no information about hole A. So STATEMENT (2) alone is not sufficient.

If we use STATEMENTS (1) and (2), then both holes together will drain $\frac{1}{24} + \frac{1}{42}$ or $\frac{7 + 4}{6 \times 28}$ or $\frac{11}{168}$ of the tank each minute. Therefore, it will take $\frac{168}{11}$ or $15\frac{3}{11}$ minutes for the tank to be empty. So STATEMENTS (1) and (2) together are sufficient, but neither statement alone is sufficient.

90. (E) STATEMENTS (1) and (2) are equivalent, since $x - y = 6$ if and only if $2x - 2y = 2(x - y) = 2 \cdot 6 = 12$. Each statement tells us only what $x - y$ is, and we have no other information. Therefore, each statement alone is insufficient. But since the two statements are the same, even together they are not sufficient.

91. (A)

STATEMENT (2) alone is not sufficient, since we must know how close the circles are and we know only the radius of each circle.

STATEMENT (1) alone is sufficient. The centers of the two circles are closer than the sum of the radii. (So we can form a triangle with DF as one side and the two other sides with length 2 and R respectively; but this means that the third vertex of the triangle will be on both circle E and circle C.)

So STATEMENT (1) alone is sufficient, but STATEMENT (2) alone is not sufficient.

92. (D) It is sufficient to be able to find his total income for the years 1967 through 1969 since we divide the total income by 3 to obtain the average income.

STATEMENT (1) alone is sufficient. Since we know his income for 1967, we can find his income in 1968 and 1969 by using STATEMENT (1). Therefore, we can find the total income. STATEMENT (2) alone is sufficient. Add the combined income from 1968 and 1969 to the income from 1967 (which is given), and we have the total income.

Therefore, STATEMENTS (1) and (2) are each sufficient.

93. **(B)**

STATEMENT (1) alone is not sufficient. $y = z$ does not imply $x = 90°$. For example, in an equilateral triangle, $x = y = z$ and $x = 60°$. STATEMENT (2) alone is sufficient. Pythagoras' theorem says x is a right angle if and only if $(AC)^2 + (BC)^2 = (AB)^2$.

94. **(A)**

STATEMENT (1) alone is sufficient. If $P =$ Paul's height, then we can write a proportion $\frac{P}{6} = \frac{9}{10}$ since their shadows are proportional to their heights. $\left[\text{Thus, } P = \frac{54}{10} = 5.4 \text{ feet.} \right]$ STATEMENT (2) alone is not sufficient. The distance they are apart does not give us any information about their heights.

Therefore, STATEMENT (1) alone is sufficient, but STATEMENT (2) alone is not sufficient.

95. **(E)**

STATEMENT (1) alone is not sufficient. Note that $4 = (-2)^2 > 1 = (-1)^2$ but $-2 < -1$.

STATEMENT (2) alone is not sufficient. If $x + 3$ is greater than $y + 2$, then x can be less than y or greater than y. For example, ½ is greater than 0, and ½ + 3 is greater than 0 + 2. However, ½ is less than 1, while ½ + 3 is greater than 1 + 2.

STATEMENTS (1) and (2) together are not sufficient. For example, −½ is less than ¼, −½ + 3 is greater than 2 + ¼, and $(-½)^2 = ¼$ is greater than $1/16 = (¼)^2$. Also, ¼ is less than 2, $(¼)^2$ is less than 2^2, and 2 + 3 is greater than ¼ + 2. So STATEMENTS (1) and (2) together are not sufficient.

Section V   Writing Ability

96. **(B)** The linking verb *looks* requires the adjective *good* and not the adverb *well*.

97. **(E)** No error.

98. **(D)** The *number* of hours should be used instead of *amount*, as the unit *hours* is mentioned.

99. **(A)** The past perfect *had met* is required, since the action preceded past action.

100. **(C)** The participle *realizing* dangles, as *my confidence* cannot do the realizing.

101. **(A)** The expression *have a loan of* is nonstandard for borrow.

102. **(C)** The verb *are* should be *is*, as the subject, *the governor*, is singular; *together with his wife etc.* is parenthetical.

103. **(B)** The required noun is *effects*, i.e., *the results of* and not *affects* which is a verb only.

104. **(E)** No error.

105. **(D)** The singular pronoun *one* requires the singular *his* and not the plural *their*.

106. **(B)** The verb must be the third person singular *understands* to agree with the singular *Neither* (one).

107. **(A)** The past conditional requires the past perfect *had come* in the conditional clause.

108. **(C)** The pronoun *which* must refer to a specific word; in this case it has no clear antecedent.

109. **(B)** The required conjunction is *than* and not the adverb *then*.

110. **(E)** No error.

111. **(C)** The adverb *hardly* already carries a negative connotation and therefore does not take the negative *not*.

112. **(E)** No error.

113. **(B)** The standard idiom is *different from.* (This would require other changes in the sentence as well.)

114. **(A)** *Data* is a plural noun and requires the plural auxiliary *have.*

115. **(B)** The subjunctive requires the use of the base form of the verb; *be told* and not the present form *is told.*

116. **(C)** The word *irregardless* is nonstandard for *regardless.*

117. **(A)** *Provided* is standard usage and not *Providing.*

118. **(E)** No error.

119. **(A)** The noun is *advice* and not *advise.*

120. **(D)** The participle *lying* is required and not *laying.*

121. **(C)** The plural subject *you and I* requires the plural verb *are.*

122. **(B)** The pronoun *he* has no clear antecedent and therefore we do not know who *shipped out the defective batch;* George or Crosby.

123. **(D)** The compound verb idea *noticed* and *called for* cannot be separated by a semicolon or any other punctuation mark.

124. **(E)** No error.

125. **(C)** *Me* is required as the object following the prepositional phrase *except for.*

126. **(A)** She felt bad. The adjective is required following the linking verb *felt* and not the adverb *badly.*

127. **(A)** The colon (:) should not be used after *are* when presenting a list.

128. **(D)** People are *healthy* but the climate is *healthful.*

129. **(B)** The word *scarcely* has a negative connotation and must be followed by *any* and not *no.*

130. **(E)** No error.

Section VI   Business Judgment

131. **(B)** Declining sales of Pandora's New York State subsidiary was the *Major Factor* prompting a decision of whether to alter the existing pricing strategy or to consider other alternatives.

132. **(A)** The determination of a viable pricing strategy for the American products is the *Major Objective* in this case.

133. **(E)** That the plant is located in the U.S. is an issue, not that it is located in New York State.

134. **(B)** Because the U.S. product price was well above that of the U.K., U.K. wholesalers were able to market their product in the U.S. and absorb the cost of shipping and duties.

135. **(C)** The U.K. company's capacity situation is a *Minor Factor.*

136. **(B)** According to the passage, only alternative III was considered. If the U.S. plant were closed, exports from the U.K. would increase. Applying sanctions to wholesalers would cause more problems and probably affect U.K. distribution as well.

137. **(B)** See answer 134 **(B)** above.

138. **(A)** Part of the blame was placed on the advertising agency that "convinced" Smith to set a premium price on the U.S. product.

139. **(C)** These factors were given in paragraphs 1 and 7.

140. **(B)** Smith did not want to "throw away" the advertising. See the last paragraph.

141. **(B)** The workers had no loyalty to the company from the "north." This is a *Major Factor* as far as their will to work is concerned.

142. **(D)** This was an assumption initially taken by Cappa upon which he developed his managerial style. It was an erroneous conclusion.

143. **(A)** Motivating the workers is Cappa's *Major Objective*.

144. **(B)** Low productivity, caused mainly by lack of motivation, is a *Major Factor*.

145. **(D)** Cappa's desire to institute a bonus system (that failed) was not supported by any evidence that it could succeed.

146. **(B)** Since worker productivity was linked to a bonus system, poor worker output could be attributed (from facts in the passage) to lack of worker commitment.

147. **(A)** Answers II and III are generalized situations that are not necessarily supported by the case. It is clear, however, that answer I is a conclusion supported by facts in the passage.

148. **(E)** Cappa used all three. See paragraphs 11, 12, and 14.

149. **(B)** Cappa wanted to manage a company on his own to prove his ability. See paragraphs 3–5.

150. **(A)** The workers resented imposed discipline.

Section VII   Case Evaluation

151. **(D)** This statement *weakens the conclusion* as Sheparton can claim that he was not aware that he was on private property. It does not, however, *disprove the conclusion* because it does not relate to the damage caused.

152. **(B)** This statement *strengthens the conclusion* in that it shows that the owner of the property took reasonable action to prevent trespassing. However, no mention is made of actions taken to protect his goods which were destroyed.

153. **(C)** This *clearly disproves the conclusion* as it shows that Murchison had not taken adequate precautions to protect his very inflam-

mable goods, a prerequisite condition for claiming damages.

154. **(A)** This clearly establishes that Sheparton has knowingly trespassed and had acted out of lack of care for the property and thus *clearly proves the conclusion*.

155. **(E)** The fact that Sheparton was injured by the explosion is *irrelevant to the conclusion* which fixes liability for damage to property and goods only.

156. **(B)** The fact that Murchison had ordered the electricity cut illustrates the precaution he took to protect his goods. But in order to win damages, Murchison needs to establish adequate measures to prevent trespass as well. This statement, therefore, only *strengthens the conclusion*.

157. **(E)** The fact of where Sheparton was apprehended has no bearing on the case. His presence on the property is established in the text.

158. **(C)** This fact *clearly disproves the conclusion* as the old bakery, being condemned for demolition, could not have been "suitably registered premises" and thus Murchison cannot claim damages from anyone.

159. **(A)** The presence of the night watchman shows that Murchison had taken adequate and reasonable action to prevent trespassing and protect his goods. The fact that Sheparton was told to leave by the watchman establishes that he was aware that he was trespassing on private property. These two facts together *clearly prove the conclusion*.

160. **(C)** The fact that the side gate was open shows that Murchison had not taken adequate precautions to prevent trespass. The many "No Trespassing" signs would not be considered adequate warning for small children, who like Sheparton, are illiterate. The statement *clearly disproves* the conclusion.

161. **(D)** This statement *weakens the conclusion* in that it gives Pimpang grounds to claim prior provocation for its action. The exten-

sive military maneuvers could have been seen by the apprehensive Pimpang as a threat of military action. However, the law stipulates *direct threat*.

162. **(E)** This statement is totally *irrelevant to the conclusion* as the villagers did not constitute a military force, armed or unarmed.

163. **(C)** This statement *clearly disproves* the conclusion. The stealing of the cattle by an organized unit of the military makes it a military action *to gain control of property*. Thus Dimpang is clearly the aggressor.

164. **(D)** Colonel Bong's intentions by themselves are not enough to disprove the conclusion. However, the activities that he had carried out to justify invasion, although undetailed, would *weaken the conclusion* by opening to question the nature of the mentioned incidents and consequently the nature of the Pimpang action.

165. **(C)** This statement *clearly disproves* the conclusion. Since the Pimpang commandos did not cross into Dimpang territory, their actions cannot count as provocation. Further, we can infer from this statement that the Dimpang troops fired on and killed the Pimpang soldiers on Pimpang territory, thus making the former clearly aggressors according to the principles quoted.

166. **(B)** This fact establishes that Dimpang had no intentions of invading Pimpang. This does not prove the conclusion but *strengthens it* as it does not change the fact that Pimpang's actions were provocation.

167. **(A)** This statement *clearly proves the conclusion* since it establishes that the Pimpang force acted first, establishing them as aggressor and the Dimpang action as retaliation. The actual size of the military unit is irrelevant.

168. **(E)** The pronouncements about "the unity of the Pang Peninsula" are irrelevant to the course of events upon which the conclusion is based. Further, we are not told the nature of these pronouncements regardless of who made them.

169. **(A)** According to just the facts presented in the text it is clear that Dimpang is not the aggressor, provocation having been established. This statement therefore *clearly proves the conclusion*.

170. **(C)** Since the force was not of the Pimpang military, Dimpang cannot justify its action as retaliation to provocation. Thus its action is clearly aggression according to the law quoted. This statement *clearly disproves the conclusion*.

171. **(B)** This statement *reinforces the conclusion* in that it establishes the truth of Sterling's words about not having any *major mechanical problems*. However, by itself it does not establish that Sterling did not either conceal other information or mislead Moss in other ways, which would be needed to *clearly prove the conclusion*.

172. **(D)** This statement *weakens the conclusion* because Sterling concealed this information which relates directly to the sale. But as we have no evidence that Sterling knew that his car had a faulty gear, it cannot be reasoned that it clearly disproves the conclusion.

173. **(D)** This statement *weakens the conclusion*. Sterling lied to Moss in a matter connected to the sale of the car. It is reasonable to assume that his intentions were to prevent Moss from handling the car and discovering any defects. But since we have no direct evidence of Sterling's intentions, we cannot infer that this statement *disproves the conclusion*.

174. **(E)** The fact that Moss and Sterling live in different parts of town disproves Sterling's statement that they are neighbors but has *no relevance* at all to the conclusion. (In any case, if Sterling were using a lie to deceive or mislead, it would be ineffective because Moss would know if they were neighbors or not.)

175. **(C)** This is an easy question. Obviously, if Sterling knew in advance that the gear was faulty, he knowingly concealed it from Moss. This statement therefore *clearly disproves the conclusion*.

614 • FIVE SAMPLE GMATs WITH ANSWERS AND ANALYSIS

176. **(E)** Sterling's need for the money is *irrelevant to the conclusion*. We can assume from this statement that Sterling may be a disreputable person, but this misstatement has little bearing on the sales agreement.

177. **(E)** This statement is also *irrelevant to the conclusion* because we are not told the result of the test.

178. **(C)** This statement *clearly disproves* the conclusion because the car, having a mechanical fault (even if Sterling, on expert advice, believed it to be minor), did not meet the specification of "perfect shape" that Sterling expressed to Moss prior to the sale.

179. **(A)** If, to the best of Sterling's knowledge, the car had no faults, then regardless of what happened after the sale, the sale is valid and thus this statement *clearly proves the conclusion.*

180. **(E)** Although this statement would seem to prove the conclusion, it is in effect *irrelevant to the conclusion*, which is based on events that took place prior to the sale.

181. **(C)** This statement *clearly disproves the conclusion*. Burke will lose because his dissatisfaction with the contracted price is no grounds for *relief from performance.*

182. **(E)** Whether Jospe told the truth or not about his vacation is not relevant to the subject of the agreement and thus *not relevant to the conclusion.*

183. **(A)** Since the renovation of the old house was the subject of the contract, its total destruction renders renovation according to Jospe's plans impossible. This statement therefore *clearly proves the conclusion.*

184. **(B)** While this statement does not clearly establish impossibility of performance, we can infer that should Burke sell the property, which he is entitled to do, the purpose of the contract, i.e., the renovation of Burke's house, will be frustrated. Since there is no evidence that Burke is selling the property specifically in order to rescind his agreement with Jospe, this statement *strengthens the conclusion* without proving it.

185. **(D)** Burke's nonapplication for a building permit does not render the performance impossible once a building permit has been attained; it merely delays Jospe's performance of his part of the contract. Thus it does *not clearly prove the conclusion.* On the other hand, we are not told Burke's motives for not applying for the permit and cannot conclude that *"he has knowingly contrived the circumstances,"* which would *clearly disprove the conclusion.* Since the attainment of the permit was in Burke's hands, it was his responsibility and thus it *weakens the conclusion* that Burke will win the case.

186. **(B)** The change in the municipal zoning laws will make residential building illegal from September 1 only; thus performance of the contract is possible up to that date. However, there is no guarantee that the building will be finished by that date, despite Jospe's assurance, and thus part of the performance could be illegal. This statement therefore *strengthens the conclusion* but does not clearly prove it.

187. **(E)** Burke's marital status has no bearing on the contractual agreement and thus is *not relevant to the conclusion.*

188. **(E)** Jospe's foreknowledge regarding the zoning laws is *irrelevant to the conclusion.* Although his ethical conduct may be called into question, the law under application specifically refers to "knowledge in advance" of "the party requesting relief from performance," i.e., Burke. Furthermore, in fairness to Jospe, the statement says that Jospe knew that the *"zoning laws may be changed."*

189. **(C)** This statement *clearly disproves the conclusion*, as Burke knowingly contrived the circumstances which made performance of the renovation impossible. He did it because he wanted to rescind the contract for renovation.

190. **(A)** This statement *clearly proves the conclusion* as it establishes impossibility of performance on the grounds that Jospe is obviously incompetent to perform in the capacity of builder in their contractual agreement.

Evaluating Your Score

Tabulate your score for each section of Sample Test 5 according to the directions on pages 4–5 and record the results in the Self-scoring Table below. Then find your rank for each score on the Self-scoring Scale and record it in the appropriate blank.

Self-scoring Table

PART	SCORE	RANK
1		
2		
3		
4		
5		
6		
7		

Self-scoring Scale

ACHIEVEMENT

PART	POOR	FAIR	GOOD	EXCELLENT
1	0–12	13–17	18–20	21–25
2	0–15	16–21	22–25	26–30
3	0–12	13–17	18–20	21–25
4	0–7	8–10	11–12	13–15
5	0–17	18–24	25–28	29–35
6	0–10	11–14	15–16	17–20
7	0–20	21–28	29–34	35–40

Study again the Review sections covering material in Sample Test 5 for which you had a rank of FAIR or POOR.

To obtain an approximation of your actual GMAT score see page 5.

SEVEN

A LIST OF SCHOOLS REQUIRING THE GMAT

The following list represents graduate schools of business which require GMAT scores as part of their admissions procedure. All the schools included are members of the American Assembly of Collegiate Schools of Business.

Adelphi University
School of Business Administration
Garden City, NY 11530

Advanced Management Institute
at Lake Forest College
Lake Forest, IL 60045

American Graduate School of International Management
Thunderbird Campus
Glendale, AZ 85306

The American University
School of Business Administration
Washington, DC 20016

Arizona State University
College of Business Administration
Tempe, AZ 85281

Atlanta University
School of Business Administration
Atlanta, GA 30314

Auburn University
School of Business
Auburn, AL 36830

Augusta College
Department of Business Administration
Augusta, GA 30904

Babson College
Babson Park, MA 02157

Baldwin-Wallace College
Division of Business Administration
Berea, OH 44017

Ball State University
College of Business
Muncie, IN 47306

Baylor University
Hankamer School of Business
Waco, TX 76706

Bentley College
Waltham, MA 02154

Bloomsburg State College
School of Business
Bloomsburg, PA 17815

Boise State University
School of Business
1910 College Boulevard
Boise, ID 83725

Boston College
School of Management
Chestnut Hill, MA 02167

Boston University
School of Management
685 Commonwealth Avenue
Boston, MA 02215

Bowling Green State University
College of Business Administration
Bowling Green, OH 43403

Bradley University
College of Business Administration
Peoria, IL 61625

Brigham Young University
Graduate School of Business
Provo, Utah 84602

Bryant College
Smithfield, RI 02917

Butler University
College of Business Administration
Indianapolis, IN 46208

California State College, Bakersfield
School of Business and
    Public Administration
9001 Stockdale Highway
Bakersfield, CA 93309

California State College, Dominguez Hills
School of Management
Dominguez Hills, CA 90747

California State College, San Bernardino
School of Administration
5500 State College Parkway
San Bernardino, CA 92407

California State College, Stanislaus
Division of Business Administration
Turlock, CA 95380

**California Polytechnic State University,
    San Luis Obispo**
School of Business and Social Sciences
San Luis Obispo, CA 93407

**California State Polytechnic University,
    Pomona**
School of Business Administration
Pomona, CA 91768

California State University, Chico
School of Business
Chico, CA 95929

California State University, Fresno
School of Business and Administrative
    Sciences
Fresno, CA 93740

California State University, Fullerton
School of Business Administration and
    Economics
Fullerton, CA 92634

California State University, Hayward
School of Business and Economics
Hayward, CA 94542

California State University, Long Beach
School of Business Administration
Long Beach, CA 90840

California State University, Los Angeles
School of Business and Economics
Los Angeles, CA 90032

California State University, Northridge
School of Business Administration
    and Economics
Northridge, CA 91330

California State University, Sacramento
School of Business and
    Public Administration
6000 Jay Street
Sacramento, CA 95819

Canisius College
School of Business Administration
Buffalo, NY 14208

Capital University
Graduate School of Administration
Columbus, OH 43209

Carnegie-Mellon University
Graduate School of Industrial
    Administration
Pittsburgh, PA 15213

Case Western Reserve University
School of Management
Cleveland, OH 44106

Central Michigan University
School of Business Administration
Mt. Pleasant, MI 48859

Central Missouri State University
School of Business and Economics
Warrensburg, MO 64093

Central State University
School of Business
Edmond, OK 73034

Chaminade University of Honolulu
Department of Business Administration
3140 Waialae Avenue
Honolulu, HI 96816

City University of New York
The Bernard M. Baruch College
School of Business and Public
    Administration
17 Lexington Avenue
New York, NY 10010

Clarion State College
School of Business Administration
Clarion, PA 16214

Clark University
Department of Management
Worcester, MA 01610

Clemson University
College of Industrial Management and
    Textile Science
Clemson, SC 29631

Cleveland State University
The James J. Nance College of Business
    Administration
Cleveland, OH 44115

College of St. Thomas
Department of Business Administration
St. Paul, MN 55105

College of William and Mary
School of Business Administration
Williamsburg, VA 23185

Colorado State University
College of Business
Fort Collins, CO 80523

Columbia University
Graduate School of Business
New York, NY 10027

Cornell University
Graduate School of Business and Public
    Administration
Ithaca, NY 14853

Creighton University
College of Business Administration
Omaha, NE 68178

Dartmouth College
The Amos Tuck School of Business
    Administration
Hanover, NH 03755

DePaul University
College of Commerce
Chicago, IL 60604

Dowling College
Business Administration Programs
Oakdale, NY 11769

Drake University
College of Business Administration
25th and University
Des Moines, IA 50311

Drexel University
College of Business and Administration
Philadelphia, PA 19104

Drury College
Breech School of Business Administration
Springfield, MO 65802

Duke University
Graduate School of Business Administration
Durham, NC 27706

Duquesne University
Graduate School of Business and
    Administration
Pittsburgh, PA 15219

East Carolina University
School of Business
Greenville, NC 27834

East Tennessee State University
College of Business
Johnson City, TN 37601

East Texas State University
College of Business Administration
Commerce, TX 75428

Eastern Illinois University
School of Business
Charleston, IL 61920

Eastern Kentucky University
College of Business
Richmond, KY 40475

Eastern Michigan University
College of Business
Ypsilanti, MI 48197

Eastern New Mexico University
College of Business
University Station No. 19
Portales, NM 88130

Eastern Washington University
School of Business and Administration
Cheney, WA 99004

Emory University
Graduate School of Business
    Administration
Atlanta, GA 30322

Emporia State University
Division of Business and Business Education
Emporia, KS 66801

Florida Atlantic University
College of Business and Public Administration
Boca Raton, FL 33432

Florida International University
School of Business and Organizational
    Sciences
Tamiami Campus
Miami, FL 33199

Florida State University
College of Business
Tallahassee, FL 32306

Florida Technological University
College of Business Administration
P.O. Box 25000
Orlando, FL 32816

Fordham University
College of Business Administration
Bronx, NY 10458

Furman University
Department of Economics and
    Business Administration
Greenville, SC 29613

Gannon College
Division of Business Administration
Erie, PA 16501

George Mason University
School of Business Administration
4400 University Drive
Fairfax, VA 22030

George Washington University
School of Government and Business
    Administration
Washington, DC 20052

Georgetown University
School of Business Administration
Washington, D.C. 20057

Georgia College
Department of Business Administration and
    Economics
Campus Box 554
Milledgeville, GA 31061

Georgia Institute of Technology
College of Industrial Management
225 North Avenue, NW
Atlanta, GA 30332

Georgia Southern College
School of Business
Statesboro, GA 30458

Georgia State University
College of Business Administration
University Plaza
Atlanta, GA 30303

Gonzaga University
School of Business Administration
Spokane, WA 99258

Governors State University
College of Business and
   Public Service
Park Forest South, IL 60466

Grand Valley State Colleges
F. E. Seidman Graduate College of
   Business and Administration
Allendale, MI 49401

Harvard University
Graduate School of Business
   Administration
Soldiers Field
Boston, MA 02163

Hofstra University
School of Business
1000 Fulton Avenue
Hempstead, NY 11550

Howard University
School of Business and Public
   Administration
Washington, DC 20059

Humboldt State University
School of Business and Economics
Arcata, CA 95521

Idaho State University
College of Business
Pocatello, ID 83209

Illinois Institute of Technology
Stuart School of Management and Finance
Chicago, IL 60616

Illinois State University
College of Business
Normal, IL 61761

Indiana State University
School of Business
Terre Haute, IN 47809

Indiana University
The Graduate School of Business
Bloomington, IN 47401

Iona College
School of Business Administration
New Rochelle, NY 10801

Jackson State University
School of Business and Economics
Jackson, MS 39217

John Carroll University
School of Business
Cleveland, OH 44118

Kansas State University
College of Business Administration
Manhattan, KS 66506

Kent State University
Graduate School of Business
   Administration
Kent, OH 44242

LaSalle College
School of Business Administration
Philadelphia, PA 19141

Lehigh University
College of Business and Economics
Bethlehem, PA 18015

Lindenwood Colleges
Department of Business Administration
St. Charles, MO 63301

Long Island University
Brooklyn Center
School of Business Administration
Brooklyn, NY 11201

Long Island University
C. W. Post Center
School of Business Administration
Greenvale, NY 11548

Louisiana State University
College of Business Administration
Baton Rouge, LA 70803

Louisiana Tech University
College of Administration and Business
Box 5796, Tech Station
Ruston, LA 71272

Loyola College
Department of Business Administration
4501 North Charles Street
Baltimore, MD 21210

Loyola Marymount University
College of Business Administration
Los Angeles, CA 90045

Loyola University
School of Business Administration
Lewis Towers
820 North Michigan Avenue
Chicago, IL 60611

Loyola University
College of Business Administration
New Orleans, LA 70118

Manhattan College
School of Business
Riverdale, NY 10471

Mankato State University
College of Business
Mankato, MN 56001

Marist College
Department of Business and Economics
North Road
Poughkeepsie, NY 12601

Marquette University
The Robert A. Johnston College of
Business Administration
Milwaukee, WI 53233

Marshall University
College of Business and Applied Science
Huntington, WV 25701

Massachusetts Institute of Technology
Alfred P. Sloan School of Management
Cambridge, MA 02139

McNeese State University
School of Business
Lake Charles, LA 70609

Memphis State University
College of Business Administration
Memphis, TN 38152

Miami University
School of Business Administration
Oxford, OH 45056

Michigan State University
The Graduate School of Business
Administration
East Lansing, MI 48824

Michigan Technological University
School of Business and Engineering
Administration
Houghton, MI 49931

Middle Tennessee State University
School of Business
Murfreesboro, TN 37132

Mississippi College
School of Business and Public Administration
Clinton, MS 39058

Mississippi State University
College of Business and Industry
Mississippi State, MS 39762

Monmouth College
Department of Business Administration
West Long Branch, NJ 07764

Moorhead State University
Business, Industry, and Applied Programs
Moorhead, MN 56560

Morehead State University
School of Business and Economics
Morehead, KY 40351

Morgan State University
School of Business and Management
Baltimore, MD 21239

Mount Saint Mary's College
Department of Business
Emmitsburg, MD 21727

Murray State University
College of Business and Public Affairs
Murray, KY 42071

New Hampshire College
Manchester, NH 03104

New Mexico State University
College of Business Administration and
    Economics
Las Cruces, NM 88003

New York Institute of Technology
Division of Business and Management
1855 Broadway
New York, NY 10023

New York University
College of Business and Public
    Administration
Washington Square
New York, NY 10003

New York University
Graduate School of Business Administration
100 Trinity Place
New York, NY 10006

Nicholls State University
College of Business Administration
Thibodaux, LA 70301

North Texas State University
College of Business Administration
Denton, TX 76203

Northeast Louisiana University
College of Business Administration
Monroe, LA 71209

Northeast Missouri State University
Business Division
Kirksville, MO 63501

Northeastern University
College of Business Administration
Boston, MA 02115

Northern Arizona University
College of Business Administration
C.U. Box 15066
Flagstaff, AZ 86011

Northern Illinois University
College of Business
DeKalb, IL 60115

Northern Michigan University
School of Business and Management
Marquette, MI 49855

Northrop University
College of Business and Management
1155 West Arbor Vitae Street
Inglewood, CA 90306

Northwest Missouri State University
Department of Business and Economics
Maryville, MO 64468

Northwestern State University of Louisiana
College of Business
Natchitoches, LA 71457

Northwestern University
Graduate School of Management
Leverone Hall
2001 Sheridan Road
Evanston, IL 60201

Oakland University
School of Economics and Management
Rochester, MI 48063

Ohio State University
College of Administrative Science
Columbus, OH 43210

Ohio University
College of Business Administration
Athens, OH 45701

Oklahoma City University
School of Management and Business Sciences
Oklahoma City, OK 73106

Oklahoma State University
College of Business Administration
Stillwater, OK 74074

Old Dominion University
School of Business Administration
Norfolk, VA 23508

Oregon State University
School of Business
Corvallis, OR 97331

Pace University
Lubin School of Business Administration
New York, NY 10028

Pacific Lutheran University
School of Business Administration
Tacoma, WA 98447

Pan American University
School of Business Administration
Edinburg, TX 78539

The Pennsylvania State University
College of Business Administration
106 Business Administration Building
University Park, PA 16802

Pennsylvania State University,
    Capitol Campus
Master of Administration Program
Middletown, PA 17057

Pepperdine University
School of Business and Management
Los Angeles, CA 90044

Philadelphia College of Textiles and Science
School of Business Administration
Philadelphia, PA 19144

Polytechnic Institute of New York
Department of Management
Brooklyn, NY 11201

Portland State University
School of Business Administration
P.O. Box 751
Portland, OR 97207

Prairie View A & M University
College of Business
Prairie View, TX 77445

Providence College
Department of Business Administration
Providence, RI 02918

Purdue University
School of Management
Krannert Graduate School of Management
West Lafayette, IN 47907

Rensselaer Polytechnic Institute
School of Management
Troy, NY 12181

Rider College
School of Business Administration
Lawrenceville, NJ 08648

Rochester Institute of Technology
College of Business
Rochester, NY 14623

Rollins College
Roy E. Crummer School of Finance
    and Business Administration
Winter Park, FL 32789

Roosevelt University
Walter E. Heller College of Business
    Administration
430 South Michigan Avenue
Chicago, IL 60605

Rutgers The State University
Graduate School of Business
    Administration
Newark, NJ 07102

Rutgers University, Camden
Department of Business and Economics
Camden, NJ 08102

Saginaw Valley State College
School of Business and Management
2250 Pierce Road
University Center, MI 48710

Saint Bonaventure University
School of Business Administration
St. Bonaventure, NY 14778

Saint Cloud State University
College of Business
Saint Cloud, MN 56301

St. John's University
College of Business Administration
Utopia and Grand Central Parkways
Jamaica, NY 11439

St. Joseph's College
Department of Business Administration
Philadelphia, PA 19131

Saint Louis University
School of Business and Administration
St. Louis, MO 63108

St. Mary's University
School of Business and Administration
One Camino Santa Maria
San Antonio, TX 78284

Samford University
School of Business
Birmingham, AL 35209

San Diego State University
School of Business Administration
San Diego, CA 92110

San Francisco State University
School of Business
1600 Holloway Avenue
San Francisco, CA 94132

San Jose State University
School of Business
San Jose, CA 95192

Savannah State College
Division of Business Administration
Savannah, GA 31404

Seattle University
Albers School of Business
Seattle, WA 98122

Seton Hall University
W. Paul Stillman School of Business
South Orange, NJ 07079

Shippensburg State College
School of Business
Shippensburg, PA 17257

Southeastern Massachusetts University
College of Business and Industry
North Dartmouth, MA 02747

Southeastern Oklahoma State University
School of Business and Industry
Durant, OK 74701

Southern Illinois University at Carbondale
College of Business and Administration
Carbondale, IL 62901

Southern Illinois University at Edwardsville
School of Business
Edwardsville, IL 62026

Southern Methodist University
School of Business Administration
Dallas, TX 75275

Stanford University
Graduate School of Business
Stanford, CA 94305

State University of New York at Albany
School of Business
Albany, NY 12222

State University of New York at Binghamton
School of Management
Binghamton, NY 13901

State University of New York at Buffalo
School of Management
Crosby Hall, Library Circle
Buffalo, NY 14214

Stephen F. Austin State University
School of Business
Nacogdoches, TX 75962

Suffolk University
College of Business Administration
47 Mt. Vernon Street
Boston, MA 02108

Syracuse University
School of Management
116 College Place
Syracuse, NY 13210

Temple University
School of Business Administration
Philadelphia, PA 19122

Tennessee Technological University
College of Business Administration
Cookeville, TN 38501

Texas Christian University
M. J. Neeley School of Business
Fort Worth, TX 76129

Texas Eastern University
School of Business Administration
Tyler, TX 75701

Thomas College
West River Road
Waterville, ME 04901

Trinity University
Faculty of Business and Management
    Studies
San Antonio, TX 78284

Troy State University
School of Business
Troy, AL 36081

Tulane University
Graduate School of Business
    Administration
New Orleans, LA 70118

United States International University
School of Business and Management
San Diego, CA 92131

University of Akron
College of Business Administration
Akron, OH 44325

University of Alabama
College of Commerce and Business
    Administration
Graduate School of Business
University, AL 35486

University of Alabama in Birmingham
School of Business
Birmingham, AL 35294

University of Alaska
School of Management
Fairbanks, AK 99701

University of Alaska, Anchorage
School of Business and Public Administration
3221 Providence Drive
Anchorage, AK 99504

University of Arizona
College of Business and Public
    Administration
Tucson, AZ 85721

University of Arkansas
College of Business Administration
Fayetteville, AR 72701

University of Arkansas at Little Rock
College of Business Administration
Little Rock, AR 72204

University of Baltimore
School of Business
Baltimore, MD 21201

University of Bridgeport
College of Business Administration
Bridgeport, CT 06602

University of California
School of Business Administration
    Graduate School of Business
    Administration
Berkeley, CA 94720

University of California, Irvine
Graduate School of Administration
Irvine, CA 92717

University of California, Los Angeles
Graduate School of Management
Los Angeles, CA 90024

University of Chicago
Graduate School of Business
5836 South Greenwood Avenue
Chicago, IL 60637

University of Cincinnati
College of Business Administration
Cincinnati, OH 45221

University of Colorado
Graduate School of Business
    Administration
Boulder, CO 80309

University of Connecticut
School of Business Administration
Storrs, CT 06268

University of Dallas
Graduate School of Management
University of Dallas Station
Irving, TX 75061

University of Dayton
School of Business Administration
Dayton, OH 45469

University of Delaware
College of Business and Economics
Newark, DE 19711

University of Denver
Graduate School of Business and Public
  Management
University Park
Denver, CO 80208

University of Detroit
College of Business and Administration
Graduate School
McNichols Road at Livernois
Detroit, MI 48221

University of Evansville
School of Business Administration
Evansville, IN 47702

University of Georgia
College of Business Administration
Athens, GA 30602

University of Hawaii
College of Business Administration
2404 Maile Way
Honolulu, HI 96822

University of Houston
College of Business Administration
4800 Calhoun Street
Houston, TX 77004

University of Idaho
College of Business and Economics
Moscow, ID 83843

University of Illinois at Chicago Circle
College of Business Administration
Box 4348
Chicago, IL 60680

**University of Illinois at Urbana-
  Champaign**
College of Commerce and Business
  Administration
Urbana, IL 61801

University of Iowa
College of Business Administration
Iowa City, IA 52242

University of Kansas
School of Business
Lawrence KS 66045

University of Kentucky
College of Business and Economics
Lexington, KY 40506

University of Louisville
School of Business
Louisville, KY 40208

University of Lowell
College of Management Science
Lowell, MA 01854

University of Maine at Orono
College of Business Administration
Orono, ME 04473

University of Maryland
College of Business and Management
College Park, MD 20742

University of Massachusetts
School of Business Administration
Amherst, MA 01002

University of Miami
School of Business Administration
Coral Gables, FL 33124

The University of Michigan
Graduate School of Business
  Administration
Ann Arbor, MI 48109

University of Michigan, Dearborn
School of Management
4901 Evergreen Road
Dearborn, MI 48128

University of Minnesota
Graduate School of Business
  Administration
Minneapolis, MN 55455

University of Minnesota, Duluth
School of Business and Economics
Duluth, MN 55812

University of Mississippi
School of Business Administration
University, MS 38677

University of Missouri, Columbia
College of Business and Public
  Administration
Columbia, MO 65201

University of Missouri, Kansas City
School of Administration
5100 Rockhill Road
Kansas City, MO 64110

University of Missouri, St. Louis
School of Business Administration
8001 Natural Bridge Road
St. Louis, MO 63121

University of Montana
School of Business Administration
Missoula, MT 59801

University of Nebraska, Lincoln
College of Business Administration
Lincoln, NE 68588

University of Nebraska, Omaha
College of Business Administration
Omaha, NE 68101

University of Nevada, Las Vegas
College of Business and Economics
Las Vegas, NV 89154

University of Nevada, Reno
College of Business Administration
Reno, NV 89557

University of New Hampshire
Whittemore School of Business and
  Economics
Durham, NH 03824

The University of New Mexico
The Robert O. Anderson Graduate
  School of Business and Administrative
  Sciences
Albuquerque, NM 87131

University of New Orleans
College of Business Administration
New Orleans, LA 70122

University of North Carolina, Chapel Hill
Graduate School of Business
  Administration
Chapel Hill, NC 27514

**The University of North Carolina,
  Charlotte**
College of Business Administration
UNCC Station
Charlotte, NC 28223

**University of North Carolina,
  Greensboro**
School of Business and Economics
Greensboro, NC 27412

University of North Dakota
College of Business and Public
  Administration
Grand Forks, ND 58201

University of Northern Iowa
College of Business and Behavioral
  Sciences
Cedar Falls, IA 50613

University of Notre Dame
College of Business Administration
Notre Dame, IN 46556

University of Oklahoma
College of Business Administration
Norman, OK 73019

University of Oregon
Graduate School of Management
  and Business
Eugene, OR 97403

University of Pennsylvania
The Wharton School
3620 Locust Walk
Philadelphia, PA 19174

University of Pittsburgh
Graduate School of Business
Pittsburgh, PA 15260

University of Portland
School of Business Administration
Portland, OR 97203

University of Puget Sound
School of Business and Public
  Administration
Tacoma, WA 98416

University of Rhode Island
College of Business Administration
302 Ballentine Hall
Kingston, RI 02881

University of Richmond
School of Business Administration
University of Richmond, VA 23173

University of Rochester
Graduate School of Management
Rochester, NY 14627

University of San Diego
School of Business Administration
San Diego, CA 92110

University of San Francisco
College of Business Administration
San Francisco, CA 94117

University of Santa Clara
Graduate School of Business and
  Administration
Santa Clara, CA 95053

University of South Carolina
Graduate School of Business
Columbia, SC 29208

University of South Dakota
School of Business
Vermillion, SD 57069

University of South Florida
College of Business Administration
4202 Fowler Avenue
Tampa, FL 33620

University of Southern California
Graduate School of Business
  Administration
University Park
Los Angeles, CA 90007

University of Southern Mississippi
College of Business Administration
Hattiesburg, MS 39401

University of Tennessee, Chattanooga
School of Business Administration
Chattanooga, TN 37401

University of Tennessee, Knoxville
College of Business Administration
Knoxville, TN 37916

University of Tennessee, Nashville
Division of Business Administration
Nashville, TN 37203

University of Texas, Arlington
College of Business Administration
Arlington, TX 76019

University of Texas, Dallas
School of Management and Administration
P.O. Box 688
Richardson, TX 75080

University of Texas, San Antonio
College of Business
San Antonio, TX 78285

University of Toledo
College of Business Administration
Toledo, OH 43606

University of Tulsa
College of Business Administration
Tulsa, OK 74104

University of Utah
College of Business
Salt Lake City, UT 84112

University of Vermont
Business Administration Department
Burlington, VT 05410

University of Virginia
The Colgate Darden Graduate School
  of Business Administration
P.O. Box 6550
Charlottesville, VA 22906

University of Virginia
McIntire School of Commerce
Monroe Hall
Charlottesville, VA 22903

University of Washington
School and Graduate School of Business
   Administration
Seattle, WA 98195

University of Wisconsin, Eau Claire
School of Business
Eau Claire, WI 54701

University of Wisconsin, LaCrosse
School of Business Administration
La Crosse, WI 54601

University of Wisconsin, Madison
Graduate School of Business
Madison, WI 53706

University of Wisconsin, Milwaukee
School of Business Administration
Milwaukee, WI 53201

University of Wisconsin, Oshkosh
College of Business Administration
Oshkosh, WI 54901

University of Wisconsin, Whitewater
College of Business and Economics
Whitewater, WI 53190

University of Wyoming
College of Commerce and Industry
Laramie, WY 82070

Utah State University
College of Business
Logan, UT 84322

Valdosta State College
School of Business Administration
Valdosta, GA 31601

Vanderbilt University
Graduate School of Management
Nashville, TN 37203

Virginia Commonwealth University
School of Business
Richmond, VA 23284

**Virginia Polytechnic Institute and
   State University**
College of Business
Blacksburg, VA 24061

Wake Forest University
Babcock Graduate School of Management
Winston-Salem, NC 27109

Washington State University
College of Economics and Business
Pullman, WA 99163

Washington University
The Graduate School of Business
   Administration
St. Louis, MO 63130

Wayne State University
School of Business Administration
Detroit, MI 48202

West Georgia College
School of Business
Carrollton, GA 30117

West Texas State University
School of Business
Canyon, TX 79016

West Virginia College of Graduate Studies
Division of Business and Management
2300 MacCorkle Avenue, S.E.,
Charleston, WV 25304

West Virginia University
College of Business and Economics
Morgantown, WV 26506

Western Carolina University
School of Business
Cullowhee, NC 28723

Western Connecticut State College
School of Business and Public Administration
Danbury, CT 06810

Western Illinois University
College of Business
Macomb, IL 61455

Western Kentucky University
Bowling Green College of Business and
   Public Affairs
Bowling Green, KY 42101

Western Michigan University
College of Business
Kalamazoo, MI 49001

Wichita State University
College of Business Administration
Wichita, KS 67208

Widener College
Center of Management and Applied
 Economics
Chester, PA 19013

Willamette University
Atkinson Graduate School of Administration
Salem, OR 97301

Woodbury University
Los Angeles, CA 90017

Wright State University
College of Business and Administration
Dayton, OH 45435

Xavier University
College of Business Administration
Cincinnati, OH 45207

Youngstown State University
School of Business Administration
Youngstown, OH 44555

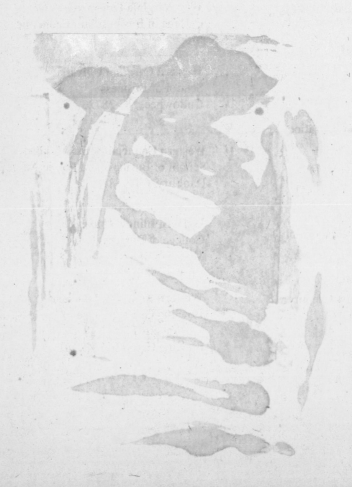